Decentralizing the Online Experience With Web3 Technologies

Dina Darwish
Ahram Canadian University, Egypt

IGI Global
PUBLISHER of TIMELY KNOWLEDGE

A volume in the Advances in Web Technologies
and Engineering (AWTE) Book Series

Published in the United States of America by
IGI Global
Engineering Science Reference (an imprint of IGI Global)
701 E. Chocolate Avenue
Hershey PA, USA 17033
Tel: 717-533-8845
Fax: 717-533-8661
E-mail: cust@igi-global.com
Web site: http://www.igi-global.com

Library of Congress Cataloging-in-Publication Data

CIP Pending
ISBN: 979-8-3693-1532-3
EISBN: 979-8-3693-1533-0

This book is published in the IGI Global book series Advances in Web Technologies and Engineering (AWTE) (ISSN: 2328-2762; eISSN: 2328-2754)

British Cataloguing in Publication Data
A Cataloguing in Publication record for this book is available from the British Library.

Advances in Web Technologies and Engineering (AWTE) Book Series

Ghazi I. Alkhatib
The Hashemite University, Jordan
David C. Rine
George Mason University, USA

ISSN:2328-2762
EISSN:2328-2754

Mission

The **Advances in Web Technologies and Engineering (AWTE) Book Series** aims to provide a platform for research in the area of Information Technology (IT) concepts, tools, methodologies, and ethnography, in the contexts of global communication systems and Web engineered applications. Organizations are continuously overwhelmed by a variety of new information technologies, many are Web based. These new technologies are capitalizing on the widespread use of network and communication technologies for seamless integration of various issues in information and knowledge sharing within and among organizations. This emphasis on integrated approaches is unique to this book series and dictates cross platform and multidisciplinary strategy to research and practice.

The **Advances in Web Technologies and Engineering (AWTE) Book Series** seeks to create a stage where comprehensive publications are distributed for the objective of bettering and expanding the field of web systems, knowledge capture, and communication technologies. The series will provide researchers and practitioners with solutions for improving how technology is utilized for the purpose of a growing awareness of the importance of web applications and engineering.

Coverage

- Security, integrity, privacy, and policy issues
- Web systems engineering design
- Data and knowledge validation and verification
- Integrated Heterogeneous and Homogeneous Workflows and Databases within and Across Organizations and with Suppliers and Customers
- Radio Frequency Identification (RFID) research and applications in Web engineered systems
- Virtual teams and virtual enterprises: communication, policies, operation, creativity, and innovation
- Competitive/intelligent information systems
- IT readiness and technology transfer studies
- Web systems performance engineering studies
- Metrics-based performance measurement of IT-based and web-based organizations

IGI Global is currently accepting manuscripts for publication within this series. To submit a proposal for a volume in this series, please contact our Acquisition Editors at Acquisitions@igi-global.com or visit: http://www.igi-global.com/publish/.

The Advances in Web Technologies and Engineering (AWTE) Book Series (ISSN 2328-2762) is published by IGI Global, 701 E. Chocolate Avenue, Hershey, PA 17033-1240, USA, www.igi-global.com. This series is composed of titles available for purchase individually; each title is edited to be contextually exclusive from any other title within the series. For pricing and ordering information please visit http://www.igi-global.com/book-series/advances-web-technologies-engineering/37158. Postmaster: Send all address changes to above address.

Titles in this Series

For a list of additional titles in this series, please visit: http://www.igi-global.com/book-series/advances-web-technologies-engineering/37158

Digital Technologies, Ethics, and Decentralization in the Dgital Era
Balraj Verma (Chitkara Business School, Chitkara University, India) Babita Singla (Chitkara Business School, Chitkara University, Punjab, India) and Amit Mittal (Chitkara Business School, Chitkara University, Punjab, India)
Engineering Science Reference • © 2024 • 365pp • H/C (ISBN: 9798369317624) • US $300.00

Infrastructure Possibilities and Human-Centered Approaches With Industry 5.0
Mohammad Ayoub Khan (University of Bisha, Saudi Arabia) Rijwan Khan (ABES Institute of Technology, India) Pushkar Praveen (Govind Ballabh Pant Institute of Engineering and Technology, India) Agya Ram Verma (Govind Ballabh Pant Institute of Engineering and Technology, India) and Manoj Kumar Panda (Govind Ballabh Pant Institute of Engineering and Technolog, India)
Engineering Science Reference • © 2024 • 318pp • H/C (ISBN: 9798369307823) • US $300.00

Internet of Behaviors Implementation in Organizational Contexts
Luísa Cagica Carvalho (Instituto Politécnico de Setúbal, Portugal) Clara Silveira (Polytechnic Institute of Guarda, Portugal) Leonilde Reis (Instituto Politecnico de Setubal, Portugal) and Nelson Russo (Universidade Aberta, Portugal)
Engineering Science Reference • © 2023 • 471pp • H/C (ISBN: 9781668490396) • US $270.00

Supporting Technologies and the Impact of Blockchain on Organizations and Society
Luís Ferreira (Polytechnic Institute of Cávado and Ave, Portugal) Miguel Rosado Cruz (Polytechnic Institute of Viana do Castelo, Portugal) Estrela Ferreira Cruz (Polytechnic Institute of Viana do Castelo, Portugal) Hélder Quintela (Polytechnic Institute of Cavado and Ave, Portugal) and Manuela Cruz Cunha (Polytechnic Institute of Cavado and Ave, Portugal)
Engineering Science Reference • © 2023 • 337pp • H/C (ISBN: 9781668457474) • US $270.00

Concepts, Technologies, Challenges, and the Future of Web 3
Pooja Lekhi (University Canada West, Canada) and Guneet Kaur (University of Stirling, UK & Cointelegraph, USA)
Engineering Science Reference • © 2023 • 602pp • H/C (ISBN: 9781668499191) • US $360.00

Perspectives on Social Welfare Applications' Optimization and Enhanced Computer Applications
Ponnusamy Sivaram (G.H. Raisoni College of Engineering, Nagpur, India) S. Senthilkumar (University College of Engineering, BIT Campus, Anna University, Tiruchirappalli, India) Lipika Gupta (Department of Electronics and Communication Engineering, Chitkara University Institute of Engineering and Technology, Chitkara University, India) and Nelligere S. Lokesh (Department of CSE-AIML, AMC Engineering College, Bengaluru, India)
Engineering Science Reference • © 2023 • 336pp • H/C (ISBN: 9781668483060) • US $270.00

IGI Global
PUBLISHER of TIMELY KNOWLEDGE

701 East Chocolate Avenue, Hershey, PA 17033, USA
Tel: 717-533-8845 x100 • Fax: 717-533-8661
E-Mail: cust@igi-global.com • www.igi-global.com

Editorial Advisory Board

Table of Contents

Detailed Table of Contents

The potential of Web 3.0 to bring about a substantial paradigm shift and disrupt the current landscape is comparable to the disruptive nature and paradigm shift brought about by Web 2.0. The core principles underpinning Web 3.0 are decentralization, openness, and enhanced consumer utility. Web 3.0, commonly referred to as Web 3, represents the subsequent phase in the evolutionary trajectory of the internet. Envision a novel iteration of the internet that possesses the capability to precisely translate textual input and comprehend spoken language, regardless of the medium employed. Furthermore, this hypothetical internet iteration would offer an unprecedented level of personalization in the content consumed by users. In the context of the internet's evolutionary trajectory, we are on the cusp of embarking upon a novel era. The term "Web 3.0" has been coined. The concept of Web 3.0 refers to the next generation of the world wide web, characterized by advanced technologies and functionalities that aim to enhance user experiences and enable more intelligent and personalized interactions. This chapter discusses the Web 3 definition, technologies and tools, as well as its benefits for individuals and companies.

The term "web3 development" refers to the practice of creating and building applications, platforms, and technologies that are designed to operate on the decentralized web, also known as web 3. This new paradigm of web development aims to leverage blockchain technology, decentralized networks, and cryptographic protocols to enable greater user control, privacy, and security. Web 3 development refers to the systematic creation of applications, platforms, and decentralized systems that leverage blockchain technology, cryptocurrencies, and decentralized networks. This procedure additionally involves implementing these applications and platforms. This chapter discusses the web 3 development importance and the driving forces behind web 3 development.

A blockchain functions as a decentralized network, serving both as a digital ledger and a mechanism for securely transferring assets without the need for a central authority. Much like the internet facilitates the digital flow of information, blockchain empowers the digital exchange of various value units. The tokenization of various assets, including currencies and real-world applications, is a feasible endeavor within the realm of blockchain networks. This technology not only facilitates secure value transfers but also maintains a persistent record of transactions, establishing a singular version of truth referred to as the network state. This chapter provides a succinct overview of blockchain, highlighting its defining characteristics that position it as a prominent and transformative technology.

Digital wallets are of utmost importance in transforming the online experience as they serve as the core constituents of decentralized ecosystems. This study explores the operational mechanisms of different types of wallets, encompassing hardware wallets and software-based solutions, in order to elucidate their distinctive characteristics and security implications. Moreover, the chapter offers a comprehensive examination of decentralized transactions, elucidating the profound impact that blockchain technology may have in cultivating trust, enhancing security, and promoting transparency. By examining real-world illustrations and analyzing case studies, readers will acquire a comprehensive comprehension of how wallets and transactions serve as the fundamental infrastructure for a novel epoch of online engagement. This transformative development is reshaping the manner in which individuals interact with digital assets and engage in decentralized networks.

In the internet's evolution, cryptocurrencies and decentralized platforms represent a significant shift. This chapter explores this shift, emphasizing Ethereum's role in Web 3. As we move from centralized to decentralized systems, Ethereum emerges as a "world computer." This chapter explores Ethereum's blockchain and smart contract technology. It clarifies Ethereum and Ether (ETH), highlighting their impact on DeFi and NFTs. Ethereum offers opportunities but also faces scalability and fee challenges. The chapter provides a balanced view, exploring these issues and Ethereum's potential to alter the internet and finance. Readers will understand Ethereum's Web 3 role, its industry implications, and developments enhancing its ecosystem.

Web 3 is considered the next generation of the internet. Decentralized autonomous organizations (DAOs) are considered the next avatar of organizations run digitally over blockchain-led technology platforms. Business logic and rules for running the organization are programmed in distributed applications (dApps) and executed using smart contracts. Token-based rights allow owing members to vote, participate in governance, and direct how the organization will be run. While DAOs are facing several legal and regulatory challenges on one side and fighting with technical vulnerabilities and hacks on the other side, future research in this field appears promising. There is an enormous need for education and awareness of the functioning of these emerging models, which can be dealt with using a multi-faceted approach. Decentralized governance can have a massive societal impact and lead to an equitable world. It drives financial inclusion and puts automatic decision-making at the fore.

Blockchain networks often require data to and from the outside world, especially when offering services such as in the financial domain. Blockchain oracles are critical infrastructure layers that bridge the blockchain network so that smart contracts get rich data to process transactions or execute business logic. Blockchain oracles are classified into various types depending on the data facility offered. Some popular oracle networks include chainlink, brand protocol, and provable. This chapter explains how oracles work, such as fetching and delivering data, data verification and aggregation, and reward mechanisms. It also briefly discusses on their applications, such as price feeds for DeFi applications, event triggers used in insurance and gambling contracts, identity/reputation management for NFTs, and aggregating of IoT sensor data. Security and decentralization are discussed. The chapter ends with a discussion of future research trends and the integration of artificial intelligence and machine learning, event-driven architectures, and recent advancements.

The evolution of blockchain technology, notably exemplified by Bitcoin, heralded a new era where smart contracts have taken center stage. Smart contracts are ingenious self-executing contracts that empower automatic enforcement of contractual terms, eliminating the need for intermediaries or trusted third parties. Consequently, smart contracts offer multifaceted benefits, including streamlined administrative procedures, cost savings, enhanced operational efficiency, and risk reduction. This chapter aims to provide the pivotal technical aspects of smart contracts and their significance within the blockchain technology landscape. The authors begin by elucidating fundamental concepts, structural intricacies, and the working principles of smart contracts. Subsequently, they delve into the technological platforms that

how to benefit from Web 2.0 tools. With Web 2.0 tools, various tools have been introduced for use in interactive presentations, animations, videos, concept maps, and measurement and evaluation. It is thought that lessons taught with Web 2.0 tools increase students' motivation, permanent learning occurs, and contribute to collaborative learning, and students will actively participate in the process.

In the rapidly evolving landscape of Web 3, where the very fabric of the internet undergoes profound transformation, the paramount significance of privacy and security emerges as the guiding light of this new era. This chapter encapsulates a multifaceted exploration of the importance of privacy and security in Web 3, delving into its historical context, technological foundations, challenges, and ethical considerations. From the retrospective examination of the web's evolution from Web 1 to Web 3, with its emphasis on decentralization and user-centric control, to the in-depth analysis of key technologies like blockchain, smart contracts, and privacy-enhancing tools, this chapter uncovers the critical infrastructure of a more secure and private digital world. The challenges and threats that loom in this decentralised landscape, from regulatory and legal considerations to security vulnerabilities, were elucidated, highlighting the need for transparent and ethical development practices. Real-world case studies serve as poignant illustrations of both the transformative potential and pitfalls of Web 3, providing valuable lessons for future research. In conclusion, the call for action resonates with readers, urging them to stay informed, vigilant, and engaged in the Web 3 era. Advocating for privacy, supporting ethical development, engaging in regulatory discussions, and actively educating and innovating are the pathways that contribute to safer and more private Web 3. In essence, this chapter is a holistic journey through the nuances of Web 3, underscoring its transformative potential and pivotal role of privacy and security in shaping a digital future that empowers individuals and safeguards their rights in the digital realm.

This chapter delved into the multifaceted benefits and challenges characterizing the Web 3 paradigm. Web 3, operating on decentralized networks, fortifies digital ecosystems against cyber threats and unauthorized access, exemplified by the resilience of Bitcoin's decentralized blockchain. Rooted in blockchain technology, web 3 introduces transparency to transactions, fostering trust and eliminating intermediaries. User empowerment takes center stage as Web 3 enables unprecedented control over digital assets through blockchain-based smart contracts. Tokenization stimulates collaboration, fostering a more inclusive digital economy, while interoperability connects diverse blockchain networks seamlessly. The metaverse's integration into Web 3 faces challenges due to a lack of industry standards, exposing users to potential financial security risks. Scalability, regulatory uncertainty, and environmental impact present hurdles, emphasizing the need for innovative solutions.

Preface

The terms *"Web 1.0" and "Web 2.0"* denote distinct periods in the evolutionary trajectory of the World Wide Web, characterized by the adoption and advancement of diverse technologies and formats. The term *"Web 1.0"* generally encompasses the time span from 1989 to 2004, during which websites primarily comprised static pages and the majority of individuals engaged with online platforms as consumers rather than creators of content. *Web 2.0* is founded on the concept of "the web as a platform" and revolves around the dissemination of user-generated content across various online platforms such as forums, social media, networking sites, blogs, and wikis, among other digital services. The user's text is not sufficient to be rewritten in an academic manner. The emergence of Web 2.0 is commonly acknowledged to have commenced circa 2004 and has persisted until near time.

Web 3 can be differentiated from Tim Berners-Lee's 1999 concept of the Semantic Web. In 2006, Berners-Lee provided a description of the Semantic Web as an integral element of Web 3.0, distinct from the connotation of Web3 within the realm of blockchain applications.

The term *"Web 3.0"* was introduced by Gavin Wood, the founder of Polkadot and co-founder of Ethereum, in 2014. It denotes a decentralized online ecosystem that operates on blockchain technology. The concept of Web3 experienced a surge in popularity during the year 2021. There was a notable surge in interest observed towards the conclusion of 2021, primarily driven by the enthusiasm of cryptocurrency enthusiasts and the substantial investments made by prominent technologists and corporations. In October 2021, representatives of Andreessen Horowitz, a venture capital firm, undertook a visit to Washington, D.C. with the purpose of advocating for the notion as a prospective resolution to the ongoing deliberations surrounding the regulation of the internet, which policymakers have been actively addressing.

Web 3, alternatively referred to as Web 3.0, is the proposed concept for a new version of the World Wide Web, encompasses various principles including decentralization, blockchain technologies, and token-based economics. Certain technologists and journalists have drawn a comparison between it and Web 2.0, positing that data and content are concentrated within a limited number of companies colloquially known as "Big Tech". The term "Web3" was introduced in 2014 by Gavin Wood, one of the co-founders of Ethereum. Subsequently, in 2021, this concept garnered significant attention from cryptocurrency enthusiasts, prominent technology corporations, and venture capital firms. The inception of the Web3 concepts can be traced back to the year 2013.

The fundamental characteristics of *Web 3.0*, including decentralization and permissionless systems, will afford users significantly enhanced autonomy in managing their personal data. This measure has the potential to mitigate the practice of data extraction, which refers to the collection of information from internet users without their explicit consent or fair compensation. Additionally, it could address the network effects that have facilitated the rise of technology giants as quasi-monopolies, primarily driven by exploitative advertising and marketing strategies.

In order to comprehend the positioning of Web 3, it is imperative to contemplate the impetus behind the pursuit of a more inclusive marketplace for computational resources. The forces propelling the transition towards hybrid, multi-cloud infrastructures align with the underlying drivers of Web 3, encompassing security, reliability, risk management, portability, interoperability, and cost management. As cloud architectures are being refactored to accommodate this transition, Web 3 emerges as the logical progression of the computing infrastructure we currently depend on, transitioning from virtual machines (VMs) to containers and eventually to serverless functions.

First, let us examine the concept of *decentralization*. In contemporary times, the ownership and regulation of the digital infrastructure supporting widely frequented online platforms and social spaces predominantly lie within the purview of corporate entities, subject to varying degrees of governmental oversight. This phenomenon can be attributed to the fact that constructing network infrastructure in this manner was the most straightforward approach. It involves an individual or entity investing funds to establish servers and configure the necessary software for online access, subsequently offering these services either for a fee or free of charge, contingent upon compliance with their stipulated regulations.

In the present era, alternative choices are available to us, with blockchain technology being a notable example. *Blockchain* is an emerging technology that facilitates the secure storage and retrieval of data on the internet. It is founded upon the fundamental principles of encryption and distributed computing.

Encryption refers to the process of securing data stored on a blockchain, ensuring that only authorized individuals can access it. This safeguard remains intact even if the data is stored on a third-party computer system, such as those owned by governmental entities or corporations.

Introduction to *Web 3 Wallets*, also known as decentralized wallets, have emerged as a crucial component in the realm of blockchain technology. These wallets enable users to securely store, manage, and interact.

Web 3 Wallets have established a novel benchmark within the industry by introducing innovative methods for individuals to possess and monetize their content, identity, and assets as we transition into the forthcoming era of the internet. In essence, *Web 3 Wallets* serve as a means to utilize hardware or software for the purpose of not only accessing funds, but also facilitating seamless interaction with decentralized applications. Moreover, they function as a conduit to bank less financial services, enable the collection of non-fungible tokens (NFTs), facilitate the establishment of on-chain identity, foster collaboration within communities, and offer a significantly broader range of applications compared to conventional wallets currently available.

Similar to the way individuals possess a physical wallet for the purpose of storing paper currency, digital wallets serve the function of storing and providing access to one's digital currency. Moreover, *Web 3 Wallets* possess the capacity to securely store digital assets, including non-fungible tokens (NFTs), while also facilitating user engagement with Decentralized Applications (dApps). This is accomplished entirely without the involvement of an intermediary.

Wallets do not physically store cryptocurrencies; rather, they retain the necessary information for accessing digital funds in the form of cryptocurrencies.

A cryptocurrency wallet comprises three primary constituents:

- ***The public key*** is a cryptographic identifier that corresponds to an address used for the purpose of sending and receiving transactions.

- ***The private key*** must be maintained in strict confidentiality and should not be revealed or disclosed. The purpose of this mechanism is to authenticate and authorize new transactions, thereby granting access to financial resources.
- ***The seed phrase*** is employed for the purpose of generating multiple private keys. Functioning as *a root key*, it serves as a gateway to the remaining keys and addresses several issues within a user's wallet. Furthermore, this process has the potential to generate novel private keys.

Within the realm of Web 3, there are various categories of wallets that are present. Each of these options has its own set of advantages and can be beneficial depending on one's specific objectives in terms of data and financial management. It is advisable to conduct an assessment to determine the most suitable type of wallet for individual needs and preferences.

Gaining a comprehensive understanding of Web 3 assets can be facilitated by examining the historical context and delving into the foundational principles of the internet. The contemporary internet infrastructure is characterized by high speed connectivity, facilitated by the deployment of advanced technologies such as 5G networks and the availability of online streaming services.

Web 3.0 will prioritize the provision of technological functionalities, specifically:

- The concept of blockchain is a decentralized digital ledger system.
- ***Smart contracts*** are self-executing contracts with the terms of the agreement directly written into code.
- Cryptocurrency is a digital or virtual form of currency that utilizes cryptography for secure financial transactions and control the creation of new units.
- The concept of decentralization refers to the distribution of power and authority away from a central authority or governing body.
- ***Artificial intelligence (AI)*** refers to the field of computer science that focuses on the development of intelligent machines capable of performing tasks that typically require human intelligence.
- ***Machine learning*** is a field of study that focuses on the development of algorithms and statistical models that enable computer systems to learn and improve from experience, without being explicitly programmed.

Web 3.0 is anticipated to engage with the aforementioned technologies in a cohesive manner. Individuals who wish to make forward-looking investments can consider purchasing Web3 cryptocurrency assets, as these tokens and blockchain technologies serve as the foundational elements of the Web 3.0 ecosystem.

Multiple cryptocurrencies, such as ApeMax, Ethereum, and Solana, among others, provide support for Web3 technology. The purpose of these cryptocurrencies is to facilitate and interact with decentralized applications, smart contracts, and achieve interoperability within the Web3 ecosystem.

Decentralized Finance (DeFi) refers to a financial system that operates on a decentralized network, such as a blockchain, rather than relying on traditional centralized intermediaries. The emergence of *Decentralized Finance (DeFi)* has established itself as a significant entity within the Web3 ecosystem. *Decentralized Finance (DeFi)* enables individuals to enhance their access to financial services, facilitates cross-border transactions, and offers avenues for generating returns through novel mechanisms such as liquidity mining and staking. DeFi protocols provide financial services such as lending, borrowing, and trading by utilizing smart contracts and blockchain technology, thereby eliminating the necessity for conventional intermediaries. The substantial expansion of decentralized finance (DeFi) has played a pivotal role in the emergence and advancement of Web 3.

Non-fungible tokens (NFTs) are digital assets that represent ownership or proof of authenticity of a unique item or piece of content, which differ from cryptocurrencies such as Bitcoin.

The emergence of *Non-Fungible Tokens (NFTs)* has garnered significant global interest, fundamentally transforming the notions of digital ownership and creativity. These distinct digital assets, which are encoded on the blockchain, have the capacity to symbolize a wide range of items, including artwork, music, virtual real estate, and in-game items. *Non-fungible tokens (NFTs)* provide creators with the opportunity to directly monetize their artistic creations, while also allowing collectors to establish and validate their ownership and the authenticity of the acquired assets. The proliferation of *NFT* marketplaces, collaborative efforts, and digital collectibles has propelled the integration of Web3 into the mainstream, garnering attention from artists, collectors, and enthusiasts on a global scale.

Another significant concept pertaining to web3 that necessitates discussion is the *Metaverse*. The term "*Metaverse*" encompasses the forthcoming advancement of the internet's user interface, referred to as web3. This interface facilitates our interaction with the virtual realm, enables communication with fellow users, and allows for the manipulation of data.

The term "Metaverse" is derived from the combination of the words "meta" and "universe," and it was initially introduced in the science fiction novel Snow Crash, published in 1992.

The *Metaverse* refers to a network comprising multiple three-dimensional virtual worlds that are primarily designed to facilitate social interactions and connections among users. In the realms of futurism and science fiction, there exists frequent depictions of a theoretical manifestation of the Internet as a unified and comprehensive virtual realm, made possible through the utilization of virtual and augmented reality headsets.

In the event that one has not been exposed to the extensive publicity surrounding it, the concept of the metaverse entails the development of an internet iteration that is notably more immersive, socially-oriented, and enduring compared to the familiar version we currently utilize and appreciate. The utilization of technologies such as virtual reality (VR) and augmented reality (AR) will facilitate a heightened level of engagement, allowing individuals to interact with the digital realm in a more organic and immersive manner. This may involve the utilization of virtual hands to physically manipulate objects, as well as the utilization of vocal commands to issue instructions to machines or engage in communication with other individuals. The *Metaverse* can be conceptualized as the medium by which individuals will interact with web3 tools and applications.

It is feasible to develop web3 applications without incorporating the *Metaverse*, as exemplified by Bitcoin. However, it is widely believed that Metaverse technology and experiences will significantly influence the manner in which numerous applications engage with our daily life.

The emergence of virtual world platforms such as Second Life has facilitated the creation of diverse Metaverses that have gained widespread popularity. One aspect of certain iterations of the *Metaverse* involves the amalgamation of virtual and physical spaces, as well as the integration of virtual economies. The association of virtual reality technology with the development of the *Metaverse* is frequently observed as a means to enhance immersion.

The term in question, employed for the purpose of public relations, has been known to embellish the advancements made in diverse technologies and projects. The social media and video game industries encounter various challenges, wherein the issues of privacy, addiction, and safety emerge as significant concerns within the realm of Metaverses.

The *Decentralized Autonomous Organization (DAO)* is a concept within the web3 framework that refers to a collective, company, or group that operates based on predetermined rules and regulations that are encoded into a blockchain. In the context of a *decentralized autonomous organization (DAO)* shop, the blockchain would serve as a repository for the prices of all items and information regarding the beneficiaries of business pay-outs. The shareholders within the *Decentralized Autonomous Organization (DAO)* possess the authority to exercise their voting rights in order to modify pricing structures or determine the allocation of funds.

Nevertheless, it is imperative to note that the alteration of rules is contingent upon obtaining the necessary authorization, thereby rendering it impossible for any single individual to effect such changes autonomously. Furthermore, it is important to note that individuals who possessed the tangible infrastructure, such as the proprietors of servers or the owners of the establishments where the earnings were stored, were unable to exert any form of intervention, such as absconding with the accumulated profits.

Significantly, *decentralized autonomous organizations (DAOs)* have the potential to completely eliminate the necessity of intermediaries typically involved in organizational operations, including bankers, lawyers, accountants, and landlords.

While the focus of this section primarily revolves around *Ethereum*, it is important to know the main concepts that are applicable to smart contracts, and cryptocurrencies.

The existence of the field of blockchain development can be primarily attributed to the implementation of *smart contracts*.

The primary innovation introduced by *Ethereum* in 2013 was the facilitation of developers to create concise segments of code, referred to as smart contracts, which could be deployed onto the Ethereum network to operate autonomously from their creators. Smart contracts in *Ethereum* are typically coded using Solidity, which is a high-level programming language specifically developed for execution on the *Ethereum Virtual Machine*.

A *smart contract* is a computer program that specifies a collection of regulations, commonly referred to as a "contract," which is capable of autonomously executing the predefined rules upon being invoked by a user within the blockchain network. Specifically, after the deployment of a smart contract, it will consistently operate in the same manner, without the possibility of modification or unauthorized manipulation by malicious entities.

The term *'Altcoins'* is derived from the combination of the words 'alternative' and 'coins,' indicating that they serve as alternative options to Bitcoin. Altcoins emerged as a result of the accomplishments attained by Bitcoin. The developers recognized the inherent potential of the blockchain technology that serves as the foundation for Bitcoin, and subsequently devised novel cryptocurrencies, each possessing distinct attributes and intended applications. The main well known *Altcoins* are:

- ***Litecoin (LTC)*** is a decentralized digital currency that operates on a peer-to-peer network. Its primary objective is to enhance the transaction speed and scalability issues that are inherent in Bitcoin.
- ***Ripple (XRP)*** has gained significant recognition due to its ongoing legal dispute with the Securities and Exchange Commission (SEC) that commenced in late 2020. The Ripple ledger is a digital payment protocol that has been specifically developed to facilitate expedited and cost-effective international transactions.
- ***Cardano (ADA)*** is a blockchain platform that places significant emphasis on security and scalability, employing a research-driven methodology.

- ***Polkadot (DOT)*** is a blockchain platform that facilitates interoperability among different blockchains, allowing for smooth transfers of data and assets.

These are merely a few examples of alternative cryptographic assets, provided here in a concise manner. It is imperative to consistently conduct thorough research prior to making any financial investments.

Throughout the course of your exploration into the realm of cryptocurrencies, you will encounter a diverse array of token types. Among these, the primary applications of digital tokens can be categorized into utility, security, and decentralized finance (DeFi).

The inherent nature of a blockchain is such that it does not engage in communication with external data sources, instead solely serving as a repository for retaining historical user data within the blockchain network.

Blockchain Oracle refers to the intermediary software that facilitates communication between a blockchain and external, off-chain data sources. The integration of off-chain data facilitated by blockchain oracles has significantly advanced the Web3 sector, opening up novel possibilities in decentralized finance and various other domains. The profitability of deploying a blockchain oracle can be realized by individuals who possess or have the ability to access valuable data.

The term *"Oracle"* is widely used and encompasses a wide range of meanings within the industry. There exists a plethora of blockchain oracle protocols available for selection. The *Chainlink* protocol is widely adopted across various layers. Blockchains and the corresponding protocols operating within them, making it the default choice. It should be noted that each oracle option presents distinct prerequisites and protocols for transferring a user's valuable data from Web2 to Web3. While there may be slight variations in the process for each protocol, node hosts encounter comparable challenges. These challenges include the management of routine API maintenance, ensuring efficient and secure data transfer, and acquiring the necessary technical expertise to establish and oversee a node for a blockchain oracle protocol. Application Programming Interfaces (APIs) are utilized by blockchain oracles to establish connections and extract information from external sources. This acquired data is subsequently employed to initiate the execution of smart contracts or modify the state of a blockchain-based application.

The utilization of Web 3.0 extends beyond cryptocurrency, encompassing a wide range of applications. The spectrum of technologies encompasses artificial intelligence and metaverse-like applications, as well as non-fungible tokens and decentralized finance. Consequently, corporations are modifying their operational strategies and transforming the dynamics of consumer engagement with digital content.

Despite being in its nascent phase, the development of Web 3.0 is experiencing significant and rapid expansion. According to estimates, the market size of Web 3.0, which is currently valued at approximately $3 billion in 2023, is projected to reach and exceed $100 billion within the next decade. Certain businesses have already implemented their Web 3.0 applications, whereas others are currently in the process of investigating the potential of this technology for various purposes such as marketing, sales, contracts, and other related applications.

However, similar to any emerging technology, Web3 is not devoid of its own set of challenges and limitations. In order to fully realize the potential of Web3, it is imperative to address various challenges pertaining to scalability, interoperability, and regulatory concerns.

In order to ascertain the most prominent vulnerabilities within Web3 projects, it is imperative to first comprehend the conceptualization of vulnerabilities. The issue pertaining to vulnerability within the realm of cyber security for Web3 solutions stems from the intricate nature of vulnerabilities. The proliferation of Web3 projects has resulted in an unparalleled surge in the prevalence of security concerns.

The primary challenge in ensuring the security of Web3 primarily revolves around the acquisition of specialized expertise. Bug bounty programs have demonstrated their efficacy in detecting vulnerabilities in Web3 systems. However, it is worth noting that a number of cybersecurity experts tend to discredit Web3 and blockchain technologies, perceiving them as fraudulent endeavors.

Web3 is anticipated to have a substantial impact on the forthcoming trajectory of electronic commerce, with the capacity to fundamentally transform the manner in which goods and services are exchanged over the internet. The advent of the digital era has ushered in numerous captivating transformations in the realm of online shopping and business operations.

It is anticipated that in the forthcoming decade, a wide range of industries, encompassing retail and e-commerce, media and entertainment, healthcare, technology, and energy, among others, will embrace the utilization of Web3.0 blockchain technology within their operational frameworks. The development and implementation of Web3.0 are closely intertwined with the utilization of blockchain technology, although its reliance on cryptocurrencies is not an essential requirement. Based on a multitude of research studies, it is anticipated that Web3.0 technology will imminently attain its adoption tipping point, leading various industries such as aircraft maintenance and food safety to tokenize their applications. The blockchain technology has demonstrated its efficacy in enhancing the security of cryptocurrencies and non-fungible tokens (NFTs), thereby positioning itself to revolutionize future web technologies across various industries.

This book titled *Decentralizing the Online Experience With Web3 Technologies* is giving focus on Web 3 main concepts, technologies and tools, and the driving forces behind the Web 3 growth. Also, this book concentrates on the recent developments and trends in the Web 3, including several emerging topics in this area, and illustrates their importance.

This book is composed of seventeen chapters; ranging from introducing Web 3, its technologies, and tools, the Driving Forces Behind Web3's Growth, Blockchain basics, Wallets and transactions, Crypto coins and Ethereum, Defi, NFTs, Metaverse, DAOs, Smart contracts, Oracles, Web3 Applications, Web3 Use Cases, Web3 Benefits and Challenges, as well as discussing the future of Web3.

The intended audience of this book comprises students who are pursuing undergraduate or postgraduate studies, as well as professionals and researchers engaged in the domains of information technology, business and management, education, media and communications, social sciences, and humanities, and are interested in staying abreast of the latest advancements in Web 3.0.

Dina Darwish
Ahram Canadian University, Egypt

Chapter 1
Web 3:
Definition, Technologies, and Tools

Dina Darwish
Ahram Canadian University, Egypt

ABSTRACT

The potential of Web 3.0 to bring about a substantial paradigm shift and disrupt the current landscape is comparable to the disruptive nature and paradigm shift brought about by Web 2.0. The core principles underpinning Web 3.0 are decentralization, openness, and enhanced consumer utility. Web 3.0, commonly referred to as Web 3, represents the subsequent phase in the evolutionary trajectory of the internet. Envision a novel iteration of the internet that possesses the capability to precisely translate textual input and comprehend spoken language, regardless of the medium employed. Furthermore, this hypothetical internet iteration would offer an unprecedented level of personalization in the content consumed by users. In the context of the internet's evolutionary trajectory, we are on the cusp of embarking upon a novel era. The term "Web 3.0" has been coined. The concept of Web 3.0 refers to the next generation of the world wide web, characterized by advanced technologies and functionalities that aim to enhance user experiences and enable more intelligent and personalized interactions. This chapter discusses the Web 3 definition, technologies and tools, as well as its benefits for individuals and companies.

INTRODUCTION

Web 3.0 is designed to yield sustainable outcomes by leveraging distributed ledger technology and smart contracts, thereby enabling its decentralized structure. Additionally, it reduces expenses by eliminating intermediaries, manual intervention, and the need for arbitration. Web 3.0 provides a significantly more personalized browsing experience for all users. In the future, websites will possess the capability to adapt seamlessly to various devices, geographical locations, and individual accessibility requirements. Additionally, web applications will exhibit enhanced responsiveness to our unique usage behaviors.

The proponents of Web 3.0 assert that its advent will yield significant enhancements to our daily existence, citing three justifiable rationales. In this study, we aim to investigate the effects of climate change on biodiversity in a tropical Enhancing the Personalization of Web Browsing Experience The

DOI: 10.4018/979-8-3693-1532-3.ch001

convenience of promptly accessing a specific offer for a desired or necessary item, which might have otherwise gone unnoticed, cannot be disregarded, despite occasional feelings of intrusiveness associated with such advertisements. The user's text is too short to rewrite in an academic manner. As previously stated, employing a natural language search engine yields significant efficacy. The advantages extend beyond the consumer, as the learning curve becomes virtually non-existent. Additionally, businesses are progressively capable of optimizing their websites for search engines through a more natural approach, rather than relying on intricate keyword techniques.

The advent of the multidimensional Web 3.0 holds the potential to extend its benefits beyond traditional websites, as it empowers web applications to offer users significantly enhanced and immersive experiences. Take into consideration a cartographic service such as Google, which has expanded its capabilities to encompass not only the basic functionality of locating places, but also includes features such as route optimization, recommendations for accommodations, and real-time traffic information. In the context of the Web 2.0 era, it was not feasible to accomplish this task.

The emergence of Web 3.0 is expected to encompass the following characteristics:

- The utilization of open-source software is anticipated for the construction of content platforms.
- The adoption of a trustless approach, wherein Zero Trust principles are universally embraced, will result in the extension of network security measures to the periphery.
- The distributed nature of interaction among devices, users, and services will enable their communication and collaboration without requiring approval from a central authority.
- The utilization of blockchain technology will facilitate direct communication between users in the forthcoming phase of the internet. Users will engage in communication by actively participating in a Decentralized Autonomous Organization (DAO), which is a collective entity governed and owned by its community members.
- The user's data will be safeguarded through a network of publicly accessible smart contracts. The contracts will be stored within a blockchain, which is a decentralized network governed by nodes.

The tracking of all transactions will be facilitated through the utilization of a distributed ledger system that employs blockchain technology, thereby ensuring a decentralized approach to data transfers. The utilization of open-access smart contracts will alleviate individuals from the necessity of depending on a centralized entity, such as a financial institution, for the preservation of data integrity. The metaverse is expected to yield substantial revenue growth for the entertainment industry. The utilization of blockchain technology will facilitate the instantaneous creation of digital goods and non-fungible tokens (NFTs), thereby ensuring the safeguarding of intellectual property and personally identifiable information (PII) for consumers. The data of users can be monetized.

This chapter discusses the importance of Web 3, its technologies and tools. And how Web 3 benefits the companies and individuals. The main topics to be covered in this chapter includes the following;

- Definition of Web 2
- Definition of Web 3
- Difference between Web 1, Web 2 and Web 3
- The technologies of Web 3
- The comparative advantages of Web 3 in relation to its preceding iterations
- The concept of Web 3 within the realm of cryptocurrency

- Blockchain security
- Layers of Web 3
- The functioning mechanism of Web 3
- The main applications of Web 3
- The advantages and disadvantages of Web 3
- The importance of Web 3 and its tools
- The Future trends for Web 3
- The future scopes of Web 3 for the enterprises

Also, this chapter is organized as follows; the first section contains the background, then, the second section includes the main focus of the chapter, including the main topics mentioned in the previous section, then finally, comes the conclusion section.

BACKGROUND

Despite the absence of a formal definition, Web 3.0 exhibits several distinctive attributes; *Decentralization* stands as a fundamental principle within the context of Web 3.0. In the context of Web 2.0, computer systems are designed to retrieve data from a specific, stationary location, often referred to as a server, by utilizing the Hypertext Transfer Protocol (HTTP) and accessing unique web addresses. The decentralization of information is a key characteristic of Web 3.0, as it enables the simultaneous storage of data in multiple locations. In this paradigm, information retrieval is based on content rather than relying on a single centralized location. By dismantling the extensive databases currently maintained by internet giants such as Meta and Google, individuals would be empowered to a greater extent. Web 3.0 will empower users to engage in the sale of their personal data via decentralized data networks, thereby guaranteeing their retention of ownership control. The aforementioned data will be generated by a diverse range of high-performance computing resources, including but not limited to mobile phones, desktop computers, household appliances, automobiles, and sensors.

Web 3.0, characterized by decentralization and *open source software*, will exhibit trustlessness, enabling participants to engage in direct interactions without relying on a trusted intermediary. Additionally, it will be permissionless, granting individuals unrestricted access without requiring authorization from any governing entity. This implies that Web 3.0 applications, commonly referred to as dApps, will function on blockchains, decentralized peer-to-peer networks, or a combination of both. Such decentralized applications are commonly known as dApps.

Artificial intelligence (AI) and machine learning have the potential to enhance the capabilities of machines to understand information in a manner that is comparable to human comprehension. This advancement is anticipated to be facilitated by the Semantic Web and technologies based on natural language processing, leading to the emergence of Web 3.0. Web 3.0 is anticipated to incorporate machine learning, a branch of artificial intelligence (AI) that emulates human learning through the utilization of data and algorithms, progressively enhancing its precision. Rather than solely focusing on targeted advertising, which currently constitutes the majority of existing endeavors, these capabilities will lead to expedited and more pertinent outcomes across various domains such as medical advancements and novel materials. The advent of Web 3.0 has resulted in enhanced connectivity and ubiquity, enabling greater accessibility of content and information across various applications. Furthermore, the proliferation of internet-connected devices has further contributed to this phenomenon. The Internet of Things represents a prominent illustration in this context.

Web3 technology is frequently linked to *cryptocurrencies and non-fungible tokens (NFTs)*; however, it possesses the capacity to fundamentally transform our perspective on enterprise computing. A novel cohort of infrastructure is currently emerging, employing consensus, verification, and transparency mechanisms to tackle the foremost challenges in contemporary enterprise computing. In order to comprehend the positioning of Web3, it is imperative to contemplate the impetus behind the pursuit of a more inclusive marketplace for computational resources.

The forces that underlie the adoption of hybrid, multi-cloud infrastructures are aligned with the driving factors behind the emergence of Web3. These factors include *security, reliability, risk management, portability, interoperability, and cost management*. As cloud architectures are being refactored to accommodate this transition, the emergence of Web3 is observed as the subsequent advancement in the computational infrastructure that we currently depend on, progressing from virtual machines (VMs) to containers and eventually to serverless functions.

A paper (Schürmann, & Möller, 2017) describes Web 3.0's major principles and technologies. The authors emphasize the importance of decentralization, interoperability, and semantic technologies for Web 3.0. The authors review Web 3.0 research and development, including projects such as Ethereum and IPFS. In the paper, research (Schlebusch, 2018) summarizes literature and technologies to suggest a definition for Web 3.0. Blockchain and other distributed ledger technologies allow decentralized, trustless user-system interactions, which the author believes defines Web 3.0. The author explores Web 3.0's privacy, security, and governance concerns.

Research (Berners-Lee et al., 2001) envisions Web 3.0, a future web with personalized and decentralized content. The future generation of the web should utilize intelligent agents to comprehend and process user choices and deliver personalized services, according to the authors. Semantic web technologies are also stressed in the article for this aim. Another research (Mougayar, 2016) examines Web 3.0, as a blockchain-enabled decentralized computing paradigm. The author claims that Web 3.0 shifts from centralized, siloed platforms to decentralized networks that facilitate peer-to-peer interactions and value sharing. Author examines Web 3.0's effects on banking, healthcare, and media. A research (Mashinsky, & Krug, 2020) discusses Web 3.0 development using machine intelligence. The authors believe that intelligent agents would interpret and analyze massive volumes of data in Web 3.0, allowing more personalized and efficient services in banking, healthcare, and transportation. This paper (Kim, & Kahng, 2020) addresses the evolution of web from Web 1.0 through Web3.0 and blockchain technology's importance. The authors suggest that Web 3.0 shifts from centralized, closed systems to decentralized, open platforms that allow peer-to-peer interactions and value exchange. This paper (Kreminski, 2019) examines Web 3.0's future via decentralization, interoperability, and intelligence. The author claims that Web3.0 shifts from centralized, profit-driven Web 2.0 to an open, collaborative, user-centric web with governance, regulatory, and sustainability challenges. Another paper (Giaccardi, & Zaga, 2021) mentioned that Web 3.0 may affect social networks through decentralization, interoperability, and user empowerment. Web 3.0 might make social networks more open, democratic, and user-centric, enabling peer-to-peer interactions and value sharing, according to the authors. The paper also examines Web 3.0's privacy, security, and user control difficulties and potential for social network architecture. This research (Mehrpouyan, & Sadeghian, 2021) explores the effects of Web 3.0 on e-commerce, emphasizing decentralization, interoperability, and trust. Web 3.0 might make e-commerce more decentralized, open, and trustworthy, enabling peer-to-peer interactions and value sharing, according to the authors.

This paper (Ball, 2022) addresses Web 3.0's influence on media, concentrating on decentralization, interoperability, and user empowerment. Web 3.0 might make media more open, democratic, and user-centric, enabling new content creation, distribution, and monetization, according to the author. Another research (Jánszky, & Pinker, 2021) describes Web 3.0's features, technologies, and applications. Web 3.0, powered by technologies such as blockchain, AI, and IoT, shifts from a web of documents to a web of data and applications, according to the authors. A research (Flynn, & Ferreira, 2021; Nasar, & Kausar, 2019; Kausar, & Nasar, 2021) discusses decentralized apps (dApps) to promote Web 3.0 development. DApps, which use blockchain and other decentralized technologies, may disrupt businesses and allow new peer-to-peer interaction and value exchange, according to the authors.

The global society is progressing towards an Internet landscape wherein individuals possess full autonomy over their data and privacy, while simultaneously affording companies the option to either capitalize on or abstain from such exploitation. The feasibility of these advancements will be facilitated by the implementation of blockchain technology. Consequently, the advent of web 3.0 is expected to expedite the equitable and transparent utilization of user data, encompassing personalized search outcomes, cross-platform software development resources, and three-dimensional visual representations. In the coming years, it is anticipated that the internet will undergo further advancements to enhance its immersive and engaging qualities.

MAIN FOCUS OF THE CHAPTER

Definition of Web 2

The term "Web 2.0" refers to a concept that emerged in the early 2000s, which represents a shift in the way the internet is used and experienced. The evolution from Web 1.0 to Web 2.0 is characterized by a shift from a limited number of content creators catering to a larger audience, to a scenario where numerous individuals generate a significantly greater amount of content for an increasingly diverse and expanding audience. Web 2.0 places a greater emphasis on active participation and contribution compared to the predominantly passive act of reading in Web 1.0.

The primary areas of focus for this particular form of Internet are user-generated content (UGC), usability, interaction, and enhanced connectivity with other systems and devices. In the context of Web 2.0, the centrality of the user experience is paramount. Consequently, this particular Web form was responsible for facilitating the establishment of social media platforms, fostering collaborations, and nurturing communities. Web 2.0 is widely recognized as the prevailing approach to web engagement for a significant portion of contemporary users. Web 2.0 is commonly characterized as the "participatory social Web," in contrast to Web 1.0 which was commonly known as the "read-only Web." The advancement and integration of web browser technologies, particularly JavaScript frameworks, have contributed to the enhancement and expansion of Web 2.0 in relation to its predecessor.

The characteristic attributes commonly associated with Web 2.0 can be categorized as follows:

- The system incorporates dynamic content that responds to user input.
- The utilization of sophisticated application programming interfaces (APIs) is employed.

- This platform promotes individual utilization and facilitates various modes of engagement such as podcasting, social media integration, tagging, blogging, commenting, curating through RSS, social networking, and web content evaluation.
- The platform provides users with the capability to collectively retrieve and categorize data, thereby facilitating the process of information sorting at no cost.
- The utilization of advanced application programming interfaces (APIs) is implemented.
- The utilization of developed information is pervasive across society at large, rather than being limited to specific communities.

Definition of Web 3

The individual responsible for the creation of the World Wide Web, Tim Berners-Lee, initially labelled Web 3.0 as the Semantic Web. He envisioned an intellectually advanced, self-reliant, and accessible Internet that harnessed the capabilities of artificial intelligence and machine learning. This envisioned Internet would operate as a "global brain," proficiently comprehending and interpreting content in both conceptual and contextual manners. The failure of this idealized version can be attributed to technological limitations, specifically the high cost and complexity associated with translating human language into machine-readable format. The subsequent enumeration comprises a set of characteristic features commonly associated with Web 3.0. The semantic web represents a significant advancement in the realm of internet technology, facilitating the generation, dissemination, and interlinking of digital content through the utilization of search and analytical mechanisms. Rather than relying on numerical values and specific terms, the focus is primarily on the comprehension and interpretation of words.

The system employs machine learning and artificial intelligence techniques. The ultimate outcome entails the emergence of Web 3.0, which exhibits enhanced intelligence and increased responsiveness to user requirements. When these concepts are combined with Natural Language Processing (NLP), the outcome is a computational system that employs NLP techniques.

This statement demonstrates the interconnectedness facilitated by the Internet of Things (IoT), wherein diverse devices and applications are linked together. The implementation of this procedure is facilitated by the utilization of semantic metadata, enabling the effective utilization of all accessible data resources. Furthermore, the internet can be accessed by individuals from any location and at any given moment, even in the absence of a computer or other technologically advanced device. The platform offers users the option to engage in either public or private interactions, safeguarding them from potential risks associated with intermediaries. This ensures the provision of "trustless" data.

Three-dimensional (3-D) graphics are employed. Indeed, the aforementioned phenomenon is readily apparent in the domains of e-commerce, virtual tours, and computer gaming. Facilitating participation without necessitating authorization from a governing body is a notable advantage. The action is conducted without proper authorization.

This concept has practical relevance in the following contexts:

- ***Metaverses*** refer to expansive virtual environments that are rendered in three dimensions, offering boundless possibilities for exploration and interaction.
- ***Blockchain-based video games*** align with the principles of non-fungible tokens (NFTs) as they empower users to establish genuine ownership over in-game assets. This application utilizes zero-

knowledge proofs and enhanced measures for safeguarding personal data, thereby addressing the concerns surrounding digital infrastructure and privacy.

- ***The concept of financial decentralization*** refers to the distribution of financial decision-making authority and control away from a central authority to various entities or Examples of this application include peer-to-peer digital financial transactions, smart contracts, and cryptocurrencies.
- ***Autonomous decentralized organizations (ADOs)*** refer to entities that operate with a high degree of self-governance and distribute decision-making authority across multiple nodes or participants. The ownership of online communities is vested in the community itself.

Difference between Web 1, Web 2 and Web 3

This section aims to explore the distinctions among Web 1.0, Web 2.0, and Web 3.0, with a focus on their respective characteristics and functionalities. Figure 1 shows the evolution of the web, and Table 1 illustrates the differences between Web 1, Web 2, and Web 3.

Figure 1. The evolution of the web

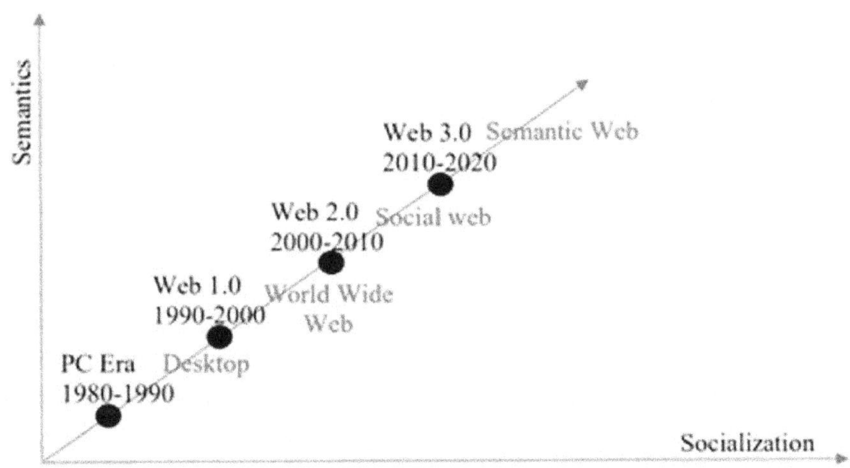

Table 1. The difference between Web 1.0, Web 2.0, and Web 3.0

	Web 1.0	*Web 2.0*	*Web 3.0*
Naming	known as the first generation of the World Wide Web, refers to the initial stage of the internet	refers to the second generation of the World Wide Web, characterized by the shift from static web	known as the third generation of the World Wide Web, refers to the envisioned evolution of the internet
Content	Static	Dynamic	Intelligent
User role	Passive	Active	Collaborative
Data	HTML	XML, AJAX, JSON	Semantic Web
Web technologies	In the 1990s, despite its limited information and minimal user interaction, it emerged as the inaugural and most dependable internet platform.	The internet has become significantly more interactive due to advancements in web technologies, including but not limited to Javascript, HTML5, CSS3, and the emergence of Web 2.0.	Web 3.0 represents a significant milestone in the progression of the Internet, facilitating its capacity to comprehend data in a manner akin to human cognition.
Interaction with users	Previously, the concept of user pages or the ability to comment on articles did not exist.	The proliferation of social networks and the production of user-generated content have experienced significant growth due to the increased ability to distribute and share data.	The proposed system will leverage AI technology, Machine Learning, and Blockchain to deliver intelligent applications to users.
Search capabilities	The lack of algorithms to scan websites in Online 1.0 posed a challenge for consumers in their search for valuable information.	Several notable web inventors, such as Jeffrey Zeldman mentioned earlier, played a pioneering role in developing the suite of technologies utilized in the current era of the internet.	This capability will facilitate the intelligent generation and dissemination of customized content to each individual user on the internet.
Focus	Company	Community	Individual

The Technologies of Web 3

The transition from Web 2.0 to Web 3.0 is occurring gradually and without significant attention from the general populace. Web 3.0 applications exhibit a similar visual and experiential interface to their 2.0 counterparts, yet they possess a fundamentally distinct underlying infrastructure. The future of Web 3.0 entails the development of universal applications that possess the capability to be accessed and utilized by a diverse array of devices and software types. This advancement is expected to enhance the convenience of both commercial and leisure activities. The emergence of technologies like distributed ledgers and blockchain storage will facilitate the decentralization of data and the creation of a transparent and secure ecosystem. This development will challenge the centralized nature, surveillance practices, and exploitative advertising prevalent in Web 2.0. In the context of a decentralized web, the empowerment of individuals to exercise rightful control over their data is anticipated to occur through the displacement of centralized technology companies by decentralized infrastructure and application platforms. In order to gain a deeper understanding of the intricacies and nuances of Web 3.0, it is imperative to examine its fundamental technologies.

1. ***Semantic web***. The concept of the *semantic web* refers to a framework that enables the sharing and integration of data across different platforms and applications. The integration of the "*semantic web*" is an essential element within the framework of Web 3.0. The term "Semantic Web" was introduced by Tim Berners-Lee in order to denote a network of information that can be processed and interpreted by machines. Could you please clarify the meaning of that statement in simpler

terms? What is the precise meaning of the term "semantics"? What is the differentiation between the statement "I have a strong affection for Bitcoin" and the expression "I love Bitcoin"? While there are differences in the syntax between the two phrases, their semantics exhibit similarity. Semantics pertains to the interpretation of meaning and emotional expression conveyed by statements, and both of the aforementioned sentences convey identical emotions in the given example. The two fundamental pillars of Web 3.0 consist of the semantic web and artificial intelligence. The utilization of the semantic web holds the potential to facilitate the process of imparting meaning to data, thereby enabling artificial intelligence (AI) to advance in its ability to generate practical applications that can effectively leverage the available data resources. The central idea revolves around the establishment of a comprehensive network of knowledge across the internet, which will facilitate the comprehension of word meanings and facilitate the generation, dissemination, and interconnection of content through search and analysis. The advent of Web 3.0 is expected to enhance data communication capabilities through the utilization of semantic metadata. Consequently, the user experience advances to a heightened level of connectivity that effectively utilizes all available data.

2. ***Blockchain*** is widely recognized as a prominent component of Web3, owing to its pivotal role in facilitating the functioning of Bitcoin and several other cryptocurrencies. Nevertheless, blockchain technology may be used across several domains, including accountancy, data storage, and communication. The technology in question is a decentralized digital ledger that has a high level of resistance against unauthorized access. If one has the fallacy that the blockchain is impervious to breaches, it is evident that there is a significant knowledge gap about this technology that needs to be addressed. Enrolling in a blockchain programming bootcamp might be beneficial in addressing knowledge gaps. By establishing a comprehensive knowledge foundation at now, individuals may enhance their preparedness for the broad use of blockchain technology.
3. ***Smart contracts*** are self-executing agreements with the terms of the agreement directly written into code. These contracts are stored on a blockchain and automatically execute when certain conditions are met. Smart contracts are software programs that autonomously execute and carry out the necessary steps to fulfil a contractual agreement. In order to develop smart contracts, it is necessary to acquire proficiency in Solidity and get familiarity with the Ethereum blockchain, since it served as the pioneering platform for the emergence of smart contracts.
4. ***The Internet of Things (IoT)*** is a network of interconnected devices that are capable of collecting and exchanging data over the internet. The Internet of Things (IoT) facilitates the interconnection of commonplace entities, including lights, sensors, vehicles, and other things, with the internet, enabling the seamless flow of data and the execution of many functionalities. The use of this technology is now being implemented across several sectors, including healthcare, transportation, and finance. The combined use of IoT and blockchain has the potential to safeguard both organizations and people from many types of damage. The use of blockchain technology may effectively enhance the security of Internet of Things (IoT) devices by implementing robust security protocols, including the deployment of secure smart contracts and the creation of immutable data records.
5. ***Cloud computing*** refers to the practice of using a network of remote servers, often hosted on the internet, to store, manage, and process data. Cloud computing involves the provision of distant services, such as data storage and computer power, via internet connectivity. Cloud computing has become an increasingly indispensable technology for organizations, owing to its notable attributes of flexibility and dependability. Consequently, it has become imperative for individuals to acquire knowledge and skills in cloud computing, as it plays a pivotal role in supporting and facilitating

everyday company operations. This makes it a significant technology to prioritize learning in the year 2023.

6. ***Edge computing*** refers to a distributed computing paradigm that involves processing and analyzing data at or near the source of data generation, rather than relying on a centralized cloud infrastructure. The term "edge" refers to devices that are situated in close proximity to either the data source or the end user. Edge computing is sometimes misconstrued as being synonymous with cloud computing; however, it is, in fact, a distinct and separate concept. Edge computing refers to the practice of executing computational tasks on devices located at the periphery of a network. Edge computing may be conceptualized as an advancement over cloud computing, since it provides a more optimized approach for data processing and analysis. Both cloud and edge computing will play a crucial role in Web3. However, the use of edge computing is essential for the purpose of compressing substantial volumes of data, hence enhancing computational efficiency and reducing loading times.
7. ***Three-dimensional graphics***, commonly referred to as *3D graphics*, are a form of computer-generated imagery that simulates the appearance of the reality. The future of the internet will be significantly impacted by the emergence of Web 3.0, which represents a transition from the current two-dimensional web to a more immersive and realistic three-dimensional cyberworld. Web 3.0 websites and services, encompassing domains such as e-commerce, online gaming, and the real estate market, extensively employ three-dimensional design elements. Despite its initial peculiarity, it is an undeniable fact that a considerable number of individuals from various parts of the globe are presently engaging in interactions within this particular setting. As an illustration, let us consider online gaming platforms such as Second Life or World of Warcraft, wherein participants exhibit a greater degree of concern for the welfare of their virtual avatars as opposed to their real-life counterparts.
8. ***Artificial Intelligence (AI)*** refers to the field of computer science that focuses on the development of intelligent machines capable of performing tasks that require human intelligence. Artificial intelligence will enable websites to effectively filter and provide users with the most accurate and reliable information. During the contemporary era of Web 2.0, organizations have initiated the practice of actively seeking customer feedback as a means to gain a deeper comprehension of the quality of a product or asset. Take into consideration a platform such as Rotten Tomatoes, wherein individuals have the ability to assign ratings and provide critiques for films. Movies that receive higher ratings are frequently considered to be of high quality. Compilations of this nature enable us to bypass the inclusion of subpar information and promptly access the superior data. However, it is widely acknowledged that human recommendations are not infallible. A collective of individuals may form an alliance with the intention of providing unwarranted favorable evaluations for a film in order to artificially boost its ratings. Artificial intelligence possesses the capability to acquire the ability to differentiate between high-quality and low-quality data, thereby enabling the provision of reliable and trustworthy information.
9. The term "***ubiquitous***" refers to something that is present or found everywhere, or The term "ubiquitous" pertains to the notion of simultaneous existence or presence in multiple locations, commonly referred to as omnipresence. The functionality in question is currently accessible within the framework of Web 2.0. Take into consideration social media platforms like Instagram, wherein individuals capture photographs using their mobile devices and subsequently upload and disseminate them on the internet, thereby establishing ownership over said images as their intellectual

property. Once uploaded, the image attains ubiquity, thereby becoming universally accessible. The ubiquity of mobile devices and internet connectivity will enable universal access to the Web 3.0 experience, transcending geographical and temporal constraints. The internet's accessibility has evolved beyond the confines of desktop computers during the Web 1.0 era and smartphones during the Web 2.0 era. The entity in question will possess unlimited power. Due to the pervasive connectivity of various objects through the Internet of Things (IoT), it is plausible to designate Web 3.0 as the interconnected web encompassing all entities and locations.

10. ***Decentralized Finance (DeFi).*** Decentralized Finance (DeFi) is a well recognized term within the Web3 community, garnering significant attention and interest. Decentralized Finance (DeFi) aims to fundamentally transform the manner in which individuals engage in the acquisition of goods and services. Due to the use of smart contracts, decentralized finance (DeFi) enables both enterprises and individuals to conduct transactions autonomously, eliminating the need for intermediary entities. The concepts of Web3 and blockchain gained significant prominence due to their association with decentralized finance (DeFi), indicating a discernible trajectory towards the adoption of a token-based economic framework in the foreseeable future. What is the rationale behind this? DeFi transactions are executed using algorithms that possess the characteristics of traceability, transparency, and security over the whole of the blockchain network.
11. ***Non-Fungible Tokens (NFTs)*** are digital assets that are unique and indivisible, making them distinct from other cryptocurrencies like Bitcoin or Ethereum. NFTs are built on blockchain technology, which ensures an NFT refers to a distinct cryptographic token that encompasses exclusive information, which can only be accessed by the individual who has the NFT. Assets, such as music, graphics, and gaming elements, may be represented by them. Non-fungible tokens (NFTs) are poised to see a surge in popularity and use due to their increasing adoption within the realm of video games.

The utilization of the Spatial Web, also known as Web 3.0, in its initial phases is already evident, despite its futuristic nature. The present moment necessitates business executives to acquire a comprehensive understanding of the forthcoming computer era, its implications on enterprises, and the potential for generating novel value as it progresses. Furthermore, individuals must be equipped to comprehend the manner in which certain well-established and innovative Web 3.0 business models will accumulate value in the forthcoming years through an analysis of current and pragmatic Web 3.0 business models. The following sections enumerate several approaches.

The act of creating and distributing a native asset. The operation of the network necessitates the presence of these indigenous assets, which obtain their worth from the security they offer. By furnishing a sufficiently enticing motivation for sincere miners to contribute their computational resources, the expense for malevolent entities to execute an assault escalates in proportion to the value of the indigenous asset. Furthermore, the augmented security engenders a heightened desire for the currency, thereby propelling its price and value. Consequently, a comprehensive evaluation and quantification of the value of these indigenous resources has been conducted.

Constructing a network through the act of retaining the indigenous asset. Several initial cryptocurrency network companies were primarily driven by the objective of enhancing the profitability and financial viability of their networks. The business model that emerged can be succinctly described as "expanding their native asset treasury and cultivating the ecosystem." Blockstream, being a prominent maintainer of Bitcoin Core, leverages its BTC balance sheet to create value. In a similar vein, ConsenSys has experienced substantial growth, expanding its workforce to encompass a significant number of employees, who are actively engaged in the development of essential infrastructure for the Ethereum network.

Tokens. ETH, short for Ethereum, is a decentralized, open-source blockchain platform that enables the creation of tokens. The user seeks to enhance the value of their Ethereum (ETH) holdings by leveraging the ecosystem. Payment tokens are digital or virtual representations of currency that can be used to facilitate transactions. These tokens are typically issued by a central authority. The emergence of token sales has led to the development of blockchain initiatives that center their business models on payment tokens within networks. These initiatives frequently establish two-sided marketplaces and mandate the utilization of a native token for all transactions. Based on the underlying assumptions, it can be posited that as the network's economy expands, there will be an increase in demand for the native *payment token* that is subject to restrictions, consequently leading to an appreciation in the token's value.

The act of incinerating or destroying tokens. The direct distribution of earnings to token holders may not always be feasible for corporations, communities, and initiatives that utilize tokens. The concept of buybacks and *token burns* has garnered significant attention as a prominent feature within the Binance ecosystem. Binance Coin (BNB) is a digital cryptocurrency that operates on the Binance blockchain. The acronym "MKR" refers to MakerDAO, a decentralized autonomous organization that operates on. The term "tokens" refers to discrete units or symbols that hold meaning within a specific context The project engages in the repurchase and subsequent burning of native tokens acquired from the public market, as revenue is generated through Binance trading fees and MakerDAO stability fees. This practice leads to a reduction in token supply and a subsequent rise in token price.

Taxes can be imposed on speculative activities. The subsequent iteration of business models focused on the establishment of the financial framework for these indigenous assets, encompassing exchanges, custodians, and providers of derivatives. All of these platforms were developed with a singular objective in mind: to offer services to individuals seeking to engage in speculation on these high-risk assets. Due to the open and permissionless nature of the underlying networks, it is not possible for organizations such as Coinbase to establish a monopolistic position by offering "exclusive access." However, these companies can still maintain a competitive advantage over time through their liquidity and strong brand presence, which serve as barriers to entry for potential competitors.

The Comparative Advantages of Web 3 in Relation to Its Preceding Iterations

Due to the absence of intermediaries in Web 3.0, the control over user data will no longer be exerted. This approach reduces the probability of censorship by governmental or corporate entities, as well as mitigates the impact of denial-of-service (DoS) attacks. As an increasing number of products are connected to the internet, the availability of larger datasets provides algorithms with a greater amount of information to evaluate. This will enable them to provide more precise information that is customized to meet the specific needs of each user. Prior to the emergence of Web 3.0, the process of locating the most precise outcome on search engines posed a formidable challenge. Over time, there has been an improvement in their capacity to identify search results that are semantically relevant by taking into account search context and information. Consequently, the convenience of web browsing is enhanced, enabling individuals to access the precise information they need with considerable ease.

The provision of customer service plays a crucial role in ensuring a favorable user experience on websites and web applications. Nevertheless, a considerable number of prosperous web enterprises encounter challenges when attempting to expand their customer support operations as a result of the substantial costs involved. Users can enhance their engagement with support personnel by utilizing intelligent chatbots that have the capability to interact with multiple consumers concurrently, a functionality made feasible by the implementation of Web 3.0.

The Concept of Web 3 Within the Realm of Cryptocurrency

In the context of Web 3.0, cryptocurrency is a topic that is commonly referenced. The reason for this is that a significant number of the protocols associated with Web 3.0 are heavily dependent on cryptocurrencies. In contrast, it provides a financial motivation (in the form of tokens) for individuals interested in participating in the creation, governance, contribution, or enhancement of any of the projects. Web 3.0 tokens refer to digital assets that are intrinsically linked to the concept of establishing a decentralized Internet. These protocols have the potential to offer a range of services, including computation, bandwidth, storage, identification, hosting, and other online services that were previously offered by cloud providers.

An example of a protocol that operates on the Ethereum platform is Livepeer. This protocol facilitates the creation of a marketplace where video infrastructure providers and streaming applications can interact. In a similar vein, Helium employs mechanisms to motivate consumers and small enterprises to contribute and validate wireless connectivity, as well as transmit device data across the network by leveraging blockchain technology and tokens. Individuals have the opportunity to generate income by engaging in the protocol through a diverse range of avenues, encompassing both technical and non-technical means. The service's consumers generally remunerate for utilizing the protocol, akin to compensating a cloud provider such as Amazon Web Services. Similar to various types of decentralization, unnecessary and often inefficient intermediaries are eradicated.

Moreover, the development of Web 3.0 will be significantly dependent on nonfungible tokens (NFTs), digital currencies, and other entities within the blockchain ecosystem. One notable example is Reddit, which is currently endeavoring to establish a presence in the realm of Web 3.0. This is being pursued through the development of a system that utilizes cryptocurrency tokens, enabling users to effectively exert control over specific aspects of the online communities in which they actively engage. The underlying notion entails users utilizing "community points," which they would accrue through their contributions on a designated subreddit. The user subsequently formulates arguments based on the aggregate number of upvotes or downvotes received by a specific post. The concept can be understood as a blockchain-based adaptation of the Reddit Karma system.

These points can effectively function as voting shares, granting users who have made substantial contributions a greater influence in decisions that impact the community. Due to the utilization of blockchain technology, the possession of these points grants their owners enhanced authority, rendering them impervious to arbitrary confiscation while concurrently facilitating comprehensive monitoring capabilities. In all fairness, the aforementioned use case represents a singular instance of a corporate adaptation of the Web 3.0 concept termed Decentralized Autonomous Organizations (DAOs). DAOs employ tokens as a means to facilitate a more equitable distribution of ownership and decision-making power.

Blockchain Security

Concerns about data security need to be addressed as more businesses investigate the usage of Blockchain technology. This will guarantee that sensitive information is kept private. When adopting a Blockchain solution for an organization, there are a number of different security measures that need be taken into consideration. Identity and access management, often known as IAM, is essential for ensuring that the system is only accessible to people who have been authorized to do so. In order to sign transactions and access data, private keys are required, hence proper key management is also quite important.

It is essential to give careful thought to data privacy in order to prevent unauthorized parties from gaining access to sensitive information. Establishing encrypted communication between nodes is necessary in order to protect against activities such as eavesdropping and man-in-the-middle attacks.

Auditing of smart contracts is also vital to preventing flaws in the smart contracts themselves, which might be exploited by attackers. When it comes to launching and maintaining their Blockchain apps, businesses may benefit from the assistance of a genuine smart contract auditing service. Last but not least, the need that several parties sign off on each transaction is one way that transaction endorsement may assist strengthen the security of a Blockchain.

The use of blockchain technology is growing in popularity across a variety of sectors, including banking and finance, healthcare, and supply chain management, and others. Learners who are interested might even sign up for training to become Blockchain Solution Architects in order to master the fundamentals of blockchain architecture and how to create applications using it.

The need for efficient penetration testing services is only going to increase as the usage of blockchain technology becomes more widespread. Blockchain penetration testing helps evaluate the level of security provided by Blockchain apps and locates any flaws that might be exploited by malicious actors.

An efficient Blockchain penetration test will include crucial components such as functional testing, performance testing, API testing, security testing, and integration testing. Ethical hackers do a test of a system called a penetration test, in which they look for and try to exploit any flaws they find. This assists in locating and fixing any vulnerabilities before they may be used by thieves.

Tools Used to Test Blockchain Security

There are a variety of methods for assessing Blockchain security that are now available on the market. The following is a quick rundown of some of the most well-liked available choices:

- Truffle is a popular Ethereum development framework that comes with a set of tools for testing and debugging smart contracts. Truffle was developed by the Truffle Project.
- Ganache is a personal Ethereum blockchain that may be used for testing and development. Ganache was developed by the Ganache team. It comes with a user interface that allows users to communicate with smart contracts.
- TestRPC is a simulator for Ethereum smart contracts that is built on top of the Node.js platform. You are able to put your contracts through their paces on a simulated version of Ethereum's network.
- Myth X: An investigation into the safety of smart contracts
- SWC-registry is an inventory of test cases and a categorization system for smart contracts.
- Oyente is a tool for doing static analysis.
- Manticore is a tool for the execution of symbols.
- The static smart contract security analyzer is known as SmartCheck.
- A security checkup is what Securify 2.0 is all about.
- Solgraph is an application that produces a DOT graph and identifies possible flaws in network security.

- Octopus is a framework for doing security analyses.
- The Solidity security blog includes a comprehensive list of vulnerabilities, attacks linked to cryptography, weaknesses, and preventive methods.

These are only some of the most well-known techniques for assessing the security of blockchains. There are a great deal more obtainable, each of which comes with a different set of qualities and characteristics. The exact requirements of your project will dictate how you should go about selecting the appropriate tool for your needs.

Layers of Web 3

The concept of Web 3.0 encompasses multiple layers that contribute to the evolution of the internet. Web 3.0 is driven by the integration of four novel layers of technological advancements:

1. The advent of web 2.0 brought about a transformation in the commoditization of personal computer technology within data centers. In contrast, web 3.0 extends this paradigm by shifting the locus of data centers towards the periphery, a concept known as *edge computing*, thereby placing computational power directly within our grasp.
2. In the context of Web 3.0, the decentralized data network empowers users with ownership over their data. *Decentralized data* networks enable various data generators to engage in the sale or sharing of their data without relinquishing ownership or depending on intermediaries.
3. The field of *artificial intelligence* and machine learning has witnessed significant advancements, enabling algorithms to reach a level of sophistication where they are capable of generating valuable predictions and occasionally performing life-saving actions.
4. The concept of *blockchain* refers to a decentralized technology that employs smart contracts for the purpose of executing transactions. The smart contracts in question establish the underlying meaning and functionality of a web 3.0 application. Consequently, individuals seeking to create a blockchain application are required to utilize the shared state machine. Figure 2 shows web 3 layers.

Figure 2. Web 3 layers

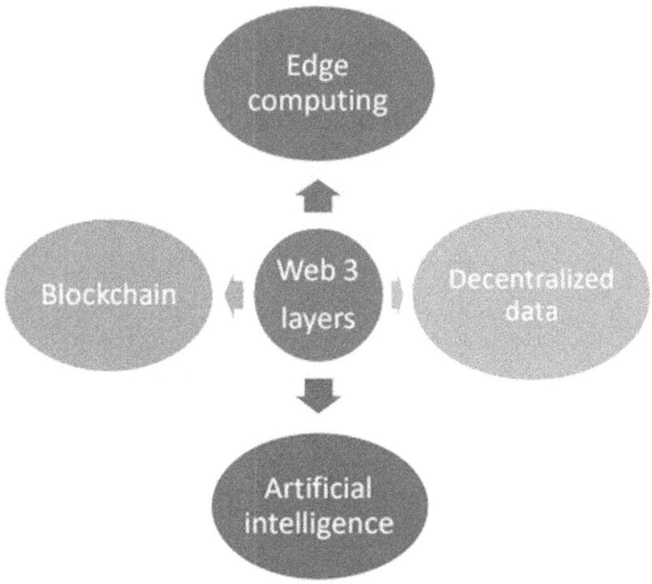

The Functioning Mechanism of Web 3

The user's data is stored within their cryptocurrency wallet on the web3 platform. In the context of web3, users will engage with applications and communities by means of their digital wallets. Notably, upon logging off, users will have the ability to retain possession of their personal data. As the possessor of the data, you possess the theoretical agency to determine whether to derive monetary value from it.

Once the guiding principles have been established, we can proceed to examine how specific web3 development features are designed to achieve these objectives.

Data ownership: The act of utilizing a platform such as Facebook or YouTube entails the collection, possession, and monetization of user data by these corporations. The user's data is stored within their cryptocurrency wallet utilizing the web3 technology. In the context of web3, users will engage with applications and communities by means of their digital wallets. Notably, upon logging off, users will have the ability to retain possession of their personal data. As the proprietor of the data, one possesses the theoretical prerogative to determine whether to derive monetary value from it.

Pseudonymity, which encompasses privacy and data ownership, is an inherent characteristic of wallet systems. The wallet functions as a means of identification on the web3 platform, thereby presenting challenges in establishing a direct link between the wallet and the user's real-world identity. Hence, despite the potential for individuals to monitor wallet transactions, the ability to discern the specific identity of a given wallet remains elusive. While the personal information remains concealed, the behavior remains observable.

There exist certain services that facilitate the connection between customers and their cryptocurrency wallets, which are employed for illicit activities. Nevertheless, one's identity remains concealed for everyday purposes.

While wallets enhance the privacy of bitcoin transactions, privacy-oriented cryptocurrencies such as Zcash and Monero offer a higher degree of anonymity to transactions. The utilization of blockchains in privacy coins enables the tracking of transactions by observers, while precluding their ability to access information pertaining to the wallets involved. Web3 is anticipated to incorporate decentralized autonomous entities that will operate applications known as DAOs. Consequently, the decision-making process has shifted from a centralized authority to individuals who possess governance tokens. These tokens can be obtained through active participation in the maintenance of decentralized programs or through their purchase.

Within the organizational structure of a conventional corporation, the Chief Executive Officer (CEO) assumes the crucial role of executing alterations that have been duly sanctioned by the shareholders. The participants who possess tokens in a Decentralized Autonomous Organization (DAO) have the authority to cast votes on proposed modifications. If these modifications are successfully approved, they are promptly integrated into the DAO's code through the utilization of a smart contract. The source code of a decentralized autonomous organization (DAO) is made accessible to all participants due to its democratized nature.

The Main Applications of Web 3

The main applications of Web 3.0 are of significant importance in various domains. Web 3.0, leveraging blockchain as its fundamental technology, facilitates the emergence of a diverse array of novel applications and services, exemplified by the subsequent instances:

Non-fungible tokens (NFTs) are a type of digital token that possess distinct and non-interchangeable characteristics. These tokens are securely stored within a blockchain network, accompanied by a cryptographic hash.

Decentralized finance (DeFi) leverages decentralized blockchain technology as the underlying framework to enable the provision of financial services beyond the limitations imposed by traditional centralized banking infrastructure. This emerging use case for Web 3.0 showcases the utilization of decentralized blockchain technology in facilitating decentralized finance.

Cryptocurrency, a novel form of currency that aims to differentiate itself from conventional fiat money, is being forged within the realm of Web 3.0 applications, exemplified by cryptocurrencies such as Bitcoin.

Decentralized applications (dApps) refer to software programs that operate in a decentralized manner and are recorded on an immutable ledger. These platforms are constructed on the foundation of blockchain technology and employ smart contracts to streamline the provision of services.

Cross-chain bridges. In the era of Web 3.0, the proliferation of blockchains has given rise to a multitude of interconnected networks. Cross-chain bridges have emerged as a means of establishing connectivity between these distinct blockchain systems.

Decentralized Autonomous Organizations (DAOs) have the potential to assume the responsibilities of governing bodies in the context of Web 3.0, providing a framework for structured and decentralized governance. Figure 3 illustrates main Web 3 applications.

Figure 3. Main applications of Web 3

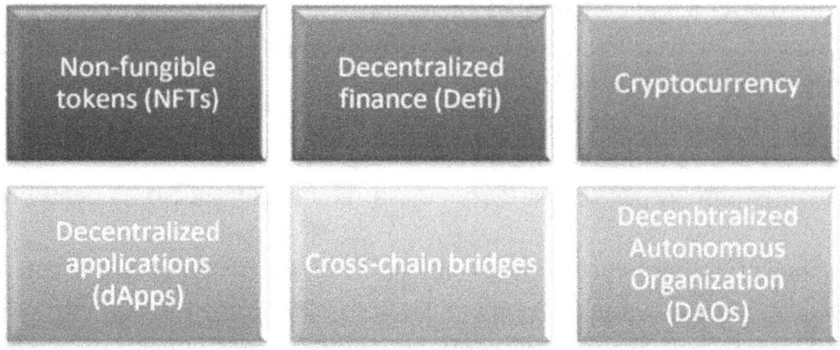

The Advantages and Disadvantages of Web 3

The present section aims to explore the advantages and disadvantages associated with the implementation of Web 3.0. There are several advantages:

- Data encryption is the most advantageous measure for end-users in the context of data security.
- The accessibility of data will be facilitated by the decentralized nature of data storage, enabling users to retrieve data under any circumstances. Users will be provided with multiple backup options to assist them in the event of a server failure.
- The majority of blockchain systems are created by non-profit organizations, which offer an open-source blockchain platform facilitating collaborative design and development.
- The data will be accessible from various locations and across multiple devices.
- Web 3.0 demonstrates utility in facilitating problem-solving endeavors and facilitating the generation of extensive knowledge.

There are several drawbacks associated with this phenomenon.

- In order to enhance global accessibility of technology, it will be necessary to broaden the capabilities and qualities of the devices.
- Websites constructed using web 1.0 technology will inevitably become outdated upon the complete integration of web 3.0 within the Internet.
- The technology of Web 3.0 exhibits greater levels of intelligence, efficiency, and accessibility when compared to its predecessors. Nevertheless, the current state of technology is not yet suitable for widespread implementation.
- Given the increased accessibility to users' personal information and the diminished level of privacy associated with web 3.0, the significance of reputation management is expected to be heightened.

The Importance of Web 3 and Its Tools

When designing Web 3.0, it is important to consider various factors such as artificial intelligence (AI), the semantic web, and the omnipresent qualities. The underlying justification for the development of artificial intelligence (AI) arises from the imperative to provide users with expedited access to data that is both more precise and reliable. A website that utilizes artificial intelligence (AI) should possess the capability to analyze and categorize data, subsequently presenting information that is deemed relevant and valuable to individual visitors. When users select websites as results, social bookmarking can potentially provide more effective outcomes compared to Google as a search engine. Nevertheless, it is within the capacity of human beings to exert influence over these results. To achieve outcomes akin to those of social media and social bookmarking platforms, while mitigating the presence of adverse feedback, the implementation of artificial intelligence (AI) could be explored. This could involve leveraging AI algorithms to discern authentic results from counterfeit ones.

The integration of virtual assistants into devices and third-party applications is gaining popularity, and there are plans to introduce them into artificially intelligent websites as well. The objective of the semantic web is to establish a framework for the systematic organization and storage of data, enabling the impartation of meaning to specific information for the purpose of instructing a system. To enhance the production and dissemination of high-quality content, it is imperative for a website to possess the ability to comprehend language in a manner akin to human comprehension. The ability of artificial intelligence to transform information into knowledge is contingent upon its comprehension of said information.

Web 3.0 capitalizes on the utilization of artificial intelligence, machine learning, and blockchain technology. The attainment of effective communication in practical contexts is anticipated. The ownership of data will be vested in individuals, who will receive compensation commensurate with their internet usage duration. The utilization of blockchain technology holds promise for the future, as it has the potential to enhance the security and protection of user data and privacy. Therefore, assuming favorable circumstances, Web 3.0 has the potential to become the predominant paradigm of the internet in the future.

Initially, it is imperative to acquire a non-fungible token (NFT) domain name. Subsequently, the creation of a website can be undertaken. It is essential to bear in mind that the website must be developed using one of the three available methods:

- Utilize pre-existing templates available on website builders.
- The website can be hosted using the InterPlanetary File System Protocol (IPFS).
- Navigate to a currently available Web 3.0 website.

The significance of Web 3.0 lies in its implications and impact on various domains.

The subsequent elements are several pivotal facets of Web 3.0 that contribute to the delineation of the anticipated characteristics of the third iteration of the internet.

- Web 3.0 is anticipated to exhibit a *decentralized nature*, distinguishing it from the preceding two iterations of the web that were characterized by predominantly centralized governance and applications. The utilization of a decentralized approach, devoid of a central governing body, will facilitate the functioning of various applications and services.
- The utilization of *blockchain technology* enables the creation and implementation of decentralized applications and services. In contrast to a centralized database infrastructure, blockchain employs a distributed approach for the dissemination of data and connections among various services. In a decentralized setting, blockchain technology can provide an unalterable record of transactions and activities, thereby aiding in the verification of authenticity.

- ***Cryptocurrency integration***: The utilization of cryptocurrencies, serving as a substitute for traditional fiat currencies, constitutes a fundamental element within the framework of Web 3.0 services.
- One crucial element of Web 3.0 pertains to increased automation, primarily facilitated by *artificial intelligence (AI).*

Compilation of Top Tools for Web 3.0

The exploration of web3 entails promptly consulting a comprehensive compilation of web 3.0 tools in order to identify the most suitable options for one's web3 project. However, it is crucial to consider the functionalities when searching for web3 tools. The inquiry pertains to the identification of web 3.0 tools. This analysis would demonstrate that web3 tools possess a broader scope beyond their function as mere tools for constructing web3 applications. The strength of the overall web3 community can be defined by the individual functionalities of web3 tools. The prevalence of smart contracts in web3 technology has led to a significant concentration of web3 tools focused on smart contract development. Presented below is an outline delineating the foremost web3 tools that warrant your attention.

1. WatchData

Another notable web 3.0 tool and application that can be categorized as a layer 1 connection platform is WatchData (WatchData, 2023). The core concept behind the design of WatchData revolves around its functionalities as a blockchain application programming interface (API) for web3. Creating and operating blockchain applications is of paramount importance to numerous developers in the blockchain field, as this toolkit provides robust assistance in these endeavors. One notable benefit of WatchData is its ability to seamlessly integrate real-time blockchain data with minimal complexities. WatchData facilitates the adaptable conversion of unprocessed and disorganized blockchain data into coherent and significant datasets. Furthermore, the implementation of the data verification process within the WatchData Powered API can significantly contribute to the assurance of data accuracy during interactions.

2. Chainstack

Chainstack (Chainstack, 2023) is a cloud-agnostic blockchain platform that offers a comprehensive suite of tools and services. Chainstack is considered to be a highly dependable choice among the top web 3.0 tools available, particularly for individuals who aspire to become web3 professionals. The utilization of this option shows potential in facilitating expedited and uninterrupted connectivity to web3 infrastructure. Chainstack has the potential to serve as a fundamental framework for the development of future web applications that possess characteristics of openness, trustlessness, and resilience.

Users have the opportunity to optimize the utilization of scalable application programming interfaces (APIs), tools, and services available on Chainstack. This platform enables the enhancement of numerous innovative projects across various domains such as non-fungible tokens (NFTs), gaming, decentralized finance (DeFi), analytics, and other sectors. The Chainstack Marketplace provides a comprehensive selection of developer tools, applications, and services that are conducive to the development of innovative decentralized applications (dApps).

3. Etherspot

Etherspot (Etherspot, 2023) is a decentralized finance (DeFi) platform that operates on the Ethereum blockchain. Etherspot can be described as a software development kit (SDK) that facilitates the creation of blockchain applications. It functions as a framework for blockchain development and offers compatibility with chains that adhere to the Ethereum Virtual Machine (EVM) standards. The functionality is achieved through the establishment of direct state channel bridges, which enable the smooth integration of user interactions across various wallets and blockchain networks. Consequently, this tool is regarded as one of the leading web 3.0 tools due to its development functionalities, which have the potential to enhance user adoption while also reducing time and cost expenditures. One notable advantage of Etherspot is its ability to leverage the most prominent attributes that arise within the Ethereum multiverse. For instance, Etherspot offers various features such as ENS integration, Meta transactions, NFT support, batched transactions, payment channels, and more, enabling users to optimize their experience on the platform.

4. Solidity

Solidity (Solidity, 2023) is a programming language that is primarily used for developing smart contracts on the Ethereum blockchain. The discussion of widely used web3 tools would be insufficient without acknowledging Solidity, the programming language utilized for smart contracts. The programming language in question is a contract-oriented language that has been specifically developed for the purpose of designing and deploying smart contracts on the Ethereum blockchain. Solidity exhibits notable resemblances to Python, JavaScript, and C++ programming languages, facilitating the creation of intelligent contracts on blockchain networks that are compatible with the Ethereum Virtual Machine (EVM). One notable benefit of Solidity as a web3 tool pertains to its ability to provide access to a vast web3 ecosystem, which encompasses an extensive array of developer support resources.

5. Hardhat

The term "hardhat" (Hardhat, 2023) refers to a type of protective headgear commonly worn in industrial areas. The compilation of responses pertaining to the question "What are the tools associated with Web 3.0?"The act of closely observing would naturally encompass the inclusion of the television program titled "Hardhat." The provided tool is a comprehensive development environment for Ethereum, which facilitates the processes of testing, compiling, deploying, and debugging decentralized applications (dApps) built on the Ethereum platform. In addition to providing essential tools for facilitating the web3 development process, Hardhat also incorporates automation features that yield advantages for developers. The salient characteristics of Hardhat pertain to its inclusion of a pre-configured local Ethereum environment and its provision of Solidity debugging capabilities accompanied by stack traces.

6. Eternal

The term "eternal" (Eternal, 2023) refers to something that is without end or everlasting. Ethernal has emerged as a prominent addition to the repertoire of popular web3 tools due to its distinctive functionality. The inclusion of a block explorer for private chains is a fundamental necessity within the web3 technology stack, due to its significant capabilities and status as an open-source tool. Hence, it is convenient for developers to effectively monitor the functioning of Hardhat, Ganache, and other development environments. Simultaneously, the block explorer also facilitates the functionality of public chains. The explorer can establish a connection with any EVM-based chain, facilitating the automatic synchronization of all blocks, contracts, and transactions with Ethernal. The straightforward user interface also facilitates the identification of pertinent information, such as emitted events and function invocations.

7. Foundry

The term "foundry" (Foundry, 2023) refers to a facility or workshop where metal is melted and poured. One notable inclusion among the top web3 tools is Foundry, a highly efficient and versatile development toolkit designed specifically for Ethereum decentralized applications (dApps). Foundry, a platform built on the Rust programming language, offers significant advantages in terms of enhancing the flexibility of Ethereum development environments. Foundry is notably included in the web 3.0 tools list due to its capacity to effectively assist developers across various use cases. It is noteworthy that developers have the capability to engage in Foundry development without the need for external libraries or configurations. The Foundry framework facilitates various functionalities, including the ability to perform function fuzzing during testing, overriding the virtual machine state, and documenting debug information in logs while tests are being executed.

8. Metamask

Metamask (Metamask, 2023) is a browser extension that serves as a digital wallet for managing cryptocurrencies and interacting. One cannot compile a comprehensive compilation of the most notable web 3.0 tools without acknowledging the inclusion of Metamask, a blockchain wallet that operates within a web browser. The browser extension has the potential to function as a means of access to the extensive decentralized application (dApp) ecosystem of Ethereum. Metamask, as a cryptocurrency wallet, possesses functionalities that facilitate the utilization of decentralized applications (dApps) within the Ethereum ecosystem. Metamask users have the capability to establish connections with Ethereum-based decentralized applications (dApps) and utilize their coins for various purposes such as participating in games or engaging in token staking within governance mechanisms. The cryptographic wallet assumes a crucial function in facilitating the connection between users and the web3 community.

9. NFT. Storage

NFT. Storage (NFT. Storage, 2023) is a platform that facilitates the storage and retrieval of non-fungible tokens. Currently, NFT. Storage is experiencing a surge in popularity. The service in question is a storage solution intended for the long-term preservation of data associated with non-fungible tokens (NFTs), with a specific focus on facilitating off-chain storage. Storage is its utilization of IPFS for the purpose of data addressing. Furthermore, the utilization of IPFS URLs and distinct identifiers for non-fungible tokens (NFTs) can also be observed. Consequently, it can facilitate the trustless verification of the content associated with non-fungible tokens (NFTs). The provision of concise documentation for NFT. Storage is of utmost significance as it facilitates the seamless utilization of this platform in web3 projects.

10. Wagmi

The phrase "Wagmi" (Wagmi, 2023) stands out as a compelling option within the prominent selections of web 3.0 tools and applications for developers specializing in web3. The provided framework comprises a collection of React Hooks that encompass the necessary functionalities for interacting and operating within Ethereum-based environments. The typical functionalities of Wagmi encompass establishing connections with wallets, interacting with contracts, signing messages, and displaying information regarding balance or ENS status. Simultaneously, Wagmi has the capability to uphold persistence, caching, and request deduplication. In addition, Wagmi also includes a test suite that is functional when used with the forked Ethereum network.

The Future Trends of Web 3

Web3 builds online spaces using blockchain, NFTs, cryptocurrencies, and DAOs. Decentralized internet spaces let people manage assets and data. Web3 supports decentralized digital democracies. Web3 empowers people and reinvents digital interactions with businesses and services. Current web3 developments may predict 2023 industry growth. Web3's rise may be confirmed by industry trends.

1. Priority Sustainability

Web3 sustainability challenges exist. Blockchain, which powers web3, presents fossil fuel energy worries. Web3 sustainability best practices and initiatives are 2023 trends. Cambridge University's Bitcoin Energy Consumption Index says Bitcoin uses 84 terra-watt hours per year. Bitcoin consumes more energy than some nations annually, which is dangerous. Web3 struggles with environmentalism and unequal resource use. Reducing app, process, and system energy use will shape web3. Interestingly, Ethereum Merge launched web3 sustainability. The Merge converts Ethereum from energy-intensive Proof of Work to Proof of Stake. The September 2022 Ethereum Merge predicted 98% energy savings. Regenerative finance use cases were promoted by the WEF Crypto Sustainability Coalition.

2. Regulations Rising

The description of web3 blockchain advances suggests 2023 regulatory involvement. Web3 transformed various sectors. Thus, governments are more inclined to limit web3's social, environmental, and economic impacts. Wyoming regulates web3 affiliation. Web3 enterprises may get tax breaks and other benefits. Colorado accepts cryptocurrencies for taxes and fees. Interesting, in 2023 web3 advances may affect non-US nations. Dubai is a web3 powerhouse. India and China were working on amendments related to web3 legislation in 2023.

3. Revised Reserve Proof View

After FTX, a large centralized crypto exchange, failed, 2022 was a bad year for crypto and blockchain. blockchain and web3's flexibility solved the issue rapidly via Proof of Reserves. Trust in bitcoin transactions with valuables will affect web3. The Proof of Reserves audit tool verified exchanges had enough reserves for user deposits and liquidity. Crypto exchanges use Proof of Reserves to avoid liability. Thus,

Proof of Liabilities is another intriguing web3 innovation. Centralized exchange confidence and growth increase with Reserves inspections. Several Proof of Reserves and Proof of Liabilities ideas have been attempted. Check Merkle tree reserves for asset backup. Decentralized on-chain and off-chain reserve verification oracles may boost centralized exchange credibility.

4. Decentralized Metaverse

In web3, metaverse is trendy. Facebook and Microsoft are planning internet evolution. The web3 metaverse would diverge greatly from tech giants' vision. Instead of centralized immersive platforms, the metaverse should be a shared environment with many views. Decentralized metaverses rule Sandbox and Decentraland. Ethereum stores data for decentralized metaverse systems. Decentralized metaverse systems permitted only approved users to change, remove, or add pieces. Lack of central metaverse data server ownership means no censorship. Facebook always controlled metaverse platforms. Web3 blockchain decentralized virtual environments are trendy in 2023. New leaders will build decentralized metaverses.

Popular decentralized metaverse platforms and metaverse project funding grew in 2023. McKinsey said 66% of people supported metaverse routines in June 2022. Metaverse ventures received $120 billion in the first five months of 2022. Only $57 billion went to metaverse projects in 2021. Web3 trends highlight brand and investor efforts to link the real and virtual worlds. Starbucks, Nike, Adidas, and Gucci use metaverses. Web3 may see metaverse innovation in 2023 as decentralized metaverse platforms gain prominence.

5. Effective Nonfungible Tokens

Web3's next big trend is utility-based NFTs. NFT tokens identify blockchain assets. Unique assets fit NFTs. In digital art, most NFTs are discussed. NFT artwork inspired Bored Ape Yacht Club and Rare Pepes in 2021. NFT artwork made artists and traders millions. However, 2023 web3 developments indicate that non-fungible tokens may be used for more than digital artwork ownership. NFTs will thrive on a decentralized network, say Web3 specialists. Data, IP, and assets may be tokenized. NFTs may be digital product and service keys. Web3 advances suggest deploying NFTs as product and service access smart contracts. Additionally, non-fungible tokens may unlock metaverse virtual settings. NFT utility would alter big expectations in 2023. NFTs' function in web3 will be explored by specialists. Owner incentives and other benefits from utility NFTs may impact digital asset perceptions.

The Future Scopes of Web 3 for the Enterprises

The proliferation of Application Programming Interfaces (APIs) leads to a diminished sense of control. In the pursuit of decentralized computation, enterprises encounter a significant obstacle: the relinquishment of control. As one increases the extent to which their computer is accessed, their level of control over its operational location diminishes. Moreover, as the dependence on third-party application programming interfaces (APIs) and shared data among partners increases, the level of control over the code and data governing one's business diminishes. However, the lack of control over a particular factor does not necessarily imply an inability to reduce or manage associated risks. Welcome to the world of trustlessness. Similar to Bitcoin, the concept of trustlessness refers to the ability to place trust in a decentralized computing platform without the need for prior trust in any of its individual participants. This facilitates an enhancement in the level of transparency and traceability for data utilized in artificial intelligence (AI) and other forms of automated processing, even in the absence of knowledge or trust in the other entities involved.

Transparent Web3 protocols enable users to place trust in the code, data, and outcomes furnished by their computational infrastructure. The increasing demand for trustless computation is readily apparent in domains characterized by a risk level that surpasses the capacity for trust, such as public application programming interfaces (APIs), regulated sectors, and fundamental financial safeguards. As the expectations for businesses to engage in collaborative efforts with trading partners and customers intensify, Web3 has the potential to offer the necessary trust and transparency.

The Future of Enterprise in the Next Five Years

The advent of cloud computing has brought about a significant paradigm shift in the construction of systems within organizational settings. Looking ahead, it is anticipated that the next 5-10 years will witness a substantial surge in the development of systems situated outside organizational boundaries. Based on the research conducted by IDC, it is projected that a significant majority of enterprises, approximately 80%, will become participants in industry ecosystems over the next five years. These ecosystems will necessitate a dependence on decentralized Web3 code. The source of information is the IDC FutureScape (IDC FutureScape, 2023) report titled "Worldwide Future of Industry Ecosystems 2023 Predictions." As the significance of APIs in business operations increases, technology teams will be required to package the unique contributions of their company into microservices (APIs) that can be made available to external parties. Additionally, these teams will need to utilize the microservices provided by other organizations.

As the application programming interfaces (APIs) currently available assume a pivotal role in facilitating the extensive functionality of various enterprises, the notion of trust will necessitate a transformation. Trustless compute plays a fundamental role in ensuring the sustained operation and security of businesses within our society. Web3 incorporates a transparent, immutable, and self-evident layer of trust within the design and operation of its APIs. Ecosystems foster interdependence among their constituent elements, necessitating the establishment of trust.

Industry ecosystems can be defined as the intricate network of enterprises, institutions, and interested parties that engage in collaborative and competitive activities within a particular industry. Emerging technologies such as Web3 and decentralization play a crucial role in fostering innovation and facilitating the expansion of these ecosystems. In light of the growing trend of collaborative efforts among organizations to generate customer value, the imperative for trust, transparency, and security in data sharing and processes becomes increasingly paramount. The decentralized nature of Web3 facilitates the establishment of trust in data and processes both within and outside independent organizations, thereby facilitating seamless collaboration within industry ecosystems. By integrating technologies such as cryptographic identity, consensus mechanisms, and coordination protocols, these ecosystems can effectively facilitate the seamless exchange of information and transactions among various participants, thereby ensuring the reliability and authenticity of data and processes.

The Role of Decentralization and Trust in the Enterprise

The adoption of decentralization by enterprises is a logical progression, as it facilitates the involvement of multiple providers, potentially enabling them to contribute their own computing resources. Nevertheless, in the context of workloads being executed on a decentralized network, organizations are faced with the challenge of establishing trust within a widespread network of service providers, which may not be feasible to thoroughly evaluate on an individual basis. Web3 plays a pivotal role in establishing trust and transparency within a decentralized environment.

In an era characterized by the prevalence of low-code and open-source solutions, wherein originality is scarce and components are frequently repurposed and integrated, the need to ensure accuracy and reliability becomes progressively crucial when dealing with data and processes originating from unfamiliar origins. Concerns such as data security, privacy, and trust can be effectively addressed through the implementation of verified computation, transparent protocols, and immutable records.

CONCLUSION

The transition to Web 3.0 refers to the ongoing evolution of the internet towards a more advanced and sophisticated version of the World Wide Web. The implementation of web 3.0 tools and applications may appear implausible to a significant number of individuals, particularly those grappling with the complexities of blockchain technology and cryptocurrency. Ten years ago, experts in the field of technology expressed concerns regarding the emergence of a novel type of digital currency that facilitated decentralized transactions between individuals. Presently, cryptocurrencies have emerged as a prominent subject of discourse within global conversations pertaining to the domains of economy and finance. Likewise, the current discourse surrounding web3 may appear incongruous at present. Contrarily, it is imperative to comprehend that web3 has already manifested itself in one form or another. An illustration of web3 applications can be seen in the form of cryptocurrencies that operate without any centralized authority. One may also explore instances of NFT ownership and NFT trading, as well as examine metaverse platforms, to gain insight into the transformative capacity of web3 in reshaping global dynamics. In a short period, the global community will observe the transformative potential of the decentralized web in reshaping traditional notions of asset ownership, digital identity, and security through the emergence of web 3.0.

Web 3.0, also referred to as Web 3, encompasses the theoretical framework for the forthcoming iteration of the internet, wherein a substantial majority of users will be interconnected through a decentralized network and possess the ability to retrieve and manage their personal data. This chapter provided insights into the technologies that are expected to progress and undergo transformation in the forthcoming years. Web 3.0 is anticipated to encompass a range of emerging technologies such as intelligent systems, semantic web, decentralization, metaverse, and digital assets. The potential success of Web 3.0 requires further examination. However, it is widely acknowledged by analysts that the prioritization of data security will be paramount. Consequently, there would be a significant demand for professionals specializing in security and corresponding security systems. Moreover, there will be a surge in the demand for professionals specializing in blockchain development. Web 3.0 trends demonstrate its youth and technological evolution. Key Web3 developments are also its biggest issues. Decentralizing metaverse platforms, increasing NFT value, and regulating—2023 is huge for web3. Web3 would prioritize user trust and centralized crypto exchange sustainability. Web3 knowledge prepares for future tech.

REFERENCES

Ball, M. (2022). *Web 3.0 and the Future of Media*. The Metaverse.

Berners-Lee, T., Hendler, J., & Lassila, O. (2001). Web3.0: A vision for personalized, decentralized web. In *Proceedings of the 12th international conference on World Wide Web* (pp. 1-4). Academic Press.

Chainstack. (2023). https://chainstack.com/

Eternal. (2023). https://eternal.gg/

Etherspot. (2023). https://etherspot.io/

Flynn, B., & Ferreira, E. (2021). Web 3.0: Decentralized Apps and the Future of the Web. *IEEE Software*, *38*(5), 78–85.

Foundry. (2023). https://www.foundry.com/

Giaccardi, E., & Zaga, C. (2021). Web 3.0 and the Future of Social Networks. *Journal of Computer-Mediated Communication*, *26*(2), 89–102.

Hardhat. (2023). https://hardhat.org/

IDC FutureScape. (2023). https://www.idc.com/events/futurescape

Jánszky, S. G., & Pinker, A. (2021). *Web 3.0: The Next Generation of the Internet*. The Futures Agency.

Kausar MA, & Nasar M (2021). SQL versus NoSQL databases to assess their appropriateness for big data application. *Recent Advances in Computer Science and Communications, 14*(4), 1098–1108.

Kim, H., & Kahng, M. (2020). Web 3.0: From Web to Blockchain. *IEEE Internet Computing*, *24*(5), 10–16.

Kreminski, M. (2019). The Future of the Web: Decentralization, Interoperability, and Intelligence. XRDS: Crossroads. *The ACM Magazine for Students*, *26*(2), 10–14.

Mashinsky, A., & Krug, J. (2020). *Web 3.0: The Age of Machine Intelligence*. Celsius Network.

Mehrpouyan, H., & Sadeghian, M. A. (2021). Web 3.0: A New Era for E-commerce. *International Journal of Business and Management*, *16*(5), 1–11.

Metamask. (2023). https://metamask.io/

Mougayar, W. (2016). *The Rise of Web 3.0: Emerging Patterns in Decentralized Computing*. Coin Desk Research.

ADDITIONAL READING

Nasar, M., & Kausar, M. A. (2019). Suitability of infuxdb database for iot applications. *International Journal of Innovative Technology and Exploring Engineering*, *8*(10), 1850–1857. doi:10.35940/ijitee.J9225.0881019

Schlebusch, P. (2018). Towards a Definition of Web 3.0. *Journal of Information Technology Theory and Application*, *19*(2), 5–26.

Schürmann, S., & Möller, K. (2017). *Web 3.0 – An Overview*. Technical Report.

Solididty. (2023). https://soliditylang.org/

Storage, N. F. T. (2023). https://nft.storage

Wagmi. (2023). https://wagmi.sh/

WatchData. (2023). https://www.watchdata.com/

KEY TERMS AND DEFINITIONS

Ethereum Name Service (ENS): Your web 3 username, a name for all your cryptocurrency addresses, and decentralized websites.

Hypertext Transfer Protocol (HTTP): Is an application protocol that runs on top of the TCP/IP suite of protocols, which forms the foundation of the internet.

IDS (International Data Corporation) FutureScape: DC examines consumer markets by devices, applications, networks, and services to provide complete solutions for succeeding in these expanding markets.

InterPlanetary File System Protocol (IPFS): Is a distributed file storage protocol that allows computers all over the globe to store and serve files as part of a giant peer-to-peer network.

Personally Identifiable Information (PII): Any representation of information that permits the identity of an individual to whom the information applies to be reasonably inferred by either direct or indirect means.

User-Generated Content (UGC): Is original, brand-specific content created by customers and published on social media or other channels.

Chapter 2
The Driving Forces Behind Web 3 Growth

Dina Darwish
Ahram Canadian University, Egypt

ABSTRACT

The term "web3 development" refers to the practice of creating and building applications, platforms, and technologies that are designed to operate on the decentralized web, also known as web 3. This new paradigm of web development aims to leverage blockchain technology, decentralized networks, and cryptographic protocols to enable greater user control, privacy, and security. Web 3 development refers to the systematic creation of applications, platforms, and decentralized systems that leverage blockchain technology, cryptocurrencies, and decentralized networks. This procedure additionally involves implementing these applications and platforms. This chapter discusses the web 3 development importance and the driving forces behind web 3 development.

INTRODUCTION

The term Web 2.0 encompasses the phenomenon whereby a multitude of individuals contribute an increased amount of material to cater to a growing audience, according to Simplilearn (Simplilearn, 2023). Web 1.0 is characterized by a limited number of content creators who provide material intended for a wider audience. Web 2.0 places more emphasis on user engagement and active participation compared to its predecessor, Web 1.0, which primarily centered on passive consumption of content.

The user's experience plays a pivotal role in the context of Web 2.0. This phenomenon pertains to the establishment of social media platforms, collaborative efforts, and the development of communal networks. In contemporary society, a significant proportion of individuals see Web 2.0 as the prevailing paradigm for engaging with online platforms.

Web 3, also referred to as Web3.0 (Edelman, 2021; Alford, 2021; Khoshafian, 2021), is a notion for a new version of the World Wide Web that integrates principles such as decentralization, blockchain technology, and token-based economics (Fenwick & Jurcys, 2022). Some engineers and journalists have made the comparison between it and Web 2.0, in which they claim that data and information are

DOI: 10.4018/979-8-3693-1532-3.ch002

centralized in a small number of businesses that are collectively referred to as "Big Tech."(Mak, 2021). In 2014, Gavin Wood, a co-founder of Ethereum, came up with the name "Web3," and by 2021, cryptocurrency enthusiasts, big technological businesses, and venture capital firms were showing interest in the concept .(Mak, 2021; Read, 2021). The ideas of Web3 were introduced for the first time in the year 2013 (Bodrenko_1, 2013; Bodrenko_2, 2013). Concerns have been raised about the potential for a smaller number of investors and people to accumulate an excessive amount of wealth (Kastrenakes, 2021), as well as the potential for an increased breach of personal privacy as a result of increased data collecting (NRP, 2021).

According to an article published in TechoPedia (TechnoPedia, 2023), Web3 is seen as the subsequent stage of the World Wide Web (WWW). This platform offers users the opportunity to engage with a novel user interface that provides access to a diverse range of resources, including papers, apps, and multimedia content. The concept of Web 3 is still undergoing development, resulting in a lack of consensus over its precise definition. The terminology surrounding the subject matter remains uncertain, since prominent analysis organizations like as Forrester, Gartner, and IDC exhibit inconsistency in their use of either "Web3" or "Web 3.0."

However, it is important to note that Web 3.0 is expected to revolve on the concept of decentralization and is anticipated to include advanced blockchain technology. In addition, the implementation will use machine learning and artificial intelligence techniques to enhance the intelligence and adaptability of the web interface.

In the realm of web development, the significant influence of Web3 cannot be disregarded. The emergence of this novel paradigm signifies a substantial transformation in the construction and engagement of online apps. The emergence of a new phase in the development of the Internet, sometimes denoted as Web 3.0, envision a virtual domain whereby the information you engage with is tailored specifically to your own tastes and areas of interest.

There is an expectation that Web 3.0 will be affected by:

- The use of open-source technologies will be employed in the construction of content platforms.
- The adoption of a trustless approach, whereby Zero Trust, would lead to the extension of network security measures to the edges.
- The distributed nature of interaction among devices, users, and services enables the possibility of operating without the need for clearance from a centralized authority.

The use of blockchain technology will facilitate direct communication between users in the next phase of the internet. Communication among individuals will be facilitated by their participation in a Decentralized Autonomous Organization (DAO), which is a collective entity governed and owned by its community members. The user's data will be safeguarded by a network of publicly accessible smart contracts. The contracts will be kept inside a blockchain, a decentralized network that will be controlled by nodes.

The following predictions pertain to the expected future developments of Web 3:

- The recording of all transactions will be monitored on a distributed ledger that employs blockchain technology, while the transport of data would be decentralized.

- The implementation of universally accessible smart contracts would alleviate individuals from the need of depending on a centralized entity, such as a financial institution, for the preservation of data integrity.
- The metaverse is expected to provide substantial revenue growth for the entertainment industry.
- The use of blockchain technology would enable customers to expeditiously generate digital products and non-fungible tokens (NFTs), therefore safeguarding intellectual property and personally identifiable information (PII).
- The data of users may be monetized.

The inquiry pertains to the precise definition and potential transformative impact of Web 3.0. If one is enthusiastic in comprehending this subject, they have arrived at the appropriate location.

This chapter discusses the importance of web 3 development and the driving forces behind web 3. The main topics to be covered in this chapter includes the following;

- The web 3 definition
- The key components of web 3 development services
- The benefits of web 3 development services
- How can web 3 help businesses
- The key driving technologies and factors behind the growth of the Web 3.0 market
- Some specific examples of how Web 3.0 is being used today
- Web 3 security threats
- The Web 3 advantages and disadvantages
- The Web 3 Accessibility
- The Web 3 and Education
- The Web 3 and current businesses
- The Web 3 and economy and society
- The Web 3 and regulation
- Web3 effect on the next industrial revolution

Also, this chapter is organized as follows; the first section contains the background, then, the second section includes the main focus of the chapter, including the main topics mentioned in the previous section, then finally, comes the conclusion section.

BACKGROUND

Cambridge Dictionary (Cambridge Dictionary, 2021) defines "driving forces" as "someone or something that can make things happen". The internet is entering a new development phase with significant advantages. The worldwide debate about internet improvements is vast. The intelligent Web—semantic web, micro-formats, natural language search, data-mining, machine learning, recommendation agents, and artificial intelligence technologies—focuses on machine-facilitated information understanding to improve user productivity and experience. According to Garrigos-Simon, Lapiedra-Alcamí, and Ribera (Garrigos-Simon et al., 2012), Web 3.0 allows intelligent computers to read, analyze, and modify cyberspace data, allowing consumer and corporate customization. Today's technology helps users access, change, adapt, and use the internet to meet their requirements. Web 3.0 was enabled by broadband, mobile Internet, and mobile devices. Web 3.0 will be more connected, open, and intelligent with semantic Web technologies, distributed databases, natural language processing, machine learning, reasoning, and autonomous agents (García, 2008). Lee (Lee, 2006) said, "people keep asking what Web 3.0 is and the Web is only going to get more revolutionary". Some Web 3.0 features: Semantic online improves online technologies to generate, disseminate, and connect content by searching and analyzing word meaning, not keywords or numbers; AI merges this with NLP. In Web 3.0, computers can examine data like humans for faster, more relevant results.

Web 3.0 websites and services match customer demands with 3D visuals. Computer games, ecommerce, geographical settings, and museum tours employ 3D visuals. Information is linked via semantic metadata. Thus, the user experience is more integrated and uses all accessible data. All devices are web-connected, several applications may access the content, and services are available everywhere (Lee, 2006). Rudman and Bruwer (Rudman & Bruwer, 2016) list identifiers, structures, and languages as Web 3.0 technologies. URIs and URLs let other computers use resources. Structures include metadata, RDF, RDFS, and intelligent agents. Simple object access protocol, structured query language, OWL, and RDF query language are languages. RDF's flexible schema may hold data types not expected at schema creation. RDF may establish web-like data links that relational or object-relational databases cannot (Lassila & Hendler, 2007). Big data, cloud computing, interoperability, intelligent agents, collaborative filtering, and smart mobility comprise Web 3.0, or the semantic web. The semantic web, openness, interoperability, global data repository, 3-D virtualization, and distributed cloud computing separate Web 2.0 from Web 3.0.

The Significance of Web3 development in Contemporary Digital Landscape. The technology in question is said to have a transformative impact on our online interactions, particularly in the realm of web applications' future. Therefore, it is important to understand the significance of this matter. Let us go into the relevance of this matter. The notion of decentralization. The notion of decentralization is a fundamental element of Web3. In contrast to the conventional online paradigm characterized by the concentration of power among a small number of dominant technology corporations, Web3 aims to restore authority to individual users. The primary focus is in the reclamation of ownership and control pertaining to our data, privacy, and digital identities. The advent of Web3 technology alleviates concerns over the potential exploitation, commercialization, or unauthorized use of individuals' personal data by major corporate entities. The current trend represents a notable transition towards an internet that prioritizes user needs and emphasizes the protection of privacy.

Web3 uses blockchain technology as a means to foster transparency. Web3 apps guarantee the security, immutability, and universal accessibility of data by using a decentralized ledger to record transactions and information. The enhanced level of transparency obviates the need for middlemen and mitigates the potential for fraudulent activities. Web3 offers a heightened degree of trust in online transactions, whether it involves validating the legitimacy of digital assets or monitoring the movement of cash within a decentralized financial ecosystem. In contrast, Web3 presents a platform that facilitates content production while also enabling individuals to assert control, ownership, and monetization privileges. In addition to establishing the foundation for non-fungible tokens (NFTs), blockchain technology and cryptocurrencies play significant roles in driving improvements in web3.

Web3 presents a vast array of opportunities for groundbreaking advancements in several domains. Presently, developers are afforded the prospect of constructing decentralized apps (dApps). Decentralized applications (dApps) provide not only robust security and transparency but also exhibit distinctive attributes and functions. The use of smart contracts enables developers to generate self-executing agreements and automated procedures, so bringing about a transformative impact on several sectors like banking, supply chain, healthcare, among others. Web3 harnesses the capabilities of blockchain technology and enables developers to envision new possibilities for the internet, therefore expanding its limits.

Financial inclusion refers to the accessibility and availability of financial services to individuals and communities, particularly those who have been historically excluded from the formal financial system. It encompasses several aspects. Web3, specifically within the domain of decentralized finance (DeFi), had the capacity to facilitate financial inclusivity and foster economic empowerment on a worldwide level. Web3 technology facilitates the provision of financial services to those who lack access to traditional banking services, including the unbanked and underbanked populations. Individuals have the ability to engage in lending, borrowing, and investing endeavors without being dependent on conventional financial institutions.

The process of democratizing finance has the capacity to fundamentally transform the worldwide economy and provide prospects for persons who were once marginalized from the conventional financial framework. Also, Web3 facilitates the development of cooperation and community-driven activities.

Machine learning and AI drive Web 3.0 (Hussain, 2012). Web 3.0 will link data from diverse sources and systems to address Web 2.0's structure and organization (Yen, et al., 2015). Every organization's think tank must make rapid, ongoing decisions internationally, regardless of size or style. Managers in today's tough business climate must make operational, tactical, and strategic decisions. To win consumers' hearts, managers must handle many risks from growing consumer expectations in every industry swiftly and prudently. Managers require a lot of information to analyze and make excellent judgements to build productive solutions. Since its creation, the Web has been a key source of information for managers, making it easier to learn about client goods (Web 1.0) and consumer beliefs (Web 2.0). These advances boosted information availability and made it tougher for managers to find important data and organize it from many sources and formats. Web 1.0 links sites to information, Web 2.0 links individuals, and Web 3.0 links data to produce knowledge. Web 3.0 search engines should leverage user profiles to provide results. Web 3.0 search engine pages will be topic-based. Reading, assessing, and recognizing semantic word directions links knowledge (Almeida, et Al., 2013).

An instance of a company, Nike (Nike, 2023), is in the process of developing a platform that provides support for Web 3. SWOOSH (swoosh, 2023) establishes a novel and all-encompassing digital community and platform that serves as a hub for Nike's virtual innovations. This initiative aims to foster inclusivity, while simultaneously providing players with enhanced assistance and contributing to the advancement of the sporting domain. The collaborative method also fosters inclusion and diversity within the community.

MAIN FOCUS OF THE CHAPTER

The Web 3 Definition

The term "Web3 Development" refers to the practice of creating and building applications, platforms, and technologies that are designed to operate on the decentralized web, also known as Web3. This new paradigm of web development aims to leverage blockchain technology, decentralized networks, and cryptographic protocols to enable greater user control, privacy, and security.

Web3 development refers to the systematic creation of applications, platforms, and decentralized systems that leverage blockchain technology, cryptocurrencies, and decentralized networks. This procedure additionally involves implementing these applications and platforms. Web3 applications, as opposed to traditional Web2 applications, are specifically engineered to enhance the openness, transparency, and user-centric nature of the internet. Traditional Web2 applications are characterized by a centralized structure wherein a sole authority is responsible for their management.

The Key Components of Web 3 Development Services

The fundamental components comprising Web3 development services are:

1. ***Cryptocurrencies.*** The incorporation of cryptocurrencies such as Bitcoin and Ethereum is a prevalent aspect of Web3 development. Cryptocurrencies enable the facilitation of financial transactions in a decentralized manner, eliminating the necessity for intermediaries or geographical limitations. Digital assets play a crucial role in facilitating the functioning of Web3 applications, enabling the provision of incentives to users, facilitating financial transactions, and ensuring the effective governance of decentralized networks.
2. ***Blockchain Technology.*** Blockchain technology enables secure and transparent peer-to-peer transactions, serving as a fundamental component of Web3 development. The blockchain operates as a decentralized ledger that documents and authenticates every transaction across a network of computers, eliminating the necessity for intermediaries in the procedure.
3. ***Decentralized Networks.*** Web3 applications operate on decentralized networks, wherein data and control are distributed across multiple nodes. This design ensures the absence of a singular point of failure, thereby enhancing security, resilience, and resistance to censorship.

The benefits of web 3 development services

The utilization of Web3 development services possesses the capacity to facilitate numerous benefits for your organization. Let us examine several of the most significant advantages:

1. ***Improved transparency.*** The advent of Web3 technology enables the real-time visibility of transaction records and data, thereby facilitating heightened transparency. As a result of this phenomenon, corporations are presented with the prospect of gaining the trust and support of their clientele and other relevant parties, thereby fostering a climate of increased transparency and accountability.
2. ***Empowering user ownership.*** In contrast to conventional Web2 applications, which frequently involve centralized entities retaining user data, Web3 applications enable users to exercise full control and ownership over their data. This objective is achieved by providing users with enhanced and direct accessibility to the administrative interface of the application. The aforementioned approach, which places emphasis on the end user, aligns with the principles of data sovereignty and privacy.
3. ***Enhanced Security***. Enhanced security in Web3 applications is achieved through the utilization of advanced cryptographic techniques and decentralized networks, which collectively enhance the applications' robustness against hacking attempts. The distribution of data across multiple nodes, as opposed to a single node, significantly reduces the probability of a data breach or a single point of failure.

4. ***Innovation and Disruption.*** Web3 technology has facilitated novel prospects for innovation and disruption in various business sectors, which were previously inaccessible. The Web3 ecosystem presents novel opportunities for enterprises to reimagine their products and services, encompassing decentralized finance (DeFi), non-fungible tokens (NFTs), and decentralized applications (DApps).
5. ***Cost Efficiency***. The utilization of Web3 development services has the potential to diminish the necessity for intermediaries, leading to a decrease in costs related to the engagement of intermediaries and third-party services. Organizations have the capacity to enhance their operational efficiency and streamline their processes through the utilization of technological advancements such as smart contracts and decentralized networks. Figure 1 illustrates the benefits of web 3 development services.

Figure 1. Benefits of web 3 development services

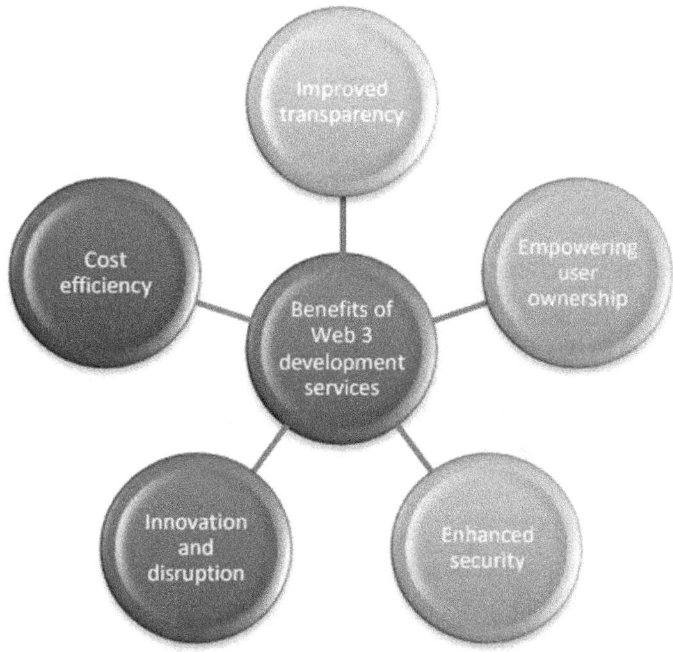

How Can Web 3 Help Businesses

The Significance of Web3 Development Services in Enhancing Company Success can be summarized as follows:

1. ***Content creation and distribution***. The emergence of Web3 development services holds the capacity to disrupt traditional methods of content generation and dissemination. The utilization of decentralized content platforms enables the elimination of intermediaries and the adoption of tokenization as a payment mechanism for artists' contributions. Contemporary artists have the ability to establish direct channels of communication with their audiences.

2. ***Decentralized Finance (DeFi).*** Decentralized Finance (DeFi) refers to the potential application of Web3 development services in the creation of platforms for decentralized financial systems. These platforms offer financial services that operate independently of traditional intermediaries commonly involved in such transactions. By embracing decentralized finance (DeFi), businesses can facilitate peer-to-peer lending, decentralized exchanges, and automated asset management. This adoption of DeFi presents opportunities for diversifying income streams and exploring novel possibilities.
3. ***Data security and privacy.*** primary objective of Web3 development is to enhance data security and privacy. Firms can enhance the security of sensitive information by employing encryption techniques and utilizing decentralized networks, thereby preventing unauthorized access and ensuring the integrity of data. This allows the companies to adhere to stringent regulations regarding data protection.
4. ***Governance and consensus.*** The emergence of Web3 technology enables the utilization of decentralized governance frameworks, wherein decision-making authority is distributed among network participants. Business enterprises can enhance equitable governance and consensus by implementing transparent voting mechanisms and smart contracts, thereby promoting community engagement and instilling trust in the organization.
5. ***Supply chain management.*** The full utilization of blockchain technology has the potential to introduce a transformative phase in supply chain management, which can be significantly enhanced through the development of Web3. Firms possess the capability to discern and track each stage of the supply chain through the establishment of ledgers that exhibit both visibility and irreversibility. This enables companies to ensure the legitimacy of their products, mitigate occurrences of counterfeit goods, and enhance customer trust.

The Key Driving Technologies and Factors Behind the Growth of the Web 3.0 Market

The significance of integrating Web3 development services is expected to increase for companies aiming to thrive in the digital era, given the persistent evolution of the digital landscape. Business enterprises possess the capacity to explore novel market opportunities, enhance security measures, promote transparency initiatives, and empower individuals by leveraging blockchain technology, cryptocurrencies, and decentralized network architectures. By utilizing Web3 development services, individuals and organizations can gain a competitive edge and position themselves for future opportunities.

Regarding the technologies driving the Web 3 growth, there exist; Blockchain, Artificial intelligence and machine learning. Blockchain is a crucial technological advancement in the context of Web 3.0. It functions as a decentralized and transparent ledger, facilitating safe and reliable transactions without the involvement of middlemen. The use of blockchain technology has the promise of significantly transforming several domains, including banking, healthcare, and supply chain management. This technology facilitates transactions that are both safe and transparent, surpassing the levels of fraudulence and manipulation seen in existing Web 2.0 platforms.

Web 3.0 is anticipated to integrate advanced artificial intelligence and machine learning techniques, potentially enabling enhanced customization of user experiences in the online realm. For instance, artificial intelligence systems has the capacity to analyze user behavior and preferences in order to provide personalized suggestions and search results. The notion of the "Semantic Web" is anticipated to be a prominent aspect of Web 3.0. The primary objective of the Semantic Web is to provide enhanced search capabilities and interactions with technology by establishing uniform, computer-interpretable data formats. Proponents argue that this development has the potential to enhance the effectiveness and cognitive capabilities of information processing. However, apprehensions have been voiced over the heightened understanding of the underlying meaning or "semantics" of the data handled by these computational systems. Several key factors contribute to the emergence and growth of the Web 3.0 market are:

- ***Increased security.*** Web 3.0 employs encryption mechanisms to safeguard users' data and transactions, thereby enhancing the security of the platform in comparison to the current iteration of the web. Individuals who express concerns regarding the security and confidentiality of their data will perceive this particular attribute as indispensable. Due to the comprehensive recording of all transactions on the blockchain, Web 3.0 is anticipated to exhibit a heightened degree of transparency in comparison to the current iteration of the web. Users will experience enhanced ease in monitoring their personal data and transactions, thereby ensuring protection against any potential misuse or exploitation.
- ***Scalability.*** The concept of scalability in Web 3.0 pertains to its ability to accommodate a larger volume of users and transactions in comparison to the current iteration of the web. The acquisition of a substantial volume of data or processing power is imperative for the optimal functioning of applications such as gaming and decentralized finance (DeFi).
- ***Decentralization.*** Web 3.0 is founded upon the utilization of decentralized technologies, such as blockchain, enabling users to exert enhanced authority over their data and safeguard their privacy. Web 3.0, alternatively referred to as the third iteration of the World Wide Web, is a term used to describe the next stage in the evolution of the internet. This presents a clear juxtaposition to the current state of the internet, which predominantly exhibits centralization, wherein a small number of large corporations possess the majority of data and influence.
- ***Innovation.*** Given the nascent stage of Web 3.0, a substantial scope for innovation exists within this platform. This phenomenon is attracting individuals who are aspiring to become software developers and entrepreneurs with a keen interest in developing novel and engaging applications.

These aforementioned factors are among the key elements that are facilitating the growth of the Web 3.0 industry. In the foreseeable future, it is expected that there will be a significant increase in expansion due to the continuous advancement of technology. Figure 2 illustrates the technologies driving the growth of Web 3, and figure 3 shows the key driving factors behind the growth of Web 3.

Figure 2. The technologies that drive the web 3 growth

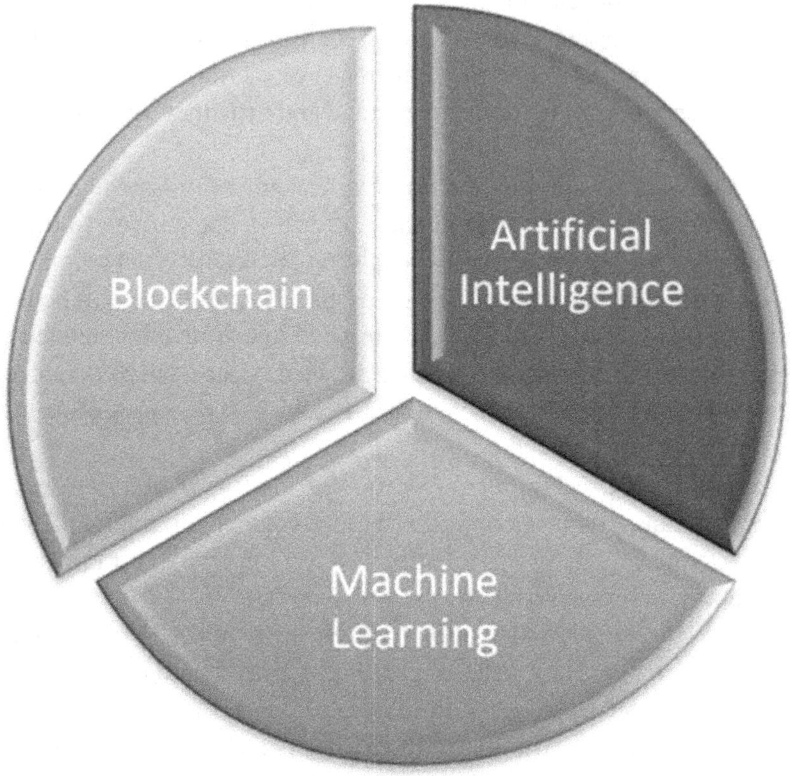

Figure 3. The key driving factors behind the growth of web 3

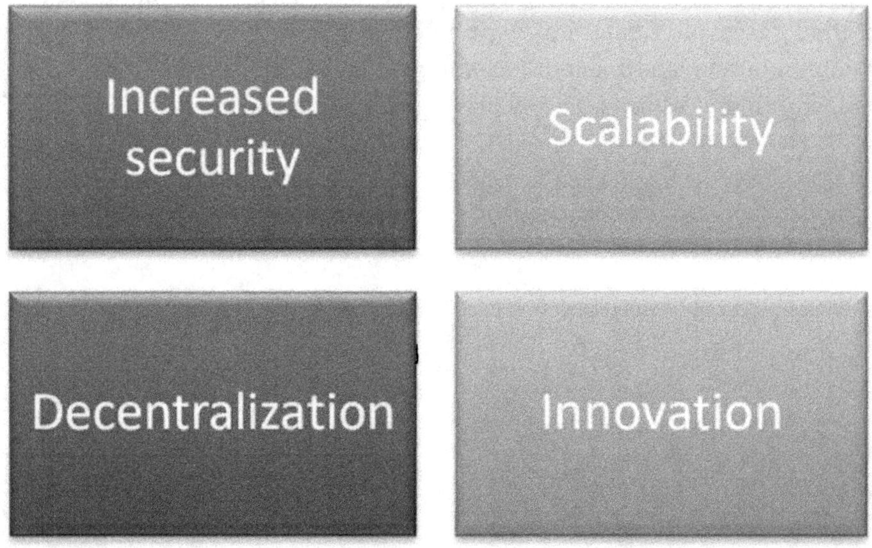

Some Specific Examples of How Web 3.0 Is Being Used Today

Outlined below are several specific examples that illustrate the practical application of Web 3.0 in contemporary society:

- ***Decentralized finance, commonly abbreviated as DeFi***, pertains to a financial framework that operates on the principles of blockchain technology. The utilization of decentralized finance (DeFi) obviates the necessity of an intermediary entity, such as a financial institution, thereby empowering individuals to independently engage in lending, borrowing, and investment activities.
- ***Non-fungible tokens (NFTs)*** are unique digital assets that possess inherent indivisibility, rendering them incapable of being substituted or interchanged with alternative entities. The utilization of non-fungible tokens (NFTs) as a means of representing ownership for digital artworks, virtual collectibles, and virtual assets within gaming contexts is a widely observed practice.
- ***The metaverse*** refers to a digital realm that is presently under development through the utilization of blockchain technology. The space in question serves as a venue for individuals to interact socially, engage in productive tasks, and participate in leisurely pursuits, including gaming.
- ***Decentralized autonomous organizations***, commonly referred to as DAOs, are entities that are administered exclusively through the utilization of computer code. Decentralized systems are characterized by the absence of a central authority or governing body, instead relying on predefined rules encoded within their structure. Consequently, these systems operate without being subject to the control or influence of any specific individual or organization.

These are only a few examples of the myriad applications currently leveraging the capabilities of Web 3.0. In the foreseeable future, it is plausible to expect the emergence of additional advanced applications as a direct consequence of the continuous advancement of technology.

Web 3 Security Threats

Although all technologies have security vulnerabilities, Web3's principles make it safer than Web 2.0. Security difficulties exist with Web3 and Web 2.0, bitcoin, and IPFS. These and other difficulties are slow to fix with Web3's network consensus. Main security concerns:

- ***No API encryption or verification***; Most individuals know not to provide unverified requesters personal info. Unauthenticated API requests and answers are typical for Web3 apps.
- ***Data is accessible to all network nodes on decentralized Web3***. Web3 front-ends must leverage user-friendly Web 2.0 technology. Web3 front-ends query the back-end for business logic and data.
- ***Many Web3 API requests are unsigned***. They are prone to on-path assaults, data interception, and other vulnerabilities like unencrypted, unsigned HTTP Web 2.0 applications. Although "implicit trust" exists, Web3 application data is typically unreliable.
- ***Hacking smart contracts***; Like any programming, smart contract security weaknesses may compromise user data or cash. The 2019 investigation found poorly structured Ethereum smart contracts that threatened $4 million Ether. In December 2021, hackers stole $31 million via misconfigured smart contracts. A faulty algorithm undervalued TerraUSD $50 billion in May 2022.

- ***Privacy concerns with decentralized data storage***; Blockchains store and access data on every node, unlike Web 2.0 databases. Data raises security and privacy concerns.
- ***Mobile wallet and account theft.*** Media reports on bitcoin and NFT wallet assaults abound. Hackers steal or phish private keys routinely. Private keys kept on devices may be stolen. Most attackers target bitcoin since DApps and Web3 utilize it. Web3 may affect other software.
- ***Bridge and protocol assaults***. Not all of Web3 is blockchain. Blockchain contains Internet-like protocols (7 OSI Levels). Many blockchains have "bridges," enabling cross-blockchain transactions. These methods are weak. The Wormhole bridge stole $320 million in cryptocurrencies in February 2022.
- ***Slow updates.*** Web3 makes security updates hard. Web3's decentralized network consensus needs network permission for all modifications. This may be Web3's largest security danger.
- ***Building secure apps is difficult***, and the inability to swiftly repair gaps after discovery makes them worse.
- ***Normal Web 2.0 dangers***. Credential theft and cross-site scripting affect Web3 front-ends regardless of the backend. Bots, API attacks, code injection, and other threats may affect apps and users.

Web3 app and infrastructure security best practices are:

- ***API request signature/encryption***; Popular HTTP request and response TLS increased Web 2.0 security. Web3 DApp API queries and answers are encrypted and signed to protect application data.
- ***Web 2.0 security measures like WAF***; Enterprises have decades of Web 2.0 security expertise. It suggests that systems have long protected user passwords, code injection, cross-site scripting, and other dangers. WAFs, bot control, and API security prevent many front-end assaults.
- ***Perform code testing before deployment***. This stage is crucial for Web 2.0, yet many organizations ignore it to launch and iterate rapidly. Later versions of new features or goods may remedy security issues.
- ***Web3 is harder***. Decentralized app updates and additions take longer than Web 1.0 and 2.0 owing to network consensus. Early security flaw detection is best. Code auditing becomes twice as important.

The Web 3 Advantages and Disadvantages

Web 3.0 Advantages:

Web 3.0 merits and downsides are hard to judge since most of its components are new or under development, and supporters minimize their shortcomings. However, a user-governed decentralized web offers advantages:

- Privacy and control. Internet consumers will regain their data from central sources.
- Openness. Web 3.0 improves transaction and decision visibility.
- Resilience. Single points of failure are less likely in decentralized applications.
- Smart personalization and prediction. Prediction and personalization using AI and ML will boost online responsiveness.

- Decentralized money. This will enable middleman-free purchasing, selling, and borrowing.
- Personalization and commerce in Web 3.0 may help companies interact with consumers.

Web 3.0 Disadvantages

Web 3.0's main drawbacks should concern enterprise leaders. The list includes:

- Complex. Decentralized networks and smart contracts are difficult to manage and understand for IT and internet users.
- Safety. These complex underlying technologies make Web 3.0 security problematic. Smart contract hacks and blockchain and cryptocurrency exchange security breaches make national news.
- Regulation worries. No central authority renders regulatory and compliance measures that safeguard online commerce and other web activities ineffective or nonexistent.
- Tech needs. Blockchain and dApps need expensive technological upgrades and energy usage that is ecologically and financially harmful.

The Web 3 Accessibility

Web accessibility, or eAccessibility, allows people with physical disabilities, situational issues, and socioeconomic bandwidth and speed limits to access and use websites. Good site design, construction, and revision provide more users equal content and usefulness. Blind individuals using text-to-speech software and devices benefit from semantic HTML, captions, and link names. Text and images may be enlarged to help low-vision readers. Underlined and colored links aid colorblind users.

Web accessibility meets these needs:

- Visual disorders include blindness, low vision, poor eyesight, and colorblindness.
- Parkinson's disease, muscular dystrophy, cerebral palsy, and stroke may induce hand tremors, muscle slowness, loss of fine muscle control, and more.
- Auditory: Deafness, hearing loss, and hard of hearing;
- Visual strobe or flashing causes photo epileptic seizures.
- Learning problems (dyslexia, dyscalculia), cognitive impairments (PTSD, Alzheimer's), and developmental "maturity" affect memory, attention, problem-solving, and reasoning.

Disability access applies to all types. Situational impairment may be a hindrance. Web accessibility should account for users' numerous constraints. In 2018, 93% of online accessibility practitioners globally have no professional web accessibility training, according to WebAIM.

Web Browsing Aids

The following assistive technologies aid impaired web users:

- Screen reader software may interpret selected monitor components or the complete computer content for blind and vision-impaired users using synthesized voice.

- Braille terminals may show text as braille characters using a refreshable braille display and keyboard or braille keyboard.
- Screen magnification software helps visually impaired people read.
- Speech recognition software can receive oral commands and transform dictation into grammatically correct text, making it useful for those with mouse or keyboard issues.
- Motor control impaired people may type more accurately using keyboard overlays.
- Subtitle or sign language videos for deaf people.

Key Web Accessibility Aspects

Accessible websites need many components.

1. Web page or web application content contains text, images, and audio and code or markup for organization, display, etc.

2.Web browsers, media players, "user agents"

3. Screen readers, keyboards, switches, scanning software, etc.
4. Web users' knowledge, experiences, and adaptations
5. designers, programmers, authors, etc., including disabled content contributors

6.Site-building software

7. HTML/CSS validators, accessibility tools, etc.

Web developers create content using authoring and assessment tools. Web browsers, media players, assistive technologies, and other "user agents" provide information access.

The Web 3 and Education

Schooling is shifting with Web3. Web3 decentralized apps provide learn-to-earn, community learning platforms that reward skill improvement, unlike web2, which prioritizes individual, centralized learning. Web3 and real-time education and blockchain activities provide users tokens for hard work and skill advancement based on their credentials. Without searching, Web 3.0 makes material available. Advanced or innovative education relies on digital learning. Education is vital to human pleasure, yet present paradigms impede learning for most people worldwide. Web3 and education emphasize environmental awareness and technology-enhanced learning. Decentralized blockchain technology enables verifiable transactions, private IP ownership, and creative empowerment.

Education Benefits of Web 3 Adoption

Web3 and education let people to own, control, and monetize their content and data, enabling new income streams. Web 3.0 simplifies information retrieval, which has several benefits:

1. ***Improved accessibility.*** Educational DAOs will allow decentralized ed3. Education centers may be there. Students may study any subject in any community. DAOs aid individualized learning. Teachers have greater leeway to teach individually. DAOs may tailor education to students.

2. ***Enhancing conventional education***. Web3 ed3 incorporates competency-based learning. Student learning may occur in DAOs, web3, education platforms, the workplace, and peer learning. Students may effortlessly switch between conventional and Web3 learning. Internet users may learn anytime. It would also identify talent before tests. Competency-based learning may turn these experiences into a standard degree. It will provide cumulative credit for work, school, business, military service, and more.
3. ***Personalized Education***. Educational semantics or Web 3.0 helps students choose vocations and education. Web apps assess our internet usage and online behaviors to adapt to our device, location, etc. Location-based services transmit data. Web 3.0 may provide appropriate information depending on the student's learning goal and location. Personal learning assistants solely give learning objective-related information. Educational Web 3.0 allows students choose their future, which is vital as an expert knowledge affects many aspects of their life.
4. ***Transparency.*** Web3's market pricing and network transparency helps talent grow. Web 3.0 incorporates the blockchain for decentralization and transparency. DAOs may increase governance transparency by giving significant funders a proportional say in curriculum and delivery. Blockchain technology revolutionizes payment processing, property and land title administration, intellectual property protection, digital IDs, cryptocurrencies, and NFTs. Ed3 will offer accessible educational models that may help students make money while studying. Bounties let them demonstrate their abilities to companies. This moves education from skills-based to competency-based. Web3 architecture allows students access free, open education from foreign universities. As students learn at their own pace, blockchain may authenticate credentials and make them accessible to employers. Kids may impress companies by completing bounties instead of academics. Many web2 platforms promote education equity.

Web 3 Integration Issues in Education

Web3 envisions the future internet. Users take ownership of their internet content, assets, and identities. Web3 technology in education may confront several problems, including:

1. Metaverse participation requires expensive, uncomfortable VR equipment.
2. Improve software security, scalability, and interoperability.
3. We can't move avatars or other assets between virtual worlds without interoperability.
4. ***Avatars*** for every location are unrealistic and not how we interact.
5. ***Developer prejudice and opinion*** may affect data tagging. Small changes might remove essential data or add developer-only data.
6. ***Censorship and privacy*** must be addressed since so much personal data will be exposed online.
7. ***Misreading internet habits*** and preferences may prohibit user-selected material.

Current learning concentrates on the 'institution'. In pre-school, secondary, high school, and university, institutions choose what students learn, how they study, and how long they have to show they are ready for the next step.

Traditional Schooling

Institutions usually provide value by offering:

- Diplomas and degrees are socially accepted proof of competence. Certain jobs need certificates. Employers prefer skilled applicants who completed 8 semesters at a university and received an undergraduate degree over those who dropped out after 7.5.
- Filtering: Universities' competitive admissions process attracts smart employees. Due to the rigorous admission process, entering a prominent university displays intelligence. Companies hire for skills, intelligence, and effort.
- Social life and peer learning: Institutions help students form strong bonds in school and college. We build professional and lifelong networks in school and college.

With Web 3, a fundamental transformation is taking place that is lowering the position of the institution at the center of our education system and providing the agency to the "learner." Web 3's tools, possibilities, and infrastructure will empower learners to select what, how, and when to study.

Web 3's Educational Influence

Education has become Ed 1, Ed 2, and Ed3, but it's roughly a decade behind the Web. Ed1 concentrated on institutions and schools transmitting knowledge offline and making certain material online, whereas Ed2 focused on Khan Academy, Coursera, EdX, Outschool, and Udemy giving accreditation and peer cooperation to global learners. We are in Ed 2 and the next few subjects will determine Ed 3.

1. Decentralization

In Web 3, blockchains can establish work and history, thus no organization will possess credentials. Students may create learning portfolios with collaborative projects, peer mentoring, internships, and university courses. The blockchain-validated learning passport would comprise micro-credentials, educational NFTs, experience letters, awards, research papers, and testimonials.

2. DAOs as University Alternatives

Schools and universities will take time to share their power and value in the value chain, but MOOCs have begun. DAOs are strong communities redefining social and financial incentives. Future education DAOs will allow students to join a community of like-minded individuals with financial incentives. Activities like managing interest-based groups, helping others, and working on group projects will be recorded on-chain as effort.

3. Earn and Develop

Nearly 40% of 1,000 U.S. teens wanted to be YouTube or Instagram influencers. Youth from UK. similar response rate. No astronaut, lawyer, or doctor like our era, just a Youtuber. The label may switch to NFT artists if this number climbs. Platforms for students to make money and reputation will grow. Traditional education is structured for 20-25 years of school, 25 years of work and family, and retirement. Influencers, gamers, interns, and entrepreneurs generate money online at 13-14 years old. 'Learning while they earn'. Increasing numbers of people are using gap years to pursue interests and improve skills. 'Learning while earning'. Many platforms encourage this. S Balaji, former Coinbase CTO and Web 3 pioneer, established 1729.com, a newsletter that funds assignments and training. Site users may earn tokens/cryptocurrency. Kids and adolescents use these ideas on web 3 game platforms like Decentraland and Fortnite. Native payment options that let youngsters earn while playing games or taking courses will grow.

4. More Microschools and Homeschools

When students have more choice over their education, micro-schools and home schools will proliferate. Micro-schools and learning pods have become popular homeschooling options in the two Covid-induced years. This increase is anticipated to decrease when we return to normality after COVID-19. However, unhappiness among all education ecosystem stakeholders—parents, students, instructors, and institution administrators—is at an all-time high, and many will not return to the existing system if they discover a model that works. More resources are available to tailor and build a learning path for your child and family. Web 3 will simplify and legitimize sideline homeschooling.

5. Metaverse/Microsoft Mesh Improves Online

Web 3 and Metaverse are different yet linked. Metaverse foundations will benefit education in Spatial Computing, Creator economy, Discovery, and Experience. Business will be more transparent and user-centric with web 3.0. Everything wrong with company data handling will change. Blockchain will be introduced by traditional and creative companies. A Blockchain makeover will make your apps transparent and accessible.

Web 3.0 Components

Blockchain technology alone cannot achieve Web 3.0 Blockchain's goals. Multiple technologies must collaborate and lead. Web 3.0 will be semantic and decentralized using new technologies. Augmented and virtual reality and high-fidelity 3D images will connect digital internet interfaces with reality. The Web will permeate physical objects' internet-connected computer interfaces as IoT devices employ 5G networks. Everything from phones to watches, cars to drones, fridges to ovens will be internet-connected. AI lets computers assess and learn on the fly, allowing user-centric interactions. To improve customer experience, chatbots and machine learning algorithms will examine structured and unstructured data.

Web 3.0 Characteristics

- ***Against Monopoly, Pro-Privacy.*** Web 3.0 will be anti-monopoly and pro-privacy. Centralized user data management won't be encouraged. Privacy and decentralization will dominate. Users will control data display, removing tech companies' monopoly and lowering data privacy assaults.
- ***Highly Safe.*** The new Web 3.0 will be safer. Decentralization and dispersion make network access difficult for hackers.

- ***Data Ownership.*** Tech giants used user data until recently. Blockchain-powered Web 3.0 allows customers complete data control. Complete network data encryption. Users may opt to share information with corporations and advertising agencies and benefit.
- ***Interoperability.*** Consumers might access app data without a platform in Web 3.0. This fixes Web 3.0's device inaccessibility.
- ***Blockchain without permission.*** Centralization is unneeded on Web 3.0 blockchain. Anyone may join the network and generate an address. This will remove gender, economic, orientation, geography, and other social obstacles. It will allow speedy, cheap cross-border digital asset and wealth transfers.

Our daily lives depend on social media. It may affect communication, community building, and connection. Web 3.0 social media enhances user engagement. Contracting Web3 game development services may enable gamification, decentralization, data ownership, and privacy.

The Web 3 and Current Businesses

Web 3.0 changes social media app development. It gives data control to individuals, preventing narrative spinning and data abuse like the Facebook Cambridge Analytics Scandal. Benefits of Web 3.0 are:

1. Social Media

- No central data collection or use authority
- Asset incentives empower users.
- Protect user privacy.
- No longer possible to impersonate.

2. Exchange Currency

Money exchange centralization fails. Disaster struck Mt Gox, which lost $460 million in bitcoins. Hackers cannot attack decentralized exchanges. Web 3.0 will see decentralized exchanges for efficient trade without hackers or transparency issues.

- Currency Exchange Benefits of Web 3.0
- Economical and fast transactions
- Hard to hack
- Excellent hardware wallet compatibility
- Users handle their funds completely.

3. Messaging Platforms

Messenger has always mattered. Because we can remember, we've used Facebook Messenger and WhatsApp for personal and Slack and Telegram for work. While messaging service complaints are down, users still risk dangerous message transmission and reliance on hackable centralized infrastructure. Web

3.0 messaging apps like ySign, Obsidian, and e-Chat employ Blockchain to preserve user privacy and security. Web 3.0 Messaging App Benefits are:

- Complete privacy
- Inability to advertise with data
- Send assets safely and swiftly.
- Fast transactions

4. Store Data

Normal users save data in Google Drive or iCloud. Companies need a more reliable and scalable central data storage solution. Most data storage operations are centralized, thus data may be manipulated or sold for advertising. Victims include Uber, LinkedIn, and T-Mobile. Web 3.0's distributed storage fixes this. It encrypts and shares files and data between peer-to-peer nodes. Web 3.0 Data Storage Benefits are:

- Works well with blockchain systems
- Strong encryption protects transmitted data
- No central authority
- Works with IoT

5. A Streaming Service

One of our fastest-growing industries is streaming. Netflix and Spotify dominate entertainment. While one of the most successful companies, streaming services are accused of utilizing data for advertising and underpaying writers. Blockchain addresses Web 3.0 problems with decentralization and smart contracts.

Web 3.0 Streaming Benefits are:

- Content creators may be transparent.
- Smart contracts reduce copyright issues.
- Less absurd content and streaming limitations.

6. Insurance

Insurance and banking have long been condemned for profiteering. Blockchain's decentralization and transparency improved their image. The technology will eliminate fraud and allow Web 3.0 insurance claims. It will also realize Open Banking, a longstanding goal. Benefits of Web 3.0 Insurance are:

- Almost no scams
- Improve customer experience
- Smooth international payments
- Banks conduct transparent internal audits.
- Future payments are being altered via Web3.

7. Browser

Google Chrome and Firefox rule Web 2.0. The Web 3.0 ideology needs decentralization. Next-generation web browsers should prevent data leakage and commercial use. Web 3.0 browsers should encrypt and reimburse users for sharing data. Benefits of Web 3.0 Browsers are:

- Internet users may browse quietly.
- Few security holes
- Data sales may generate money.
- Fast and safe

Web 3.0 Blockchain dApps would open and transparent the web. Blockchain-powered apps will empower individuals with data and disrupt the corporate corporations' grip. Web 3.0 uses decentralized blockchain technology. After Web 3.0, companies that use consumer data will disappear and those that operate in the background will grow. In an open financial and data world, firms must adapt. Web 3.0 will assist tiny enterprises most since digital behemoths will lose their monopoly and established brands will have to reinvent to survive.

Semantic Technology creates machine-processable languages for sophisticated, self-describing linkages to describe and link online data. If this technology is added to the Web, robots will understand humans well. Every human-web contact will satisfy users. Web 3.0 will transform digital interaction for everyone. Web 3.0 blockchain will effect established and creative businesses. Web 2.0 to Web 3.0 will take time. Companies will have time to evaluate decentralization and transparency. Web 3.0 is approaching; organizations must prepare.

The Web 3 and Economy and Society

We expect decentralized Web 3.0 to transform the economy and society. New ecosystems will enable direct physical-digital interactions between individuals and enterprises. This may develop new business models, income streams, investment instruments, and strategic partnerships. Corporate leaders see the potential of Web 3.0 technology investments, which have increased. Web 3.0 development will also be affected by AI, IoT, and 5G. These technologies will enable decentralized applications and services that boost industrial security, efficiency, and transparency.

During COVID-19, several companies converted to remote work and online sales, driving digital technology adoption. Digital transformation solutions for remote collaboration and e-commerce are popular. The global digital transformation sector will grow 15.5% to $6.8 trillion by 2026. Digital transformation is integrating digital technology into all aspects of a business to boost efficiency, customer experience, and performance. Manufacturing, healthcare, retail, and finance employ digital technology, driving digital transformation. Cloud computing, big data analytics, AI, and IoT promote digital transformation. Metaverse users may connect with one other and digital goods, and the sector is expected to reach $758.6 billion by 2026. The following Web 3.0 economic indicators matter:

- As more people learn about web 3.0 technologies like blockchain and decentralized finance, user numbers will rise. Interest in the decentralized web and industrial adoption of these technologies will drive this trend.

- More emerging and frontier technologies are expected in web 3.0. Examples include digital twins, federated learning, and advanced computing.
- A vibrant entrepreneurial ecosystem: Web 3.0 has helped entrepreneurs and scaleups develop decentralized technologies and apps.
- As more people utilize web 3.0, transactions on these platforms will increase. DeFi, cryptocurrency, and decentralized marketplace transactions are included.
- As their potential is seen, web 3.0 investments will climb. Venture capitalists, institutional, and private investors invest. Web 3.0 may increase M&A activity as it evolves.

Demand for decentralized applications, digital assets, NFTs, DeFi, and CeFi platforms drives.

Web 3.0. Defi is blockchain-based financial applications and services without intermediaries, whereas CeFi offers centralized financial services. DeFi and CeFi promote digital assets, financial products, and markets. New business ecosystems will need Web 3.0 infrastructure like decentralized storage and computation. These platforms will enable new business models and use cases by supporting dApps and services. AI, IoT, and 5G or 6G networks will enable web 3.0 create new business ecosystems. These technologies will enable decentralized applications and services that boost industrial security, efficiency, and transparency.

Web 3.0 combines blockchain, AI, robots, AR, VR, XR, 3D printing, 5G and 6G networks, the IoT, next-generation computing, quantum computing, DNA computing, neuromorphic computing, and edge computing. These technologies should create a decentralized, autonomous web where individuals own their data and digital identities. Blockchain supports decentralized applications and digital assets in Web 3.0. Robots, AR/VR/XR, and 3D printing will increase physical interactions with the digital world while AI automates processes and decision-making. 5G and 6G networks will provide faster, more reliable connection, while IoT will connect more devices. Quantum, DNA, neuromorphic, and edge computing will improve system power and capabilities. All of these technologies should improve online efficiency, security, and decentralization.

The web 3.0-powered metaverse will increase social interaction, entertainment, and commerce, altering society and the economy. One of the metaverse's largest ramifications is its potential to establish new social interactions and groups. Users may host and attend virtual events and communicate with people worldwide in new and intriguing ways. A developed metaverse ecosystem will leverage web 3.0 architecture and enable immersive and interactive story, gaming, and other digital content, affecting entertainment and media. Metaverse may boost e-commerce virtual marketplaces and digital goods. Metaverse may potentially create new customer and partner interactions, corporate structures, and revenue streams. Growing metaverse may help economy by creating jobs for entrepreneurs and small business owners. These include design, development, content, and community administration.

Using blockchain to create new business ecosystems, Web 3.0 will alter businesses and digitalize them. Cryptocurrencies demonstrate how web 3.0 is creating new business opportunities. These currencies offer fast, secure, and transparent transactions and DeFi. E-commerce and omnichannel marketing will be affected by Web 3.0. These systems will enable social media, email, and SMS customer communication, enabling unprecedented personalization and engagement opportunities.

Challenges

Web 3.0 will face privacy, cyber, regulatory, legal, and ESG challenges. Web 3.0 may improve privacy and security, but without adequate management, it might be a major liability. Web 3.0's role as a digital trust gateway requires proactive digital ethics and cyberdefense by business and government leaders. Since decentralized systems may not be protected by law, regulatory and legal difficulties may arise. Decentralized systems may hurt the environment and society, and industry-specific indicators are being produced, ESG concerns may arise.

To address these concerns, the industry must work with regulators and politicians to adopt appropriate policies. Research and development are needed for ESG problems, system security, privacy, and trust. The web 3.0 digital literacy and fluency must increase so key stakeholders and business leaders can make informed decisions on a cutting-edge approach.

Opportunities

Despite its issues, Web 3.0 provides many opportunities if we operate internationally, multi-stakeholder, and cooperatively. Opportunities include data democracy, digital ethics and cyber resilience, social entrepreneurship, digital and financial inclusion, and driving the UN SDG 2030 agenda and 2050 Net Zero Coalition. Web 3.0 may promote Human Rights if utilized properly.

The Web 3 and Regulation

Digital regulation is the range of tools government, regulators, businesses, and other organizations use to manage the impact of digital technology and activities on individuals, firms, the economy, and society. Standards, self-regulation, conduct norms, and basic laws. These treatments promote market-unattainable consequences. Non-regulatory tools may augment or replace regulation. Industry standards reflect global technological expertise and best practices. For fast-moving digital marketplaces, the government will try new methods to update their initiatives. Digital activities need specific control. Digital enterprises and applications are innovative, yet these features may challenge how we handle consumer and social issues. These traits may include;

- Personal data collection, processing, and portability
- Digital content oversight, verification, and responsibility
- Strong data analytics/algorithms and transparency
- Digital business size, scope, and network effects
- Digital service interruptions are simple and anonymous.
- Global data and digital reach
- The value of digital networks and infrastructure

Companies may collect massive amounts of personal data on global internet applications, evaluate it using algorithms, and exploit it for commercial purposes. This pushes companies to enter health, banking, advertising, and communications, offering data for numerous applications. The regulatory strategy must be broad, flexible, and adaptable, guided by consistency and clear principles, to solve these difficulties. Web3, the decentralized web, uses blockchain and other trustless technologies. Web3 has no central authority like Google, Facebook, or Amazon, so users may better control their data and identities with greater privacy and security. Web3 protocols encrypt and anonymize data to prevent unauthorized access. Without regulations, businesses and individuals suffer in this industry. Regulation may provide Web3 ecosystem developers, users, and stakeholders clear standards. A secure and dependable technological environment may promote transparency, accountability, consumer protection, and innovation. Regulation may also attract institutional investors that require safety rules. This may increase industrial capital, financing growth and development. But government and regulation have always challenged decentralized systems. They may impede speech and creativity. It also indicates government control, which contradicts decentralization.

Government regulations may hinder Web3 development in several ways. Traditional regulatory mechanisms are hard to enforce on Web3 owing to its decentralization. Web3 startups and organizations struggle to comply with various laws due to cost and complexity. This may hinder smaller firms and raise legal ambiguity and risk. When laws are unclear or change often, they might inhibit industry growth. Business, investor, and user doubts in the sector may hinder growth and progress. Overregulation that restricts developers' flexibility to experiment and innovate might also make Web3 development slower by creating a risk-averse atmosphere. Therefore, governments must balance user protection and innovation in their legislation.

DEXes like Uniswap are adapting to these restrictions and improving compliance. Centralized exchanges like CoinEx are complying with local government rules to become the blockchain infrastructure and the gateway for regular investors to the Web3 ecosystem. It employs a strong and specialized compliance and risk management staff to safeguard its users. To comply with regulations and maintain industry-leading security, the firm is aggressively obtaining new compliance licenses. Government and regulation provide both possibilities and risks to Web3 growth. These entities may limit Web3's expansion, but their potential must be considered. Finding the correct balance between innovation and regulation is important. How the sector engages with regulatory authorities while maintaining its goal of an open, transparent, and decentralized internet may determine Web3's destiny.

The Effect of Web 3 on the Next Industrial Revolution

The metaverse has garnered significant attention primarily due to its consumer-oriented aspects. However, it is important to recognize that Web3 also holds immense potential for individuals engaged in commercial and industrial contexts. In summary, the following points emerge:

- The ***metaverse*** has garnered significant attention, with much of the focus being on the potential benefits it may bring to consumers in the future. However, it is important to recognize that the primary source of value creation in the metaverse currently lies within the industrial sector.
- The utilization of ***digital twins*** is a potent approach for the surveillance, administration, and proactive manipulation of operational activities within physical industrial establishments.
- The emergence of ***the industrial metaverse*** is facilitated by advancements in technology and infrastructure, alongside the growing trend towards collaborative ecosystems.

There is a persistent and notable level of media attention directed towards the metaverse. In recent years, there has been a notable focus on the consumer and entertainment aspects. Numerous businesses are currently poised to integrate their goods and services into the metaverse, recognizing the imperative of formulating a metaverse strategy in anticipation of its widespread adoption as a corporate norm. The gaming community anticipates a heightened level of immersion in the near future as virtual and augmented reality technology and software continue to advance. The forthcoming integration of scent and touch capabilities is expected to further enhance the overall gaming experience, allowing players to engage more deeply with the virtual environment. In recent times, non-fungible tokens (NFTs) have garnered significant media coverage, with particular emphasis on prominent enterprises. There is an increasing recognition among companies, governments, and service providers of the potential offered by the metaverse in terms of facilitating collaboration and interaction within a digital realm. EY is actively adopting the concept of the metaverse and recognizing its potential benefits for both the clientele and the workforce. This phenomenon is evident in various endeavors such as EY wavespace, the EY metaverse lab, and the EY Talent Tree, alongside the immersive Web3 educational platform referred to as "EY Metaversity" (EY Metaversity, 2023).

Certain experts in the field contend that the industrial metaverse holds the highest potential for value creation, notwithstanding the fact that stakeholders are also enthused about the consumer and business prospects of the metaverse. Investigating the potential implications of the metaverse on business could serve as a catalyst for fostering innovation, enhancing operational processes, mitigating risks, boosting productivity, and achieving cost savings within industrial enterprises, which currently form the fundamental framework of our tangible economy.

Currently, we find ourselves situated within the epoch of the Internet of Things (IoT), with projections indicating a considerable proliferation of interconnected devices reaching approximately 30 billion by the year 2030. The potential benefits derived from these advancements will increase as artificial intelligence (AI) continues to advance in sophistication. This progress is facilitated by a resilient mobile infrastructure that enables the rapid transfer of vast quantities of data. The utilization of digital twins represents a robust approach to leverage the real-time data derived from the physical realm, enabling the generation of insightful analyses and predictions pertaining to future events.

Digital Twin Characteristics

- A digital twin refers to a virtual model or replica of a physical object or system, which is constructed using real-time data obtained from interconnected devices or sensors. The virtual entities exhibit a striking resemblance in their actions, reactions, and behaviors to their real-world counterparts, and this resemblance becomes more refined over time.
- In the realm of business, the utilization of analysis and modelling techniques serves the purpose of assessing performance, conducting hypothesis testing through simulations, and identifying potential areas for enhancement. By means of a captivating and immersive encounter, the various parties invested in the company are able to comprehend the unfolding events and discern their personal implications. Enhanced access to real-time information empowers decision makers to make more informed decisions, thereby facilitating the implementation of physical interventions and enabling the monitoring of progress through iterative feedback mechanisms.

The concept of the metaverse is frequently discussed in a future-oriented manner, representing a collective aspiration that has not yet been fully realized. It symbolizes a destination that remains beyond our current reach. Nevertheless, there has been a notable trend of corporate entities venturing into the metaverse, with a specific focus on the industrial domain. Industrial organizations perceive this technology as one that will yield immediate and future value. Non-fungible tokens (NFTs) have the potential to serve as smart contracts for the protection of patents and intellectual property rights. Additionally, augmented reality (AR), virtual reality (VR), and Metaverse platforms are emerging as foundational elements in augmented Building Information Modelling (BIM) software. This integration facilitates enhanced team collaboration, mitigates the need for expensive modifications, and enhances safety measures. Non-fungible tokens (NFTs) have the potential to serve as intelligent agreements for the protection and enforcement of patents and intellectual property rights. Several prominent stakeholders in the industrial sector have already initiated metaverse projects and are actively integrating them into their operations to optimize their business processes. This analysis examines the utilization of digital twins and immersive technologies by leading global industrial firms to effectively manage and enhance their operational processes. Additionally, it explores the dissemination of their research findings to a wider audience.

The Boeing Company (Boeing, 2023) is a prominent multinational corporation in the aerospace industry. Boeing is employing mixed reality technology at its future factory to enhance the digital information beyond the confines of two-dimensional displays, thereby enabling a more immersive and three-dimensional encounter. This encompasses the utilization of immersive three-dimensional engineering and holographic goggles. The primary objective of the aircraft manufacturer is to develop digital replicas of aircraft, known as digital twins, and integrate them into the manufacturing system. This integration enables the execution of simulations utilizing both the physical aircraft and its digital counterpart.

Nokia, (Nokia, 2023) is a multinational telecommunications and information technology corporation, has established a factory of the future at its Oulu 5G plant. This facility is responsible for the production of 1,000 base stations per day, encompassing both 4G and 5G technologies. In conjunction with automation and other digital solutions, Nokia achieved a productivity enhancement of more than 30 percent, halved the time required to bring products to market, and achieved substantial cost savings in the millions of euros annually. These outcomes were attributable to the central emphasis placed on the concept of a digital twin. Nokia is motivated to extend its offerings to industrial clientele by leveraging its existing accomplishments, aiming to furnish them with access to the company's expertise and technological advancements.

In the automotive automobiles and commercial vehicles, the automotive corporation established a comprehensive system of digital replicas, known as digital twins, with the purpose of generating a virtual representation of the company's facilities and production lines. Real-world counterparts have been equipped with sophisticated data collection capabilities in order to supply their digital counterparts with a vast amount of data points on a daily basis. According to estimates, the corporation is projected to realize cost savings exceeding US$300 million by the year 2025. The organization anticipates that efficiency enhancements will positively impact its environmental footprint.

There are multiple occurrences of service providers operating within an industry and offering digital twin technology and other solutions to manufacturers operating across the entirety of that sector. General Electric (General Electric, 2023) asserts that digital twins constitute a crucial component of the broader digital transformation landscape. The company offers industrial clients solutions aimed at enhancing operational efficiency.

CONCLUSION

There exist several examples demonstrating that the integration of several disruptive technologies in the industry is not merely a speculative notion, but rather a current reality. These advancements are facilitated by the progress in computer hardware, cloud computing, fifth-generation wireless networks, artificial intelligence, and web3 technologies. The confluence of these technological advancements enables the analysis of data at accelerated rates and larger scales. The convergence of success criteria exemplifies the operational dynamics of the metaverse, wherein the actualization of its potential is contingent upon the collective interaction of all participants. Furthermore, individuals will experience enhanced opportunities for equitable participation in organizational processes, alongside increased prospects for career progression within a work setting that values the contributions of all employees. The forthcoming state of the technologies related to Web 3 will be characterized by a heightened focus on value creation, surpassing the sole pursuit of monetary benefits.

REFERENCES

Alford, H. (2021). *Crypto's networked collaboration will drive Web 3.0*. TechCrunch.

Almeida, F., Santos, J. D., & Monteiro, J. A. (2013). E-Commerce business models with the context of Web 3.0 paradigm. *International Journal of Advanced Information Technology*, *3*(6), 1–12. doi:10.5121/ijait.2013.3601

Boeing. (2023). https://www.Boeing.com/

Cambridge Dictionary. (n.d.). https://dictionary.cambridge.org/dictionary/english/driving-force

Edelman, G. (2021). *What Is Web3, Anyway?* Wired.

Fenwick, M., & Jurcys, P. (2022). *The Contested Meaning of Web3 and Why it Matters for (IP)*. Lawyers. doi:10.2139/ssrn.4017790

García, F. A. C. (2008). *The third generation web is coming*. https://methainternet.wordpress.com/2008/01/25/the-third-generation-web-is-coming/

Garrigos-Simon, F. J., Lapiedra-Alcamí, R., & Ribera, T. B. (2012). Social networks and Web 3.0: Their impact on the management and marketing of organizations. *Management Decision*, *50*(10), 1880–1890. doi:10.1108/00251741211279657

General Electric. (2023). https://www.ge.com/

Hussain, F. (2012). E-learning 3.0=E-learning 2.0 + Web 3.0? *Proceedings of the IADIS International Conference on Cognition and Exploratory Learning in Digital Age*, 11-17.

Kastrenakes, J. (2021). *Jack Dorsey says VCs really own Web3 (and Web3 boosters are pretty mad about it)*. The Verge.

Khoshafian, S. (2021). *Can the Real Web 3.0 Please Stand Up?* RTInsights.

Lassila, O., & Hendler, J. (2007). Embracing Web 3.0. *IEEE Internet Computing*, *11*(3), 90–93. doi:10.1109/MIC.2007.52

Lee, T. B. (2006). *Data growth and Web 3.0*. Retrieved March 10, 2018, from http://www.expertsystem.com /web-3-0/

Mak, A. (2021). *What Is Web3 and Why Are All the Crypto People Suddenly Talking About It?* Slate.

MetaversityE. (2023), https://www.ey.com/en_eg

Nike. (2023). https://www.nike.com/

ADDITIONAL READING

Read, M. (2021). *Why Your Group Chat Could Be Worth Millions*. Intelligencer.

Rudman, R., & Bruwer, R. (2016). Defining Web 3.0: Opportunities and challenges. *The Electronic Library*, *34*(1), 132–154. doi:10.1108/EL-08-2014-0140

Yen, N. Y., Zhang, C., Waluyo, A. B., & Park, J. J. (2015). Social media services and technologies towards Web 3.0. *Multimedia Tools and Applications*, *74*(14), 5007–5013. doi:10.1007/s11042-015-2461-4

KEY TERMS AND DEFINITIONS

Augmented Reality (AR): Is an interactive experience that enhances the real world with computer-generated perceptual information. Using software, apps, and hardware such as AR glasses, augmented reality overlays and digital content onto real-life environments and objects.

Building Information Modelling (BIM): Is the foundation of digital transformation in the architecture, engineering, and construction (AEC) industry.

Decentralized Applications (DApps): Are digital applications or programs that run on a decentralized network, rather than a single computer or server.

Decentralized Finance (DeFi): Is an emerging model for organizing and enabling cryptocurrency-based transactions, exchanges, and financial services.

Environmental, Social, and Corporate Governance (ESG): Is a set of aspects considered when investing in companies, that recommends taking environmental issues, social issues, and corporate governance issues into account.

Interplanetary File System (IPFS): Is a distributed file storage protocol that allows computers all over the globe to store and serve files as part of a giant peer-to-peer network.

Massive Open Online Courses (MOOC): Are free online courses available for anyone to enroll. MOOCs provide an affordable and flexible way to learn new skills.

Non-Fungible Tokens (NFTs): Are blockchain-based tokens that each represent a unique asset like a piece of art, digital content, or media.

Post-Traumatic Stress Disorder (PSTD): Is a disorder that that develops in some people who have experienced a shocking, scary, or dangerous event.

United Nations Sustainable Development Goals (UN SDGs): Also known as Global Goals, were adopted by the United Nations in 2015 as a universal call to action to and poverty, protect the planet, and ensure that by 2030 all people enjoy peace and prosperity.

Virtual Reality (VR): A computer-generated environment with scenes and objects that appear to be real, making the user feel they are immersed in their surroundings. This environment is perceived through a device known as Virtual Reality headset or helmet.

Web Accessibility in Mind (WebAim): Is to expand the potential of the web for people with disabilities.

Web Application Firewall (WAF): Helps protect web applications by filtering and monitoring HTTP traffic between a web application and the internet.

World Wide Web (WWW): Commonly known as the web, is an information system enabling information to be shared over the internet through simplified ways.

Chapter 3
Blockchain Basics:
A Deep Dive Into the Blocks, Chains, and Consensus

Muhammad Ahmed
Superior University, Lahore, Pakistan

Adnan Ahmad
COMSATS University Islamabad, Lahore, Pakistan

Furkh Zeshan
https://orcid.org/0000-0002-2960-9632
COMSATS University Islamabad, Lahore, Pakistan

Hamid Turab
https://orcid.org/0000-0002-2280-2704
COMSATS University Islamabad, Lahore, Pakistan

ABSTRACT

A blockchain functions as a decentralized network, serving both as a digital ledger and a mechanism for securely transferring assets without the need for a central authority. Much like the internet facilitates the digital flow of information, blockchain empowers the digital exchange of various value units. The tokenization of various assets, including currencies and real-world applications, is a feasible endeavor within the realm of blockchain networks. This technology not only facilitates secure value transfers but also maintains a persistent record of transactions, establishing a singular version of truth referred to as the network state. This chapter provides a succinct overview of blockchain, highlighting its defining characteristics that position it as a prominent and transformative technology.

DOI: 10.4018/979-8-3693-1532-3.ch003

INTRODUCTION

In recent years, there has been a significant surge in the application of Information and Communication Technologies (ICT) for swift, efficient, and secure data transfer among diverse devices globally. The rise of the internet has enabled a digital exchange of information between various parties, primarily conducted through online financial transactions where users send and receive payments. Traditionally, this system of communication and transaction relies on a centralized third-party verification entity, as depicted in Figure 1. Such an entity is responsible for ensuring the secure transfer and accurate recording of data across multiple accounts. Nonetheless, this method poses several challenges when dealing with the transmission of information through an open network (Sunyaev & Sunyaev, 2020). Therefore, the issues such as potential fraud by the trusted third party, vulnerability to cyber-attacks, which could lead to a single point of failure, delays introduced by third-party involvement, and the need for assured transaction validation arise. The exclusive reliance on a solitary third-party controller raises significant concerns regarding both trust and operational efficiency. Traditional methodologies are heavily contingent upon this third-party framework, introducing substantial apprehensions related to the potential compromise of privacy and anonymity. Consequently, there exists an urgent requirement for the establishment of a decentralized system capable of ensuring robust security for transaction management and contract execution, particularly within the realm of device communication. The implementation of a communication protocol that guarantees data protection, integrity, authenticity, irrefutability, and confidentiality becomes imperative, especially when dealing with the diverse range of data generated by smart devices (Ahmadi et al., 2014; Li et al., 2019). Hence, Distributed Ledger Technology (DLT), commonly recognized as blockchain, emerges as a plausible solution to address these challenges, as depicted in Figure 2. The genesis of this concept can be attributed to an individual or group operating under the pseudonym Satoshi Nakamoto, who introduced the groundbreaking Bitcoin, which is the pioneer in decentralized digital currency (Cosares et al., 2021; Gandal et al., 2021; Nakamoto, 2008). The widespread adoption of Bitcoin is reflected in its transaction volumes. This technology offers a decentralized network that is capable of generating and managing smart contracts within IoT-enabled smart applications, enhancing security and eliminating central points of vulnerability.

Figure 1. Traditional system

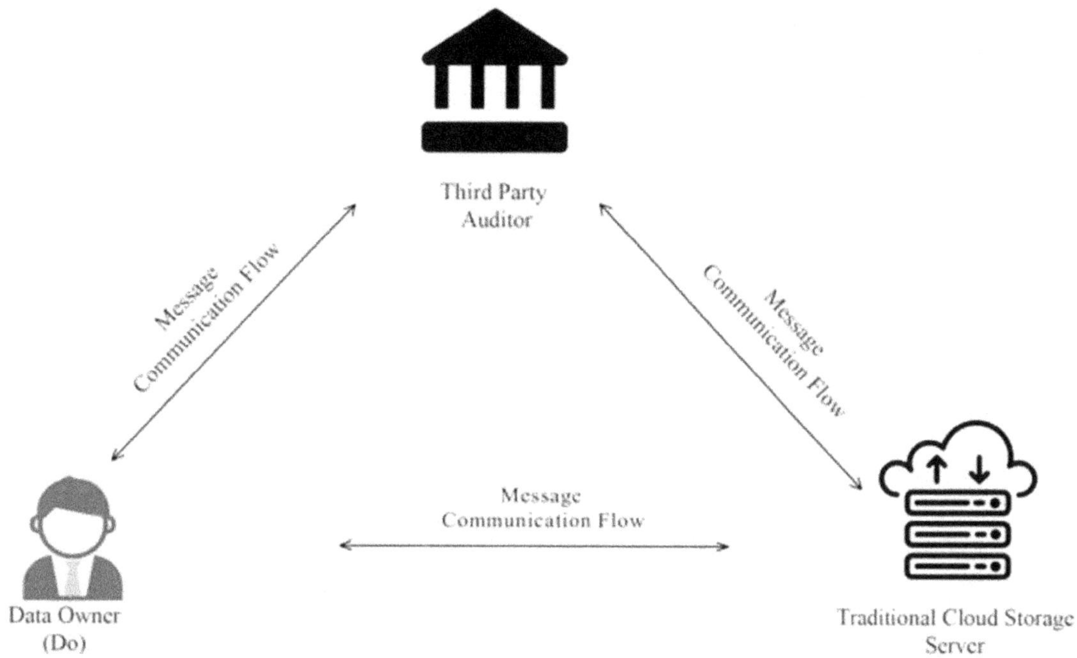

Such applications are not immune to network threats, including but not limited to DDoS attacks, malware, and brute force attacks (Aslan et al., 2023). To counter these threats, blockchain technology is proposed as a robust solution. It fortifies the system's security and privacy and is characterized by its features: scalability, adaptability, dependability, authorization capabilities, data integrity, identity management, non-repudiation, authentication, and accountability. Recent advancements in information technology infrastructure, along with the revitalization of previously sidelined technologies, have been propelled by innovative improvements and the gradual rise of cohesive, analytic platforms. Artificial intelligence (AI), particularly with its significantly enhanced machine learning (ML) and deep learning (DL) algorithms, is currently drawing considerable interest (McConaghy, 2016). In the era of digitalization, with technologies at the edge becoming increasingly influential, we are witnessing unprecedented levels of interconnectivity and deep-rooted integration across digital networks and devices. Concepts like the Internet of Things (IoT) and cyber-physical systems (CPS) are gaining traction and popularity. One of the emerging trends is the amalgamation of various established technologies the blockchain technology, for instance, is a prime example of this trend, merging multiple groundbreaking technologies into a singular, influential framework projected to have profound and far-reaching effects (Khettry et al., 2021). Blockchain stands out as one of the leading security technologies within the distributed software systems of today. At its core, it leverages the principles of the cryptocurrency network to ensure confidentiality and privacy for its users, employing cryptographic methods to secure communications between nodes in a network. This network is essentially a series of digital signatures connected in a mesh-like structure. A key attribute of blockchain is its nature as a decentralized platform for computation and information exchange. This allows for various authoritative entities to come together, forging a unified platform to bolster security and privacy across numerous transactions. Such a collaborative environment enables these entities to develop applications that are crucial for strategic decision-making within business intelligence and management, as well as in engineering domains (Abou Jaoude & Saade, 2019). However, exploration of blockchain technology the whole chapter divided into its evolution through various stages, from Blockchain 1.0 to the current Blockchain 5.0. Examining the scope and characteristics of blockchain, which uncovers key concepts and terminology crucial to understanding this innovative technology. The workings of a blockchain are demystified, accompanied by an exploration of public, private, hybrid, and consortium blockchains.

Figure 2. Distributed system

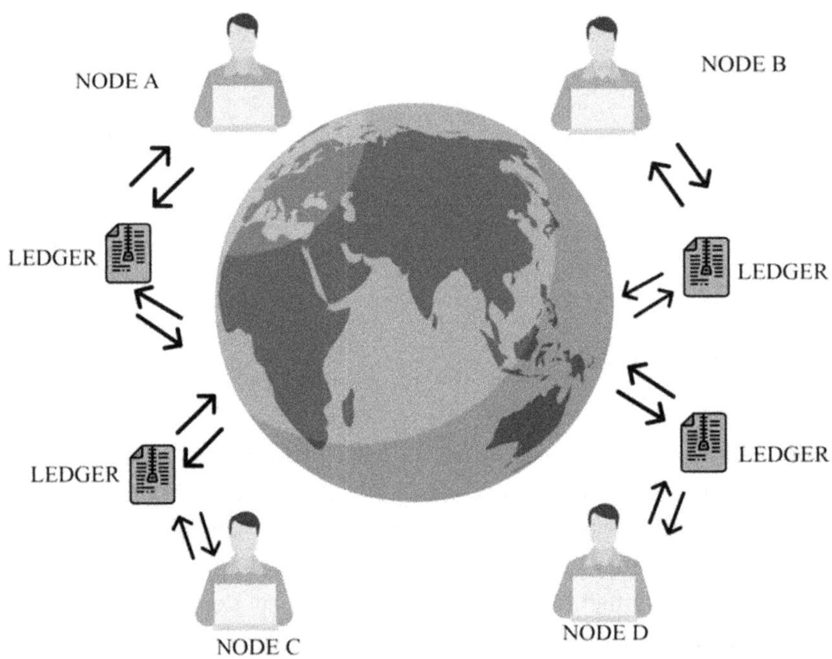

This investigation delves into the examination of support levels for smart contracts, elucidating their importance. The discourse navigates through the terrain of blockchain platforms, exploring the various types and accentuating their respective runtime environments. The foundational medium of blockchain, namely consensus mechanisms, is studied, encompassing an in-depth analysis of Proof of Work and Practical Byzantine Fault Tolerance. A thorough SWOT analysis has been conducted to provide insights into the strengths, weaknesses, opportunities, and threats existing in the field of blockchain. This exploration determines with a reflective examination of the deep significance and inherent potential of blockchain technology in the current vibrant landscape.

BLOCKCHAIN TRENDS AND DEVELOPMENT IMPLICATIONS

The progress of blockchain technology is continuously advancing and witnessing a rise in the popularity of decentralized systems. The current advancements in blockchain technology encompass various areas such as cryptocurrencies, decentralized finance, non-fungible tokens, and decentralized autonomous organizations. The study of their influence on the broader of blockchain development is delineated in Table 1.

1. Cryptocurrencies and Decentralized Finance (DeFi)

Cryptocurrencies have undergone a dramatic transformation that goes beyond simple digital forms of currency. Resulting in the emergence of groundbreaking financial systems typified by the growth of Decentralized Finance (DeFi). DeFi operates independently, breaking away from traditional financial systems and avoiding the need for third parties. It achieves this by utilizing blockchain technology. As a result, smart contracts streamline financial procedures such as lending, borrowing, and trading. However, this decentralized, and peer-to-peer idea not only promotes financial inclusiveness, but also empowers people with unparalleled control over their assets (Makarov & Schoar, 2022). The consequences for blockchain development are substantial, necessitating the establishment of robust smart contract infrastructure, secure blockchain networks. Advancements in consensus algorithms and cross-chain interoperability to meet the demands of DeFi protocols. The integration of decentralized oracles for providing real-world data to smart contracts is also recognized as pivotal in DeFi development. As cryptocurrencies continue to reshape the financial landscape. A comprehensive understanding and ongoing research into the intricate dynamics of DeFi remain imperative for both academia and industry (Chen, 2018).

2. Non-Fungible Tokens (NFTs)

Non-Fungible Tokens (NFTs) organize the unique digital assets, that signify ownership of distinct items. In contrast to transposable assets like cryptocurrencies, Non-Fungible Tokens (NFTs) lack divisibility and cannot be exchanged on a one-to-one basis. Ensuring that the scarcity and authenticity of the subsequent digital asset. Each NFT is marked by cryptographic verification. These digital tokens have gained importance for representing various digitized real-world items, involving art, music, virtual real estate, and more (Makarov & Schoar, 2022). The ownership and transaction history of NFTs so the blockchain is tightly recorded. Establishing a transparent and unalterable ledger. NFTs have introduced a novel proportion to digital ownership and provenance. Permitting creators and collectors to establish verifiable and unique digital ownership rights. Consequently, NFTs have got significant attention in the field of art, entertainment, and digital commerce. Reshaping conventional notions of value and ownership in the digital era (Nobanee & Ellili, 2023).

3. Decentralized Autonomous Organizations (DAOs)

Decentralized Autonomous Organizations (DAOs) present an advanced paradigm for organizational governance in the field of blockchain technology. These entities operate independently, governed by rules encoded as computer programs. It is typically executed using smart contracts. Eliminating the necessity for a central governing authority and DAOs classify themselves through their decentralized structure. Instead, decision-making authority is distributed among active members, they often employ token-based voting systems to determine collective choices. The autonomy of DAOs is underpinned by the transparent and open-source nature of their code. It ensures availability to all participants for a broad understanding of organizational processes. However, consensus mechanisms facilitating decision-making on significant matters with DAOs play a crucial role in asset and fund management. Despite their potential to reshape governance structures, DAOs face challenges which include security vulnerabilities in smart contracts. The compulsion to navigate complex legal and regulatory landscapes. The ongoing evolution of blockchain technology. Governance models continues to exert influence on the trajectory and applications of DAOs across different industries (Bellavitis et al., 2023).

4. Development Implications

Secure blockchain networks and a robust smart contract architecture are essential for the development of DeFi protocols. The collective need for scalable and interoperable solutions has led to improvements in consensus algorithms and cross-chain interoperability. The rising popularity of NFTs highlights the necessity for blockchain networks that can securely handle high transaction volumes. To tackle congestion and reduce associated high fees, scalability solutions like layer 2 protocols are being investigated. Therefore, there is a growing focus on environmentally sustainable blockchain development, driven by concerns about specific consensus mechanisms.

Table 1. Blockchain trends

Blockchain Trend	Description
Cryptocurrencies and DeFi	• Digital assets denominated in virtual tokens. • Native tokens serve as the principal store of value and medium of exchange within blockchain networks. • Transaction fees (gas fees) compensate validators who maintain the decentralized network (Chen, 2018). • Decentralized Finance (DeFi) enables the creation of user generated currencies and financial services on blockchain.
Nonfungible Tokens (NFTs)	• Distinct, noninterchangeable tokens recorded on a blockchain. Used for digital ownership, offering verifiable and traceable proof of ownership. • Applied in various creative fields, including digital art, music, collectibles, and more (Chohan & Paschen, 2023). • Can represent ownership in digital and physical realms, including access passes to events.
Decentralized Autonomous Organizations (DAOs)	• Organizations managed entirely through smart contracts on a blockchain (Kaplan & Haenlein, 2010). • Programmed aspects of organizational structure, governance, and activities (Lumineau et al., 2021). • Enable secure and automated governance processes, including membership based on NFTs. • Facilitate decentralized collaboration, fundraising, and decision-making (Levis et al., 2021).

BLOCKCHAIN EVOLUTION

The foundational architecture of blockchain technology is currently undergoing multiple iterations, aiming to offer a diverse range of applications, as illustrated in Figure 3. Presenting a diversity of perspectives, blockchain development stages (1.0 to 5.0) have already been proposed, covering functionality, applicability range, features, strengths, flaws, problems, and security concerns. However, blockchain 5.0, the most recent version, has continuously been actively developed to enhance its appropriateness for different types of businesses. Figure 3 depicts the primary phases of blockchain evolution in terms of applications, consensus techniques, and features (from 1.0 to 5.0).

1. Blockchain 1.0

Satoshi Nakamoto invented Bitcoin, a crypto-currency which is prominent, during the initial developmental phase known as blockchain 1.0 (Nakamoto, 2008). Blockchain 1.0 is a widely used version of Bitcoin, a fast-expanding digital payment system that has been adopted by financial sector worldwide (Buterin, 2019; Sagirlar et al., 2018). As a result, issues about compatibility and adaptation with blockchain1.0 have been mentioned as key hurdles to widespread use.

2. Blockchain 2.0

Blockchain 2.0 presents a smart contract is executable user program that operates upon the Ethereum blockchain ecosystem and can perform a variety of automated tasks and make legal decisions. Smart contract simple user programs that run on the blockchain to execute different automated operations and make lawful decisions (Kiayias et al., 2020). These are the programs that are available to operate independently, adhering to pre-programmed timing, efficiency, decision, and verification logic and criterion standards. Blockchain network's applications (contracts) make use of user identities to keep personal information private (Kosba et al., 2016). Therefore, Ethereum (Lotti, 2016; Magaki et al., 2016) is the most popular and widely used program which is blockchain 2.0 based for securely writing and executing smart contracts.

3. Blockchain 3.0

The difficulty of storing large amounts of data and the dependency on public networks are two of the key flaws of blockchain technology (1.0 and 2.0). Bitcoin and Ethereum are two public platforms where data is created and recorded on the blockchain regularly; as a result, data must be kept in a bunch of locations, including data systems and cloud storage (Milutinovic et al., 2016). To address this problem, the development of blockchain 3.0 emerged, aiming to effectively store substantial volumes of data and legitimize multiple communication methods. Additionally, decentralized systems are connected through system calls, granting developers the flexibility to compose application code in diverse programming languages. Although decentralized networks offer various advantages, it is important to acknowledge that they face a range of security challenges. These challenges include issues related to user authentication, authorization, and data access control (Muzammal et al., 2019).

4. Blockchain 4.0

The next phase in the progressive evolution of major blockchain iterations, advancing from 1.0 to 3.0, focuses on addressing the practical limitations of real-life applications. In this progression, blockchain 4.0 aims to overcome industrial constraints by enabling the creation and execution of real-world applications in a decentralized and secure manner (Niranjanamurthy et al., 2019). This marks a transformative shift, allowing industries and businesses to revamp their entire framework and operations compared to traditional self-recording systems. The transformation is facilitated by adopting a decentralized database characterized by a distributed and immutable ledger, distinctive features of blockchain 4.0. The rise of Industrial 4.0, a technological wave fostering connectivity between individuals and machines, leads to significant industry growth and productivity breakthroughs that benefit both people and the environment simultaneously (Nofer et al., 2017). The integration of Industry 4.0 and blockchain 4.0 gives rise to a new paradigm, built on reliable networks that eliminate the need for intermediary entities. Concurrently, manual operations undergo transformation into interconnected systems through the deployment of automated and autonomous technologies. This convergence places emphasis on integrating smart contracts into industrial processes, reducing reliance on paper-based contracts, and managing the network through consensus (Noyes, 2016; O'Dwyer & Malone, 2014). Financial services (Panarello et al., 2018), Internet of Things (Paul; Paul et al., 2014), Transportation and Logistics (Puthal & Mohanty, 2018), SG (Reed, 2014; Reyna et al., 2018), and E-Health (Sagirlar et al., 2018) are only a few examples of such companies that have recently integrated a combination of blockchain 4.0 with Industry 4.0 into their company processes.

5. Blockchain 5.0

By standardizing and simplifying the digital future generation, blockchain 5.0 aims to meet the needs of the next generation of business leaders. In this revolutionary context, blockchain 5.0, It's critical to construct the next generation of decentralized Web 3.0 apps while assuring the confidentiality, security, and interoperability of data by combining Artificial Intelligence (AI) and Distributed Ledger Technology (DLT). In the emerging era of blockchain 5.0, a huge number of researchers is already making significant strides toward success by adopting this approach (Sharma et al., 2017).

Figure 3. Blockchain evolution

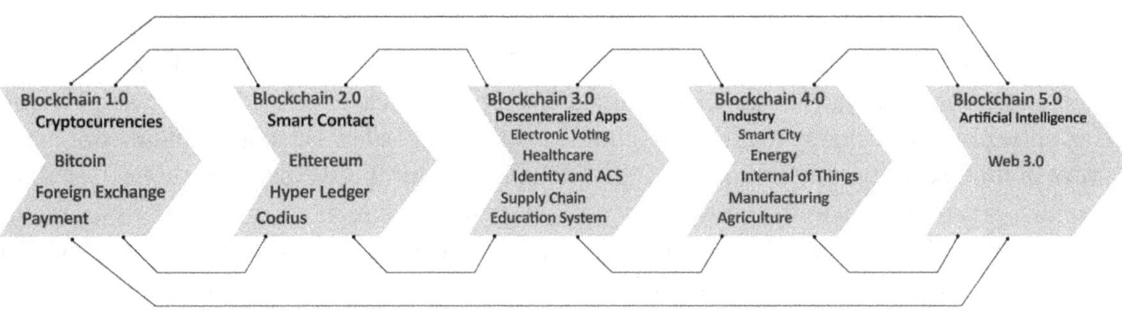

SCOPE OF THE BLOCKCHAIN

This technology is utilized to provide improved authorization, accountability, and authentication, collectively known as AAA, along with integrity, security, and non-repudiation. Centralized systems may not offer these features as effectively and efficiently [8,9]. Blockchain combines three distinct technological areas: public-key cryptography, a peer-to-peer network, and programming. It has transformed the field of digital currency by eliminating the need for intermediary specialists in registration and distribution processes. Its most notable contribution is Bitcoin, a form of cryptocurrency, which operates as a public ledger for all network transactions. It addresses issues such as double-spending and unauthorized access, thereby enhancing network security and privacy. This technology has wide-ranging applications, including smart grids, voting systems, financial services, and supply chain management, demonstrating significant potential (Kshetri & Voas, 2018; Wang & Yang, 2021). When incorporated into digital transactions, blockchain provides several benefits, such as time and cost savings related to the validation and processing of transactions. Functioning on a distributed ledger improves operational efficiency, security, and resilience against cyber threats. It emerges as a highly dependable technology for monitoring digital assets, introducing heightened security, and enhancing privacy within organizational infrastructures (Cosares et al., 2021; Laroiya et al., 2020).

Future Applications of Blockchain

The future applications of blockchain area various sectors, as discussed below:

1. **Digital Advertising:** The digital advertising sector is currently seizing with challenges such as fraudulent domains and dense data practices. Blockchain presents a solution by presenting transparent and immutable data records, thus fostering trust in areas where it was previously lacking.
2. **Cybersecurity:** Blockchain's public ledgers keep the data that is both verified and encrypted, making it resistive to tampering and excluding the need for third authority.
3. **Single Failure Points:** As a decentralized framework, blockchain drives without third-party intermediaries, reduction the risk of a single point of failure and ensuring that transaction data is verifiable and reliable.
4. **Supply Chain Management:** Blockchain's record-keeping on a public, distributed ledger provides heightened transparency and efficiency, reducing human errors and delays. It also facilitates detailed tracking of costs and processes throughout the supply chain.
5. **Cloud Storage:** Blockchain strengthens the protection and resilience of cloud storage, guarding against hacking, data loss, and human errors. This improvement makes cloud services more secure against various types of cyber-attacks.

CHARACTERISTICS OF BLOCKCHAIN

The defining characteristics of blockchain technology, which confer substantial advantages across various applications due to the qualities outlined in Figure 4.

1- Persistency: Persistency refers to the unchanging nature of blockchain records. Unlike centralized systems where data can be tampered with, the blockchain's ledger is immutable, ensuring that once data is entered, it cannot be altered, thus providing transparent and secure records (Viriyasitavat & Hoonsopon, 2019).

2- Decentralization: Where traditional systems depend on a single entity for transaction validation, potentially creating a point of vulnerability, blockchain operates on a decentralized model. This allows a network of nodes that may not necessarily trust one another to engage in trust-free interactions, making collective, rational decisions (Eyal & Sirer, 2014).

3- **Digitization:** Blockchain technology eliminates the need for paper-based records by digitizing all data. This information is methodically stored in the blockchain's sequential blocks (Hanna, 1995).

4- **Distributed Ledger:** The ledger on a blockchain is duplicated across the network, publicly recording each transaction and participant's details. Every node has the capability to independently verify the information without relying on a central authority, ensuring the continuity of network function even if some nodes fail (Fan & Chai, 2018; Fernandez-Carames & Fraga-Lamas, 2019).

5- **Consensus Driven:** The consensus process in blockchain is a method through which nodes in the network quickly reach an agreement. This is critical when multiple nodes are involved in validating transactions, ensuring unanimous approval before a transaction is considered finalized (Lashkari & Musilek, 2021).

6- **Cryptographic Security:** Blocks on the blockchain are secured using cryptographic techniques, making alterations and unauthorized access extremely challenging. This cryptographic sealing improves the system's resilience against failures and removes single points of failure (Delgado-Segura et al., 2018).

KEY CONCEPTS AND TERMINOLOGY

Blocks and Chains

Blockchain technology originates its name from its foundational structure, characterized by "blocks" of data linked together in a "chain." Each block contains a set of transactions or data entries. When a new block is added to the chain, it references the previous block, creating a chronological and immutable record of transactions. Blocks function as containers for data and are often limited in size to ensure efficient processing and validation. The process of chaining blocks within a blockchain system maintains the integrity of data, as altering a single block requires changes to subsequent blocks, a computationally infeasible task due to the consensus mechanisms implemented in blockchain networks.

Figure 4. Blockchain characteristics

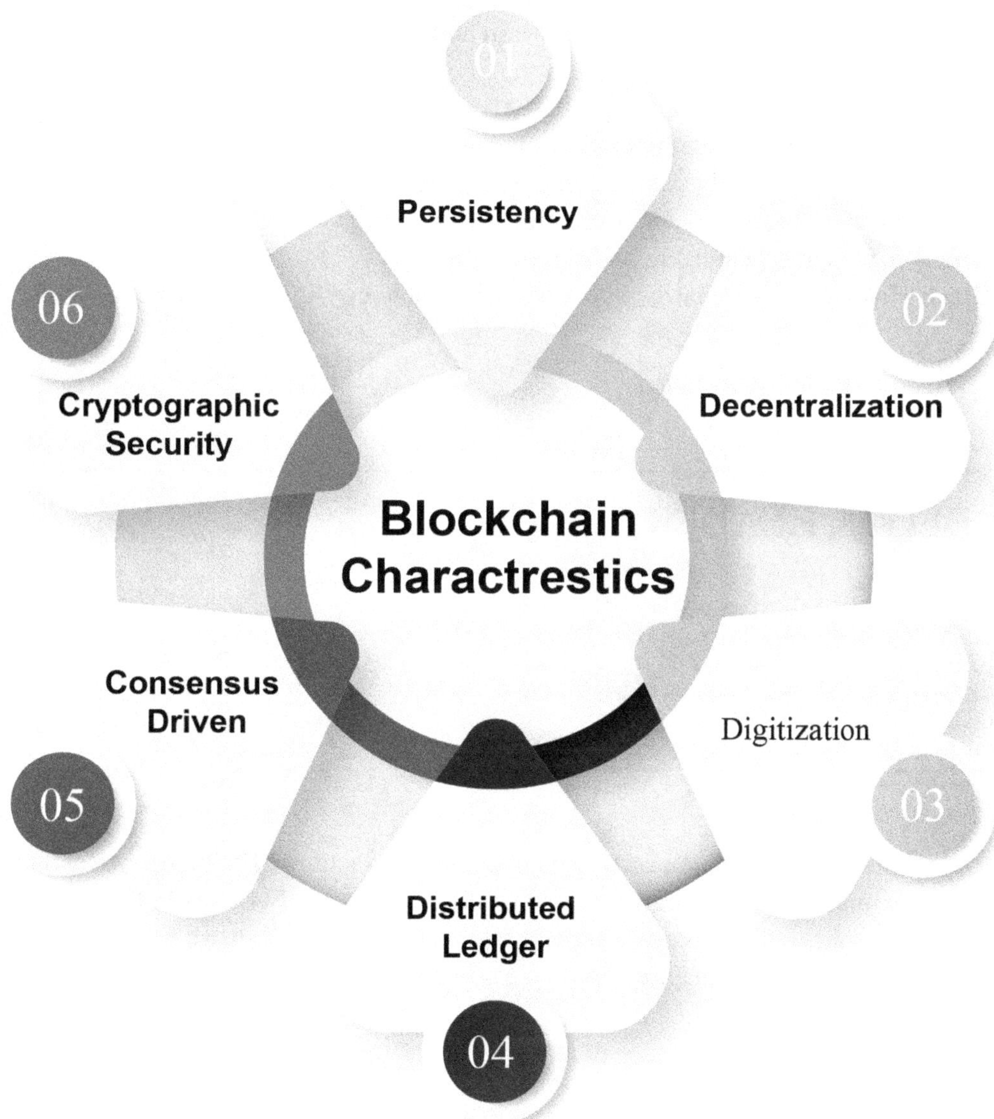

This concept of blocks and chains fosters transparency and security, as all participants in the network can verify the transaction history, making it challenging for a single entity to manipulate or alter data without the consensus of the network. Upon closer inspection of a block, numerous interconnected components are visible, including block version, Merkle tree root hash, timestamp, n-bits, token, and parent block hash. A block comprises a block header, as depicted in Figure 5. The block header includes the following information:

1- **Block Version:** This denotes the rules of validation set for the block (Singh et al., 2021).
2- **Merkel's Tree Root Hash:** Merkle trees employ a technique to store information within the block using hashes. The Merkle tree enables the storage of multiple blocks with their corresponding hashes.

This technique serves to verify whether a transaction can be included in a block or not (Bosamia & Patel, 2018; Wei et al., 2020).

3- Timestamp: The universal time, which is shown in hours, minutes and seconds e.g. January 1, 2022 (Di Pierro, 2017).

4- n-Bits: n-Bits is a numeric value of a target hash that must be less than or equal to in order for a new block to be awarded to the miner (Zhang et al., 2018).

5- Tokens: A 4-byte field, typically commencing with 0 and incrementing with each hash calculation, serves as a repository for statistical information regarding the elapsed time between four successive hash values (Breitner & Heninger, 2019).

6- Parent Block Hash: A 256-bit hash value referencing the preceding block (Khettry et al., 2021).

Figure 5. Blockchain header information

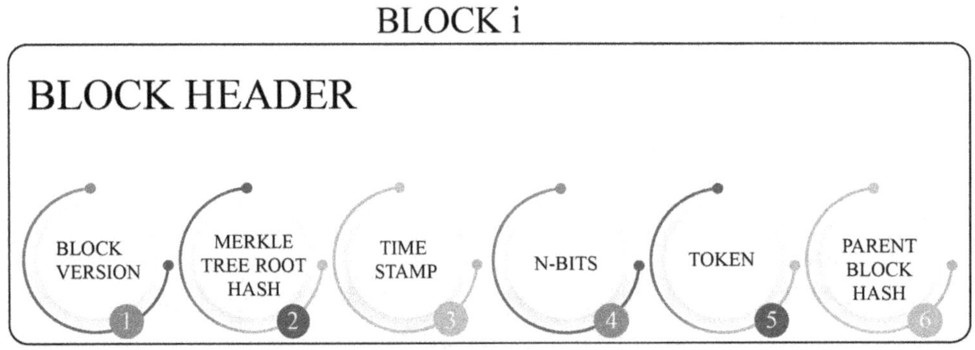

The block body is made up of a transaction counter and transactions. The block size and transaction size govern the maximum number of transactions that may be contained in a block. Blockchain employs asymmetric cryptography as a technique to authenticate transactions (Eberhardt & Tai, 2017), and lacking trust environment, a digital signature based on asymmetric cryptography is utilized.

WORKING OF A BLOCKCHAIN

A blockchain is like a digital ledger that holds information and is shared among nodes in a network. One key difference between a blockchain and a regular database is how they organize data. A blockchain is a shared and unchangeable ledger, as the name suggests, where data is structured into blocks. On the other hand, a database organizes data into tables. In a blockchain, these blocks are linked together in a chain, with each block containing data and being connected to the previous ones. The primary type of information stored on a blockchain is transactions, though various other types of information can also be stored on the network (Bamakan et al., 2020; Omar et al., 2021).

1. **Enabling a transaction:** When a new transaction is introduced into the blockchain network, all the required information undergoes double encryption using both public and private keys.

2. **Transaction Verification:** The transaction is distributed to a globally dispersed network of peer-to-peer computers. Subsequently, all nodes on the network validate the transaction, verifying factors such as the availability of an adequate amount of ether for the transaction to take place.
3. **Creation of a New Block**: Within a standard blockchain network, numerous nodes simultaneously verify multiple transactions. After a transaction is confirmed as legitimate, it is included in the chain.
4. **Consensus Algorithm:** Nodes constituting a block continually seek to integrate it into the blockchain network. However, permitting each node to independently add blocks can disrupt the seamless operation of the blockchain. In response, nodes utilize a consensus mechanism, ensuring that every new block added to the blockchain reflects the universally agreed-upon truth among all nodes. Only a valid block securely attaches to the blockchain. The designated node, commonly known as a "miner," receives a reward for successfully adding a block. The consensus algorithm generates a hash code essential for the addition of the block to the blockchain.
5. **New Block added to the Blockchain:** After the newly generated block acquires its hash value and undergoes verification, it is poised for inclusion in the blockchain. Each block encompasses the hash value of the preceding block, establishing a cryptographic linkage between blocks to form a cohesive blockchain. The new block is then appended to the open end of the blockchain.
6. **Transaction Finalized:** Upon the addition of the block to the blockchain, the transaction concludes, and its details are permanently recorded within the blockchain. Subsequently, anyone can retrieve and verify the transaction particulars.

Consider the example of Jhon and Tim in the blockchain network. Jhon initiates a transaction, intending to send 10 BTC to Tim. The verification message is broadcasted to all nodes, checking crucial parameters such as Jhon's balance and the registration status of both nodes. Once verified, the transaction becomes part of a new block, and the Proof-of-Work consensus algorithm is employed to ensure authenticity. After successful mining, the new block is added to the blockchain, marking the completion of the transaction. Tim receives the 10 BTC, and transaction details are permanently recorded. This transparent and verifiable ledger allows any network participant to confirm transactions, preventing double spending. Future transactions involving Jhon can be scrutinized by nodes, ensuring her financial capacity, and maintaining the integrity of the blockchain as depicted in Figure 6.

Figure 6. Working process

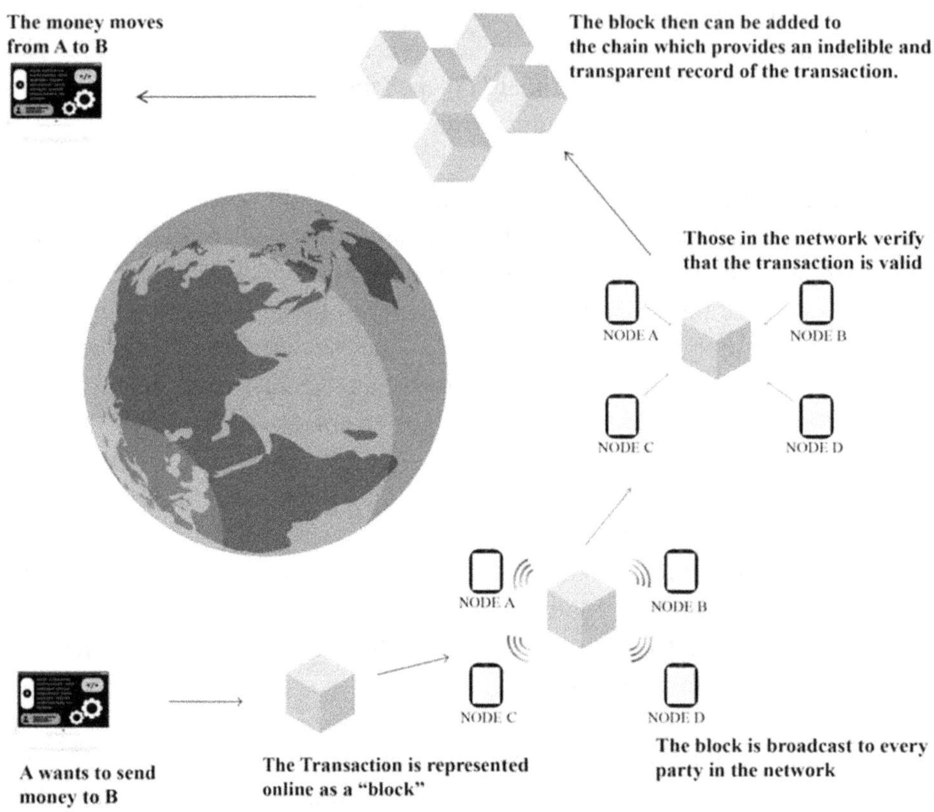

TYPES OF BLOCKCHAINS

The fundamental purpose of blockchain is to facilitate transactions within a network, leading to its widespread adoption in various scenarios. Blockchain and ledger technology are utilized to ensure secure data handling in diverse applications. The establishment of a multichain system is one method employed to prevent unauthorized access to sensitive data, confining its availability solely to authorized entities within an organization. The choice of the appropriate blockchain type depends on the specific requirements of the organization. In comprehensive exploration, there are four prevalent types of blockchain systems currently in use: public blockchain, private blockchain, hybrid blockchain, and consortium blockchain (Hedayati & Hosseini, 2021; Zheng et al., 2017). Basic properties of these blockchain types are explained below (Bhutta et al., 2021; Idrees et al., 2021; Kim, 2020; Liu et al., 2021; Shoker, 2021; Wüst & Gervais, 2018; Ziegler et al., 2021).

1- **Consensus Determination:** In a public blockchain, every node has the opportunity to engage in the consensus process. Conversely, a private chain is entirely controlled by a single organization, which has the authority to determine the final consensus. In a hybrid blockchain, a combination of public and private elements may collaborate to validate the block. In a consortium blockchain, only a subset of nodes is tasked with validating the block (Bamakan et al., 2020).

2- **Read Permission:** Transactions on a public blockchain are accessible to the public. In contrast, transactions in a private blockchain, hybrid blockchain, or consortium blockchain may either be public or restricted, depending on the specific design and purpose of the blockchain network (Patel et al., 2020).
3- **Immutability:** Records in a public blockchain are distributed across a wide array of participants, making tampering with transactions nearly impossible. In contrast, transactions within a private blockchain, hybrid blockchain, or consortium blockchain can be more susceptible to tampering, as there is only a restricted number of participants involved (Omar et al., 2021).
4- **Efficiency:** A public blockchain network, marked by a large number of nodes, encounters extended transaction and block transmission times. As a result, transaction throughput is limited, and latency becomes notable. Conversely, consortium blockchain, hybrid blockchain, and private blockchain, with fewer validators, may demonstrate more efficient transaction processing (Omar et al., 2021).
5- **Centralized:** The paramount distinction among the four types of blockchains lies in their degree of decentralization. A public blockchain is characterized by full decentralization, while hybrid and consortium blockchains exhibit a partial centralization. In contrast, a private blockchain is entirely centralized, as it is managed by a single party (Sengupta et al., 2020).
6- **Consensus Process:** Everyone in the world could join the consensus process of the blockchain. Consensus process depend upon the types of blockchain (Viriyasitavat & Hoonsopon, 2019). Therefore, a public blockchain is accessible to the global populace, drawing a substantial number of users.

However, many varieties of blockchain are investigated, which are classified according to the blockchain's uses as shown in Figure 7.

Figure 7. Types of blockchain system

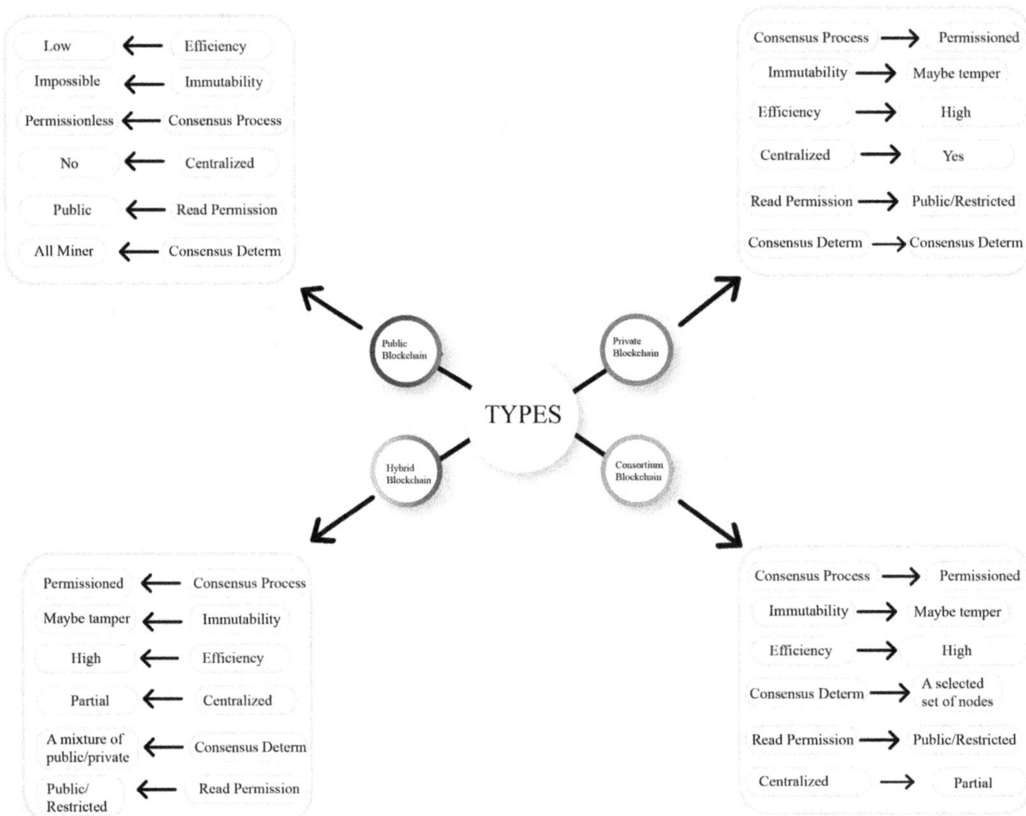

1- Public Blockchain

Public blockchain is open to the whole public. The participant and validator roles in public blockchain are unrestricted. The primary advantage of this type of blockchain is that no single entity has complete control over the network (Xu et al., 2017). Therefore, it safeguards the security of the data and contributes to the immutability of the information. In a fully distributed public blockchain, all nodes connecting to it have equal power. Real-world applications of public blockchain are exemplified by Bitcoin, Ethereum, and Litecoin. A public blockchain is being used in real-world settings by Bitcoin, Ethereum, and Litecoin. Anyone with an internet connection may observe and track transactions in these blockchain networks. Here some advantages and disadvantages of public blockchain are respectively: decentralized network, transparency, trusty chain, unchangeable and unbreakable technology and other hand it takes heavy energy consumption in mining process (Ali et al., 2018).

2- Private Blockchain

As the name implies, this type of blockchain requires participants to be invited before they can join. Only individuals within the blockchain ecosystem have access to view all transactions. These blockchains are more centralized and regulated compared to public blockchains. Due to their centralized nature, they can be managed and regulated by an entity that ensures governance over participants (Dinh et al., 2017). These blockchains may or may not include a token, depending on the blockchain owner's preferences (Ismailisufi et al., 2020). In private blockchain, a network administrator oversees user permissions if a specific user demands more authority on the fly. Typically, they are employed in private businesses to keep sensitive information about the company (Johnson et al., 2001). Here some advantages and disadvantages of private blockchain are respectively; the speed of a private blockchain is a significant because private blockchain have fewer members, it takes the network less time to establish an agreement (Kim, 2020). Thousands of transactions can be processed per second on private blockchain because private blockchain networks have a smaller number of members, which results in a faster agreement time among participants. Private blockchain are also significantly more scalable than public blockchain, the network can execute more transactions because few nodes are authorized and accountable for data management. It is centralized and the decision-making process is substantially speedier. However, one of the most significant downsides of private blockchain is its centralization. Private blockchains automatically become centralized due to a private network. Another issue with private blockchain is security. Malicious actors have an easier time gaining control of the network when there are fewer nodes. A private blockchain, on the other hand, is significantly more vulnerable to being hacked or may change the data (Ali et al., 2018).

3- Hybrid Blockchain

This type of blockchain is a combination of public and private blockchain. As a result, certain nodes will be permitted to take part in transactions; and the other nodes oversee ensuring that the consensus process runs well. This is a hybrid blockchain that combines the advantages of both private and public blockchain. However, all nodes may access the blockchain here, the degree of information that can be obtained depends on which node is accessing that data. There are generally two categories of users on this blockchain. The first is the user who has complete authority over the blockchain and determines the level of security for a certain user, while the others just access it (Chalaemwongwan & Kurutach, 2018). Here some advantages and disadvantages of hybrid blockchain are respectively: one of the most significant benefits of hybrid blockchain is that it functions in a closed environment, which prevents outside hackers from mounting a 51% attack on the network. It also protects personal information while permitting third-party communication, transactions are cheap and fast, and the network scales are better than a public blockchain network. However, this type of blockchain isn't completely visible because information may be buried and upgrading is difficult, and users have few incentives to join or contribute to the network.

4- Consortium Blockchain

A consortium blockchain, is like a hybrid blockchain in that it combines private and public blockchain features, is the fourth type of blockchain. However, in that, it entails diverse organizational members cooperating on a decentralized network. A consortium blockchain is essentially a private blockchain with restricted access to a specified group, which eliminates the risks associated with a blockchain managed by a single company. In a consortium blockchain, preset nodes manage consensus techniques. It has a validator node that handles transaction initiating, receiving, and validation. Member nodes can receive or initiate transactions. Compared to a public blockchain network, a consortium blockchain is more secure, scalable, and efficient. Furthermore, a consortium blockchain exhibits less transparency compared to a public blockchain. In the event of a member node being infiltrated, it remains susceptible to hacking, and adherence to the blockchain's rules can potentially render the network inoperable (Kang et al., 2017). Blockchain can be categorized based on the degree of support for smart contracts, yielding the following insights (Hileman & Rauchs, 2017);

SMART CONTRACT SUPPORT LEVELS

1- **Stateless Blockchain:** In a Stateless Blockchain system, the primary emphasis is on optimizing transactions and the core chain functionality, which involves verifying transactions through hash computations. This type of blockchain operates independently of the smart contract logic layer and is not influenced by potential bugs or vulnerabilities in smart contract code.
2- **Stateful Blockchain:** In contrast, Stateful Blockchains provide extensive support for smart contracts and transaction computation. They have the ability to execute smart contracts and manage complex business logic. Additionally, Stateful Blockchains optimize and maintain logical states, ensuring the integrity and functionality of contracts and transactions.

BLOCKCHAIN PLATFORM

Blockchain technology is undergoing rapid evolution and maturation as its adoption continues to expand. The inaugural blockchain-powered platform, Bitcoin, was introduced in 2009, transforming the exchange of digital cryptocurrency by eliminating the need for a central authority. Bitcoin utilizes peer-to-peer distributed technology and incorporates robust cryptographic protocols and hash functions, rendering it highly resistant to counterfeiting. The creation of new coins in the Bitcoin network relies on a process called mining, which involves solving computational hashes and verifying transactions to receive rewards (Benji & Sindhu, 2019).Over the past decade, numerous blockchain platforms have emerged, sharing similarities with Bitcoin but incorporating additional functionalities. These blockchain platforms serve as the core infrastructure of blockchain networks and offer essential services to participating nodes. The comparison of different blockchain platforms shown in Table 2.

TYPES OF BLOCKCHAIN PLATE FORM

Four widely utilized blockchain platforms are currently in use, namely: Hyperledger Fabric, Ripple, R3 Corda, and Ethereum (Lemieux, 2016; Mingxiao et al., 2017).

1- **Hyperledger Fabric:** Hyperledger serves as an all-encompassing umbrella organization established by the Linux Foundation, bringing together various individual platforms. Throughout its evolution, Hyperledger has embraced a permissioned distributed ledger approach, enabling validators to be both whitelisted and blacklisted over time (Androulaki et al., 2018). During its initial phases, Bitcoin served as the primary term encompassing both electronic currency and blockchain technology. Hyperledger's development language base has transitioned from Erlang and Elixir to more widely adopted open-source languages such as Java and Scala. Remarkably, the framework has adopted an Unspent Transaction Output (UTXO) model, where unspent outputs can serve as new transactional inputs, a model paradoxically foundational to Bitcoin. In its latest iteration, Hyperledger integrates code from a cloned version of Bitcoin, incorporating segments from both IBM's platform and Ethereum. Fabric, a component of Hyperledger, is structured with three distinct states: Smart contracts, Transaction ordering, and Transaction validation. Authenticated users, supported by managed IDs, can engage in designated actions.

2- **Ripple:** Ripple operates as a permissioned enterprise blockchain platform, having previously existed in an alternative form known as Ripple pay which established formally in 2012 (Armknecht et al., 2015; Benji & Sindhu, 2019). Centrally focused on financial applications, Ripple employs a system that integrates currency exchange, real-time gross settlement (RTGS), and a remittance network to facilitate its functionalities [5]. A distinctive feature setting Ripple apart from other discussed platforms is its current abstention from utilizing smart contracts.

3- **R3 Corda:** R3 Corda CEV emerged as a distributed ledger product in 2014 (Benji & Sindhu, 2019). The acronym CEV was initially coined to encapsulate pivotal aspects of their business concept: crypto, consulting, exchanges, and ventures. This terminology emerged as a result of roundtable discussions that involved various entities operating in the cryptocurrency domain. Therefore, participants from several distributed ledger organizations, including Ripple and Ethereum, actively engaged in three distinct roundtable sessions.

4- **Ethereum:** In 2013, Ethereum had its genesis under the development of Vitalik Buterin, emerging as a project derived from the Satoshi Nakamoto bitcoin initiative, a trait shared with several platforms to be examined (Oliva et al., 2020). Marking its official debut in 2015, Ethereum solidified its presence in the cryptocurrency landscape. However, it achieved widespread recognition and prominence only in April 2016, following the announcement of the establishment of the Distributed Autonomous Organization (DAO).

BLOCKCHAIN RUNTIME ENVIRONMENT

Smart contracts and managing blockchain transactions securely play a pivotal role in the blockchain runtime environment. This environment typically incorporates a secure operating system. A dedicated programming language, runtime libraries, and necessary supporting libraries.

1- **Cryptographic Services:** This layer has important cryptographic algorithms which include hash functions and digital signatures.

2- **Smart Contract Module:** This module facilitates the integration of business logic. Primarily significant for Stateful Blockchains. It supports various programming languages like Go, Solidity, Java, Rust, C++, and some others.

3- **Secondary Storage:** On blockchain platform is critical handling extensive transaction volumes on blockchain secondary storage. It provides a secure, reliable, and scalable solution for collecting block data. It is shown in the distributed ledger. In this layer includes Level DB, Rocks DB, H2 Database, MongoDB, and other distributed data systems.

4- **Memory Store:** The Blockchain Memory Store layer is responsible for provisionally storing recent transactions. It's also provide facilitating quick data access and efficient transaction processing. It employs data structures like Merkle Trees, Tries, Acyclic Directed Graphs, and Associative Arrays.

5- **Consensus Protocol Module:** The Consensus Protocol Module includes the processes for attaining consensus among nodes which maintained the validity and authenticity of transactions. This consensus is essential for recording transactions in the distributed ledger. The blockchain consensus protocols including Proof of Work (PoW) (Yli-Huumo et al., 2016), Proof of Stake (PoS) (Young, 2018), Raft(Huang et al., 2019), Practically Byzantine Fault Tolerance (PBFT) (Li et al., 2020; Zyskind & Nathan, 2015), and others.

Table 2. Comparison of different blockchain platform

S.#	Blockchain Platform	Year	Hash Function	Data Structure		Secondary Storage	Consensus Protocol	Types	Design	Permission Level	Programming Languages
1	Hyperledger Fabric	2016	SHA3 SHAKE256	Bucket-tree, Merkle Tree		RocksDB	PBFT, Raft, PoW, PoS	Consortium	Stateful	Permissioned	Go, JavaScript, Java
2	Ripple	2012	SHA2-512	Merkle Tree, Knowledge Grap		RocksDB, NuDB	RPCA, PoW, PoS	Consortium	Stateless	Permissioned	C++, JavaScript
3	Corda R3	2015	SHA-256	Merkle tree		H2 database	Validity consensus	Consortium	Stateful	Permissioned	Java, Kotlin
4	Ethereum	2015	Keccak256	Trie		LevelDB, RocksDB	PoW, PoS	Public	Stateful	Permissionless	Go, C++, Rust, Solidity

CONSENSUS MECHANISMS OF BLOCKCHAIN

A consensus mechanism serves as a fault-tolerant mechanism within blockchain systems, facilitating the essential agreement among distributed processes, particularly within cryptocurrencies, regarding a singular data value. Fundamental to blockchain technology, consensus algorithms play a central role in safeguarding the tamper-proof nature and decentralization of the blockchain. Despite the absence of a central authority for validation and verification, every transaction within the blockchain is perceived as secure and authenticated, owing to the efficacy of consensus mechanisms. The pivotal element in any blockchain network is the consensus protocol, the linchpin enabling this security. Therefore, here are some consensus mechanism which are most commonly used algorithms like proof of work (PoW) (Yli-Huumo et al., 2016), proof of stake (PoS) (Young, 2018), practical byzantine fault tolerance (PBFT) (Zyskind & Nathan, 2015). A comparison of the most important consensus algorithms is also presented in Table 3.

1- Proof of Work

Proof of Work (PoW) serves as the underlying mechanism for mining in Bitcoin (Yli-Huumo et al., 2016). It functions as a data structure responsible for gathering and broadcasting all transactions to every node within the peer-to-peer network for validation. Upon successful verification of transactions and solving the cryptographic puzzle, a node transmits the resulting block to the blockchain network. Subsequent mining nodes carefully examine the block to verify the submitter's honesty. Unanimous agreement among miners, determined by a majority vote, is essential for the block to be appended to the blockchain, and the submitter is rewarded with compensation. This consensus mechanism proves challenging to manipulate unless malicious actors gain control over more than half of the mining nodes. Despite its effectiveness, a drawback of this approach is the substantial consumption of processing resources in attempting to solve the mathematical challenge.

2- Proof of Stake

Proof of Stake (PoS) stands as the second most widely adopted alternative to Proof of Work (PoW) among consensus mechanisms, offering several advantages in terms of energy efficiency, time efficiency, cost-effectiveness, and computing power requirements. In this consensus process, the creation of the next block in the chain is determined through a randomized approach. Unlike PoW, PoS involves validators instead of miners. Users can choose to stake their tokens to become validators, requiring them to lock their funds for a specific duration to facilitate the generation of a new block (Young, 2018). The likelihood of a user constructing a new block and becoming a validator is highest for the individual with the largest stake, and the duration of the stake depends on that user.By allowing only selected validators to construct a block, this consensus method conserves the energy of other validators in the network. PoS proves to be highly beneficial as it imposes penalties on validators for errors during block formation, leading to the removal of their stakes. Consequently, validators are incentivized to be truthful, and they receive compensation for their honesty. In contrast to PoW, where miners collect transaction fees, in PoS, other validators verifying and validating the block receive these fees (Gaži et al., 2019).

3- Byzantine Fault Tolerance

Byzantine fault tolerance (BFT) represents a crucial aspect within distributed systems. Ensuring that nodes within a network can achieve a consensus on a shared value. Even when facing node failures or the dissemination of inaccurate information. In decentralized systems, the incorporation of a BFT mechanism introduces an additional layer of reliability, safety, and resilience (Muratov et al., 2018). The primary objective of deploying a BFT mechanism; in such systems is to strengthen against potential system failures. This is achieved through a collective decision-making process. It involves both active nodes and those that may be faulty. The primary goal is to diminish the influence of faulty nodes on the system's overall integrity. By leveraging BFT, these decentralized systems can maintain a higher level of trust and robustness. It's guaranteeing that the network remains functional and agreeable. It may even be in the presence of adversarial components. This approach is particularly valuable in the environment. Where trust is distributed, and the reliability of individual nodes cannot be taken for granted.

4- Practical Byzantine Fault Tolerance

Byzantine Fault Tolerance (BFT) delineates the capability of a distributed system to sustain functionality despite component failures. It presents a viable solution to challenges inherent in distributed systems. In contrast to conventional methods, PBFT(Li et al., 2020; Zyskind & Nathan, 2015) introduces a consensus mechanism grounded in Byzantine Fault Tolerance principles for blockchain consensus. It diverges from reliance on resource-based approaches. In this procedural paradigm, nodes collectively participate in the selection and consensus-building process to designate a leader. The designated leader within the blockchain network validates the transactions and disseminates a block to all participating nodes. The commitment of a transaction to a new block only materializes when two-thirds of the mining nodes affirm its integrity. The fluidity of leadership, characterized by regular selection and replacement of leaders. That's mitigates the perception of centralization in this strategy. While Practical Byzantine Fault Tolerance (PBFT) has demonstrated heightened transactional speed in comparison to preceding methods. It concerns about scalability emerge due to the associated elevated communication costs. Despite the profound significance of cryptocurrencies. In the numerous enterprises choose not to integrate them into their blockchain frameworks. The selection of a consensus algorithm may vary depending on the nature of the blockchain. It takes into account factors such as enterprise nodes versus miners. Furthermore, the allocation of the financial burden may rest solely on a single organization or be distributed among multiple entities.

Table 3. Blockchain consensus comparison

Consensus Mechanism	Node Identity	Language Used	Execution Environment	Energy Efficient	Recourse Consumption	Cost	Throughput	Limitation
PoW	Public	Golang, C++, Solidity	Native, Ethereum virtual machine (EVM)	High Power	High CPU	High	Low	Less secure, high-power consumption
PoS	Public	Michelson	Native holders	Yes	Fast	Medium	Low	Highest paid stake of Consensus control
BFT	Private	Any Language	Nill	Yes	High CPU	Low	High	Semi trusted, less scalable
PBFT	Private	Golang, Java	Docker Tool	Yes	High Bandwidth	Low	High	Communication overhead

BLOCKCHAIN TECHNOLOGY IN VARIOUS REAL-LIFE APPLICATIONS

Blockchain technology has emerged as a transformative tool with widespread applications. It includes various fields, including finance, governance, healthcare, IoT, supply chain management, record keeping, and digital identity. This section delves into the foundational principles of blockchain and its practical implementations in these domains. By furnishing a secure, transparent, and decentralized framework. Blockchain faces critical challenges related to data confidentiality, trust, and accountability. The discussion investigates the distinctive features of blockchain that render it suitable for diverse applications. It is emphasizing its potential to enhance efficiency, reduce fraud, and bolster overall system reliability.

1. Financial Applications

Blockchain facilitates secure and transparent financial transactions. It is through the utilization of distributed ledgers. An integral component in this process is the role played by smart contracts, which automate procedures, diminishing reliance on intermediaries. Consequently, accelerate transactions, reduce costs, and advance financial inclusivity. Particularly in regions with limited access to conventional banking services and transformative impact on the financial sector extends across various domains which includes investment funds, cryptocurrency exchanges, stock markets, insurance, credit records, and mass funding. The advantages inherent in the incorporation of blockchain within financial applications are considerable (Mishra & Kaushik, 2023). The system ensures expeditious, dependable, and cost-effective transactions facilitated by distributed ledgers. Smart contracts streamline processes, diminishing reliance on intermediaries and augmenting financial inclusivity. Especially in regions with constrained access to traditional banking services. The blockchain's reliability is fortified by its controllable, non-tampering blocks, establishing a secure and transparent environment. In instances of system failures, recoverability is assured. Nonetheless, these advantages are accompanied by challenges that integration of the complete blockchain structure into banking systems presents complexities. Real-world applications often necessitate a certain level of centralization. Furthermore, as the volume of blocks increases, the verification time of the system experiences escalation. It is potentially impeding the overall process. Despite these challenges, the prospective benefits position blockchain as a compelling solution for the transformation of financial transactions and services (Kumar et al., 2022).

2. Governance Applications

Blockchain plays a pivotal role in governance by ensuring transparency, traceability, and accountability. The utilization of distributed ledgers for voting systems and record-keeping serves to mitigate the risks associated with fraud and manipulation. Consequently, bolstering public trust in governmental processes and cultivating a more democratic and participatory system. Blockchain technology is making notable advancements in diverse governance applications, addressing challenges across sectors such as voting, land transactions, tax regulation, education, government services, inheritance, charities, labor rights, and authentication. It leverages distributed ledgers to minimize the susceptibility to fraud and manipulation. Ultimately fortifying public trust in governmental processes (Tan et al., 2022). The advantages of blockchain governance are conspicuous, providing a transparent, reliable, and verifiable system. Additionally, it ensures data security, even in the event of natural disasters, effectively preserving assets, reporting, availability, and collateral management at a reduced cost. However, challenges persist in the implementation of blockchain governance. Internet-based systems are susceptible. It is potentially compromising data security. The addition of blocks may lead to system slowdowns. Therefore, its key privacy in all cases can be challenging. Furthermore, the presence of selfish miners poses a risk to the overall integrity of the system. Despite these challenges, the implementation of blockchain in governance applications holds the promise of fostering a more democratic. Its participatory system through its transformative impact on transparency and accountability.

3. Healthcare Applications

Blockchain, with its secure and interoperable characteristics. It proves highly suitable for healthcare applications. The storage of patient records on a decentralized ledger establishes a singular source of truth which ensures the accuracy and accessibility of data. This systematic approach enhances data sharing among healthcare providers. Thereby elevating the quality of patient care. The utilization of blockchain not only improves the security of patient data but also facilitates the comprehensive storage or analysis of health information. It enables private and auditable sharing of healthcare data. Thus, it leads to expedited and cost-effective transactions. The establishment of trustful and transparent healthcare systems resulting from blockchain implementation contributes to a secure and scalable storage platform (Wenhua et al., 2023). However, challenges persist in the adoption of blockchain technology within the healthcare sector. While blockchain effectively prevents unauthorized access, technical failures may inadvertently release confidential data. Moreover, the successful implementation of blockchain in healthcare necessitates mandatory training for patients and their integration into the system. Despite these challenges, blockchain harbors immense potential to revolutionize healthcare processes. Offering enhanced data sharing among healthcare providers and ultimately augmenting patient care through streamlined and secure systems (Ramzan et al., 2022).

4. IoT Applications

Blockchain serves to enhance the security of IoT devices through the establishment of a decentralized and immutable record of device interactions. This proactive measure effectively diminishes the risk of unauthorized access and ensures the integrity of data generated by IoT devices. The implementation of smart contracts facilitates automated and secure transactions between devices. Obviating the need for intermediaries and further mitigating the risk of unauthorized access. In applications such as cloud storage, data backup, IoT management, messaging, and cloud computing. Blockchain affords advantages such as data consistency and expeditious verification of operations. These benefits contribute to heightened productivity and increased flexibility. Diminished costs by eliminating the necessity for third-party agents (Abdelmaboud et al., 2022). The utilization of open-source code in blockchain fosters the development of dynamically evolving systems. However, challenges persist in the form of cost and capacity constraints, potential data manipulation. The vulnerability of cloud servers to attacks during downtime, and the risk of data theft, which could compromise the overall system. Despite these challenges, the adoption of blockchain in IoT applications holds the promise of creating more secure, efficient, and streamlined systems for managing interconnected devices in the digital landscape.

5. Supply Chain Management Applications

Blockchain's transparency and traceability bring considerable benefits to supply chain management by recording every transaction in a secure and irreversible ledger. This guarantees the authenticity of products, reduces fraud, and enables more efficient tracking of goods from manufacturing to distribution. The advantages of blockchain in supply chain management are diverse, especially in applications such as digital supply chain, supply chain quality management, pharmaceutical supply chain, electronic open-source traceability of wood, blockchain system for drug traceability and regulation, traceability of counterfeit medicine supply chain, and establishing proof of ownership in the supply chain. These advantages include reduced costs, increased efficiency, secure and easily accessible healthcare information, real-time automatic updates, and a decentralized processing network that eliminates the need to trust a single computer, database, or institution. Despite these benefits, challenges persist in proving the cost-effectiveness of blockchain, building robust security mechanisms to protect patient data from leaks, and addressing regulatory issues and technical challenges associated with its implementation. Nevertheless, the adoption of blockchain in supply chain management applications holds the promise of revolutionizing the industry by establishing a secure, transparent, and efficient framework for managing the flow of goods across various sectors (Queiroz et al., 2020).

6. Record Keeping Applications

Blockchain's tamper-resistant attributes make it highly suitable for record-keeping applications, ensuring the integrity and authenticity of documents and records while minimizing the risk of data manipulation. This quality finds applications in various sectors, including legal, educational, and governmental record-keeping systems. Specific applications, such as the blockchain-based flight data recorder, record-keeping, distributed operating systems, and blockchain computing, benefit from advantages such as cost savings, increased efficiency, reduced risk, flexibility, and competitive advantage (Lemieux et al., 2019). However, challenges persist in ensuring the security of data stored on the blockchain, particularly without sufficient layers of security, which may expose the data to hacking risks. Additionally, concerns related to inconsistency and inefficiency, associated costs, security vulnerabilities, and potential liability issues, including HIPAA violations in certain contexts, must be carefully addressed. Despite these challenges, the implementation of blockchain in record-keeping applications offers a promising solution for enhancing data integrity and authenticity in various sectors, paving the way for more efficient and secure record-keeping systems (Wang et al., 2020).

7. Digital Identity Applications

Blockchain serves as a secure and decentralized solution for digital identity management. Empowering individuals with control over access to their personal information and mitigating the risks of identity theft and unauthorized access. It has widespread applications in various digital identity contexts, including identity management, cloud identity management, self-sovereign identity, smart contract-based PKI and identity systems, and identity and smart contract management systems (Yang & Li, 2020). The advantages of utilizing blockchain in digital identity applications are evident. It is especially in the realm of Bitcoin transactions. Personal information is securely managed. It provides users with the freedom of payment and transparent information sharing during Bitcoin transactions accompanied by low transaction fees. However, challenges and considerations exist. Such as the lack of physical form in Bitcoins and potential unexploited technical flaws. Additionally, issues related to synthetic identity and identity verification processes warrant careful attention. Despite these considerations, the implementation of blockchain in digital identity applications holds the promise of significantly enhancing security (Zwitter et al., 2020).

SWOT ANALYSIS OF BLOCKCHAIN

Blockchain has garnered significant attention in the modern world as an emerging technology comparable to the internet. This section evaluates the technology using a SWOT analysis, a crucial component of a strategic plan that empowers sectors like healthcare, food, automotive, and financial industries to address potential hurdles associated with blockchain implementation in the specified domains. SWOT analysis is used to analyze an industry's strengths, weaknesses, opportunities, and threats. The study is appropriate for a strategic planning process to effectively prepare industries before pursuing an opportunity or reducing hazards. Both emerging and established sectors can use the research as a tool to evaluate the level of competition in their respective marketplaces. Industrial executives evaluate the future potential of new business models in their industries using a SWOT analysis before changing their present business strategy. It is possible for industries to address the potential drawbacks of blockchain, smart contracts, and cryptocurrencies within their appropriate domain by conducting a SWOT analysis, which is a hallmark of a strategic planning The SWOT analysis is a systematic planning tool for evaluating those four parts of an association, project, or business venture (Wüst & Gervais, 2018). Table 4, Shows the detailed SWOT analysis of blockchain.

Table 4. SWOT analysis of blockchain

Strengths	Weaknesses	Opportunities	Threats
• Complete transparency • Bypassing intermediaries • Verifiable audit trail • Enhanced efficiency and productivity in business processes • Decentralized methodology • High-quality and infallible data • Improved efficiency • Reduced costs • Mitigated risks • Enhanced security • Independence from third-party reliance • Resilience (elimination of Single Point of Failure) • Swiftness • Openness • Trust within trustless networks • Uncompromised privacy	• Difficulty in accessing • Managing changes • Integrating with existing legacy systems • Absence of standardized practices • Limited capacity and processing speed •Ownership-related challenges • Adoption of nascent technology (not fully developed) • Ensuring scalability • Cybersecurity measures against malicious actors • Storage constraints • Technological maturity concerns	• Implementation of automated processes • Optimization of business procedures • Removal of the need for trust • Accelerated (international) payment transfers • Enhanced customer experience • Improved quality of products and services • Innovation across various industries, with a particular impact on banking • Immediate settlements • Utilization of KYC databases • Emergence of new intermediaries • Independence from rating agencies • Potential opportunities in IoT (Internet of Things) • Application of programmable control mechanisms • Integration of smart contracts in the insurance sector • Streamlining of banking processes	• Extensive research requirements • Diminishing traditional banking employment opportunities • Government readiness for adoption • Substantial investments needed for implementation • Significant regulatory implications • Overhyped expectations • Legal, regulatory, and compliance considerations • Privacy and security concerns • Time-consuming negotiation processes • Uncertainty regarding the overall impact

CONCLUSION

This chapter provided a comprehensive exploration of blockchain technology, tracing its evolution from Blockchain 1.0 to the current Blockchain 5.0. The discussion delves into the fundamental characteristics, scope, and mechanisms of blockchain, elucidating its role in securely tokenizing and transferring a wide range of assets. The examination of smart contract support, diverse blockchain types, and consensus mechanisms highlights the versatility of this transformative technology. Beyond its technical facets, the motivation to adopt blockchain arises from its potential to redefine trust and transparency. Blockchain represents more than a digital ledger; it signifies a paradigm shift in how value is securely exchanged. Considering its implications, the appeal of blockchain lies in its capacity to establish a decentralized, tamper-resistant foundation for transactions, fostering real-time transparency for all participants. Looking ahead, the drive to integrate blockchain into diverse sectors stems from its promise to reshape industries and catalyze innovation, ushering in a decentralized, transparent, and secure future. The journey into blockchain is not merely a technological exploration but a venture into reimagining trust and exchange in the digital landscape.

REFERENCES

Abdelmaboud, A., Ahmed, A. I. A., Abaker, M., Eisa, T. A. E., Albasheer, H., Ghorashi, S. A., & Karim, F. K. (2022). Blockchain for IoT applications: Taxonomy, platforms, recent advances, challenges and future research directions. *Electronics (Basel)*, *11*(4), 630. doi:10.3390/electronics11040630

Abou Jaoude, J., & Saade, R. G. (2019). Blockchain applications–usage in different domains. *IEEE Access : Practical Innovations, Open Solutions*, *7*, 45360–45381. doi:10.1109/ACCESS.2019.2902501

Ahmadi, M., Moghaddam, F. F., Jam, A. J., Gholizadeh, S., & Eslami, M. (2014). A 3-level re-encryption model to ensure data protection in cloud computing environments. *2014 IEEE Conference on Systems, Process and Control (ICSPC 2014).*

Ali, M. S., Vecchio, M., Pincheira, M., Dolui, K., Antonelli, F., & Rehmani, M. H. (2018). Applications of blockchains in the Internet of Things: A comprehensive survey. *IEEE Communications Surveys and Tutorials*, *21*(2), 1676–1717.

Androulaki, E., Barger, A., Bortnikov, V., Cachin, C., Christidis, K., De Caro, A., Enyeart, D., Ferris, C., Laventman, G., & Manevich, Y. (2018). Hyperledger fabric: a distributed operating system for permissioned blockchains. *Proceedings of the Thirteenth EuroSys Conference.*

Armknecht, F., Karame, G. O., Mandal, A., Youssef, F., & Zenner, E. (2015). Ripple: Overview and outlook. *Trust and Trustworthy Computing: 8th International Conference, TRUST 2015, Heraklion, Greece, August 24-26, 2015, Proceedings, 8.*

Aslan, Ö., Aktuğ, S. S., Ozkan-Okay, M., Yilmaz, A. A., & Akin, E. (2023). A comprehensive review of cyber security vulnerabilities, threats, attacks, and solutions. *Electronics (Basel)*, *12*(6), 1333.

Bamakan, S. M. H., Motavali, A., & Bondarti, A. B. (2020). A survey of blockchain consensus algorithms performance evaluation criteria. *Expert Systems with Applications*, *154*, 113385. doi:10.1016/j.eswa.2020.113385

Bellavitis, C., Fisch, C., & Momtaz, P. P. (2023). The rise of decentralized autonomous organizations (DAOs): A first empirical glimpse. *Venture Capital*, *25*(2), 187–203. doi:10.1080/13691066.2022.2116797

Benji, M., & Sindhu, M. (2019). A study on the Corda and Ripple blockchain platforms. Advances in Big Data and Cloud Computing: *Proceedings of ICBDCC18.*

Bhutta, M. N. M., Khwaja, A. A., Nadeem, A., Ahmad, H. F., Khan, M. K., Hanif, M. A., Song, H., Alshamari, M., & Cao, Y. (2021). A survey on blockchain technology: evolution, architecture and security. *IEEE Access : Practical Innovations, Open Solutions*, *9*, 61048–61073.

Bosamia, M., & Patel, D. (2018). Current trends and future implementation possibilities of the Merkel tree. *International Journal on Computer Science and Engineering*, *6*(8), 294–301.

Breitner, J., & Heninger, N. (2019). Biased nonce sense: Lattice attacks against weak ECDSA signatures in cryptocurrencies. *International Conference on Financial Cryptography and Data Security.*

Buterin, V. (2019). *On public and private blockchains (2015).* https://blog. ethereum. org/2015/08/07/on-public-and-private-blockchains

Chalaemwongwan, N., & Kurutach, W. (2018). Notice of Violation of IEEE Publication Principles: State of the art and challenges facing consensus protocols on blockchain. *2018 International Conference on Information Networking (ICOIN)*.

Chen, Y. (2018). Blockchain tokens and the potential democratization of entrepreneurship and innovation. *Business Horizons*, *61*(4), 567–575.

Chohan, R., & Paschen, J. (2023). NFT marketing: How marketers can use nonfungible tokens in their campaigns. *Business Horizons*, *66*(1), 43–50. doi:10.1016/j.bushor.2021.12.004

Cosares, S., Kalish, K., Maciura, T., & Spieler, A. C. (2021). Blockchain applications in finance. In *The Emerald Handbook of Blockchain for Business* (pp. 275–291). Emerald Publishing Limited. doi:10.1108/978-1-83982-198-120211022

Delgado-Segura, S., Pérez-Sola, C., Navarro-Arribas, G., & Herrera-Joancomartí, J. (2018). Analysis of the Bitcoin UTXO set. International Conference on Financial Cryptography and Data Security, Di Pierro, M. (2017). What is the blockchain? *Computing in Science & Engineering*, *19*(5), 92–95.

Dinh, T. T. A., Wang, J., Chen, G., Liu, R., Ooi, B. C., & Tan, K.-L. (2017). Blockbench: A framework for analyzing private blockchains. *Proceedings of the 2017 ACM International Conference on Management of Data*.

Eberhardt, J., & Tai, S. (2017). On or off the blockchain? Insights on off-chaining computation and data. *European Conference on Service-Oriented and Cloud Computing*.

Eyal, I., & Sirer, E. G. (2014). Majority is not enough: Bitcoin mining is vulnerable. *International Conference on Financial Cryptography and Data Security*.

Fan, X., & Chai, Q. (2018). Roll-DPoS: a randomized delegated proof of stake scheme for scalable blockchain-based internet of things systems. *Proceedings of the 15th EAI International Conference on Mobile and Ubiquitous Systems: Computing, Networking and Services*.

Fernandez-Carames, T. M., & Fraga-Lamas, P. (2019). A review on the application of blockchain to the next generation of cybersecure industry 4.0 smart factories. *IEEE Access : Practical Innovations, Open Solutions*, *7*, 45201–45218.

Gandal, N., Hamrick, J., Moore, T., & Vasek, M. (2021). The rise and fall of cryptocurrency coins and tokens. *Decisions in Economics and Finance*, *44*(2), 981–1014. doi:10.1007/s10203-021-00329-8

Gaži, P., Kiayias, A., & Zindros, D. (2019). Proof-of-stake sidechains. *2019 IEEE Symposium on Security and Privacy (SP)*.

Hanna, G. (1995). Challenges to the importance of proof. *For the Learning of Mathematics*, *15*(3), 42–49.

Hedayati, A., & Hosseini, H. A. (2021). A Survey on Blockchain: Challenges, Attacks, Security, and Privacy. *International Journal of Smart Electrical Engineering*, *10*(03), 141–168.

Hileman, G., & Rauchs, M. (2017). *Global Blockchain Benchmarking Study: 2017*. Cambridge Centre for Alternative Finance.

Huang, D., Ma, X., & Zhang, S. (2019). Performance analysis of the raft consensus algorithm for private blockchains. *IEEE Transactions on Systems, Man, and Cybernetics. Systems*, *50*(1), 172–181. doi:10.1109/TSMC.2019.2895471

Idrees, S. M., Nowostawski, M., Jameel, R., & Mourya, A. K. (2021). Security aspects of blockchain technology intended for industrial applications. *Electronics (Basel)*, *10*(8), 951. doi:10.3390/electronics10080951

Ismailisufi, A., Popović, T., Gligorić, N., Radonjic, S., & Šandi, S. (2020). A private blockchain implementation using multichain open source platform. *2020 24th International Conference on Information Technology (IT)*.

Johnson, D., Menezes, A., & Vanstone, S. (2001). The elliptic curve digital signature algorithm (ECDSA). *International Journal of Information Security*, *1*(1), 36–63.

Kang, J., Yu, R., Huang, X., Maharjan, S., Zhang, Y., & Hossain, E. (2017). Enabling localized peer-to-peer electricity trading among plug-in hybrid electric vehicles using consortium blockchains. *IEEE Transactions on Industrial Informatics*, *13*(6), 3154–3164. doi:10.1109/TII.2017.2709784

Kaplan, A. M., & Haenlein, M. (2010). Users of the world, unite! The challenges and opportunities of Social Media. *Business Horizons*, *53*(1), 59–68. doi:10.1016/j.bushor.2009.09.003

Khettry, A. R., Patil, K. R., & Basavaraju, A. C. (2021). A detailed review on blockchain and its applications. *SN Computer Science*, *2*(1), 1–9. doi:10.1007/s42979-020-00366-x PMID:34723205

Kiayias, A., Miller, A., & Zindros, D. (2020). Non-interactive proofs of proof-of-work. *International Conference on Financial Cryptography and Data Security*.

Kim, J. (2020). Blockchain technology and its applications: Case studies. *Journal of System and Management Sciences*, *10*(1), 83–93.

Kosba, A., Miller, A., Shi, E., Wen, Z., & Papamanthou, C. (2016). Hawk: The blockchain model of cryptography and privacy-preserving smart contracts. *2016 IEEE Symposium on Security and Privacy (SP)*.

Kshetri, N., & Voas, J. (2018). Blockchain in developing countries. *IT Professional*, *20*(2), 11–14.

Kumar, S., Kumar, B., Nagesh, Y., & Christian, F. (2022). Application of blockchain technology as a support tool in economic & financial development. *Manager-The British Journal of Administrative Management*.

Laroiya, C., Saxena, D., & Komalavalli, C. (2020). Applications of blockchain technology. In *Handbook of research on blockchain technology* (pp. 213–243). Elsevier. doi:10.1016/B978-0-12-819816-2.00009-5

Lashkari, B., & Musilek, P. (2021). A comprehensive review of blockchain consensus mechanisms. *IEEE Access : Practical Innovations, Open Solutions*, *9*, 43620–43652. doi:10.1109/ACCESS.2021.3065880

Lemieux, V., Hofman, D., Batista, D., & Joo, A. (2019). *Blockchain technology & recordkeeping*. ARMA International Educational Foundation.

Lemieux, V. L. (2016). Trusting records: Is Blockchain technology the answer? *Records Management Journal*, *26*(2), 110–139. doi:10.1108/RMJ-12-2015-0042

Levis, D., Fontana, F., & Ughetto, E. (2021). A look into the future of blockchain technology. *PLoS One*, *16*(11), e0258995. doi:10.1371/journal.pone.0258995 PMID:34788307

Li, A., Tan, S., & Jia, Y. (2019). A method for achieving provable data integrity in cloud computing. *The Journal of Supercomputing*, *75*(1), 92–108. doi:10.1007/s11227-015-1598-2

Li, W., Feng, C., Zhang, L., Xu, H., Cao, B., & Imran, M. A. (2020). A scalable multi-layer PBFT consensus for blockchain. *IEEE Transactions on Parallel and Distributed Systems*, *32*(5), 1146–1160. doi:10.1109/TPDS.2020.3042392

Liu, C., Zhang, X., & Medda, F. (2021). Plastic credit: A consortium blockchain-based plastic recyclability system. *Waste Management (New York, N.Y.)*, *121*, 42–51. doi:10.1016/j.wasman.2020.11.045 PMID:33348229

Lotti, L. (2016). Contemporary art, capitalization and the blockchain: On the autonomy and automation of art's value. *Finance and Stochastics*, *2*(2), 96–110.

Lumineau, F., Wang, W., & Schilke, O. (2021). Blockchain governance—A new way of organizing collaborations? *Organization Science*, *32*(2), 500–521. doi:10.1287/orsc.2020.1379

Magaki, I., Khazraee, M., Gutierrez, L. V., & Taylor, M. B. (2016). Asic clouds: Specializing the datacenter. *2016 ACM/IEEE 43rd Annual International Symposium on Computer Architecture (ISCA)*.

Makarov, I., & Schoar, A. (2022). *Cryptocurrencies and decentralized finance (DeFi)*. Academic Press.

McConaghy, T. (2016). *How blockchains could transform artificial intelligence*. Dataconomy.

Milutinovic, M., He, W., Wu, H., & Kanwal, M. (2016). Proof of luck: An efficient blockchain consensus protocol. *Proceedings of the 1st Workshop on System Software for Trusted Execution*.

Mingxiao, D., Xiaofeng, M., Zhe, Z., Xiangwei, W., & Qijun, C. (2017). A review on consensus algorithm of blockchain. *2017 IEEE International Conference on Systems, Man, and Cybernetics (SMC)*.

Mishra, L., & Kaushik, V. (2023). Application of blockchain in dealing with sustainability issues and challenges of financial sector. *Journal of Sustainable Finance & Investment*, *13*(3), 1318–1333.

Muratov, F., Lebedev, A., Iushkevich, N., Nasrulin, B., & Takemiya, M. (2018). YAC: BFT consensus algorithm for blockchain. *arXiv preprint arXiv:1809.00554*.

Muzammal, M., Qu, Q., & Nasrulin, B. (2019). Renovating blockchain with distributed databases: An open source system. *Future Generation Computer Systems*, *90*, 105–117. doi:10.1016/j.future.2018.07.042

Nakamoto, S. (2008). Bitcoin: A peer-to-peer electronic cash system. *Decentralized Business Review*, 21260.

Niranjanamurthy, M., Nithya, B., & Jagannatha, S. (2019). Analysis of Blockchain technology: Pros, cons and SWOT. *Cluster Computing*, *22*(6), 14743–14757. doi:10.1007/s10586-018-2387-5

Nobanee, H., & Ellili, N. O. D. (2023). Non-fungible tokens (NFTs): A bibliometric and systematic review, current streams, developments, and directions for future research. *International Review of Economics & Finance*, *84*, 460–473. doi:10.1016/j.iref.2022.11.014

Nofer, M., Gomber, P., Hinz, O., & Schiereck, D. (2017). Blockchain. *Business & Information Systems Engineering*, *59*(3), 183–187. doi:10.1007/s12599-017-0467-3

Noyes, C. (2016). Bitav: Fast anti-malware by distributed blockchain consensus and feedforward scanning. *arXiv preprint arXiv:1601.01405.*

O'Dwyer, K. J., & Malone, D. (2014). *Bitcoin mining and its energy footprint.* Academic Press.

Oliva, G. A., Hassan, A. E., & Jiang, Z. M. (2020). An exploratory study of smart contracts in the Ethereum blockchain platform. *Empirical Software Engineering*, *25*(3), 1864–1904. doi:10.1007/s10664-019-09796-5

Omar, I. A., Jayaraman, R., Salah, K., Yaqoob, I., & Ellahham, S. (2021). Applications of blockchain technology in clinical trials: Review and open challenges. *Arabian Journal for Science and Engineering*, *46*(4), 3001–3015. doi:10.1007/s13369-020-04989-3

Panarello, A., Tapas, N., Merlino, G., Longo, F., & Puliafito, A. (2018). Blockchain and iot integration: A systematic survey. *Sensors (Basel)*, *18*(8), 2575. doi:10.3390/s18082575 PMID:30082633

Patel, V., Khatiwala, F., Shah, K., & Choksi, Y. (2020). A review on blockchain technology: Components, issues and challenges. *ICDSMLA*, *2019*, 1257–1262. doi:10.1007/978-981-15-1420-3_137

Paul, G., Sarkar, P., & Mukherjee, S. (2014). Towards a more democratic mining in bitcoins. *International Conference on Information Systems Security.*

Puthal, D., & Mohanty, S. P. (2018). Proof of authentication: IoT-friendly blockchains. *IEEE Potentials*, *38*(1), 26–29.

Queiroz, M. M., Telles, R., & Bonilla, S. H. (2020). Blockchain and supply chain management integration: A systematic review of the literature. *Supply Chain Management*, *25*(2), 241–254. doi:10.1108/SCM-03-2018-0143

Ramzan, S., Aqdus, A., Ravi, V., Koundal, D., Amin, R., & Al Ghamdi, M. A. (2022). Healthcare applications using blockchain technology: Motivations and challenges. *IEEE Transactions on Engineering Management.*

Reed, S. L. (2014). Bitcoin cooperative proof-of-stake. *arXiv preprint arXiv:1405.5741.*

Reyna, A., Martín, C., Chen, J., Soler, E., & Díaz, M. (2018). On blockchain and its integration with IoT. Challenges and opportunities. *Future Generation Computer Systems*, *88*, 173–190. doi:10.1016/j.future.2018.05.046

Sagirlar, G., Carminati, B., Ferrari, E., Sheehan, J. D., & Ragnoli, E. (2018). Hybrid-iot: Hybrid blockchain architecture for internet of things-pow sub-blockchains. *2018 IEEE International Conference on Internet of Things (iThings) and IEEE Green Computing and Communications (GreenCom) and IEEE Cyber, Physical and Social Computing (CPSCom) and IEEE Smart Data (SmartData).*

Sengupta, J., Ruj, S., & Bit, S. D. (2020). A comprehensive survey on attacks, security issues and blockchain solutions for IoT and IIoT. *Journal of Network and Computer Applications*, *149*, 102481.

Sharma, P. K., Moon, S. Y., & Park, J. H. (2017). Block-VN: A distributed blockchain based vehicular network architecture in smart city. *Journal of Information Processing Systems*, *13*(1), 184–195.

Shoker, A. (2021). Blockchain technology as a means of sustainable development. *One Earth*, *4*(6), 795–800. doi:10.1016/j.oneear.2021.05.014

Singh, P., Sammanit, D., Krishnan, P., Agarwal, K. M., Shaw, R. N., & Ghosh, A. (2021). Combating challenges in the construction industry with blockchain technology. In *Innovations in Electrical and Electronic Engineering* (pp. 707–716). Springer. doi:10.1007/978-981-16-0749-3_56

Sunyaev, A., & Sunyaev, A. (2020). Cloud computing. *Internet Computing: Principles of Distributed Systems and Emerging Internet-Based Technologies*, 195-236.

Tan, E., Mahula, S., & Crompvoets, J. (2022). Blockchain governance in the public sector: A conceptual framework for public management. *Government Information Quarterly*, *39*(1), 101625. doi:10.1016/j.giq.2021.101625

Viriyasitavat, W., & Hoonsopon, D. (2019). Blockchain characteristics and consensus in modern business processes. *Journal of Industrial Information Integration*, *13*, 32–39. doi:10.1016/j.jii.2018.07.004

Wang, H., Moon, S., & Han, N. (2020). A study on the applications of blockchain transactions and smart contracts in recordkeeping. *Journal of Korean Society of Archives and Records Management*, *20*(4), 81–105.

Wang, H., & Yang, D. (2021). Research and Development of Blockchain Recordkeeping at the National Archives of Korea. *Computers*, *10*(8), 90. doi:10.3390/computers10080090

Wei, P., Wang, D., Zhao, Y., Tyagi, S. K. S., & Kumar, N. (2020). Blockchain data-based cloud data integrity protection mechanism. *Future Generation Computer Systems*, *102*, 902–911. doi:10.1016/j.future.2019.09.028

Wenhua, Z., Qamar, F., Abdali, T.-A. N., Hassan, R., Jafri, S. T. A., & Nguyen, Q. N. (2023). Blockchain technology: Security issues, healthcare applications, challenges and future trends. *Electronics (Basel)*, *12*(3), 546. doi:10.3390/electronics12030546

Wüst, K., & Gervais, A. (2018). Do you need a blockchain? *2018 Crypto Valley Conference on Blockchain Technology (CVCBT)*.

Xu, L., Shah, N., Chen, L., Diallo, N., Gao, Z., Lu, Y., & Shi, W. (2017). Enabling the sharing economy: Privacy respecting contract based on public blockchain. *Proceedings of the ACM Workshop on Blockchain, Cryptocurrencies and Contracts*.

Yang, X., & Li, W. (2020). A zero-knowledge-proof-based digital identity management scheme in blockchain. *Computers & Security*, *99*, 102050.

Yli-Huumo, J., Ko, D., Choi, S., Park, S., & Smolander, K. (2016). Where is current research on blockchain technology?—A systematic review. *PLoS One*, *11*(10), e0163477. doi:10.1371/journal.pone.0163477 PMID:27695049

Young, S. (2018). Changing governance models by applying blockchain computing. *Catholic University Journal of Law and Technology*, *26*(2), 87–128.

Zhang, X., Qin, R., Yuan, Y., & Wang, F.-Y. (2018). An analysis of blockchain-based bitcoin mining difficulty: Techniques and principles. *2018 Chinese Automation Congress (CAC)*.

Zheng, Z., Xie, S., Dai, H., Chen, X., & Wang, H. (2017). An overview of blockchain technology: Architecture, consensus, and future trends. *2017 IEEE International Congress on Big Data (Big Data Congress)*.

Ziegler, T., Shneor, R., Wenzlaff, K., Wang, B., Kim, J., Paes, F. F. d. C., Suresh, K., Zhang, B. Z., Mammadova, L., & Adams, N. (2021). The global alternative finance market benchmarking report. *Available at SSRN 3771509*.

Zwitter, A. J., Gstrein, O. J., & Yap, E. (2020). Digital identity and the blockchain: Universal identity management and the concept of the "Self-Sovereign" individual. *Frontiers in Blockchain*, *3*, 26. doi:10.3389/fbloc.2020.00026

Zyskind, G., & Nathan, O. (2015). Decentralizing privacy: Using blockchain to protect personal data. *2015 IEEE Security and Privacy Workshops*,

KEY TERMS AND DEFINITIONS

Blockchain: Is a decentralized and distributed digital ledger that securely and immutably records of transactions across a network of computers.

Consensus Mechanisms: Refers to protocols used to achieve agreement among nodes in a decentralized network.

Decentralization: Refers to the distribution of power and control throughout a network, therefore eliminating the necessity of central authority and fostering a system that is more robust and democratic.

Distributed Ledger: Refers to a synchronized and replicated digital database that contains data which is shared and disseminated over multiple computers.

Peer-to-Peer Network: Refers to a distributed network where peers interact directly with one another, without the need for a central server.

Smart Contracts: Refer to self-executing contracts with the terms of the agreement directly written into code, enabling automated and trustless execution of contractual clauses.

Transactions: Refer to exchanges of value recorded on a blockchain, typically involving the execution of smart contracts.

Chapter 4
Wallets and Transactions

Pankaj Bhambri
https://orcid.org/0000-0003-4437-4103
Guru Nanak Dev Engineering College, Ludhiana, India

ABSTRACT

Digital wallets are of utmost importance in transforming the online experience as they serve as the core constituents of decentralized ecosystems. This study explores the operational mechanisms of different types of wallets, encompassing hardware wallets and software-based solutions, in order to elucidate their distinctive characteristics and security implications. Moreover, the chapter offers a comprehensive examination of decentralized transactions, elucidating the profound impact that blockchain technology may have in cultivating trust, enhancing security, and promoting transparency. By examining real-world illustrations and analyzing case studies, readers will acquire a comprehensive comprehension of how wallets and transactions serve as the fundamental infrastructure for a novel epoch of online engagement. This transformative development is reshaping the manner in which individuals interact with digital assets and engage in decentralized networks.

1. INTRODUCTION TO WEB 3 WALLETS

In the rapidly evolving landscape of decentralized technologies, Web3 wallets have emerged as transformative tools, operating within the framework of blockchain to grant users unprecedented control over their digital assets and identities (Rumbelow, 2023). This chapter aims to provide a comprehensive exploration of Web3 wallets, shedding light on their evolution from conventional digital wallets and elucidating their pivotal role in the broader Web3 ecosystem.

1.1. Problem Statement: The Need for Decentralized Control

Traditionally, digital interactions and financial transactions have been mediated by centralized entities, introducing issues of control, privacy, and security. The reliance on intermediaries such as banks for transactions and record-keeping poses challenges to user autonomy and the secure management of digital assets.

DOI: 10.4018/979-8-3693-1532-3.ch004

1.2 Proposed Solution: Web 3 Wallets as Decentralized Gateways

In response to these challenges, the emergence of Web3 wallets signifies a paradigm shift towards decentralization. Unlike traditional wallets that primarily store currency, Web3 wallets serve as gateways to the blockchain, enabling secure interactions with decentralized applications (dApps) and the broader blockchain ecosystem (Tondon and Bhambri, 2017). Their defining characteristics include user control, privacy, and ownership of digital assets through cryptographic keys.

1.3 Defining Web 3 Wallets

To navigate the evolving decentralized online experience, it is crucial to define the multifaceted nature of Web3 wallets. This definition encompasses various types, including browser-based, mobile, and hardware wallets, each designed to cater to different user preferences and security needs (Henry and Shannon, 2023; Huang et al., 2023).

1.4 Evolution from Traditional to Web 3 Wallets

Web3 wallets represent a fundamental evolution from traditional wallets associated with centralized financial systems. This transition empowers users with unprecedented control over their funds and digital identities, leveraging blockchain technology to manage various cryptocurrencies and interact directly with decentralized applications (Cassatt, 2023; Patiño-Martínez and Paulo, 2023).

1.5 Importance in Decentralized Ecosystems

At the core of decentralized systems lies the principle of empowering individuals with control over their digital assets and data. Web3 wallets play a pivotal role in realizing this vision by providing secure and user-friendly means to manage cryptographic keys, enabling access to dApps, and facilitating peer-to-peer transactions on blockchain networks (Hundreds, 2023).

In addition to enabling user control, Web3 wallets contribute significantly to the overall security and integrity of decentralized ecosystems (Singh et al., 2013). By securely storing private keys and facilitating cryptographic signatures for transactions, these wallets enhance the trustworthiness of interactions within decentralized networks (Bouzid et al., 2023). The robust security measures implemented in Web3 wallets mitigate the risk of unauthorized access and fraudulent activities, ensuring the reliability of blockchain-based transactions.

2. TYPES OF WEB 3 WALLETS

Web3 wallets come in various forms, each tailored to meet specific user preferences and security needs. Browser-based wallets operate within web browsers, offering convenience and accessibility for users engaging with decentralized applications online (Connolly, 2023). Mobile wallets, designed for smartphones, provide flexibility and on-the-go access to digital assets. Hardware wallets prioritize security by storing cryptographic keys offline, protecting them from potential online vulnerabilities. Paper wallets involve the physical representation of keys on paper, offering an additional layer of offline security.

Social wallets leverage social media platforms for user authentication and engagement (Arroyo, 2023). Each type caters to different user requirements, reflecting the evolving landscape of Web3 and the diverse ways individuals choose to interact with decentralized technologies.

2.1 Browser-based Wallets: Seamless Integration for Web-Centric Transactions

Browser-based wallets operate within web browsers, offering a user-friendly interface for managing cryptographic keys and executing cryptocurrency transactions. These wallets, often in the form of browser extensions or plugins, seamlessly integrate with the user's online experience. By securely storing private keys, enabling transactions, and facilitating interaction with decentralized platforms directly from web browsers, they lower entry barriers to blockchain technology. This inclusivity fosters a more user-centric approach, simplifying participation in decentralized ecosystems (Pejic, 2023).

2.2 Mobile Wallets: On-the-Go Access and User Empowerment

Designed for smartphones, mobile wallets provide on-the-go access to blockchain functionalities. Featuring intuitive interfaces, these wallets empower users to send and receive cryptocurrencies, interact with dApps, and monitor digital asset portfolios (Bhambri et al., 2009). Leveraging mobile device capabilities like biometric authentication and QR code scanning enhances security and streamlines the user experience. Mobile wallets play a vital role in expanding accessibility to decentralized technologies, enabling users to participate in blockchain networks anytime, anywhere, contributing to the widespread adoption of decentralized applications and digital assets.

2.3 Hardware Wallets: Offline Security and Convenient Access

Resembling USB devices or smart cards, hardware wallets prioritize security by operating offline (Bhambri et al., 2019). The private keys, crucial for authorizing cryptocurrency transactions, remain within the hardware wallet, resistant to online hacking attempts. Users initiate transactions through a computer or mobile device, with the hardware wallet securely signing them. This isolation from online connections and dedicated security features makes hardware wallets an attractive choice for secure and convenient storage and access to digital assets, especially in the realm of decentralized finance and blockchain technology.

2.4 Paper Wallets: Enhanced Security Through Offline Storage

Generated through dedicated software, a paper wallet involves the physical representation of cryptographic key information, often in the form of QR codes (Defidao et al., 2023). Serving as a secure means to store cryptocurrency offline, paper wallets minimize exposure to online vulnerabilities such as hacking and malware. Despite the advent of more user-friendly options, paper wallets remain a viable choice for individuals prioritizing maximum security. Users must exercise caution, ensuring the safekeeping of the physical document to prevent the irreversible loss of funds.

2.5 Social Wallets: Community-Centric Engagement and Trust

Distinguished by their focus on community dynamics, social wallets leverage social networks to enhance user engagement within blockchain ecosystems (Lopez, 2023). These wallets integrate social features, allowing users to connect and transact with peers seamlessly. Social wallets foster a sense of community and trust, enabling users to send and receive digital assets within their social circles. The concept of social recovery, where trusted contacts assist in key recovery, adds an additional layer of security through social verification. Aligning with the collaborative and decentralized ethos of Web3, social wallets intertwine social relationships with digital asset management on the blockchain, simplifying the user experience.

3. KEY FEATURES OF WEB 3 WALLETS

Web3 wallets exhibit key features that are integral to their role in decentralized ecosystems, aligning closely with security measures, user privacy and control, interoperability with dApps, and cross-platform functionality. One of the foremost considerations in Web3 wallet design is security. These wallets employ advanced cryptographic techniques to secure users' private keys, ensuring that unauthorized access is extremely difficult (Kaur et al., 2012). Multi-signature authentication, biometric verification, and the integration of hardware wallets are among the security measures that fortify the protection of digital assets. By prioritizing security, Web3 wallets contribute to the overall robustness of decentralized ecosystems, fostering user trust and confidence in the blockchain space. User privacy and control are paramount in Web3 wallet design philosophy. Unlike centralized systems where user data is often stored and controlled by third parties, Web3 wallets empower users with complete ownership of their data (Kraski and Shenkarow, 2023). Users retain control over their private keys, digital identities, and transactional information, aligning with the principles of self-sovereignty. This emphasis on privacy and control distinguishes Web3 wallets from traditional models, offering users a level of autonomy that is fundamental to the decentralized ethos. Interoperability with dApps is another key feature of Web3 wallets. These wallets are designed to seamlessly integrate with a diverse array of dApps, allowing users to interact with various blockchain-based services without the need for multiple accounts or complicated authentication processes. This interoperability enhances the user experience, making it more intuitive and encouraging widespread adoption of decentralized technologies. Cross-platform functionality further enhances the versatility of Web3 wallets. Users can access their digital assets and interact with decentralized applications across different devices and platforms, including web browsers, mobile devices, and even hardware wallets. This flexibility is crucial for accommodating the diverse preferences and lifestyles of users, making Web3 wallets accessible to a broad audience and facilitating the integration of blockchain technology into everyday digital interactions.

4. CRYPTOGRAPHIC FOUNDATIONS OF WEB 3 TRANSACTIONS

The cryptographic foundations of Web3 transactions are fundamental to ensuring the security, integrity, and privacy of interactions within decentralized ecosystems. At the heart of this foundation is the use of public and private keys, which form the basis of user identities and cryptographic authentication. Public keys, which are shared openly, act as addresses to receive funds or communications, while private keys, known only to the user, serve as the means of unlocking access to their assets or confirming transactions (Lekhi and Kaur, 2023). This asymmetric key pair system is a cornerstone of blockchain security, allowing users to prove ownership and control over their digital assets without exposing sensitive information. Smart contract interactions further extend this cryptographic foundation by introducing programmable, self-executing contracts that operate based on predefined conditions. These contracts, stored on the blockchain, are secured by cryptographic principles, ensuring transparency and immutability in the execution of predefined rules and agreements. Digital signatures play a crucial role in Web3 transactions, providing a secure way to verify the authenticity and integrity of messages or transactions on the blockchain. When a user initiates a transaction or interacts with a smart contract, they use their private key to create a digital signature. This signature, unique to the transaction and the user, is then verified by the network using the corresponding public key. The use of digital signatures ensures that transactions are tamper-resistant, and the provenance of every action on the blockchain can be traced back to the rightful owner. Encryption methods further fortify the cryptographic foundations by safeguarding the confidentiality of sensitive data. In Web3 transactions, especially in the context of privacy-focused blockchains or applications, encryption is employed to secure the content of messages, ensuring that only authorized parties can decipher and access the information (Duffey, 2023). This is particularly pertinent in scenarios where privacy is a paramount concern, such as in financial transactions or sensitive data exchanges.

5. DECENTRALIZED IDENTITY AND AUTHENTICATION

Web3 wallets not only store cryptographic keys but also serve as custodians of decentralized identities, enabling users to have self-sovereign control over their personal information. Authentication processes within Web3 wallets leverage this decentralized identity model, ensuring secure access to digital assets and participation in blockchain transactions. By seamlessly integrating decentralized identity solutions, such as self-sovereign identity systems, Web3 wallets enhance user privacy, reduce reliance on centralized authorities for authentication, and foster a trustless environment (Neto, 2023). This synergy between decentralized identity and wallets not only bolsters the security of transactions but also aligns with the overarching ethos of decentralization, where users have full control over their digital personas, contributing to a more resilient and user-centric paradigm for online interactions.

5.1 Self-Sovereign Identity

In a decentralized context, self-sovereign identity empowers users with the autonomy to manage and share their identity attributes without relying on centralized authorities. This paradigm shift ensures that individuals have granular control over the disclosure of specific details, enhancing privacy and reducing the risk of identity theft. By leveraging decentralized technologies such as blockchain, self-sovereign identity enables users to hold and manage their digital credentials, creating a portable and interoperable identity layer. This approach not only strengthens user security but also promotes a more inclusive and user-centric authentication process, as individuals can selectively disclose relevant identity information for seamless interactions within decentralized ecosystems (Morales de Medrano, 2023). In essence, self-sovereign identity is a cornerstone in the move towards decentralized authentication, offering a more secure, privacy-preserving, and user-controlled model for asserting one's digital identity across the online landscape.

5.2 Multi-Factor Authentication

In the context of decentralized systems, where individuals have greater control over their digital identities, Multi-factor authentication (MFA) serves as an additional layer of defense against unauthorized access and potential security breaches (Bhambri and Thapar, 2009). By requiring users to provide multiple forms of verification, such as passwords, biometrics, or device-based authenticators, MFA significantly reduces the risk of identity compromise. In the realm of decentralized identity, where users maintain ownership of their personal data on blockchain networks, MFA acts as a robust safeguard, ensuring that only authorized individuals can access and control their digital personas. This multi-layered approach not only aligns with the overarching principles of user empowerment and privacy in decentralized ecosystems but also contributes to the establishment of a more resilient and secure foundation for the authentication processes integral to Web3 technologies.

5.3 Biometric Integration

By incorporating biometric measures, such as fingerprint or facial recognition, into the authentication process, decentralized identity platforms enhance the security and user-friendliness of digital interactions. Biometric integration adds an extra layer of personalization, making it significantly more challenging for unauthorized entities to gain access to an individual's decentralized identity. This not only bolsters the overall security of decentralized ecosystems but also streamlines the user experience by providing a seamless and intuitive means of identity verification. In a decentralized context, where the emphasis is on user empowerment and privacy, biometric integration aligns with the principles of self-sovereign identity, ensuring that individuals retain control over their personal information while benefiting from the heightened security and convenience afforded by biometric authentication methods (Vero, 2023).

5.4 Identity on the Blockchain

In decentralized ecosystems, establishing and verifying user identity without reliance on central authorities is a fundamental challenge. Leveraging blockchain technology for identity management introduces a paradigm shift by enabling users to have self-sovereign control over their digital identities. Through decentralized identity and authentication mechanisms, users can anchor their identity on the blockchain, creating a tamper-resistant and verifiable record of personal information (Dezfouli, 2023). This not only enhances security by minimizing the risk of data breaches but also streamlines the authentication process, as users can selectively share cryptographic proofs of their identity without divulging sensitive details. As a result, the integration of identity on the blockchain becomes a linchpin for trust and privacy in decentralized environments, promoting user empowerment and paving the way for innovative applications in areas such as secure access to services, decentralized finance, and digital ownership.

6. TRANSACTION LIFECYCLE IN WEB 3

In the context of Web3 wallets, understanding the transaction lifecycle is pivotal for users to navigate the intricacies of blockchain interactions. The lifecycle typically involves initiating a transaction, broadcasting it to the network, confirmation through consensus mechanisms, and the finality of the transaction. Web3 wallets play a central role in each of these stages by serving as the tool through which users initiate transactions, sign them with their private keys, and monitor the status and confirmation (George et al., 2023). The integration of Web3 wallets with decentralized applications ensures a seamless user experience, where users can effortlessly trigger transactions directly from their wallets, interacting with smart contracts and blockchain networks without relying on centralized intermediaries.

Web3 wallets incorporate features that allow users to set transaction fees, understand gas costs, and ensure the timely processing of transactions (Bhambri et al., 2008). The lifecycle also addresses the critical aspect of transaction finality, assuring users that once a transaction is confirmed, it becomes an immutable part of the blockchain. This reliability is crucial for users to trust the decentralized systems and understand the outcome of their interactions. As the Web3 landscape evolves, innovations in the transaction lifecycle will likely further streamline processes, enhance user control, and contribute to the maturation of decentralized economies by optimizing the interaction between wallets and the broader transactional ecosystem.

7. INTEGRATION OF WALLETS WITH DECENTRALIZED APPLICATIONS

The interaction between wallets and dApps is symbiotic, serving as the linchpin for a user-friendly and efficient decentralized experience. The functionality of Web3 wallets encompasses the initiation and confirmation of transactions. When integrated with dApps, these wallets become the conduit through which users effortlessly access and engage with decentralized services. This integration not only streamlines the user experience but also ensures that transactions within the decentralized ecosystem are secure, leveraging the cryptographic foundations (Bansal et al., 2012). Moreover, the integration fosters trust by allowing users to seamlessly interact with a variety of decentralized applications without compromising the security of their private keys, thus promoting the widespread adoption and utility of both wallets and decentralized applications in the evolving landscape of Web3 technologies.

7.1 Seamless User Experience

A seamless user experience ensures that the interaction between users and dApps, facilitated by Web3 wallets, is intuitive and efficient. When users can seamlessly connect their wallets to various decentralized applications without encountering friction, it enhances accessibility and encourages broader participation in the decentralized ecosystem. This integration involves user-friendly interfaces, simplified authentication processes, and interoperability standards that enable wallets to smoothly interact with diverse dApps, promoting a cohesive and user-centric environment. By prioritizing a seamless user experience, the integration of wallets with decentralized applications becomes a catalyst for mainstream adoption, empowering users to explore and engage with the decentralized web effortlessly.

7.2 Wallet Connect Protocols

Wallet connect protocols serve as the linchpin for establishing a secure and efficient communication channel between users' Web3 wallets and diverse decentralized applications. By adopting standardized connection methods, such as QR code scanning or deep linking, wallet connect protocols eliminate friction in the user on-boarding process. Users can effortlessly link their wallets to dApps, allowing for the secure transfer of transaction requests and data. This integration not only enhances user experience but also opens up a realm of possibilities for developers, enabling them to create sophisticated and interconnected decentralized ecosystems (Goswami, 2023). The use of wallet connect protocols ensures that users retain control over their private keys while enjoying a seamless and intuitive interaction with a diverse array of decentralized applications, thereby fostering widespread adoption and usability in the decentralized landscape.

7.3 Access Control and Permissions

As users engage with diverse dApps, each with its unique functionality and purpose, the seamless integration of wallets becomes pivotal in managing access and permissions effectively (Russo, 2023). Web3 wallets serve as the linchpin, facilitating secure and permissioned interactions between users and decentralized platforms. Through cryptographic signatures and private key management, wallets ensure that users retain granular control over the actions they authorize within dApps, ranging from simple transactions to more complex operations like smart contract interactions. This integration not only enhances the security of user data and assets but also empowers individuals by allowing them to dictate the extent of their engagement with various decentralized services (Lee, 2023). In essence, the harmonious interplay between access control mechanisms and wallet integration contributes to a more user-centric and secure decentralized experience, fostering trust and reliability in the broader Web3 landscape.

8. SECURITY BEST PRACTICES FOR WEB 3 WALLETS

Security is paramount when it comes to Web3 wallets, given their central role in safeguarding users' cryptographic keys and facilitating secure transactions on decentralized networks. Implementing robust security best practices is crucial to protect users from potential threats and vulnerabilities. One fundamental aspect is the adoption of cold storage strategies, which involve keeping private keys completely offline, disconnected from the internet. This minimizes the risk of exposure to online threats such as hacking and phishing attacks, providing an extra layer of protection for users' digital assets.

Another essential practice is the meticulous management of recovery phrases and backup mechanisms. Users should be educated on the importance of securely storing their recovery phrases, often consisting of a series of words, as these phrases serve as the ultimate backup to regain access to their wallets in case of loss or compromise. Encouraging users to keep multiple secure copies of their recovery phrases in different physical locations enhances the resilience of their accounts (Abrol et al., 2005). Additionally, incorporating multi-signature authentication, where a transaction requires multiple private key signatures for validation, adds an extra layer of security, reducing the risk associated with a single point of failure. Smart contract vulnerabilities represent a critical concern, and developers of Web3 wallets must conduct thorough code audits and testing to identify and address potential weaknesses (Lisdorf, 2023).

Regular software updates and patches are essential to patch any discovered vulnerabilities promptly. Educating users about potential phishing attacks is equally vital, emphasizing the importance of verifying the legitimacy of websites and applications before entering sensitive information. Implementing hardware-based security, such as utilizing hardware wallets, adds an extra layer of protection against online threats by isolating the private keys from potentially compromised devices. By incorporating the following security practices, overall security posture of users in decentralized environments can be enhanced in web3 wallets:

- Two-Factor Authentication (2FA): Encourage users to enable two-factor authentication (2FA) for an additional layer of security. By requiring users to provide a secondary form of verification, such as a code from a mobile app or a physical token, even if the primary credentials are compromised, unauthorized access becomes significantly more challenging.
- Regular Security Audits: Emphasize the importance of regular security audits for both wallet developers and users. Developers should conduct periodic audits of their codebase to identify and address potential vulnerabilities. Users, on the other hand, should routinely review their security settings, check for any suspicious activities, and update their wallet software promptly.
- Secure Connection Practices: Highlight the significance of using secure and encrypted connections when interacting with Web3 wallets. Users should avoid accessing their wallets on public Wi-Fi networks or unsecured internet connections, as these may expose them to potential man-in-the-middle attacks. Secure connections, such as Virtual Private Networks (VPNs) or HTTPS, enhance the overall security of transactions and interactions (YILDIZ, 2023).
- Timely Logout and Session Management: Encourage users to log out of their Web3 wallets after completing transactions or when not in use. Implementing automatic logout features and robust session management mechanisms can help mitigate the risk of unauthorized access, especially on shared or public devices.
- Privacy-Centric Practices: Promote privacy-centric practices, such as using dedicated devices or virtual machines for Web3 wallet activities. This approach helps minimize the risk of cross-site scripting (XSS) attacks or other forms of malware that may compromise the security of the wallet. Users should also be cautious about sharing wallet-related information on social media or public forums.
- Continuous User Education: Continual education is key to maintaining a secure Web3 environment. Regularly update users on emerging security threats and best practices. Provide resources, tutorials, and guides to help users stay informed about the latest developments in Web3 security and empower them to make informed decisions.
- Decentralized Identity Solutions: Explore decentralized identity solutions as an additional layer of security. Technologies such as decentralized identifiers (DIDs) and verifiable credentials enhance user control over identity and reduce reliance on centralized authentication methods. Integrating these solutions into Web3 wallets can contribute to a more secure and privacy-focused user experience.

9. REGULATORY CONSIDERATIONS AND COMPLIANCE

As decentralized systems gain prominence, regulators around the world are grappling with the need to establish legal frameworks that ensure the responsible use of these technologies while safeguarding users and preventing illicit activities.

One primary concern is compliance with anti-money laundering (AML) and know your customer (KYC) regulations. Web3 wallets, being gatekeepers to digital assets, need to implement robust identification processes to verify the identities of users, preventing anonymous and potentially illicit transactions. This presents a challenge, as the foundational principle of many blockchain networks is pseudonymity (Gupta and Bhambri, 2012). Striking a balance between privacy and regulatory compliance becomes paramount in the design and operation of these wallets.

Moreover, the global regulatory landscape is diverse and complex, with different countries adopting varied approaches toward crypto-currencies and decentralized technologies. Web3 wallet developers must navigate this intricate terrain, ensuring their products align with regional legal requirements. This involves staying abreast of evolving regulations, engaging with regulatory bodies, and implementing features that enable compliance without compromising the decentralized ethos.

Ensuring the security of transactions and user data in compliance with privacy regulations is another key consideration. As personal and financial data traverse decentralized networks, wallets must adhere to data protection laws to maintain user trust and meet legal standards.

10. FUTURE TRENDS AND INNOVATIONS IN WEB 3 WALLETS

The future trajectory of Web3 wallets is poised for transformative advancements, driven by ongoing innovations and emerging trends that aim to redefine the landscape of decentralized digital interactions. Here are some key trends shaping the future of Web3 wallets:

- Continuous Enhancement of User Experience: The relentless pursuit of improving user experience remains a central focus in the evolution of Web3 wallets. Ongoing efforts in user interface design, intuitive user experiences, and streamlined onboarding processes aim to mitigate the complexities associated with cryptographic keys and blockchain interactions. The goal is to make Web3 wallets more accessible to a broader audience, fostering mass adoption by offering a user experience comparable to that of traditional applications.
- Integration with Emerging Technologies: The integration of Web3 wallets with emerging technologies is a noteworthy trend that promises to expand their functionality and use cases. Artificial Intelligence (AI) and the Internet of Things (IoT) are anticipated to play pivotal roles in shaping the next generation of wallets. Potential AI-driven features may include personalized financial insights, predictive analytics for transaction patterns, and enhanced security measures through adaptive learning algorithms. Moreover, IoT integration could enable wallets to interact with physical devices, unlocking new possibilities for decentralized applications in areas such as smart homes, supply chain management, and more. These advancements underscore the potential for Web3 wallets to evolve beyond transactional tools, becoming integral components of a technologically interconnected world.

- Cross-Chain Interoperability: Cross-chain interoperability stands out as a crucial future trend for Web3 wallets. As blockchain ecosystems continue to diversify, users increasingly engage with multiple blockchain networks. Wallets that seamlessly navigate and interact across these diverse chains will become indispensable, allowing users to manage various assets and engage with a wide range of decentralized applications. This interoperability not only enhances user convenience but also contributes to the overall cohesion and efficiency of the decentralized ecosystem (Lewis, 2023).
- Governance Features within Web3 Wallets: The rise of decentralized autonomous organizations (DAOs) has led to the emergence of governance features within Web3 wallets. These features empower users to actively participate in decision-making processes related to the development and evolution of underlying blockchain protocols. The trend aligns with the core principles of decentralization, distributing power among network participants and fostering a more democratic and community-driven approach to blockchain development.

11. CASE STUDIES AND USE CASES

Numerous case studies showcase the successful implementation of Web3 wallets across diverse industries. One notable example is the adoption of MetaMask, a popular browser extension wallet, in the decentralized finance (DeFi) space. MetaMask allows users to seamlessly connect to various DeFi platforms, facilitating the management of assets and participation in decentralized lending and trading. Another success story is the widespread use of hardware wallets like Ledger and Trezor, providing robust security solutions for storing private keys offline and ensuring the safekeeping of cryptocurrencies (Pelfrey, 2023). These implementations underscore the versatility of Web3 wallets and their adaptability to different use cases, contributing to the broader adoption of blockchain technologies.

11.1 Impact on Specific Industries

Web3 wallets have demonstrated a transformative impact on specific industries, particularly in areas where decentralized technologies bring novel solutions. In the realm of supply chain management, wallets integrated with blockchain technology provide transparent and traceable records of the production and distribution process. For example, VeChainThor Wallet has been employed to enhance transparency in supply chains, ensuring the authenticity of products through immutable blockchain records. In the gaming industry, wallets like Fortmatic and Bitski have enabled users to truly own and trade in-game assets across different platforms, fostering a new era of digital ownership. These instances illustrate how Web3 wallets are not just transactional tools but pivotal enablers of decentralized applications, offering tangible benefits in sectors ranging from finance to healthcare.

11.2 User Adoption Stories

User adoption stories serve as compelling evidence of the practical impact of Web3 wallets on individuals. One noteworthy narrative is the rise of decentralized autonomous organizations (DAOs) facilitated by wallets like MyEtherWallet and Trust Wallet. Users participating in DAOs leverage these wallets to vote on governance proposals, showcasing the democratic and inclusive nature of decentralized systems.

Additionally, the adoption of web-based wallets like Coinbase Wallet and Rainbow by mainstream users highlights the growing acceptance of decentralized technologies beyond the crypto enthusiast community (Ottina et al., 2023). As more individuals experience the ease of use and enhanced security provided by Web3 wallets, the shift towards decentralized ecosystems gains momentum. These user adoption stories underscore the importance of user-friendly interfaces, seamless integration with applications, and the overall positive impact Web3 wallets have on democratizing access to blockchain technologies.

12. CHALLENGES AND OPPORTUNITIES

The deployment of Web3 wallets and transactions presents a landscape of both challenges and opportunities.

12.1 Scalability Issues

One of the primary challenges facing Web3 wallets is scalability. As decentralized ecosystems grow, the demand for efficient and scalable wallet solutions increases exponentially. Blockchain networks, especially those with high transaction volumes, may face congestion and slower transaction processing times. This can result in a less-than-optimal user experience, hindering the widespread adoption of decentralized applications. To address this challenge, developers and stakeholders in the Web3 space are actively exploring and implementing solutions such as layer 2 scaling solutions (e.g., sidechains, state channels), consensus algorithm enhancements, and advancements in blockchain interoperability. These innovations aim to improve the throughput and speed of transactions, ensuring that Web3 wallets can seamlessly handle the increasing demands of a growing user base.

12.2 User Education and On-Boarding

User education and on-boarding present another significant challenge for Web3 wallets. The decentralized nature of blockchain technology introduces complexities that may be unfamiliar to the average user (Bathla et al., 2007). Concepts such as private key management, gas fees, and decentralized governance can be intimidating for those new to the space. Enhancing user education and on-boarding processes is crucial for driving mainstream adoption. Wallet developers and the broader blockchain community have the opportunity to create user-friendly guides, tutorials, and interactive resources to demystify these concepts. Moreover, integrating educational components directly into wallet interfaces can empower users with the knowledge they need to navigate decentralized ecosystems confidently. Collaboration between wallet providers, industry organizations, and educational institutions can contribute to a more informed and empowered user base, unlocking the full potential of Web3 technology.

12.3 Potential Solutions and Innovations

In addressing scalability issues, ongoing research and development efforts are focused on scaling solutions that can enhance the efficiency of blockchain networks. Layer 2 scaling solutions, like Optimistic Rollups and zk-rollups, aim to process transactions off-chain or in a more optimized manner, reducing congestion on the main blockchain. Additionally, advancements in blockchain consensus algorithms, such as proof-of-stake (PoS) and sharding, hold promise for scalability improvements. To tackle user education and onboarding challenges, wallet providers can prioritize user experience (UX) design, creating interfaces that guide users through key concepts in a clear and intuitive manner. Gamification and incentive programs can also be leveraged to encourage users to learn and engage with Web3 technologies. Collaborative efforts within the blockchain community, including partnerships with educational institutions and initiatives to promote digital literacy, can contribute to a more educated and inclusive Web3 ecosystem (Panda et al., 2023). Ultimately, by addressing these challenges and leveraging innovative solutions, Web3 wallets can play a pivotal role in realizing the broader vision of a decentralized and user-centric internet.

CONCLUSION

The role of wallets in shaping the Web3 landscape is nothing short of transformative. Web3 wallets serve as the linchpin of decentralized ecosystems, providing users with the means to manage their digital assets, access decentralized applications, and assert control over their online identities. The shift from traditional, centralized models to decentralized paradigms hinges on the capabilities and security features of these wallets. By offering users a secure and user-friendly interface to interact with blockchain technology, Web3 wallets democratize access to the benefits of decentralization. They empower individuals to be the custodians of their own data, fostering a sense of self-sovereignty that is foundational to the ethos of Web3.

Looking ahead, the evolving role of wallets in decentralized ecosystems promises continued innovation and integration with emerging technologies. As the Web3 landscape matures, wallets are likely to become even more versatile, offering advanced features such as enhanced privacy measures, artificial intelligence integration, and seamless interoperability across different blockchain networks. The evolution of these wallets will not only streamline user experiences but also contribute to the scalability and adoption of decentralized technologies on a global scale. Additionally, the role of wallets in governance structures within decentralized ecosystems may become more pronounced, as users actively participate in decision-making processes related to the development and maintenance of blockchain networks. In essence, the future holds exciting possibilities for Web3 wallets, positioning them as dynamic tools that not only facilitate transactions but also play a central role in shaping the trajectory of decentralized technologies in the years to come.

REFERENCES

Abrol, N., Shaifali, Rattan, M., & Bhambri, P. (2005). Implementation and performance evaluation of JPEG 2000 for medical images. *International Conference on Innovative Applications of Information Technology for Developing World.*

Arroyo, A. (2023). *Beyond Realms: Navigating the Metaverse and Web3.* Academic Press.

Bansal, P., Bhambri, P., & Gupta, O. P. (2012). *GOR Method to Predict Protein Secondary Structure using Different Input Formats.* Paper presented at the International Conference on Advanced Computing and Communication Technologies, Delhi, India.

Bathla, S., Jindal, C., & Bhambri, P. (2007, March). Impact of Technology On Societal Living. In *International Conference on Convergence and Competition* (p. 14). Academic Press.

Bhambri, P., Hans, S., & Singh, M. (2008, November). Bioinformatics - Friendship between Bits & Genes. In *International Conference on Advanced Computing & Communication Technologies* (pp. 62-65). Academic Press.

Bhambri, P., Hans, S., & Singh, M. (2009). Inharmonic Signal Synthesis & Analysis. *Technia-International Journal of Computing Science and Communication Technologies, 1*(2), 199-201.

Bhambri, P., Sinha, V. K., & Jaiswal, M. (2019). Change in iris dimensions as a potential human consciousness level indicator. *International Journal of Innovative Technology and Exploring Engineering, 8*(9S), 517–525. doi:10.35940/ijitee.I1082.0789S19

Bhambri, P., & Thapar, V. (2009, May). *Power Distribution Challenges in VLSI: An Introduction*. Paper presented at the International Conference on Downtrend Challenges in IT.

Bouzid, A., Narciso, P., & Wood, S. (2023). *NFTs for Business: A Practical Guide to Harnessing Digital Assets*. APress.

Cassatt, A. (2023). *Web3 Marketing: A Handbook for the Next Internet Revolution*. Wiley.

Defidao, Lee, D. K. C., Guan, C., & Ding, D. (2023). *Global Web3 Eco Innovation*. Singapore University of Social Sciences.

Dezfouli, M. (2023). *Ultraverse City: Delve into a world where the boundaries between reality and fantasy are blurred*. Academic Press.

Duffey, C. (2023). *Decoding the Metaverse: Expand Your Business Using Web3*. Kindle Edition.

George, A. S. H., George, A. S., & Hameed, A. S. (2023). *The Web3 Revolution: Navigating the Future of Decentralized Networks*. Book Rivers.

Gupta, O. P., & Bhambri, P. (2012). Protein Secondary Structure Prediction. *PCTE Journal of Computer Sciences, 6*(2), 39–44.

Henry, C. D., & Shannon, L. (2023). *Virtual Natives: How a New Generation is Revolutionizing the Future of Work, Play, and Culture*. Wiley.

Huang, H., Wu, J., & Zheng, Z. (Eds.). (2023). *From Blockchain to Web3 & Metaverse*. Springer. doi:10.1007/978-981-99-3648-9

Hundreds, B. (2023). *NFTs Are a Scam / NFTs Are the Future: The Early Years: 2020-2023*. MCD.

Kaur, J., Bhambri, P., & Goyal, F. (2012). Phylogeny: Tree of Life. *International Conference on Sports Biomechanics, Emerging Technologies and Quality Assurance in Technical Education*, 350-354.

Kraski, J., & Shenkarow, J. (2023). *The Future of Community: How to Leverage Web3 Technologies to Grow Your Business*. Wiley.

Lee, W. (2023). *Beginning Ethereum Smart Contracts Programming: With Examples in Python, Solidity, and JavaScript*. APress.

Lekhi, P., & Kaur, G. (Eds.). (2023). *Concepts, Technologies, Challenges, and the Future of Web 3*. IGI Global. doi:10.4018/978-1-6684-9919-1

Lewis, G. (2023). *Web 3.0: Simple Guide*. Kindle Edition.

Lisdorf, A. (2023). *Still Searching for Satoshi: Unveiling the Blockchain Revolution*. Academic Press.

Lopez, R. A. (2023). *The rise of the metaverse: A must-have guide on How virtual reality, augmented reality, and mixed reality are transforming the way we work, learn, and play in the world of artificial intelligence*. Academic Press.

Neto, J. B. S. (n.d.). *The Next Phase of Blockchain: From Cryptocurrencies to Smart Contracts and a Decentralized Future*. Academic Press.

Ottina, M., Steffensen, P. J., & Kristensen, J. (2023). *Automated Market Makers: A Practical Guide to Decentralized Exchanges and Cryptocurrency Trading*. APress.

Panda, S. K., Mishra, V., Dash, S. P., & Pani, A. K. (Eds.). (2023). *Recent Advances in Blockchain Technology: Real-World Applications: 237 (Intelligent Systems Reference Library)*. Springer. doi:10.1007/978-3-031-22835-3

Patiño-Martínez, M., & Paulo, J. (Eds.). (2023). Distributed Applications and Interoperable Systems. In *23rd IFIP WG 6.1 International Conference, DAIS 2023, Held as Part of the 18th International*. Springer.

Pejic, I. (2023). *Big Tech in Finance: How To Prevail In the Age of Blockchain, Digital Currencies and Web3*. Kogan Page.

Pelfrey, K. (2023). *The Pathway to Blockchain & Web3: Next Waves for Developers in Tech*. Academic Press.

Rumbelow, J. (2023). *Building With Ethereum: Products, Protocols, and Platforms*. APress.

Russo, D. (2023). *Pioneering Sustainable Supply Chain Solutions: Green Chain Revolution*. Academic Press.

Singh, S., Kakkar, P., & Bhambri, P. (2013). A Study of the Impact of Random Waypoint and Vector Mobility Models on Various Routing Protocols in MANET. *International Journal of Advances in Computing and Information Technology*, *2*(3), 41–51.

Tondon, N., & Bhambri, P. (2017). Novel Approach for Drug Discovery. *International Journal of Research in Engineering and Applied Sciences*, *7*(6), 28–46.

Vero, K. (2023). *From Pixels to Portals: Exploring the Future of the Metaverse through the Evolution of Videogames*. Academic Press.

Yildiz, H. (2023). *The Web3, Metaverse and AI Handbook: How to leverage new technologies to create unique brands and drive new lanes of revenue*. Academic Press.

KEY TERMS AND DEFINITIONS

Blockchain: Blockchain is a decentralized and distributed digital ledger technology that enables secure and transparent record-keeping of transactions across a network of computers. It consists of a chain of blocks, each containing a list of transactions, linked together through cryptographic hashes. The decentralized nature of blockchain ensures that no single entity has control over the entire chain, enhancing security and reducing the risk of tampering. This technology is widely associated with cryptocurrencies like Bitcoin but has applications beyond finance, such as supply chain management, voting systems, and smart contracts.

Decentralized Transactions: Decentralized transactions are financial or data exchanges that take place without the involvement of a central authority or middleman. Transactions in a decentralized system occur directly between users on a peer-to-peer network, usually with the assistance of blockchain technology. This obviates the need for a central authority, like as a bank or government, to validate and authorize transactions. Decentralized transactions are commonly linked to cryptocurrencies such as Bitcoin and platforms based on blockchain technology. In these systems, a distributed ledger guarantees transparency, security, and agreement among participants in the network.

Digital Wallets: Digital wallets are electronic platforms that enable users to securely store and oversee their financial data, including credit card numbers, bank account information, and other payment methods, in a virtual version. These wallets provide electronic transactions, such as online purchases, mobile payments, and in-app transactions, without the requirement of actual currency or cards. Digital wallets commonly employ encryption technology to bolster security and may also offer supplementary functionalities like loyalty cards, coupons, and ticket storage. Notable instances are Apple Pay, Google Pay, and PayPal.

Online Experience: It pertains to the digital contact and engagement that users have while handling their financial transactions and electronic wallets on the internet. The term refers to the complete process that individuals go through when using online platforms to carry out a range of financial tasks, including making payments, moving funds, monitoring account balances, and using digital wallets. The online experience strives to offer users a smooth, efficient, and safe environment for carrying out financial transactions via digital channels. This entails utilizing electronic wallets, which are digital instruments or software that allow users to store and oversee their payment data, hence simplifying online transactions effortlessly.

Security: It pertains to the specific safeguards and protocols put in place to protect digital wallets and financial transactions from unauthorized access, fraudulent behavior, and destructive activities. This encompasses the utilization of encryption methods to safeguard confidential data; authentication measures to guarantee that only authorized individuals may have access to the wallet, and secure procedures for executing transactions in order to avoid unauthorized financial transfers and tampering with data. The purpose of security measures is to establish a reliable setting where users can securely keep their digital assets and carry out financial transactions in the digital realm.

Trust: It pertains to the level of confidence and dependence placed on a digital wallet or payment system to securely and accurately manage financial transactions. Users have confidence in the wallet's ability to protect their funds, provide secure transactions, and uphold the confidentiality of their sensitive information. Trust is essential for promoting consumer acceptance and maintaining the authenticity of financial transactions in the digital domain, where dependence on technology and online platforms is inherent. Security features, clear policies, and a proven history of dependability all contribute to establishing trust in digital wallets and transactional systems.

WalletConnect Protocols: WalletConnect is a publicly available protocol that facilitates secure connection between decentralized applications (DApps) and mobile bitcoin wallets. Users can engage with DApps on their desktop browsers while ensuring the secure storage of their private keys on their mobile wallets. The protocol facilitates a connection by means of QR code scanning and employs end-to-end encryption to guarantee the security of user payments. WalletConnect has emerged as a widely adopted standard in the blockchain and cryptocurrency industry, serving to improve the user-friendliness and security of decentralized apps.

Chapter 5
Crypto Coins and Ethereum: Pioneering Decentralized Finance

Kaushikkumar Patel
https://orcid.org/0009-0005-9197-2765
TransUnion LLC, USA

ABSTRACT

In the internet's evolution, cryptocurrencies and decentralized platforms represent a significant shift. This chapter explores this shift, emphasizing Ethereum's role in Web 3. As we move from centralized to decentralized systems, Ethereum emerges as a "world computer." This chapter explores Ethereum's blockchain and smart contract technology. It clarifies Ethereum and Ether (ETH), highlighting their impact on DeFi and NFTs. Ethereum offers opportunities but also faces scalability and fee challenges. The chapter provides a balanced view, exploring these issues and Ethereum's potential to alter the internet and finance. Readers will understand Ethereum's Web 3 role, its industry implications, and developments enhancing its ecosystem.

1. INTRODUCTION

The digital age, marked by relentless innovation and transformative shifts, has witnessed the internet's evolution as a central force driving these changes. From its early days, when the internet was a mere repository of static web pages under the Web 1.0 paradigm, it transitioned into the interactive and user-centric era of Web 2.0. This phase was characterized by dynamic websites, social media platforms, and a surge in user-generated content, fundamentally altering how individuals and businesses interacted online. Now, as the digital landscape readies itself for another monumental shift, the promise of Web 3.0 emerges. This new era, often referred to as the decentralized web, is poised to challenge and redefine traditional online structures, offering users unprecedented control, security, and transparency.

At the heart of the Web 3.0 narrative is the groundbreaking concept of cryptocurrencies and the decentralized platforms on which they operate. Among these, Ethereum has distinguished itself as a trailblazer, setting the stage for a new wave of decentralized applications and solutions. Unlike conventional currencies, which are typically overseen by central banks or financial institutions, cryptocurrencies

DOI: 10.4018/979-8-3693-1532-3.ch005

thrive in a decentralized environment. This decentralization ensures that transactions are transparent, secure, and free from unilateral control or manipulation.

Ethereum's significance extends beyond its role as a cryptocurrency. Often referred to as the "World Computer," Ethereum represents a visionary leap in blockchain technology. While Bitcoin, the first-generation blockchain, introduced the world to decentralized digital currency, Ethereum expanded upon this foundation. It offered a platform that was not only transactional but also programmable, enabling the development and deployment of complex Decentralized Applications (dApps). These dApps, anchored on Ethereum's blockchain, operate autonomously, free from centralized control, ensuring their integrity and security.

One of Ethereum's most notable contributions to the blockchain realm is the introduction of smart contracts. These are not mere contracts in the traditional sense but programmable contracts that automatically execute when predefined conditions are met. By eliminating intermediaries, smart contracts offer a streamlined, transparent, and efficient transaction process. Such innovations have spurred developments in various sectors. For instance, the realm of decentralized finance (DeFi) is witnessing a renaissance, with traditional financial instruments being reimagined on the blockchain. Similarly, the burgeoning world of non-fungible tokens (NFTs) is challenging conventional notions of digital ownership and authenticity.

Yet, the journey of Ethereum, like any pioneering technology, has been punctuated with challenges. Scalability concerns, fluctuating transaction fees, and debates over energy consumption have often clouded discussions around its potential. However, the proactive and forward-thinking Ethereum community is not one to rest on its laurels. With initiatives like the Ethereum 2.0 upgrade on the horizon, there is a concerted effort to address existing challenges and optimize the platform for the future.

In this chapter, titled "Crypto Coins and Ethereum," readers are invited on an exploratory journey into the world of Ethereum. Through a comprehensive examination of its origins, technological foundations, real-world applications, and future trajectories, this chapter aspires to offer a panoramic view of Ethereum's transformative impact on the Web 3.0 ecosystem. By charting its past successes, present innovations, and future potential, the chapter endeavors to present Ethereum as a cornerstone of the next phase of internet evolution.

2. LITERATURE REVIEW

The transformative potential of cryptocurrencies and blockchain technology has garnered significant attention in both academic and industry circles. As the digital landscape evolves, understanding the nuances, challenges, and opportunities presented by these technologies becomes paramount. This literature review delves deep into the myriad facets of the cryptocurrency world, with a particular emphasis on Ethereum, its innovations, and its implications for the future of decentralized systems.

2.1 The Genesis of Cryptocurrencies and Blockchain

a. Birth of a New Paradigm: The inception of blockchain technology marked a significant shift in the digital landscape, introducing a decentralized system anchored by a distributed ledger. This revolutionary technology ensures that every transaction is transparent, immutable, and secure, effectively decentralizing power and control (Oliva, G. A., 2020). The decentralized nature of blockchain offers a solution to the double-spending problem without the need for a trusted authority or central server, making it a groundbreaking innovation in the realm of digital currencies (Sheridan, D., 2022).

b. Bitcoin: The Pioneer: Bitcoin, conceptualized by the enigmatic Satoshi Nakamoto in 2009, emerged as the first application of this technology, marking the dawn of the cryptocurrency age (Sheridan, D., 2022). As the inaugural and most renowned cryptocurrency, Bitcoin's primary innovation lay in its utilization of blockchain technology, enabling peer-to-peer transactions without the need for intermediaries (Vijayalakshmi, J., 2017). Beyond its role as a digital currency, Bitcoin's decentralized nature challenged traditional financial systems and introduced the concept of trustless transactions, where trust between parties is established by cryptographic proof rather than central intermediaries (Korpal, G., 2022).

2.2 Comparative Analysis of Major Cryptocurrencies

a. Exploring the Landscape: In addition to Bitcoin, other significant cryptocurrencies like Ripple (XRP), Litecoin, and Cardano have contributed to the diversity of the crypto ecosystem. Each of these cryptocurrencies brings unique features and technological innovations, such as Ripple's focus on cross-border payments and Litecoin's emphasis on faster transaction processing (Gandal, N., 2021).

b. Ethereum's Distinct Position: Ethereum stands out in this landscape due to its Turing-complete blockchain and the introduction of smart contracts, enabling a wide range of decentralized applications beyond mere currency transactions. This section compares Ethereum's capabilities with other major cryptocurrencies, highlighting its unique role in advancing decentralized applications and smart contracts (Gilbert, S., 2022).

2.3 Ethereum: Beyond Mere Transactions

c. Ethereum's Vision: While Bitcoin introduced the world to cryptocurrencies, Ethereum, envisioned by Vitalik Buterin, expanded the horizons of what blockchain could achieve (Gandal, N., 2021). Unlike Bitcoin, Ethereum was designed as a platform to facilitate decentralized applications (dApps), offering a broader range of functionalities. Ethereum's blockchain is Turing complete, allowing developers to create more complex and diverse applications, from games to social networks (Gilbert, S., 2022).

d. Smart Contracts: The Game Changer: Central to Ethereum's innovation is the smart contract - self-executing contracts with the agreement's terms directly inscribed into lines of code (Liu, Z., 2021). These contracts, once activated on the Ethereum blockchain, operate autonomously, ensuring that all predefined conditions are met before execution (Gilbert, S., 2022). Smart contracts have the potential to automate a wide range of processes, from simple transactions to complex multi-party agreements, making them a cornerstone of the Ethereum ecosystem (Petcu, A., 2023).

2.4 The Rise of Decentralized Finance (DeFi) on Ethereum

a. Democratizing Finance: Ethereum's platform has been instrumental in the birth and growth of the decentralized finance (DeFi) sector. DeFi projects on Ethereum aim to recreate traditional financial tools in a decentralized environment, eliminating the need for intermediaries (Béres, F., 2021). This democratization of finance has the potential to increase financial inclusivity, offering services like lending, borrowing, and insurance to a broader audience without the need for traditional banking systems (Murray, A., 2023).

b. Expanding Horizons: From lending and borrowing platforms to decentralized exchanges and stablecoins, Ethereum's DeFi ecosystem showcases the vast potential of blockchain in reshaping the financial landscape (Zheng, J., 2023). With the introduction of yield farming and liquidity mining, DeFi platforms have introduced innovative mechanisms to incentivize user participation and liquidity provision, further driving the growth of the sector (Buterin, V., 2016).

2.5 Non-Fungible Tokens (NFTs): A New Digital Asset Class

a. 4.1. The Uniqueness of NFTs: Non-fungible tokens (NFTs) have carved a niche in the digital asset space (Yavuz, E., 2018). Unlike traditional cryptocurrencies, NFTs are distinct, ensuring each token's uniqueness. This uniqueness has made NFTs particularly valuable for representing one-of-a-kind assets like art, collectibles, and even real estate (Bambacht, J., 2022).

b. Ethereum's Role in the NFT Revolution: Ethereum's blockchain has become the primary platform for creating and trading NFTs, influencing diverse sectors ranging from art and music to gaming and collectibles (Singh, S., 2023). With the ability to embed metadata and provenance directly into the token, NFTs on Ethereum offer a level of authenticity and ownership previously unattainable in the digital realm (PrasadRao, K. V., 2018).

2.6 Challenges and Evolution in the Ethereum Ecosystem

a. Addressing the Hurdles: Ethereum, despite its innovations, has faced challenges. Scalability concerns, volatile transaction fees, and the environmental impact of mining have been significant issues (Cong, L. W., 2023). Additionally, the regulatory landscape's fluidity has raised concerns about consumer protection and potential misuse (Luong, D. H., 2019). The platform's consensus mechanism, while secure, has faced criticism for its energy-intensive nature, leading to calls for more sustainable alternatives (Arslan, E., 2021).

b. The Anticipated Ethereum 2.0: The Ethereum community's commitment to evolution is evident in the much-anticipated Ethereum 2.0 upgrade. This upgrade, which includes a shift from a Proof of Work (PoW) to a Proof of Stake (PoS) consensus mechanism, promises enhanced energy efficiency and transactional throughput (Allen, D. W., 2023). The introduction of sharding and other consensus mechanisms in Ethereum 2.0 aims to address the platform's scalability concerns, ensuring that it remains competitive in the ever-evolving blockchain landscape (Ranganthan, V. P., 2018).

The literature encompassing cryptocurrencies and Ethereum offers a comprehensive view of a rapidly evolving digital frontier. From the foundational principles of decentralized currencies to the cutting-edge innovations in DeFi and NFTs, the journey of exploration is both enlightening and challenging. The references detailed in this review serve as a compass, guiding readers through the intricate maze of blockchain innovations, challenges, and future prospects. As the domain continues to evolve, staying abreast of the latest research, debates, and technological advancements will be crucial for anyone vested in the future of digital assets and decentralized platforms.

3. ETHEREUM'S ECOSYSTEM AND ITS COMPONENTS

Ethereum's ecosystem represents a comprehensive suite of decentralized services and applications, underpinned by the blockchain's inherent security and transparency. This ecosystem is not just a network for cryptocurrency exchange but a foundational platform for a wide array of decentralized applications (dApps) that extend the functionality of the blockchain to virtually any industry. The ecosystem thrives on its community of developers, entrepreneurs, and users, all contributing to an ever-expanding innovation landscape. With its native cryptocurrency, Ether, Ethereum facilitates not only value transfer but also the deployment and operation of complex contractual agreements encoded into smart contracts (Gandal, N., 2021). To provide a clear overview of the diverse elements within Ethereum's ecosystem, Table 1, named 'Key Components of Ethereum's Decentralized Ecosystem' has been included for a concise and comprehensive illustration.

3.1 Ethereum Virtual Machine (EVM)

c. The Heart of Ethereum: At the center of Ethereum's technological prowess is the Ethereum Virtual Machine (EVM), a powerful, decentralized computing engine that executes smart contracts. The EVM abstracts the underlying hardware of the Ethereum network, providing a layer that allows developers to write applications in high-level programming languages. This abstraction is crucial as it ensures that applications can run on any node of the network without compatibility issues, fostering a unified and cohesive ecosystem (Gilbert, S., 2022).
d. Interoperability and Consistency: The EVM's design is instrumental in maintaining the interoperability and consistency that are hallmarks of the Ethereum network. By ensuring that every smart contract is executed in the same way on every node, the EVM upholds the principles of decentralization and trustlessness. This consistency is vital for developers and users alike, as it guarantees that contracts will behave predictably, which is essential for the security and reliability of decentralized applications (Liu, Z., 2021).

3.2 Smart Contracts: Ethereum's Defining Feature

a. Autonomy and Trustlessness: Smart contracts are self-operating contracts with the terms of the agreement directly written into code. These contracts execute and enforce themselves based on a set of conditions, without the need for external enforcement or intermediation. This feature not only reduces the potential for disputes but also significantly lowers transaction costs by removing the need for trusted intermediaries. Smart contracts are immutable once deployed, which means they cannot be altered, providing a level of security and trust that traditional contracts cannot match (Petcu, A., 2023).

b. Use Cases and Applications: The applications of smart contracts are vast and varied. They serve as the backbone for decentralized finance (DeFi) platforms, which offer financial services without the need for traditional financial intermediaries. Smart contracts also enable the creation and exchange of non-fungible tokens (NFTs), which have revolutionized the digital art and collectibles markets. Beyond these, smart contracts are being explored for use in supply chain management, voting systems, and automated legal agreements, showcasing their potential to transform numerous sectors (Béres, F., 2021).

3.3 Decentralized Applications (dApps)

a. Redefining Online Interactions: Decentralized applications (dApps) are a radical departure from traditional applications, as they are not controlled by a single entity but operate on a peer-to-peer network. This architecture not only prevents any single point of failure but also ensures that dApps are resistant to censorship and external control. The open-source nature of dApps aligns with the ethos of transparency and collective development that is central to the Ethereum community (Murray, A., 2023).

b. Categories and Growth: The diversity of dApps on Ethereum is a testament to the platform's flexibility and the creativity of its community. Categories of dApps range from games and marketplaces to social networks and autonomous organizations. The growth of dApps has been exponential, with Ethereum's smart contract functionality enabling developers to build applications that are not just decentralized but also interoperable, allowing for composability where dApps can seamlessly integrate and build upon each other's features (Zheng, J., 2023).

3.4 Gas and Transaction Fees

a. The Fuel for Ethereum: Gas is a unique concept to Ethereum, representing the unit of measure for the computational effort required to execute operations. Users must pay gas for every transaction, including smart contract executions and transfers of Ether. This mechanism prevents network abuse by making it costly to perform actions that could overload the system. Gas prices are determined by supply and demand between the network's miners, who process transactions, and users, creating a dynamic market for computational resources (Buterin, V., 2016).

b. Challenges and Implications: Despite its intended purpose, the gas system has been a double-edged sword. During times of network congestion, gas prices can soar, leading to a scenario where only users willing to pay high fees can afford to transact, which raises questions about the network's inclusivity. These challenges have sparked debates within the community about the need for a more scalable and cost-effective solution, which Ethereum 2.0 seeks to provide. The high gas fees have also spurred the development of Layer 2 scaling solutions, which aim to alleviate the pressure on the main Ethereum blockchain by handling transactions off-chain (Yavuz, E., 2018).

3.5 Ethereum 2.0: The Next Evolutionary Step

a. Addressing the Scalability Conundrum: Ethereum 2.0 represents a significant overhaul of the network, with scalability at the forefront of its objectives. By introducing sharding, the network will be broken down into smaller, more manageable pieces, which can process transactions and smart contracts in parallel. This fragmentation is expected to drastically increase the network's capacity and transaction speed, addressing one of the most significant bottlenecks of the current Ethereum infrastructure (Bambacht, J., 2022).
b. Transition to Proof of Stake (PoS): The transition to a Proof of Stake (PoS) consensus mechanism is perhaps the most revolutionary aspect of Ethereum 2.0. PoS changes the way the network reaches consensus by allowing users to "stake" their Ether as a form of economic commitment to the network's integrity. This mechanism is not only more energy-efficient than the current Proof of Work (PoW) system but also opens up new avenues for user participation in network security. The shift to PoS is expected to reduce the overall energy consumption of the Ethereum network by a significant margin, addressing one of the most critical environmental concerns associated with blockchain technology (Singh, S., 2023).

The Ethereum ecosystem is a dynamic and evolving landscape that has significantly impacted the broader blockchain and cryptocurrency space. Its components, from the EVM to smart contracts and dApps, have laid the groundwork for a decentralized future where applications are not bound by the limitations of traditional infrastructures. As Ethereum continues to evolve, particularly with the advent of Ethereum 2.0, it stands at the cusp of addressing its most significant challenges, paving the way for broader adoption and innovation. The ecosystem's growth and the community's commitment to continuous improvement reflect a shared vision of a decentralized, secure, and efficient digital world (PrasadRao, K. V., 2018).

Table 1. Key components of Ethereum's decentralized ecosystem

Ethereum's Ecosystem	Description
Ethereum Virtual Machine (EVM)	The core processing engine of Ethereum, enabling the execution of smart contracts across a decentralized network.
Smart Contracts	Autonomous contracts with terms directly written into code, allowing for self-executing and self-enforcing agreements.
Decentralized Applications (dApps)	Applications that run on a P2P network rather than a single computer, removing single points of failure and resisting censorship.
Gas and Transaction Fees	The pricing mechanism for executing transactions and smart contracts, representing the computational effort required.
Ethereum 2.0	A major upgrade aimed at improving scalability and efficiency, transitioning from Proof of Work to Proof of Stake consensus.
Scaling Challenges	Demands effective strategies for auto-scaling and understanding service interdependencies to prevent bottlenecks.

4. ETHEREUM'S INFLUENCE ON THE FINANCIAL LANDSCAPE

Ethereum's emergence as a foundational technology for decentralized finance (DeFi) has been transformative for the financial sector. By utilizing blockchain's decentralization, Ethereum has disrupted traditional financial operations, offering an alternative that is not only transparent and efficient but also operates without central authorities. To better understand Ethereum's transformative role in finance, refer to Table 2, named 'Ethereum's Disruptive Impact on the Financial Sector' which summarizes its key influences and contributions.

a. **Decentralized Finance (DeFi) Platforms:** The proliferation of DeFi platforms on Ethereum has been a cornerstone of its financial influence. These platforms have redefined financial transactions, enabling peer-to-peer exchanges, lending, and borrowing without the need for banks or brokers. The automation of complex financial contracts through smart contracts has reduced the need for intermediaries, cutting costs and increasing transaction speeds. This has not only democratized financial services but has also led to innovative financial products and mechanisms such as yield farming and liquidity mining, which have attracted significant capital inflows into the Ethereum ecosystem (Gilbert, S., 2022).
b. **Tokenization of Assets:** Ethereum's smart contracts have unlocked the potential for tokenizing a wide array of assets, including real estate, art, and commodities. This tokenization process has created new markets and liquidity for assets previously considered illiquid. By fractionalizing ownership, Ethereum has enabled smaller investors to participate in markets traditionally dominated by large players, thereby democratizing wealth creation and investment opportunities. This has also led to the development of new financial instruments and investment platforms that leverage these tokenized assets for generating returns (Murray, A., 2023).
c. **Stablecoins and Payment Systems:** Stablecoins on Ethereum have become a vital component of the cryptocurrency ecosystem, offering price stability in a market known for its volatility. These digital assets, pegged to stable reserves like fiat currencies or commodities, have become a medium of exchange, a unit of account, and a store of value. They are increasingly being used for remittances, payments, and as a gateway for traditional investors entering the cryptocurrency space. The integration of stablecoins into payment systems and online commerce is an ongoing trend that could redefine money transfer and payment processing (Bambacht, J., 2022).
d. **Governance and DAOs:** The concept of decentralized governance has been brought to life through Ethereum's DAOs. These entities operate on rules encoded as computer programs, cutting out the bureaucracy and politics of traditional organizational governance. DAOs have been used for venture capital funding, collective investments, and community-driven decision-making. They represent a radical shift in how organizations can be structured and managed, potentially influencing corporate governance beyond the blockchain space (Luong, D. H., 2019).
e. **Impact on Traditional Banking and Insurance:** Ethereum's DeFi applications are not just a competitive threat but also an innovation catalyst for traditional banking and insurance sectors. By offering alternatives to savings accounts, loans, and insurance policies, DeFi platforms are forcing these institutions to reassess their business models. Some banks have begun to integrate blockchain technology to streamline operations and develop new products, while insurers are exploring smart contracts for automating claims processing (Vijayalakshmi, J., 2017).

f. **Challenges and Regulatory Scrutiny:** The rapid growth of Ethereum's financial applications has not gone unnoticed by regulators worldwide. Concerns over consumer protection, financial stability, and the potential for illicit activities have led to calls for clearer regulatory frameworks. The DeFi space, in particular, faces challenges around compliance with existing financial regulations, including AML and KYC requirements. The outcome of these regulatory discussions will significantly impact the adoption and development of Ethereum-based financial services (Zavratnik, J., 2022).
g. **Scalability and Infrastructure Development:** As Ethereum's influence grows, so does the strain on its network. High transaction fees and network congestion have highlighted the need for scalability solutions. The ongoing development of Ethereum 2.0, with its transition to a Proof of Stake consensus mechanism and the introduction of sharding, promises to address these issues, potentially leading to wider adoption and an even more significant impact on the financial landscape (Fantazzini, D., 2022).

Ethereum's role in the financial sector has been groundbreaking, offering a glimpse into a future where financial services are more accessible, efficient, and equitable. Its ability to facilitate the creation, exchange, and management of digital assets has laid the groundwork for a new financial paradigm. As the platform continues to evolve and address its challenges, its influence is poised to expand, reshaping the financial landscape in ways that are only beginning to be understood.

Table 2. Ethereum's disruptive impact on the financial sector

Ethereum's Innovations	Implications and Developments
DeFi Platforms	Enabled peer-to-peer financial services like exchanges, lending, and borrowing directly on the blockchain, reducing reliance on traditional financial intermediaries.
Tokenization of Assets	Created new markets and liquidity for traditionally illiquid assets, allowing fractional ownership and investment from a broader range of investors.
Stablecoins and Payment Systems	Introduced digital assets pegged to stable reserves, facilitating remittances and payments, and acting as a bridge for traditional finance into cryptocurrencies.
Governance and DAOs	Pioneered decentralized governance models, leading to new forms of collective investment and decision-making structures.
Traditional Banking and Insurance Impact	Pushed traditional financial institutions to innovate and adapt to blockchain technology's capabilities, particularly in streamlining operations and product offerings.
Regulatory Scrutiny	Prompted discussions for clearer regulatory frameworks to address concerns over consumer protection and financial stability.
Scalability and Infrastructure	Highlighted the need for network improvements to support growing demand, leading to significant developments like Ethereum 2.0.

5. ETHEREUM AND THE DIGITAL ART REVOLUTION

The emergence of Ethereum has not only disrupted traditional financial systems but has also left an indelible mark on the art industry, particularly through the introduction and proliferation of non-fungible tokens (NFTs). These unique digital tokens, which represent ownership of a specific item or piece of content, have transformed the digital art scene by providing a means to prove provenance and ensure authenticity.

Table 3, named 'Ethereum's Role in Shaping the Digital Art Ecosystem' offers a summarized view of how Ethereum has revolutionized the digital art world, highlighting its major impacts and developments.

a. **NFT Marketplaces:** The rise of NFTs has led to the development of dedicated marketplaces on the Ethereum network, such as OpenSea, Rarible, and Foundation. These platforms have become hubs for artists to mint and sell their digital works directly to a global audience, bypassing traditional art dealers and galleries. The decentralized nature of these marketplaces ensures that artists retain a greater degree of control over their work and benefit from direct engagement with their patrons (Wang, Q., 2022). Moreover, these platforms have introduced novel auction mechanisms and showcased the potential for dynamic pricing models based on demand and rarity.
b. **Artist Empowerment:** Ethereum's smart contracts have been a game-changer for artists, enabling them to embed royalties into their digital works. This means that artists can receive a commission automatically every time their art is resold on the secondary market, a feature that is particularly attractive in the digital realm where copies can be easily made and distributed. This empowerment has led to a new wave of digital artists entering the space, attracted by the prospect of a more equitable system where they can reap ongoing benefits from their original creations (Zavratnik, J., 2022).
c. **Collectors and Speculation:** The NFT craze has attracted a diverse group of collectors, ranging from traditional art aficionados to cryptocurrency enthusiasts and investors looking to diversify their portfolios. The speculative nature of the market has seen some NFTs sell for millions of dollars, with the record sale of Beeple's digital collage at Christie's auction house being a watershed moment for the industry. This has sparked a debate on the intrinsic value of digital art and the speculative bubble that seems to be forming around these assets (Vijayalakshmi, J., 2017).
d. **Cultural Impact:** The influence of NFTs extends beyond the art market to broader cultural and social domains. Mainstream adoption by celebrities, musicians, and athletes has brought NFTs into the public eye, challenging preconceived notions about the ownership and value of digital assets. The NFT trend has also led to innovative collaborations between artists and technologists, exploring the boundaries of interactive and multimedia art forms (Fantazzini, D., 2022).
e. **Environmental Concerns:** The environmental impact of NFTs, particularly in relation to the energy consumption associated with Ethereum's proof-of-work consensus mechanism, has been a point of contention. Critics argue that the carbon footprint of minting and transacting NFTs is unsustainable. In response, the Ethereum community is actively working towards the Ethereum 2.0 upgrade, which promises to significantly reduce the network's energy consumption by shifting to a proof-of-stake model (Urquhart, A., 2022).
f. **Authenticity and Provenance:** One of the most significant contributions of Ethereum to the digital art world is the ability to verify the authenticity and trace the provenance of artworks. The blockchain's immutable ledger ensures that once an artwork is registered as an NFT, its history and transfers of ownership are permanently recorded and publicly accessible. This has provided a solution to the art world's persistent problem of forgeries and disputes over ownership (Wang, Q., 2022).
g. **Challenges and Criticisms:** Despite the enthusiasm surrounding NFTs, the market is not without its challenges. Issues such as copyright infringement, the potential for market manipulation, and the creation of artificial scarcity have all been points of critique. Additionally, the high volatility

of the market poses risks for both artists and collectors, with some warning of a bubble akin to the dot-com bust or the tulip mania (Zavratnik, J., 2022).

In summary, Ethereum's role in the digital art revolution is multifaceted and profound. It has enabled the creation of a new marketplace that is global, open, and direct, empowering artists and challenging traditional art market structures. While the NFT phenomenon has introduced novel ways for artists to monetize their work and for collectors to invest in digital art, it also raises important questions about sustainability, value, and equity in the art world. As the technology matures and the market stabilizes, Ethereum's influence on the digital art revolution is likely to grow, fostering further innovation and potentially reshaping the cultural landscape.

Table 3. Ethereum's role in shaping the digital art ecosystem

Impact Area	Description
NFT Marketplaces	Platforms on Ethereum for artists to mint and sell digital works, enabling global reach and direct patronage.
Artist Empowerment	Smart contracts allow artists to receive automatic royalties, fostering a sustainable creator economy.
Collectors and Speculation	A new class of digital art collectors has emerged, fueling market growth and speculation.
Cultural Impact	Mainstream adoption of NFTs is influencing popular culture and redefining digital ownership.
Environmental Concerns	The energy-intensive nature of NFT transactions has sparked a push towards more sustainable practices.
Authenticity and Provenance	Blockchain technology provides a verifiable record of an artwork's history and authenticity.
Challenges and Criticisms	Issues such as copyright infringement, market volatility, and artificial scarcity are prevalent concerns.
NFT Marketplaces	Platforms on Ethereum for artists to mint and sell digital works, enabling global reach and direct patronage.

6. CHALLENGES AND SOLUTIONS

Ethereum's ascent in the blockchain space has been transformative, introducing programmability and complex applications. Yet, it faces significant challenges such as scalability, energy consumption, and a steep learning curve for new users. These issues are pivotal for Ethereum's sustainability and growth, affecting transaction speeds, environmental impact, and user adoption. The community's response involves a mix of technical upgrades, like the transition to Ethereum 2.0 with its Proof of Stake consensus, and educational outreach to demystify blockchain technology. Solutions are being developed with a focus on enhancing the network's efficiency and fostering a regulatory environment conducive to innovation. The collective effort to overcome these hurdles is crucial for maintaining Ethereum's role at the forefront of the blockchain revolution. The complexities and the innovative solutions in Ethereum's journey are encapsulated in Table 4, named 'Balancing Act: Addressing Ethereum's Challenges with Innovative Solutions' providing a quick reference to the main challenges and their corresponding solutions.

a. Scalability

i. Challenge: Ethereum's current architecture can handle only around 15-30 transactions per second, which is insufficient for global-scale applications. This limitation leads to network congestion, resulting in slow transaction times and exorbitant gas fees during periods of high demand.
ii. Solution: The Ethereum community is exploring several scalability solutions. Sharding is a key feature of the upcoming Ethereum 2.0 upgrade, which aims to partition the network into multiple shards, each capable of processing transactions and smart contracts independently. Layer 2 solutions, such as Optimistic and ZK-Rollups, bundle numerous transactions off-chain and submit a single proof to the main chain, significantly reducing the burden on the network. These solutions, in conjunction, are expected to increase Ethereum's transaction throughput by several orders of magnitude.

b. Energy Consumption

i. Challenge: The current PoW mechanism is energy-intensive, as it requires a global network of miners to solve complex mathematical puzzles to validate transactions and create new blocks. This process has drawn criticism for its environmental impact due to the massive amounts of electricity consumed.
ii. Solution: Ethereum's shift to a PoS consensus mechanism with Ethereum 2.0 is poised to reduce the network's energy consumption by up to 99%. In PoS, validators are chosen to create new blocks based on the number of coins they hold and are willing to "stake" as collateral, rather than on computational power. This shift not only mitigates the environmental impact but also lowers the barrier for participation in network security.

c. Security

i. Challenge: Smart contracts on Ethereum are immutable and, once deployed, cannot be altered. This immutability, while a feature, can also be a drawback if the contract contains vulnerabilities or bugs, as these cannot be patched easily.
ii. Solution: The Ethereum community emphasizes rigorous smart contract auditing by independent third parties before deployment. Tools and practices such as formal verification, which mathematically proves the correctness of contract code, and the establishment of standard coding practices, are becoming more prevalent. Additionally, decentralized autonomous organizations (DAOs) and multisig wallets are being used to manage and mitigate the risks of contract vulnerabilities.

d. Interoperability

i. Challenge: The blockchain space consists of numerous isolated networks, each with its own protocols and tokens. The lack of interoperability hinders the seamless exchange of assets and information across different blockchains.

ii. Solution: Interoperability protocols, such as Polkadot and Cosmos, are being developed to enable different blockchains to communicate with each other. Ethereum's own efforts, like the development of wrapped tokens and the introduction of blockchain bridges, facilitate the transfer of value between Ethereum and other chains, promoting a more interconnected blockchain ecosystem.

e. User Experience

i. Challenge: The complexity of the Ethereum network and its dApps can be daunting for non-technical users. The user experience is often hindered by complex wallet setups, transaction processes, and the understanding of gas fees.
ii. Solution: Projects are focusing on enhancing the user interface and simplifying the user journey. Wallet providers are integrating user-friendly features, such as human-readable addresses, while dApp developers are working on abstracting the complexities of blockchain interactions, making them more intuitive. Educational initiatives are also crucial in bridging the knowledge gap for new users.

f. Regulation

i. Challenge: The decentralized nature of Ethereum and its applications operates in a regulatory grey area. The absence of a clear legal framework for digital assets creates uncertainty for both users and developers, potentially stifling innovation and adoption.
ii. Solution: Active engagement with policymakers and regulatory bodies is crucial to develop a legal framework that can accommodate the unique aspects of blockchain technology. Efforts from organizations such as the Blockchain Association and the Chamber of Digital Commerce aim to educate regulators and shape policies that foster innovation while protecting consumers and maintaining market integrity.

g. Testing Complexities

i. Challenge: Microservices require a shift from traditional testing strategies due to their distributed nature. Ensuring quality demands testing each service in isolation and in conjunction with others, simulating real-world conditions and accounting for unpredictable network factors.
ii. Solution: A multi-level testing strategy is essential, including unit testing, integration testing, contract testing, and end-to-end testing. Service virtualization can simulate components to ensure more realistic and comprehensive testing. Chaos engineering, where the system is intentionally stressed in production to uncover weaknesses, also contributes to a robust testing strategy.

h. Performance Monitoring

i. Challenge: In a microservices architecture, understanding the intricate performance metrics of each service and the system as a whole is crucial. This includes monitoring the runtime behavior of services, analyzing response times, and ensuring system health. The distributed nature of the architecture makes pinpointing bottlenecks and performance issues challenging.
ii. Solution: Specialized application performance monitoring (APM) tools that provide deep insights into service performance are essential. Implementing distributed tracing with tools like Jaeger or Zipkin can track a request's journey through various services, helping identify performance bottlenecks and optimization opportunities. These tools, combined with real-time monitoring and alerting systems, ensure performance issues are quickly identified and addressed.

The challenges facing Ethereum are significant, yet they are matched by the determination and ingenuity of the blockchain community. Each solution brings Ethereum closer to its goal of a decentralized, secure, and scalable platform for global applications. The evolution of Ethereum is a testament to the collaborative spirit of the open-source community, with developers, validators, and users working together to address these challenges. As these solutions are implemented, they not only resolve existing issues but also lay the groundwork for future innovations, ensuring Ethereum's position as a leading force in the blockchain space.

Table 4. Balancing act: Addressing Ethereum's challenges with innovative solutions

Challenges in Ethereum's Ecosystem	Proposed and Ongoing Solutions
Scalability and Network Congestion	Ethereum 2.0 Upgrade (Sharding, PoS)
High Energy Consumption	Transition to Proof of Stake
Steep Learning Curve	Educational Initiatives & Resources
Security Vulnerabilities	Enhanced Smart Contract Auditing
Regulatory Uncertainty	Engagement with Policy Makers
High Transaction Fees	Layer 2 Scaling Solutions
Network Upgrades and Forks	Community Consensus Mechanisms
Interoperability with Other Chains	Cross-Chain Bridges and Protocols
Decentralization vs. Usability	User-Friendly Decentralized Apps
Data Privacy Concerns	Zero-Knowledge Proofs & Encryption

7. FUTURE RESEARCH DIRECTIONS

The rapid evolution of blockchain technology and the Ethereum ecosystem presents numerous opportunities for in-depth research. The expanded subsections provide a more detailed roadmap for future investigations in this dynamic field. To encapsulate the potential avenues for future exploration in this field, Table 5, named 'Future Research Directions in Ethereum and Blockchain Technology' is presented, outlining the key areas ripe for academic and industry research.

a. **Scalability and Efficiency:** Research into scalability solutions for Ethereum is critical as the platform grows. Studies could compare the efficiency of various layer 2 scaling solutions, such as rollups and sidechains, and their integration with the main Ethereum blockchain. The impact of these solutions on the user experience, particularly regarding transaction speed and cost, is another vital research area. Additionally, the security implications of such scaling solutions, including potential vulnerabilities and attack vectors, should be thoroughly explored (Gilbert, S., 2022), (Zheng, J., 2023) and (PrasadRao, K. V., 2018).
b. **Interoperability and Cross-Chain Technologies:** The ability of different blockchain networks to communicate and transfer value is essential for a truly interconnected ecosystem. Future research could focus on the development of decentralized bridges and their security models, ensuring the safe and reliable transfer of assets between chains. Studies might also explore the economic models underlying these bridges, including incentive structures and fee mechanisms, to ensure their long-term sustainability and adoption (Béres, F., 2021) and (Ranganthan, V. P., 2018).
c. **Decentralized Finance (DeFi) Mechanisms:** DeFi's rapid growth necessitates a deeper understanding of its mechanisms and potential risks. Research could investigate the stability of various DeFi protocols during extreme market conditions, exploring the effectiveness of their governance models and the resilience of their underlying smart contracts. Additionally, the potential for DeFi to contribute to financial inclusion, especially in underbanked regions, is an area ripe for exploration (Petcu, A., 2023), (Yavuz, E., 2018) and (Fantazzini, D., 2022).
d. **Regulatory and Ethical Implications:** The intersection of blockchain technology with global regulatory frameworks presents complex challenges. Future studies could analyze the impact of specific regulatory actions on the innovation and growth of the crypto space. Ethical considerations, such as the right to financial privacy versus the need for transparency in combating illicit activities, also present a rich field for academic inquiry (Korpal, G., 2022), (Buterin, V., 2016) and (Vijayalakshmi, J., 2017).
e. **Environmental Impact and Sustainability:** The shift from PoW to PoS in Ethereum 2.0 offers a case study in blockchain sustainability. Research could assess the actual environmental benefits of this transition, examining the energy consumption patterns of validators in the new PoS system. Studies might also explore the role of carbon credits and renewable energy sources in creating a more sustainable blockchain ecosystem (Sheridan, D., 2022), (Singh, S., 2023) and (Allen, D. W., 2023).
f. **Security and Cryptographic Advances:** As blockchain technology advances, so do the threats against it. Future research could focus on the development and implementation of quantum-resistant cryptographic algorithms to secure blockchain against emerging computational threats. The integration of privacy-enhancing technologies, such as zk-SNARKs and zk-STARKs, into public blockchains could also be a significant area of study, balancing the need for privacy with the transparency that blockchains provide (Oliva, G. A., 2020), (Allen, D. W., 2023) and (Luong, D. H., 2019).
g. **Social and Economic Impact:** The widespread adoption of cryptocurrencies could have profound social and economic effects. Research could explore the impact of cryptocurrencies on traditional financial systems, analyzing how banks and financial institutions adapt to this new paradigm. The potential of blockchain technology to drive economic empowerment and reduce inequality could also be a focus, particularly in developing economies (Gandal, N., 2021), (Bambacht, J., 2022) and (Urquhart, A., 2022).

h. **Technological Convergence:** The convergence of blockchain with other cutting-edge technologies could lead to transformative applications. Future research could explore the integration of blockchain with the Internet of Things (IoT), examining the security and scalability challenges of managing decentralized networks of devices. The potential for AI to optimize blockchain network performance and smart contract functionality is another promising research direction (Liu, Z., 2021), (Cong, L. W., 2023) and (Wang, Q., 2022).

i. **User Experience and Adoption:** For blockchain to reach mainstream adoption, the user experience must be addressed. Research could focus on the design of more user-friendly wallets and interfaces, reducing the barriers to entry for non-technical users. Studies might also investigate the psychological factors that influence the adoption of cryptocurrencies and how educational initiatives can increase public understanding and trust in blockchain technology (Arslan, E., 2021) and (Zavratnik, J., 2022).

j. **Governance and Decentralized Autonomous Organizations (DAOs):** The governance of decentralized networks is an emerging field of study. Research could examine the efficacy of DAOs in managing complex ecosystems, comparing their performance to traditional organizational structures. The legal status of DAOs and their ability to enter into binding contracts could also be explored, along with the social dynamics and decision-making processes within these novel organizations (Petcu, A., 2023) and (Ranganthan, V. P., 2018).

The path ahead for research in the domain of Ethereum and cryptocurrencies is both broad and deep. Each of these potential research directions not only offers the opportunity to advance the field but also to address the pressing challenges that come with the adoption of these technologies. As Ethereum continues to evolve and find its place in the broader context of Web3, the insights gained from such research will be invaluable in guiding its development and ensuring its relevance and utility in an increasingly decentralized world.

Table 5. Future research directions in Ethereum and blockchain technology

Research Area	Key Focus
Scalability and Efficiency	Exploring layer 2 solutions, user experience, and security implications.
Interoperability and Cross-Chain Technologies	Development of decentralized bridges and their economic and security models.
Decentralized Finance (DeFi) Mechanisms	Stability of DeFi protocols, governance models, and financial inclusion.
Regulatory and Ethical Implications	Impact of regulations on crypto innovation and ethical considerations of privacy.
Environmental Impact and Sustainability	Assessing the environmental benefits of Ethereum 2.0 and sustainable practices.
Security and Cryptographic Advances	Quantum-resistant cryptography and privacy-enhancing technologies.
Social and Economic Impact	Cryptocurrency's effect on traditional finance and its role in economic empowerment.
Technological Convergence	Integration of blockchain with IoT and AI for optimized performance.
User Experience and Adoption	Designing user-friendly interfaces and understanding psychological adoption factors.
Governance and DAOs	Efficacy of DAOs, legal considerations, and organizational dynamics.

8. CONCLUSION

The exploration of crypto coins, focusing on Ethereum, reveals a transformative landscape where finance and technology converge to challenge traditional paradigms. Ethereum emerges not merely as a cryptocurrency but as a foundational technology for Web3, heralding a new era of decentralized applications. The journey through Ethereum's ecosystem, from its smart contract functionality to its pivotal role in the DeFi and NFT spaces, underscores its potential to redefine user interaction with online platforms, emphasizing autonomy and security.

Despite the promise, Ethereum, like any burgeoning technology, faces significant challenges. Scalability, energy consumption, and regulatory hurdles are but a few of the obstacles that must be navigated. Yet, the ongoing transition to Ethereum 2.0 and the broader community's commitment to innovation offer pathways to overcoming these barriers, suggesting a resilient and adaptable framework for the future.

As the chapter concludes, it is evident that Ethereum and crypto coins are not mere speculative instruments but are integral to the fabric of a decentralized online experience. They serve as catalysts for a shift towards a more equitable and user-centric internet, one where value, ownership, and control rest with the users themselves. The implications of this shift are profound, promising a more inclusive financial system and a digital realm where privacy and agency are paramount.

The discourse on Ethereum and its role in Web3 is far from complete. It is a narrative in progress, with each development, each solution, and each challenge adding depth to the conversation. This chapter has laid the groundwork for understanding the complexities and the potential of Ethereum, providing a springboard for further inquiry and participation in the unfolding story of Web3.

As the digital landscape continues to evolve, Ethereum stands as a testament to the power of decentralized technologies to empower individuals and reshape industries. It is a beacon for innovation, a challenge to the status quo, and a vision of what the internet can become. The journey is ongoing, and the future, much like the blockchain, is being written one block at a time.

REFERENCES

Allen, D. W., & Potts, J. (2023). Web3 toolkits: A user innovation theory of crypto development. *Journal of Open Innovation*, *9*(2), 100050. doi:10.1016/j.joitmc.2023.100050

Arslan, E., & Güzel, G. (2021). Development of crypto coins and their place in the economy. [PAP]. *PressAcademia Procedia*, *14*(1), 80–83. doi:10.17261/Pressacademia.2021.1491

Bambacht, J., & Pouwelse, J. (2022). Web3: A decentralized societal infrastructure for identity, trust, money, and data. *arXiv preprint arXiv:2203.00398.* https://arxiv.org/abs/2203.00398

Béres, F., Seres, I. A., Benczúr, A. A., & Quintyne-Collins, M. (2021, August). Blockchain is watching you: Profiling and deanonymizing ethereum users. In *2021 IEEE international conference on decentralized applications and infrastructures (DAPPS)* (pp. 69-78). IEEE. https://ieeexplore.ieee.org/abstract/document/9566179/

Buterin, V. (2016). Ethereum: platform review. *Opportunities and Challenges for Private and Consortium Blockchains, 45.* https://files.gitter.im/cyberFund/cyber.fund/P8Xb/314477721-Ethereum-Platform-Review-Opportunities-and-Challenges-for-Private-and-Consortium-Blockchains-_1_.pdf

Cong, L. W., Tang, K., Wang, Y., & Zhao, X. (2023). *Inclusion and democratization through web3 and defi? initial evidence from the ethereum ecosystem* (No. w30949). National Bureau of Economic Research. https://www.nber.org/papers/w30949

Fantazzini, D. (2022). Crypto-coins and credit risk: Modelling and forecasting their probability of death. *Journal of Risk and Financial Management, 15*(7), 304. doi:10.3390/jrfm15070304

Gandal, N., Hamrick, J. T., Moore, T., & Vasek, M. (2021). The rise and fall of cryptocurrency coins and tokens. *Decisions in Economics and Finance, 44*(2), 981-1014. https://link.springer.com/article/10.1007/s10203-021-00329-8

Gilbert, S. (2022). *Crypto, web3, and the Metaverse. Bennett Institute for Public Policy.* Policy Brief. https://www.bennettinstitute.cam.ac.uk/wp-content/uploads/2022/03/Policy-brief-Crypto-web3-and-the-metaverse.pdf

Korpal, G., & Scott, D. (2022). *Decentralization and web3 technologies.* https://attachment.victorlampcdn.com/article/content/20220824/drewscott_gkorpal_web3.pdf

Liu, Z., Xiang, Y., Shi, J., Gao, P., Wang, H., Xiao, X., & Hu, Y. C. (2021). Make web3. 0 connected. *IEEE Transactions on Dependable and Secure Computing, 19*(5), 2965–2981. doi:10.1109/TDSC.2021.3079315

Luong, D. H. (2019). *The Ethereum blockchain: Use cases for social finance applications.* https://trepo.tuni.fi/bitstream/handle/123456789/27245/Luong.pdf?sequence=4

Murray, A., Kim, D., & Combs, J. (2023). The promise of a decentralized internet: What is Web3 and how can firms prepare? *Business Horizons, 66*(2), 191–202. doi:10.1016/j.bushor.2022.06.002

Oliva, G. A., Hassan, A. E., & Jiang, Z. M. (2020). An exploratory study of smart contracts in the Ethereum blockchain platform. *Empirical Software Engineering, 25*(3), 1864–1904. doi:10.1007/s10664-019-09796-5

Petcu, A., Pahontu, B., Frunzete, M., & Stoichescu, D. A. (2023). A Secure and Decentralized Authentication Mechanism Based on Web 3.0 and Ethereum Blockchain Technology. *Applied Sciences (Basel, Switzerland), 13*(4), 2231. doi:10.3390/app13042231

PrasadRao. K. V., RadhaKrishna, P. K. S., Teja, G. M. C., & Panda, S. K. (n.d.). *Blockchain based Smart Contract deployment on Ethereum Platform using Web3. js and Solidity.* https://www.researchgate.net/profile/Mani-Gaddam/publication/356988224_Blockchain_based_Smart_Contract_deployment_on_Ethereum_Platform_using_Web3js_and_Solidity/links/61f079e0dafcdb25fd501ebb/Blockchain-based-Smart-Contract-deployment-on-Ethereum-Platform-using-Web3js-and-Solidity.pdf

Ranganthan, V. P., Dantu, R., Paul, A., Mears, P., & Morozov, K. (2018, October). A decentralized marketplace application on the ethereum blockchain. In *2018 IEEE 4th International Conference on Collaboration and Internet Computing (CIC)* (pp. 90-97). IEEE. https://ieeexplore.ieee.org/abstract/document/8537821/

Sheridan, D., Harris, J., Wear, F., Cowell, J., Jr., Wong, E., & Yazdinejad, A. (2022). Web3 challenges and opportunities for the market. *arXiv preprint arXiv:2209.02446.* https://arxiv.org/abs/2209.02446

Singh, S., & Bharti, M. (2023). *Building and Deploying Modern Web 3.0 Blockchain Application*. http://www.ir.juit.ac.in:8080/jspui/handle/123456789/9834

Urquhart, A. (2022). Under the hood of the Ethereum blockchain. *Finance Research Letters*, *47*, 102628. doi:10.1016/j.frl.2021.102628

Vijayalakshmi, J., & Murugan, A. (2017, February). Crypto Coins: The Future of Transactions. In *Proceedings of International Conference on Communication, Computing and Information Technology*. https://www.researchgate.net/profile/Dr-J-Vijayalakshmi/publication/333310695_Crypto_Coins_The_Future_of_Transactions/links/5e4b792ea6fdccd965aef3b9/Crypto-Coins-The-Future-of-Transactions.pdf

Wang, Q., Li, R., Wang, Q., Chen, S., Ryan, M., & Hardjono, T. (2022). Exploring web3 from the view of blockchain. *arXiv preprint arXiv:2206.08821*. https://arxiv.org/abs/2206.08821

Yavuz, E., Koç, A. K., Çabuk, U. C., & Dalkılıç, G. (2018, March). Towards secure e-voting using ethereum blockchain. In *2018 6th International Symposium on Digital Forensic and Security (ISDFS)* (pp. 1-7). IEEE. https://ieeexplore.ieee.org/abstract/document/8355340/

Zavratnik, J. (2022). *Analysis of web3 solution development principles* (Master's thesis, Universitat Politècnica de Catalunya). https://upcommons.upc.edu/handle/2117/379908

Zheng, J., & Lee, D. K. C. (2023). Understanding the Evolution of the Internet: Web 1.0 to Web3. 0, Web3 and Web 3. *Handbook of Digital Currency: Bitcoin, Innovation, Financial Instruments, and Big Data*. https://papers.ssrn.com/sol3/papers.cfm?abstract_id=4431284

KEY TERMS AND DEFINITIONS

Blockchain: A decentralized digital ledger that records transactions across multiple computers in a way that prevents alteration.

Consensus Mechanism: A system used in blockchain networks to achieve agreement on a single data value or a single state of the network among distributed processes or multi-agent systems.

Cryptocurrency: A digital or virtual currency secured by cryptography, operating independently of a central bank.

Decentralized Applications (dApps): Digital applications or programs that exist and run on a blockchain or P2P network of computers instead of a single computer.

Decentralized Finance (DeFi): Financial services, including lending, borrowing, and trading, provided on a decentralized network, typically on blockchain technology.

Ethereum: A decentralized platform that enables smart contracts and decentralized applications (dApps) to be built and operated without downtime, fraud, control, or interference.

Fork: A change in protocol causing the blockchain to diverge into two separate paths, either temporarily or permanently.

Gas (Ethereum): A unit that measures the amount of computational effort required to execute operations on the Ethereum network.

Interoperability: The ability of different blockchain systems to work together and share information.

Ledger: The record-keeping system of a blockchain, where all transactions are recorded.

Liquidity Mining: A process in DeFi where users provide liquidity to a pool and receive rewards in return, often in the form of tokens.

Mining: The process of validating transactions and adding them to a blockchain ledger, often involving solving complex computational problems.

Non-Fungible Tokens (NFTs): Unique digital assets that represent ownership of specific items or content, verified using blockchain technology.

Proof of Stake (PoS): A type of consensus mechanism used by blockchains that allows participants to validate transactions and create new blocks based on the number of coins they hold and are willing to "stake" for network security.

Proof of Work (PoW): A consensus mechanism in a blockchain that requires participants to perform a computationally difficult task to validate transactions and create new blocks.

Sharding: A method used in blockchain technology to increase the number of transactions a network can process by splitting the network into smaller, more manageable parts.

Smart Contract: A self-executing contract with the terms of the agreement directly written into lines of code.

Token: A unit of value issued by a project, representing some asset or utility in its blockchain.

Wallet (Cryptocurrency): A digital tool that allows users to store, send, and receive cryptocurrencies.

Yield Farming: A strategy used in DeFi to maximize returns by moving assets across different lending markets to take advantage of varying interest rates.

Chapter 6
Revolutionizing Finance With Decentralized Finance (DeFi)

Vijaya Kittu Manda
https://orcid.org/0000-0002-1680-8210
PBMEIT, India

Arnold Mashud Abukari
Tamale Technical University, Ghana

Vivek Gupta
https://orcid.org/0000-0002-1101-1886
Indian Institute of Management, Lucknow, India

Madavarapu Jhansi Bharathi
https://orcid.org/0000-0001-8478-6626
University of the Cumberlands, USA

ABSTRACT

Decentralized finance is an innovative use of blockchain technology in financial services. Because of its transparency and lack of intermediaries, it brings several advantages to the traditional finance ecosystem. Features like tokenization, total value locked (TVL), oracles, and data aggregation help in building a variety of DeFi products and services. Decentralized apps (dApps) run autonomously atop distributed ledger networks. Decentralized stablecoins, decentralized exchanges (DEX), decentralized credit and lending, derivates, and even decentralized insurance are offered on DeFi platforms. The chapter takes through three forms of decentralized insurance models. Case studies and examples for successful and unsuccessful claims are explored. However, the implementation of DeFi comes with its challenges and regulatory hurdles. Similarly, governance and security aspects are of increased importance.

DOI: 10.4018/979-8-3693-1532-3.ch006

INTRODUCTION

The concept of finance evolved over centuries, with rapid progress happening in the last two decades in the form of Financial Technologies (FinTech). The traditional financial system is often run by exchanges and intermediaries, such as banks, stockbrokers, stock exchanges, and insurance companies. Apart from charging a fee, these intermediaries often set the rules for how the financial services are offered. This method of providing financial services is called Centralized Finance (CenFi).

CenFi has been famous for centuries, but it comes with severe disadvantages. The intermediaries have central control over the transaction, charge high transaction fees, and often have a say on the exchange rates at which the transaction happens. A 2021 McKinsey report estimated that the global financial services sector earns around 2-3% of global GDP in revenues. The list included all types of financial services, such as banking, lending, investment, and insurance. Financial transactions are prone to data breaches, security issues and vulnerabilities, and potential forgery of transactions. Research shows that the traditional system delays international transactions and leads to global inequality (Kaur et al., 2023b).

A growing number of disruption technologies such as Blockchain and Distributed Ledger Technologies (DLT), Artificial Intelligence, Big Data, and Cloud computing are emerging and attempting to re-vitalize finance by bringing in features that shift power and authority from central intermediaries to the customers, thereby disrupting the business of the intermediaries.

Decentralized Finance (DeFi) is an emerging ecosystem comprising a wide range of complex financial applications built using Blockchain and associated technology so that financial services are offered by using existing and new financial instruments in an open, decentralized manner on a trustworthy network without using any central financial intermediary (Gramlich et al., 2023). This means the traditional supply and demand matching functions currently handled by banks, lenders, payment service providers, or investment companies will be done by decentralized protocols and smart contracts in an open, interoperable, transparent, and automated manner (Zetzsche et al., 2020). DeFi is considered a financial revolution, a financial inclusion movement to build an open, democratic, permission-free, and censorship-free blockchain-based economic infrastructure rather than relying on centralized intermediaries and institutions. DeFi is found to open doors for new entrepreneurial opportunities.

The inspiration for building the decentralized financial infrastructure could have come from how the electronic mail (email) system works. When it is possible to send an email to anyone in the world, why not be able to send money to anyone in the world in the same way?

Like a typical financial service provider, DeFi offers financial services such as loans, payments, decentralized markets, and derivatives. Removing intermediaries and retaining trust gives customers control over their finances. The DeFi applications offer services such as lending, borrowing, exchange, monetary banking (such as the issuance of stablecoins), tokenization, or other financial instruments such as insurance, derivatives, and prediction markets. DeFi enjoys the blessings of Blockchain and benefits from the transparent and trust less network features. DeFi is not a specific project, but a collection of ideas and projects built on blockchain technology.

The name Decentralized Finance or DeFi was coined in a Telegram group comprising software engineers and entrepreneurs struggling to propose a name for a service that offers blockchain-based financial services without the need for traditional intermediary financial institutions. A transition from a conventional financial system to a DeFi requires many infrastructure changes to be done apart from getting approval from various stakeholders. Though the financial intermediaries are left out of the DeFi system, there is still a need to stay connected with the real financial world for data, such as exchange rates and prices.

The DeFi (Decentralized Finance) market is experiencing significant growth and innovation. Figure 1 shows that the number of unique addresses buying and selling DeFi assets has risen globally. The top five countries where DeFi transactions happen are the U.S., UK, Germany, Canada, and Russia.

Figure 1. Number of unique addresses that either bought or sold DeFi assets between December 2017 and January 2023
Data Source: Statista; Data is till January 9, 2023

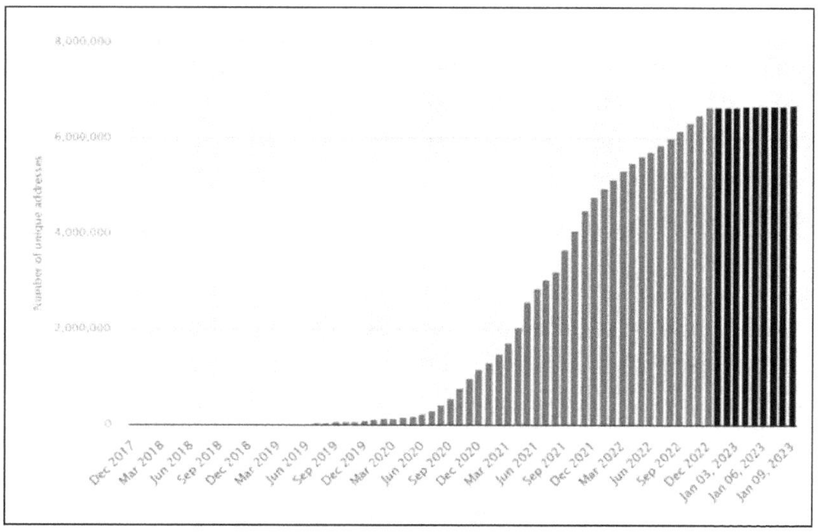

Many DeFi activity was originally on Ethereum chains but later expanded to non-Ethereum chains. The number and variety of DApps-based DeFi financial and investment products are increasing.

Several Blockchain-based classification frameworks were built in the past few years. The two dimensions of such a systematic classification have a level of analysis (Users and society, DeFi applications, Blockchain infrastructure, and Financial Industry) as one dimension and Activities (Design and features, Measures and value, and Management and organization) on the other (Gramlich et al., 2023).

DeFi can work closely with other technologies, such as the Metaverse and Web 3.0, giving both opportunities and threats to the banking industry (Marx, 2022).

Protocols

Protocols describe and provide smart contract-based services. Providing essential building blocks, such as swapping assets or allocating liquidity efficiently, they can be reused and combined in many ways. These protocols give users access to digital assets, such as tokens, and expose them to the cryptocurrency market. However, the security of the DeFi protocols can be compromised by not only software vulnerabilities but also unforeseen movements in the cryptocurrency market or arbitrage and speculation opportunities. These situations have been of interest to researchers (Tolmach et al., 2021).

Tokenization

Tokenization uses computer programs to create digital representations of a non-crypto asset, such as a loan or shares. The digital representations will be in the form of a crypto token. It contains information about the tokenized asset and its ownership, with a service layer embedding the platform rules and governance. Through tokenization, transactions involving money, financial, and real assets can be automated, allowing the contingent transfer and combination of claims via smart contracts (Aldasoro et al., 2023). It connects traditional financial systems with the digital asset ecosystem (Carapella et al., 2023).

Example: Dinari Securities Backed Tokens, or dShares, allows investors outside the U.S. to use cryptocurrencies to buy shares of some of the largest U.S. companies and exchange-traded funds. The stocks are tokenized securities backed by one-to-one real-world shares purchased by Dinari. Because the system works on Blockchain, anyone can monitor every transaction. In the initial phase, the platform allowed tokens to be sold back to Dinari. The company's broader goal is to allow them to be widely used as collateral for loans or to swap for other security tokens in the crypto market.

Tokenization involves three key elements: assets, ledgers, and tokens. The process of tokenization of an asset involves five steps:

1. A blockchain (such as a private permissioned blockchain or permissionless Blockchain)
2. A reference asset (such as a building ownership, or a digital artwork)
3. A mechanism to assess the value of the reference asset (such as an appraisal by a professional appraiser of buildings, or past sales of similar works, artist reputation, and market demand)
4. A means to store and provide custody for the reference asset (such as in a digital vault)
5. A mechanism to facilitate redemptions of the token and the reference asset (such as transfer of digital assets from wallet to another though an exchange).

Most tokenization is being developed, financed, and run by small venture-capital-backed crypto companies. Some financial companies such as Santander, JP Morgan, and Franklin Templeton have announced plans to use the concept.

Advantages of Tokenization

1. **Fractional ownership**: Facilitates participation from retail and small investors.
2. **Efficiency enhancement**: Streamlines transactions, contracts, interest, and dividend execution and minimizes intermediary involvement.
3. **Improved transparency**: Offers greater visibility into the asset history and transactions.

Total Value Locked (TVL)

Total Value Locked (TVL) measures the amount of capital locked inside each DeFi protocol. For a protocol, the more value is locked in, the better. The locked capital offers services such as market making, lending, asset management, and arbitraging across the ecosystem, earning yields for the capital providers (Stepanova & Eriņš, 2021).

The TVL levels will be volatile as the capital can be prone to temporary incentives, such as liquidity mining programs, or for external reasons, such as smart contract bugs. Hence, TVL should not be considered as a reliable metric. Table 1 shows TVL having reached it peaks in 2023 (DeFi Llarma, 2023).

Table 1. TVL over the past few years

Year	TVL
2018	644.83k
2019	591.09m
2020	15.00b
2021	164.00b
2022	38.50b
Mid Nov-2023	44.97b

Data Source: DeFi Llarma

Oracles and Data Aggregation

Oracles in Greek mythology are known to have infinite knowledge and wisdom because of their close relationships with the gods of Mount Olympus and, hence, used to help travelers with key information. Oracles in Blockchain is an essential, trusted partner for data inputs and helps connect smart contracts to access real-world off-chain data and events. If Oracles are not there, smart contracts would only have access to on-chain data and would be unable to interact with the outside world (i.e., from anywhere else). Oracles can send or receive information from blockchains in either direction. DeFi Oracles are a link solution that bridges the on-chain and off-chain environments (Suarez Barcia, 2023).

Some examples of Oracles are:

1. Price feeds for cryptocurrency prices
2. Event oracles for sport/election results
3. Blockchain explorers for on-chain data
4. Randomness beacons for random number generation

An Oracle Problem questions how one brings information from outside the trusted blockchain environment onto the trust-less Blockchain in a trusted manner (Bartholic et al., 2022).

Major DeFi oracles like Chainlink aim to be highly decentralized, with many independent node operators running the infrastructure. This helps ensure that the data provided remains accurate and censorship-resistant. Popular oracles will aggregate data from multiple sources and cross-check results to provide smart contracts with a single agreed-upon data feed. This adds redundancy and consensus around the results. Well-designed oracles use economic incentives and penalties to motivate node operators to report accurate, honest data. Handling incentives correctly is essential for security and reliability. As a vital bridge between on and off-chain, oracles introduce new attack surfaces that require consideration of robust infrastructure, economic incentives, and redundancy in data feeds.

Liquidity Pools

A liquidity pool is a pool of cryptocurrency assets that facilitates trading on DeFi protocols. Liquidity pools are made up of two or more cryptocurrencies that users deposit. A user can trade one cryptocurrency for another by adding liquidity to the pool. The liquidity providers are then rewarded with a portion of the trading fees.

Lido DAO, Rocket Pool, Frax Share, Ankr Network, and Stride are the top five Liquid staking governance tokens (Coingecko, 2023).

Yield Farming/Liquidity Mining

Yield Farming refers to deploying assets into decentralized finance protocols to provide liquidity and earn outsized rewards. By leveraging automated market-making formulas and arbitrage opportunities between platforms, yield farmers seek to profit from high initial issuance rates as new DeFi projects launch and incentivize initial liquidity provision (McGhin et al., 2021).

Yield Farming involves depositing tokens into liquidity pools and helps facilitate trading on decentralized exchanges (DEXs). Users earn rewards in the form of tokens in return for providing liquidity. The quantum of rewards earned depends on the liquidity provided and the trading activity on the DEX.

Yield Aggregators automatically deposit user funds into different liquidity pools that offer the highest yields. These platforms automate the yield farming process and help users earn better returns than traditional methods. By automatically re-investing, users do not have to manually track their investments and let the platforms auto-compound and maximize returns. This can be time-consuming and error-prone.

The advantages of Yield Farming are that they are convenient, efficient, and allow the spreading of risk by diversification across different liquidity pools. However, they come with risks, such as smart contract risk (the protocol code could have bugs/errors) and impairment loss (the price of tokens in the pool moves against the investor).

Aave, Compound, Yearn Finance, Pickle Finance, Cream Finance, Alpha Homora, Curve Finance, and Balancer are some famous companies in this activity.

Flash Loans

Flash loans are leveraged capital deployment by leveraging the programmatic capabilities of smart contracts on distributed ledger networks. Flash loans allow arbitrageurs to capitalize upon temporary inefficiencies in asset prices across uncommissioned liquidity pools. This is done by automating the issuance of short-term credit taken and repaid within the same blockchain transaction. While the permissionless and collateral-free nature of such loans has enabled a range of experimental financial applications, establishing new avenues for capital optimization, it has also raised concerns regarding potential systemic risks to protocol stability should flash loans be subverted for destabilizing market manipulation. Considerable work is still to be done to ensure adequate safeguarding of DeFi protocols against such threats through restrictions that curb only benign contract execution while permitting ongoing innovation within this space.

Lossless/Lossy Loans

Lossless loans are structured such that the lender's principal is fully preserved and only the yield from interest accumulates. Mechanisms like over-collateralization, where the collateral pledged far exceeds the loan amount, are used in this. Lossy loans, on the other hand, expose the lender's capital to potential impairment if the borrower defaults or collateral value decreases. Such loans may be under-collateralized, attached to volatile assets, or feature liquidation protocols wherein collateral is automatically liquidated on a collateralization ratio breach, even if the resulting price falls short of the debt obligation. While riskier, lossy loans potentially offer borrowers more attractive borrowing terms. From lenders' perspective, substantial risks and trades exist between lossless and lossy strategies when allocating capital through DeFi lending protocols.

Cross-Chain Swaps/Bridges

Cross-chain asset mapping services, such as a cross-chain asset exchange, can map encrypted assets on one Blockchain to tokens on another for chain interoperability.

On-Chain/Off-Chain Assets

Assets that exist natively on a blockchain network are called on-chain assets. Examples of on-chain assets include cryptocurrencies like Bitcoin, Ethereum, and stablecoins that are minted on-chain. These assets have their ownership and transaction details recorded on the Blockchain. These assets can be seamlessly integrated into DeFi applications without intermediaries. These transactions are transparent, immutable, and decentralized.

Assets that represent real-world value but are not directly stored on a blockchain are called off-chain assets. Examples of off-chain assets include fiat currencies, real estate, commodities, and stocks. In DeFi, off-chain assets are typically represented on-chain through tokenized versions. They allow various real-world assets to be represented and invested in via DeFi, thereby expanding the usage potential of DeFi. The risks involved with off-chain assets are that their value depends on the performance and existence of the underlying off-chain asset. There may be risks around custody and settlement between on/off chains. More intermediation is required compared to purely on-chain assets.

Liquid Staking

Staking is the process of locking up cryptocurrency assets to participate in the security of a blockchain network. Liquid staking allows users to stake their cryptocurrencies while still maintaining liquidity. This is done using a third-party service that mints a new token representing the user's staked cryptocurrency. The user can then use this token to trade or lend while still earning staking rewards.

DeFi PRODUCTS AND SERVICES

The Top DeFi categories according to Coingecko 2023 data are (Lim, 2023):

1. Decentralized exchanges (DEXs) (39.7% market share)
2. Oracles (16.9%)
3. Liquid staking (14.2%)
4. Lending
5. Derivatives
6. Yield Aggregators
7. Insurance
8. Asset Management and
9. Fixed Interest

The top 3 categories make up 70.7%. In 2022 Q2, Liquid staking overtakes lending as the third biggest in the DeFi ecosystem. The liquid staking governance token performance is a prime reason for the DeFi sector market cap jumping 65.2% in 2023 Q1, translating to $29.6 billion in gains. Crypto spot trading volumes are up 18.1%, reaching $2.8T in 2023 Q1, with DEXs outpacing CEXs' quarterly growth (CoinGecko, 2023). Popular Blockchains that support DeFi are Ethereum, Binance Smart Chain, Solana, Cardano, Avalanche, Polygon, and Fantom (Kaur et al., 2023a). DeFi can be implemented using smart contracts (Friesendorf & Blütener, 2023a). These are best implemented on the Ethereum ecosystem, and a basic understanding of the Blockchain architecture is a pre-requisite. Table 2 shows some popular DeFi products and services.

Table 2. Popular DeFi products and services

Category	Popular DeFi Products/Services
Decentralized Applications (dApps)	Uniswap, MakerDAO, Aave, Compound, Balancer, 1inch, Axie Infinity, OpenSea
Decentralized Stablecoins	DAI, FRAX, USDC, Liquity USD (LUSD), MakerDAO, Synthetix,UMA
Decentralized Exchanges (DEX)	Uniswap, PancakeSwap, SushiSwap, Curve Finance, dYdX, 1inch, Kyber Network, Bancor, 0x
Decentralized Credit	Compound, MakerDAO, Aave, Nuo Network, Rootstock, Dharma Protocol, BlockFi, Genesis Capital
Lending	Aave, MakerDAO, Compound, Nuo Network, Cred, Ethlend, Salt Lending
Derivatives	dYdX, Melon Protocol, Uma Project, Quadrant Protocol, Set Protocol, Opyn, Synthetix, bZx Protocol, Moloch DAO
Decentralized Insurance	Nexus Mutual, Etherisc, InsurAce, Opyn, Dydx Protocol, Boulder Mutual, Cover Protocol, Arceus
Decentralized autonomous organizations (DAOs)	ConstitutionDAO, MakerDAO, Aragon, DAOstack, Metacartel DAO, MolochDAO, Gitcoin, BurnerDAO, PleasrDAO

Data Source: Author compilation

Decentralized Applications (dApps)

Decentralized Applications (dApps, DApp, Dapp, or dapp), constitute a nascent class of software programs designed to operate autonomously atop distributed ledger networks without centralized governance or administration. Through an open architecture accessible to any party Internet-connected, dApps allow for novel peer-to-peer use cases spanning DeFi, governance, and digital social cooperation. Ethereum is the distributed ledger technology (DLT) that has the largest DApp market.

Types of dApps

Decentralized applications exist along a spectrum from centralized to fully decentralized architectures. Centralized dApps primarily use a centralized server, database, and user interfaces with limited distributed features. For example, the backend relies on a single company's servers rather than a distributed network. Semi-decentralized dApps use elements of both centralized and decentralized structures, such as smart contracts interacting with off-chain databases or servers controlled by a single entity. Meanwhile, fully decentralized dApps use smart contracts or distributed technologies for all primary functions without relying on centralized intermediaries. The code and agreements run on a distributed network, such as Ethereum, with no single point of control or ownership over the application. This architecture aims to maximize the security, resilience, transparency, and accessibility of dApps through fully autonomous operation across nodes of a public multi-stakeholder network.

Decentralized Stablecoins

Within the field of decentralized finance, protocol-backed stablecoins use autonomous incentive mechanisms have arisen as an innovative means of engendering price stability independently of centralized fiscal or monetary interventions, with projects like DAI pioneering Permissionless stablecoin issuance through smart contracts and community governance (Saengchote et al., 2023).

Decentralized Exchanges (DEX)

Decentralized Exchanges (DEXs) allow customers to trade cryptocurrencies or digital currencies without a central authority or an intermediary (Aspris et al., 2021). DEX is a cryptocurrency exchange or digital currency exchange (DCE) variant. A typical cryptocurrency exchange can be a centralized exchange or a decentralized exchange. These exchanges allow customers to add or withdraw funds in fiat money to the account and use them for trading in cryptocurrencies. Some DEX, such as Etherdelta, IDEX, and HADAX, do not store customer funds on the exchange but facilitate peer-to-peer cryptocurrency trading. DEX is generally resistant to security problems that affect other exchanges. Despite being loaded with features, their overall trading volumes are low but slowly increasing. The number of DEXs worldwide shows their increased acceptance by the trader community. There will be low transaction costs for a partially filled and filled order book (Pop et al., 2018).

Uniswap is the most popular and most significant DEX. It is a decentralized platform with the exchange running on a Blockchain-based network like Ethereum (Lo & Medda, 2022). The smart contracts allow traders to get the assets of the trade directly into their wallets automatically without any manual interference. This eliminates many intermediates who often charge fees for offering their services.

An Automated Market Maker (AMM) matches buyers and sellers of cryptocurrencies through smart contracts (Frtisch et al., 2022). Decentralized Derivatives Exchanges are variants of DEX that allow users to trade derivatives contracts on cryptocurrencies and other assets.

Decentralized Credit

Decentralized Credit is a financial system that enables people and businesses to take out loans and lend money without needing a centralized organization like a bank. Blockchain and smart contracts can be used to do this. Ripple and Stellar are popular distributed credit networks. Decentralized Lending and Borrowing Platforms are a variant of Decentralized Credit because they allow cryptocurrencies to be borrowed or lent.

Decentralized Credit has the potential to make credit more accessible and affordable and to reduce the risk of fraud and abuse. The wide adoption of the technology depends on how effectively it can overcome challenges.

Decentralized Credit comes with some advantages:

1. Increased access to credit
2. Lower interest rates
3. Increased transparency
4. Reduced fraud

Challenges of Decentralized Credit

Here are some of the challenges of decentralized credit:

1. **Security**: The security of blockchain technology is still evolving. There is always a risk of hacking or fraud. Most decentralized credit networks do not preserve user privacy. Some others are not be truly decentralized. Hence, researchers have built some alternatives that adhere to a universal composability framework and can identify malicious network actors (Panwar et al., 2019).
2. **Regulation**: The regulatory environment for decentralized credit is still unclear, which could hinder its adoption.
3. **Scalability**: Decentralized credit systems can be slow and expensive to operate, which could limit their reach.

Lending

MakerDAO, Compound, and Aave are popular names in the credit/lending field. Established in 2015, MakerDAO is a platform for customers to save, borrow/lend, and stake coins. DAI is its internal currency and a decentralized stablecoin. Using smart contracts built on the Ethereum platform, DAI attempts to maintain its value close to the U.S. dollar.

Compound Finance started to compensate lenders and borrowers on its platform with its COMP token in addition to the regular interest payments to lenders. Loans on Compound are typically for short periods, averaging 31 days, and most of the borrowing is for yield farming. Concentration and interconnectedness in Compound are key reasons for systemic risk (Saengchote, 2023).

Derivatives

Derivatives in traditional finance are one of the largest traded assets on stock exchanges. A derivative derives its value from some underlying asset – such as an index, stock, commodity, or interest rate. The product is often used either for hedging or for speculative trading.

Yield and Synthetix are popular names in the derivatives field.

Decentralized Insurance

Decentralized insurance eliminates the need for a central intermediary such as traditional insurance companies. Individuals contribute small amounts to a shared fund called an insurance pool. An algorithm determines payouts based on pre-defined conditions coded into smart contracts. The smart contract automatically pays the claimant from the shared fund if a claim is valid according to the rules. No single entity controls the funds or makes subjective decisions. The code guarantees the payments. These two features allow for lowering costs while providing transparency, removing bias, and creating a more accessible way for individuals to help each other in need. This model can lower costs, making claims processing more efficient and transparent. Despite its early stages, experts believe Decentralized Finance has the potential to revolutionize the insurance industry. There are three popular decentralized insurance models. There are three popular decentralized insurance models.

- Peer-to-peer insurance
- Parametric insurance
- Mutual insurance

Decentralized Insurance Protocols

Decentralized Insurance Protocols allow users to purchase insurance against a variety of risks, such as smart contract hacks and theft. They deal with risk transfer between interested parties. Some prominent smart contract-based insurance protocols include Nexus Mutual, Etherisc, InsurAce, Nsure, Cozy Finance, Unslashed Finance, and Risk Harbor. Some of these protocols are not fully decentralized and might thus pose some risk and shock propagation and might not work in situations where the insurance protocols become illiquid. Some enhanced implementations to overcome these disadvantages are evolving (Nadler et al., 2022).

Nexus Mutual

Nexus Mutual was established in 2017 as a peer-to-peer discretionary mutual (and not as an insurance company because of regulatory reasons; mutuals are outside the ambit of insurance regulations). The company is regarded as the first DeFi Insurance Company. They use a native token called NXM token. The company initially considered selling earthquake insurance via smart contracts, but the idea did not work out. So, the business model was quickly changed to provide cover from smart contract risks. It is a community-owned and governed platform, and NXM tokens are used to participate in governance, purchase cover, and earn rewards. Nexus Mutual went to add an exchange cover, lender cover, and DeFi cover to its products suite.

To purchase cover from Nexus Mutual, users need to stake NXM tokens. Depending on the risk of the underlying asset, NXM is required to purchase cover. For example, covering for a low-risk asset like Ethereum will require less NXM than covering for a high-risk asset, such as a new DeFi protocol. If a claim is filed against Nexus Mutual, it is assessed by a group of community members called the Claims Committee. The Claims Committee decides whether to pay the claim and, if so, how much.

Etherisc

Etherisc is an open-source, decentralized platform that uses blockchain technology to transform how insurance is conceptualized and delivered. Etherisc works as a DAO and uses smart contracts to define policy parameters, underwrite risk pooling mechanisms, and handle premium settlement and claims adjudication. The economic model helps shift demand and supply by reducing transactional costs (Sheth & Subramanian, 2019). Etherisc wishes to streamline insurance transactional processes and disintermediate traditional insurance firms as trusted third parties. With its unique functioning, Etherisc aims to make insurance more accessible and secure for both individuals and businesses.

InsurAce

InsurAce is an Ethereum-based decentralized insurance platform that uses blockchain technology to modernize the (re)insurance business model. It uses intelligent smart contracts to automate underwriting, risk transfer, and claim settlements between insurers, brokers, and policyholders. InsurAce aims to streamline inefficiency and reduce premium costs vis-a-vis disintermediating legacy firm roles. InsurAce's parametric structure also ostensibly affords flexibility, catering to diversified risk categories. It uses an approach called the proof of insurance that acts as a risk assessment system. The system requires that policyholders stake their premiums in a special token called RAI (Risk Assessment Index) during the underwriting process. This stake acts as collateral, and in the event of a claim, the RAI is used to calculate the payout. While remaining in prototype phases addressing challenges of integrating actuarial vetting on-chain, InsurAce shows potential to upend incumbent insurers with transparent peer-to-business and peer-to-peer models if scalably executed according to compliance.

Smart Contracts in Decentralized Insurance

Different types of smart contracts are used to facilitate various aspects of decentralized insurance.

Parametric or "if-this-then-that" contracts are used to insulate against events where payouts are automatically triggered based on predetermined parameters. For example, a parametric contract could insure farmers against drought by paying out if rainfall in a given region falls below a certain threshold within a set period. The measurement and payout would be automated through embedded oracles that check publicly available rainfall data.

Another type is mutualized loss coverage contracts, where participants pool funds to insure against shared risks. If a covered event occurs, funds from the pool are automatically paid out to affected participants proportional to their stake. This allows for spreading risks and costs across a large number of policyholders. Smart mutuals have been created to insure items like flight delays or provide health coverage.

Indemnity-style smart contracts can also be used to insure against direct losses. These evaluate claims individually to determine payout eligibility and amount rather than relying solely on market-linked triggers. Claimants would need to provide verifiable proof-of-loss documents for the contract to process a payout automatically. Indemnity contracts require more complex programming to assess fault and claim validity on a case-by-case basis.

Reinsurance smart contracts allow insurers to transfer portions of their risks to other parties in return for a portion of the premiums paid. This helps mitigate concentrated exposures and improves balance sheets. Decentralized reinsurance markets using smart contracts are in the early stages of development.

Additional smart contract types explored for decentralized insurance include usage-based coverage tied to IoT sensors, micro-coverage for insuring small, frequent losses, and multi-tiered layered contracts combining features from different models. As the sector matures, more innovative contract designs are expected to emerge that preserve the benefits of transparency, trust, and automation inherent to blockchain technology.

Insurance comprises a complex set of business processes and no wonder a blockchain-based decentralized insurance system will comprise several smart contracts. These include:

1. **Premium smart contracts** handle the collection of premium payments from policyholders. They can automatically withdraw premiums on a set schedule.
2. **Claim assessment smart contracts** encode the rules for assessing and validating claims. They can access data inputs like IoT sensor feeds or other oracle services to check conditions and determine payouts automatically.
3. **Payout smart contracts** release approved claim payments once claim assessment smart contracts validate them. This enables instant, transparent payouts without manual intervention.
4. **Underwriting smart contracts** set the rates and risk models for pricing insurance coverage based on data feeds, statistics, and algorithms encoded into them. This enables customized, dynamic pricing.
5. **Governance smart contracts** control roles, responsibilities, and decision-making powers in a decentralized autonomous organization that serves as the virtual insurance carrier.
6. **Reinsurance smart contracts** connect pooled capital across multiple carriers for reinsurance to spread risk. This allows for a larger shared coverage capacity.

CASE STUDIES OF DECENTRALIZED INSURANCE CLAIMS

Successful Claims

John was in a car accident and suffered injuries. His smart contract vehicle sensors logged the incident details on-chain. His medical records validated that his injuries matched the accident. The smart contract automatically processed his medical expense claim against the decentralized risk pool. Within 10 minutes, the entire claim amount was deposited into John's digital wallet.

Unsuccessful Claims

Emily reported water damage to her home from a burst pipe. Photos showed only minor damage, but she claimed $10,000 in repairs. The smart contract accessed her home's IoT water sensor records, which did not detect abnormal water usage or leaks on her reported date. Prior insurance fraud was also discovered. The smart contract denied the claim, citing a lack of evidence and past fraudulent activity. Emily was refunded her premium, less network transaction fees.

FUTURE OF DECENTRALIZED INSURANCE

Emerging Trends in Decentralized Insurance

The future of decentralized insurance depends on four major factors - further decentralization, automation, usage-based models, and global accessibility.

1. Increased usage of smart contracts and blockchain technology will help automate underwriting, claims handling, and payouts, reducing costs and turning insurance into an actual asynchronous peer-to-peer system.
2. Continued growth and improvements in decentralized insurance protocols like Nexus Mutual, Cover Protocol, and BHCPool allow for more nuanced policies and coverages developed directly by participants.
3. Integrating decentralized identity and reputation systems helps assess risks better using on-chain identity and behaviour data rather than relying purely on self-reported information.
4. Adoption of decentralized data ecosystems that provide independent, verifiable sources of information for assessing risk and determining payouts for parametric/usage-based policies.
5. The development of loss prevention services through decentralized sensor networks and IoT devices provides incentives to reduce claims.
6. Usage-based and usage-insured policies have become more popular, covering risks proportional to verifiable usage or exposure rather than broad liability-style coverage.
7. Due to high costs, there will be a growth in decentralized risk pools for highly specialized, niche, or geo-specific risks that traditional insurers do not address.
8. There will be a maturation of jurisdiction-free policies operating across borders according to terms of smart contracts rather than individual country regulations.

Decentralized Autonomous Organizations (DAOs)

Inspired by self-organization, DAO is a type of organization that operates autonomously without any centralized organization controlling it or outsiders intervening in its operations flow. The organization's management and operational rules are run on a Blockchain and enforced through smart contracts. DAOs generally on a five-tier architectural mode:

1. Basic Technology comprising Internet Protocol, Blockchain, Big Data, and Artificial Intelligence

2. Governance Operations comprising of Consensus Mechanism, Smart Contracts, Digitalization, Intelligent Matching, On/Off-Chain Collaboration
3. Incentive Mechanism comprising of Token Incentive, issue/circulation, locking/recycling, value management, and reputation system
4. Organizational form comprising of Multi-centered stereoscopic network, small number of basic terms, and large-scale community autonomy
5. Manifestation comprising digital currencies, systems/organizations, intelligent machines, distributed decentralization, and distributed polycentric.

The DAO

Launched in May 2016 by members of the Ethereum community, The DAO is the world's first DAO project. It is an investor-directed venture capital fund that allows token holders to vote on proposals and funding decisions. The DAO raised more than 150 million dollars by selling tokens when launching, making it the most prominent crowdfunding fundraising campaign of all time. The DAO's smart contract code was exploited, allowing an attacker to withdraw millions of dollars' worth of Ether. This highlighted weaknesses in relying solely on code for governance without sufficient safety measures or human oversight. While the Ethereum community voted to revert the transactions in the hard fork, it underscored challenges around developing fully decentralized models at the smart contract level. The failure of The DAO experiment has turned into a lesson that decentralized governance requires careful consideration of both technical design and economic incentives.

Olympus DAO

Olympus DAO is a DAO that creates a decentralized and censorship-resistant reserve currency called OHM. It is the first to propose protocol-owned liquidity (POL). OHM is designed to be a stablecoin. This means that its value is pegged to a fixed amount of fiat currency, such as the U.S. dollar. Olympus DAO uses a bonding mechanism to mint new OHM tokens. When users bond their cryptocurrency, they receive OHM tokens at a discount. This discount incentivizes users to bond their cryptocurrency and helps stabilize OHM's price. Olympus DAO also uses a staking mechanism to reward users for holding OHM tokens. Users who stake their OHM tokens receive additional OHM tokens as a reward. This reward is proportional to the amount of OHM tokens the user is staking. As a result of staking and bonding, the Olympus DAO protocol allows for the direct ownership of liquidity and treasury assets. Olympus DAO aspires to create a stable and censorship-resistant reserve currency that anyone, anywhere in the world, can use.

Decentralized Autonomous Corporations (DACs)

Decentralized autonomous corporations (DACs) are an evolving organizational model in which peer-to-peer corporations will not have a central leadership or hierarchical structure (Wang et al., 2019). DACs have the potential to transform traditional corporate models into democratic and distributed organizations powered by organizational entrepreneurship and innovations (Bellavitis et al., 2023). It enforces corporate governance using Blockchain and related technologies (Kaal, 2020). Instead, they leverage cryptographic tokens and on-chain governance to facilitate distributed control and decision-making among stakeholders. It uses secure multiparty computation - a secure multiparty protocol for authorizing transactions (Wright, 2020). Proposals are voted on by token holders and executed automatically through embedded code, bringing advantages such as enhanced transparency, reduced transaction costs, and bureaucratic inefficiencies. However, DACs also present technical and social challenges because of their complete decentralization. Codifying all governance into contracts is difficult, and ongoing participation cannot be assumed. Human biases may still affect outcomes despite anonymity. Therefore, DACs now often incorporate some degree of centralized guidance to address short-term coordination needs. Future innovations could see hybrid models balancing the strengths of decentralization with centralized stewardship to optimize functionality at scale.

GOVERNANCE

Governance on a Decentralized platform is its decision-making ability. Decision-making covers all aspects, including the fee to be charged for the products being supplied. The governance in DeFi is first run by a program owned by a single individual. With the growth of the network, the authority will eventually be transferred to the community. Thus, the community takes over the decision-making authority. Such a type of transition and functioning turns into the form of a Decentralized Autonomous Organization (DAO). On a DAO, the rules and regulations are written in the computer code itself, which issues governance tokens, allowing currency holders to vote for decisions.

Working of DAOs

Individuals can join a DAO by holding a specific blockchain token. The tokens confer voting rights to members that are used to propose and vote on potential actions through on-chain governance mechanisms. These may include funding initiatives, changing operational parameters encoded in the DAO's smart contracts, or electing representatives to specified decision-making roles. Approved actions are automatically executed via smart contracts. As distributed digital entities without legacy corporate forms, DAOs aim to build more collaborative, transparent organizational models enabled by cryptography and consensus-based protocols. Opportunities exist to coordinate resources and crowd-source ideas. However, concerns remain regarding the lack of recourse, accountability, and technical security vulnerabilities.

CASE STUDIES OF DEFI GOVERNANCE

Uniswap

Uniswap is made substantial contribution for the development of the automated liquidity protocol system. Their role in establishing structures for governed decentralized exchange within the emerging DeFi ecosystem is invaluable. By facilitating an initial decentralized governance mechanism tied to its native UNI token, Uniswap has enabled open participation in collective decision-making regarding protocol upgrades and parameter adjustments. This nascent experiment in governed liquidity provisioning through an on-chain token-based framework provides valuable insights into models for porous, inclusive governance within permissionless financial networks.

Aave

The permissionless lending market Aave underpins its governance model with the LEND token, later renamed AAVE, to enable on-chain coordination and community steering of the protocol's evolutionary trajectory. By allocating voting power proportionate to token holdings and executing governance votes on-chain, Aave has pioneered a permissionless framework for democratically directing risk parameter modifications, system updates, and strategic intent for its innovative, tokenized credit provision platform within the nascent decentralized finance sector.

MakerDAO

MakerDAO has established one of the earliest examples of strong decentralized governance within open finance through its foundation upon the MKR token. Holders of MKR exercise voting powers to shape risk variables, collateral types, and upgrade proposals for the project's smart contracts, facilitating borderless stablecoin issuance. The frontier governance system incorporates elements of liquid democracy. It has withstood challenges such as Black Thursday, demonstrating how on-chain coordination mechanisms may engender resilience in autonomous organizations operating as monetary and credit market protocols. MakerDAO, therefore, provides valuable insights into implementing governed frameworks for permissionless financial systems at the Internet scale.

Challenges of DeFi Governance

Various governance challenges observed in DeFi include:

1. Because protocols are autonomous and permissionless, there is no central authority to shepherd development or make definitive decisions. This makes coordination difficult and can lead to strategic hurdles.
2. Proposals require community consensus, but stakeholders may have varying or competing objectives, making agreement complex.
3. Network effects also concentrate power, as larger token holders control protocol evolution. In many applications, governance tokens are distributed through initial coin offerings (ICOs) or airdrops, leading to unequal voting power distribution. This can result in a small group of users having disproportionate influence over decision-making processes.
4. On-chain voting is still nascent, and participation is often skewed, raising questions about accurate democratic representation. In addition, it is often unclear how the results of these votes are implemented. This can lead to user mistrust and a lack of accountability among governance participants.
5. Human biases and exploitable behaviours also translate to on-chain discussions and outcomes.
6. There are DeFi fixed standards. Most DeFi applications have their own governance models and decision-making processes, which can lead to ecosystem fragmentation. This can make it difficult for users to participate in governance and result in inconsistent outcomes across different applications.

The rapid growth of the DeFi ecosystem has magnified these issues, as protocols now manage billions in digital assets. Effective governance will require continued innovation in socio-technical solutions that balance decentralization with the need for timely, informed leadership to shepherd sustainable development. Future advancement may draw from decentralized autonomous organizations, quadratic voting, and futarchy concepts.

Voter Apathy

Voter apathy has emerged as a significant issue/challenge plaguing governance in DeFi protocols. On-chain voting processes often see only a tiny fraction of token holders participating in governance polls. The disinterest in voting stems from various reasons, such as the complexity of navigating voting interfaces, lack of tangible incentives, and not understanding proposed changes. It essentially concentrates power in the hands of a few whales or a small percentage of users who can sway outcomes. Low voter turnouts make protocols vulnerable to influence campaigns or attacks.

Many governance systems require users to hold a certain number of tokens to be eligible to vote, and the voting process itself can be pretty technical. This can make it difficult for users to participate in governance, resulting in a lack of engagement from the broader community.

In some cases, there is a lack of transparency in the governance process, while in some cases, it is unclear how decisions are being made and how the outcomes of votes are being implemented. This can lead to user mistrust and a lack of motivation to participate in the governance process.

Efforts are needed to educate users and simplify their participation. Projects are seen experimenting with proposals like quadratic voting and weighing votes by personal stakes. Engaging informal community opinion leaders also shows promise. Overcoming apathy will help optimize decentralized decision-making.

Thus, the hour needs to develop more user-friendly governance models and promote transparency. These improve DeFi governance, making it more accessible and inclusive for all users.

SECURITY ISSUES

Because of the immense value that smart contracts and DeFi services provide, they are increasing security targets. Security breaches would result in the theft of digital financial assets worth billions of dollars. The threats can arise because of logic flaws to achieve arbitrage at a low cost, such as in the case of bZx DeFi protocol breach in February 2020, the UniswapV1 re-entrancy vulnerability in April 2020, True Seigniorage Dollar (TSD) attack in 2021, Cream Finance attack in October 2021, Terra LUNA crash in 2022, Smart contract attack on Yearn Finance in 2023, amongst others (Qian et al., 2023). Increased attacks are one reason DeFi TVL decreased from $200 billion in April 2022 to $80 billion in July 2022. This drastic fall motivated researchers to systematically analyze the topic (Li et al., 2022).

The Terra-Luna crash exposes some of the risks in DeFi, making anomaly detection an important requirement of the system, for which deep learning can help (Song et al., 2023).

DeFi security developers work on different strategies and tools to protect the DeFi ecosystem from security attacks. One such strategy is to monitor each transaction in the pending transaction pool to detect potential attacks (Deng et al., 2023).

While much of the safety and security issues are handled by Blockchain, DeFi is prone to crucial loss, the honesty of service providers, and the intrusion on systems, which motivates the use of threshold signature schemes, which threshold signature schemes attempt to address (Shi et al., 2022).

DeFi offers a high degree of leverage. When these funds are used as collateral for other transactions, an undue risk emerges, leading to distress and instability in the marketplace and panic. Defi uses oracles extensively. If the data stream is compromised, manipulated, or rendered inaccurate, it can lead to the system's application layer dealing with corrupt data.

Case Studies of DeFi Security Breaches

The DAO Hack: In the spring of 2016, anonymous hackers stole around $50 million worth of Ether from "The DAO", a decentralized venture capital fund based on Ethereum Blockchain. DAO had an investment of $168 million at that time. The DAO had used smart contracts to manage investments from token holders, but hackers exploited a vulnerability to drain funds from its accounts. It highlighted issues with smart contract security and prompted a contentious hard fork to return some of the stolen funds, splitting the Ethereum blockchain. The hack showed the risks of decentralization and spurred more work on security best practices (Mehar et al., 2021).

The Poly Network Hack: In August 2021, a hacker exploited a vulnerability to steal over $600 million from Poly Network, a decentralized finance protocol. The hacker could drain crypto assets from Poly Network's systems by exploiting weaknesses in its smart contracts. Unlike other attacks, the hacker claimed that it was done for fun and to improve security and has returned most of the stolen funds. The incident highlighted the risks of DeFi apps and pushed the industry to improve security practices and auditing.

The Wormhole Hack: In February 2022, hackers exploited a bug in the Wormhole cryptocurrency platform, a bridge that allows transfers between blockchains like Ethereum and Solana. They were able to steal around $320 million worth of cryptocurrency. A $10 million bounty was offered for money returned through the Wormhole. Eventually, the community came together to propose forfeiting the stolen assets to make users whole again. The incident exposed security flaws in blockchain bridges and taught the consequences of unaudited smart contracts. Since then, new technologies have been built to identify crypto-jackers and trace out the hijackers (Subburaj et al., 2023).

LEGAL AND REGULATORY ASPECTS

Legal and regulatory uncertainty is one reason challenging the adoption of DeFi. This is a crucial area with scope for future research (Gramlich et al., 2023). Regulations on DeFi services and products are still unclear, and Governments and Regulators are still contemplating how to regulate them and to what extent they should be regulated. Further, at what level should the regulations be implemented, and how should they be enforced? How can individuals be made responsible and liable? The U.S. and Europe have begun some steps towards this (Friesendorf & Blütener, 2023c).

These financial products are not yet regulated, meaning they might pose unknown risks and little or no protection from potential financial losses to their stakeholders. Research on customer acceptance, ability, willingness, and preferences for and against DeFi is still nascent (Friesendorf & Blütener, 2023b).

According to Compound founder Robert Leshner, institutional investors love the idea of DeFi but want to use it to trade traditional assets such as stocks, bonds, and currencies, not cryptocurrencies (Aleks, 2023).

Importance of DeFi Regulations

Regulating DeFi is essential for various reasons:

1. **Protect consumers:** Regulating DeFi exchanges, lending protocols, and platforms provides needed consumer protection against fraud, hacking, and loss of funds. It establishes guidelines for safeguards and disclosures.
2. **Prevent illicit activity:** Without proper oversight and know-your-customer practices, DeFi applications could enable money laundering, terrorist financing, tax evasion, and other illegal uses more easily. Regulations aim to curb criminal abuse.
3. **Maintain financial stability:** Rapid growth and new risks introduced by DeFi warrant monitoring to identify and deal with any threats to broad financial stability, like risks of bank runs or contagion effects.
4. **Ensure equitable access:** Clear regulatory ground rules regarding securities, licensing, and eligibility can foster wider adoption of DeFi by reducing uncertainty and making the sector more approachable/inclusive to retail investors and traditional financial players.
5. **Spur continued innovation:** Certainty around applicable rules and guidelines for new business models can encourage further development and investment in DeFi as companies have a compliant framework to operate. This balances oversight with allowing technology progress.

CONCLUSION

With several futuristic features, Decentralized Finance (DeFi) has all the ingredients necessary to become the future of banking and financial services (BFS). As part of the Web 3 ecosystem, it works on top of blockchain and related technologies to revolutionary various financial services such as decentralized stablecoins, decentralized credit, lending, derivatives, and insurance, amongst others. DeFi plays a vital role in decentralized autonomous organizations and decentralized autonomous corporations. Governance plays an essential role in the functioning of DAO. The chapter ends with discussing security issues and legal and regulatory aspects.

REFERENCES

Aldasoro, I., Doerr, S., Gambacorta, L., Garratt, R., & Wilkens, P. K. (2023). *The tokenisation continuum*. BIS. https://www.bis.org/publ/bisbull72.htm

Aleks, G. (2023, September 13). *Compound founder Robert Leshner says 'institutions aren't coming' to DeFi*. DLNews. https://www.dlnews.com/articles/defi/robert-leshner-says-institutional-investors-arent-coming-to-defi/

Aspris, A., Foley, S., Svec, J., & Wang, L. (2021). Decentralized exchanges: The "wild west" of cryptocurrency trading. *International Review of Financial Analysis*, *77*, 101845. doi:10.1016/j.irfa.2021.101845

Bartholic, M., Laszka, A., Yamamoto, G., & Burger, E. W. (2022). A Taxonomy of Blockchain Oracles: The Truth Depends on the Question. *2022 IEEE International Conference on Blockchain and Cryptocurrency (ICBC)*, 1–15. 10.1109/ICBC54727.2022.9805555

Bellavitis, C., Fisch, C., & Momtaz, P. P. (2023). The rise of decentralized autonomous organizations (DAOs): A first empirical glimpse. *Venture Capital, 25*(2), 187–203. doi:10.1080/13691066.2022.2116797

Carapella, F., Chuan, G., Gerszten, J., Hunter, C., & Swem, N. (2023). Tokenization: Overview and Financial Stability Implications. *Finance and Economics Discussion Series, 60*, 1–29. doi:10.17016/feds.2023.060

CoinGecko. (2023, July 17). *2023 Q1 Crypto Industry Report*. https://www.coingecko.com/research/publications/2023-q1-crypto-report

Coingecko. (2023, September 9). *Top Liquid Staking Governance Tokens Coins by Market Cap*. https://www.coingecko.com/en/categories/liquid-staking-governance-tokens

DeFi Llarma. (2023). *DeFi Llarma*. https://defillama.com/

Deng, X., Zhao, Z., Beillahi, S. M., Du, H., Minwalla, C., Nelaturu, K., Veneris, A., & Long, F. (2023). A Robust Front-Running Methodology for Malicious Flash- Loan DeFi Attacks. *2023 IEEE International Conference on Decentralized Applications and Infrastructures (DAPPS)*, 38–47. 10.1109/DAPPS57946.2023.00015

Friesendorf, C., & Blütener, A. (2023a). Decentralized Finance: Concept and Characteristics. In Decentralized Finance (DeFi) (pp. 29–36). Springer Nature Switzerland. doi:10.1007/978-3-031-37488-3_3

Friesendorf, C., & Blütener, A. (2023b). Decentralized Finance: Empirical Analysis of Customer Willingness. In Decentralized Finance (DeFi) (pp. 75–94). Springer Nature Switzerland. doi:10.1007/978-3-031-37488-3_10

Friesendorf, C., & Blütener, A. (2023c). Decentralized Finance: Regulation. In Decentralized Finance (DeFi) (pp. 55–59). Springer Nature Switzerland. doi:10.1007/978-3-031-37488-3_7

Frtisch, R., Käser, S., & Wattenhofer, R. (2022). The Economics of Automated Market Makers. *Proceedings of the 4th ACM Conference on Advances in Financial Technologies*, 102–110. 10.1145/3558535.3559790

Gramlich, V., Guggenberger, T., Principato, M., Schellinger, B., & Urbach, N. (2023). A multivocal literature review of decentralized finance: Current knowledge and future research avenues. *Electronic Markets, 33*(1), 11. doi:10.1007/s12525-023-00637-4

Kaal, W. A. (2020). Decentralized Corporate Governance via Blockchain Technology. *Annals of Corporate Governance, 5*(2), 101–147. doi:10.1561/109.00000025

Kaur, G., Habibi Lashkari, A., Sharafaldin, I., & Habibi Lashkari, Z. (2023a). DeFi Platforms. In Understanding Cybersecurity Management in Decentralized Finance (pp. 57–70). Springer International Publishing. doi:10.1007/978-3-031-23340-1_3

Kaur, G., Habibi Lashkari, A., Sharafaldin, I., & Habibi Lashkari, Z. (2023b). The Origin of Modern Decentralized Finance. In Understanding Cybersecurity Management in Decentralized Finance (pp. 1–28). Springer International Publishing. doi:10.1007/978-3-031-23340-1_1

Li, W., Bu, J., Li, X., Peng, H., Niu, Y., & Zhang, Y. (2022). A survey of DeFi security: Challenges and opportunities. *Journal of King Saud University. Computer and Information Sciences*, *34*(10), 10378–10404. doi:10.1016/j.jksuci.2022.10.028

Lim, Y. Q. (2023, June 26). *DeFi Ecosystem: Categories by Market Share*. https://www.coingecko.com/research/publications/defi-categories-market-share

Lo, Y. C., & Medda, F. (2022). Do DEXs work? Using Uniswap V2 to explore the effectiveness of decentralized exchanges. *Journal of Financial Market Infrastructures*. doi:10.21314/JFMI.2022.004

MarxF. (2022). *Banking without banks? An analysis of the opportunities and threats for commercial banks resulting from DeFi, Metaverse, and Web 3.0*. doi:10.13140/RG.2.2.36020.01923

McGhin, T., Eyal, I., Mirhoseini, Z. S., Zhang, J., & Juels, A. (2021). Smart contracts for fair exchange: Applications to trade finance. ACM Transactions on Economics and Computation.

Mehar, M. I., Shier, C. L., Giambattista, A., Gong, E., Fletcher, G., Sanayhie, R., Kim, H. M., & Laskowski, M. (2021). Understanding a Revolutionary and Flawed Grand Experiment in Blockchain: The DAO Attack. In Research Anthology on Blockchain Technology in Business, Healthcare, Education, and Government (pp. 1253–1266). IGI Global. doi:10.4018/978-1-7998-5351-0.ch069

NadlerM.BekemeierF.SchärF. (2022). *DeFi Risk Transfer: Towards A Fully Decentralized Insurance Protocol*. doi:10.48550/ARXIV.2212.10308

Panwar, G., Misra, S., & Vishwanathan, R. (2019). BlAnC: Blockchain-based Anonymous and Decentralized Credit Networks. *Proceedings of the Ninth ACM Conference on Data and Application Security and Privacy*, 339–350. 10.1145/3292006.3300034

Pop, C., Pop, C., Marcel, A., Vesa, A., Petrican, T., Cioara, T., Anghel, I., & Salomie, I. (2018). Decentralizing the Stock Exchange using Blockchain An Ethereum-based implementation of the Bucharest Stock Exchange. *2018 IEEE 14th International Conference on Intelligent Computer Communication and Processing (ICCP)*, 459–466. 10.1109/ICCP.2018.8516610

Qian, P., Cao, R., Liu, Z., Li, W., Li, M., Zhang, L., Xu, Y., Chen, J., & He, Q. (2023). *Empirical Review of Smart Contract and DeFi Security: Vulnerability Detection and Automated Repair* (arXiv:2309.02391). arXiv. http://arxiv.org/abs/2309.02391

Saengchote, K. (2023). Decentralized lending and its users: Insights from compound. *Journal of International Financial Markets, Institutions and Money*, *87*, 101807. doi:10.1016/j.intfin.2023.101807

Saengchote, K., Putniņš, T., & Samphantharak, K. (2023). Does DeFi remove the need for trust? Evidence from a natural experiment in stablecoin lending. *Journal of Behavioral and Experimental Finance*, *100858*, 100858. Advance online publication. doi:10.1016/j.jbef.2023.100858

Sheth, A., & Subramanian, H. (2019). Blockchain and contract theory: Modeling smart contracts using insurance markets. *Managerial Finance*, *46*(6), 803–814. doi:10.1108/MF-10-2018-0510

Shi, Y., Liang, J., Li, M., Ma, T., Ye, G., Li, J., & Zhao, Q. (2022). Threshold EdDSA Signature for Blockchain-based Decentralized Finance Applications. *25th International Symposium on Research in Attacks, Intrusions and Defenses*, 129–142. 10.1145/3545948.3545977

Song, A., Seo, E., & Kim, H. (2023). Anomaly VAE-Transformer: A Deep Learning Approach for Anomaly Detection in Decentralized Finance. *IEEE Access : Practical Innovations, Open Solutions*, *11*, 98115–98131. doi:10.1109/ACCESS.2023.3313448

StepanovaV.ErinšI. (2021). Review of Decentralized Finance Applications and Their Total Value Locked. *TEM Journal*, 327–333. https://doi.org/ doi:10.18421/TEM101-41

Suarez Barcia, L. (2023). Decentralized Finance Oracles. *Journal of New Finance*, *3*(1). Advance online publication. doi:10.46671/2521-2486.1016

Subburaj, T., Shilpa, K., Sultana, S., Suthendran, K., Karuppasamy, M., Arun Kumar, S., & Jyothi Babu, A. (2023). Discover Crypto-Jacker from Blockchain Using AFS Method. In K. A. Reddy, B. R. Devi, B. George, K. S. Raju, & M. Sellathurai (Eds.), *Proceedings of Fourth International Conference on Computer and Communication Technologies* (*Vol. 606*, pp. 145–156). Springer Nature Singapore. 10.1007/978-981-19-8563-8_15

TolmachP.LiY.LinS.-W.LiuY. (2021). Formal Analysis of Composable DeFi Protocols (arXiv:2103.00540). doi:10.1007/978-3-662-63958-0_13

Wang, S., Ding, W., Li, J., Yuan, Y., Ouyang, L., & Wang, F.-Y. (2019). Decentralized Autonomous Organizations: Concept, Model, and Applications. *IEEE Transactions on Computational Social Systems*, *6*(5), 870–878. doi:10.1109/TCSS.2019.2938190

Wright, C. S. (2020). Decentralized Autonomous Corporations. In X.-S. Yang, S. Sherratt, N. Dey, & A. Joshi (Eds.), *Fourth International Congress on Information and Communication Technology* (*Vol. 1027*, pp. 153–167). Springer Singapore. 10.1007/978-981-32-9343-4_14

Zetzsche, D. A., Arner, D. W., & Buckley, R. P. (2020). Decentralized Finance. *Journal of Financial Regulation*, *6*(2), 172–203. doi:10.1093/jfr/fjaa010

KEY TERMS AND DEFINITIONS

Decentralized Finance (DeFi): A financial system that is built on blockchain technology with an aim to remove intermediaries like banks and financial institutions during financial transactions. DeFi protocols allow users to borrow, lend, trade, and invest assets directly with each other, often using smart contracts.

Decentralized Insurance (DeFi): A peer-to-peer insurance system built on blockchain technology. DeFi insurance protocols allow users to create and purchase insurance policies without relying on traditional insurance companies. Claims are typically governed by smart contracts and decided by a community of stakeholders.

Financial Derivatives: Financial contracts whose value is derived from the underlying value of another asset, such as a stock, bond, or commodity. In DeFi, derivatives can be used for hedging, speculation, and leverage.

Flash Loan: A type of uncollateralized loan in DeFi where a borrower can access a pool of funds for a short period (usually seconds) without any upfront collateral. Flash loans are often used for arbitrage opportunities or complex DeFi transactions.

Insurance Claim: A request for compensation made by a policyholder to an insurance company after a covered event, such as a loss or damage. In DeFi insurance, claims are typically submitted and adjudicated through smart contracts and community governance.

Liquid Staking: A process of staking cryptocurrencies to earn rewards while still maintaining some degree of liquidity. Liquid staking platforms issue derivative tokens that represent staked assets, which can be traded or used in other DeFi applications.

Liquidity Pool: A collection of cryptocurrencies deposited into a smart contract to facilitate trading. Liquidity pools are used by decentralized exchanges (DEXs) to allow users to buy and sell cryptocurrencies without relying on a central order book.

Network Protocol: A set of rules that govern the communication and interaction between nodes in a blockchain network. Different protocols have different features and functionalities, such as consensus mechanisms, transaction formats, and smart contract capabilities.

Offchain Assets: Assets that exist outside of a blockchain network, such as fiat currency, real estate, or intellectual property. Offchain assets can be represented and traded on blockchain networks using tokenization.

Onchain Assets: Assets that exist natively on a blockchain network, such as cryptocurrencies, stablecoins, and non-fungible tokens (NFTs). Onchain assets are secured by the blockchain's distributed ledger and can be directly transferred between users.

Chapter 7
NFTs:
Transforming Digital Ownership in the Web 3 Era

Pankaj Bhambri
https://orcid.org/0000-0003-4437-4103
Guru Nanak Dev Engineering College, Ludhiana, India

ABSTRACT

This chapter delves into the revolutionary landscape of non-fungible tokens (NFTs) and their profound impact on reshaping digital ownership within the framework of Web 3 technologies. NFTs have emerged as a unique form of digital asset, utilizing blockchain technology to certify and authenticate ownership of digital content, be it art, music, virtual real estate, or other digital assets. The chapter provides a comprehensive exploration of the underlying technology that powers NFTs, elucidating the role of smart contracts and decentralized ledgers in ensuring the scarcity and provenance of these digital assets. The chapter further delves into the economic and cultural implications of the NFT phenomenon, examining the way in which these tokens have disrupted traditional models of intellectual property and content monetization. It explores the democratizing potential of NFTs, allowing creators to directly engage with their audiences and enabling new forms of digital expression.

1. INTRODUCTION

In the era of Web3, characterized by a focus on decentralization, the emergence of Non-Fungible Tokens (NFTs) has become a significant catalyst for change. These tokens facilitate the ownership of digital assets in a manner that is distinct, verifiable, and indivisible. The chapter explores the complexities of blockchain technology, smart contracts, and tokenization to elucidate the decentralized framework offered by NFTs for the verification and exchange of digital material (Zohar, 2015). The discourse delves into the varied uses of NFTs, encompassing domains such as art, collectibles, digital real estate, and more. It highlights the significance of NFTs in transforming the online realm, facilitating novel economic frameworks, and empowering both artists and users within the decentralized environment. Figure 1 demonstrates the examples of fungible and non-fungible tokens. Each NFT possesses a distinct functionality

DOI: 10.4018/979-8-3693-1532-3.ch007

or characteristic that cannot be compared to other NFTs. NFTs are tokens that serve as representations of digital art, real estate, or valuable gemstones such as diamonds.

Figure 1. Examples of fungible and non-fungible tokens

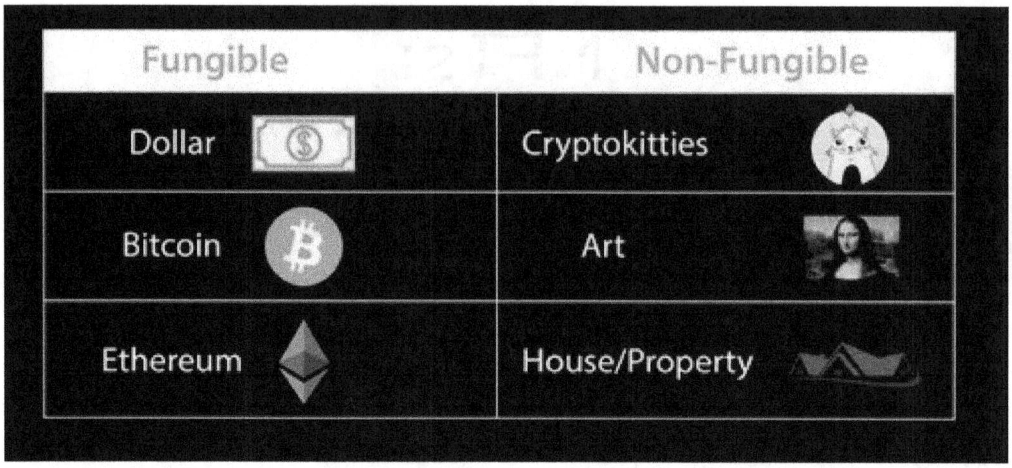

By employing astute analyses and concrete illustrations, the chapter elucidates the capacity of NFTs to act as agents of transformative change in our understanding, valuation, and transaction of digital assets within the dynamic domain of Web3 technologies.

1.1 Definition of NFTs

NFTs embody distinctive digital assets that possess the qualities of indivisibility, distinctiveness, and distinguishability from one another within the context of a blockchain ecosystem. In contrast to fungible crypto-currencies like Bitcoin or Ethereum, NFTs include a unique identifier, rendering them irreplaceable and distinctive, hence precluding one-to-one exchangeability. NFTs utilize blockchain technology, commonly adhering to established protocols such as ERC-721 or ERC-1155, to guarantee the verifiable ownership, authenticity, and provenance of digital assets. These assets encompass a wide range of digital content, including but not limited to digital art, collectibles, virtual real estate, and in-game items. Brief differences between the fungible and non-fungible tokens are shared in Table 1.

Table 1. Differences between fungible and non-fungible tokens

Parameters	Fungible	Non-Fungible
Exchangability	Fungible tokens can be exchanged with other tokens of the same type	Non-Fungible tokens cannot be exchanged with similar type NFT's. For eg:- A car cannot be exchanged with another car
Uniformity	All Fungible tokens are identical to each other	NFT's are unique and not similar to each other
Fractionalisation	Fungible tokens can be divided into smaller units. For eg: a $100 note can be exchanged with another $100 or two $50 tokens	NFT's cannot be divided but are one entire unit

Blockchain technology ensures the secure recording of ownership and transaction history of NFTs, thereby establishing a visible and unalterable ledger. This innovative concept has significantly transformed the concept of digital ownership by facilitating producers and users to generate genuine scarcity and uniqueness inside the digital domain. As a result, it has brought about a fundamental change in our understanding, exchange, and valuation of digital assets in the era of Web3.

1.2 Evolution of Digital Ownership

Originally bound to centralized models, the notion of digital ownership has transformed, expanding beyond its traditional association with conventional intellectual property to encompass a broader scope inside the decentralized environment. The introduction of blockchain technology, particularly with the rise of NFTs and smart contracts, has resulted in a transformation of the concept of digital ownership. This transformation is characterized by a trend towards decentralized systems that offer transparency and verifiability. The progression described has enabled individuals to acquire, exchange, and generate financial value from a diverse range of digital assets, encompassing distinctive digital artwork and collectibles, as well as real-world items that have been tokenized (Narayanan et al., 2016; Pilkington, 2016). The convergence of blockchain, encryption, and decentralized technologies has significantly transformed the discourse surrounding digital ownership, presenting novel opportunities for robust and immutable governance in the era of Web3.

1.3 Significance in the Web 3 Context

NFTs, which leverage blockchain technology and smart contracts, offer unprecedented levels of transparency, immutability, and distinctiveness inside the digital domain. In the era of Web3, NFTs transcend their tokenized nature and represent a paradigm shift that enables individuals to genuinely possess and verify digital property. This encompasses a wide range of items, including artwork, collectibles, virtual real estate, and in-game assets. This innovative technology possesses the capacity to revolutionize various industries through the provision of a decentralized and transparent ecosystem. This ecosystem facilitates the exchange of digital assets, establishes ownership, and determines the genuine worth of such assets for producers and users alike.

2. FOUNDATIONS OF NFTS

NFTs represent unique and indivisible digital assets, often leveraging blockchain standards like ERC-721 or ERC-1155, which grant each token a distinct identity and verifiable scarcity. The central idea pertains to the establishment of a robust and transparent framework that enables the verification of ownership and genuineness of digital assets, including various forms such as artwork, music, virtual properties, and in-game objects. Smart contracts, embedded within the blockchain, underpin the functionality of NFTs, ensuring programmable and trustless execution of transactions. The advent of this revolutionary technology has significantly disrupted conventional conceptions of digital property rights. It has enabled creators and collectors to establish verifiable ownership of their digital assets. Furthermore, decentralized platforms and marketplaces have emerged to facilitate the exchange and monetization of these distinctive digital assets. Consequently, this development has ushered in a novel era of digital ownership within the broader Web3 environment.

2.1 Blockchain Technology Overview

Blockchain technology is a decentralized and distributed ledger system that facilitates the secure and transparent recording of transactions over a network of computers. Fundamentally, a blockchain is comprised of a sequence of blocks, wherein each block encompasses a collection of transactions, interconnected through cryptographic hashes. The immutability of blockchain is a prominent characteristic, whereby the addition of a block to the chain renders past transactions highly resistant to modification, hence safeguarding the integrity of the entire ledger. Consensus mechanisms, such as Proof of Work (PoW) or Proof of Stake (PoS), are utilized to authenticate and reach a consensus over the current state of the blockchain. This technological advancement obviates the necessity of middlemen across diverse sectors, offering a trustless and highly efficient means of executing transactions. Blockchain finds applications beyond crypto-currencies, extending to fields like supply chain management, healthcare, finance, and more, offering a revolutionary approach to data management and trust in the digital age.

2.2 Smart Contracts and NFT Standards

Smart contracts and NFT standards, such as ERC-721 and ERC-1155, play a crucial role in decentralized ecosystems by enabling the generation, transfer, and administration of distinct digital assets on blockchain networks. Smart contracts are a type of self-executing code that is kept on a blockchain. These contracts serve the purpose of automating and enforcing the terms of agreements. By doing so, they facilitate transparent and tamper-proof execution of established conditions. In the context of NFTs, ERC-721 and ERC-1155 are pivotal standards that define how these unique, indivisible digital assets are created and interact within decentralized applications (dApps). ERC-721, the first widely adopted NFT standard, ensures the uniqueness and ownership of each token, making it ideal for digital art and collectibles. In contrast, ERC-1155 presents a more adaptable methodology by enabling the generation of both fungible and non-fungible tokens within a singular contract, hence augmenting operational effectiveness and mitigating blockchain congestion (Swan, 2015; Mougayar, 2016). These standards have a significant impact on facilitating a diverse range of applications, including the ownership of digital art and gaming assets, as well as the tokenization of real-world assets. This paves the way for a new era characterized by digital ownership and decentralized applications.

2.3 Tokenization of Digital Assets

The concept of tokenization in the context of digital assets pertains to the procedure of utilizing blockchain technology to establish digital tokens that reflect ownership or entitlements to both physical and virtual assets. These tokens are assets that can be programmed and utilize blockchain technology, enabling the division of ownership and the capacity to transfer assets securely and transparently. Tokenization facilitates the transformation of previously less liquid assets, like as real estate or art, into divisible and tradable units, hence enhancing liquidity and expanding accessibility to a wider array of investors. The utilization of smart contracts facilitates the automation of multiple facets of asset management, encompassing the allocation of dividends, granting of voting rights, and adherence to regulatory obligations, inside the tokenization process. The aforementioned disruptive strategy serves to democratize access to investments and also brings about efficiency, transparency, and security to the ownership and transfer of assets within the dynamic realm of decentralized finance and Web3 technologies.

3. LITERATURE REVIEW

As NFTs continue to gain prominence, this literature review establishes a foundation for understanding the multifaceted impact of NFTs on digital ownership within the context of the Web3 era. Further research is needed to explore the evolving landscape of NFTs and their implications for various industries and user experiences.

3.1 NFTs and Digital Ownership in the Web 3 Era

In recent years, the emergence of Web3 technologies has significantly transformed the landscape of digital ownership, with Non-Fungible Tokens (NFTs) standing out as a key innovation. NFTs are unique cryptographic tokens that represent ownership of specific digital or physical assets, often stored on blockchain platforms. This literature review explores existing research on NFTs, examining their impact on digital ownership and their role in the evolving Web3 ecosystem.

3.2 NFTs and Blockchain Technology

Blockchain technology serves as the foundation for NFTs, providing a secure and transparent decentralized ledger for recording ownership. Antonopoulos (2014) emphasized the importance of blockchain in establishing trust and eliminating intermediaries in digital transactions. The immutability and transparency of blockchain contribute to the authenticity of NFTs, ensuring the integrity of digital ownership records.

3.3 Digital Ownership and NFTs in the Creative Industries

Research has highlighted the transformative impact of NFTs on the creative industries, particularly in art and music. A study by Zohar and Abbe (2020) explored how NFTs enable artists to tokenize their work, creating new revenue streams and establishing direct relationships with their audiences. The study emphasized the potential for NFTs to democratize the art market and empower creators.

3.4 Challenges and Critiques of NFTs

While NFTs offer exciting possibilities, researchers have also identified challenges and critiques associated with their adoption. Swan (2015) discussed the environmental concerns related to energy-intensive blockchain networks, raising questions about the sustainability of NFTs. Additionally, debates around copyright issues and the potential for digital asset theft have been subjects of scholarly discourse (Jones et al., 2021).

3.5 NFTs Beyond Art: Real-World Applications

Beyond the creative industries, NFTs have found applications in diverse sectors. Tapscott and Tapscott (2016) argued that NFTs could revolutionize supply chain management by providing transparent and traceable ownership records for physical goods. This expands the scope of NFTs beyond the digital realm, showcasing their potential to reshape traditional industries.

3.6 Web3 and the Future of Digital Ownership

The integration of NFTs into the Web3 era signifies a paradigm shift in how individuals interact with digital assets. Grigg (2018) conceptualized Web3 as a user-centric, decentralized web experience enabled by blockchain technologies. NFTs, as integral components of Web3, play a pivotal role in reshaping the dynamics of digital ownership, fostering a more inclusive and equitable online environment.

4. DECENTRALIZED OWNERSHIP AND PROVENANCE

Decentralized ownership ensures that individuals have direct control over their digital possessions, be it crypto-currency, NFTs, or other tokenized assets. Simultaneously, provenance, as facilitated by blockchain's immutable ledger, establishes an unalterable record of the origin, history, and ownership transitions of these digital assets (Tondon and Bhambri, 2017). The integration of this combination not only serves as a protective measure against fraudulent activities and unauthorized alterations but also cultivates a sense of confidence in the realm of digital transactions and the genuineness of digital artifacts. Consequently, it has the potential to reshape the current state of digital ownership and facilitate the development of a fairer and more transparent online environment.

4.1 Immutable Ledger and Transparency

An immutable ledger denotes a distributed and impervious repository of transactions, wherein once data is documented, it remains unmodifiable or removable. This functionality is accomplished by employing cryptographic hashing and consensus techniques that are inherent in blockchain protocols. The preservation of the ledger's immutability guarantees a significant degree of integrity and trustworthiness in digital transactions. In contrast, transparency entails the provision of readily available and easily accessible information to all pertinent stakeholders. Transparency is an inherent characteristic within the realm of blockchain technology, mostly owing to the distributed nature of the ledger. This decentralized structure enables participants within the network to have the ability to observe and authenticate transactions in real-time (Buterin, 2017; Croman et al., 2016). The amalgamation of an unchangeable ledger and the attribute of transparency facilitates a novel framework of responsibility, diminishing the likelihood of deceitful activities, guaranteeing the authenticity of information, and augmenting the overall confidence in decentralized systems. The aforementioned attribute possesses extensive ramifications in diverse sectors, encompassing finance, supply chain, healthcare, and other domains. It provides a reliable and transparent basis for the advancement of digital interactions in the age of Web3.

4.2 Proof of Authenticity

The establishment of provenance for a digital asset is of utmost importance in many fields including art, collectibles, and digital media. To address this difficulty, Proof of Authenticity offers a viable solution. By leveraging blockchain technology, namely through the implementation of technologies such as NFTs and cryptographic hashing, the Proof of Authenticity protocol establishes a robust and transparent ledger that documents the origin, ownership, and chronological sequence of transactions about a given asset. The cryptographic proof possesses characteristics of immutability, timestamping, and public accessibility, hence facilitating users in verifying the genuineness of a digital asset by tracing its complete historical record on the blockchain. As the digital landscape evolves, Proof of Authenticity becomes a foundational concept, empowering creators and owners to assert the legitimacy of their digital possessions in a trustless and decentralized manner.

4.3 Advantages of Traditional Ownership Models

Unlike traditional ownership records that can be forged or tampered with, NFTs leverage blockchain technology to create an immutable and transparent ledger. This feature guarantees a verifiable and traceable record for every digital asset, providing a degree of authenticity that was previously difficult to attain in the digital domain.

One notable benefit is the programmability aspect of NFTs facilitated by smart contracts. Smart contracts facilitate the implementation of self-executing agreements that incorporate predetermined rules, thereby automating diverse facets of ownership, including but not limited to royalties, resale conditions, and revenue distribution. This feature revolutionizes the way artists, content creators, and even game developers can monetize their work. NFTs allow for the automatic and transparent distribution of royalties to creators every time the digital asset is sold or used, eliminating the need for intermediaries and ensuring a fair compensation structure.

NFTs also introduce the concept of fractional ownership, allowing multiple individuals to own a share of a digital asset. This democratizes access to valuable digital content and enables a broader audience to participate in the ownership and appreciation of digital art, music, or other forms of digital media. This fractional ownership model can be particularly empowering for emerging artists and creators, as it provides new avenues for monetization and exposure.

Furthermore, NFTs address the issue of interoperability by providing a standardized format for digital ownership. This means that NFTs can be easily transferred and traded across different platforms and marketplaces, fostering a more interconnected and dynamic digital economy. Traditional ownership models often face challenges when it comes to transferring and proving ownership outside of specific contexts, and NFTs provide a solution to this limitation.

5. NFT USE CASES

NFTs have attracted considerable attention owing to their distinctive capacity to symbolize ownership and establish the authenticity of digital assets on the blockchain. The utilization of NFTs encompasses a wide array of sectors, leading to a paradigm shift in our understanding, exchange, and engagement with digital assets. Within the domain of art and entertainment, NFTs serve as a means of empowering creators through the establishment of a secure and transparent framework for the tokenization and sale of their artistic endeavors. This, in turn, facilitates the cultivation of a direct and mutually beneficial connection between creators and their audiences. Moreover, NFTs are bringing about a significant transformation in the gaming sector by facilitating the authentic ownership and exchange of in-game assets across diverse platforms. Beyond the creative sphere, NFTs find applications in real estate, proving ownership and facilitating transparent transactions. The technology has also extended to virtual goods, identity verification, and even environmental initiatives, showcasing the versatility and potential societal impact of NFTs in the Web3 era.

5.1 Digital Art and NFTs

NFTs provide a blockchain-based solution to the long-standing challenge of establishing provenance and ownership in the digital art world. Through tokenization, digital artworks become unique, indivisible assets, allowing artists to authenticate and monetize their creations directly on decentralized platforms (Eyal et al., 2014; Garzik, 2014). The inherent immutability of blockchain technology guarantees a visible and traceable record of ownership, thereby mitigating concerns about piracy and unauthorized replication (Zyskind et al., 2015). Moreover, NFTs enable artists to embed programmable smart contracts; ensuring creators receive a percentage of sales in perpetuity. This transformative synergy between digital art and NFTs not only redefines the economics of the art market but also democratizes access for artists, fostering a global, decentralized ecosystem where creativity and ownership are seamlessly intertwined.

5.2 Collectibles and Memorabilia

Collectibles and memorabilia hold a significant place in various cultures, serving as tangible representations of historical moments, cultural phenomena, and personal memories. These items, whether they be vintage toys, sports memorabilia, or historical artifacts, often evoke nostalgia and sentimentality, fostering a connection between individuals and their past. In the digital age, the concept of collectibles has expanded into the virtual realm, with NFTs playing a pivotal role. NFTs enable the ownership and authentication of digital collectibles, allowing users to buy, sell, and trade unique items in the form of blockchain-based assets. This transformation has not only digitized the traditional notion of collecting but has also introduced new opportunities for artists, creators, and enthusiasts to engage with and showcase their work in decentralized digital marketplaces (Gervais et al., 2016).

The convergence of collectibles and memorabilia with blockchain technology and NFTs has brought about a paradigm shift in the perception and engagement of individuals with digital assets. With NFTs, individuals can own and trade unique digital items, ranging from virtual art pieces and music albums to in-game items and virtual real estate. The blockchain ensures the provenance and authenticity of these digital collectibles, providing a secure and transparent ledger of ownership (Bathla et al., 2007). This fusion of technology and collectibles has not only created new avenues for artists and content creators to monetize their work but has also democratized access to unique and valuable digital assets, allowing a global audience to participate in the ownership and appreciation of digital memorabilia. As the Web3 era unfolds, the concept of collectibles and memorabilia is undergoing a transformative shift, bringing together the tangible and digital worlds in a way that resonates with both collectors and enthusiasts alike (Poon and Dryja, 2016).

5.3 Tokenized Real Estate and Virtual Assets

By leveraging blockchain's capabilities, these tokenized assets enable the fractionalization of traditionally illiquid and high-entry-barrier assets like real estate, artwork, or virtual items in digital environments (Singh et al., 2013). Tokenization involves representing ownership or rights to these assets through blockchain-based tokens, providing a more accessible and efficient means for individuals to invest in or trade portions of these assets (Zohar, 2015). This innovation not only democratizes access to investment opportunities but also enhances liquidity in markets that were historically limited by geographic constraints and regulatory hurdles. Moreover, the transparency, security, and programmability of smart contracts inherent in blockchain technology contribute to a more seamless and trustless process for transactions and ownership transfers, ultimately reshaping the landscape of asset ownership and investment in the digital age.

5.4 NFTs in Gaming and Virtual Worlds

By leveraging blockchain technology, NFTs enable gamers to truly own in-game assets, such as characters, items, and skins, as these digital assets are tokenized and recorded on a decentralized ledger. This not only enhances player autonomy and control over their virtual possessions but also opens up new avenues for the creation of unique, scarce, and tradable items (Szabo, 1997). Gamers can buy, sell, and trade NFTs both within and outside gaming ecosystems, fostering a vibrant digital economy. Additionally, NFTs introduce the concept of 'play-to-earn,' where players can earn real-world value through their in-game achievements and assets. This transformative intersection of NFTs and gaming not only enhances the gaming experience but also blurs the lines between the virtual and real worlds, creating a dynamic and participatory gaming ecosystem."

6. NFT MARKETPLACES

NFT marketplaces are digital platforms that facilitate the creation, buying, selling, and trading of unique digital assets represented by NFTs (Brown and Jones, 2018). These marketplaces leverage blockchain technology, often built on platforms like Ethereum, to ensure the authenticity, scarcity, and ownership of digital content. Popular NFT marketplaces include OpenSea, Rarible, and Mintable (Tapscott and Tapscott, 2016). These platforms act as decentralized market hubs where artists, creators, and collectors can engage in transactions without relying on traditional intermediaries.

6.1 User Experience and Interface

The user experience in NFT marketplaces is crucial for fostering widespread adoption (Gupta and Bhambri, 2012). These platforms typically feature intuitive interfaces that allow users to easily browse, discover, and interact with NFTs. Users can showcase their digital assets, explore curated collections, and participate in auctions or fixed-price sales. A seamless and user-friendly interface is essential for both creators uploading their work and collectors navigating the marketplace (Wood, 2014). Many platforms incorporate user profiles, customizable galleries, and social features to enhance the overall experience and encourage community engagement.

6.2 Legal and Regulatory Considerations

As the NFT space continues to grow, legal and regulatory considerations become increasingly important (Ethereum Project, 2022). NFT marketplaces must address issues related to intellectual property rights, copyright, and ownership verification. Ensuring that creators receive fair compensation and that buyers have legitimate ownership claims is crucial (Finney, 2004). Moreover, there is an increasing prevalence of adherence to regional and international legislation in the realm of NFTs, particularly regarding anti-money laundering (AML) and know-your-customer (KYC) obligations. NFT marketplaces need to implement robust legal frameworks and adhere to industry best practices to navigate potential legal challenges and ensure a secure and trustworthy environment for users.

7. SMART CONTRACTS AND PROGRAMMABLE OWNERSHIP

Smart contracts and programmable ownership are highly innovative features of blockchain technology, specifically NFTs, which introduce novel perspectives on digital assets and ownership.

7.1 Programmability of NFTs

Traditional ownership of digital assets often lacks flexibility and control, but with smart contracts, NFTs can embody programmable features. These smart contracts allow for the implementation of specific rules and conditions governing the use and transfer of NFTs. For instance, creators can embed rules specifying how the digital asset can be utilized, transferred, or even replicated. This programmability adds a layer of dynamism to ownership, enabling creators to express and enforce specific terms and conditions associated with their digital creations.

7.2 Conditional Transfers and Automated Royalties

Smart contracts facilitate conditional transfers, hence enabling the automated execution of predetermined activities upon the fulfillment of specific conditions (Bhambri et al., 2019; Abrol et al., 2005). Within the realm of NFTs, it can be observed that the transfer of ownership can be subject to particular circumstances, hence enabling a form of conditional ownership that was previously unattainable. Moreover, the integration of automated royalty systems within smart contracts can guarantee that creators are entitled to a predetermined percentage of all future sales or use of their NFTs. This not only empowers creators by automating revenue streams but also ensures a fair and transparent compensation system, directly facilitated by the self-executing nature of smart contracts.

7.3 NFTs in Decentralized Finance (DeFi)

Smart contracts enable the integration of NFTs into financial instruments and protocols, allowing users to collateralize their digital assets for loans or participate in decentralized exchanges (Heilman et al., 2015) This intersection of NFTs and DeFi unlocks liquidity for NFT holders, transforming these unique digital assets into fungible tokens for financial transactions. The capacity to program smart contracts enhances the development of intricate financial instruments, hence enabling novel opportunities for innovation in the decentralized financial domain.

8. INTEROPERABILITY AND STANDARDS

The decentralized nature of Web3 technologies calls for seamless interactions between different blockchain networks and dApps (Dai and Vasileiou, 2020). This is where interoperability becomes crucial.

8.1 Interoperability Challenges and Solutions

Interoperability challenges arise because different blockchain networks may have distinct architectures, consensus mechanisms, and smart contract languages (Kaur et al., 2012). This diversity can hinder the smooth transfer and recognition of NFTs across platforms. To address this, developers and blockchain communities are actively working on interoperability solutions. Interoperability protocols, such as cross-chain bridges and standards like the Interledger Protocol (ILP), are being developed to facilitate the transfer of NFTs across disparate blockchains (Nakamoto, 2008). Additionally, middleware solutions are emerging to create a layer of abstraction, enabling decentralized applications to interact seamlessly with various blockchain networks.

8.2 Emerging NFT Standards

The Ethereum blockchain has witnessed extensive acceptance of established standards, namely ERC-721 and ERC-1155. However, emerging NFT standards are being proposed and developed to cater to the evolving needs of the Web3 ecosystem. These standards aim to address issues like gas fees, scalability, and environmental concerns. For example, Layer-2 scaling solutions and more energy-efficient consensus mechanisms are being explored. The development of these standards contributes to a more sustainable and user-friendly NFT ecosystem.

8.3 Cross-Chain NFTs

Cross-chain NFTs enable NFTs to move seamlessly between different blockchain networks, allowing users to access and trade digital assets across ecosystems (Tapscott and Tapscott, 2016). Various projects are experimenting with cross-chain solutions, including interoperability protocols and bridges that connect blockchains. These endeavors aim to create a unified experience for users and expand the reach and utility of NFTs beyond individual blockchain silos (Zheng et al., 2018). The success of cross-chain NFTs is closely tied to the establishment of interoperability standards, ensuring a harmonious and secure transfer of digital assets across diverse blockchain environments.

9. CULTURAL IMPACT OF NFTS

The cultural impact of NFTs extends beyond the realm of digital ownership, influencing various aspects of identity, empowerment, and social dynamics. One notable facet is the intersection of NFTs and digital identity. NFTs provide a unique and immutable representation of digital assets on the blockchain, linking them to individuals or entities. This association contributes to the establishment of digital identity in the Web3 era, where ownership and authenticity are verifiable and traceable. NFTs enable creators and users to express their identity through the digital assets they own, fostering a sense of individuality and uniqueness in the virtual space (Catalini and Gans, 2016).

Moreover, NFTs play a pivotal role in the empowerment of creators and users. Traditionally, artists and content creators have faced challenges in asserting control over their work and receiving fair compensation. NFTs disrupt this paradigm by allowing creators to tokenize their digital assets, establishing clear ownership, and providing a direct means for monetization through blockchain-based marketplaces. This empowerment extends to users who can actively participate in supporting and engaging with the content they appreciate. The decentralized nature of NFT transactions ensures that creators and users have a more direct and transparent relationship, circumventing traditional intermediaries.

The social and cultural implications of NFTs are profound. NFTs enable a democratization of value in the digital space, allowing diverse forms of art, culture, and expression to flourish (Grinberg, 2012). Artists from different backgrounds and regions can gain recognition and support on a global scale (Bhambri and Thapar, 2009). This democratization also extends to the cultural significance of digital assets, as NFTs provide a mechanism for communities to collectively assign and acknowledge value. The social aspect of ownership and interaction within NFT communities fosters a sense of belonging and shared cultural experiences.

10. CHALLENGES AND CONSIDERATIONS

Addressing the various challenges is crucial for the sustainable and equitable development of decentralized systems.

10.1 Scalability Issues

Scalability is a paramount concern in decentralized ecosystems, especially as NFTs gain popularity. The existing blockchain infrastructure encounters constraints about the velocity of transactions and overall throughput. As the demand for NFT transactions increases, scalability issues can result in network congestion and higher transaction fees. Solutions like layer 2 scaling solutions, sharding, and optimized consensus algorithms are being explored to enhance scalability without compromising the decentralization ethos.

10.2 Environmental Concerns

There have been concerns raised regarding the environmental implications of blockchain networks, namely those that employ proof-of-work (PoW) consensus processes. The energy-intensive characteristic of PoW can potentially lead to a substantial carbon footprint (Androulaki, 2018). The adoption of energy-efficient consensus techniques such as proof-of-stake (PoS) or the investigation of environmentally sustainable blockchain solutions becomes crucial. Striking a balance between decentralization and environmental sustainability is a key consideration in the Web3 era.

10.3 Security and Ownership Risks

While blockchain technology offers robust security features, the growing sophistication of cyber threats poses a constant challenge. NFT platforms must address vulnerabilities in smart contracts, wallet security, and decentralized applications. Additionally, the issue of digital ownership risks arises, as users may face challenges proving ownership of NFTs in legal frameworks. Implementing secure coding practices, conducting regular audits, and exploring decentralized identity solutions can mitigate these risks.

10.4 Accessibility and Inclusivity

Ensuring that Web3 technologies, including NFTs, are accessible and inclusive is a critical consideration (Antonopoulos, 2014). Factors such as user-friendly interfaces, educational resources, and affordable access to technology need attention. Accessibility challenges extend beyond technical aspects to socio-economic barriers, potentially excluding certain demographics from participating in the decentralized ecosystem (Bhambri et al., 2008). Developing initiatives that promote inclusivity, education, and broad access to Web3 technologies is essential for realizing the full potential of decentralized systems.

11. FUTURE TRENDS AND INNOVATIONS

As blockchain networks mature and scalability improves, NFTs are likely to become more versatile and efficient (Bansal et al., 2012). This may involve the development of new token standards, enhanced interoperability between different blockchain platforms, and improved mechanisms for creating and managing NFTs. The goal would be to make NFTs more accessible, cost-effective, and environmentally sustainable.

The incorporation of nascent technologies, like as Augmented Reality (AR) and Virtual Reality (VR), has the potential to fundamentally transform the user experience inside the NFT ecosystem (Narayanan et al., 2016). Imagine a future where NFT owners can showcase their digital assets in immersive virtual environments or use AR applications to interact with their tokenized collectibles in the physical world. This integration not only enhances the aesthetic appeal of NFTs but also opens up new possibilities for creative expression and engagement.

Furthermore, the role of community governance is anticipated to be crucial in influencing the development of NFT ecosystems. The decentralized nature of blockchain allows for more inclusive decision-making processes, where token holders have a say in the development and governance of the platforms they participate in. This democratization of decision-making fosters a sense of community ownership, ensuring that the NFT ecosystem evolves in a way that aligns with the collective interests and values of its participants. Decentralized Autonomous Organizations (DAOs) could emerge as powerful entities, providing a framework for decentralized governance within NFT communities.

12. CONCLUSION

In conclusion, the exploration of NFTs in the ongoing evolution of Web3 reveals a transformative force that extends far beyond mere digital ownership. NFTs have emerged as a pivotal element in transforming our understanding and engagement with digital assets, presenting novel dimensions of ownership, genuineness, and worth. The utilization of NFTs has extended beyond conventional limitations, exerting influence on various industries like art, gaming, entertainment, and other domains. NFTs leverage blockchain technology and smart contracts to establish an unalterable and transparent ledger, thereby guaranteeing the origin and limited availability of digital assets. This mechanism cultivates a perception of reliability and exclusivity within the digital domain.

Looking ahead, the role of NFTs in shaping digital ownership is poised for continued innovation and integration. The decentralized nature of NFTs aligns with the core principles of Web3, emphasizing user empowerment, privacy, and security. As the technology matures, NFTs are likely to play a crucial role in broader applications, including DeFi, supply chain management, and digital identity. Moreover, the ongoing development of cross-chain interoperability and standards such as ERC-1155 opens new possibilities for a seamless and interconnected NFT ecosystem.

The future promises a landscape where NFTs not only represent ownership but also serve as dynamic entities with programmable functionalities, allowing for complex interactions and smart contract-driven capabilities. The potential for NFTs to empower content creators, enable new economic models, and redefine the concept of ownership in the digital age is vast. The ongoing exploration of NFTs by sectors indicates that these tokens will retain their prominent position in the Web3 revolution, leading to a fundamental change in our understanding, exchange, and assessment of digital assets. The continuous development of NFTs provides evidence of the significant impact that blockchain technology has in influencing the trajectory of digital ownership and decentralized experiences.

REFERENCES

Abrol, N., Shaifali, Rattan, M., & Bhambri, P. (2005). Implementation and performance evaluation of JPEG 2000 for medical images. *International Conference on Innovative Applications of Information Technology for Developing World.*

Androulaki, E., Barger, A., Bortnikov, V., Cachin, C., Christidis, K., De Caro, A., ... Yellick, J. (2018). Hyperledger Fabric: A Distributed Operating System for Permissioned Blockchains. In *Proceedings of the Thirteenth EuroSys Conference* (pp. 30:1-30:15). 10.1145/3190508.3190538

Antonopoulos, A. M. (2014). *Mastering Bitcoin: Unlocking Digital Cryptocurrencies.* O'Reilly Media.

Bansal, P., Bhambri, P., & Gupta, O. P. (2012). *GOR Method to Predict Protein Secondary Structure using Different Input Formats*. Paper presented at the International Conference on Advanced Computing and Communication Technologies, Delhi, India.

Bathla, S., Jindal, C., & Bhambri, P. (2007, March). Impact of Technology On Societal Living. In *International Conference on Convergence and Competition* (pp. 14). Academic Press.

Bhambri, P., Hans, S., & Singh, M. (2008, November). Bioinformatics - Friendship between Bits & Genes. In *International Conference on Advanced Computing & Communication Technologies* (pp. 62-65). Academic Press.

Bhambri, P., Hans, S., & Singh, M. (2009). Inharmonic Signal Synthesis & Analysis. *Technia-International Journal of Computing Science and Communication Technologies, 1*(2), 199-201.

Bhambri, P., Sinha, V. K., & Jaiswal, M. (2019). Change in iris dimensions as a potential human consciousness level indicator. *International Journal of Innovative Technology and Exploring Engineering, 8*(9S), 517–525. doi:10.35940/ijitee.I1082.0789S19

Bhambri, P., & Thapar, V. (2009, May). Power Distribution Challenges in VLSI: An Introduction. *International Conference on Downtrend Challenges in IT*, 63.

Brown, C., & Jones, D. (2018). Securing Web3 Wallets: Best Practices for Users. *Journal of Blockchain Technology*, *5*(2), 112–130.

Buterin, V. (2017). Ethereum: A Next-Generation Smart Contract and Decentralized Application Platform. *Ledger*, *1*, 63–75. doi:10.5195/ledger.2017.23

Catalini, C., & Gans, J. S. (2016). *Some Simple Economics of the Blockchain*. MIT Sloan Research Paper No. 5191-16.

Croman, K., Decker, C., Eyal, I., Gencer, A. E., Juels, A., Kosba, A. E., . . . Wattenhofer, R. (2016). On Scaling Decentralized Blockchains. In *International Conference on Financial Cryptography and Data Security* (pp. 106-125). Academic Press.

Dai, W., & Vasileiou, I. (2020). Exploring the Security Landscape of Web3 Wallets. *International Journal of Cybersecurity*, *14*(3), 245–263.

Ethereum Project. (2022). *Ethereum White Paper*. Retrieved from https://ethereum.org/whitepaper/

Eyal, I., & Sirer, E. G. (2014). Majority is not enough: Bitcoin mining is vulnerable. In *International conference on financial cryptography and data security* (pp. 436-454). Academic Press.

Finney, H. (2004). *Reusable Proof of Work (RPOW)*. Retrieved from https://www.finney.org/~hal/rpow/

Garzik, J. (2014). *BIP 32: Hierarchical Deterministic Wallets*. Retrieved from https://github.com/bitcoin/bips/blob/master/bip-0032.mediawiki

Gervais, A., Karame, G. O., Wüst, K., Glykantzis, V., Ritzdorf, H., & Capkun, S. (2016). On the Security and Performance of Proof of Work Blockchains. In *Proceedings of the 2016 ACM SIGSAC Conference on Computer and Communications Security (CCS '16)* (pp. 3-16). 10.1145/2976749.2978341

Grigg, I. (2018). *Web3: A Platform for Decentralized Applications*. Retrieved from https://medium.com/@i.m.grigg/web3-a-platform-for-decentralised-applications-17a46b2caf1

Grinberg, R. (2012). Bitcoin: An Innovative Alternative Digital Currency. *Hastings Science & Technology Law Journal*, *4*, 159–207.

Gupta, O. P., & Bhambri, P. (2012). Protein Secondary Structure Prediction. *PCTE Journal of Computer Sciences*, *6*(2), 39–44.

Heilman, E., Kendler, A., Zohar, A., & Goldberg, S. (2015). Eclipse Attacks on Bitcoin's Peer-to-Peer Network. In *24th USENIX Security Symposium (USENIX Security 15)* (pp. 129-144). USENIX.

Jones, A. (2021). NFTs: Ownership, Distribution, and the Digital Frontier. *Journal of Digital Media & Policy*, *13*(1), 7–23.

Kaur, J., Bhambri, P., & Goyal, F. (2012). Phylogeny: Tree of Life. *International Conference on Sports Biomechanics, Emerging Technologies and Quality Assurance in Technical Education*, 350-354.

Mougayar, W. (2016). *The Business Blockchain: Promise, Practice, and Application of the Next Internet Technology*. John Wiley & Sons.

Nakamoto, S. (2008). *Bitcoin: A Peer-to-Peer Electronic Cash System*. Retrieved from https://bitcoin.org/bitcoin.pdf

Narayanan, A., Bonneau, J., Felten, E., Miller, A., & Goldfeder, S. (2016). *Bitcoin and Cryptocurrency Technologies: A Comprehensive Introduction*. Princeton University Press.

Pilkington, M. (2016). Blockchain Technology: Principles and Applications. *Research Handbook on Digital Transformations*, 225-253.

Poon, J., & Dryja, T. (2016). *The Bitcoin Lightning Network: Scalable Off-Chain Instant Payments*. Retrieved from https://lightning.network/lightning-network-paper.pdf

Singh, S., Kakkar, P., & Bhambri, P. (2013). A Study of the Impact of Random Waypoint and Vector Mobility Models on Various Routing Protocols in MANET. *International Journal of Advances in Computing and Information Technology*, *2*(3), 41–51.

Swan, M. (2015). *Blockchain: Blueprint for a New Economy*. O'Reilly Media.

Szabo, N. (1997). Formalizing and Securing Relationships on Public Networks. *First Monday*, *2*(9). Advance online publication. doi:10.5210/fm.v2i9.548

Tapscott, D., & Tapscott, A. (2016). *Blockchain revolution: how the technology behind Bitcoin is changing money, business, and the world*. Penguin.

Tondon, N., & Bhambri, P. (2017). Novel Approach for Drug Discovery. *International Journal of Research in Engineering and Applied Sciences*, *7*(6), 28–46.

Wood, G. (2014). Ethereum: A Secure Decentralised Generalised Transaction Ledger. *Ethereum Project Yellow Paper*, *151*. Advance online publication. doi:10.1007/s10203-008-0041-7

Zheng, Z., Xie, S., Dai, H., Chen, X., & Wang, H. (2018). An Overview of Blockchain Technology: Architecture, Consensus, and Future Trends. In *2017 IEEE International Congress on Big Data (Big Data Congress)* (pp. 557-564). Academic Press.

Zohar, A. (2015). Bitcoin: Under the hood. *Communications of the ACM*, *58*(9), 104–113. doi:10.1145/2701411

Zohar, A., & Abbe, A. (2020). The Tokenization of Assets and Potential Implications for Artists. *International Journal of Blockchain and Cryptocurrency*, *1*(1), 67–81.

Zyskind, G., Nathan, O., & Pentland, A. (2015). Decentralizing Privacy: Using Blockchain to Protect Personal Data. In 2015 IEEE Security and Privacy Workshops (pp. 180-184). IEEE.

KEY TERMS AND DEFINITIONS

Blockchain: Blockchain is a decentralized and distributed digital ledger technology that enables secure, transparent, and tamper-resistant record-keeping of transactions across a network of computers. It serves as the underlying technology for various applications beyond its original use case as the foundation for cryptocurrencies like Bitcoin.

Cryptocurrency: Cryptocurrency is a form of digital or virtual currency that uses cryptography for security and operates on decentralized networks, typically based on blockchain technology. Unlike traditional currencies issued by governments and central banks, cryptocurrencies rely on cryptographic techniques to secure transactions, control the creation of new units, and verify the transfer of assets.

Decentralized Finance: Decentralized Finance, often abbreviated as DeFi, refers to a financial ecosystem built on blockchain and cryptocurrency technologies that aims to recreate and enhance traditional financial systems, such as banking, lending, and trading, in a decentralized and permissionless manner. DeFi eliminates the need for traditional intermediaries like banks and financial institutions, allowing users to engage in financial activities directly with one another through smart contracts and decentralized applications (DApps).

Digital Assets: Digital assets refer to any form of content or data that exists in a digital format and holds economic value or represents ownership.

Digital Ownership: Digital ownership refers to the concept of having rights and control over digital assets or content. In the context of the internet and digital technologies, ownership traditionally meant having a copy or access to a file, but digital ownership has evolved with the advent of blockchain and Web3 technologies.

Interoperability: Interoperability refers to the ability of different systems, devices, or software applications to seamlessly exchange and interpret data or perform functions in a coordinated and effective manner. It ensures that disparate systems can work together, share information, and operate cohesively, even if they are developed by different vendors or utilize different technologies.

Tokenization: Tokenization is the process of converting rights to an asset into a digital token on a blockchain. In the context of blockchain and decentralized technologies, tokens represent a unit of value or ownership for a specific asset or utility. These digital tokens are stored on a blockchain, providing a secure and transparent record of ownership and transactions.

Chapter 8
Building Blocks, Opportunities, and Challenges of Metaverse in Web 3.0

Vijaya Kittu Manda
https://orcid.org/0000-0002-1680-8210
PBMEIT, India

ABSTRACT

The Metaverse is an immersive virtual world facilitated by virtual reality (VR) and augmented reality (AR). It is a backbone technology for Web 3 in which users interact using avatars in a digital content environment. Metaverse as a platform enriches Web 3 with its decentralized, interactive, and immersive experiences, allowing newer forms of collaboration, innovation, and entrepreneurship. A quick historical background and its evolution are discussed. Being a content-rich environment, upgraded high-speed connectivity is necessary. Internet 3.0, decentralization, and VR/AR technologies will help build the foundation. Metaverse requires special hardware, software, content, networking, and governance. The Metaverse promises economic models in which cryptocurrencies and Metaverse Coins are traded. Metaverse is still evolving as research is increasing and associations are focusing on standards. Robust governance and regulations are still nascent. Certain negative aspects include privacy and security, addiction, cyberbullying, and disinformation, about which users must be cautious.

INTRODUCTION

The Metaverse is a virtual digital environment in which people appear as digital avatars and interact with software and each other using objects in both virtual and real worlds. It is an online environment and a parallel digital universe where people play games, work, learn, meet, and socialize. It is an infinitely and constantly expanding virtual world with new features, dimensions, and technologies.

Metaverse allows people to buy and sell digital assets. Digital assets are those that do not have a physical form but are only used or experienced online, such as software, subscription, or membership

DOI: 10.4018/979-8-3693-1532-3.ch008

to online services such as music. Cryptocurrencies are often the preferred currency for transacting these digital assets.

Metaverse has no space and location limits. This turns out to be a for-it advantage. In contrast, there is the possibility of missing content because of an unstable internet connection which is a disadvantage.

HISTORICAL BACKGROUND

There are several definitions for the term "Metaverse" (Ritterbusch & Teichmann, 2023). Being evolving and because of the lack of sufficient standards on the topic, there is no single authoritative definition. "Metaverse" is a crossword that comprises two words – "Meta" from Greek to mean "with," "after," "beyond," or "transcendency." "Verse" means "universe." So, Metaverse roughly means a "new universe" or a "third space." Another version is a philosophical view that defines the Metaverse as a "metaphysical," meaning "to stimulate different people's understanding, imagination, and innovation" of the Metaverse.

Metaverse is not a straightforward technological development but an evolution with progress happening in bits and pieces. It is the culmination of various technologies that saw small feature enrichments developed over time. Ivan Sutherland's paper, *A Framework for Virtual Reality* (1965), was the first to discuss an "ultimate display" – a head-mounted device that can help traverse a virtual world (simulation environment) created by computer software. It can provide sensory experiences in a way that is indistinguishable from reality. This idea laid the foundation for virtual reality (VR) and has influenced the development of VR technology over the years. The same year, Morton Hellig built a VR prototype called Sensorama Simulator that provided a multi-sensory experience. William Gibson's novel *Neuromancer* (1984) mentions about cyberspace. The first formal use of the term "Metaverse" is in Neal Stephenson's science fiction novel *Snow Crash* (1992). Several movies showed traits of the Metaverse, including *Johnny Mnemonic* (1995), *The Matrix* (1999), and *Ready Player One* (2018).

The development of the internet has brought Metaverse to a more reality. *Second Life* (2003) by Linden Lab is the first virtual world. Though the intention was not to create a game, it largely appears to be a massively multiplayer online role-playing game. The first augmented reality (AR) game, *Pokémon Go*, was released in 2006. The first virtual reality (VR) headset, Oculus Rift, was released in 2012. Facebook acquired Oculus Rift in 2014 for $2 billion. In 2018, Fortnite, a popular video game, introduced a "Party Royale" mode that allowed players to socialize in a virtual world.

The term *Metaverse* gained popularity after Mark Zuckerberg, on October 28, 2021, announced the name change of the popular social media platform Facebook to Meta Platforms. The name change reflects potential changes and extensions in social media with virtual and augmented reality (FB, 2021). It expressed commitment and a changing focus towards building a futuristic platform. Meta went on to build its Metaverse world called *Horizon Worlds*.

Microsoft soon followed with the Activision Blizzard acquisition in 2022 for $68.7 billion. The move was seen as a major investment in the Metaverse, and the company hoped the move would accelerate its adaptation and readiness to the new technology. Microsoft Mesh, released in March 2023, is a mixed-realty collaboration platform featuring customizable avatars, objects, and environments and integrates well with other Microsoft products, such as HoloLens and AltspaceVR.

The Metaverse became a hot topic at the World Economic Forum (WEF) Annual Meeting 2022 in Davos, Switzerland. Several workshops and sessions dedicated to it are featured at the event. It became the first major venue, reflecting the importance of the platform. It became a stage for global collaborations between governments, businesses, and civil society to ensure that the Metaverse is developed responsibly and maximizes its potential benefits.

Though still in its early stages of development, the Metaverse is already gaining increasing attention from businesses and investors. Alphabet (formerly Google) has built a VR platform, *Daydream,* an AR glass called *Google Glass, a* virtual field trip app called *Google Expeditions*, and *Google Maps AR*. Google also organically tried growing by making acquisitions, such as *The Void,* in 2020.

Roblox has built one of the largest social platforms that allows users to build 3D games and virtual worlds. Epic Games' Unreal Engine is one of the most widely used real-time 3D creation platforms, and their MetaHuman Creator tool is advancing virtual avatars. The Sandbox is developing a virtual world platform focused on user-generated content and token-based economies. Unity Technologies provides another leading real-time 3D development platform on which many metaverse platforms are built. Nvidia contributes through its graphics processing hardware and AI platforms that help power sophisticated virtual environments.

Several thousands of companies globally have invested money and resources and have built tools and platforms for the Metaverse in various applications. Together, these companies are advancing different building blocks to contribute to the evolution of shared interactive virtual worlds.

Evolution of Metaverse

The evolution of the Metaverse can be tracked in three distinct phases (Filipova, 2023).

The first and current ongoing developments in Metaverse (during 2021 – 2024) will be called the "Emerging Metaverse." This phase is inspired by the Web 3.0 app-based market and technologies. Direct opportunities would be limited because the market will begin to explore and experiment with use cases. In most cases, the opportunities will appear indirectly from technologies that are not explicitly developed for the Metaverse.

The second phase will witness exponential developments between 2025 – 2029 and be considered the "Advanced Metaverse." While technology convergence happens during this period, new technologies emerge, especially in navigation around physical and digital spaces, sensing and mapping people, places, things, and processes. The combinative approach is to be followed in this phase. It is expected that the Metaverse will have infrastructure capabilities, such as interoperability frameworks, protocols, and registries, at the end of this phase.

The developments from 2029 and beyond will be in the third stage, "Mature Metaverse," which will feature interconnected worlds, completely interoperable ecosystems, and immersive experiences in new virtual economies. The Metaverse will be more clearly defined and easier to navigate for organizations and individuals. This will be driven by advances in foundational technologies (5G, computer vision, immersive tech, digital currencies) and the maturation of inspirational use cases and applications. As a result, the systems needed for a mature metaverse will be well-understood, creating significant opportunities for infrastructure vendors to compete to build the backbone of this transformative and potentially ubiquitous system.

APPLICATIONS

The Metaverse is a promising new technology that has several diversified applications.

Entertainment and Gaming

Metaverse allows one to host and attend virtual theme parks and movies, leading to newer forms of entertainment that can be experienced without actually moving out of the home.

Metaverse has infinite virtual worlds, allowing multiple players to have a real-time immersive and realistic interaction playing virtual games – both educational and social games. Players interact with each other within the game in a way that was not possible earlier.

Roblox Corporation, the makers of the popular *Minecraft,* envisioned that the Metaverse would be a reality several years ago. It is slowly moving its player and developer community towards the Metaverse, calling it – human co-experience. Microsoft.

Popular games on the Metaverse include Axie Infinity, Sandbox Game, Decentraland, UFO Gaming, Polkacity, Revomon, Vulcan Forged, Mobox, Star Atlas, StarMon, Bloktopia, Blockchain Monster Hunt, SolChicks, Ember Sword, Cryptovoxels, Somnium Space, NFT Worlds, Alien Worlds, Farmers World, Upland, amongst others.

Meta Horizons World is an online game developed by Meta Platforms to work on Oculus Rift S and Meta Quest 2 headsets. It was released in December 2021, and by February 2022, it had 300,000 estimated users. The game was unlocked for various geographies over time. Meta also released Ouro Interactive, a first-party studio, in August 2023 to allow building games that can be played in Horizon Worlds.

Illuvium is a role-playing game where players collect Illuvial, a form of NFT. The collections from the game can also be used to trade at external NFT marketplaces.

Table 1 lists the top 5 companies and major metaverse platforms or games in the region.

Table 1. Countries and leading Metaverse platform/game

Country	Metaverse Platform/Game
U.S.A.	Roblox, Fortnite, and Decentraland
China	Tencent, Sword and Fairy, Honour of Kings, Genshin Impact, Moonlight Blade, New Gods, NetEase
South Korea	MapleStory, Axie Infinity, Illusion Connect, Closers, Sudden Attack, KartRider, Elyon, Epic Seven, Black Desert Mobile
Japan	Sword Art Online, Dragon Quest Walk, Pokemon Go, Beat Saber, Final Fantasy XIV, VRMMO Project Sense, Cool Japan VR, VR Zone Shinjuku
Germany	The Sandbox, Decentraland, Somnium Space, Cryptovoxels, Minecraft, Core, Axie Infinity

UK, France, and Italy from Europe, and the Philippines, Thailand, and Vietnam from Southeast Asia are other countries that are witnessing increased Metaverse gaming. Metaverse is found to reduce the user-developer gap in game development by intertwining, making the player the co-creator, and using "serious game" approaches (Volk, 2008).

Virtual Events

Virtual events such as concerts, conferences, trade shows, and sporting events can be hosted in the Metaverse. The events can be attended by a wider audience from any place in the world because there will not be any space constraints in the virtual world. The viewers do not need to travel, thereby saving time and money. The events can also make events more accessible to people with disabilities. AnyTechMeta is a company that conducts virtual events.

Education/Teaching

An Educational Metaverse is called an Edu-Metaverse. Metaverse can give location and time independence and possibly higher learning outcomes than typical purely physical or digital teaching. It fosters the students with accessibility, diversity, equality, and humanity, especially in campus life (Seitova & Malik, 2023). Metaverse in Education Market is expected to grow at 37.7% CAGR – from $3.9 billion in 2023 to $19.3 billion by 2028, according to market research firm Markets And Markets.

LeewayHertz feels that integrating VR, AR, and other immersive technologies opens new possibilities by helping build virtual settings for educators and students to work and study together. Academic research, too, agrees with this. University 5.0 brings in 3D virtual classrooms of Metaverse where user data is stored on cloud storage, and Blockchain is used for quality, safe, and secure user data management in online education. This leads to new learning possibilities such as greater engagement, learning by doing, and getting familiar with foreign and multicultural educational systems can be achieved (Mourtzis et al., 2023).

Educators have experimented with combining a learning environment implemented in Unity3D Game Engine with a traditional Moodle-based Learning Management System and found positive outcomes (De Marco et al., 2023). It improves the quality of e-learning (Muhammad Khan & Ullah Khan, 2023) and will be an interesting platform for qualitative and quantitative evaluation of students (Bartels & Hahne, 2023).

Research shows that Metaverse platforms like Gather can enhance lesson planning outcomes, foster engagement, and provide a valuable alternative to traditional videoconferencing tools in teacher preparation education (H.-J. Chen, 2023).

Immersive classes are more appealing and cause more interaction than a typical traditional classroom. Students could use the Metaverse to explore historical landmarks, conduct experiments, or collaborate with other students on projects.

Governments and institutions should invest in Metaverse-based educational programs to impart virtual training by providing immersive and interactive experiences and ensuring digital literacy for all. Similarly, there is a need to encourage skill development and certification within the Metaverse, creating opportunities for career advancement and personal growth.

Remote Work

Employers can create virtual workplaces that allow them to work together from virtual offices and interact with clients in virtual meetings from anywhere, transcending physical boundaries. This could be a more efficient and productive way to work, especially for businesses with remote employees. Virtual offices are likely to replace the norm in the future. It also facilitates digital transformation and contributes to Industry 5.0 (Agarwal & Alathur, 2023). Spatial, VRChat, Engage, Mozilla Hubs, and Somnium Space are some metaverse virtual office solution providers.

Social Networking

Over the years, online social environments have evolved from personal computer-based to mobile and now to Metaverse. Being immersive in nature, Metaverse appears like a social network place with people sitting next to each other, though, in reality, they could be continents away. Their rich social interactions with each other will be more engaging, immersive, and realistic way. Meta says that the Metaverse is the next revolutionary form of social connections and the internet.

Second Life is a Metaverse where users interact with each other in digital avatar mode. They can make purchases of goods and services using its internal in-world currency called Linden Dollars. Sandbox, a virtual game, allows users to monetize and earn NFTs, which can be used to buy or sell digital assets.

Marketing and Shopping

The Metaverse is turning into a new social media model for product promotion (Ni et al., 2023). As a result of the multimodal sensory interaction offered by AR, retail product presentations are more realistic compared to the text and images currently used in web-based e-commerce websites (Shen et al., 2021). Consumer intention to buy is activated through a psychological process, bringing benefits beyond those associated with traditional online shopping (C. Chen et al., 2023).

Several retailers have begun transitions to virtual commerce. Walmart and Roblox are experimenting with virtual merchandise stores to provide a rich experience for Generation Z. Alibaba, and Ikea experimented with virtual commerce Metaverses in certain geographies.

Branding and Advertising

Brands such as fashion brands and marketers can leverage Metaverse to showcase their products (Mogaji, Dwivedi, et al., 2023). The luxury sector reinforces the perception of scarcity, accelerates the "artification" process, and communicates the ancestral heritage uniquely and innovatively (Murtas et al., 2023). Advertisements are more personalized and immersive, allowing advertisers to target and better impact the products and services.

Virtual Marketplaces and Electronic Commerce

Virtual stores allow visitors to walk into the shopping mall and buy products and services just as one shops at a grocery or a convenience store. Payment for the products is made using cryptocurrencies, and the real physical goods will be home-delivered. Payments are encouraged to be done in cryptocurrency format.

Real Estate

Metaverse has applications in both traditional and digital real estate (Ante et al., 2023). It allows traditional real estate companies to host virtual replicas/staging of real estate properties, thereby benefiting property marketing and leasing process. Prospective buyers from any part of the world can explore the property by going through an immersive property tour before deciding to visit the real site and consider purchasing the property. Virtual auctions and property showcases within the Metaverse transform the traditional sales process. Virtual property management in the Metaverse streamlines operations, offering a central hub for landlords and tenants to interact seamlessly (El Jaouhari et al., 2023).

Both Metaverse and Web 3 foster real estate tokenization by converting property ownership rights into Blockchain digital tokens, thereby increasing market efficiency, enhancing liquidity, diversifying opportunities, accessibility, and inclusivity, and increasing transparency (Jack, 2023). Technological advancements in tokenization and NFTs will open doors for newer legal challenges (Alcón, 2023).

Tourism

Metaverse can give an immersive preview and a virtual experience of tourist destinations and thereby increase destination awareness. It can help in trip planning by providing improved interaction and engagement. So, it is a tool that improves tourist behavior and experience before, during, on-site, and after traveling (Buhalis et al., 2023). An interplay was observed between Metaverse and smart city tourism (Um et al., 2022). It became an urban tourist attraction and a significant element in various exhibitions (Zhang & Quoquab, 2023). Virtual locations that may have real-world counterparts can be toured. Metaverse cognitive processing positively influenced metaverse tourist responses, including satisfaction and loyalty (Jafar & Ahmad, 2023).

Healthcare and Wellness

Virtual doctors, virtual therapy sessions, and virtual yoga classes are hosted on the Metaverse, eliminating the need to travel to the doctor or wait for long hours to get a doctor's appointment. This is especially useful to people in rural areas where access to healthcare is difficult. Early studies have shown that a metaverse platform is a good alternative service-delivery model for group genetic counseling (Yoo et al., 2024).

INFRASTRUCTURE AND TECHNOLOGY

Building the Foundation

Creating a Metaverse requires a robust and scalable technological infrastructure. Key components include:

Internet 3.0

The Metaverse necessitates an evolved internet infrastructure that supports massive data transfer, low latency, and high bandwidth. Governments, tech giants, and startups must collaborate to build this new internet.

Decentralization

A decentralized architecture based on blockchain technology is essential to ensure the Metaverse's resilience and independence from single points of failure. Blockchain will provide security, trust, and transparency in transactions and interactions within the Metaverse.

VR/AR Technology

Virtual Reality (VR) and Augmented Reality (AR) are pivotal for immersive experiences in the Metaverse. Companies should continue to develop advanced VR/AR hardware and software, making them more accessible to the general population.

CONNECTIVITY

5G, 6G, and Beyond

Connecting and participating in real-time with 3D graphics and extensive data requires reliable, low-latency, high-speed data transfer, energy-efficient, and massive connectivity (Muhammad Khan & Ullah Khan, 2023). These internet speeds should be available to everyone, including those from rural and currently inaccessible areas, for the Metaverse to become commonly and evenly available. Features such as eMBB, nMTC, and uRLLC that come with 5G make it a dependable backbone of the Metaverse. XR research towards this started in 2019, during which 23 R17 5G evolution standard projects were presented (Njoku et al., 2022). While investments in 5G infrastructure must continue, research into even faster and more reliable network technologies is being explored. 6G networks can give superior network connectivity of approximately 1 Tb/s and maximize the user quality of service (QoS), such as 1-microsecond latency (or near-zero latency), far superior to 5G. Mobile Edge Computing MEC) combines cloud computing with the internet service environment at the network's edge (Aslam et al., 2023). 6G will also become necessary to work with other technologies such as Blockchain, AI, Edge computing / Edge AI, IoE, Cloudification, and Open RAN. Research has to overcome certain limitations that are currently hampering the progress of 6G. The list includes limited backward compatibility, lack of standards, accountability, resilience, privacy reservation, and energy inefficiency (Siniarski et al., 2016). VR Hive, 6G Life, and Luxembourg Metaverse are the names of some 6G Metaverse projects.

Satellite Internet

Global accessibility through satellite internet coverage must be extended to remote and underserved areas. Companies should collaborate on projects to provide affordable satellite internet services worldwide.

BUILDING A METAVERSE

Developing a metaverse environment is a complex and challenging task, but it is also an exciting opportunity to create something truly new and innovative. Here are some of the key components to consider:

Hardware: Accessing and traversing the Metaverse requires various hardware devices, such as VR headsets, AR glasses, and haptic gloves. These devices will allow users to interact in a more immersive and realistic virtual world. Perhaps the devices are inspired by Neo's plug-in jack in *The Matrix,* goggles, and public booths that Hiro used in *Snow Crash* or the special lenses mentioned in Charlie Brooker's *Black Mirror*. A VR headset covers the eyes and stops outside light from entering, giving a virtual reality experience. Meta's Oculus system, Samsung's Gear, Google's Daydream, and PlayStation are some examples of VR devices. AR glasses or AR headsets give augmented reality with which real-world objects are visible, but data, images, and video appear on the glasses. Apple and Facebook are actively working in this area.

Software: The Metaverse will need a powerful and stable software platform to support the real-time rendering of 3D environments and objects. The software helps in user interaction, communication, and collaboration. Software tools required for building Metaverse includes game engines, 3D modelling and animation software, web development tools, AR/VR development tools, and blockchain development tools.

Content: The Metaverse will involve graphic-rich content and high level of user interaction. So, it will deal with a lot of varieties and quantity of content. Content formats include 3D models, textures, animations, and sound effects. This content will be used to create virtual worlds, objects, and experiences for the Metaverse users to interact.

Networking: The Metaverse environment will require high-speed and low-latency networks. 5G or 6G networks support such requirements and provide real-time communication and interaction for users. This network will also need to be secure to protect user data and privacy.

Governance: The Metaverse requires strong governance standards to make it safe and secure for its users. So, developing policies and procedures for things like user behavior, content moderation, and data privacy are required.

Apart from these key components, many other factors will need to be considered when developing a metaverse environment. The selection of tools will depend on the target audience, the desired features, the budget, and the timeline.

INTEGRATION WITH OTHER TECHNOLOGIES

Metaverse embraces and is a close friend of various other disruptive Industry 4.0 technologies such as Artificial Intelligence (AI), Cloud computing, the Internet of Things (IoT), and Blockchain (such as Cryptocurrencies and digital tokens). These technologies together will be the face of Web 3.

Closeness With Web 3

Most researchers say Metaverse is a part of the broader Web 3. Both Metaverse and Web 3 have a shared vision of creating an immersive, decentralized, and user-centric digital environment. The similarities between the two can be studied in six areas:

1. **Decentralization**: Both emphasize decentralization, creating a trust-less, user-controlled systems. Metaverse can benefit from decentralization wherein a single entity does not control virtual worlds, assets, and experiences but exists on a distributed server and node network.
2. **Digital Ownership:** Web 3 technologies, such as non-fungible tokens (NFTs) and decentralized identifiers (DIDs), enable users to have true ownership of their digital assets and identities. NFT will be the biggest form of currency in the Metaverse. Several user surveys done for this purpose confirmed this. Users will own limited edition virtual items such as avatars and other digital possessions. These ownership concepts are in line with the Web 3 infrastructure wherein users are allowed to carry their digital assets across various metaverse environments.

3. **Interoperability:** Interoperability is an important aspect of the Metaverse and Web 3. Web 3 envisions a web where data and assets can flow seamlessly between applications and platforms. Similarly, the Metaverse aims to allow users to move between different virtual worlds and experiences without friction. Integrating Web 3 protocols can facilitate this seamless movement of data and assets within the Metaverse.
4. **Digital Identity:** Both concepts involve the management of digital identities. In Web 3, users have decentralized identities tied to cryptographic keys, enhancing privacy and security. In the Metaverse, users need persistent digital identities to navigate virtual spaces and interact with others. These digital identities can be tied to Web 3 identity solutions, ensuring user control and security.
5. **Economy and Transactions:** Web 3 introduces decentralized financial systems and cryptocurrencies. They can be used within the Metaverse for transactions, purchases, and economic activities. This enables the creation of a unified digital economy within the Metaverse. Users can easily be able to buy, sell, and trade both physical and virtual goods and services using Web 3-based tokens.
6. **Security and Privacy:** Both Web 3 and the Metaverse gives importance to security and privacy. Blockchain and cryptographic technologies in Web 3 are used to improve the security strength of digital assets and transactions. These security features can be integrated into the Metaverse to protect user data and assets from potential threats.

Artificial Intelligence (AI)

Metaverse and Artificial Intelligence (AI) together can help in close-to-reality situations where recorded or predictable situations are of less use, such as simulations of aircraft, medical surgeries, and war scenarios to train armed forces in posing.

AI is capable of performing tasks that typically require human intelligence. AR can seamlessly integrate by superimposing digital information from the digital and physical worlds. Together, AI and AR can enhance human-computer interaction in the Metaverse. AI-powered virtual assistants, for example, could provide visual cues to help guide users through virtual environments (Chenna, 2023).

AI can help in designing and building the Metaverse. There is a possibility that AI might appear as a human-like robot or an avatar. AI can help collaborate with humans in real and Metaverse environments.

Digital Currencies and Blockchain Tokens

Many Metaverse platforms began offering their own digital currencies and tokens to provide highly secure and seamless trading of digital real estate, avatars, and many more objects. The blockchain ledger is often used to create a secure and transparent system for transactions in the Metaverse. Decentralized Finance (DeFi) offers innovative economic models that can help in Metaverse.

Internet of Things (IoT)

IoT focuses on interconnected hardware. IoT and the Metaverse have some specific applications, especially in industrial environments. AR glasses are part of IoT hardware components in an IoT network. A popular industrial Metaverse Platform, embedded in Industry 4.0, could collect maintenance information from an IoT network, process it, and transmit it to a maintenance worker wearing AR glasses (Ritterbusch & Teichmann, 2023).

METAVERSE ECONOMIC MODELS

A. Digital Economy

Cryptocurrency Integration

Cryptocurrencies enable frictionless transactions, secure ownership of virtual assets, and facilitate in-world commerce. They empower users with financial sovereignty and drive interoperability between different metaverse ecosystems, fostering vibrant and sustainable virtual economies in the evolving landscape of the Metaverse. The Metaverse should have a unified cryptocurrency that facilitates transactions and incentivizes content creators and service providers. This currency should be decentralized and interoperable with other cryptocurrencies.

Almost all Metaverse platforms have their native currency called Metaverse Coins. Some of these are traded and invested over cryptocurrency exchanges. MANA (Decentraland), HFC (High Fidelity), Meta Masters Guild (that bridges gaming and the Blockchain), CLA (Calvaria immersive horror experiences), TDOG (Tamadoge, a meme-inspired metaverse coin), APE (ApeCoin), VRCH (VRChat), CUBE (Somnium Space), SAND (The Sandbox), ROBLOX (Roblox), IMVU, MJ (Mojo), STA (Staramba), are some popular names.

Creator Economy

Encourage the growth of the creator economy within the Metaverse, where individuals can monetize their skills and content. Smart contracts can ensure fair compensation and revenue sharing among participants.

B. Universal Basic Income (UBI)

Metaverse UBI

Consider implementing a Universal Basic Income within the Metaverse, where users receive a stipend for their participation. This could reduce economic inequality and ensure broader access to Metaverse services.

Resource Allocation

Develop algorithms and systems to allocate resources, such as land and digital assets, fairly and equitably, preventing excessive concentration of wealth.

RESEARCH ON METAVERSE

Being an evolving and emerging technology, Metaverse is a topic of both academic and industry research interest. Much of the research is interdisciplinary, connecting various aspects - computer science, education, business and management, and others (Kim, 2023). Further, several other technologies, such as cryptocurrencies and artificial intelligence, are coming closer and have applications in Metaverse owing to the technology being part of Web 3. Most research studies focused on two challenges – social implications comprising social and economic issues and technical implications comprising open standards and hardware (Ritterbusch & Teichmann, 2023). As a new and unique environment, some studies focus on the user interface design aspects. Psychology-related studies focus on the social and ethical implications of the Metaverse, while management-related studies focus on economic and business models for the Metaverse. Overall, the depth and breadth of Metaverse research is still insufficient and is unevenly distributed (Feng et al., 2022) .

Interoperability and Standards

While several forums are established to work on interoperability and standards, academic researchers are working on their own way to address issues hampering progress in this area. One issue identified hampering the progress is the need for high-performance client terminals and a long response time in some cases. Researchers have proposed an interoperable Split-Protocol with role changeover capabilities to address this issue to help Metaverse systems be more resilient and highly available (Rawal et al., 2022).

Ownership

The concept of ownership in the context of Metaverse is complex. Users can own various digital assets, such as avatars, clothing, and virtual real estate. It is an unlimited space. Because it is backed by Blockchain, cryptography can easily verify and secure ownership. This feature makes ownership of digital assets at par with ownership of physical assets. Users can buy or win NFTs and become owners of collectibles (such as in-game collectibles), improving their avatar abilities or personalizing experience.

Ownership in the Metaverse raises several legal, social, and economic questions. It challenges traditional notions of property rights and ownership, making it a subject of researchers' interest. Key aspects include legal frameworks, intellectual property rights, governance rights, and social and economic implications.

Advancements in Technologies

Researchers are working on advancements in VR/AR technologies, mainly hardware. Similarly, technology frameworks for 3D Virtual Worlds that bring Metaverse and Human-Computer Interaction are being developed (Y. Wang et al., 2022).

Virtual Economies and Social Applications

In a virtual world powered by blockchain technology, digital ownership becomes a reality, enabling users to create, buy, sell, and trade digital assets such as virtual real estate, digital art, and even in-game items—newer forms of entrepreneurship and collaboration. Users can start businesses in the virtual world, offering services or selling digital products to other users. Brands also have opportunities to create virtual stores and experiences, which can generate revenue. These economic activities are facilitated by cryptocurrencies and non-fungible tokens (NFTs), which enable secure and transparent transactions. Virtual communities can collaborate on projects, engage in social activities, and even conduct governance through decentralized autonomous organizations (DAOs).

Regarding Consumer Behavior Research and Virtual Commerce Application Design, some researchers suggest that future research trends on the topic will be around a diversity of boundary factors and that of immersive technology, organic behavior-design research circle, paying attention to virtual consumption, and paying attention to Metaverse evolution trends (Shen et al., 2021).

Social Interaction

Research on social interactions explores how people communicate, connect, and form communities within virtual and augmented reality environments. Because of new possibilities for social interaction, blending the digital and physical worlds and enabling users to engage with others in immersive and interactive ways. Some researcher interests in this area include virtual communities, nonverbal communication, immersive experiences, application-specific interactions in educational or professional spaces, and ethical considerations.

Privacy and Security

Metaverse and Web 3 promote the concept of decentralization, transparency, and secured infrastructure. The platforms give more control over user data and privacy. These decentralized social networks can provide a more transparent and secure alternative to traditional platforms, which often monetize user data and have been criticized for their privacy practices. In the Metaverse, users interact with digital avatars, which can potentially expose personal information if not appropriately managed. Users act responsibly and must be able to trust the platforms they interact with, knowing their information is protected and secure.

Developers and companies must employ robust encryption techniques, secure data storage, and strict access controls. Moreover, privacy-preserving technologies, such as zero-knowledge proofs and Tornado Cash's anonymous transactions, should be integrated into these systems to protect users' identities and transactions.

Accessibility and Human-Computer Interaction

Accessibility involves ensuring that the Metaverse is accessible to individuals with disabilities and the marginalized population (Abendschein et al., 2023). It promotes inclusivity for all. The Metaverse could be expensive to develop and maintain. This could limit its accessibility to some users, and hence, designers must consider how interactions can be designed to minimize the disadvantage (Parker et al., 2023). This is truer in the context of social media interactions, where many users will be interacting simultaneously. Having metaverse content development standards can help in such practical situations (Jeong et al., 2023).

Cultural Preservation

Preservation of cultural heritage is a goal of various governments globally. The Metaverse encourages this by allowing users to explore and celebrate diverse cultures. The digital reconstruction of ancient archaeological sites is an example of how lost heritage is given a digital projection (Alkhatib et al., 2023). Some Metaverse cultural creations are:

1. The Palace of Knossos (an ancient Minoan palace reconstructed using 3D scanning technology)
2. The Colosseum in Rome (developed by the Italian Institute of Technology)
3. The Great Wall of China (Alibaba Group, China Central Television (CCTV), Synthesia, Vanke, and GreatWorks)
4. The Parthenon in Athens (Ancient Rome Virtual Reality (ARVR)
5. The Department of Computer Science and Engineering at the University of Minnesota)
6. The Rosetta Stone (by the British Museum)
7. The Palmyra, Syria (built in collaboration with the Institute for Digital Archeology of the University of California, Berkeley, Tsinghua University in Beijing, and Dubai Future Foundation).

METAVERSE STANDARDS

Standardization is essential for the Interoperable Metaverse, especially because of the rapid pace at which new technologies are evolving, and to ensure that Metaverse is interoperable (Hyun, 2023). The current Metaverse suffers from poor user experience and poor corporate cooperation, partly because of a lack of standardization. Standardizing Metaverse can eliminate confusion among producers and consumers and make it an open, equitable, and ubiquitous information space (Havele et al., 2022). Some prominent associations working in this area are:

1. Metaverse Standards Forum (MSF)
2. XR Association
3. SpatialWeb Foundation
4. Decentraland Foundation
5. Somnium Space Association
6. Blender Development Fund
7. World Wide Web Consortium (W3C)
8. Open Metaverse Interoperability Group (OMIG)
9. Decentralized Identity Foundation (DIF)
10. The Khronos Group
11. OpenXR Consortium
12. Immersive Digital Experiences Alliance (IDEA)
13. The Metaverse Alliance
14. IEEE Global Initiative on Ethics of Extended Reality (XR)

GOVERNANCE AND REGULATION

It is generally said that technology moves quicker than the slower pace of regulation. The Metaverse poses several regulatory challenges, such as protecting user privacy and security and using them responsibly and ethically. Thus, Mark Zuckerberg called upon everyone involved to build the Metaverse responsibly right from the beginning.

Establishing Ethical Guidelines

Digital Bill of Rights

A set of fundamental digital rights should be established, ensuring privacy, security, and freedom of expression within the Metaverse. Governments, NGOs, and technology companies must collaborate to draft and uphold these rights.

Content Moderation

Guidelines for content moderation should be transparent and consistent, balancing free speech and preventing harm. An independent body with representatives from various stakeholders should oversee content moderation.

Anti-Monopoly Measures

Healthy Market Competition

Governments should enact and enforce antitrust legislation to prevent monopolistic control of the Metaverse, fostering competition and innovation among technology companies.

Interoperability Standards

Develop and implement open standards that enable interoperability between different Metaverse platforms, allowing users to move seamlessly.

Data Privacy and Security

Regulating becomes essential because there will be increased digital profiling, decreased privacy, infringement of human dignity, and deep fakes by wrongdoers will be assisted by artificial intelligence (Filipova, 2023).

User Ownership

Users should have full ownership and control over their data. Data privacy laws should be strengthened, and users should have the right to consent or withdraw their data from the Metaverse at any time.

Cybersecurity

Stringent cybersecurity measures are essential to protect users from cyber threats.

NEGATIVE ASPECTS

Like every technology with positive and negative dimensions, the Metaverse can pose some challenges. These include some Web 2.0 era issues related to online – such as hate speech, social media addiction, and potentially creating new monopolies by companies like Meta (formerly Facebook). Metaverse can emerge into a new fraud marketplace (Smaili & De Rancourt-Raymond, 2022), posing newer challenges to organizations, regulatory bodies, and financial authorities. It can create newer job roles and professions to contain the menace. Promoting responsible use of the Metaverse and providing resources for managing screen time, cyberbullying, and addiction is necessary. Similarly, there is a need to explore therapeutic applications of the Metaverse, such as virtual support groups and mental health services.

Privacy and Security

The Metaverse could pose a threat to privacy and security. Users could be tracked and monitored in the Metaverse, and their personal data could be stolen. While the possibilities are fewer in a Web 3.0 environment compared to a Web 2.0, it cannot be said that the Metaverse is a totally safe environment on privacy and security counts. Users must take their own cautionary view before entering the Metaverese. There is an increased push for platforms to clear user data regularly, such as search keywords and website surfing patterns, among others. Users need to have a degree of control as to how and what data is shared amongst the platforms. When signing up for a service on a platform, it is important to consider the level of data privacy provided and the duration for which this information will be utilized.

Addiction

Being the immersive social media version, the Metaverse can be addictive, affecting individual and group psychology (Bojic, 2022) and mental health (Usmani et al., 2022). Research suggests that the intensity of addiction will be more significant in new media. An Immersive Time (ImT) is what happens when a user spends conscious, deliberate, and dedicated time on the Metaverse while using accessories and a headset (Mogaji, Wirtz, et al., 2023). According to Gartner, 30 percent of people will spend 2 hours a day in a Metaverse by 2027 for work, entertainment, gaming, and socialization. Users could spend excessive amounts of time in the Metaverse, neglecting their real-world relationships and responsibilities. Consequently, there will be social isolation, sleep deprivation, physical inactivity, insecurity, anxiety, depression, and behavioral addiction (Ochoa et al., 2023).

Cyberbullying

The Metaverse could become a platform for cyberbullying in which technology will be used to harass or bully-victims, causing psychological and physical damage. Cyberbullying is likely high in anonymous metaverses, necessitating a more respectful culture (Upadhyay et al., 2023). Traditional press coverage on the concepts began covering stories and began giving precautionary and solution suggestions (Yıldız & Tanyıldızı, 2022). Several conceptual models, such as the stress-strain models, were proposed to explain the relationship between technostress elements and cyberbullying (Qasem et al., 2022).

Disinformation

The Metaverse could be used to spread disinformation, exposing users to false or misleading information and fake news. This poses additional need for detection and information security (J. Wang et al., 2023).

CONCLUSION

The Metaverse is a promising new technology with the potential to revolutionize how we interact with the internet and each other. It will be one of the foundation technologies for Web 3. Metaverse adoption increases as the technology evolves through the emerging, advanced, and mature stages. Several challenges need to be addressed before the Metaverse becomes a mainstream technology. Despite the challenges posed, the potential benefits are significant and overweight.

As Metaverse begins to form more concrete shape and mass adoption, it is increasingly become important to remain vigilant considering the ethical, regulatory, and societal challenges that may arise. The full features of the Metaverse can become useful to the lives of everyone with the help of innovation and to have shared values and aspirations.

Funding: There is no specific funding by any agency for this research work.
Conflicts of Interest: The author declares no specific conflict of interest.

REFERENCES

AbendscheinR.DesaiS.AstellA. J. (2023). Towards Accessibility Guidelines for the Metaverse: A Synthesis of Recommendations for People Living With Dementia. doi:10.25972/OPUS-32019

Agarwal, A., & Alathur, S. (2023). *Metaverse revolution and the digital transformation: Intersectional analysis of Industry 5.0. Transforming Government: People*, Process and Policy. doi:10.1108/TG-03-2023-0036

Alcón, A. P. (2023). The acquisition (or not) of property in the metaverse: The tokenization of real estate assets. *Revista de Derecho Civil, 10*(2), 163–185.

Alkhatib, Y. J., Forte, A., Bitelli, G., Pierdicca, R., & Malinverni, E. (2023). Bringing Back Lost Heritage into Life by 3D Reconstruction in Metaverse and Virtual Environments: The Case Study of Palmyra, Syria. In L. T. De Paolis, P. Arpaia, & M. Sacco (Eds.), *Extended Reality* (Vol. 14219, pp. 91–106). Springer Nature Switzerland. doi:10.1007/978-3-031-43404-4_7

Ante, L., Wazinski, F.-P., & Saggu, A. (2023). Digital real estate in the metaverse: An empirical analysis of retail investor motivations. *Finance Research Letters, 58*, 104299. doi:10.1016/j.frl.2023.104299

Aslam, A. M., Chaudhary, R., Bhardwaj, A., Budhiraja, I., Kumar, N., & Zeadally, S. (2023). Metaverse for 6G and Beyond: The Next Revolution and Deployment Challenges. *IEEE Internet of Things Magazine, 6*(1), 32–39. doi:10.1109/IOTM.001.2200248

Bartels, N., & Hahne, K. (2023). Teaching Building Information Modeling in the Metaverse—An Approach Based on Quantitative and Qualitative Evaluation of the Students Perspective. *Buildings*, *13*(9), 2198. doi:10.3390/buildings13092198

Bojic, L. (2022). Metaverse through the prism of power and addiction: What will happen when the virtual world becomes more attractive than reality? *European Journal of Futures Research*, *10*(1), 22. doi:10.1186/s40309-022-00208-4

Buhalis, D., Leung, D., & Lin, M. (2023). Metaverse as a disruptive technology revolutionising tourism management and marketing. *Tourism Management*, *97*, 104724. doi:10.1016/j.tourman.2023.104724

Chen, C., Zhang, K. Z. K., Chu, Z., & Lee, M. (2023). Augmented reality in the metaverse market: The role of multimodal sensory interaction. *Internet Research*. Advance online publication. doi:10.1108/INTR-08-2022-0670

Chen, H.-J. (2023). Gather in the metaverse: Learning outcomes, virtual presence, and perceptions of high- and low-achieving pre-service teachers of English as a Foreign Language. *Education and Information Technologies*. Advance online publication. doi:10.1007/s10639-023-12135-3

Chenna, S. (2023). Augmented Reality and AI: Enhancing Human-Computer Interaction in the Metaverse. SSRN *Electronic Journal*. doi:10.2139/ssrn.4324629

De Marco, E. L., Longo, A., & Zappatore, M. (2023). Game Engine Platforms Supporting Metaverse-Linking Process: A Proposed Case Study on Virtual 3D Printing. In L. T. De Paolis, P. Arpaia, & M. Sacco (Eds.), *Extended Reality* (Vol. 14218, pp. 198–209). Springer Nature Switzerland. doi:10.1007/978-3-031-43401-3_13

El Jaouhari, A., Arif, J., Samadhiya, A., Kumar, A., & Trinkūnas, V. (2023). Are we there Or Do we have more to do? Metaverse in Facility Management and Future Prospects. *International Journal of Strategic Property Management*, *27*(3), 159–175. doi:10.3846/ijspm.2023.19516

FB. (2021, October 28). *Introducing Meta: A Social Technology Company*. https://about.fb.com/news/2021/10/facebook-company-is-now-meta/

Filipova, I. A. (2023). Creating the Metaverse: Consequences for Economy, Society, and Law. *Journal of Digital Technologies and Law*, *1*(1), 7–32. doi:10.21202/jdtl.2023.1

Havele, A., Polys, N., Benman, W., & Brutzman, D. (2022). The Keys to an Open, Interoperable Metaverse. *The 27th International Conference on 3D Web Technology*, 1–7. 10.1145/3564533.3564575

Hemphill, T. A. (2023). The 'Metaverse' and the challenge of responsible standards development. *Journal of Responsible Innovation*, *10*(1), 2243121. doi:10.1080/23299460.2023.2243121

Hyun, W. (2023). Study on standardization for Interoperable Metaverse. *2023 25th International Conference on Advanced Communication Technology (ICACT)*, 319–322. 10.23919/ICACT56868.2023.10079642

Jack, W. (2023, July 18). *Tokenization of Real Estate: The Ultimate Guide to Invest in Tokenized Real Estate*. https://faun.pub/tokenization-of-real-estate-the-ultimate-guide-to-invest-in-tokenized-real-estate-59c5c89f3658

Jafar, R. M. S., & Ahmad, W. (2023). Tourist loyalty in the metaverse: The role of immersive tourism experience and cognitive perceptions. *Tourism Review*. Advance online publication. doi:10.1108/TR-11-2022-0552

Jeong, W.-J., Oh, G.-S., Oh, S.-H., & Whangbo, T.-K. (2023). Establishment of Production Standards for Web-based Metaverse Content: Focusing on Accessibility and HCI. *Journal of Web Engineering*. Advance online publication. doi:10.13052/jwe1540-9589.2181

Kim, H. (2023). An Analysis of Domestic and International Research Trends on Metaverse. *Journal of the Korean Society for Library and Information Science*, *57*(3), 351–379. doi:10.4275/KSLIS.2023.57.3.351

Mogaji, E., Dwivedi, Y. K., & Raman, R. (2023). Fashion marketing in the metaverse. *Journal of Global Fashion Marketing*, 1–16. doi:10.1080/20932685.2023.2249483

Mogaji, E., Wirtz, J., Belk, R. W., & Dwivedi, Y. K. (2023). Immersive time (ImT): Conceptualizing time spent in the metaverse. *International Journal of Information Management*, *72*, 102659. doi:10.1016/j.ijinfomgt.2023.102659

Mourtzis, D., Angelopoulos, J., & Panopoulos, N. (2023). Metaverse and Blockchain in Education for collaborative Product-Service System (PSS) Design towards University 5.0. *Procedia CIRP*, *119*, 456–461. doi:10.1016/j.procir.2023.01.008

Muhammad Khan, F., & Ullah Khan, I. (2023). *The Game-Changing Impact of 5G and Metaverse on the Future of E-Learning*. https://www.researchgate.net/publication/368397907

Murtas, G., Pedeliento, G., & Mangiò, F. (2023). Luxury fashion brands at the gates of the Web 3.0: An analysis of early experimentations with NFTs and the metaverse. *Journal of Global Fashion Marketing*, 1–25. doi:10.1080/20932685.2023.2249476

Ni, P., Zhu, J., & Wang, G. (2023). Activity-Oriented Production Promotion Utility Maximization in Metaverse Social Networks. *IEEE/ACM Transactions on Networking*, 1–15. doi:10.1109/TNET.2023.3309624

Njoku, J. N., Ifeanyi Nwakanma, C., & Kim, D.-S. (2022). The Role of 5G Wireless Communication System in the Metaverse. *2022 27th Asia Pacific Conference on Communications (APCC)*, 290–294. 10.1109/APCC55198.2022.9943778

Ochoa, A. M. M., Corgo, S. R., & Cristóbal, I. D. (2023). Metaverse and mental health, what about the future? *European Psychiatry*, *66*(S1). Advance online publication. doi:10.1192/j.eurpsy.2023.1171

Parker, C., Yoo, S., Lee, Y., Fredericks, J., Dey, A., Cho, Y., & Billinghurst, M. (2023). Towards an Inclusive and Accessible Metaverse. *Extended Abstracts of the 2023 CHI Conference on Human Factors in Computing Systems*, 1–5. 10.1145/3544549.3573811

Qasem, Z., Hmoud, H. Y., Hajawi, D., & Al Zoubi, J. Z. (2022). The Effect of Technostress on Cyberbullying in Metaverse Social Platforms. In A. Elbanna, S. McLoughlin, Y. K. Dwivedi, B. Donnellan, & D. Wastell (Eds.), *Co-creating for Context in the Transfer and Diffusion of IT* (Vol. 660, pp. 291–296). Springer International Publishing. doi:10.1007/978-3-031-17968-6_22

Rawal, B. S., Mentges, A., & Ahmad, S. (2022). The Rise of Metaverse and Interoperability with Split-Protocol. *2022 IEEE 23rd International Conference on Information Reuse and Integration for Data Science (IRI)*, 192–199. 10.1109/IRI54793.2022.00051

Ritterbusch, G. D., & Teichmann, M. R. (2023). Defining the Metaverse: A Systematic Literature Review. *IEEE Access : Practical Innovations, Open Solutions*, *11*, 12368–12377. doi:10.1109/ACCESS.2023.3241809

Seitova, D., & Malik, G. (2023). Unlocking the Metaverse: Revolutionizing Resource Learning for Future Students. *International Journal of Educational Technology and Artificial Intelligence*, *2*(2). https://topazart.info/e-journals/index.php/ijetai/article/view/34

Shen, B., Tan, W., Guo, J., Zhao, L., & Qin, P. (2021). How to Promote User Purchase in Metaverse? A Systematic Literature Review on Consumer Behavior Research and Virtual Commerce Application Design. *Applied Sciences (Basel, Switzerland)*, *11*(23), 11087. doi:10.3390/app112311087

Siniarski, B., Alwis, C. D., Gür, G., & Liyanage, M. (2016). *Need of 6G for the Metaverse Realization.* Academic Press.

Smaili, N., & De Rancourt-Raymond, A. (2022). Metaverse: Welcome to the new fraud marketplace. *Journal of Financial Crime*. Advance online publication. doi:10.1108/JFC-06-2022-0124

Um, T., Kim, H., Kim, H., Lee, J., Koo, C., & Chung, N. (2022). Travel Incheon as a Metaverse: Smart Tourism Cities Development Case in Korea. In J. L. Stienmetz, B. Ferrer-Rosell, & D. Massimo (Eds.), *Information and Communication Technologies in Tourism 2022* (pp. 226–231). Springer International Publishing. doi:10.1007/978-3-030-94751-4_20

Upadhyay, U., Kumar, A., Sharma, G., Gupta, B. B., Alhalabi, W. A., Arya, V., & Chui, K. T. (2023). Cyberbullying in the Metaverse: A Prescriptive Perception on Global Information Systems for User Protection. *Journal of Global Information Management*, *31*(1), 1–25. doi:10.4018/JGIM.325793

Usmani, S. S., Sharath, M., & Mehendale, M. (2022). Future of mental health in the metaverse. *General Psychiatry*, *35*(4), e100825. doi:10.1136/gpsych-2022-100825 PMID:36189180

Volk, D. (2008). Co-creative game development in a participatory Metaverse. *Proceedings of the Tenth Anniversary Conference on Participatory Design 2008*, 262–265.

Wang, J., Makowski, S., Cieslik, A., Lv, H., & Lv, Z. (2023). Fake News in Virtual Community, Virtual Society, and Metaverse: A Survey. *IEEE Transactions on Computational Social Systems*, 1–15. doi:10.1109/TCSS.2022.3220420

Wang, Y., Siau, K. L., & Wang, L. (2022). Metaverse and Human-Computer Interaction: A Technology Framework for 3D Virtual Worlds. In J. Y. C. Chen, G. Fragomeni, H. Degen, & S. Ntoa (Eds.), *HCI International 2022 – Late Breaking Papers: Interacting with eXtended Reality and Artificial Intelligence* (Vol. 13518, pp. 213–221). Springer Nature Switzerland. doi:10.1007/978-3-031-21707-4_16

Yıldız, İ., & Tanyıldızı, N. İ. (2022). An Analysis of News Containing Cyberbullying in the Metaverse. In G. Sarı (Ed.), Advances in Social Networking and Online Communities. IGI Global. doi:10.4018/978-1-6684-5426-8.ch012

Yoo, B., Kim, A., Moon, H. S., So, M.-K., Jeong, T.-D., Lee, K. E., Moon, B.-I., & Huh, J. (2024). Evaluation of Group Genetic Counseling Sessions via a Metaverse-based Application. *Annals of Laboratory Medicine*, *44*(1), 82–91. doi:10.3343/alm.2024.44.1.82 PMID:37665289

Zhang, J., & Quoquab, F. (2023). Metaverse in the urban destinations in China: Some insights for the tourism players. *International Journal of Tourism Cities*. doi:10.1108/IJTC-04-2023-0062

KEY TERMS AND DEFINITIONS

Augmented Reality (AR): AR is a technology that brings digital information to the real world. It value adds upon the physical environment and creating a more immersive experience.

Avatar: An avatar is a digital representation of a user or character in a virtual world or game.

Headset: A headset is a wearable hardware device that users will wear to watch and experience virtual and augmented reality. The device usually includes a display, tracking sensors, and input controls so that the user will be able to interact with virtual environments in an immersive manner.

Metaverse: Metaverse is a virtual world where users can interact with one another and with digital objects and environments, creating a sense of presence and immersion through advanced technologies such as virtual reality and augmented reality.

Mixed Reality (MR): An MR is a combination of AR and VR, where the digital and physical worlds are blended together to create a more immersive and interactive experience.

Roblox: Roblox is a user-generated gaming platform that has evolved into a metaverse where users can create, play, and explore virtual worlds and experiences.

Second Life: Second Life is a virtual world platform that allows users to create avatars and engage in a range of social and creative activities. The platform was launched in 2003 and was one of the first virtual worlds to gain mainstream attention. Second Life has been used to explore a range of social, educational, and business applications, and is seen as a precursor to the metaverse.

Unity3D: A cross-platform game engine that enables developers to create interactive 3D experiences, including metaverse applications and virtual reality experiences.

Virtual Reality: Virtual reality refers to the use of computer technology to create a simulated environment that can be experienced by a user. Virtual reality typically involves the use of a headset or other display device that allows the user to see and interact with a virtual environment in a more immersive way.

Virtual World: A virtual world is a computer-based simulated environment that allows users to interact with each other and digital objects in a virtual space.

Chapter 9
The Future of Decentralized Governance With DAO and Web 3

Bikkina Srinivas
Vingas Industries Private Limited, India

U. V. Adinarayana Rao
GITAM School of Business, GITAM University (Deemed), India

ABSTRACT

Web 3 is considered the next generation of the internet. Decentralized autonomous organizations (DAOs) are considered the next avatar of organizations run digitally over blockchain-led technology platforms. Business logic and rules for running the organization are programmed in distributed applications (dApps) and executed using smart contracts. Token-based rights allow owing members to vote, participate in governance, and direct how the organization will be run. While DAOs are facing several legal and regulatory challenges on one side and fighting with technical vulnerabilities and hacks on the other side, future research in this field appears promising. There is an enormous need for education and awareness of the functioning of these emerging models, which can be dealt with using a multi-faceted approach. Decentralized governance can have a massive societal impact and lead to an equitable world. It drives financial inclusion and puts automatic decision-making at the fore.

INTRODUCTION

Background on Emerging Web 3 Technologies and Blockchain

Web3 and blockchain are key emerging technologies that can potentially revolutionize the functioning of the internet. As the next generational step in the information age, Web3 is a vision for a new iteration of the internet (Sheridan et al., 2022). It is designed to be more decentralized, secure, and private than the current web. Web3 is expected to be built on several technologies, including blockchain, a distributed

DOI: 10.4018/979-8-3693-1532-3.ch009

ledger technology that allows for safe, tamper-proof, and transparent transactions without intermediaries (Gupta & Sadoghi, 2019).

Web3 brings in many features necessary for the next generation of web users. Considering the growing importance of personal data privacy, Web3 users are expected to have more control over their data and how it will be used. Web3 emphasizes decentralized applications (dApps) as a critical feature (Korpal & Scott, 2022). These applications are built on blockchain technology and will not be controlled by any single entity but by their users. Similarly, smart contracts are another critical feature of Web3. These self-executing contracts are stored on the blockchain. They can be executed automatically without the need for intermediaries.

Blockchain disrupts traditional business systems by eliminating middlemen and central platforms. This paves the way to a "platform-as-a-service" era (Trabucchi et al., 2020). It works by creating a chain of blocks that are linked together. Each block contains a record of transactions that have taken place. Network participants verify transactions on the blockchain but cannot tamper with it, making blockchain very secure and transparent.

The Web3 involves several emerging technologies – Blockchain, Extended AR/VR, and Artificial Intelligence. These technologies are expected to work in collaboration with each other, bringing about value. So, they can potentially revolutionize how businesses are run, especially in financial services. Digital assets and tokens are expected to change the way payments are made. The new technologies also facilitate newer governance models, changing how organizations will be governed. A brief overview of these is presented here:

1. **Decentralized Finance (DeFi):** The entire DeFi ecosystem is called the "Lego of finance" as a metaphor for its composibility (Popescu, 2020). DeFi has several applications based on Blockchain technology, allowing users to lend, borrow, trade, and invest assets without intermediaries (Meyer et al., 2021).
2. **Non-Fungible Tokens (NFTs):** NFTs are unique digital assets. They convert ownership of digital items such as art, music, and collectibles into tokenized form. The ownership details of these are stored on a tamper-proof blockchain ledger. NFT is currently in its 2.0 version, which focuses on interoperability, programmability, and scalability (Guidi & Michienzi, 2023).
3. **Decentralized Autonomous Organizations (DAOs)**: DAOs are new-generation organizations coordinated and governed by their members using blockchain technology (Hassan & De Filippi, 2021). DAOs have exciting use cases in crowdfunding, NFT-powered investment, dApp governance, proposal execution, and decentralization in the Metaverse.

Decentralization as the Defining Principle of Web 3

Decentralization is the foundation of Web3. It presents a paradigm shift in how information is disseminated and interacted online. It moves away from the traditional centralized Web2 model, where a few powerful entities control the flow of information and services. Web3 attempts to empower users by allowing them to manage the data and digital assets fully. This gives greater autonomy, security, and transparency and keeps the web user truly at the centre of the ecosystem. Decentralized networks and blockchain technology form the backbone of this new ecosystem, enabling the creation of open, censorship-resistant, and trustless systems. By eliminating intermediaries, Web3 fosters a more equitable and democratic digital landscape where everyone has an equal voice and stake in the network.

The decentralized architecture of Web3 will benefit a wide range of industries and sectors - from how finances are offered to how users make social media posts. For example, decentralized finance (DeFi) applications allow users to borrow, lend, and trade assets without involving intermediaries, delivering quickly and at a reduced cost. Decentralized social media platforms give users more control over their data and enable them to connect, communicate, interact, and share with other users without a central authority.

Defining DAOs and Their Role in Decentralized Governance

DAOs are digital entities (such as firms, corporations, and organizations) that operate through Smart contracts on Blockchain networks (Napieralska & Kępczyński, 2023a). The business and operational rules for running the organization are coded in a program, such as a Decentralized Application (dApp or DApp). They are characterized by their ability to self-govern and self-regulate in an automated manner without the interference of intermediaries or centralized authorities. DAOs are run by their owners (members), who make decisions through a consensus-based voting system. This decentralized governance model allows for a more democratic and transparent decision-making process because all members will have an equal say in the direction and management of the organization. Organizations will receive good corporate governance practices. They will maintain transparent accountability practices. Overall, they function better compared to the traditional corporate models.

Role and Potential of DAOs

DAOs have multiple dimensions in the context of decentralized governance. Firstly, they provide a framework for decentralized decision-making. Members can reach a consensus on various issues online - from financial decisions to strategic planning. Secondly, DAOs allow the creation of decentralized communities. In this, members can collaborate and engage in discussions while having a stake in the decision-making process. This fosters a sense of ownership and accountability among the members. This can lead to more effective and sustainable decision-making. Hence, the fate and future of the organization and its functioning are collectively in the hands of its members.

In addition, DAOs can serve as a tool for decentralized finance (DeFi) and decentralized data management (that allows for decentralized data searches, distributed authorization mechanisms, and Smart contract exploitation) (Zichichi et al., 2022). They can issue tokens representing ownership or assets, which can be traded on decentralized exchanges. This enables the creation of decentralized financial systems that are not controlled by any single entity. Furthermore, DAOs can also manage and store data decentralized, ensuring that a single entity does not control data and is accessible to all members.

DAO or DAC?

DAC is a Decentralized Autonomous Corporation (Wright, 2020). Many people use them interchangeably, while few term DAC to be a DAO that makes profits for its shareholders. By attributing the word "Corporation", a DAO will probably obtain a legal framework like a Limited Liability Company (LLC). The LAO (TheLAO, 2023) is a for-profit, legally compliant US venture capital fund that runs on the principles of a DAO. It is a Delaware limited liability company primarily administered through an online distributed application ("DApp") and related Smart contracts. It was launched in late April 2020 and is backed by over 130 projects across the Ethereum and blockchain ecosystem. At least for now, there is no clear differentiation between a DAO and a DAC.

Benefits of Decentralized Governance

Several decentralized governance models have recently been developed - reputation-based systems, liquid democracy, and DAO (Surve & Khandelwal, 2023). DAOs and decentralized governance are interconnected concepts. DAOs serve the organizational structure for which the decentralized governance mechanisms are used in decision-making. Combining these two concepts contributes to developing more open, transparent, and community-driven systems in the Blockchain space. The advantages of Decentralized Governance are best studied in four areas:

1. Transparency and accountability
2. Democracy and inclusion
3. Efficiency and effectiveness
4. Innovation and creativity

Transparency and accountability are fundamental principles in decentralized governance. These two ensure the responsible and ethical functioning of the local government structures.

Transparency refers to the open and accessible flow of information. Citizens will be able to understand decision-making processes and access government data. It fosters trust and informed civic participation. DAO rules are programmed into smart contracts. The rules are openly shown and available for members to scrutinize. Accountability is the obligation of the officials to answer for their actions and decisions. DAOs come with features related to accountability to ensure that the elected representatives and oversight bodies are accountable for their activities in the decentralized system.

DAOs have the power to reduce corruption because of the sound governance principles that the system promotes. This helps in efficient public service delivery. Shareholders will have complete control over the working of DAO. No government will influence its activities. Decentralized governance systems will help local authorities make decisions quickly and easily. Because the activities are transparent and accountable, these decisions will be equitably and responsive and benefit the community. DAOs encourage public engagement and ensure that elected officials remain accountable to their constituents. This strengthens the democratic foundations of decentralized governance.

DAOs promote a democratic and inclusive form of governance compared to traditional hierarchical structures. DAOs promote the participation of stakeholders in decision-making through an on-chain voting system. This removes participation barriers and gives all members an equal say regardless of factors like gender, age, or socioeconomic status. Additionally, on-chain governance introduces transparency, where all proposals and votes are public. These systems will build trust.

Smart contracts help DAOs to operate with higher efficiency and effectiveness. They automate workflows and execute organizational decisions by executing transactions and implementing administrative rules and operational logic (Chao et al., 2022). Actions get triggered automatically through coded rules and parameters. This removes the need for human interpretations. It is faster and reduces operating costs as well. Data records are held on distributed ledgers and provide a single source of truth. Member coordination will improve. Token-based economies further align incentives to maximize collective benefit. Removing central control and intermediaries through decentralization allows DAOs to streamline processes and optimize stakeholder resource allocation. Overall, DAO comes with features that lead to a new generation of organizational economics and transform organizations to be democratic and distributed (Bellavitis et al., 2023).

Example

Aragon is a popular project that started to create decentralized organizations. It runs on the Ethereum blockchain and is governed by smart contracts. It provides a framework and tools for creating and managing DAOs, enabling a transparent and accountable decision-making process. Members can easily participate in proposals and case votes without any barriers. It has a no-code setup with easy minting and token distribution, making deployment easy.

EVOLUTION OF DAOS

Early Blockchain Experiments With DAOs

Blockchain technology and smart contracts have evolved over time. They are critical pillars in the development of distributed governance models in the form of DAOs (Rikken et al., 2019). The concept of self-governance organizational models are trending now. Some such recent phenomenon are the Cyber Movement Organizations (CMOs) on the internet, and Distributed Artificial Intelligence (DAI).

"The DAO" is one of the first experiments of the concept that followed the DAO approach. It was able to raise funds successfully. Unfortunately, it got hacked resulting in a huge loss to its stakeholders. The incident has highlighted the risks associated with the DAO model. The failure led to experimenting with different methods and models to make the concept robust. Smart contract security practices and governance token design are upgraded and more powerful. Several newer forms of DAOs, such as liquid democracies to cooperative organizations run through on-chain voting, emerged. Some famous examples of such platforms are Daohaus, Colony, and Aragon. Since numerous DAO platforms have evolved, researchers have worked on a decision model for selecting the right DAO platform (Baninemeh et al., 2023).

Another set of parallel DAOs emerged in the form of grant-awarding DAOs like Gitcoin and Moloch using novel quadratic voting and continuous liquid democracy tools.

Growing Use of DAO Models for Funding Projects

DAO funding models have gained traction for supporting collaborative projects. Rather than relying on traditional venture capital, DAOs allow like-minded communities to self-organize and crowdfund initiatives through blockchain-based governance. Notable examples include Gitcoin granting over $100 million to open-source software development and Moloch facilitating funding for public goods. Another active area is decentralized scientific research DAOs such as ResearchHub, which crowdsource hypotheses testing. This suggests that DAOs can effectively distribute knowledge creation and problem-solving resources beyond geography, affiliations, or investment thesis constraints.

DAO, however, would be limited because of scalability and other blockchain limitations. Increasing member (userbase) counts will impact the coordination efficiency of the system. Novel methods experimenting with off-chain organization and on-chain settlements may address this. The legal status also lacks regulatory clarity, and regulatory sandboxes have helped evaluate compliance models. Furthermore, funding sustainability necessitates continual value accrual to token holders, which projects must strategize. Long-tail distributions in proposal voting also accentuate winner-take-all dynamics requiring thoughtful incentive rebalancing. Despite challenges, the participatory and liquid funding presented by DAOs has the potential to support a diversity of open initiatives that are difficult to finance otherwise, especially as blockchain capabilities mature.

Newer DAOs were able to address and resolve some of the challenges that old DAOs used to suffer. Visible updates can be seen in governance scalability, addressing security vulnerabilities, legal and regulatory compliance, user experience and adoption and, to some extent, governance participation.

WORKING OF A DAO

Technical Architecture: Smart Contracts, Governance Tokens

Smart contracts are at the core of a DAO's technical architecture (Napieralska & Kępczyński, 2023b). Smart contracts are self-executing, programmable agreements that run on blockchain platforms. Ethereum is one such platform that supports the necessary scripting languages and consensus algorithms.

They automatically execute actions according to predefined rules and eliminate the need for intermediaries. Examples of these rules are codified governance mechanisms like voting and proposal processes. Smart contracts will define the organization's rules, roles, and decision-making processes within a DAO. These contracts facilitate transparent and trustless operations. With this, the organization follows the predefined rules without human intervention. Several tools and accelerators are available to deal with the managerial challenges of redesigning decentralized business models (Saurabh et al., 2023). Few other researchers proposed a five-layered architecture (Wang et al., 2019). Smart contracts can programmed to handle various business functions and logics - such as fund management, voting mechanisms, and the distribution of governance tokens.

Governance tokens are digital assets that allow holders (owners) to get involved in the organizational decision-making processes (Rutskiy et al., 2023). These tokens provide members ownership stakes and voting weight proportional to their holdings. Since they represent voting power, they allow stakeholders to influence the organization's direction and policies. Governance tokens democratize the decision-making within a DAO. Thus, the outcome will emerge as a collective effort rather than being centralized in a few hands. These tokens are often distributed through token sales or airdrops as incentives for participation, and the number of tokens held typically determines the weight of one's vote. This aligns incentives while allowing open and pseudonymous participation. Code upgrades and changes require on-chain governance votes by token holders. So, they exert influence on the functioning of the DAO.

The technical architecture of a DAO combines these two elements to create a decentralized, self-governing entity. Smart contracts manage the allocation and distribution of governance tokens while defining the rules for voting and decision-making. When proposals or changes are introduced, token holders can cast their votes through the Smart Contract, and the results are executed automatically according to the rules set in the code.

Layer 2 solutions are expanding their capacity and scalability for real-world deployment (Unnikrishnan & Victer Paul, 2022). Interoperable standards are also vital in realizing the vision of a decentralized web where value and data can flow freely across disjointed systems. Frontend interfaces leverage Web 3 technologies to provide user-friendly access to these permissionless backend structures.

Web 3 technologies, including blockchain and decentralized storage, are pivotal in ensuring these systems' transparency, security, and immutability. With Web 3, data is stored across a distributed network of nodes, reducing the risk of censorship and centralization. This architecture enables DAOs to operate autonomously without reliance on centralized servers or institutions.

Governance Processes: Voting and Decision Making, On-Chain Coordination

On-chain voting protocols are embedded in DAO frameworks using purpose-built Smart contracts. Voting mechanisms steer strategic direction and enable collaborative decision-making at scale (Dimitri, 2023). Proposals can cover changes to system parameters, funding initiatives, operations, and risks. Several voting mechanisms now exist, allowing platforms to select the most suitable ones (Kurniawan, 2022). Members weighted votes based on crypto-economic incentives using governance tokens like time-locks, quadratic voting, or liquid democracy (Li et al., 2023). Mechanisms used for on-chain voting and decision-making within DAOs are:

1. Token-weighted Voting
2. Quadratic Voting
3. Delegated Voting
4. Futarchy
5. Threshold Voting and
6. Conviction Voting

While expanding participation, challenges remain around coordination efficiency as voter turnouts and proposal quality impact outcomes. Research explores mitigations like vote delegation, quadratic funding pools, and off-chain deliberation before on-chain settlements. Social voting patterns like herding must also be addressed to optimize informed consensus.

New schemes experiment with token curation rewards and prediction markets to crowdsource proposal evaluation. Continual liquid feedback systems gather opinions throughout proposal lifecycles rather than single votes. Stake-weighted poll features on DAO forums facilitate discussion proportional to member investments.

On-chain treasury management contracts automate funding allocation according to voting results while upholding transparency. Capital is dispersed via crypto-economic assurances like staged releases. Interoperable wallet integrations enhance access.

The iterative innovations balance coordination and protection against manipulation or disproportional influence as blockchain governance matures. With careful design grounded in mechanism design theory, DAO processes can optimize open collaboration at the Internet scale. The features of DAO make it work like a modernized form of corporate governance (Tokmakov, 2019).

Financial Model: Initial Funding, Revenues, and Treasury Management

DAOs are commonly bootstrapped through cryptoeconomic mechanisms like initial coin offerings (ICOs) or launchpad fundraising rounds (Myalo, 2019). This enables communities to crowdfund the initial project development capital and operations. Compliant public sales of governance tokens following regulatory guidelines assist financing.

Revenue streams then aim to sustain the DAO long-term. For protocols, transaction fees from network usage fill treasuries. Applications may earn subscription revenues or take cuts from bundled services. Non-profits seek grants. Regardless, income accrues token value through buy-backs or burn mechanisms.

Modern treasury funds are governed by token holders using on-chain smart contract voting. Some commonly used techniques in this area are:

1. Multi-signature wallets
2. Ringfence reserves
3. Risk management controls

Transparency puts the organizational mission first over individuals' self-interests. Staged funding models are used to disburse capital proportionally. The fund management is linked to milestones inorder to balance risk versus rewards. DAOs come with stronger treasury management capabilities. This helps in long-term sustainability and stay resileient, especially when facing tough situations. While challenges remain regarding revenue dependency, security assurances, and regulatory ambiguity, continuous innovation helps to DAOs to stay reliabile and helps in strengthening them as decentralized organizations.

Modern alternative financing system include competitive grant programs awarded to projects. New capital allocation methods allow the optimization of resource distribution. Social impacts is given more importance over simplistic profit motives. DAOs also explore hybrid ownership, transferring partial administrative control to for-profit subsidiaries pursuing larger-scale missions.

USE CASES OF DAOS IN WEB3

Decentralized Finance (DeFi) Protocols

Decentralized Finance (DeFi) protocols are essential components of DAOs in a Web3 economy. They reflect the early success cases of DAOs. As decentralized lending, trading, and savings services are powered by smart contracts and governed through token holders, DeFi DAOs demonstrate scalable financial products functioning without intermediaries. DAOs help in the governance and decision-making processes of DeFi platforms. Community members members can thus vote on crucial matters and direct the flow and working of the organization. Some common topics on which voting is done include protocol upgrades, changes to economic parameters, and the addition or removal of assets. This democratic approach improves transparency and inclusivity and allows for better alignment with the decentralized philosophy of Web3.

Investment DAOs

Investment DAOs allows members to collate crypto funds and allocate them to ventures or assets through a democratic process. This form of community-led investing empowers a community of investors to make investment decisions collectively. They allow for a decentralized approach to portfolio management. This not only democratizes investment opportunities but also fosters a sense of community ownership and accountability. DAO projects are found to reduce information asymmetry and lead to better market pricing compared to non-DAO projects. The efficiency is better with increasing liquidity and age (Perez Riaza & Gnabo, 2023).

Grant-Making DAOs

Grant-making DAOs (or simply Grant DAOs or Philanthropy DAOs) have emerged as innovative funding models, particularly for open-source projects such as philanthropy and funding initiatives. These are considered the future of giving (Braeckman, 2022). These DAOs enable communities to collectively decide on allocating funds for various projects, promoting transparency and reducing reliance on centralized authorities. This model enhances the efficiency of grant distribution to individuals and organizations and ensures that the community's values align with the projects receiving support. DAOs are not just for commercial organizations but also non-profit organizations.

Examples include Gitcoin supporting public goods through a Decentralized Autonomous Community (DAC) structure (Gitcoin, 2023). Social DAOs aim to strengthen online collaboration using decentralized technologies. Platforms like Pleasr allow peer-to-peer coordination on creative, social impact initiatives through blockchain-based collective decision-making. DAOmatch maintains a list of DAOs accepting applications for grants and funding (DAOmatch, 2023).

Social DAOs

Social DAOs leverage decentralized governance structures to enable community-driven decision-making in social platforms. From content moderation to feature development, social DAO users collectively shape the platform's direction. This empowers users and cultivates a sense of ownership and responsibility within the community. Some Music DAOs are set to revolutionize the industry with Listen-To-Earn and yet aspire to incentivize artists and content creators (Behal, 2022).

Service DAOs

Service DAOs coordinate to provide services or products. These DAOs have found applications where community members collectively manage and govern service providers. These DAOs enhance trust and transparency, as users have a direct say in the decision-making processes related to service offerings, quality standards, and dispute resolutions.

For example, 0xmons levels game assets production through modular membership roles and voting, validating new means of distributed workforce collaboration.

Crowdfunding of Apps/Projects

Crowdfunding DAOs facilitate development funding through open democratic participation on platforms like DAOStack, allowing token holders to support projects directly in exchange for ownership.

Through token-based voting mechanisms, project backers in a DAO collectively decide on funding allocations, milestones, and project developments. This approach mitigates risks associated with centralized fundraising platforms and ensures that backers directly influence project outcomes.

Decentralized Autonomous Companies (DACs)

Decentralized autonomous companies represent an innovative organizational structure. These companies are governed through smart contracts and cryptocurrencies. DACs represent a broader application of DAOs in the formation and operation of fully decentralized companies. DACs use smart contracts and "tokenomics" to create organizations without traditional hierarchical structures. Smart contracts take care of all activities - from governance to revenue distribution. They promote efficiency, transparency, and community-driven decision-making.

Some examples of DACs are as follows. Uniswap, BitDAO, and MakerDAO from the finance and investment segments, DeepDAO, and Friends With Benefits from Arts and Media, and AssangeDAO and FreeRossDAO from other segments.

Decentralized Knowledge-Sharing Platforms

The Knowledge Sharing 3.0 generation involves semantic knowledge-sharing mechanisms (Zhang et al., 2020). Technologies like blockchain play a critical role here. "Steem" is a decentralized knowledge platform that uses DAO principles. On this platform, users can share content and build communities with remuneration for contributions and mediating. Information is spread through decentralized consensus. This model ensures that decisions regarding platform features, content moderation, and incentives are made collectively. These features align with the platform's evolution with the needs and preferences of its user base.

Decentralized Social Organizations

Certain programs are seen using DAO as a means to achieve societal benefits. DAOs are reshaping social organizations by enabling decentralized governance structures for clubs, associations, and communities. Applications of these models range from event planning to resource allocation. Members of Social DAOs can collaboratively make decisions, have stronger community engagement and bonding, and take shared responsibility.

Examples of Social DAOs include Supernova, which backs advocacy work on universal basic incomes through community funding. Environmental DAO (EnviroDAO) funds carbon removal projects selected by voting members in a decentralized, incentivized manner. Several DAOs run on social impact and ecological and environmental space (Davis, 2021).

CHALLENGES AND OPPORTUNITIES

Being emerging models, DAOs will have to encounter, address, and resolve several challenges in their journey (Wang et al., 2019). The challenges can be at four levels:

1. Legal and regulatory challenges
2. Scalability and security challenges, especially in largescale DAOs
3. Technical vulnerabilities and hacks
4. The need for education and awareness, especially about governance and security

Addressing these challenges will be crucial to facilitating the responsible growth of DAOs and unlocking their positive societal impacts.

Legal and Regulatory Challenges

DAOs are decentralized entities. So, they pose unique challenges in terms of legal and regulatory frameworks. The absence of a centralized authority makes establishing legal accountability and liability difficult. Traditional legal structures are ill-equipped to handle the decentralized nature of DAOs, leading to ambiguity in jurisdiction and legal recourse. Concerns about taxation and potential liability for members could also be raised. They are not subject to physical or economic constraints (Chao et al., 2022).

Furthermore, legal ambiguities arose in most cases because most DAOs were operating in legally grey areas. Unlike traditional organizational structures, DAOs lack agreed jurisdictional oversight (Cloots, 2019). One reason for this could be because DAOs aim to be globally accessible. After all, DAOs depend on blockchain, which itself transcends geographical boundaries. So, establishing jurisdiction becomes a complex task.

Further, legal recognition varies vastly by geography. For example, US and EU regulations diverge on the classification of digital tokens, complicating cross-border DAOs (European Securities and Markets Authority., 2021). Resolving legal status and applicable laws is critical for DAOs' legitimacy and long-term viability.

Regulatory bodies worldwide are grappling with classifying and regulating DAOs (Ushida & Angel, 2021). Striking a balance between fostering innovation and protecting stakeholders is crucial for the sustainable growth of DAOs.

Contract enforcement and dispute resolution within DAOs present significant challenges. The absence of intermediaries calls for Smart contract development that is technically sound and legally enforceable. Striking this delicate balance requires collaboration between legal experts and blockchain developers to create a framework that aligns with existing legal systems. If DAOs become regulated, they must have 'sufficient decentralization' to not lose their properties. This leads to the need to assess DAOs on five parameters - Token-weighted voting, Infrastructure, Governance, Escalation, and Reputation (Axelsen et al., 2022).

Some recommendations and strategies to address these include:

1. Engaging legal experts
2. Exploring hybrid models
3. Advocating for regulatory clarity

Scalability and Security Challenges

Large, decentralized networks face issues aggregating participants' preferences and efficiently reaching consensus (Christidis & Devetsikiotis, 2016). Scaling DAOs can lead to increased coordination difficulties. This jeopardizes decision-making quality because, with increased participation, reaching a consensus among diverse stakeholders with varying interests can become time-consuming and complex. This leads to suboptimal or stalled outcomes unfit for greater responsibilities. Effective governance structures and consensus mechanisms must be implemented to streamline decision-making and prevent gridlock in DAO operations.

Scalability becomes more important as the DAO increases in size (such as a vast number of participants and transactions) and complexity (such as an increase in underlying business logic). The blockchain network's capacity and efficiency must be constantly monitored to prevent congestion and to ensure that its operations are going smoothly.

A balancing act is required to achieve scalability while maintaining decentralization. Researchers proposed several technical solutions to achieve this. Quadratic voting is a popular mechanism to optimize preference elicitation in large groups (Weyl, 2017). Security concerns would come up as the size of the system increases because of potential vulnerabilities in smart contracts and blockchain infrastructure. The examples of high-profile hacks on DAOs have highlighted the need for stronger security measures. Ensuring the integrity and confidentiality of transactions within a DAO is imperative for building trust among participants.

Some recommendations and strategies to address these include:

1. Integration of Layer 2 solutions, such as sidechains or state channels
2. Implement rigorous security protocols, including regular code audits, penetration testing, and formal verification techniques.

Technical Vulnerabilities and Hacks

DAOs, like any system/structure, are not immune to technical vulnerabilities and hacks. Smart contracts are the backbone of DAO governance and could have coding errors or bugs that can be exploited to manipulate the organization's operations or to divert funds. The immutability of blockchain technology makes it difficult to reverse such attacks. Here, the feature itself turned into a painpoint. This can potentially lead to significant financial losses and reputational damage to DAOs.

DAO suffered from extensive technical vulnerabilities in the past. The operational and adoption capabilities, especially integrity and functionality, are well tested with DAOs, which led to its emerging stronger and better. The irreversible and autonomous nature of smart contracts amplifies the impact of coding errors or vulnerabilities. Security audits and rigorous testing are essential to identify and rectify potential weaknesses before deployment.

There are several high-profile hacks wherein millions are stolen. These incidents highlight the risks of dependencies on blockchain infrastructure and Smart contracts. The DAO and Poly Network attacks are some outstanding examples of this. While bringing desirable attributes, the complexity of DAOs provides more attack surfaces requiring robust defense.

Developers must continuously update and patch smart contracts to stay ahead of the evolving security threats. DAOs require a collective effort from the community to address and mitigate vulnerabilities promptly. Advances in cybersecurity must keep pace with increasingly sophisticated exploits.

Some recommendations and strategies to address these include:

1. Incentivize security researchers to identify and report vulnerabilities.
2. Use multi-signature wallets
3. Develop and maintain Emergency response plans

Need for Education and Awareness

A few educational gaps and awareness levels around DAOs exist. The field is nascent, and the quantum of knowledge is small. There is a need for standardized knowledge of governance best practices, smart contract development, and social engineering. Coordinating and active participation is difficult without a sufficient understanding of decentralized technologies. This may discourage some while it can also attract bad actors who can bring in more challenges and choas.

The widespread adoption of DAOs depends on public understanding and education. The concept of decentralized governance and token-based ownership can be complex and unfamiliar to many individuals. This sometimes works negative as it creates barrier for the entry of potential participants. Educational efforts are necessary to raise awareness about DAOs. The courses can discuss about the benefits and potential risks, about bring trust. Encouragement for improving access to high-quality education on Blockchain and DAO engineering can help.

Awareness of the potential benefits and risks associated with DAO participation is essential. Participants must be equipped to make informed decisions. Building a community that understands the DAO vocabulary encourages a collaborative environment for innovation and growth.

Some recommendations and strategies to address these include:

1. Community outreach to conduct educational campaigns
2. Preparing documentation and tutorials
3. Partnerships and collaborations with educational institutions

Path for Overcoming the Challenges

A multi-dimensional approach is needed for DAOs to realize their vision of decentralized cooperation. Continued progress on the legal, coordination, security, and education fronts will help alleviate ambiguity and risk, improving the trust necessary for larger-scale, impactful DAOs. With a collaborative effort, challenges can be navigated to realize benefits like increased access, inclusion, and efficiency of socially impactful organizations, respecting principles like autonomy, transparency, and individual participation. Ongoing research on scalable governance protocols is very much the need of the hour.

FUTURE OF DECENTRALIZED GOVERNANCE

Societal Impact and Creating an Equitable World

One of the most promising aspects of DAOs is their potential to create a more just and equitable world (Surve & Khandelwal, 2023). By removing intermediaries and enabling direct participation, DAOs empower individuals to have a say in decision-making that affects their lives. This can lead to improved representation of marginalized communities and increase diversity in decision-making bodies.

Furthermore, DAOs can provide opportunities for financial inclusion. Financial inclusion focuses on providing valuable and affordable access to financial products and services by financial institutions, individuals, and firms so that their financial needs can be addressed. While considerable progress has been made so far, traditional financial systems are lagging, making many people inaccessible or exclusionary. Studies have already shown that financial technologies improve financial inclusion. DAOs offer inclusive alternatives that can provide financial services to underserved individuals around the globe. This has the potential to bridge the wealth gap and enable economic empowerment for the unbanked.

DAOs can accelerate innovation and cooperative efforts between geographically dispersed individuals. As a unique socio-technical model driven by open-source protocols and digital coordination, DAOs allow global networks of diverse actors to pool their various skills and assets to jointly create solutions applicable to some of humanity's most pressing problems. Examples include distributed efforts to mitigate anthropogenic climate change, alleviate socioeconomic deprivation, and enhance international healthcare access through innovative combinatorial contributions.

Future Research Directions

As an emerging technology in its early stages, the scope and dimensions of DAO are not yet fixed but are constantly evolving. Hence, there is much scope for research in this area. Several research directions can be explored, especially in DAO governance, from a management theory perspective and a technical implementation perspective.

Firstly, improving member participation and voting mechanisms is important. DAOs can utilize voting systems such as the quadratic voting (Weyl, 2017) or futarchic voting to guarantee equitable representation and distribution of decision-making authority among their members. Proposed by Robin Hanson, an economist, Futarchy is an untried form of government model in which "the basic rule of government would be: when a betting market estimates that a proposed policy would increase expected national welfare, that proposal becomes law."

Secondly, developing effective reputation systems is believed to help strengthen the DAO governance process. Reputation systems can promote trust, incentivize participation, and hold individuals accountable for their actions. Exploring innovative ways to design reputation systems that can capture both qualitative and quantitative factors will be valuable.

Research should be focused on creating scalable and adaptable governance frameworks. As DAOs grow in size and complexity, it becomes essential to design governance mechanisms that are efficient, flexible, and able to handle dynamic changes.

Finally, clearly mentioned decentralized dispute resolution and conflict management mechanisms will improve the DAO governance. Implementing automated dispute resolution protocols and decentralized arbitration systems can ensure transparency, fairness, and efficiency in resolving conflicts.

CONCLUSION

The Web3 ecosystem is formed by the cohesion of a bunch of emerging technologies. These technologies together promote for newer forms of governance systems. Decentralized Autonomous Organizations (DAOs) involve individual and group efforts and are run using blockchain-based rules. The rules are coded in the smart contracts and are automatically exceuted with little or no human intervention. This makes them distrinct from the traditional hierarchical management structures. The transition to decentralization aims to increase transparency, democracy, and efficiency compared to existing centralized models.

Early blockchain experiments with DAOs show their potential for coordination. The growing use of DAO models now funds diverse projects through group contribution and governance. Successful existing

DAOs, including Aave, Compound, and MakerDAO, govern decentralized finance protocols through on-chain voting. The technical operation relies on Smart contracts to automate governance processes and manage collective treasuries derived from member activity or initial funding.

DAOs provide innovative solutions across many use cases. In decentralized finance, they govern lending platforms, stablecoins, and exchanges. Investment DAOs collectively manage and allocate funds. Grant-making DAOs crowdsource ideas and distribute resources. Social DAOs organize communities and civic participation. Other areas include crowdfunding, services, knowledge platforms, and companies governed as DAOs.

DAOs may face scalability, security, and complexity challenges that threaten their adoption. Legal ambiguity also remains around virtual organizations. However, continued innovation aims to address such issues and realize a future with widespread decentralized institutions. If perfected, DAOs may transform governance, finance, and social organization models to empower individuals globally. Further development needs education and multi-stakeholder cooperation to realize such potential responsibly.

REFERENCES

Axelsen, H., Jensen, J. R., & Ross, O. (2022). When is a DAO Decentralized? *Complex Systems Informatics and Modeling Quarterly*, *31*(31), 51–75. doi:10.7250/csimq.2022-31.04

Baninemeh, E., Farshidi, S., & Jansen, S. (2023). A decision model for decentralized autonomous organization platform selection: Three industry case studies. *Blockchain: Research and Applications*, *4*(2), 100127. doi:10.1016/j.bcra.2023.100127

Behal, P. (2022). Listen-To-Earn: How Web3 Can Change the Music Industry. SSRN *Electronic Journal*. doi:10.2139/ssrn.4150998

Bellavitis, C., Fisch, C., & Momtaz, P. P. (2023). The rise of decentralized autonomous organizations (DAOs): A first empirical glimpse. *Venture Capital*, *25*(2), 187–203. doi:10.1080/13691066.2022.2116797

Braeckman, Y. (2022, February 18). *Philanthropy DAOs—The future of giving?* Medium.Com. https://medium.com/impact-shakers/philanthropy-daos-the-future-of-giving-608cc7a829b4

Chao, C.-H., Ting, I.-H., Tseng, Y.-J., Wang, B.-W., Wang, S.-H., Wang, Y.-Q., & Chen, M.-C. (2022). The Study of Decentralized Autonomous Organization (DAO) in Social Network. *The 9th Multidisciplinary International Social Networks Conference*, 59–65. 10.1145/3561278.3561293

Christidis, K., & Devetsikiotis, M. (2016). Blockchains and Smart contracts for the Internet of Things. *IEEE Access : Practical Innovations, Open Solutions*, *4*, 2292–2303. doi:10.1109/ACCESS.2016.2566339

Cloots, A. S. (2019). Blockchain and the Law: The Rule of Code. *The Cambridge Law Journal*, *78*(1), 213–217. doi:10.1017/S0008197319000084

DAOmatch. (2023). *Grants & Funding from DAOs*. https://daomatch.xyz/grants-investments

Davis, M. (2021). *10 DAOs to Follow in the Social Impact and Environmental Space*. https://www.onegreenplanet.org/human-interest/10-daos-to-follow-in-the-social-impact-space/

Dimitri, N. (2023). Voting in DAOs. *Distributed Ledger Technologies: Research and Practice*, *3624574*(4), 1–12. Advance online publication. doi:10.1145/3624574

European Securities and Markets Authority. (2021). *TRV, ESMA Report on Trends, Risks and Vulnerabilities* (Vol. 1). Publications Office. https://data.europa.eu/doi/10.2856/723305

Gitcoin. (2023). *Gitcoin Grants*. https://grants.gitcoin.co/

Guidi, B., & Michienzi, A. (2023). From NFT 1.0 to NFT 2.0: A Review of the Evolution of Non-Fungible Tokens. *Future Internet*, *15*(6), 189. doi:10.3390/fi15060189

Gupta, S., & Sadoghi, M. (2019). Blockchain Transaction Processing (pp. 366–376). doi:10.1007/978-3-319-77525-8_333

Hassan, S., & De Filippi, P. (2021). Decentralized Autonomous Organization. *Internet Policy Review*, *10*(2). Advance online publication. doi:10.14763/2021.2.1556

Korpal, G., & Scott, D. (2022). *Decentralization and web3 technologies*. https://attachment.victorlampcdn.com/article/content/20220824/drewscott_gkorpal_web3.pdf

Kurniawan, W. (2022). *Voting Mechanism Selection for Decentralized Autonomous Organizations*. https://secureseco.org/wp-content/uploads/2022/08/Voting_Mechanism_Selection_for_Decentralized_Autonomous_Organizations-3-1.pdf

Li, C., Xu, R., & Duan, L. (2023). Liquid Democracy in DPoS Blockchains. *Proceedings of the 5th ACM International Symposium on Blockchain and Secure Critical Infrastructure*, 25–33. 10.1145/3594556.3594606

Meyer, E., Welpe, I. M., & Sandner, P. (2021). Decentralized Finance—A systematic literature review and research directions. SSRN *Electronic Journal*. doi:10.2139/ssrn.4016497

Myalo, A. S. (2019). Comparative Analysis of ICO, DAOICO, IEO and STO. Case Study. *Finance: Theory and Practice*, *23*(6), 6–25. doi:10.26794/2587-5671-2019-23-6-6-25

Napieralska, A., & Kępczyński, P. (2023a). Smart contracts and Web 3: From Automated Transactions to DAOs. In P. Lekhi & G. Kaur (Eds.), Advances in Web Technologies and Engineering. IGI Global. doi:10.4018/978-1-6684-9919-1.ch008

Napieralska, A., & Kępczyński, P. (2023b). Smart contracts and Web 3: From Automated Transactions to DAOs. In P. Lekhi & G. Kaur (Eds.), Advances in Web Technologies and Engineering. IGI Global. doi:10.4018/978-1-6684-9919-1.ch008

Perez Riaza, B., & Gnabo, J.-Y. (2023). Decentralized Autonomous Organizations (DAOs): Catalysts for enhanced market efficiency. *Finance Research Letters*, *58*, 104445. doi:10.1016/j.frl.2023.104445

Popescu, A.-D. (2020). Decentralized Finance (DeFi) – The Lego of Finance. *Social Sciences and Education Research Review*, *7*(1), 321–349.

Rikken, O., Janssen, M., & Kwee, Z. (2019). Governance challenges of blockchain and decentralized autonomous organizations. *Information Polity*, *24*(4), 397–417. doi:10.3233/IP-190154

Rutskiy, V., Muda, I., Joudar, F., Ilia, F., Lyubaya, S., Kuzmina, A., & Tsarev, R. (2023). DAO Tokens: The Role for the Web 3.0 Industry and Pricing Factors. In R. Silhavy & P. Silhavy (Eds.), *Networks and Systems in Cybernetics* (Vol. 723, pp. 595–604). Springer International Publishing. doi:10.1007/978-3-031-35317-8_54

Saurabh, K., Rani, N., & Upadhyay, P. (2023). Towards blockchain led decentralized autonomous organization (DAO) business model innovations. *Benchmarking*, *30*(2), 475–502. doi:10.1108/BIJ-10-2021-0606

Sheridan, D., Harris, J., Wear, F., Cowell, J., Jr., Wong, E., & Yazdinejad, A. (2022). *Web3 Challenges and Opportunities for the Market* (arXiv:2209.02446). arXiv. http://arxiv.org/abs/2209.02446

Surve, T., & Khandelwal, R. (2023). The Development of Decentralized Governance Models for Web 3 Ecosystems. In P. Lekhi & G. Kaur (Eds.), Advances in Web Technologies and Engineering. IGI Global. doi:10.4018/978-1-6684-9919-1.ch006

TheLAO. (2023). *The LAO*. https://thelao.io/

Tokmakov, M. A. (2019). Corporate Governance Modernization: Legal Trends and Challenges. *SHS Web of Conferences, 71*, 04011. 10.1051/shsconf/20197104011

Trabucchi, D., Moretto, A., Buganza, T., & MacCormack, A. (2020). Disrupting the Disruptors or Enhancing Them? How Blockchain Reshapes Two-Sided Platforms. *Journal of Product Innovation Management*, *37*(6), 552–574. doi:10.1111/jpim.12557

Unnikrishnan, K. N., & Victer Paul, P. (2022). A Survey on Layer 2 Solutions to Achieve Scalability in Blockchain. In R. R. Rout, S. K. Ghosh, P. K. Jana, A. K. Tripathy, J. P. Sahoo, & K.-C. Li (Eds.), *Advances in Distributed Computing and Machine Learning* (Vol. 427, pp. 205–216). Springer Nature Singapore. doi:10.1007/978-981-19-1018-0_18

Ushida, R., & Angel, J. (2021). Regulatory Considerations on Centralized Aspects of DeFi Managed by DAOs. In M. Bernhard, A. Bracciali, L. Gudgeon, T. Haines, A. Klages-Mundt, S. Matsuo, D. Perez, M. Sala, & S. Werner (Eds.), *Financial Cryptography and Data Security. FC 2021 International Workshops* (Vol. 12676, pp. 21–36). Springer Berlin Heidelberg. doi:10.1007/978-3-662-63958-0_2

Wang, S., Ding, W., Li, J., Yuan, Y., Ouyang, L., & Wang, F.-Y. (2019). Decentralized Autonomous Organizations: Concept, Model, and Applications. *IEEE Transactions on Computational Social Systems*, *6*(5), 870–878. doi:10.1109/TCSS.2019.2938190

Weyl, E. G. (2017). Quadratic Vote Buying. SSRN *Electronic Journal*. doi:10.2139/ssrn.2003531

Wright, C. S. (2020). Decentralized Autonomous Corporations. In X.-S. Yang, S. Sherratt, N. Dey, & A. Joshi (Eds.), *Fourth International Congress on Information and Communication Technology* (*Vol. 1027*, pp. 153–167). Springer Singapore. 10.1007/978-981-32-9343-4_14

Zhang, B., Li, X., Ren, H., & Gu, J. (2020). Semantic Knowledge Sharing Mechanism Based on Blockchain. In Y. Liu, L. Wang, L. Zhao, & Z. Yu (Eds.), *Advances in Natural Computation, Fuzzy Systems and Knowledge Discovery* (Vol. 1075, pp. 115–127). Springer International Publishing. doi:10.1007/978-3-030-32591-6_13

Zichichi, M., Ferretti, S., & Rodríguez-Doncel, V. (2022). Decentralized Personal Data Marketplaces: How Participation in a DAO Can Support the Production of Citizen-Generated Data. *Sensors (Basel), 22*(16), 6260. doi:10.3390/s22166260 PMID:36016019

KEY TERMS AND DEFINITIONS

Crowdfunding: On blockchain and web3-based crowdfunding platforms, projects can raise capital (funds) through the sale of crypto tokens to backers in a decentralized manner without an intermediary, providing greater transparency, security and opportunities for community governance.

DAO: The DAO is one of the first platforms that attempted the concepts of decentralized autonomous organization. It highlighted both the potential risks and challenges of governance and coordination in emerging decentralized systems without established safeguards or oversight bodies. It demonstrated a useful experiment and learning opportunity.

Decentralization: In decentralized blockchain networks and applications, no single entity controls the network or data. Instead, consensus is reached through the participation of distributed nodes securing and validating transactions on an immutable, shared record of value transfers.

Decentralized Autonomous Organization: DAOs operating on blockchain networks employ decentralized governance models where organizational rules and workflows are codified as incorruptible smart contracts rather than relying on a hierarchy. This democratizes decision making.

Decentralized Finance: DeFi is a set of open access to financial services by implementing elements like exchanges, lending protocols and stablecoins on public blockchains, removing centralized control and fees. Users can gain interest or earn yield through participating in trustless, transparent transactions.

Decentralized Governance: Web3 shifts power from platforms to users through decentralized governance facilitated by blockchain technology and economic incentives aligned through token incentives. Governance tokens enable protocol-level decision making.

Decentralized Social Media: Decentralized social applications run on peer-to-peer networks rather than centralized servers. Users own their data and digital identities, and protocols are improved through on-chain governance. Tokens align network effects toward common goals.

Governance Tokens: Holding governance tokens allows stakeholders to vote on protocol upgrades, transaction approval and more in decentralized systems. This balances centralized coordination with distributed control.

Non-Fungible Tokens: NFTs provide proof of ownership and provenance for digital creations like art, collectibles and virtual assets on the blockchain, defining a scarce digital item and enabling new models for monetizing online content.

Smart Contracts: These are programs/code that automate the workflows for transactions of value and assets on blockchain in a transparent and secure manner without intermediaries. This streamlines processes like crowdfunding, proof of work payments and distributed computing.

Chapter 10
The Critical Role of Blockchain Oracles in Web 3

Vijaya Killu Manda
https://orcid.org/0000-0003-2938-838X
GITAM School of Science, GITAM University (Deemed), India

Vedavathi Katneni
GITAM School of Science, GITAM University (Deemed), India

ABSTRACT

Blockchain networks often require data to and from the outside world, especially when offering services such as in the financial domain. Blockchain oracles are critical infrastructure layers that bridge the blockchain network so that smart contracts get rich data to process transactions or execute business logic. Blockchain oracles are classified into various types depending on the data facility offered. Some popular oracle networks include chainlink, brand protocol, and provable. This chapter explains how oracles work, such as fetching and delivering data, data verification and aggregation, and reward mechanisms. It also briefly discusses on their applications, such as price feeds for DeFi applications, event triggers used in insurance and gambling contracts, identity/reputation management for NFTs, and aggregating of IoT sensor data. Security and decentralization are discussed. The chapter ends with a discussion of future research trends and the integration of artificial intelligence and machine learning, event-driven architectures, and recent advancements.

WHAT ARE ORACLES?

The burgeoning blockchain landscape has witnessed a proliferation of heterogeneous blockchain platforms, each with a unique architecture and protocol. Unfortunately, these platforms remain mostly isolated, hindering seamless communication and interoperability. Two popular approaches currently famous for this are – the relay approach and the oracle approach.

An "Oracle", according to Greek mythology, is a person who can communicate with God. Because ordinary people sometimes cannot make decisions independently, they used to turn to oracles to help

DOI: 10.4018/979-8-3693-1532-3.ch010

communicate with God and get insights. In blockchain, "Oracles" are considered infrastructure tools and layers through which off-chain data is accessed, sourced, and verified for use by the blockchain. They are essential in blockchains such as Decentralized Finance (DeFi) because of the necessary interactions with the real world when offering financial services. No wonder they are called the 'invisible backbone' of DeFi and blockchain-based applications (Wintermeyer, 2021). Oracles are conceptual solutions offered as services. However, they are not explicit programs, codes, or data sources. They use trusted third parties that collect data from data sources, verify it, and then transmit it to the blockchain so that the smart contracts get exogenous data (data/information from the outside world) (Hassan et al., 2023). Because oracles are centralized, the dependency of blockchain on them could pose problems because they bring back the concepts of centralization and trust them back to blockchains.

Definition and Purpose of Oracles

Oracles are intermediaries that facilitate communication between a distributed application (dApps) and some external real-world data sources. They serve as trusted third-party entities that verify and validate external data, ensuring its accuracy and authenticity. Applications can get rich real-world data such as price feeds (as in stock markets or for an online store), weather updates, or event notifications (such as from an IoT sensor or a CCTV camera). dApps and blockchain networks need external data to enhance the functionality and decision-making processes as per the business logic.

There are five main advantages of using blockchain oracles:

1. **Decentralized Data Access**: Blockchain oracles will make secure and reliable external data, resources, and events available. With this, dApps can make more informed decisions and improve their functionality.
2. **Increased Trust and Security**: Oracles ensure the accuracy and authenticity of data by validating and verifying external information. Reduced risk of fraud and manipulation will hence become possible. Also, the blockchain nodes will be de-stressed because of the shift in part of their processing load.
3. **Interoperability**: Interaction with external systems and networks will be possible through blockchain oracle-enabled dApps. This promotes interoperability and collaboration between various elements and stacks of the blockchain ecosystems. This became even more important because typical blockchain systems have several fragmented and heterogeneous blockchain platforms. Blockchains implement interoperability using Naive relay and Oracle solutions (Sober et al., 2021).
4. **Feeding off-chain data to smart contracts**: The Oracle Problem is an open practical problem involving off-chain data to and from blockchains and their smart contracts. According to the oracle problem, or oracle paradox, as it is referred to in some literature, the dilemma lies in the fact that the reliability of blockchain data is threatened and compromised when data/information is introduced from the outside world. The paradox is believed to be a prime reason some businesses hesitate about smart contracts. Some mitigation strategies were proposed to counter this (Albizri & Appelbaum, 2021). "Trust, but Verify" and "from trust to truth" (Hassan et al., 2023) remain famous mantras. One example of this happens is when oracles are used to observe occurrences and provide this information to smart contracts. Researchers insist that oracles should be viewed as service organizations under the auditing standards of the AICPA and PCAOB (Sheldon, 2021).

5. **Event-Driven Functionality**: Oracles can trigger events and actions within dApps, enabling them to respond to changes in the external environment and improve their responsiveness.

Types of Blockchain Oracles

Blockchain oracles serve as intermediaries that provide external information to smart contracts on a blockchain. Several types of blockchain oracles are designed to facilitate the integration of off-chain data with on-chain smart contract execution. The choice of a specific oracle depends on the particular requirements and priorities of a given application or use case. There are several types of blockchain oracles:

1. **Centralized Oracles:** Centralized oracles are controlled by either a single entity or a small group of entities. The entity acts as the singular data source for the oracle. Because of their nature and design, they are perceived to be faster and more efficient than decentralized oracles. For example, they have single authority, more straightforward data aggregation, reduced communication overheads, simplified governance, reduced census requirements, and lower latency in data sources. However, they are less preferred because they are more vulnerable to manipulation and censorship. Applications for this type of oracles are in traditional finance, enterprise solutions, compliance areas, weather data, real estate, and entertainment.
2. **Decentralized Oracles:** These oracles are built on blockchain networks and operate decentralized, often using consensus mechanisms. They involve "distributing trust". They are run by a network of nodes, ensuring that no single entity controls the data or the validation process. They are more secure and resilient to manipulation. So, it is more challenging for malicious actors to compromise the oracle and provide false or manipulated data. They are less susceptible to a single point of failure. These are more preferred than their centralized counterparts but might suffer from consensus problems because multiple parties must agree with the outcome. Some famous decentralized oracles include Chainlink, Provable, Band Protocol, and Tellor. These oracles are used in DeFi, prediction markets, supply chain management, insurance, and gaming.
3. **Software Oracles**: Software oracles exist in the form of API Oracles and Custom Software Oracles. API Oracles retrieve data from external Application Programming Interfaces (APIs) and feed it into smart contracts (Pasdar et al., 2023). Custom Software Oracles are specifically programmed to fetch and validate external (online) data from diverse sources such as websites, web service APIs, and public databases such as online databases, servers, etc. They are connected to the internet and can fetch real-time information (such as flight information and currency prices), making them popular.
4. **Hardware Oracles or IoT Oracles:** These oracles collect data or measure something from the physical world and send it to the blockchain. Internet of Things (IoT) devices can act as oracles by capturing real-world data and sending it to smart contracts. For example, a temperature sensor transmits data to a smart contract on a blockchain. Another example is the Modular Construction (MC) industry, wherein quality assurance is monitored at the off-shore manufacturing stage (Kong et al., 2022). The supply chain industry (such as a truck transporting goods) benefits from temperature and location tracking being captured by an IoT device and feeds it to a blockchain.
5. **Consensus-Based Oracles or Schelling Point Oracles**: These Oracles rely on the Schelling points theory to identify the correct data point among various data points reported by the off-chain nodes. Participants converge on a focal point of agreement. This could involve voting mechanisms or pre-

diction markets to determine data accuracy. This is exemplified in the work undertaken on Spartan Price Oracle (SPO) to how accurate price data can be provided by an oracle (S. He, 2023).

6. **Incentivized Oracles**: These exist in two forms. Staking Oracles allows participants to stake a certain amount of cryptocurrency as collateral to vouch for the accuracy of the data they provide. If their data is proven incorrect, they may lose their staked funds. Reward-based oracles are those in which participants are rewarded with cryptocurrency for providing accurate data to smart contracts.
7. **Witnet Oracles**: Leveraging the Witnet protocol, these oracles provide decentralized data retrieval and verification services.
8. **Data Feed Oracles**: These provide off-chain data to smart contracts, like price feeds for cryptocurrencies, stocks, commodities, and indices, amongst others. Chainlink Oracle employs decentralized nodes and connects smart contracts with real-world data, offering a secure and reliable solution.
9. **Event Oracles:** Detect real-world events happening off-chain and relay them to the blockchain. For example, oracles that detect flight/shipping status updates.
10. **Compute Oracles**: Also called compute-enabled oracles, these oracles allow off-chain computations and APIs to be accessed by smart contracts. This can include running AI models, fetching maps/other data, and processing payments, which are generally impractical to run on-chain for technical, legal, or financial reasons. With this, oracles help external or off-chain computational power available to the blockchain.
11. **Scheduled Oracles**: These oracles trigger the smart contract executions based on predefined schedules rather than events. Useful for tasks like periodic payments.
12. **Ambient Oracles**: These oracles behave as gateway hosts to aggregate data by sensing, monitoring, and collecting data from IoT sensors, wearables, and other devices. The data collected can be hot (live or being streamed and hence fresh) or cold (already collected) and is provided as off-chain inputs to blockchain apps (Al Breiki et al., 2019).
13. **Cryptographic Oracles**: These oracles leverage zero-knowledge proofs and multiparty computation to keep data private while allowing contract verification.
14. **On-chain Oracles**: These oracles integrate data directly into the blockchain using methods like on-chain price aggregation.
15. **Multi-chain Oracles**: These protocols provide cross-chain data for interoperability between separate blockchains. Applications of these include in areas where data availability between a trusted blockchain and side blockchains is necessary (Mitra, 2023).
16. **Crowdsourced Oracles**: These oracles derive off-chain facts by aggregating opinions from a crowd of participators. Crowd oracles are utilized when a problem requires human input or insight rather than being solvable by machines alone. The problem is typically broken into small chunks and distributed to people to solve (Pastore et al., 2013).
17. **Inbound Oracles**: These oracles are the most popular oracles and supply/transfer external data from off-chain (real-world) to the smart contract of a blockchain.
18. **Outbound Oracles:** Smart contracts of these oracles interact with the outside world by exporting (forwarding) data and commands to the off-chain systems. An example of such a system is the opening of a smart lock.
19. **Human Oracles:** These oracles depend on the manual intervention of people with deep domain knowledge and interest. These experts have to manually verify the authenticity of information, such as the source of information of a news article, and approve it so that it can be further fed to

the smart contract. Because human processing and decision-making speed is limited, the system might work slightly slower than automated ones.

20. **Unmanned Oracles:** These oracles retrieve, process, and verify the information of some set of pre-determined rules and algorithms specific to a given domain. They run without any human intervention or control. They use a combination of data sources such as APIs and sensors and are well-suited for real-time applications such as prediction markets and decentralized exchanges.

Popular Oracle Platforms

Over the past few years, several blockchain oracle platforms have emerged. Each platform has unique features and capabilities; hence, the selection largely depends on the blockchain implementation. The top 10 popular platforms are:

1. Chainlink
2. Universal Market Access
3. API3
4. Band Protocol
5. Chronicle
6. Pyth
7. UMA
8. Nest Protocol
9. XYO Network
10. iExec RLC
11. WINkLink
12. Tellor
13. DIA

Here are some of the most popular Oracle platforms:

1. **Chainlink**: Chainlink (LINK) aspires to "connect the world to blocks" (Chainlink, 2023). They started as SmartContract.com in 2014 and were later renamed to Chainlink. They started over an Ethereum Testnet and started their mainnet in 2017. They added LINK in 2019. In 2020, they partnered with some majors such as Google Cloud, SWIFT, and other major enterprises. With over 2,000 global nodes in 2023, they became the largest in the industry. Incidentally, they are also the only company to reach a market capitalization of over a billion dollars. They are one of the most widely used blockchain oracle platforms, supporting many blockchain networks, including Ethereum, Binance Smart Chain, Solana, and Polkadot. Chainlink's decentralized network of nodes ensures that data is validated and secured, providing high reliability and trust. Its flagship product, Chainlink Price Feeds, is an industry-standard price oracle network for decentralized finance (DeFi) applications. Chainlink is also instrumental in formulating the Cross-Chain Interoperability Protocol (CCIP), a new global standard for decentralized inter-blockchain messaging, data, and token movements. Chainlinks network data is one of the most used data in research studies. They are so popular that they are consistent transmitters (receivers) of volatility innovations during the Russia-Ukraine military conflict (Kumar et al., 2023).

2. **Band Protocol**: Band Protocol was co-founded by Soravis Srinawakoon, Sorawit Suriyakarn, and Paul Nattapatsiri in 2017/2018 in Thailand. With an initial coin offering (ICO) and raised $13.5 million in 2018. In 2019, they launched their mainnet and began providing real-world data to smart contracts. By 2020, they are data providers and validators to over 100 nodes. The company is backed by global investors such as Sequoia, Dunamu & Partners, Binance, Spartan, Alphain Ventures, Woodstock, and Southeast Asia Exponential Ventures. The protocol is popular in a public blockchain called BandChain.

Their primary focus is to provide high-quality data feeds to dApps (Band Protocol, 2023). In order to ensure the accuracy and authenticity of data, the protocol uses a novel data provenance system. This makes it one of the preferred choices for applications requiring precise and reliable data. Its product range includes Cosmoscan, Band Price Feeds, Band VRF, and Band Integration Tools.

3. **Provable/Oraclize**: Oraclize is the first oracle service for blockchain. It is now a "provably honest" blockchain oracle platform/service offering a range of features, including data validation, data feeds, and event-driven functionality. It supports several blockchain networks and provides a user-friendly interface for developers to integrate oracles into their dApps. It gives cryptographic proofs on the blockchain using authenticity proofs that the network did not alter the data forwarded to the smart contract (pNetwork Team, 2015). The authenticity proofs are built using different technologies, such as auditable virtual machines and Trusted Execution Environments. Using the proofs confirms that the data is genuine and not tampered with.

Established in 2014, Oraclize was established began offering services in 2015. They began integration with Ethereum in 2018. They re-branded to Provable in 2019 after merging with a Swiss holding company called Poseidon Group (Marco, 2019). The re-branding was done to reflect a broader vision beyond just oracles, emphasizing the concept of provable truth in smart contracts.

WORKING OF ORACLES

Oracles are the bridge that connects blockchains to external data feeds and application program interfaces (API) endpoints, allowing smart contracts to access off-chain information and conditions to execute properly. Oracles functions as external services and validate the external information before sending it to the blockchain for storage. In most cases, the data validation happens in an automated manner. When automated validations cannot be done, oracles have to depend on humans to collaboratively cross-check the external information (Gennaro et al., 2022). In practical situations, APIs connect real-world data to the blockchain. Blockchain Oracle implementation methods are classified into two types (Pasdar et al., 2023):

1. **Voting-based** strategies depend on participants' stakes for outcome finalization. The parties vote on the correctness of a piece of information by betting an amount. To incentivize honest behavior, the user wins a reward if the vote aligns with the majority. Otherwise, the initial bet is lost. Voting-based systems are also popular for interoperability between heterogeneous blockchains (Sober et al., 2021).

2. **Reputation-based** ones use reputation and performance metrics with authenticity-proof mechanisms for data correctness and integrity. These rely on information provided by parties with different reputations that measure their reliability. The reputation is usually increased if the information provided is in line with the majority of the other parties and decreased otherwise.

Extensions to these are now available in which the tool utilizes reputation to measure value and as a tool to associate questions with context (Bartholic et al., 2023). Further, distributed human-based oracles such as *DeepThought* are also explored (Gennaro et al., 2022).

How Oracles Fetch and Deliver Off-Chain Data

When a smart contract needs access to off-chain data, it issues a request to the oracle nodes specifying the type of data required. The blockchain oracle nodes then use APIs or web scraping to retrieve the requested data from external sources like stock prices, weather conditions, and sports results. Multiple oracle nodes detch data independently to avoid single points of failure, dependence, or manipulation.

The introduction of a distributed oracle protocol that supports on-chain transaction executionis an advancement in this area. With this off-chain information can become dependable without the need of a trusted party as a source. Such protocols are useful in applications where the transaction is time-sensitive (expiry/timeout bassed) (L. He et al., 2021).

Data Verification and Aggregation

Data collected is to be verified before being submitted it for use by the smart contract. The oracle nodes handles the data validation part against each other and tries their best to filter out errors and outliers. Like a majority vote, a consensus algorithm determines the final data value. This process of verification and aggregation adds reliability to the off-chain data being reported on-chain.

Reward Mechanism for Oracle Nodes

Running an oracle node requires hardware resources and ongoing costs that need to be compensated. Most public oracles use a staking and reward-based model to incentivize participation. Nodes stake tokens to participate and get rewarded based on their accuracy and availability. Part of the fees paid by smart contracts for data requests are distributed as rewards to incentivize high-quality data provisioning from oracle nodes. Over time, honest and accurate nodes are rewarded while malicious nodes get their stakes slashed, allowing the oracle network to become more decentralized and resilient.

Contrasting Viewpoints

There are differing perspectives on the challenges and solutions regarding blockchain oracles. Skeptics argue that oracles introduce a single point of failure by relying on centralized data sources, compromising the immutable and trustless nature of the blockchain. However, proponents emphasize that oracles enable smart contracts to process real-world inputs, significantly expanding their utility beyond closed cryptosystems.

While critics demand fully decentralized oracle designs, others note the technology barriers. They argue that gradually improving reliability is more pragmatic. Centralized oracles prioritize stability but risk censorship. Decentralized approaches, on the other hand, aim for censorship resistance but struggle with overhead coordination.

There is little consensus about what an ideal oracle model should be. Opinions clash, and disagreement primarily lies in ensuring the right balance between decentralization, scalability, and assurance of off-chain data quality. Continuous research and market experimentation are needed to develop secure, robust, and inclusive oracle solutions that align with core values of transparency and blockchain consensus.

Applications of Oracles

Blockchain oracles play a seminal role in connecting transparent virtual economies with the external real world by bringing trusted data feeds, events, and identities onto the blockchain in a decentralized manner. This powers a new wave of decentralized applications across sectors like DeFi, gaming, insurance, and supply chain management to transform online experiences. Frameworks are now available that help in the meticulously use oracles with specific considerations on the origin of data, oracle properties, encryption method, oracle data source, validation procedures, and finally in the integration of oracles to dApps (Immunebytes, 2023; Mammadzada et al., 2020).

Price Feeds for DeFi Applications

Decentralized finance (DeFi) applications rely on price data from centralized sources like exchanges to determine values and process transactions. However, this introduces newer risks such as censorship, manipulation, or downtime because of the centralized nature. Financial networks generally use complex and a variety of private and public blockchains. They can consider using blockchain oracles to allow DeFi platforms to access reliable, uncensored price data from multiple sources in a trustless manner.

Oracles aggregate price data from trusted exchanges and relevant market data providers (S. He, 2023), compute average prices and publish them on-chain through blockchain transactions. DeFi smart contracts can natively access dynamic, decentralized price feeds without counterparty risks. Popular oracle projects like Chainlink provide decentralized price feeds through a decentralized network of independent, incentivized nodes. The multi-source nature of price data makes it resistant to manipulation and safeguards DeFi protocols from the potential failure of any single data source.

Event Triggers for Insurance/Gambling Contracts

Blockchain oracles enable integrating real-world events and data triggers into smart contracts, unlocking use cases in insurance, prediction markets, and gaming. For example, weather oracles allow the creation of financial derivatives contracts that pay based on temperature readings from various global locations. Similarly, sports betting platforms use the oracle data on game scores and match results to determine payouts for bets placed on-chain.

Insurance contracts rely on oracle-provided data around events like floods, storms, or accidents to process insurance claims efficiently (Chainlink, 2021). DeFi applications can implement automated payouts with the help of on-chain settlement that are triggered by oracle data. This removes reliance on centralized claim adjusters. This streamlines insurance processes while maintaining transparency and guaranteed payouts through smart contract programming. The trustless execution of events makes these applications censorship-resistant against any entity trying to influence outcomes.

Identity/Reputation Oracles for NFTs

Non-fungible tokens (NFTs) representing digital collectibles, art, and game items require identity and reputation systems to establish scarcity and prevent fraud. Blockchain oracles enable the authentication of the blockchain's real-world identities, attributes, and reputation scores in a decentralized way.

Identity oracles allow linking public blockchain addresses/wallets to verified identity attributes like names, photos, and social profiles. This process makes ownership attribution easy for NFT creators and buyers. These tools help establish the credibility and background of NFT traders, a crucial element for high-value marketplaces. It also disincentivizes platforms from manipulating feedback to influence NFT prices. Similarly, reputation oracles gather user feedback from likes and posts on social platforms, discussion boards, survey and feedback forms, marketplaces, and other applications to associate global reputation scores with blockchain addresses. Oracle-backed digital identities and reputation boost transparency and foster trust in online communities around NFTs and creator economies.

Aggregating IoT Sensor Data

The Internet of Things (IoT) generates vast volumes of real-time sensor data from devices across manufacturing, supply chain, agriculture, and utilities. Blockchain oracles make this unstructured IoT data accessible to decentralized applications by filtering, aggregating, and publishing it on-chain (Sadawi et al., 2022).

Oracle subscribes to temperature, humidity, and pressure data from sensors in shipping containers are some examples for this. It analyzes the streams, identifies outliers, and averages readings from multiple containers. This aggregated data is then submitted regularly to the blockchain through transactions. Supply chain dApps can access these signatures directly to track environmental conditions, detect anomalies, and automate insurance payouts or invoice settlements (ETHGlobal, 2023).

Similarly, oracles interface with equipment on production floors to retrieve vital statistics on machine performance, errors, and uptimes. The anonymized, macro-level data published on-chain trains AI/ML algorithms for predictive maintenance without revealing proprietary sensor data off-chain. This demonstrates how oracles connect real-world IoT systems and their decentralized virtual representations.

ETHICAL, LEGAL, PRIVACY, AND SECURITY CONSIDERATIONS

The security and decentralization of oracles are paramount to ensuring the integrity and robustness of blockchain-based applications. Some vulnerabilities introduced by oracles include concentration, data quality, and technical risks (Patel et al., 2023).

Regulatory and Legal Complexities

Blockchain oracles introduce regulatory and legal complexities. Applications dealing in sensitive domains like finance and insurance have to consider this with more caution because they involve personal data, and secure handling that is of greater importance. The role of oracles in capital markets require regulatory oversight to prevent manipulation and information asymmetry. Because oracles work as intermediaries between blockchains and external data sources, they must ensure fair and lawful data practices as per prevailing legislation. A healthcare oracle, for example, providing patient records to smart contracts must comply with laws such as HIPAA, FERPA, CCPA, GINA, amongst others (Flaumenhaft & Ben-Assuli, 2018).

Privacy Preservation

Oracles should employ appropriate techniques to preserve user privacy while confirming data to smart contracts. Simply publishing raw personal details on public ledgers may violate privacy norms. Techniques like zero-knowledge proofs allow verification of queries without revealing underlying data. Proper access controls and anonymization are also necessary. However, completely decentralized oracles with no central oversight bring their own accountably challenges.

Security and Reliability

From a technical perspective, oracle security and reliability are paramount. Smart contracts assume the veracity of oracle inputs, so compromised oracles could enable fraudulent transactions. The following are some active areas of research in this segment:

1. Techniques to confirm data integrity using multiparty computation
2. Trusted hardware enclaves
3. Reputation systems

However, it should be understood that completely eliminating human/system fallibility will remain challenging.

Making Oracles Tamper-Proof and Censorship-Resistant

The need for smart contracts on external data makes it necessary for system designers to focus on the security and reliability of oracles. When data provided by oracles is tampered with or censored, it can lead to serious and unwanted consequences that can result in financial losses, operational disruptions, and even reputational damage to the entire blockchain ecosystem.

Centralized oracles are more prone to manipulation, censorship, and malicious attacks, rendering them unsuitable for critical applications. They pose inherent security vulnerabilities and have limited reliable data provision. They are controlled by a single entity or a small group of entities. Developers often confine their use to some limited applications only. Some issues include single point of failure, data censorship, transparency concerns, and limited scalability.

Decentralized Oracle Networks (DONs), on the other hand, have emerged to address these concerns and bring a promising solution. DONs use a distributed network of nodes to connect data and events to smart contracts, spreading trust and decision-making across the node network more easily. Using DONs will eliminate the single failure point seen in centralized oracles.

Three aspects by which DONs vary amongst themselves are in terms of the following parameters:

1. How does the DON handle its consensus mechanisms?
2. What are their incentivization structures?
3. What is the provision of trustworthy data for smart contracts?

When developers must select a suitable DON for a given project, they should focus on security and decentralization, apart from addressing the specific needs or distinct requirements of their particular use case.

Decentralized Techniques for Consensus

DONs use consensus mechanisms to bring in data integrity and reliability before providing the data can be used by the smart contracts. So, these mechanisms focus on distributing trust and decision-making across the network of nodes. By doing so, they prevent any single entity from exerting undue influence or manipulating data. Some consensus mechanisms enhance the security of the oracle networks by involving multiple validators in the data verification process.

1. **Proof-of-Work (PoW):** PoW consensus utilizes computationally intensive algorithms to validate transactions and blocks. Nodes compete to solve puzzles and mathematical problems. The node that stands first to find a solution earns the right to add the following block to the blockchain. Such protocols give the benefit of better security and reduced need for computational power. A ranking of the top 19 most relevant blockchain consensus mechanisms has given PoW a market share of 87%(UnblockTalent, 2023).
2. **Proof-of-Stake (PoS):** PoS consensus makes the nodes stake their cryptocurrency holdings to participate in the network validation. Participation is restricted only to entities (individuals or organizations) with a legitimate stake in the blockchain (Van Molken & Molken, 2018). The validators are incentivized to provide accurate data to maintain their stake and earn rewards in this mechanism. They use negligible energy consumption and low transaction delay and have specific mobile roaming (BlockRoam) and metaverse applications (MetaShard) (Nguyen, 2023). Most modern blockchain implementations prefer or transform this method compared to PoW. PoS has a market share of 3% but is growing faster than PoW. Ethereum's switch to PoS challenged the dominance of PoS (UnblockTalent, 2023).
3. **Hybrid Consensus Mechanisms**: PoS and PoW methods might be resource-intensive in nature, slow in terms of transaction processing, and might have limited scalability (Chorey & Sahu, 2024). These needs led some DONs to employ hybrid consensus mechanisms that combine PoS and PoW elements, leveraging the strengths of both approaches to enhance security and efficiency. New protocols such as the Proof-of-Participation that implements PoS through PoW are examples (Nandwani et al., 2019).

Standardization

Standardizing oracle protocols and data formats is another challenge impacting cross-chain applications. Currently, different blockchains employ custom oracle designs with a lack of uniform standards. This creates barriers for smart contracts that require off-chain resources from multiple ledgers. Standard bodies are exploring specification development, but challenges around decentralization, governance, and adapting to rapid technological changes persist.

Universal standards would enable "money lego" type composability across blockchains via oracles as interoperable building blocks. This could accelerate innovation in multi-asset decentralized finance (DeFi) protocols and blockchain-based supply chain management spanning independent ledgers. However, censorship resistance is also a key consideration for decentralized oracle networks that avoid centralized control over specifications and reference data.

Future of Oracles

The quantum of research/academic literature on blockchain oracles is minimal (Caldarelli, 2020b). A literature review showed that only 15% of 142 journal papers studied have dealt with oracles and that only 10% deal with the limitations that they come up with (Caldarelli, 2020a). Chainlink 2.0, for example, has made substantial progress in the evolution of DONs with a specific focus on seven areas - hybrid smart contracts, abstracting away complexity, scaling, confidentiality, order-fairness for transactions, trust-minimization, incentive-based (cryptoeconomic) security (Breidenbach et al., 2021).

Emerging Debased and Research Directions

The reliability and trustworthiness of oracle data remain an ongoing debate. As blockchain applications evolve, there is increasing focus on improving oracle security, accuracy, and decentralization. Researchers are exploring new ways to design oracles using multi-signature schemes, reputation systems, and decentralized consensus protocols. Some ideas involve using trusted hardware like Intel SGX to ensure data integrity. Futuristic ideas around decentralized oracle networks aim to leverage distributed computing and cryptocurrency incentives. Overall, making oracles more robust, tamper-proof, and aligned with blockchain values is crucial for realizing the full potential of decentralized applications depending on off-chain inputs and triggers.

Integration With AI and Machine Learning

Blockchain oracles connecting off-chain data and events to smart contracts are vital to expanding decentralized applications. Recent trends are to integrate them with other emerging technologies, such as Artificial Intelligence (AI) and Machine Language (ML), to scale blockchain utilities (Papadouli & Papakonstantinou, 2023). Spherical Insights has termed that the Blockchain AI market was US$ 230.10 million in 2021 but could grow to US$ 24.06% by 2030, reflecting a potential 24.06% CAGR (Spherical Insights, 2023).

Chainlink is using AI to establish a research category focusing on connecting nodes to external data sources like AI prediction APIs. This permits smart contracts access to sophisticated models without comprising security. Advances may see AI-powered oracles autonomously identifying high-quality off-chain data feeds with minimal human configuration and automating repetitive tasks.

Enhancement of predictive analytics in financial smart contracts is an important application for this. Traditional financial instruments often rely on centralized data sources, introducing vulnerabilities and potential manipulation. Blockchain oracles integrated with AI can use predefined criteria to analyze vast datasets, predict market trends, and execute transactions autonomously. Reliance on centralized entities will hence reduce the efficiency and accuracy of financial transactions within decentralized ecosystems.

AI-based sequential decision-making (SDM) algorithms are used to build protocols such as CONDOR. The protocols are used between a smart contract and some off-chain AI-based oracles to enable smart contracts to choose among AI solution proposals while inciting those oracles to provide non-forged results (Sata et al., 2021). AI-powered oracles can contribute to decentralized platforms' identity verification and reputation systems. Machine learning algorithms in software, hardware, and inbound oracles can assess user behavior, validate identities, and assign reputation scores. This dynamic approach ensures a more robust and adaptable decentralized ecosystem that promotes trust and reliability among smart contracts and blockchain users.

Event-Driven Architectures

Some recent blockchains are using event-driven architectures that bring reactive programming to oracles. Anthropic's programmable, event-driven oracle framework utilizes a push model notifying subscribers about externally triggered contract states. Similarly, EMURGO developed a serverless oracle platform based around ephemeral workers managed through Kubernetes in response to events rather than polling (Emurgo, 2023). The efficiency of the oracle can be improved by using event-based designs. Similarly, modern techniques such as Natural language processing (NLP) are used for event detection and filtering processes. With these steps, oracles are found to reduce the workloads by moving some stress and complexities off the main blockchain. Studies show that this also has made the system work more efficiently than before (Shahbazi & Byun, 2022). Of course, making these changes will also need consideration of the system engineering process.

The traditional request-response models may face scalability challenges because dApps have become more complex and interconnected than before. Event-driven architectures address this issue by allowing systems to react to specific events or triggers. With this, the decentralized ecosystems will be more efficient and responsive. When integrated with event-driven architectures, blockchain oracles can provide real-time updates and responses to changes in external conditions. In the case of supply chain management, for example, oracles can trigger smart contracts to automatically update the blockchain when a shipment reaches a particular location or when specific conditions are met (Bhandari, 2018). This level of automation ensures a seamless and tamper-proof record of events, enhancing transparency and traceability in supply chain processes. All these are based on basic tenets of Web3 and blockchain systems.

Decentralized gaming environments are another interesting cases where oracles can demonstrate its use. Gaming extensively uses event-driven blockchain oracles (LinkedIn, 2023). When an in-game event occurs, such as completing a quest or achieving a milestone, an oracle can trigger corresponding actions within the smart contracts governing the game. This dynamic and responsive approach improves user engagement and introduces newer experiences in the Web3 gaming ecosystems. Several external third-party tools, such as Oracle Mechanism, can now extend the primary smart contract to a systemic and holonomic architecture. After making data request to the oracle mechanism, the oracle mechanism collects data from nodes and makes data aggregation before responding to the blockchain (Wang et al., 2020).

Recent Advancements

The growth and advancements in DONs will depend on the diverse consensus mechanisms beyond essential majority voting. Band Protocol, for example, uses Bayesian reasoning algorithms for oracles to evaluate the data sources and thereby factor trustworthiness (Taghavi et al., 2023). Other ideas include utilizing trust minimization protocols like Tinychain for distributed cross-checking while maintaining secrecy. Through advanced quorum implementations, Sybil resistance can be used to strengthen resilience against adversarial players (Platt & McBurney, 2023).

The concept of decentralization will continue to increase. Blockchain as a technology will continue evolving to newer generations and find more applications. Smart contracts will be increasingly used for autonomous, diverse, and secure off-chain interfacing. DONs will have to evolve to meet requirements because the demand for reliable data feeds and external information will continue to grow. Recent deployments of DONs are more successful in addressing security, scalability, and trust challenges. A significant breakthrough in this regard is the implementation of multiple oracles and consensus mechanisms within decentralized networks. This approach mitigates the risk of single points of failure and ensures data reliability to smart contracts.

The integration of cross-chain compatibility is a major step in the development of DONs. As blockchain ecosystems expand, interoperability between different chains becomes crucial for the seamless flow of information. Advanced oracle networks are designed to fetch and verify data from multiple blockchains, making smart contracts that access a broader range of information and interact with various Web3 ecosystems.

CONCLUSION

Blockchain oracles are vital links that feed external information to the blockchain network and make them more useful. Various types of oracles are seen to be providing a host of functions for blockchain applications. Oracles are primarily implemented using a voting- or reputation-based strategy and are vital in the blockchain ecosystem. They also have to handle some tasks, such as data verification and aggregation, and have a node reward mechanism. Though still an emerging technology, they can potentially improve further developments across various sectors, such as decentralized finance, supply chain, and identity management, amongst others, by bridging the gap between blockchains and external data sources. Standardization of the oracle architectures and economic models will be necessary for widespread adoption as blockchains begin to connect and collaborate with more technologies in the Web3 ecosystem.

REFERENCES

Al Breiki, H., Al Qassem, L., Salah, K., Habib Ur Rehman, M., & Sevtinovic, D. (2019). Decentralized Access Control for IoT Data Using Blockchain and Trusted Oracles. *2019 IEEE International Conference on Industrial Internet (ICII)*, 248–257. 10.1109/ICII.2019.00051

Albizri, A., & Appelbaum, D. (2021). Trust but Verify: The Oracle Paradox of Blockchain Smart Contracts. *Journal of Information Systems*, *35*(2), 1–16. doi:10.2308/ISYS-19-024

Band Protocol. (2023). *Band Protocol—Secure, Scalable Blockchain-Agnostic Decentralized Oracle*. https://www.bandprotocol.com/

Bartholic, M., Burger, E. W., Matsuo, S., & Jung, T. (2023). Reputation as Contextual Knowledge: Incentives and External Value in Truthful Blockchain Oracles. *2023 IEEE International Conference on Blockchain and Cryptocurrency (ICBC)*, 1–9. 10.1109/ICBC56567.2023.10174903

Bhandari, B. (2018). Supply Chain Management, Blockchains and Smart Contracts. SSRN *Electronic Journal*. doi:10.2139/ssrn.3204297

Breidenbach, L., Cachin, C., Coventry, A., Ellis, S., Juels, A., Miller, A., Magauran, B., Nazarov, S., Topliceanu, A., Zhang, F., Chan, B., Koushanfar, F., Moroz, D., & Tramer, F. (2021). *Chainlink 2.0: Next Steps in the Evolution of Decentralized Oracle Networks*. https://naorib.ir/white-paper/chinlink-whitepaper.pdf

Caldarelli, G. (2020a). Real-world blockchain applications under the lens of the oracle problem. A systematic literature review. *2020 IEEE International Conference on Technology Management, Operations and Decisions (ICTMOD)*, 1–6. 10.1109/ICTMOD49425.2020.9380598

Caldarelli, G. (2020b). Understanding the Blockchain Oracle Problem: A Call for Action. *Information (Basel)*, *11*(11), 509. doi:10.3390/info11110509

Chainlink. (2021, December 14). *Blockchain in Insurance*. https://blog.chain.link/blockchain-insurance

Chainlink. (2023). *Chainlink*. https://chain.link

Chorey, P., & Sahu, N. (2024). Enhancing efficiency and scalability in Blockchain Consensus algorithms: The role of Checkpoint approach. *J. Integr. Sci. Technol.*, *12*(1), 1–7.

Emurgo. (2023). *Emurgo—Supporting Adoption Of Cardano And Blockchain Tech*. https://www.emurgo.io/

ETHGlobal. (2023). *Supply Chain Dapp*. https://ethglobal.com/showcase/supply-chain-dapp-crcvh

Flaumenhaft, Y., & Ben-Assuli, O. (2018). Personal health records, global policy and regulation review. *Health Policy (Amsterdam)*, *122*(8), 815–826. doi:10.1016/j.healthpol.2018.05.002 PMID:29884294

Gennaro, M. D., Italiano, L., Meroni, G., & Quattrocchi, G. (2022). DeepThought: A Reputation and Voting-Based Blockchain Oracle. In J. Troya, B. Medjahed, M. Piattini, L. Yao, P. Fernández, & A. Ruiz-Cortés (Eds.), *Service-Oriented Computing* (Vol. 13740, pp. 369–383). Springer Nature Switzerland. doi:10.1007/978-3-031-20984-0_26

Hassan, A., Makhdoom, I., Iqbal, W., Ahmad, A., & Raza, A. (2023). From trust to truth: Advancements in mitigating the Blockchain Oracle problem. *Journal of Network and Computer Applications*, *217*, 103672. doi:10.1016/j.jnca.2023.103672

He, L., Kang, T., & Guo, L. (2021). Blockchain based Distributed Oracle in Time Sensitive Scenario. *2021 the 7th International Conference on Communication and Information Processing (ICCIP)*, 103–111. 10.1145/3507971.3507990

He, S. (2023). *Spartan Price Oracle: A Schelling-point Based Decentralized Pirce Oracle* [Master of Science, San Jose State University]. doi:10.31979/etd.y8qv-myun

Immunebytes. (2023, March 20). *Explained: Blockchain Oracles & Their Use Cases*. https://www.immunebytes.com/blog/explained-blockchain-oracles-their-use-cases/

Kong, L., Chen, C., Zhao, R., Chen, Z., Wu, L., Yang, Z., Li, X., Lu, W., & Xue, F. (2022). When permissioned blockchain meets IoT oracles: An on-chain quality assurance system for off-shore modular construction manufacture. *2022 IEEE 1st Global Emerging Technology Blockchain Forum: Blockchain & Beyond (iGETblockchain)*, 1–6. 10.1109/iGETblockchain56591.2022.10087164

Kumar, S., Patel, R., Iqbal, N., & Gubareva, M. (2023). Interconnectivity among cryptocurrencies, NFTs, and DeFi: Evidence from the Russia-Ukraine conflict. *The North American Journal of Economics and Finance*, *68*, 101983. doi:10.1016/j.najef.2023.101983

LinkedIn. (2023). *What are the benefits of decentralized gaming in Web3?* https://www.linkedin.com/advice/1/what-benefits-decentralized-gaming-web3-skills-blockchain-lqvjf

Mammadzada, K., Iqbal, M., Milani, F., García-Bañuelos, L., & Matulevičius, R. (2020). Blockchain Oracles: A Framework for Blockchain-Based Applications. In A. Asatiani, J. M. García, N. Helander, A. Jiménez-Ramírez, A. Koschmider, J. Mendling, G. Meroni, & H. A. Reijers (Eds.), *Business Process Management: Blockchain and Robotic Process Automation Forum* (Vol. 393, pp. 19–34). Springer International Publishing. doi:10.1007/978-3-030-58779-6_2

Marco, C. (2019, May 9). Provable (formerly Oraclize) joins Poseidon Group. *Cryptonomist*. https://en.cryptonomist.ch/2019/05/09/provable-oraclize-joins-poseidon-group/

Mitra, D. (2023). *Channel Coding Techniques for Scaling Modern Data-Driven Applications: From Blockchain Systems to Quantum Communications* [Doctor of Philosophy in Electrical and Computer Engineering, University of California]. https://escholarship.org/uc/item/0cp2c3tk

Nandwani, A., Gupta, M., & Thakur, N. (2019). Proof-of-Participation: Implementation of Proof-of-Stake Through Proof-of-Work. In S. Bhattacharyya, A. E. Hassanien, D. Gupta, A. Khanna, & I. Pan (Eds.), *International Conference on Innovative Computing and Communications* (*Vol. 55*, pp. 17–24). Springer Singapore. 10.1007/978-981-13-2324-9_3

Nguyen, C. T. (2023). *Proof-of-Stake-based Blockchain Frameworks for Smart Data Management* [Doctor of Philosophy, University of Technology]. https://www.proquest.com/dissertations-theses/proof-stake-based-blockchain-frameworks-smart/docview/2901815472/se-2?accountid=139958

Papadouli, V., & Papakonstantinou, V. (2023). A preliminary study on artificial intelligence oracles and smart contracts: A legal approach to the interaction of two novel technological breakthroughs. *Computer Law & Security Report*, *51*, 105869. doi:10.1016/j.clsr.2023.105869

Pasdar, A., Lee, Y. C., & Dong, Z. (2023). Connect API with Blockchain: A Survey on Blockchain Oracle Implementation. *ACM Computing Surveys*, *55*(10), 1–39. doi:10.1145/3567582

Pastore, F., Mariani, L., & Fraser, G. (2013). CrowdOracles: Can the Crowd Solve the Oracle Problem? *2013 IEEE Sixth International Conference on Software Testing, Verification and Validation*, 342–351. 10.1109/ICST.2013.13

Patel, D., Johnston, A., Stokesberry, J., Damak, M., Duran, C., Raziano, A., Wilkinson, L., & O'Neill, A. (2023). *Utility at a cost: Assessing the risks of blockchain oracles*. S&P Global.

Platt, M., & McBurney, P. (2023). Sybil in the Haystack: A Comprehensive Review of Blockchain Consensus Mechanisms in Search of Strong Sybil Attack Resistance. *Algorithms*, *16*(1), 34. doi:10.3390/a16010034

pNetwork Team. (2015, November 4). Oraclize, the provably-honest oracle service, is finally here! *Medium.Com*. https://medium.com/pnetwork/oraclize-the-provably-honest-oracle-service-is-finally-here-3ac48358deb8

Sadawi, A. A., Hassan, M. S., & Ndiaye, M. (2022). On the Integration of Blockchain With IoT and the Role of Oracle in the Combined System: The Full Picture. *IEEE Access : Practical Innovations, Open Solutions*, *10*, 92532–92558. doi:10.1109/ACCESS.2022.3199007

Sata, B., Berlanga, A., Chanel, C. P. C., & Lacan, J. (2021). Connecting AI-based Oracles to Blockchains via an Auditable Auction Protocol. *2021 3rd Conference on Blockchain Research & Applications for Innovative Networks and Services (BRAINS)*, 23–24. 10.1109/BRAINS52497.2021.9569808

Shahbazi, Z., & Byun, Y.-C. (2022). Blockchain-Based Event Detection and Trust Verification Using Natural Language Processing and Machine Learning. *IEEE Access : Practical Innovations, Open Solutions*, *10*, 5790–5800. doi:10.1109/ACCESS.2021.3139586

Sheldon, M. D. (2021). Auditing the Blockchain Oracle Problem. *Journal of Information Systems*, *35*(1), 121–133. doi:10.2308/ISYS-19-049

Sober, M., Scaffino, G., Spanring, C., & Schulte, S. (2021). *A Voting-Based Blockchain Interoperability Oracle* (arXiv:2111.10091). arXiv. doi:10.1109/Blockchain53845.2021.00030

Spherical Insights. (2023). *Global Blockchain AI Market*. https://www.sphericalinsights.com/reports/blockchain-ai-market

Taghavi, M., Bentahar, J., Otrok, H., & Bakhtiyari, K. (2023). A reinforcement learning model for the reliability of blockchain oracles. *Expert Systems with Applications*, *214*, 119160. doi:10.1016/j.eswa.2022.119160

UnblockTalent. (2023). *Top 19 global ranking of consensus mechanisms*. UnblockTalent. https://www.unblocktalent.com/topics/building-blocks/consensus/consensus-ranking/

Van Molken, R., & van Molken, R. (2018). *Blockchain across Oracle*. Packt Publishing.

Wang, Y., Liu, H., Wang, J., & Wang, S. (2020). Efficient Data Interaction of Blockchain Smart Contract with Oracle Mechanism. *2020 IEEE 9th Joint International Information Technology and Artificial Intelligence Conference (ITAIC)*, 1000–1003. 10.1109/ITAIC49862.2020.9338784

Wintermeyer, L. (2021, October 14). *Oracles: The invisible backbone of DeFi and applied Blockchain apps*. Forbes.Com. https://www.forbes.com/sites/lawrencewintermeyer/2021/10/14/cryptohacks-oraclesthe-invisible-backbone-of-defi-and-applied-blockchain-apps/

KEY TERMS AND DEFINITIONS

Application Program Interface (API): An API allows different software/services to communicate with each other. In web3, APIs facilitate communication between decentralized applications (DApps) and blockchain nodes/oracles.

Blockchain Node: A blockchain node is a computer/device that stores, validates and helps propagate transactions on a blockchain network like Ethereum. Full nodes run the blockchain client software and have a full copy of the blockchain data.

Blockchain Oracle: An oracle provides real-world data like price feeds, location coordinates etc to smart contracts on blockchains which otherwise have no way to access off-chain data. It acts as a bridge between blockchains and external data sources and APIs.

Chainlink: Chainlink is an oracle network that aggregates off-chain data and securely provides it to smart contracts on blockchains. By connecting smart contracts to existing APIs and data sources, Chainlink allows decentralized applications to access key functionalities.

Consensus Mechanisms: Consensus mechanisms ensure all nodes reach an agreement about the validity and order of transactions/blocks added to a blockchain. The two main types are Proof of Work and Proof of Stake which use different algorithms to achieve distributed consensus.

Data Aggregators: Data aggregators collect data from multiple sources, websites, APIs etc and make it available through a unified interface. In blockchain oracles, data aggregators consolidate off-chain data for smart contracts from various endpoints in a decentralized network.

Decentralized Oracle Networks: A Decentralized oracle network crowdsources data from several independent oracle nodes/providers to reduce centralization risks. It uses economic incentives, redundancies and other techniques to deliver more accurate and secure data to blockchain applications.

IoT Sensor: IoT (Internet of Things) sensors are hardware devices that detect real-world conditions like temperature, motion, pressure etc and relay this digital sensor data to other electronic devices and systems. They are an important source of off-chain data for blockchain oracles.

Proof of Stake: In Proof of Stake (PoS) protocols, the creator of the next block is chosen in a pseudorandom way, depending on how many coins they hold. This favors those with more existing wealth holding stakes in the currency. The validation process is faster with less resource intensive than Proof of Work.

Proof of Work: Proof of Work (PoW) is the original consensus algorithm where participants validate transactions by competing to solve complex cryptographic puzzles in a process called mining. The first to solve the puzzle and add the block to the chain is rewarded with coins. This process requires immense computing power.

Chapter 11
Revolutionizing Industry and Business Processes With Smart Contracts in Blockchain

L. Mary Shamala
Vellore Institute of Technology, Chennai, India

V. R. Balasaraswathi
Vellore Institute of Technology, Chennai, India

R. Gayathri
Vellore Institute of Technology, Chennai, India

ABSTRACT

The evolution of blockchain technology, notably exemplified by Bitcoin, heralded a new era where smart contracts have taken center stage. Smart contracts are ingenious self-executing contracts that empower automatic enforcement of contractual terms, eliminating the need for intermediaries or trusted third parties. Consequently, smart contracts offer multifaceted benefits, including streamlined administrative procedures, cost savings, enhanced operational efficiency, and risk reduction. This chapter aims to provide the pivotal technical aspects of smart contracts and their significance within the blockchain technology landscape. The authors begin by elucidating fundamental concepts, structural intricacies, and the working principles of smart contracts. Subsequently, they delve into the technological platforms that support smart contracts. They then provide an overview of the application landscape, with a focus on Ethereum and hyperledger fabric platforms. Finally, they address the challenges associated with smart contract technology and offer insights into potential opportunities.

DOI: 10.4018/979-8-3693-1532-3.ch011

The worldwide web is continually evolving and is now on the third wave of web services called Web 3.0. Web 3.0 is an open-source internet where consumers control information while enjoying direct access to apps, eliminating the need for intermediaries. Web 3.0 focuses on decentralization, thus Blockchain has a crucial role in its evolution. Blockchain technology has recently sparked widespread attention in research and business. As the name suggests, Blockchain is a shared software platform that enables the execution of operations without an intermediary (Khan et al, 2021). Consequently, it is possible to accomplish commercial activities cheaply and quickly. Furthermore, blockchain ensures widespread confidence because it is tough to alter any activities contained in blockchains, and all past actions are transparent and provable. Smart contract technology, deeply integrated into blockchain ecosystems, is heralding a paradigm shift in traditional industries and business operations.

Nick Szabo, a cryptographer, and Computer Engineer first put forward the concept of smart contracts in the 1990s (Szabo, 1997). Smart contracts are codes that are independently grounded on blockchains or comparable networks and enable secure and transparent execution of predetermined procedures. Smart contracts currently manage billions of dollars in worth. These self-executing contracts have revolutionized the way agreements are made and enforced, eliminating the need for intermediaries and enhancing operational efficiency across various sectors. The primary distinction between smart contracts and ordinary contracts is that smart contracts record provisions in a programming language rather than a legal language (Khan et al, 2021). In decentralized blockchains, transaction-based smart contracts are fundamentally duplicated and maintained. On the other hand, traditional contracts would delivered in a centralized fashion by an established third party leading to lengthy processing periods and higher expenses.

Smart contracts, being autonomous and state-based, have transcended the realm of programmable currency and entered a domain characterized by decentralized, autonomous, observable, verifiable, and information-sharing capabilities. They facilitate the creation of customized programming logic across the blockchain, enabling the development of programmable finance and a programmable society. Smart contracts find extensive applications including electronic payments, controlling assets, multi-signature deals, the Internet of Things, cloud computing, and the economy of collaboration (Tern, 2021). Smart contracts thus represent an essential part of Web3 Technologies, allowing for a new paradigm of automated, trustless, decentralized, and ubiquitous services and applications.

BASIC CONCEPTS OF SMART CONTRACTS

A blockchain is a distributed information storage system that archives every activity in the blockchain network. The information within it is copied and distributed across members of the network. The key characteristic of this technology is the fact it enables unverified users to securely interact and transfer transactions to one another in the absence of an intermediator. The blockchain consists of a chronological collection of blocks. A cryptographic hash identifies each of these blocks. Every single block is linked to the previous forming a block chain. A block consists of a set of operations. After a block is generated and published to an existing blockchain, its actions are irreversible or incapable of being modified (Badri et al, 2022). This serves as the basis for avoiding the risk of double spending and preserving the integrity of information (Alharby et al, 2018). Blockchains are distributed, and extremely secure thanks to cryptographic functions and enforceable consensus procedures for fresh transactions, thereby eliminating the "middleman" to generate confidence. As a result, transaction fees are much lower (both in terms of money and time) than in the standard trade system.

Smart contracts are indeed a significant development in the realm of blockchain technology. They constitute self-executing agreements in which the conditions of a buyer-seller deal are explicitly encoded into the program. Whenever the conditions specified in the code are satisfied, the smart contract conducts the agreed-upon activities immediately, without the need for intermediaries or third parties. This automation reduces the risks of errors, delays, and disputes. Smart contracts deployed on a blockchain offer a decentralized and foolproof record storing transactions and data. When a smart contract is put into action on a blockchain, the code it contains is replicated across the network of nodes, ensuring transparency and security. These smart contracts offer inventive solutions not only in the financial sector but also have a significant role in the administration of various aspects, including information, assets, contracts, oversight, and other elements within the broader social system (Lin et al, 2022).

A smart contract is formally defined as "a set of promises, specified in digital form, including protocols within which the parties perform on these promises"(Szabo, 1997). Vending machines exemplify a straightforward application of smart contracts (automated logic). Upon coin insertion, it dispenses the products automatically and gives back change if required. There is no human intervention required as the machine operates based on programmed instructions. A code manages the coin insertion event, verifies the transaction, and executes the dispensing of goods, all in compliance with legal standards. The process is tamper-proof as the executed contract operates predictably. Automation in vending machines minimizes labor expenses, eliminates human errors, or delays, and saves time efficiently.

There are many informal definitions for smart contracts in the literature such as "autonomous machines", "contracts between parties stored on a blockchain" or "any computation that takes place on a blockchain" (IO, 2017). All these definitions typically fall under one of these two distinct groups: smart legal contract and smart contract code (Wikipedia). Smart contract code is stated as "Code that is stored, verified, and executed on a blockchain" (Stark, 2017). The strength of smart contract code is dependent upon the programming language chosen to define the contract as well as the potential of blockchain. A smart legal contract entails software that executes or replaces legal agreements. Instead of technology, the potential of such a smart contract is determined through legal, business, and political systems (Choudhury et al, 2023).

Figure 1. Progress of smart contracts within the blockchain

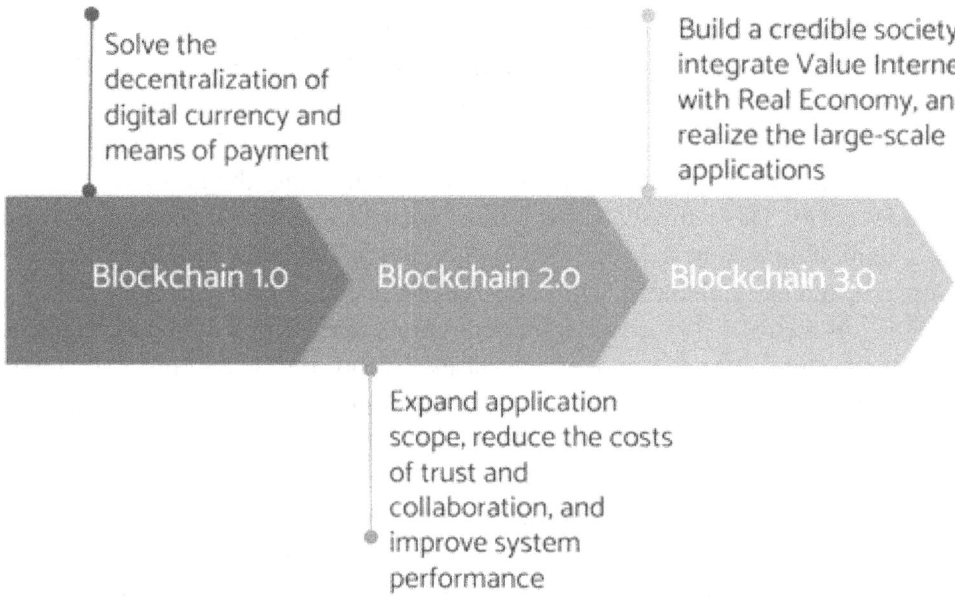

The progress underlying smart contracts is visible in three distinct stages throughout the ongoing development of Blockchain technology (Lin et al, 2022), as depicted in Figure 1. Stage 1 is Blockchain 1.0 where Bitcoin stands out as the primary representative application. Its primary use case involves facilitating digital currency transactions. The inclusion of smart contracts in Blockchain 2.0 paves the path enabling the design of distributed software applications (DApps) on the blockchain. This advancement has brought about improvements in transaction speed and system performance, while also expanding the range of functions that can be achieved. The technology has evolved beyond its initial use case in digital currencies (as seen in Blockchain 1.0) to support a more diverse range of applications and use cases. Notably, two of the most prominent development platforms in this era are Ethereum and Hyperledger Fabric. The blockchain ecosystem is continuously evolving, with new development platforms and technologies like side chains, cross-chain solutions, and Enterprise Operation Systems (EOS). The envisioned Blockchain 3.0 achieves greater autonomy through a distributed independent structure built around smart contracts, having transaction data and program rules stored within the distributed ledger. These advancements come with both high expectations and ongoing debates within the blockchain community. Blockchain 4.0 (Bodkhe, 2020), the most recent iteration of the blockchain focuses on innovation within Blockchain. Blockchain 4.0 intends to expand Blockchain into a business-useable platform for building and operating sophisticated and popular decentralized apps. Blockchain 4.0 focuses on speed, accessibility, and usage by the public. Perhaps the foremost characteristic of Blockchain 4.0 is that it can propel forward the progress of Web 3.0 (Mukherjee, 2021).

Key Features

Smart agreements or contracts constitute autonomous software programs operating on blockchain-based systems to autonomously impose, validate, or facilitate agreement or contract negotiation. They come with several notable features primarily derived from the underpinning Blockchain system (Aggarwal & Kumar, 2021). These features make smart contracts a powerful tool across a variety of uses, covering financial services, manufacturing, supply chain, and many more.

- *Automation:* Whenever specific conditions occur, smart contracts operate instantaneously. (Hewa et al, 2021). This automation reduces the need for human supervision and minimizes the potential for human errors.
- *Trust and Security:* Smart contracts run on blockchain systems, removing the dependency on a centralized agency. Moreover, all transactions are cryptographically protected. This can reduce fraud and increase confidence in the system.
- *Accuracy:* Smart contracts are executed according to the predefined rules without human involvement. This reduces the risk of human errors during the execution of agreements.
- *Immutability:* Once deployed, smart contracts are immutable. This implies that it is not possible to change or interfere with the code and data associated with the contract. It guarantees that the conditions of the agreement remain consistent as well as cannot be changed unilaterally.
- *Decentralization:* Smart contracts are carried out and verified over a distributed system of nodes. This removes the possibility of malfunction at a single point. Decentralization enhances security and ensures the continuous operation of the contract.
- *Efficiency:* Smart contracts systematize and expedite processes by automating the execution of agreements. This leads to cost savings and faster transaction times, particularly for cross-border or complex transactions.
- *Backup:* Blockchain networks typically maintain redundancy and backup mechanisms to ensure the security and availability of data. These mechanisms may involve multiple nodes independently maintaining a copy of the blockchain's ledger (Aggarwal & Kumar, 2021).
- *Versatility:* Smart contracts have numerous uses, spanning from finance sector to logistics and beyond. They are not limited to any industry.

Benefits of Smart Contracts

Smart contracts offer several advantages, including cost-efficiency, speed, and error reduction. As a result, smart contracts with significant development efficiency, inexpensive upkeep, and superior implementation efficiency complement the blockchain system flawlessly. Figure 2 highlights the benefits and ways to achieve these are discussed further (Zheng et al, 2020; Aggarwal & Kumar, 2021).

Figure 2. Advantages of smart contracts for business

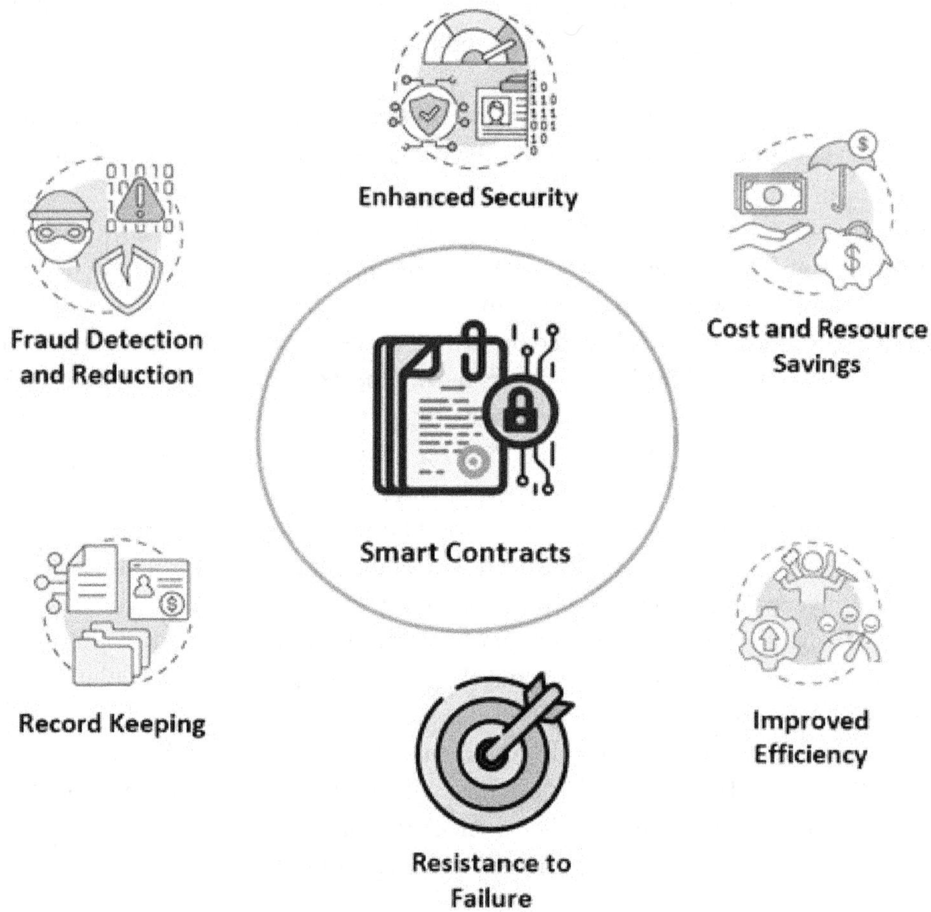

- *Enhanced Security:* Transactions and data within smart contracts are secured using cryptographic techniques, making them highly resistant to unauthorized access or tampering.
- *Cost and Resource Savings:* By reducing the need for intermediaries and automating processes, smart contracts cut down administrative and service costs. This can result in significant cost savings for businesses and individuals.
- *Efficiency of Business Processes:* Smart contracts can automate deal enforcement and remove third parties, resulting in quicker processing times.
- *Resistance to Failure:* Smart contracts are executed and verified across a network of nodes, removing central points of failure, and enhancing network security.
- *Record Keeping:* Smart contracts provide a permanent, tamper-proof record of transactions and agreements, which can be valuable for audit trails and legal purposes.
- *Fraud Detection and Reduction:* The terms and execution of smart contracts are recorded on a public blockchain, available to each network participant. This transparency fosters oversight, lowering the potential for deception or manipulation.

Role of Smart Contracts in DeFi and DAO Models

Decentralized Finance (DeFi) (Schär, 2021) is upending existing business structures and offering fresh perspectives to interactions, financing, and other areas. Smart contracts are crucial in decentralized trading systems because they enable trustless and safe currency trades. Users can trade various cryptocurrencies directly from their wallets on DeFi platforms, eliminating the need for a centralized authority such as a bank or legal entity. Smart contracts automate the management of liquidity pools, the setting of prices, and the carrying out of business, guaranteeing openness and autonomy in the whole trading cycle. Decentralized exchanges (DEX) and crowdfunding sites are two popular DeFi applications that use smart contracts.

Smart contracts are also significant for the management of Decentralized Autonomous Organizations (DAOs). A DAO is set up by an alliance of individuals who agree to follow specific guidelines to achieve a shared objective. DAOs are "consortia that are run through rules encoded as computer programs called smart contracts" (Chohan, 2017). Thus, DAO smart contracts are computer programs that incorporate democratic and managerial principles and operate upon networks of peers. To render frauds harder, DAOs provide a reliable and secure distributed ledger for routing cash transfers across the internet using reliable timestamps in a shared database. Ethereum DAO, DigixDAO, and crowdfunding are some applications that adopt the DAO Model (Singh, 2019).

OPERATION OF SMART CONTRACTS

Smart contracts are autonomous and self-executing software codes that use computing resources to enact the clauses and provisions of a certain accord or relationship. A smart contract's life cycle, like that of a regular contract, involves four operational phases (Zheng et al, 2020): generation, deployment, execution, completion, or settlement as illustrated in Figure 3.

Generation Phase: The various individuals must first negotiate their responsibilities, privileges, and constraints on contracts. An agreement might be reached after a few sessions of meetings and negotiations. Legal professionals or counselors can assist individuals in developing a preliminary contractual deal. The natural language agreement is subsequently transformed by software experts into a smart contract coded by a computer language (Thabet & Abdelbaki, 2021). Smart contract development is thus a continuous procedure that calls for numerous rounds of talks and revisions. Additionally, it is working with a variety of partners, including stakeholders, legal professionals, and programmers.

Figure 3. Lifecycle phases of a smart contract

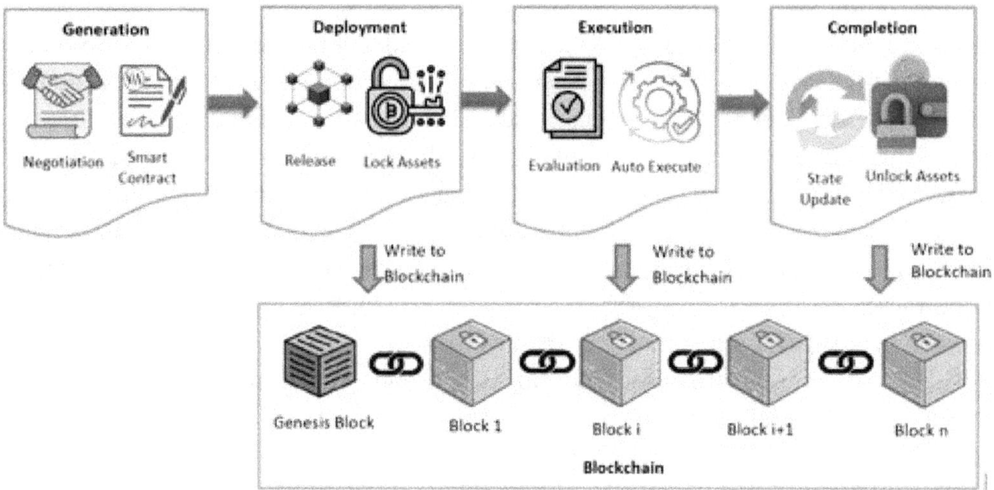

Deployment Phase: The signed contract is broadcast to each node through the distributed network for verification. The verified smart contracts are subsequently placed on blockchain-based systems. Contracts maintained on blockchains are unchangeable because of their immutability. Alterations if any necessitate the formation of a fresh contract. When contract documents go live on blockchains, everyone will gain access to the contracts via the blockchains. Furthermore, the digital belongings of everyone who signed the smart contract remain immobilized by locking the associated electronic wallets (Sillaber& Waltl, 2017; Khan, et al, 2021).

Execution Phase: The event trigger method is used to execute smart contracts. The terms and conditions will be reviewed following the smart contracts' deployment phase. When the conditions of the agreement are met, the contractual operations are immediately carried out.

Completion: Following the execution phase, completed operations and modified states of everyone involved were recorded within the blockchains. At this point, electronic belongings are being moved between the involved parties. As a result, the digital possessions of the parties concerned are now released.

Figure 4. Working principle of smart contract

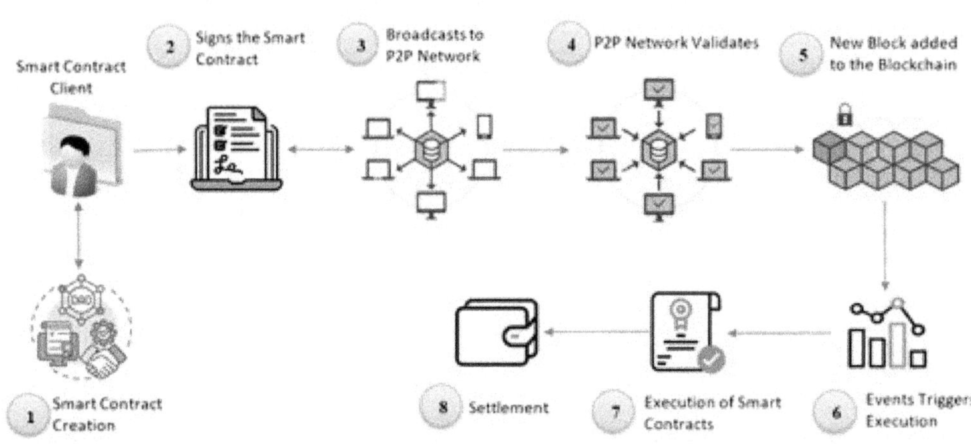

The smart contract interacts with real-world assets on the same premise as that of the 'If- Else Statement' of a computer program. When a predefined condition is met, the smart contract implements its contractual provisions. Figure 4 depicts the steps involved in the operation principle of smart contracts and is detailed below. A predefined contract is written in the native language which covers the specifics and conditions accepted by everyone involved. The software engineers write smart contracts as simple codes. The smart contract client digitally signs the smart contract and creates a new block containing this smart contract. This block is then deployed on the Blockchain network by interacting with all participants of the P2P system. Once most nodes validate the block, it gets uploaded to the Blockchain network. The codes and conditions of smart contracts are thus present on the public ledger. When an event is triggered in the contract like a share's target price is reached, then the code executes automatically. Finally, all the settlements are made quickly and efficiently and the state of all the parties involved is updated in blockchain. Meanwhile, regulators can watch the contract activities regularly on the blockchain to gain insight into the industry while protecting individuals' privacy and security.

Best Practices Involved in the Deployment of Smart Contract

Smart contracts are more commonly used in a variety of business contexts. Because smart contracts frequently deal with financial transactions, security is critical because it undermines the overall operation of any blockchain. A significant concern is that smart contracts cannot be altered once deployed as it is immutable. If something goes wrong with smart contracts after their deployment, enterprises may face software vulnerabilities, ineffective access control, and revenue loss (Hewa et al, 2021). As a result, programmers should be versed in every possible danger and adhere to best practices from the industry while developing smart contracts. This is intended to promise the blockchain network's reliability, safety, and performance. Certain important recommendations related to smart contract adoption are:

- Smart contract auditing
- Rigorous Testing before deployment
- Implementing Security protocols
- Gas consumption optimization
- Proper documentation of smart contract
- Provision/ Support for upgradation
- Compliance with regulatory standards
- Minimizing external dependency

Designers can implement smart contracts to remain secure, productive, and adaptive to potential shifts in the distributed ledger network by embracing these standards of practice.

ENABLING TECHNOLOGIES

Developers can design smart contract apps using basic user interfaces available from smart contract development platforms. Many of the existing blockchain systems can accommodate smart contracts. Here, we introduce the highlights of the leading technological platforms that support smart contracts, with a particular focus on Ethereum (Buterin, 2013), Hyperledger (Cachin, 2016), and EOS (IO, 2017). Table 1 gives a comparison of these enabling technologies in various aspects.

Ethereum (Buterin, 2013) is widely recognized for its pioneering role in enabling the creation of decentralized applications through smart contracts. It has established a robust ecosystem for Decentralized Applications (DApp) development. Launched in 2015 by Vitalik Buterin and a team of developers, Ethereum introduced the concept of programmable money, allowing developers to build a variety of applications beyond simple digital currency transactions. Ethereum's main innovation is its ability to execute smart contracts with the terms of the agreement directly written into code. These contracts run on the Ethereum Virtual Machine (EVM) and enable decentralized applications to perform various functions without the need for intermediaries. Ether is the native cryptocurrency of the Ethereum network. It serves as a medium of exchange for transactions on the platform and acts as a reward for miners who secure the network. Ethereum Improvement Proposals (EIPs) are proposals for changes or improvements to the Ethereum network. They can include upgrades, new features, or adjustments to the protocol. Ethereum was instrumental in popularizing the concept of smart contracts and continues to be a key player in the evolution of decentralized technologies.

Hyperledger Fabric (Cachin, 2016) developed under the Linux Foundation's Hyperledger project, on the other hand, is known for its focus on enterprise-grade blockchain solutions. It provides a framework for creating permissioned blockchains tailored for businesses and organizations, offering enhanced privacy and scalability features. Fabric supports smart contracts, known as Chaincode, authored in familiar programming dialects like Java, JavaScript, or Go. Chaincode is developed to encapsulate business logic and be executed in an isolated environment. Fabric provides channels, enabling private and confidential transactions between specified network members. This feature allows subsets of network participants to conduct transactions privately without sharing data with all network nodes. Transactions in Hyperledger Fabric must be endorsed by specific parties according to predefined policies before being added to the blockchain. This allows for customizable transaction validation based on business requirements. Fabric is well-suited for enterprise applications across industries such as finance, supply chain, healthcare, and more. It caters to scenarios requiring privacy, scalability, and adherence to regulatory requirements.

Table 1. Features of smart contract programming platforms

Parameters/Platform	Ethereum	Hyperledger Fabric	EOS
Language	Solidity, Serpent, Low-Level Lisp-like Language (LLL), Mutan	Java, Golang	C++
Execution Environment	Ethereum Virtual Machine (EVM)	Docker	WebAssembly
Data Model	Account-based	Key-value pair	Account-based
Consensus Algorithm	Proof of Work(PoW)	Practical Byzantine Fault Tolerance (PBFT)	Delegated Proof of Stake (DPOS) and Byzantine Fault Tolerance (BFT)
Operation Mode	Public	Private	Public
Native Cryptocurrency	Ether	None	EOS
Turing Completeness	Turing Complete	Turing Complete	Turing Complete
Application Context	General	General	General

EOS (IO, 2017) is a Blockchain protocol intended to allow for the proliferation of independent applications. It aims to provide a platform that is scalable, flexible, and user-friendly. EOS has a consensus process known as Delegated Proof of Stake, which involves token holders voting for block producers who are in charge of verifying and securing the network. This consensus model aims to achieve high transaction throughput and scalability. EOS also combines both Delegated Proof of Stake (DPOS) and Byzantine Fault Tolerance (BFT) consensus algorithms for better performance. EOS uses WebAssembly (Wasm) to allow smart contracts to be written in a variety of dialects. EOS has faced criticism related to centralization concerns due to the limited number of block producers, as well as concerns regarding its governance model and potential vulnerabilities in the network.

Table 2. Common programming languages for writing smart contracts

Language	Platform	Based On	Key Feature
Solidity	Ethereum	C++, Python, JavaScript	High-level and Turing-complete
Vyper	Ethereum	Python	More secure and readable than solidity
Cairo	StarkNet/ StarkEx	Python	Proves computational correctness
Go (Golang)	Hyperledger Fabric	C	Simple and built-in concurrency
Scilla	Zilliqa		Secure by design contract
Yul	Ethereum	JavaScript	Improved performance and lower transaction costs than solidity
Rust	Polkadot, Cosmos and Solana	C, C++	Scalable and faster
Move	Diem, Aptos and Sui	Rust	Built-in security capabilities
Haskell	Cardano	-	Imperative programming language, secure high-level functionality
Pact	Kadena	-	Immutable, Turing-incomplete; Robust, quick and secure.
Liquidity	Tezos	OCaml, Michelson	fully typed functional language

Smart contracts are typically written in a variety of computer languages commonly referred to as Smart Contract Languages (SCLs) (Dwivedi, 2021). Table 2 lists the most prevalent languages for building smart contracts. Among them, Solidity and Vyper are the finest languages for programmers trying to start building DApps with the Web3 stack. A simple example of a smart contract code for cryptocurrency named "SimpleCoin" in Solidity SCL is listed in Figure 5. Simply the contract's developer has the authority to generate or issue additional currencies. Anyone can then transfer these coins to a recipient using his or her address.

Figure 5. Sample smart contract in solidity SCL

```
1. pragma solidity ^0.8.4;
2. contract SimpleCoin {
3. address public creator;
4. mapping(address => uint) public balance;
5. event Transaction(address from, address to, uint amount);
6. constructor() {
7.          creator = msg.sender;
8.          }
9. function Create(address receiver, uint amount) public {
10.         require(msg.sender == creator;
11.         balance[receiver] += amount;
12.        }
13. error InsufficientBalance(uint requested, uint available);
14. function Send(address receiver, uint amount) public {
15.        if (amount > balances[msg.sender]) revert
16.        InsufficientBalance({
17.                requested: amount, available:
18.                balances[msg.sender]});
19.                balance[msg.sender] -= amount;
20.                balance[receiver] += amount;
21.                Transaction(msg.sender, receiver, amount);
22.        }
23. }
```

Event *Transaction* on line 5 allows customers to respond to changes in the contract. The constructor code in line 6 executes when a deal is established. The function *Create* in line 9 delivers a certain number of newly produced coins to a given address. The contract administrator can use this feature. The function *Send* in line 14 transmits a certain number of a specified number of current coins from the caller to the specified address.

BLOCKCHAIN SMART CONTRACT-BASED SOLUTIONS

Smart contracts offer a wide array of solutions across various industries due to their automated, secure, and decentralized nature. Some of the smart contract solutions that can be used in several areas as in the literature are discussed below.

Peng et al. (2023) proposed a framework for blockchain smart contracts in the agriculture food industry that seems to offer a structured approach to implementing smart contracts in this sector. This closed-loop general framework consists of five stages namely (i) analysis of information flow characteristics, (ii) intelligent model creation, (iii) technology selection, (iv) development of platform selection, and (v) application testing. The framework seems to provide a structured methodology to guide researchers and practitioners in implementing blockchain smart contracts within the agri-food industry. Its generality across different agricultural products suggests that it can be adaptable and applicable to various scenarios within this sector.

Wang et al.'s (2019) Loan on Blockchain (LoC) leverages smart contract locking and unlocking functions to automate the processing of transactions. It is a financial debt management platform built on the Hyperledger Fabric platform. Furthermore, event, oracle, and digital signatures were added to authenticate the lending company and ensure data privacy. Through implementation and performance assessments of the system, the authors showed its usage in a real-world financial lending context.

Agrawal et al. (2023) studied how blockchain powered by smart contracts improves partnerships, sharing of resources, and optimization in supply chains. They examined the flow of data among parties in a blockchain system, important structural elements, and the creation of smart contract guidelines. By implementing the generated smart contract on an Ethereum blockchain, the investigation uncovers how blockchain technology-based smart contracts reward partnerships. Furthermore, it evaluates public support for broader participation of stakeholders in stronger inclusive trade relationships and enterprise ecosystems.

Varfolomeev et al. (2021) suggested a system that clarifies the benefits of smart contracts in the context of the smart city environment's varied activities. It includes crucial information regarding this technology and its effect on the entire organizational structure of every service offered via smart governments. The article used an example of managing a real estate lease document digitally to demonstrate the benefits of blockchain technology in overcoming current obstacles in real estate.

Ferro et al. (2023) offer a new approach to digital rights management designed as part of the MediaVerse project. It suggests combining smart legal contracts and blockchain smart contracts to encourage media content dissemination while protecting intellectual property rights. Discussion for legally protected derivative works that use previous material posted to the system, involving collaborative works by several writers who communicate ownership of the work and concur on the specific earnings is dealt with. As an instance of self-determination, the effort may result in a better and more equitable revenue method for content creators.

APPLICATION LANDSCAPE OF SMART CONTRACTS

Smart contracts have diverse applications across industries, playing key roles in electronic payments, controlling assets, multi-signature agreements, the Internet of Things, cloud computing, and supply chain management (Hewa et al, 2021). Figure 6 highlights the broad spectrum of use cases of smart contracts on Blockchain.

Financial Industry

In the Financial industry, smart contracts possess the ability to reform operations such as escrow services, payment settlement, and issuance of financial instruments. They have the ability to streamline complex financial agreements, eliminating agents, saving administrative and service costs, decreasing financial risks, and speeding up the execution of transactions [19]. Smart contracts underpin various decentralized finance applications, enabling lending, borrowing, yield farming, and other financial services without traditional intermediaries. Token issuance, distributed trades, and protocols for loanable assets are the most notable Decentralised Finance (DeFi) uses of smart contracts. A few notable use cases in this domain are currency management, escrow service, insurance, stock trading, and auditing procedures.

Figure 6. Applications of smart contracts

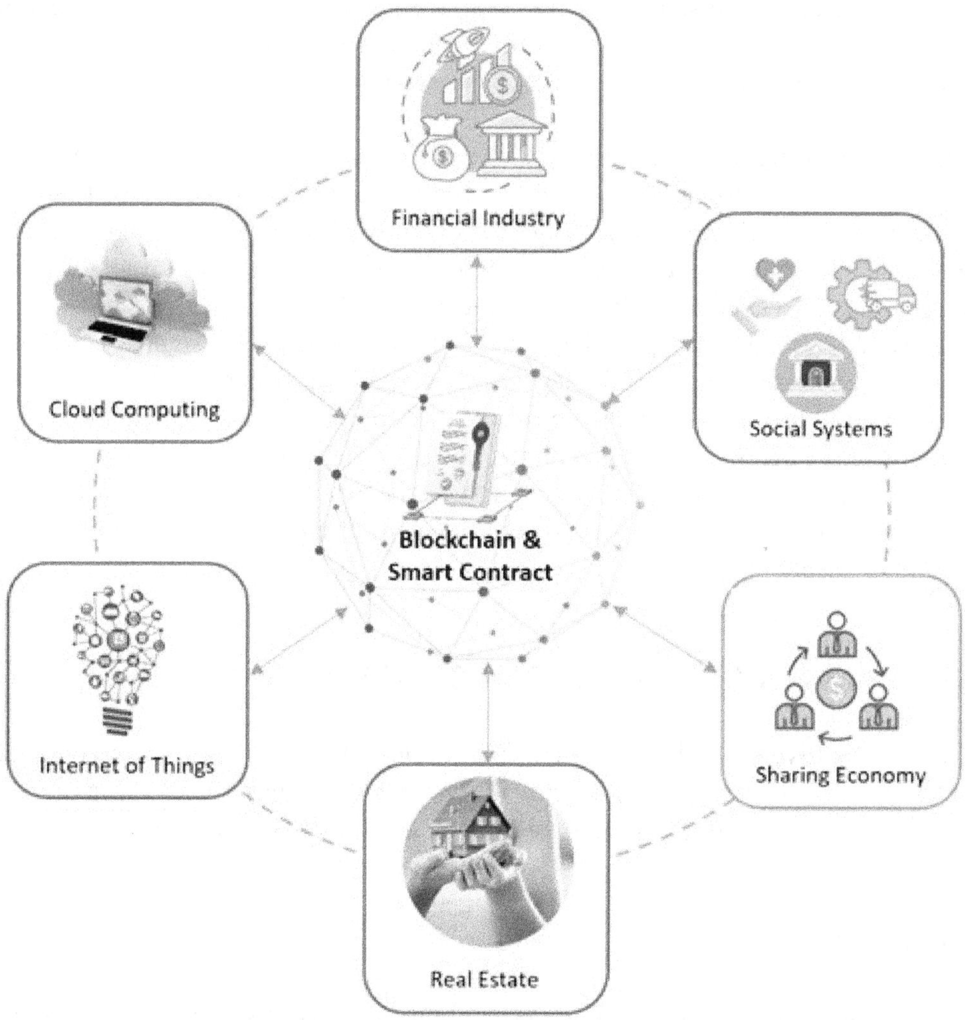

Social Systems

Smart contracts can also be applied to manage various aspects of social systems. Smart contracts along with blockchain may avoid data fraud and increase the openness of public data. For example, they can used in governance structures to automate voting and decision-making processes (Balakrishnan et al, 2023), in supply chain management to track the provenance of goods (Prause, 2019), in healthcare to manage patient records (McGhin et al, 2019; Choudhury et al, 2023), and in a wide range of other use cases (Maesa et al, 2020). Smart contracts can create transparent and secure voting systems, minimizing fraud and ensuring accurate results in elections or decision-making processes. Implementing smart contracts in supply chains enhances transparency, traceability, and efficiency. They can automate tasks like tracking goods, verifying authenticity, and managing agreements between different parties. In healthcare, smart contracts can improve patient data management, securely share medical records between institutions, automate insurance claims processing, and ensure compliance with regulations.

Real Estate

The commercial real estate market is made up of many forms of deals such as renting, leasing, and buying as well as diverse types of property such as office space, residences, and grounds. All data about property ownership, leasing, etc so on is administered by government agencies. Changing possession and leasing operations are carried out using the assistance of intermediate parties. Smart contracts can facilitate property transactions by automating the transfer of ownership, managing rental agreements, and securely storing property records on a blockchain. Smart contracts obviate the need for trusted intermediaries because the transfer itself happens automatically. The smart contracts approach is expected to completely transform the real estate trade business by providing increased security, eliminating processing fees and commissions, and reducing processing time (Hewa et al, 2021).

Decentralized Network Security

Cloud networks can be made more resilient against DDOS attacks (Mansfield-Devine, 2015) or other centralized target-based threats by smart contracts. They handle the attacks in a fully decentralized manner, distributing resources and mitigating risks. Smart Contracts can also be used to administer and enforce Service Level Agreements (SLAs) among cloud service providers and users. This ensures that agreed-upon security measures are maintained and triggers predefined actions in case of breaches or service failures (Uriarte et al, 2016). The potential benefits of integrating smart contracts into cloud computing include identity and access management, automated security protocols, secure SLAs, threat detection and response.

Internet of Things

The basic goal of the Internet of Things is to connect things to the Internet while offering consumers numerous services. The Internet of Things was initially postulated to implicitly streamline certain business operations. Hence, the potential of IoT can be realized through the incorporation of smart contracts to provide an automated solution. In the manufacturing industry, firmware upgrades in the form of smart contracts are published in blockchains dispersed across the entire network by manufacturers. Smart contracts can then send firmware upgrades to devices automatically. This method saves many resources (Zheng et al, 2020; Christidis et al, 2016). Some other use cases of smart contracts in IoT are scalable resource sharing, edge computing, unmanned aerial vehicles, and smart cities.

Sharing Economy

The concept of sharing has various advantages, such as cutting consumer expenses by sharing and reusing things, increasing the utilization of resources, enhancing customer service, and lessening environmental effects (Taeihagh, 2017). By decentralizing sharing economy systems, smart contracts can revolutionize the sharing economy. Furthermore, the convergence of the IoT with smart contracts has the potential to enhance collaborative economy systems like electronic asset management (Bodemer, 2023), collaborative automated payment networks, monetary exchange, and transport systems (Huckle et al, 2015).

These applications demonstrate the versatility and potential of smart contracts to streamline processes, reduce costs, enhance security, and create more efficient and transparent systems across diverse sectors. The key industries in which smart contracts are used are government administration, banking, supply chain management, information, and communication technology (ICT), medical care business, and energy, making up 85.63% of all applications. Table 3. gives a summary of the positive aspects of smart contracts across various industrial applications.

Table 3. Summary of smart contracts uses in various Sectors

Smart Contract Benefits	Application Industry											
	Public Sector	Supply Chain	ICT	Finance	Healthcare	Energy	Agriculture	Business	Real Estate	Education	Entertainment	Manufacturing
Trust	√	√	√	√		√	√	√				√
Transparency	√	√		√	√	√	√	√	√			
Traceability		√	√	√			√					√
Trusted Third Party	√	√	√	√	√	√	√	√	√		√	
Security	√	√	√	√		√	√	√	√	√		
Privacy	√		√	√	√	√		√		√	√	
Integrity	√			√						√		
Simple Process	√	√	√	√	√			√		√		
Less Human Error	√	√		√	√	√						
Data Sharing			√		√		√		√			
Cost efficient	√	√		√	√		√	√	√			
Time Efficient		√	√		√	√	√	√		√	√	

CHALLENGES IN SMART CONTRACT TECHNOLOGY

In this section, we address the challenges associated with smart contract technology. Scalability, privacy and security, lack of governance, and performance issues are some of the key aspects to consider in adopting smart contract-based blockchain applications.

Scalability: The sequential execution of smart contracts would limit the number of transactions executed per time quantum. Blockchain solutions may be unlikely to expand over time as the sheer quantity of smart contracts increases. Scalability remains an issue when greater transactions are to be completed on blockchain systems. For widespread use, the quickness and efficacy of processing smart contracts must be enhanced.

Security and Privacy: The majority of contemporary smart contract and blockchain platforms require privacy-protection features, particularly for financial data. Because many people prefer financial transactions, this lack of anonymity may hinder the widespread use of smart contracts (Zheng et al, 2020). Smart contract platforms have innate software weaknesses that make them vulnerable to fraud. It is possible to perform criminal actions with the help of smart contracts (Juels et al, 2016). Re-entrancy, Integer over/underflow, and Locked Ether are the most prevalent smart contract flaws. Keeping them safe from breaches, vulnerabilities, and flaws is a major task.

Inconsistency in Standardization: The absence of oversight or uniformity in standardized smart contract creation techniques, resources, and interfaces poses a challenge for programmers to produce reliable and compatible contracts. Different blockchain platforms have different smart contract languages and standards. Ensuring interoperability between various blockchains is a challenge for seamless execution across networks. Once deployed, smart contracts are immutable. Handling updates, fixes, and amendments without compromising security or functionality is a challenge.

Legal Enforcement: It is difficult to combine legal frameworks with smart contracts because these may oppose the long-lasting nature of smart contracts. Because every nation has a unique set of rules and legislation, ensuring compliance with all requirements across jurisdictions is difficult. Since legal provisions or criteria are not realizable, modeling them in smart contracts remains difficult. Further, governments have a stake in monitoring and regulating the application of blockchain technology shedding some of its nature (Khan et al, 2021).

Performance: Miners sequentially execute smart contracts. Because the quantity of smart contracts that may be executed every unit of time is restricted, serial execution has an important influence on the functioning of blockchain systems. Nevertheless, since there is shared information among smart contracts, it is difficult to operate smart contracts at once (Zheng et al, 2020).

FUTURE DIRECTIONS

Overcoming the obstacles yet capitalizing on possibilities to produce more trustworthy, successful, and intuitive systems with many purposes throughout sectors is critical to the advancement of smart contract technology. Some of the insights into research directions would be:

- Though Parallel execution of smart contracts is an identified solution for the scalability problem, future studies should focus on implementing smart contracts that are interdependent. Correspondingly, there is a need to identify and solve performance problems that will enable the use of blockchains to reach their potential needs to be undertaken (Alharby et al, 2018).
- The key to smart contract development is the disparity between information technology and operational technology. This problem could be addressed by integrating software technologies, computational languages, and artificial intelligence.
- Development and research activities are needed in smart contract assessment tools, formal verification techniques, and security reward programs. Also, creating intuitive interfaces and tools will help non-technical users create and connect to smart contracts.
- Scalability may be enhanced by incorporating layer 2 approaches, partitioning, and superior consensus mechanisms. These approaches aim to ease bottlenecks and reduce transaction costs by handling payments outside of the primary blockchain.
- Creating standards and protocols for seamless interaction between different blockchains will facilitate wider adoption.
- Collaborating with regulators to establish legal frameworks that accommodate smart contracts can boost adoption and trust.
- Progress in privacy-preserving approaches such as safe multi-party processing and zero-knowledge proofs may improve electronic contract secrecy. (Bodemer, 2023).
- Standardization of SCL, tools, and best practices efforts may aid in facilitating and managing contracts.

- Research into secure methods for introducing upgrades and amendments to deploy smart contracts without compromising security. Consider incorporating upgradeability capabilities within the smart contract to allow for future upgrades and additions without interfering with its current operation.

CONCLUSION

This chapter serves as a comprehensive resource for understanding the transformative potential of smart contracts in the blockchain ecosystem. By harnessing the capabilities of blockchain technology, smart contracts are poised to redefine the way agreements are executed and fulfilled, thereby unlocking a new era of innovation and efficiency in the business landscape. Smart contracts find extensive applications in electronic payments, financial asset handling, cloud computing, multi-signature deals, supply chain management, and the Internet of Things. The manner contracts are carried out simultaneously and depend on one another is a key challenge that must be overcome for performance optimization. Future research opportunities are available to improve performance, scalability, and integration of Artificial Intelligence in the creation of smart contracts.

REFERENCES

Aggarwal, S., & Kumar, N. (2021). Blockchain 2.0: smart contracts. In Advances in Computers (Vol. 121, pp. 301-322). Elsevier. doi:10.1016/bs.adcom.2020.08.015

Agrawal, T. K., Angelis, J., Khilji, W. A., Kalaiarasan, R., & Wiktorsson, M. (2023). Demonstration of a blockchain-based framework using smart contracts for supply chain collaboration. *International Journal of Production Research*, *61*(5), 1497–1516. doi:10.1080/00207543.2022.2039413

Alharby, M., Aldweesh, A., & Van Moorsel, A. (2018, November). Blockchain-based smart contracts: A systematic mapping study of academic research. In *2018 International Conference on Cloud Computing, Big Data and Blockchain (ICCBB)* (pp. 1-6). IEEE. https://doi.org/10.5121/csit.2017.71011

Badri, N., Nasraoui, L., & Saidane, L. A. (2022, May). Blockchain for WSN and IoT Applications. In *2022 IEEE 9th International Conference on Sciences of Electronics, Technologies of Information and Telecommunications (SETIT)* (pp. 543-548). IEEE. 10.1109/SETIT54465.2022.9875746

Balakrishnan, N., Aruna, S., Akshaya, D., Karthikeyan, P. C., & Dharshini, G. D. (2023, May). Smart Contracts and Blockchain based E-Voting. In *2023 7th International Conference on Intelligent Computing and Control Systems (ICICCS)* (pp. 1394-1399). IEEE. 10.1109/ICICCS56967.2023.10142675

Bodemer, O. (2023). *Corporate Asset Management in the Digital Age: A Blockchain Perspective*. https://doi.org/ doi:110.36227/techrxiv.24220675.v1

Bodkhe, U., Tanwar, S., Parekh, K., Khanpara, P., Tyagi, S., Kumar, N., & Alazab, M. (2020). Blockchain for industry 4.0: A comprehensive review. *IEEE Access : Practical Innovations, Open Solutions*, *8*, 79764–79800. doi:10.1109/ACCESS.2020.2988579

Buterin, V. (2013). *Ethereum whitepaper: A next-generation smart contract and decentralized application platform* [White Paper]. Ethereum.

Cachin, C. (2016, July). Architecture of the hyperledger blockchain fabric. *Workshop on distributed cryptocurrencies and consensus ledgers, 310*(4), 1-4.

Cant, B., Khadikar, A., Ruiter, A., Bronebakk, J. B., Coumaros, J., Buvat, J., & Gupta, A. (2016). *Smart Contracts in Financial Services: Getting from Hype to Reality*. Capgemini Consulting. https://www.capgemini.com/consulting-de/wp-content/uploads/sites/32/2017/08/smart_contracts_paper_long_0.p

ChohanU. W. (2017). The decentralized autonomous organization and governance issues. *Available at* SSRN 3082055. doi:10.2139/ssrn.3082055

Choudhury, T., Khanna, A., Chatterjee, P., Um, J. S., & Bhattacharya, A. (Eds.). (2023). *Blockchain Applications in Healthcare: Innovations and Practices*. John Wiley & Sons. doi:10.1002/9781394229512

Christidis, K., & Devetsikiotis, M. (2016). Blockchains and smart contracts for the internet of things. *IEEE Access : Practical Innovations, Open Solutions*, *4*, 2292–2303. doi:10.1109/ACCESS.2016.2566339

Dwivedi, V., Pattanaik, V., Deval, V., Dixit, A., Norta, A., & Draheim, D. (2021). Legally enforceable smart-contract languages: A systematic literature review. *ACM Computing Surveys*, *54*(5), 1–34. doi:10.1145/3453475

Ferro, E., Saltarella, M., Rotondi, D., Giovanelli, M., Corrias, G., Moncada, R., & Favenza, A. (2023). Digital assets rights management through smart legal contracts and smart contracts. *Blockchain: Research and Applications*, *100142*(3). Advance online publication. doi:10.1016/j.bcra.2023.100142

Hewa, T., Ylianttila, M., & Liyanage, M. (2021). Survey on blockchain based smart contracts: Applications, opportunities and challenges. *Journal of Network and Computer Applications*, *177*, 102857. doi:10.1016/j.jnca.2020.102857

Huckle, S., Bhattacharya, R., White, M., & Beloff, N. (2016). Internet of things, blockchain and shared economy applications. *Procedia Computer Science*, *98*, 461–466. doi:10.1016/j.procs.2016.09.074

IO. E. (2017). *Eos. IO technical white paper*. doi:10.1016/j.procs.2016.09.074

Juels, A., Kosba, A., & Shi, E. (2016, October). The ring of gyges: Investigating the future of criminal smart contracts. In *Proceedings of the 2016 ACM SIGSAC Conference on Computer and Communications Security* (pp. 283-295). 10.1145/2976749.2978362

Khan, S. N., Loukil, F., Ghedira-Guegan, C., Benkhelifa, E., & Bani-Hani, A. (2021). Blockchain smart contracts: Applications, challenges, and future trends. *Peer-to-Peer Networking and Applications*, *14*(5), 2901–2925. doi:10.1007/s12083-021-01127-0

Lin, S. Y., Zhang, L., Li, J., Ji, L. L., & Sun, Y. (2022). A survey of application research based on blockchain smart contract. *Wireless Networks*, *28*(2), 635–690. doi:10.1007/s11276-021-02874-x

Maesa, D. D. F., & Mori, P. (2020). Blockchain 3.0 applications survey. *Journal of Parallel and Distributed Computing*, *138*, 99–114. doi:10.1016/j.jpdc.2019.12.019

Mansfield-Devine, S. (2015). The growth and evolution of DDoS. *Network Security*, *2015*(10), 13–20. doi:10.1016/S1353-4858(15)30092-1

McGhin, T., Choo, K. K. R., Liu, C. Z., & He, D. (2019). Blockchain in healthcare applications: Research challenges and opportunities. *Journal of Network and Computer Applications*, *135*, 62–75. doi:10.1016/j.jnca.2019.02.027

Mukherjee, P., & Pradhan, C. (2021). Blockchain 1.0 to blockchain 4.0—The evolutionary transformation of blockchain technology. In *Blockchain technology: applications and challenges* (pp. 29–49). Springer International Publishing. doi:10.1007/978-3-030-69395-4_3

Peng, X., Zhao, Z., Wang, X., Li, H., Xu, J., & Zhang, X. (2023). A review on blockchain smart contracts in the agri-food industry: Current state, application challenges and future trends. *Computers and Electronics in Agriculture*, *208*, 107776. doi:10.1016/j.compag.2023.107776

Prause, G. (2019). Smart contracts for smart supply chains. *IFAC-PapersOnLine*, *52*(13), 2501–2506. doi:10.1016/j.ifacol.2019.11.582

Schär, F., & Finance, D. (2021). On Blockchain- and Smart Contract-Based Financial Markets Federal Reserve Bank of St. Louis Review. *Second Quarter*, *103*(2), 153–174. doi:10.20955/r.103.153-74

Sillaber, C., & Waltl, B. (2017). Life cycle of smart contracts in blockchain ecosystems. *Datenschutz Datensich*, *41*(8), 497–500. doi:10.1007/s11623-017-0819-7

Singh, M., & Kim, S. (2019). Blockchain technology for decentralized autonomous organizations. In *Advances in Computers* (Vol. 115, pp. 115–140). Elsevier. doi:10.1016/bs.adcom.2019.06.001

Stark, J. (2017). Making Sense of Blockchain Smart Contracts, 2016. *Acesso em, 13*. https://www.coindesk.com/markets/2016/06/04/making-sense-of-blockchain-smart-contracts/

Szabo, N. (1997). *The idea of smart contracts, in: Nick Szabo's Papers and Concise Tutorials*. https://www.fon.hum.uva.nl/rob/Courses/ InformationInSpeech/CDROM/Literature/LOTwinterschool2006/szabo.best. vwh.net/smart_contracts_2.html

Taeihagh, A. (2017). Crowdsourcing, sharing economies and development. *Journal of Developing Societies*, *33*(2), 191–222. doi:10.1177/0169796X17710072

Tern, S. (2021). Survey of smart contract technology and application based on blockchain. *Ozean Journal of Applied Sciences*, *11*(10), 1135–1148. doi:10.4236/ojapps.2021.1110085

Thabet, N. A., & Abdelbaki, N. (2021, October). Efficient querying blockchain applications. In *2021 3rd Novel Intelligent and Leading Emerging Sciences Conference (NILES)* (pp. 365-369). IEEE. https://doi.org/10.1109/NILES53778.2021.9600533

Uriarte, R. B., Tiezzi, F., & De Nicola, R. (2016). Dynamic slas for clouds. In *Service-Oriented and Cloud Computing: 5th IFIP WG 2.14 European Conference, ESOCC 2016, Vienna, Austria, September 5-7, 2016, Proceedings 5* (pp. 34-49). Springer International Publishing. 10.1007/978-3-319-44482-6_3

Varfolomeev, A. A., Alfarhani, L. H., & Oleiwi, Z. C. (2021). Secure-reliable smart contract applications based blockchain technology in smart cities environment. *Procedia Computer Science*, *186*, 669–676. doi:10.1016/j.procs.2021.04.188

Wang, H., Guo, C., & Cheng, S. (2019). LoC—A new financial loan management system based on smart contracts. *Future Generation Computer Systems*, *100*, 648–655. doi:10.1016/j.future.2019.05.040

Wikipedia. (n.d.). https://en.wikipedia.org/wiki/Smart_contract

Zheng, Z., Xie, S., Dai, H. N., Chen, W., Chen, X., Weng, J., & Imran, M. (2020). An overview on smart contracts: Challenges, advances, and platforms. *Future Generation Computer Systems*, *105*, 475–491. doi:10.1016/j.future.2019.12.019

Chapter 12
Transforming the Travel Landscape:
Smart Contracts in Tourism Management

Jeganathan Gomathi Sankar
https://orcid.org/0000-0002-5077-5109
BSSS Institute of Advanced Studies, India

Arokiaraj David
https://orcid.org/0000-0002-9591-2410
Al Tareeqah Management Studies, UAE

ABSTRACT

This chapter explores smart contract integration in tourism, examining its current state, applications, challenges, and future trajectories. Leveraging blockchain, smart contracts enhance transaction security and transparency, addressing fraud concerns. They significantly cut costs and boost efficiency in booking and payment, benefiting travelers and service providers with increased control and trust. Challenges like technical hurdles, legal considerations, and seamless system integration are viewed as opportunities for meticulous resolution. Emphasis is placed on addressing scalability, coding, legal frameworks, and user education. The chapter envisions a future where smart contracts merge with AI/ML, reshaping personalized travel services. It explores DAOs in tourism, suggesting decentralized decision-making, transparent governance, and community-driven initiatives. The chapter acknowledges limitations and advocates for ongoing monitoring due to the dynamic nature of smart contracts.

DOI: 10.4018/979-8-3693-1532-3.ch012

INTRODUCTION

A smart contract represents a revolutionary paradigm shift in contract execution, leveraging the transformative capabilities of blockchain technology. Fundamentally, a smart contract is just a computer programme that runs on a blockchain network and is self-executing. In contrast to traditional contracts, which depend on middlemen such as banks, notaries, or legal organisations to enforce and verify terms, smart contracts run independently and carry out predetermined conditions automatically. Blockchain technology is the main component that makes smart contracts possible. These contracts are built on top of blockchain, which is sometimes referred to as a distributed and decentralised ledger. The capacity of blockchain to provide a safe and unchangeable record of transactions is its distinctive characteristic.

The travel sector is only one of the many industries that smart contracts have the potential to transform. Smart contracts have the potential to automate a multitude of tasks in the travel industry, including reservation booking and payment, itinerary and accommodation management, asset rental and sharing, insurance and risk management for travel services, customer relationship management, and loyalty programmes. According to a new analysis by Allied Market Research, the travel and hospitality sector will be a major driver of the worldwide smart contracts market, which is expected to reach USD 27.5 billion by 2028. Eighty percent of travel industry executives believe blockchain technology will have a major influence over the next five years, according to another IBM poll, and smart contracts might save travel industry up to $2 billion annually through automation and fraud reduction.

Because of their potential to improve transaction efficiency, transparency, and security, smart contracts self-executing digital contracts with conditions encoded directly into code—have drawn a lot of interest. These contracts provide a viable way to simplify a number of procedures in the tourist management field, from data administration and loyalty programmes to reservations and payments (Demirel et al., 2022). In the current environment, smart contracts are being used more and more in many areas of tourist management. Smart contracts are proving their adaptability in solving industry-specific problems, from handling complicated travel schedules to automating booking procedures and securing payments (Joo et al., 2021). Smart contracts stand out as a shining example of innovation as the travel industry struggles with the demand for more smooth, safe, and effective operations. Notwithstanding the significant potential advantages of smart contracts for tourist management, there are still difficulties. Obstacles that require attention include uncertainty around regulations, integration challenges, and the necessity of extensive industry engagement. Unlocking the full potential of smart contracts and laying the groundwork for their successful deployment need an understanding of these issues (Ozdemir et al., 2020). The use of smart contracts in tourist management will affect many different stakeholders in significant ways. Increased security, expedited procedures, and better experiences all around will benefit travellers. In contrast, service providers are faced with the problem of adjusting to this new technology paradigm while weighing the possible benefits against the real-world difficulties (Karagoz Zeren & Demirel, 2020). Through an examination of their uses, difficulties, and consequences for industry stakeholders, this study aims to present a thorough overview of the situation of smart contracts in tourist management today.

BENEFITS OF SMART CONTRACTS IN TOURISM MANAGEMENT

By streamlining and automating procedures, the use of smart contracts in tourist management has several advantages and is revolutionising the sector. These agreements reduce administrative burden and expedite booking processes, guaranteeing quick and safe money transactions. Smart contracts improve security by lowering the possibility of fraud and unauthorised access by utilising blockchain's cryptographic characteristics (Luo & Zhou, 2021). Because of their decentralised structure, middlemen, service providers, and travellers may all trust one another. Automated loyalty programmes encourage client interaction, while real-time updates and notifications enhance the customer experience. Smart contracts lower costs by doing away with middlemen, increasing the efficiency of transactions. Their compliance with data privacy laws guarantees the safe treatment of private data (Antoniadis et al., 2020). Additionally, smart contracts encourage the development of novel business models in the travel industry, providing fresh approaches to the provision and use of travel services. Robust against disturbances, these agreements augment general confidence in dealings, offering a safe, clear, and effective structure for the travel sector (Demirel et al., 2022).

Enhanced Security and Transparency in Travel Transactions

The travel sector has witnessed a significant breakthrough in terms of improved security and transparency with the introduction of smart contracts into transactions. Utilising cryptographic techniques, smart contracts that run on blockchain technology offer an unmatched degree of security. Sensitive data is protected against fraud and unauthorised access by this cryptographic safeguard, which also guarantees the integrity of the data (Aghaei et al., 2021). By dispersing transaction data over a network of nodes, the decentralised aspect of blockchain technology also considerably improves security. There is a strong barrier against security breaches because of its decentralised and distributed ledger structure, which makes it extremely difficult for bad actors to alter or corrupt transaction data (Rashideh, 2020). One important feature of blockchain technology is its immutability, which means that once a transaction is recorded, it cannot be changed or removed. Through the creation of an unquestionable and impenetrable historical record, this feature strengthens the integrity of travel transactions. By doing this, confidence is built amongst all stakeholders and the interests of both travellers and service providers are protected. Furthermore, blockchain technology and smart contracts' inherent transparency are revolutionising the tourism sector. An auditable and traceable history of actions is created by recording every transaction and making it public to all authorised network members (Gupta et al., 2023). Because all parties involved can independently confirm the specifics of every transaction, this openness reduces the possibility of miscommunication, disagreements, or fraudulent activity. Additionally, it establishes a greater degree of accountability, promoting responsible and ethical practices among travel service providers (Willie, 2019). Basically, smart contract implementation guarantees a transparent and safe travel transaction framework. By doing this, the travel industry's ecosystem is made more robust and reliable while also safeguarding the interests of all players. According to Ozdemir et al. (2020), smart contracts have the potential to revolutionise the travel management industry by establishing a more streamlined, dependable, and transparent system due to their better security and transparency features.

Reduced Costs and Improved Efficiency

The application of smart contracts to the field of travel management has a revolutionary effect that is characterised by lower expenses and increased productivity. The removal of middlemen is one of the main ways to reduce costs. Several middlemen are frequently involved in traditional travel transactions, which raises prices and lengthens processing times (Kontogianni & Alepis, 2020). With smart contracts running independently on blockchain technology, these middlemen are eliminated, simplifying the entire process and cutting costs substantially. According to Mandelaliyev et al. (2020), smart contracts' automation is also essential for increasing efficiency. Because smart contracts are self-executing, they automate tasks that would otherwise require human involvement, such transaction verification, payment processing, and booking management. This not only expedites the pace of transactions but also minimizes the likelihood of errors, contributing to operational accuracy and efficiency (Aghaei et al., 2021).

In addition to their superior performance in streamlining administrative chores, smart contracts significantly reduce paperwork, time, and resource consumption associated with traditional administrative operations. According to Zheng et al. (2020), the decentralised and tamper-proof characteristics of blockchain technology guarantee the smooth execution of administrative procedures, hence optimising operations. Smart contracts provide quick and easy payment procedures in the context of financial transactions. Payment process automation guarantees quick and safe transactions, cutting down on expenses and delays. Financial transactions can be tracked more easily thanks to blockchain's transparent and auditable nature, which promotes financial responsibility and narrows the possibility of disputes. Beyond financial transactions, there are other cost savings and efficiency gains (Tolmach et al., 2021). For instance, loyalty programs can be automated through smart contracts, enhancing customer engagement without the need for additional administrative overhead. Real-time updates and notifications provided by smart contracts also contribute to a more responsive and customer-friendly environment.

Automated and Streamlined Processes

By automating and simplifying numerous procedures, the use of smart contracts in travel management is revolutionising the sector. These contracts, which use blockchain technology, automate difficult jobs like making hotel reservations, handling payments, and handling administrative duties. This removes the need for middlemen and drastically lowers operating costs (Demirel et al., 2022). By instantly informing travellers of changes to itineraries or lodgings, real-time updates and alerts improve the entire customer experience. The automation of loyalty programmes encourages consumer participation and lessens administrative workloads. Blockchain's decentralised and secure architecture guarantees effective data management while shielding sensitive data from security breaches (Karagoz Zeren & Demirel, 2020). Furthermore, smart contracts' self-executing capability guarantees that contractual conditions are carried out automatically, eliminating the need for human supervision. The transparent and unchangeable nature of blockchain streamlines dispute resolution and speeds up the process (Luo & Zhou, 2021). In addition to bringing about cost savings, this revolutionary technology guarantees quicker, more accurate, and secure procedures, which eventually improves the effectiveness of travel management globally (Demirel et al., 2022).

Facilitation of New and Innovative Travel Products and Services

The incorporation of smart contracts into travel management not only improves current procedures but also functions as a spur for the development of fresh, cutting-edge travel-related goods and services. Smart contracts create new opportunities for innovative travel-related business models and offers by automating and securing transactions on a blockchain network (Luo & Zhou, 2021). For example, the automation of loyalty programmes makes it possible to design creative incentive schemes and consumer incentives. The creation of distinctive and transparent trip packages is made possible by decentralised and tamper-proof records, which lessens the need for faith in middlemen. Additionally, smart contracts facilitate the development of novel payment structures, including tokenized assets for fractional ownership of lodging or microtransactions for customised travel experiences (Demirel & Zeren, 2021). This transformative technology fosters an environment where creative and customer-centric travel products and services can flourish, driving the industry towards new horizons of innovation and customer satisfaction.

APPLICATIONS OF SMART CONTRACTS IN TOURISM MANAGEMENT

Booking and Payment for Travel Reservations

The application of smart contracts in booking and payment for travel reservations signifies a transformative paradigm in the realm of tourism management, heralding a new era of efficiency, security, and transparency (Sankar et al., 2022). This revolutionary shift leverages the power of blockchain technology to automate and optimize the entire reservation process, offering travelers a seamless and efficient experience from accommodation selection to finalizing travel arrangements (Zeren, 2023). In the domain of booking, smart contracts act as the backbone of a streamlined reservation process. Travelers, upon selecting their accommodations or finalizing travel details, set in motion a series of predefined conditions embedded within the smart contract. These conditions act as triggers, automatically executing the booking process with precision. The result is a swift and error-free confirmation of reservations, the issuance of relevant documentation, and the seamless updating of pertinent databases. The fundamental innovation lies in the autonomous nature of these processes. The smart contract, acting as a self-executing agreement, eliminates the need for manual intervention at various stages of the booking process (Unal et al., 2020). This not only expedites the entire procedure but also significantly reduces the administrative burden on both travelers and service providers. By automating the workflow, smart contracts ensure that reservations are confirmed promptly, documentation is generated accurately, and databases are updated in real-time (Karagoz Zeren & Demirel, 2020).

Concurrently, smart contracts bring about a revolution in the payment processes associated with travel reservations. These contracts are meticulously designed to autonomously execute payment transactions based on specific conditions being met. For example, upon the confirmation of a traveler's check-in or the validation of a reservation, the smart contract seamlessly initiates the payment process. This innovative approach eliminates the need for manual oversight, expediting financial transactions and fostering a more efficient payment cycle (Demirel & Zeren, 2021). One of the primary advantages of smart contracts in payment processing is the layer of security they introduce. By automating payment transactions, smart contracts reduce the reliance on intermediaries, minimizing the potential for errors or disputes. The conditions embedded within the contract ensure that payments are executed only when specific criteria are met, adding an extra layer of validation (Karagoz Zeren & Demirel, 2020). This not only enhances the security of financial transactions but also contributes to the overall trust between stakeholders in the travel ecosystem. The integration of blockchain technology further enhances the transformative impact of smart contracts in tourism management. Blockchain, as a decentralized and tamper-proof ledger, ensures transparency and immutability in every step of the process (Zeren, 2023). From the initiation of a reservation to the execution of payments, each transaction is securely recorded on the blockchain, creating an indisputable and verifiable record of events. The transparency introduced by blockchain technology builds trust among stakeholders. Travelers, service providers, and other participants in the travel ecosystem can access real-time and accurate information securely recorded on the blockchain. This transparency not only fosters trust but also contributes to the efficiency of dispute resolution mechanisms. In case of discrepancies or disagreements, the immutable nature of the blockchain provides an indisputable record, simplifying and expediting the resolution process (Demirel & Zeren, 2021). Furthermore, the application of smart contracts and blockchain technology creates a reliable and accountable environment. Stakeholders can have confidence in the accuracy and security of the transactions, knowing that the technology ensures the integrity of the entire process. This reliability extends to every aspect of the reservation and payment cycle, reinforcing the trust between travelers and service providers.

Management of Travel Itineraries and Accommodations

Smart contracts contribute significantly to the management of travel itineraries and accommodations, revolutionizing the way these aspects are handled in the tourism industry. For travel itineraries, smart contracts act as automated agents, streamlining the entire process and providing a decentralized and secure framework. Once travelers confirm their plans, smart contracts, governed by predefined conditions, initiate a sequence of automated actions. This includes updating schedules in real-time, sending immediate notifications about any changes or modifications, and seamlessly incorporating adjustments made by travelers themselves (Tsung-Chih et al., 2023). The decentralized nature of blockchain technology ensures that this information is securely stored and accessible to all relevant parties involved in the itinerary, reducing the chances of discrepancies and enhancing collaboration (Sankar et al., 2022). In the domain of accommodations, smart contracts bring efficiency to the management of bookings and stay arrangements. These contracts automate crucial tasks like reservation confirmations, check-ins, and check-outs. Upon travelers confirming their reservations, the smart contract activates the necessary processes, facilitating a smooth and streamlined experience for both guests and accommodation providers. The transparency provided by blockchain ensures that all parties involved have access to accurate and up-to-date information, minimizing the risk of errors and enhancing overall customer satisfaction (Wang et al., 2020). The integration of smart contracts and blockchain technology introduces a level of transparency, automation, and security that significantly improves the management of travel itineraries and accommodations. The automated execution of tasks, combined with the tamper-proof recording of transactions, establishes a reliable and accountable system, offering a more efficient and trustworthy framework in the dynamic landscape of tourism management (Buonincontri & Micera, 2016). This not only simplifies processes but also contributes to a more seamless and satisfying experience for travelers and service providers alike.

Rental and Sharing of Travel Assets

Smart contracts represent a revolutionary transformation in the landscape of rental and sharing within the tourism industry, introducing a more efficient, secure, and transparent framework that reshapes the dynamics of asset utilization. In the realm of asset rental, smart contracts serve as automated orchestrators, streamlining the entire process from the initiation of agreements to the return of assets (Sankar et al., 2022). As travelers confirm their rental plans, predefined conditions within the smart contract trigger a sequence of automated actions. This encompasses the issuance of rental agreements, secure handling of payments, and real-time updates on the availability status of the asset. The automation introduced by smart contracts not only streamlines the rental process but also significantly reduces administrative overhead, providing a dynamic and responsive system that benefits both asset owners and renters (Bodkhe et al., 2019). Concurrently, smart contracts play a pivotal role in facilitating the sharing of travel assets within the broader sharing economy. Whether it involves sharing a car, accommodation, or other resources, smart contracts automate and secure the sharing process. These contracts ensure that predetermined conditions are met before assets are shared, encompassing actions such as automatically unlocking a rented car, granting access to a shared accommodation, or facilitating the exchange of various assets (Paktiti & Economides, 2023). The decentralized and transparent nature of blockchain technology, the underlying foundation of smart contracts, ensures that every transaction and agreement is securely recorded, fostering a climate of trust among participants and significantly reducing the risk of disputes. The integration of smart contracts into the rental and sharing of travel assets brings forth a multitude of advantages that extend beyond operational efficiency (Antoniadis et al., 2020). The automated execution of tasks, coupled with the tamper-proof recording of transactions on the blockchain, introduces an additional layer of security and accountability. This transformative technology creates a reliable and transparent system for both asset owners and users, instilling confidence and trust in the sharing economy within the tourism sector.

Asset rental through smart contracts initiates with travelers confirming their plans, triggering the smart contract to automatically generate and execute rental agreements. This not only expedites the process but also ensures that all parties involved have access to a secure and standardized agreement, minimizing the potential for miscommunication or disputes (Antoniadis et al., 2020). The secure handling of payments within the smart contract further enhances the reliability of the rental process. Travelers can confidently make payments knowing that the smart contract will execute the transaction only when predefined conditions, such as the initiation of the rental period, are met. This reduces the risk of payment disputes and promotes a secure financial transaction environment (Paktiti & Economides, 2023). Real-time updates on the availability status of the rented asset represent a critical feature facilitated by smart contracts. The decentralized nature of blockchain ensures that updates are securely recorded and accessible to both asset owners and renters, offering transparency and eliminating uncertainties related to asset availability. This feature not only enhances the user experience by providing accurate and immediate information but also contributes to the effective management of assets within the rental ecosystem (Demirel, 2023). In the sharing economy, smart contracts bring a transformative layer of automation and security to the sharing of travel assets. Whether it's a car, accommodation, or other resources, the automation introduced by smart contracts ensures that the sharing process adheres to predefined conditions. For example, in car sharing, smart contracts can automatically unlock the vehicle for the agreed-upon duration once the rental period begins, providing a seamless and secure experience for the user. This level of automation extends to shared accommodations, where smart contracts can grant access to the rented space upon confirmation of the reservation, eliminating the need for manual intervention. The decentralized and transparent nature of blockchain technology ensures that every shared asset and the associated agreement is securely recorded and easily traceable (Karagoz Zeren & Demirel, 2020). This transparency contributes to the establishment of trust among participants in the sharing economy, as all parties have access to a verifiable record of transactions. In the event of disputes or discrepancies, the immutable nature of the blockchain provides an indisputable history of agreements and transactions, simplifying dispute resolution processes and reducing the need for extensive mediation. The integration of smart contracts into the rental and sharing of travel assets not only streamlines operational processes but also introduces a layer of security and accountability. The tamper-proof recording of transactions on the blockchain enhances the integrity of the entire system, ensuring that data related to agreements, payments, and asset availability remains secure and unaltered. This security feature is particularly crucial in fostering trust within the sharing economy, where participants rely on transparent and secure transactions (Demirel & Zeren, 2021). Furthermore, smart contracts contribute to operational efficiency by reducing administrative overhead associated with traditional rental and sharing models (Paktiti & Economides, 2023). The automation of tasks, such as the issuance of agreements and handling of payments, eliminates the need for manual intervention, allowing asset owners and users to focus on the core aspects of their travel experience. This operational efficiency extends to the management of assets, with real-time updates on availability ensuring optimal utilization and reducing the likelihood of overbooking or scheduling conflicts.

Insurance and Risk Management for Travel Services

Insurance and risk management in the realm of travel services represent critical components in ensuring the safety, security, and well-being of both travelers and service providers. The integration of smart contracts, powered by blockchain technology, into this domain introduces a transformative approach that enhances the efficiency, transparency, and effectiveness of insurance and risk management processes within the dynamic landscape of the travel industry (Luo & Zhou, 2021). Traditional insurance processes in travel services often involve complex documentation, manual verification, and a prolonged claims settlement period. However, smart contracts bring a paradigm shift by automating and streamlining these processes, creating a more responsive and secure framework (Demirel & Zeren, 2021). When travelers engage in travel services, smart contracts automatically initiate insurance coverage based on predefined conditions. For instance, upon confirmation of a flight reservation or hotel booking, the smart contract can trigger the issuance of insurance coverage for the specified travel period. This automated approach not only expedites the insurance initiation process but also ensures that travelers are adequately covered without the need for extensive paperwork (Antoniadis et al., 2020). Moreover, the decentralized and tamper-proof nature of blockchain technology ensures the integrity of insurance agreements. Smart contracts securely record all insurance-related transactions on the blockchain, providing an auditable and transparent history of coverage. This not only reduces the risk of fraudulent claims but also enhances the trust between insurers and insured parties. The immutable nature of blockchain ensures that once an insurance agreement is established, it remains unchanged, creating a reliable and verifiable record that can be accessed by all relevant parties (Demirel & Zeren, 2021).

Smart contracts also revolutionize the claims settlement process in travel insurance. Traditionally, the claims process involves a series of manual verifications, document submissions, and a protracted period before settlements are reached (Antoniadis et al., 2020). In contrast, smart contracts automate the claims settlement process by autonomously evaluating predefined conditions. For example, in the case of a canceled flight, the smart contract can automatically trigger the claims settlement process, ensuring that eligible travelers receive compensation without unnecessary delays (Subramanian & Liu, 2021). This not only expedites the settlement period but also minimizes the administrative burden on both insurers and claimants. The integration of smart contracts in insurance and risk management for travel services extends beyond traditional coverage models. Parametric insurance, a form of insurance that pays out predetermined amounts based on measurable parameters, becomes more feasible with smart contracts. For instance, smart contracts can be programmed to trigger insurance payouts automatically based on predefined conditions such as flight delays exceeding a certain duration or specific weather-related incidents at a travel destination. This proactive and automated approach to risk management enhances the overall resilience of the travel industry by providing more responsive and adaptive insurance coverage. Additionally, smart contracts enable dynamic and real-time adjustments to insurance coverage based on evolving travel circumstances (Sedkaoui & Chicha, 2021). For example, if a traveler extends their stay or modifies their itinerary, smart contracts can automatically adjust insurance coverage to align with the updated travel plans. This level of flexibility ensures that travelers are adequately covered throughout their journey, adapting to the dynamic nature of travel services (Foggan & Cwiertny, 2018). The transparency introduced by blockchain technology also extends to the risk management aspect of travel services. Service providers, such as airlines and accommodations, can benefit from smart contracts by automating the assessment of potential risks and liabilities. Smart contracts can be programmed to evaluate various risk factors, such as weather conditions, geopolitical events, or public health alerts, and automatically trigger risk mitigation measures. This proactive risk management approach enhances the overall safety and security of travel services, minimizing potential disruptions and ensuring a more resilient industry (Dutta et al., 2023). Furthermore, the decentralized and tamper-proof nature of blockchain ensures that risk-related data is securely recorded and accessible to relevant stakeholders. This transparency fosters collaboration between different entities within the travel ecosystem, including insurers, service providers, and travelers. The shared and immutable ledger created by blockchain technology enhances the accuracy and reliability of risk-related information, enabling more informed decision-making processes (Benduch, 2019). The emergence of blockchain-based smart contracts in insurance and risk management for travel services aligns with the broader industry trends of digitization, automation, and enhanced customer experience. The efficiency gains, transparency, and adaptability introduced by smart contracts contribute to a more robust and customer-centric framework within the travel insurance and risk management landscape (Dutta et al., 2023).

Customer Relationship Management and Loyalty Programs

In the realm of tourism management, the dynamic interplay between customer relationship management (CRM) and loyalty programs takes on a transformative role, shaping the way businesses engage with travelers, foster loyalty, and enhance overall customer satisfaction (Treiblmaier & Petrozhitskaya, 2023). As the travel industry becomes increasingly competitive, the integration of CRM strategies and loyalty programs proves essential in creating personalized, memorable experiences that not only attract customers but also cultivate enduring relationships, paving the way for sustained brand loyalty.

Unified Customer Profiles for Personalization

The integration of Customer Relationship Management (CRM) and loyalty programs in the tourism industry represents a groundbreaking shift, fostering a holistic understanding of travelers through unified customer profiles. This integration blends data from CRM interactions and loyalty program participation, creating a comprehensive tapestry of individual preferences, past interactions, and engagement with loyalty incentives (Treiblmaier & Petrozhitskaya, 2023). These unified profiles offer profound insights into traveler preferences, providing businesses with a nuanced view of each customer's journey. Analyzing past interactions, purchase history, and loyalty program engagement enables businesses to tailor highly personalized experiences (Shen et al., 2016). The integration extends to strategic decision-making, empowering businesses to align offerings with emerging trends. The unified profiles streamline operations, enhancing efficiency in customer service and internal processes (Logesh et al., 2019). Ultimately, this integration propels the tourism industry into an era of customer-centricity, where personalized, insightful, and seamlessly orchestrated travel experiences are at the forefront of engagement strategies.

Targeted Marketing Strategies

The synergistic integration of Customer Relationship Management (CRM) data and insights derived from loyalty programs empowers businesses to craft precisely targeted marketing campaigns in the tourism industry. By amalgamating comprehensive customer profiles that encapsulate both CRM interactions and loyalty program participation, businesses gain a nuanced understanding of individual traveler preferences and behaviors. This wealth of information enables the design of highly personalized marketing strategies tailored to the specific needs and interests of each traveler. These targeted campaigns not only serve to retain existing travelers by highlighting tailored benefits but also effectively attract new customers by showcasing the value proposition of loyalty program participation (Treiblmaier & Petrozhitskaya, 2023). The personalized nature of these marketing efforts resonates with travelers, fostering a sense of individualized attention and enhancing engagement (Logesh et al., 2019). As a result, businesses witness heightened conversion rates, as travelers are more likely to respond positively to marketing messages that align closely with their preferences and showcase the tangible advantages of participating in loyalty programs, ultimately contributing to a more effective and efficient marketing ecosystem within the dynamic landscape of the tourism industry (Madhani, 2022).

Seamless Travel Experiences

The integration of Customer Relationship Management (CRM) and loyalty programs in the tourism industry orchestrates a seamless and gratifying travel experience for customers, ensuring a cohesive journey from the initial interaction captured in the CRM system to the rewards earned through the loyalty program. This harmonious integration creates a unified and comprehensive customer profile that serves as a dynamic roadmap for every traveler's engagement with the travel brand. Starting with the first point of contact, whether it be an inquiry, booking, or interaction with promotional material, the CRM system captures and synthesizes this information, providing businesses with a holistic view of the traveler's preferences and past interactions (Sankar et al., 2022). As the traveler progresses through the journey, from planning to booking and post-trip engagement, the integrated system ensures that every touchpoint is seamlessly connected (Thees et al., 2020). Loyalty program rewards, intricately tied to CRM data, become a natural extension of the traveler's experience, reinforcing a sense of recognition and appreciation. This cohesiveness eliminates silos in customer interactions, presenting a unified narrative that resonates with travelers incentives (Treiblmaier & Petrozhitskaya, 2023). The result is a travel experience that feels tailored and continuous, where each phase of the journey seamlessly transitions into the next. This cohesiveness significantly enhances customer satisfaction as travelers perceive a brand that not only understands their individual preferences but also seamlessly integrates those preferences into every aspect of their travel experience (Buhalis & Amaranggana, 2015). Consequently, the strengthened bond between the customer and the travel brand contributes to an enhanced overall brand image, establishing the business as one that is attentive, responsive, and committed to delivering a consistently gratifying and unified travel experience. In a competitive tourism landscape, such seamless integration becomes a powerful differentiator, fostering customer loyalty and advocacy.

Real-Time Engagement and Recognition

The synergy between integrated Customer Relationship Management (CRM) and loyalty programs facilitates real-time engagement with travelers, offering businesses a dynamic and responsive approach to customer interactions in the tourism industry. This integration allows businesses to promptly respond to various customer actions, spanning from bookings and interactions with marketing materials to active participation in the loyalty program (Coita & Ban, 2020). In the context of bookings, the integrated system ensures that businesses can swiftly acknowledge and respond to reservation requests, providing timely confirmations and relevant details. Additionally, when travelers engage with marketing materials, the integrated CRM enables businesses to respond in real-time, tailoring follow-up communications or offers based on the specific interactions. This personalized and immediate response contributes to an enhanced customer experience, demonstrating a keen understanding of individual preferences (Balcerzak et al., 2022). Participation in the loyalty program becomes a dynamic and interactive process through real-time engagement. Businesses can instantly recognize and reward loyalty program activities, whether it's accruing points or redeeming rewards. This instant acknowledgment not only adds a gamified and rewarding element to the loyalty experience but also reinforces the traveler's value to the brand. Real-time recognition within the integrated system goes beyond transactional interactions; it reflects a commitment to acknowledging and appreciating each customer's contributions to the brand journey (Karim et al., 2022). This not only enhances the overall traveler experience but also reinforces a positive brand perception, as customers feel valued and recognized in the moment. In a competitive tourism landscape, where customer expectations for personalized and timely interactions are high (Sankar & David, 2023), the real-time engagement facilitated by integrated CRM and loyalty programs becomes a powerful tool (Treiblmaier & Petrozhitskaya, 2023). It allows businesses to not only meet but exceed customer expectations, fostering loyalty, satisfaction, and a positive brand relationship (Jeganathan & Srinivasulu, 2014).

Continuous Improvement Through Data Insights

The integrated approach, combining Customer Relationship Management (CRM) and loyalty programs, forms a dynamic framework for the continual enhancement of services and loyalty program offerings within the tourism industry. Through the analysis of comprehensive data derived from both CRM interactions and loyalty program engagement, businesses gain invaluable insights that drive continuous improvement initiatives (Kachniewska, 2021). The amalgamation of CRM and loyalty program data empowers businesses to identify emerging trends in customer preferences and behavior. By scrutinizing this combined dataset, businesses can discern patterns that illuminate shifting expectations, allowing for proactive adjustments to services and offerings (Del Vecchio et al., 2018). This analytical approach ensures that the travel brand remains attuned to evolving customer desires, staying one step ahead in a dynamic market. Measuring the effectiveness of loyalty incentives becomes a strategic focus within this integrated framework. Businesses can assess the impact of loyalty program offerings on customer engagement, retention, and overall satisfaction (Baggio et al., 2020). The ability to correlate CRM data with loyalty program outcomes provides a nuanced understanding of the factors influencing customer loyalty, enabling businesses to refine their strategies for optimal results (Kachniewska, 2021). The integrated analysis of CRM and loyalty program data fosters an iterative process of refinement. By leveraging these insights, businesses can implement strategic adjustments to their services and loyalty incentives. This agility is paramount in an industry where customer expectations are subject to rapid change, ensuring that the travel brand remains adaptive and responsive to the evolving landscape (Hamid et al., 2021). In essence, the integrated approach establishes a feedback loop that drives continual improvement. The symbiotic relationship between CRM and loyalty programs creates a data-driven cycle wherein insights gleaned from customer interactions inform the refinement of loyalty incentives and services (Kachniewska, 2021). This iterative process positions the travel brand as not only responsive to current customer expectations but also as a proactive player, anticipating and meeting the evolving needs of travelers in an ever-changing tourism landscape.

CONSIDERATIONS FOR IMPLEMENTING SMART CONTRACTS IN TOURISM MANAGEMENT

Technical Challenges of Smart Contract Development

The implementation of blockchain technology and smart contracts in various industries, including the challenges associated with their technical aspects, presents a multifaceted landscape that organizations must navigate. One significant technical challenge revolves around the scalability of blockchain networks. As more transactions are added to the decentralized ledger, the network can experience bottlenecks, leading to slower transaction processing times and increased costs. Finding scalable solutions that maintain the decentralized nature of blockchain while addressing performance issues is crucial for widespread adoption. Interoperability is another technical challenge in the blockchain space (Zou et al., 2019). With various blockchain platforms and smart contract languages in existence, ensuring seamless communication and collaboration between different systems remains a hurdle. Developing standardized protocols and frameworks for interoperability is essential to foster a more interconnected blockchain ecosystem. Smart contract security is a paramount concern, given the irreversible and self-executing nature of these contracts. Vulnerabilities in the code can lead to exploitable weaknesses, potentially resulting in financial losses or other detrimental consequences (Zou et al., 2019; Vacca et al., 2021). Establishing best practices for secure smart contract development, rigorous auditing processes, and ongoing security research are critical components in mitigating these risks (Zheng et al., 2020). The energy consumption associated with some blockchain consensus mechanisms, such as proof-of-work, poses environmental concerns. Addressing the environmental impact of blockchain networks by exploring and implementing more energy-efficient consensus mechanisms is a technical challenge that aligns with broader sustainability goals (Vacca et al., 2021). Additionally, the lack of standardized regulations and legal frameworks for blockchain and smart contracts presents technical challenges related to compliance. Navigating the regulatory landscape globally, ensuring adherence to legal requirements, and developing technical solutions that facilitate compliance without compromising decentralization pose intricate challenges for organizations operating in this space (Zheng et al., 2020).

Legal and Regulatory Considerations for Smart Contracts

The integration of smart contracts in the travel industry brings forth a myriad of legal and regulatory considerations that must be carefully navigated to ensure compliance, security, and the seamless execution of transactions. One primary concern involves the recognition and enforceability of smart contracts under existing legal frameworks (Savelyev, 2017). As smart contracts operate in a digital, decentralized environment, clarifying their legal status and ensuring that they are recognized as binding agreements is crucial. Jurisdictions around the world vary in their approach to this, necessitating a harmonized and standardized understanding (Gilcrest & Carvalho, 2018). Data protection and privacy regulations also play a pivotal role in the implementation of smart contracts in the travel sector. Given that smart contracts often involve the processing of personal information, adherence to stringent data protection laws, such as the General Data Protection Regulation (GDPR), is imperative (Ferreira, 2021). Ensuring that the design and execution of smart contracts align with privacy regulations is essential to safeguarding the rights of individuals. Smart contracts that involve financial transactions may fall under the purview of financial regulations. Compliance with anti-money laundering (AML) and know your customer (KYC) regulations is paramount to prevent illicit activities within the decentralized ecosystem (Fiorentino & Bartolucci, 2021). Navigating these financial regulations requires a nuanced understanding of how smart contracts interact with traditional financial systems. The cross-border nature of the travel industry introduces an additional layer of complexity. Legal harmonization and international agreements are necessary to facilitate the recognition and enforcement of smart contracts across different jurisdictions (Sanz Bayón, 2019). Achieving a global consensus on the legal treatment of smart contracts can contribute to a more streamlined and efficient international travel ecosystem. Moreover, establishing liability and dispute resolution mechanisms is essential in the context of smart contracts. Determining responsibility in the event of contract breaches or errors in code execution requires legal frameworks that can adapt to the unique characteristics of decentralized and automated contract systems (Gilcrest & Carvalho, 2018). Implementing smart contracts that embed clear dispute resolution mechanisms can mitigate potential legal challenges.

Integration with Existing Tourism Management Systems

Integrating smart contracts into existing tourism management systems presents a set of challenges and opportunities that businesses in the travel industry must carefully address. One of the primary considerations is interoperability, ensuring that smart contracts seamlessly integrate with diverse and often legacy tourism management systems (Hamid et al., 2021). Compatibility with existing technologies, databases, and platforms is crucial to avoid disruptions in operations and to leverage the full potential of smart contract functionalities. The integration process involves connecting the decentralized nature of smart contracts with the centralized aspects of traditional tourism management systems (Demirel et al., 2022). Bridging this gap requires the development of standardized protocols and application programming interfaces (APIs) that facilitate smooth communication and data exchange between smart contracts and existing systems (Yadav et al., 2021). Establishing these integration points is fundamental for the cohesive operation of both decentralized and centralized components. Another key challenge is the adaptation of smart contracts to meet the specific requirements of tourism management processes. Customization and flexibility in smart contract development are essential to tailor these digital agreements to the nuances of booking systems, reservation databases, and other elements within the tourism industry. Aligning smart contracts with existing business logic and operational workflows ensures a more seamless integration (Karagoz Zeren & Demirel, 2020). Security considerations are paramount, especially when integrating decentralized technologies into existing systems. Ensuring the resilience of smart contracts against cyber threats, vulnerabilities, and potential attacks is crucial to maintaining the integrity of tourism management systems. Implementing robust security measures and conducting thorough audits of smart contract code are essential steps in safeguarding the entire integrated ecosystem (Yadav et al., 2021). Moreover, user education and training become essential during the integration process. Tourism management system users, including employees and customers, need to understand the functionalities, benefits, and potential risks associated with smart contracts (Karagoz Zeren & Demirel, 2020). Providing comprehensive training programs and educational resources fosters a smooth transition and enhances the overall adoption of this innovative technology. Despite these challenges, the integration of smart contracts into existing tourism management systems offers numerous advantages (Demirel et al., 2022). Streamlining and automating processes such as booking, payment, and reservation management can lead to increased efficiency, reduced costs, and enhanced customer experiences. Smart contracts have the potential to revolutionize how transactions are conducted within the travel industry, providing a decentralized, secure, and transparent framework for managing various aspects of tourism operations (Karagoz Zeren & Demirel, 2020).

FUTURE DIRECTIONS AND TRENDS IN SMART CONTRACT APPLICATIONS FOR TOURISM

Integration of Smart Contracts With Artificial Intelligence and Machine Learning

The integration of smart contracts with artificial intelligence (AI) and machine learning (ML) represents a synergistic convergence that holds immense potential for the evolution of decentralized systems. This integration introduces a new paradigm in which smart contracts can leverage the capabilities of AI and ML to enhance automation, decision-making, and adaptability within various industries, including finance, supply chain, and, notably, the travel sector (Samara et al., 2020). One of the key benefits of integrating smart contracts with AI and ML is the ability to automate complex decision-making processes (Filieri et al., 2021). Smart contracts, which are self-executing agreements, can be enriched with AI algorithms that analyze vast datasets and make intelligent decisions based on predetermined criteria. In the context of travel, this integration can streamline tasks such as dynamic pricing, personalized recommendations, and itinerary optimization (Samara et al., 2020). The predictive and adaptive nature of machine learning can be applied to enhance the functionality of smart contracts in the travel industry. By analyzing historical data, user preferences, and market trends, machine learning algorithms embedded in smart contracts can anticipate customer behavior and dynamically adjust contract terms. For example, in the booking process, smart contracts can utilize machine learning to predict peak travel times, adjust pricing accordingly, and optimize resource allocation for maximum efficiency (Solakis et al., 2022). Furthermore, AI and ML can contribute to the improvement of smart contract security. These technologies can be employed to detect anomalies and potential vulnerabilities within the decentralized ecosystem, offering proactive measures to enhance the resilience of smart contracts against cyber threats. Continuous learning from patterns of behavior and emerging risks ensures adaptive security measures. The integration of smart contracts with AI and ML also opens avenues for enhanced customer experiences in the travel industry (Filieri et al., 2021). Personalization becomes more sophisticated as smart contracts, fueled by AI-driven insights, tailor services and recommendations to individual preferences (Samara et al., 2020). This includes personalized travel itineraries, accommodation suggestions, and even real-time adjustments to travel plans based on changing circumstances. Despite these promising opportunities, challenges exist in ensuring the seamless integration of smart contracts with AI and ML. Standardizing communication protocols, creating interoperable frameworks, and addressing issues related to data privacy and ethical considerations are crucial components of this integration (Filieri et al., 2021). Collaboration between blockchain developers, AI specialists, and industry stakeholders is essential for navigating these challenges and unlocking the full potential of this transformative synergy.

Emerging Applications of Smart Contracts in Decentralized Autonomous Organizations (DAOs)

Smart contracts have ushered in transformative applications within Decentralized Autonomous Organizations (DAOs), fundamentally reshaping organizational governance and functionality. DAOs leverage smart contracts for automated governance, enabling transparent and tamper-proof decision-making through token holder voting (Dwivedi et al., 2021). These contracts play a pivotal role in decentralized funding and resource allocation, automating fundraising campaigns and transparently managing contributions. The tokenization of membership within DAOs, facilitated by smart contracts, allows for seamless ownership representation and transfer (Pranata & Tehrani, 2022). Smart contracts are integral to the development of decentralized applications (DApps) within DAO ecosystems, including decentralized finance (DeFi) protocols and applications that operate autonomously (Bellavitis et al., 2023). Automated revenue distribution among DAO members is achieved through smart contracts, ensuring fair and transparent revenue-sharing mechanisms. DAOs also leverage smart contracts for liquidity pool management in DeFi, collaborative content creation platforms, and applications in supply chain and logistics for enhanced transparency and efficiency (Pranata & Tehrani, 2022). These decentralized and autonomous entities exemplify a paradigm shift in organizational structures, harnessing the transparency, security, and automation capabilities provided by smart contracts on blockchain networks.

CONCLUSION

The integration of smart contracts into tourism management signifies a revolutionary shift in the modus operandi of the travel industry, ushering in a new era of transparency, efficiency, and stakeholder empowerment. This comprehensive research has navigated the intricate landscape of smart contracts, traversing their current state, applications, challenges, and future trajectories within the realm of travel. In synthesizing the multifaceted findings, it is evident that smart contracts offer a spectrum of advantages. Their ability to enhance security and transparency in travel transactions by leveraging blockchain's decentralized architecture addresses longstanding concerns of fraud and opacity. Simultaneously, the adoption of smart contracts contributes to substantial cost reductions and efficiency gains, streamlining processes, particularly in booking and payment procedures. Stakeholders, both travelers and service providers, stand to benefit, with increased control and trust for the former and operational efficiencies for the latter. However, this transformative journey is not devoid of challenges. Technical hurdles, encompassing scalability issues and intricate coding requirements, present formidable obstacles demanding meticulous resolution. Legal and regulatory considerations emerge as pivotal factors, highlighting the imperative for a nuanced understanding of contract enforceability, data protection, and compliance. Integrating smart contracts seamlessly into existing tourism management systems poses a complex task, necessitating efforts towards interoperability and user education. Looking forward, the fusion of smart contracts with artificial intelligence (AI) and machine learning (ML) emerges as a beacon of promise, potentially reshaping how travel services are personalized, priced, and delivered. Additionally, the exploration of decentralized autonomous organizations (DAOs) as a frontier for smart contract applications in tourism unveils the prospect of decentralized decision-making, transparent governance, and community-driven initiatives. While this research offers invaluable insights and strategic guidance for industry stakeholders, acknowledging its limitations is crucial. The rapidly evolving nature of blockchain and smart contract technologies implies the necessity for continued monitoring and adaptation. The generalized focus on applications may overlook specific nuances within different travel sectors, beckoning future research to delve deeper into sector-specific impacts. Furthermore, longitudinal studies tracking the evolution of smart contract adoption in the travel industry could provide a more nuanced understanding of the technology's dynamic landscape. In essence, the integration of smart contracts into tourism management emerges not merely as a technological advancement but as a catalyst for profound industry-wide transformation. As the travel industry navigates the complexities of the digital age, smart contracts stand as a linchpin technology, offering a decentralized, transparent, and efficient framework. The challenges identified, far from deterring progress, serve as beacons guiding stakeholders towards informed implementation. The future, shaped by the amalgamation of smart contracts with cutting-edge technologies and innovative organizational structures, holds the promise of a travel landscape that is not only technologically sophisticated but also more resilient, transparent, and responsive to the evolving needs of all stakeholders involved.

REFERENCES

Aghaei, H., Naderibeni, N., & Karimi, A. (2021). Designing a tourism business model on block chain platform. *Tourism Management Perspectives*, *39*, 100845. doi:10.1016/j.tmp.2021.100845

Antoniadis, I., Spinthiropoulos, K., & Kontsas, S. (2020). Blockchain applications in tourism and tourism marketing: A short review. Strategic Innovative Marketing and Tourism: 8th ICSIMAT. *Northern Aegean, Greece*, *2019*, 375–384.

Baggio, R., Micera, R., & Del Chiappa, G. (2020). Smart tourism destinations: A critical reflection. *Journal of Hospitality and Tourism Technology*, *11*(3), 407–423. doi:10.1108/JHTT-01-2019-0011

Balcerzak, A. P., Nica, E., Rogalska, E., Poliak, M., Klieštik, T., & Sabie, O. M. (2022). Blockchain technology and smart contracts in decentralized governance systems. *Administrative Sciences*, *12*(3), 96. doi:10.3390/admsci12030096

Bellavitis, C., Fisch, C., & Momtaz, P. P. (2023). The rise of decentralized autonomous organizations (DAOs): A first empirical glimpse. *Venture Capital*, *25*(2), 187–203. doi:10.1080/13691066.2022.2116797

Benduch, D. (2019, September). Risks And Opportunities for Tourism Using Smart Contracts. In *26th Geographic Information Systems Conference and Exhibition "GIS ODYSSEY 2019"* (p. 12). Academic Press.

Bodkhe, U., Bhattacharya, P., Tanwar, S., Tyagi, S., Kumar, N., & Obaidat, M. S. (2019, August). BloHosT: Blockchain enabled smart tourism and hospitality management. In *2019 international conference on computer, information and telecommunication systems* (CITS) (pp. 1-5). IEEE.

Buhalis, D., & Amaranggana, A. (2015). Smart tourism destinations enhancing tourism experience through personalisation of services. In *Information and Communication Technologies in Tourism 2015: Proceedings of the International Conference in Lugano, Switzerland, February 3-6, 2015* (pp. 377-389). Springer International Publishing. 10.1007/978-3-319-14343-9_28

Buonincontri, P., & Micera, R. (2016). The experience co-creation in smart tourism destinations: A multiple case analysis of European destinations. *Information Technology & Tourism*, *16*(3), 285–315. doi:10.1007/s40558-016-0060-5

Coita, D. C., & Ban, O. (2020). Revolutionizing marketing in tourism industry through blockchain technology. In Strategic Innovative Marketing and Tourism: 8th ICSIMAT, Northern Aegean, Greece, 2019 (pp. 789-797). Springer International Publishing. doi:10.1007/978-3-030-36126-6_87

Del Vecchio, P., Mele, G., Ndou, V., & Secundo, G. (2018). Creating value from social big data: Implications for smart tourism destinations. *Information Processing & Management*, *54*(5), 847–860. doi:10.1016/j.ipm.2017.10.006

Demirel, E. (2023). Application of Blockchain-Based Smart Contract in Sustainable Tourism Finance. In *Blockchain for Tourism and Hospitality Industries* (pp. 122–138). Routledge. doi:10.4324/9781003351917-9

Demirel, E., Karagöz Zeren, S., & Hakan, K. (2022). Smart contracts in tourism industry: A model with blockchain integration for post pandemic economy. *Current Issues in Tourism*, *25*(12), 1895–1909. doi:10.1080/13683500.2021.1960280

Demirel, E., & Zeren, S. K. (2021). Developing smart contracts for financial payments as innovation. In Research Anthology on Blockchain Technology in Business, Healthcare, Education, and Government (pp. 1870-1889). IGI Global. doi:10.4018/978-1-7998-5351-0.ch102

Dutta, H., Nagesh, S., Talluri, J., & Bhaumik, P. (2023). A Solution to Blockchain Smart Contract Based Parametric Transport and Logistics Insurance. *IEEE Transactions on Services Computing*, *16*(5), 3155–3167. doi:10.1109/TSC.2023.3281516

Dwivedi, V., Norta, A., Wulf, A., Leiding, B., Saxena, S., & Udokwu, C. (2021). A formal specification smart-contract language for legally binding decentralized autonomous organizations. *IEEE Access : Practical Innovations, Open Solutions*, *9*, 76069–76082. doi:10.1109/ACCESS.2021.3081926

Ferreira, A. (2021). Regulating smart contracts: Legal revolution or simply evolution? *Telecommunications Policy*, *45*(2), 102081. doi:10.1016/j.telpol.2020.102081

Filieri, R., D'Amico, E., Destefanis, A., Paolucci, E., & Raguseo, E. (2021). Artificial intelligence (AI) for tourism: An European-based study on successful AI tourism start-ups. *International Journal of Contemporary Hospitality Management*, *33*(11), 4099–4125. doi:10.1108/IJCHM-02-2021-0220

Fiorentino, S., & Bartolucci, S. (2021). Blockchain-based smart contracts as new governance tools for the sharing economy. *Cities (London, England)*, *117*, 103325. doi:10.1016/j.cities.2021.103325

Foggan, L. A., & Cwiertny, C. E. (2018). *Blockchain, smart contracts and parametric insurance: Made for each other*. Academic Press.

Ganeshkumar, C., Sankar, J. G., & David, A. (2023). Impact of Artificial Intelligence on Agriculture Value Chain Performance: Agritech Perspective. In Blockchain, IoT, and AI Technologies for Supply Chain Management (pp. 71-98). CRC Press.

Gilcrest, J., & Carvalho, A. (2018, December). Smart contracts: Legal considerations. In *2018 IEEE International Conference on Big Data (Big Data)* (pp. 3277-3281). IEEE.

Gupta, S., Modgil, S., Lee, C. K., & Sivarajah, U. (2023). The future is yesterday: Use of AI-driven facial recognition to enhance value in the travel and tourism industry. *Information Systems Frontiers*, *25*(3), 1179–1195. doi:10.1007/s10796-022-10271-8

Hamid, R. A., Albahri, A. S., Alwan, J. K., Al-Qaysi, Z. T., Albahri, O. S., Zaidan, A. A., Alnoor, A., Alamoodi, A. H., & Zaidan, B. B. (2021). How smart is e-tourism? A systematic review of smart tourism recommendation system applying data management. *Computer Science Review*, *39*, 100337. doi:10.1016/j.cosrev.2020.100337

Jeganathan, G. S., David, A., & Ganesh Kumar, C. (2022). Adaptation of Blockchain Technology In HRM. *Korea Review of International Studies*, 10-22.

Jeganathan, G. S., David, A., & Ilangovan, K. (2022). Determination of Hospitality Services Quality and Customer Satisfaction–a Holserv Approach. In *AU Virtual International Conference on" Entrepreneurship & Sustainability in Digital Era" under the theme of" Challenges of Organizational & Business Management in Dynamic Digital Dimension"* (Vol. 3, No. 1, pp. 325-334). Academic Press.

Jeganathan, G. S., & Srinivasulu, Y. (2014). Growth Drivers of Tourism Industry in India. *International Journal of Business and Management*, *2*(11), 100.

Joo, J., Park, J., & Han, Y. (2021). Applications of blockchain and smart contract for sustainable tourism ecosystems. *Evolutionary Computing and Mobile Sustainable Networks Proceedings of ICECMSN, 2020*, 773–780.

Kachniewska, M. (2021). Smart Tourism: Towards the Concept of a Data-Based Travel Experience. Handbook of Sustainable Development and Leisure Services, 289-302.

Karagoz Zeren, S., & Demirel, E. (2020). Blockchain based smart contract applications in tourism industry. *Digital business strategies in blockchain ecosystems: Transformational design and future of global business*, 601-615.

Karim, R., Ishrat, M., & Rahman, M. A. (2022). Blockchain Technology and Its Untapped Potentials in the Hospitality Industry. *Journal of Technology Management and Business*, *9*(1), 1–10. doi:10.30880/jtmb.2022.09.01.001

Kontogianni, A., & Alepis, E. (2020). Smart tourism: State of the art and literature review for the last six years. *Array (New York, N.Y.)*, *6*, 100020. doi:10.1016/j.array.2020.100020

Logesh, R., Subramaniyaswamy, V., Vijayakumar, V., & Li, X. (2019). Efficient user profiling based intelligent travel recommender system for individual and group of users. *Mobile Networks and Applications*, *24*(3), 1018–1033. doi:10.1007/s11036-018-1059-2

Luo, L., & Zhou, J. (2021). BlockTour: A blockchain-based smart tourism platform. *Computer Communications*, *175*, 186–192. doi:10.1016/j.comcom.2021.05.011

Madhani, P. M. (2022). Effective marketing strategy with blockchain implementation: Enhancing customer value propositions. *IUP Journal of Business Strategy*, *19*(1), 7–35.

Mehraliyev, F., Chan, I. C. C., Choi, Y., Koseoglu, M. A., & Law, R. (2020). A state-of-the-art review of smart tourism research. *Journal of Travel & Tourism Marketing*, *37*(1), 78–91. doi:10.1080/10548408.2020.1712309

Ozdemir, A. I., Ar, I. M., & Erol, I. (2020). Assessment of blockchain applications in travel and tourism industry. *Quality & Quantity*, *54*(5-6), 1549–1563. doi:10.1007/s11135-019-00901-w

Paktiti, M., & Economides, A. A. (2023). Smart contract applications in tourism. *International Journal of Technology Management & Sustainable Development*, *22*(2), 165–184. doi:10.1386/tmsd_00074_1

Pranata, A. R., & Tehrani, P. M. (2022). The Legality of Smart Contracts in a Decentralized Autonomous Organization (DAO). In Regulatory Aspects of Artificial Intelligence on Blockchain (pp. 112-131). IGI Global.

Rashideh, W. (2020). Blockchain technology framework: Current and future perspectives for the tourism industry. *Tourism Management*, *80*, 104125. doi:10.1016/j.tourman.2020.104125

Samara, D., Magnisalis, I., & Peristeras, V. (2020). Artificial intelligence and big data in tourism: A systematic literature review. *Journal of Hospitality and Tourism Technology*, *11*(2), 343–367. doi:10.1108/JHTT-12-2018-0118

Sankar, J.G., & Srinivasulu, Y. (2014). Growth Drivers of Tourism Industry in India. *The International Journal of Business & Management, 2*(11).

Sankar, J. G., & David, A. (2023). Measuring the Service Quality of Artificial Intelligence in the Tourism and Hospitality Industry. In Handbook of Research on Innovation, Differentiation, and New Technologies in Tourism, Hotels, and Food Service (pp. 133-155). IGI Global. doi:10.4018/978-1-6684-6985-9.ch007

SankarJ. G.DavidA.Ganesh KumarC. (2022). Adaptation of Blockchain Technology In HRM. *Available at* SSRN 4515408.

Sankar, J. G., & Kiruba Sagar, M, V. (2020). Examining the Risk Factor Associated with UTAUT MODEL. *Solid State Technology*, 1196–1198.

Sankar, J. G., Sugundan, N., & Sivakumar, S. (2018). MOOCs: A Comparative analysis between Indian scenario and Global scenario. *International Journal of Engineering & Technology, 7*(4.39), 854-857.

Sankar, J. G., Valan, P., & Siranjeevi, M. S. (2020). Various Models to Evaluate Quality in the Service Industry. In Digital Transformation and Innovative Services for Business and Learning (pp. 181-194). IGI Global.

Sanz Bayón, P. (2019). Key legal issues surrounding smart contract applications. *SSRN*, *9*(1), 63–91. doi:10.2139/ssrn.3525778

Savelyev, A. (2017). Contract law 2.0: 'Smart' contracts as the beginning of the end of classic contract law. *Information & Communications Technology Law, 26*(2), 116–134. doi:10.1080/13600834.2017.1301036

Sedkaoui, S., & Chicha, N. (2021). Blockchain-based smart contract technology application in the insurance industry: The case of "Fizzy". *MJBS*, (2).

Shen, J., Deng, C., & Gao, X. (2016). Attraction recommendation: Towards personalized tourism via collective intelligence. *Neurocomputing, 173*, 789–798. doi:10.1016/j.neucom.2015.08.030

Solakis, K., Katsoni, V., Mahmoud, A. B., & Grigoriou, N. (2022). Factors affecting value co-creation through artificial intelligence in tourism: A general literature review. *Journal of Tourism Futures*.

Subramanian, H., & Liu, R. (2021). Blockchain and smart contract: A review. *Journal of Database Management, 32*(1), vii–xxvi.

Thees, H., Erschbamer, G., & Pechlaner, H. (2020). The application of blockchain in tourism: Use cases in the tourism value system. *European Journal of Tourism Research, 26*, 2602–2602. doi:10.54055/ejtr.v26i.1933

Tolmach, P., Li, Y., Lin, S. W., Liu, Y., & Li, Z. (2021). A survey of smart contract formal specification and verification. *ACM Computing Surveys, 54*(7), 1–38. doi:10.1145/3464421

Treiblmaier, H., & Petrozhitskaya, E. (2023). Is it time for marketing to reappraise B2C relationship management? The emergence of a new loyalty paradigm through blockchain technology. *Journal of Business Research, 159*, 113725. doi:10.1016/j.jbusres.2023.113725

Tsung-ChihH.HsiehN. K.ChangC. Y.ChenT. L. (2023). Research on the Application of Smart Contracts in Travel Insurance Claims. *Available at* SSRN 4480435. doi:10.2139/ssrn.4480435

Unal, D., Hammoudeh, M., & Kiraz, M. S. (2020). Policy specification and verification for blockchain and smart contracts in 5G networks. *ICT Express, 6*(1), 43–47. doi:10.1016/j.icte.2019.07.002

Vacca, A., Di Sorbo, A., Visaggio, C. A., & Canfora, G. (2021). A systematic literature review of blockchain and smart contract development: Techniques, tools, and open challenges. *Journal of Systems and Software, 174*, 110891. doi:10.1016/j.jss.2020.110891

Velmurugan, T. A., & Sankar, J. G. (2017). A comparative study on motivation theory with Maslow's hierarchy theory and two factor theory in organization. *Indo-Iranian Journal of Scientific Research, 1*(1), 204–208.

Wang, W., Kumar, N., Chen, J., Gong, Z., Kong, X., Wei, W., & Gao, H. (2020). Realizing the potential of the internet of things for smart tourism with 5G and AI. *IEEE Network, 34*(6), 295–301. doi:10.1109/MNET.011.2000250

Willie, P. (2019). Can all sectors of the hospitality and tourism industry be influenced by the innovation of blockchain technology? *Worldwide Hospitality and Tourism Themes, 11*(2), 112–120. doi:10.1108/WHATT-11-2018-0077

Yadav, J. K., Verma, D. C., Jangirala, S., & Srivastava, S. K. (2021). An IAD type framework for Blockchain enabled smart tourism ecosystem. *The Journal of High Technology Management Research*, *32*(1), 100404. doi:10.1016/j.hitech.2021.100404

Zeren, S. K. (2023). Revolutionizing Tourism Payments: The Formation of Decentralized Tourism Financial Systems. In Blockchain for Tourism and Hospitality Industries (pp. 66-83). Routledge.

Zheng, Z., Xie, S., Dai, H. N., Chen, W., Chen, X., Weng, J., & Imran, M. (2020). An overview on smart contracts: Challenges, advances and platforms. *Future Generation Computer Systems*, *105*, 475–491. doi:10.1016/j.future.2019.12.019

Zou, W., Lo, D., Kochhar, P. S., Le, X. B. D., Xia, X., Feng, Y., Chen, Z., & Xu, B. (2019). Smart contract development: Challenges and opportunities. *IEEE Transactions on Software Engineering*, *47*(10), 2084–2106. doi:10.1109/TSE.2019.2942301

KEY TERMS AND DEFINITIONS

Blockchain Technology: A distributed and decentralized ledger enabling secure and transparent transaction recording, foundational for smart contract operations.

Continuous Improvement Through Data Insights: Iteratively enhancing tourism services by analyzing combined CRM and loyalty program data to stay responsive to evolving customer needs.

Customer Relationship Management (CRM): A business strategy managing interactions with customers, crucial in tourism for building relationships; smart contracts contribute by automating loyalty programs and enhancing engagement.

Decentralized Ledger: A distributed database across multiple nodes, ensuring secure and tamper-resistant transaction records, vital for smart contract reliability.

Operational Efficiency: The ability of smart contracts to automate tasks, reducing manual intervention, time, and resource consumption, enhancing efficiency in processes.

Real-Time Engagement and Recognition: Facilitating dynamic, immediate interactions with travelers by integrating CRM and loyalty programs in the tourism industry.

Risk Management: The identification, assessment, and mitigation of potential risks in travel services, improved by smart contracts automating insurance processes.

Seamless Travel Experiences: Integrating CRM and loyalty programs to ensure a cohesive and tailored travel journey from start to finish.

Smart Contract: A self-executing computer program on a blockchain, automating predefined conditions without intermediaries, ensuring transparency and efficiency in various industries.

Smart Contract Development Challenges: Technical hurdles in implementing blockchain and smart contracts, including scalability, interoperability, security, environmental impact, and regulatory complexities.

Targeted Marketing Strategies: Crafting precise tourism marketing campaigns based on combined CRM and loyalty program insights for attracting and retaining customers.

Unified Customer Profiles: Merging CRM and loyalty program data in tourism for detailed traveler profiles, enabling personalized services.

Chapter 13
Management Cases Studies and Technical Use Cases on Web 3

Anuradha Yadav
Dayananda Sagar College of Engineering, India

Srikantalahari Sagi
Avinash College of Commerce, India

ABSTRACT

This chapter involves numerous examples, using management cases and technology use cases, to understand the practical uses of Web 3 technologies. A discussion is had on Web 3 foundational concepts such as smart contracts, decentralized applications, decentralized identity and authentication, data privacy and control, and supply chain traceability. Then, cases related to DeFi, content monetization, decentralized exchanges, P2P lending, anonymized payments, lending platforms, stablecoins, financial inclusion and democratization, and autonomous funding are discussed. Tokenization led to the evolution of a new digital economy, and along with NFTs, the way digital art, real estate, and memorabilia are managed has changed. DAO is changing the way organizations work and are governed. Web 3 has several social applications and privacy-preserving technologies. Finally, interoperability options of Web 3 are discussed.

INTRODUCTION

Web 3.0 supports developing and deploying distributed applications (DApps) that run on decentralized networks, ensuring transparency, security, and user autonomy. A Decentralized Voting System, for example, allows the votes to be registered on a decentralized ledger, bringing about transparency (Huang et al., 2022). Cryptographic encryption allows the registration and storage of votes in a secure and hack-proof system. Web3 systems give autonomy to their users, allowing voters to cast their vote from anywhere without physical or geographical restrictions, thereby giving users autonomy.

Web3 is a technological revolution, giving several use cases in itself. However, they offer many possibilities when combined with potential applications from the management domains such as marketing,

DOI: 10.4018/979-8-3693-1532-3.ch013

finance, supply chain, and human resources as a global transition is happening towards a decentralized economy (Mathilde, 2022).

The online experience has evolved rapidly since the origins of the World Wide Web. What started as a decentralized system allowing for the free flow of information (the Web 1.0 era) has increasingly turned into a centralized under a handful of powerful corporations. Web 2.0 saw the rise of social media platforms and app ecosystems that amassed control over our data and online interactions. While this enabled new levels of connection and convenience, it has come at the cost of privacy and autonomy for users. Many technologists argue that the next generation of the internet, Web 3.0, promises a return to decentralization through technologies like Blockchain (Korpal & Scott, 2022). Decentralization is not just with technology but with how businesses are run (such as in decentralized governance) and how they are governed (such as in decentralized governance), amongst others.

Web 3 aims to put the user back in control by distributing data, infrastructure, and governance across disparate nodes rather than centralized servers. Decentralizing the online experience in this way could help address data ownership, digital surveillance, censorship, and single points of failure that have emerged under Big Tech oligopolies. This book will explore emerging Web 3 use cases that showcase the potential of decentralization to revolutionize how we connect, transact, and engage online more openly and equitably. Further, Web3 is perceived as 'self-infrastructure,' though how that happens is to be worked out (Nabben, 2023). It is to be noted that efforts are happening in intelligent and symbiotic (human-machine interaction) networks with massive interfaces and linkages as part of Web 4, the modalities of which are still to be worked out (Khaleel Ibrahim, 2021).

CASES ON THE FOUNDATIONAL CONCEPTS OF WEB 3

Blockchain technology is the foundational infrastructure supporting the decentralized vision of web3. A blockchain is a distributed digital ledger that can record transactions and track the exchange of assets across a peer-to-peer network. In web3, blockchains facilitate the transfer of cryptocurrencies, smart contracts, and self-executing programs stored on blockchain nodes. Decentralized applications are built on blockchains to remove the need for centralized institutions as intermediaries. Blockchain brings more transparency to processes since the records stored are immutable and auditable. This enhances security and trust in web3 as no single entity controls the network or can alter its transaction history.

Smart Contracts

Smart contracts are self-executing contracts that automate the execution of agreements and transactions on the blockchain. Applications include:

a. **Automated payments**: Cryptocurrencies and blockchain technology have made it possible to facilitate near-instant automated payments without intermediaries. Coinbase, for example, has built a crypto exchange and wallet platform. The platform allows users to send cryptocurrencies like Bitcoin directly to others with an address or a QR code. The transaction removes the need and dependence on traditional banking and saves both time and money on transaction fees compared to alternatives.

b. **Verifying authenticity**: Non-fungible tokens (NFTs) can be used to register digital assets on blockchains like Ethereum. They represent and establish proof of ownership. NFTs help verify the authenticity of digital art, collectibles, event tickets, and other assets converted into NFT forms. NFTs also help in supply chain management, wherein companies implement blockchain to track raw materials, parts, and finished goods as they change hands, ensuring authenticity and keep a check on counterfeiting. Luxury brands deploy similar solutions to authenticate high-value physical products.

c. **Automated legal processes in property transactions**: Conveying property in legal terms involves numerous intermediaries and paperwork that drives up costs, leading to transactional delays. Startups use blockchain-based pilot projects that run on smart contracts to automate escrow account management, title transfers, and document recording processes. This is made possible with the help of transparent programmable agreements, which are automatically enforced by the smart contracts without the need of an intermediary such as title insurance companies or closing attorneys. If tests are successful, it could streamline real estate conveyancing.

d. **Escrow services**: An escrow holds funds from a transaction in trust until pre-determined terms are met, such as, for example, the delivery of goods. Escrow services can hold crypto payments in dispute mediation or other transactions. There will be conditional release clauses using cryptocurrency wallets controlled by smart contracts. The distributed nature of blockchain prevents funds from being misused, while programs (smart contracts) enforce the agreed terms. With this, ambiguity and reducing legal costs from arbitration are reduced/eliminated.

e. **Raising funds using crowdsourcing in a decentralized manner**: Crowdfunding platforms increasingly use blockchain technology and smart contracts to power transparent fundraising. Projects are seen posting project details on a portal. The funding is done by raising cryptocurrency donations from supporters worldwide. Funds are held by the smart contract and only released to projects meeting targets. On-chain systems help track the projects and try to provide transparency to the extent possible. This enables frictionless global crowdfunding without centralized intermediation. Platforms like Kickstarter and IndieGoGo have already implemented these.

f. **Secure and transparent voting**: Blockchain has an inherent ability to record votes and balances without alteration transparently. Secure voting in corporate companies or Governments is a potential case for this. Governments globally are prototyping private blockchain voting systems allowing citizens to cast verified votes from any internet-connected device. Advanced architectures provide receipt-free and public verifiability, preventing vote buying while maintaining privacy.

g. **Automated settlement of insurance claims**: Private permissioned blockchains allow insurance providers to program claim criteria into smart contracts. The claim support documents are automatically built by connecting to IoT devices and digital records for simple automatic insurance payouts like property damage below a preset amount. Once the form is generated, a trigger will process and make an instant automated claims settlement according to policy terms without human review. This streamlines the claims process.

h. **Creation of tokens for physical and virtual assets**: The tokens can digitally represent ownership of real-world or virtual items. For example, they can track shares in private companies or gaming virtual goods, enabling fluid transactions on decentralized exchanges rather than being confined to a single proprietor platform. Tokenization opens vast opportunities for new trading models.

Decentralized Applications

Decentralized applications (DApps) have emerged as one of the central pillars of the evolving web3 infrastructure. As software programs are built on blockchain networks using smart contract functionality, DApps allow digital services and platforms to be created without reliance on centralized authorities or intermediaries. This provides advantages such as improved transparency, security, censorship resistance, and user autonomy. Decentralizing all traditional centralized applications will soon become necessary and keep everyone busy going forward (Tyagi, 2023).

Popular categories of DApps currently include decentralized finance (DeFi) applications such as Uniswap for cryptocurrency exchanges, social media platforms like Steemit, and games in the NFT space like Axie Infinity. The rise of DApps demonstrates the potential of an internet controlled and owned by users rather than large corporations. By functioning as distributed peer-to-peer systems, DApps may shape the future development of a genuinely decentralized web.

Several technical advancements are happening as the world approaches the Web3 era. Newer forms of blockchain, such as Smart Redbelly Blockchain (SRBB), were proposed to reduce congestions in Web3, thereby facilitating blockchains to be ready for realistic web application workloads (Tennakoon et al., 2023). The emergence of dApps has fostered the concept of decentralization across various services. Decentralized Function-as-a-Service (dFaaS) scalability and flexibility are achieved by using multiple cloud service providers/data centers (Karanjai et al., 2023).

Decentralized Identity and Authentication

Users can own and control their identity and personal data. This allows the system to function without depending on centralized entities like social media platforms for authentication or Know-Your-Customer (KYC) agencies. Use cases include:

a. **Better Single sign-on (SSO):** SSO allows users to securely access multiple applications and systems with a single login credentials. This improves user experience and reduces credential management overhead. However, current SSO implementations are often centrally controlled. They do not provide users ownership over their data. A decentralized approach using blockchain technology could address these issues. For example, the user's identity and credentials could be stored in an independent digital wallet controlled solely by the user. This provides true SSO while maintaining user privacy and control.

b. **Verification of certificates, licenses, and certifications**: Institutions like universities, employers, and certification bodies currently verify certificates manually. This approach is inefficient, time-consuming, and creates duplication of effort. A shared, tamper-proof digital record of credentials using blockchain could streamline verification across organizations. For instance, listing certifications on an open standard like Open Badges allows verifiers to quickly validate claims instead of contacting individual issuers. They save time and resources for all parties while preventing the falsification of records. Open Badges also has separate modules for certifying practicing evaluators (Davies et al., 2015).

c. **Self-sovereign Identity (SSI):** Revealing extensive personal details should no longer be necessary to access most online services. With SSI and verifiable credentials, users can share only identity attributes or qualifications required for a given interaction. Blockchain-backed credentials enable privacy-protecting authentication. This allows individuals to claim about themselves on a need-to-know basis. For example, a patient could access medical records from any provider using a Decentralized identifiers (DIDs) without disclosing unnecessary details. This reduces risks from centralized data holdings as in current identity systems.

SSI refers to a set of systems allowing users to own and control the tools needed to prove their identity attributes and qualifications (Chen et al., 2021). Using SSI, users will no longer rely on third-party intermediaries like governments or corporations to manage their identity data. For example, individuals can use DIDs to selectively share cryptographically verified claims about themselves. The details can be age or qualifications that are shared with an application depending on the need for a particular transaction.

Data Privacy and Control

Users have more control over their data, choosing how and when to share it, thereby addressing privacy concerns prevalent in Web 2.0. Applications include:

a. User-centric data control. Changes the way data is collected, stored, and used
b. Consent-driven data sharing allows data to be used only for the purpose for which permission is granted.
c. Transactions data is transparent to verify and track while maintaining anonymity or selectively disclosing information as needed.
d. Improved data security by using decentralized storage solutions
e. Increased transparency and trust because the blockchain enforces trust (Truong et al., 2021)
f. Reduced the reliance and dependency on centralized intermediaries
g. Enhanced interoperability between systems and platforms
h. Integrates privacy-enhancing technologies such as zero-knowledge proofs, homomorphic encryption, and decentralized identity
i. Allows users monetization of personal data, not intermediaries (Guidi & Michienzi, 2022).

Supply Chain Traceability

Blockchain in Web 3.0 allows for transparent tracking of goods, ensuring authenticity and reducing fraud in supply chains for industries like food, pharmaceuticals, and luxury goods (Dasaklis et al., 2022).

a. **Provenance and authenticity verification**: Blockchain can help verify the origin and authenticity of goods by recording critical milestones in a product's lifecycle, like manufacturing and transportation, on an immutable ledger (Cui et al., 2019). For example, luxury brands partner with blockchain companies such as Everledger. By doing this, they can curb counterfeiting by assigning unique crypto assets representing diamonds at mining. This allows anyone to verify a diamond's provenance and origins.
b. **Transparent supply chains**: Blockchain networks allow transactions to be executed without relying on explicit trust (Francisco & Swanson, 2018). Networks like VeChain bring transparency to supply chains by tracking shipments and enabling stakeholders to view data like temperature/location of

perishable goods in transit. This builds trust. For example, Walmart China uses VeChain to track pork and implement food safety tracing from farm to store.

c. **Quality assurance and compliance**: Documenting quality test results, certifications, and compliance data on distributed ledgers increases visibility and ensures standards are met (Lucena et al., 2018). An example is providing traceability of organic certification documents for fair trade coffee on a blockchain from harvest to retail.
d. **Reduced fraud and improved security**: Immutable records on shared ledgers curb the risk of data tampering in supply chains (Phan et al., 2019). Counterfeiting of diamonds, batteries, and almost any manufactured product is reduced as manufacturers integrate blockchain to issue digital passports for components at the production stage.
e. **Easier and more efficient recall processes**: By tracking products through the chain, targeted recalls can isolate affected batches, saving costs versus a broader recall. For example, a recall of lettuce contaminated in shipping can identify and pull only pallets from an implicated truck. Several use cases related to this are documented by researchers, especially in the automobile industry (Patro et al., 2021) and the pharmaceutical industry (Wu & Lin, 2019).
f. **Sustainable and ethical sourcing**: Blockchains allow documenting sourcing standards like organic/ fair trade practices end-to-end for trust. An example is the provenance of conflict-free minerals sourced ethically in DRC. It is being recorded on the blockchain for electronics makers.
g. **Real-time monitoring and predictive analytics**: Sensor data on blockchains with analytics helps proactively manage issues like adjusting production based on demand forecasts or rerouting perishables if delays are detected to avoid waste. An example is monitoring fish catch/storage temperatures on Blockchain with IoT to maximize freshness.

CASES FROM FINANCIAL APPLICATIONS

Decentralized Finance (DeFi) Platforms

Web 3.0 enables decentralized lending, borrowing, and trading through smart contracts, removing the need for traditional banks or intermediaries. Decentralized finance is considered the "true internet of money" (Harvey et al., 2021). It has the potential to introduce new financial products, such as information aggregation, which can help rebuild financial markets (Li, 2021). However, most of the products offered on these platforms are not regulated by authorities (Kwon, 2023) and hence might be extremely risky, especially when the technology is still evolving.

Though offering numerous advantages, DeFi platforms face limitations, challenges, and security issues. For example, Flash loans allow raising funds in the form of a loan in which users can raise funds and repay them in a single transaction. However, with liquidity issues or protocol attacks, hackers can exploit security issues to disrupt the system.

Content Monetization and Micropayments

Web 3.0 facilitates direct transactions between content creators and consumers. This allows for small, low-cost micropayments that are enabled with low transaction fees (Konashevych & Khovayko, 2020). Applications include content access or contributions without intermediaries.

Decentralized Exchanges (DEXs)

DEX allows individuals to trade in cryptocurrencies directly with one another and bypasses the need for intermediaries like banks, stock brokers, or traditional exchanges. This enhances financial autonomy and security while facilitating peer-to-peer transactions. For example, Uniswap facilitates instant peer-to-peer crypto trading through on-chain liquidity pools and an automated market maker, disrupting traditional exchanges through 24/7 access. The scholarly community discussed and compared features extensively on centralized and decentralized exchanges (Tsai et al., 2020; Yousaf et al., 2023). Investors are often cautioned about centralized cryptocurrency exchanges and the risks they pose. The collapse of the FTX cryptocurrency exchange (Manda & Nihar, 2023) and its aftermath (triggering a dominion effect, forcing tighter regulations, and questioning the sustainability of the cryptocurrency ecosystem) (Manda & Anuradha, 2023) is a testimony to this.

P2P Lending

Peer-to-peer lending has become a modern financial innovation. P2P platforms allow individuals to loan money to other individuals directly. When implemented on a blockchain, they bypass the traditional banking financial services system that charges fees for their services. Using online marketplaces and protocols like Maker, individuals can list loans they want to fund and set the terms, such as loan amounts, interest rates, and durations. Other individuals can then finance portions of those loans in exchange for a share of the interest payments. The Maker protocol specifically allows individuals to lock up cryptocurrency assets as collateral in smart contracts on the Ethereum blockchain. This collateral will then be used to mint Dai stablecoins autonomously. The stablecoins are issued as loans to borrowers. Borrowers can repay their loans directly through smart contracts. In this entire process, the blockchain system demonstrates the potential for trustless, global peer-to-peer lending without involving centralized intermediaries.

Anonymized Payments

Cryptocurrencies like Monero utilize privacy-enhancing technologies (PET) like ring signatures to obscure transaction details. With this, users can make fungible and untraceable value transfers on public ledgers. Blockchain is an excellent PET that helps anonymize transaction data (Averin et al., 2020) and has potential applications in allowing anonymized payments in a Web3 ecosystem.

Stablecoins for Price Stability

Stablecoins are a type of cryptocurrency in which the assets are pegged to a stable asset like fiat currency or commodities. They address the volatility concerns of traders and investors in the crypto market. They sometimes act as a bridge between the crypto and traditional financial systems. They are used in dealing with multiple currencies or payment systems because they enable faster, cheaper, and more efficient cross-border transactions. They provide a reliable medium for transactions and value storage without being affected by market fluctuations. As of January 31, 2023, the total market capitalization of stablecoins was approximately $138.4 billion.

Financial Inclusion and Democratization

DeFi democratizes financial instruments and access and has a broader positive societal impact. They eliminate geographical barriers and reduce dependency on traditional financial infrastructure. It allows individuals worldwide to access financial services and promotes financial inclusion on a global scale. DApp models of various social and financial inclusion models, such as microfinance, are being proposed (Jyothi & Supriya, 2023).

Autonomous Funding

A DAO like Moloch utilizes smart contracts to govern its decentralized fund, allocating grants through democratic member voting. This shows how blockchain removes centralized control over community resources.

CASES ON TOKENIZATION AND NON-FUNGIBLE TOKENS (NFTS)

NFTs (Non-Fungible Tokens) leverage blockchain to prove ownership and uniqueness of digital assets, revolutionizing art, gaming (including in-game items), collectibles, and even real estate. These digital assets are created, bought, and sold on the blockchain.

NFTs are criticized for their negative environmental impacts, for which certain potential workarounds are worked upon. Steps include avoiding the creation of NFTs till a purchase happens, Layer 2 and sidechains that allow the Ethereum platform interoperability, which helps move energy-intensive tasks to other systems, making donations of NFT proceeds for carbon credit, and making blockchains run on clean energy.

Tokenization of Digital Art and Collectibles

NFTs have revolutionized the art world by allowing artists to tokenize their work. The tokenized creations can be sold to collectors and receive royalty payments on future resales. They provide proof of ownership and uniqueness.

1. Popular digital collectibles such as Cryptopunks and Bored Ape Yacht Club have issued distinct limited-supply profile pictures using NFTs. Avid fans form communities to socialize, engage in derivative works, and host real-world meetups - bringing community and online identity together through shared NFT collectors.
2. Platforms like Foundation facilitate the sale and ownership certification of unique digital artworks.
3. Projects like CryptoPunks and Beeple's "Everydays: The First 5000 Days" have fetched millions in auctions, emphasizing the value of digital art as NFTs.
4. A platform like CryptoKitties popularized the concept of blockchain-backed unique digital assets through its kitschy cats, showcasing smart contracts as the technological building blocks empowering new forms of digital property.

Ownership of Gaming Assets

NFTs are transforming the concept of in-game assets. They allow the creation of unique characters and items that players can buy, sell, or trade on a decentralized marketplace, fostering a vibrant in-game economy.

NFT games like Decentraland, Axie Infinity, Gods Unchained, and The Sandbox use dApps to issue distinct, blockchain-backed tokens representing in-game creatures, body parts, and land. Players can freely trade these NFT assets on open markets, genuinely owning the items and retaining resale value. This brings absolute digital scarcity to virtual economies.

Gaming Assets

Gaming assets have become precious tradeable items within blockchain-based games. Game developers create non-fungible tokens (NFTs) to offer digitally limited quantities of unique in-game items and creatures. In games like Axie Infinity, each NFT-issued avatar or item is one-of-a-kind, providing players with actual ownership over their game holdings. These assets can be freely bought and sold on NFT marketplaces or can be earned by loyal and die-hard players. As the games become popular, the value of the rare and desirable NFT gaming assets increases substantially.

Some creatures and items were reportedly sold for tens of thousands of dollars. The most expensive game NFT sold so far is "The Merge" by Pak, which was auctioned for $91.8 million on December 2, 20211. It attracted over 30,000 bidders in the auction. By using blockchain to verify the authenticity and scarcity of virtual game items, NFTs allow gaming assets to be liquid and transferable, taking the concept of ownership within games to a new level.

Music and Creative Content

NFTs have introduced newer monetization methods for digital creative works such as music, art, and videos. They provide a way to attach absolute scarcity and ownership to digital files that would otherwise typically be endlessly reproduced. Artists can build an economy around collecting and trading such tokens by issuing limited editions of songs, images, or videos as NFTs. Fans can engage actively with works they value by acquiring NFTs representing them. Marketplaces and business models were created to focus on creative NFTs, which have emerged as a bridge between content creators and buyers. The platforms became new potential revenue streams. The tokenization of media allows for the interaction between the artist and the audience in the digital sphere.

Collectibles and Memorabilia

Collectibles, or collector's items, are objects of immense value or interest to a collector. Collectibles are a whole world in themselves and comprise trading cards, memorabilia, and one-of-a-kind artifacts. NFTs have transformed the world of collectibles by minting physical collectibles into digital NFTs. Their digital ownership details are put on a blockchain. Rare trading cards, signed jerseys, concert posters, and more can find a new lease of life through NFTs, widening their potential market and investment appeal. NFT marketplaces specializing in collectibles have seen tremendous growth, allowing pricing to be driven by open market demand. Tokenization opens up global ownership of valuable memorabilia to many more collectors. It offers a means to liquidate assets and preserve provenance for items in a wholly digital sphere.

Real Estate and Tokenization of Assets

Ownership of property assets (both physical and virtual) can be represented as NFT fractions. The advantage of fractional real estate ownership is that it allows investors to buy and trade fractions of high-value properties, increasing accessibility and liquidity to real estate investment opportunities. Investors can buy, trade, and receive rental income payments in tokens backed by slices of actual buildings and land titles, amongst other things. This includes voting rights over lease and management decisions.

Several companies are already offering these services. RealT, Propy, Meridio, Slice, Elevated Returns (tokenized luxury hotels), Harbor, Atac, BrickMark, and Ubitquity are examples of this.

CASES OF DECENTRALIZED AUTONOMOUS ORGANIZATIONS (DAOS)

Web 3.0 supports the creation of DAOs, where stakeholders can participate in decision-making processes transparently and autonomously (Kondova & Barba, 2020). Compound DAO, AssangeDAO, Bankless, and Krausehouse are the names of some popular DAOs.

DApps like Aragon and DAOstack offer decentralized governance and decision-making platforms. They enable communities to create and manage decentralized autonomous organizations (DAOs) where members can vote on proposals transparently and securely using smart contracts. DAOs are found to have poor decentralization regarding voting, but the decentralization capabilities have improved over time (Sharma et al., 2023).

Only a small number of participants actually participate in the voting process; Sybil attacks, influence concentration, and scalability limitations are certain aspects that limit the use of DAOs.

Case Study: The DAO

The DAO was launched on April 30, 2016, as a truly decentralized organization. It is expected not to have a head. So, the organization will not have managers or CEOs. It is expected to have a flat democratic structure. Their motive is to raise money through Initial Coin Offering (ICO) and let the token holders decide how the funds are to be used. In simple words, it tried to become a decentralized venture capital! The DAO raised $150 million worth of Ether, making it the most significant crowdfunding effort. Unfortunately, it suffered from "The DAO Hack," which led to a loss of a few million raised from the ICO and drained a third of its funds (Dhillon et al., 2017). Issues related to Ethereum, specifically smart contract vulnerability, were blamed. The hack became a very prominent textbook example. It even made the US Securities and Exchange Commission (SEC) say that the DAO ICO violated the laws because it sold securities without necessary approvals (SEC, 2017). The DAO episode highlighted risks associated with undiscovered software flaws in decentralized systems lacking corporate accountability structures.

Case Study: MakerDAO

MakerDAO came out in 2014 and is one of the first successful implementations of the principles of DAO. They have a governance token called MKR. Its ICO came up in 2018. Like any other DAO, MakerDAO decided that the tokenholders would decide the company's direction. Another promise it makes is lower volatility (Brennecke et al., 2022).

Case Study: Compound DAO

Compound DAO leverages the Compound protocol's success with algorithmic money markets to establish an autonomous funding venture (Compound DAO, 2023). Holding more than $1 billion of assets, Compound represents one of DeFi's most prominent projects.

Prior governance occurred through informal discussions rather than formalized structures. Compound DAO addresses this using a DAO framework governed by COMP tokens. Unlike traditional DAOs, Compound DAOs employ a unique structure where token holders vote with their economic stake rather than one token, one vote. This innovative design aligns the interests of participants with the platform's success, as those with more at stake have a more significant say in governance decisions. It allocates stablecoin reserves generated by protocol growth to fund proposals enhancing the Compound ecosystem, such as integrating new assets, developing risk tools, or researching protocol upgrades.

Grants are awarded through on-chain token-weighted voting by COMP holders. This distributes fiscal power proportionally to stake while maintaining decentralized decision-making. Compound DAO has disbursed multiple millions in grants since its launch. Its business model streamlines the autonomous management of Compound surpluses. Its robust token enjoys huge demand. The governance system allows for strategically cultivating the protocol's longevity through community-funded initiatives. However, challenges do persist around voter participation rates and proposal selection subjectivity.

Compound DAO uses a quadratic voting mechanism to balance influence. This system prevents a small group of individuals from dominating the decision-making process. It promotes a fairer, more inclusive system where minority voices can still be heard and considered. It also tends to incentivize active participation through various mechanisms, such as rewarding governance token holders for voting and engaging in the platform's activities.

Compound DAO has marked a significant evolution in DAO governance and has taken the whole concept to the next level. It demonstrated and showed how to balance various features such as decentralization, fairness, and active participation to benefit all stakeholders in the system. Its innovative approach may serve as a model for future DeFi projects, providing a robust framework for more effective and equitable decentralized decision-making processes.

CASES ON SOCIAL APPLICATIONS

Decentralized Social Media Networks

Decentralized social media network platforms like Minds, Steemit, and Mastodon are built leveraging blockchain technology. These DApps are run such that no single individual owns them and that personal data safety is offered organically by design (Manoj Kumar T et al., 2022). It allows users to control their data and content while incentivizing contributions through token rewards, disrupting the centralized model of social media platforms (Guidi, 2021). A platform like Hive allows users to own their data/ content, post updates to a blockchain-based feed, and earn rewards through engagement—providing decentralized alternatives. Online social media that runs entirely on blockchain infrastructure – called Blockchain Online Social Media (BOSM) - was proposed where content generators can even get rewarded (Guidi & Michienzi, 2022). Substantial scholarly efforts went into fake news detection using blockchain in association with other technologies (Shahbazi & Byun, 2021; Xiao et al., 2020).

Metaverse

Platforms like Decentraland and Somnium Space are building metaverse platforms using VR/AR/XR technologies. These platforms enable users to create, own, and trade virtual assets and land parcels, fostering a virtual economy and immersive social experiences within a decentralized environment. The metaverse has led to the evolution of several applications (Kirkpatrick, 2022). Blockchain and metaverse are expected to bring a higher customer experience in the Web3 era (Khaliq & Manda, 2023). Metaverse is bringing several opportunities for entrepreneurs and professionals with a whole new range of tools - from marketing to retailing to offering professional services (Momtaz, 2022).

Knowledge Marketplace

DApps like STEMx, Cent, and SkillWallet are exploring decentralized education models. They use tokenization to incentivize peer-to-peer learning, allowing students/experts to trade educational resources/ verify credentials in a shared open marketplace. Users can create and consume educational content while earning tokens or rewards, fostering a peer-to-peer learning ecosystem. However, studies say that decentralized education cannot be presumed to yield better outcomes in every context and has put doubts on its advocacy and adoption (Kameshwara et al., 2020).

Virtual Events and Entertainment Spaces

Cryptovoxels, VRChat, and similar platforms offer virtual spaces for interactive entertainment and events. These platforms enable users to socialize, attend events, and create their own experiences, blurring the lines between social interactions and entertainment in a decentralized virtual environment.

Digital Art Communities

NFT platforms like CryptoVoxels become virtual galleries housing unique digital creations, enabling artists to monetize work and fans/collectors to socialize around shared interests in 3D environments. Studies show that blockchain and metaverse are to be seen as inclusive innovations and as a means of democratizing art institutions (Damodaran, 2023).

WEB 3 AND PRIVACY

Web 3 promises a more decentralized internet where users control their data and digital identities. However, this new iteration of the web raises privacy concerns as well. With information stored on blockchains, users must know that their transactions and interactions will be public. Strong privacy protections and options for anonymity will be crucial for Web 3 adoption as people's online behaviors and connections could now be permanently tracked on distributed ledgers. Advances in privacy-preserving technologies may help alleviate these issues (Boussada et al., 2022).

Data transparency and privacy are two sides of a coin, and specific features of Web 3 conflict with these. If managed and secured incorrectly, smart contracts and immutable records can pose privacy risks. Complex ownership structures become challenging to untangle. Regulatory bodies are seen struggling to protect privacy and ensure ethical data practices.

Decentralized Identity and Self-Sovereign Identity (SSI)

Projects like uPort and Sovrin are pioneering decentralized identity solutions that empower users to securely control and manage their digital identities. These platforms use blockchain and cryptographic techniques to provide individuals with self-sovereign identities, ensuring privacy and reducing reliance on centralized authorities for identity verification. Anonymous Authentication can be done using digital credentials that may be issued and verified on zkSnarks-powered blockchains without revealing user identities. This facilitates privacy-preserving proof of qualifications/attestations for interacting anonymously.

Privacy-Preserving Cryptocurrencies

Privacy-focused cryptocurrencies like Monero and Zcash employ advanced cryptographic techniques (such as ring signatures and zero-knowledge proofs) to provide enhanced privacy and anonymity in transactions. These cryptocurrencies prioritize user privacy by obscuring transaction details and sender and receiver information, though they suffer from the remark of being the cryptocurrency of choice for cybercriminals (Koerhuis et al., 2020).

Secure Communication and Messaging

Applications such as Signal and Session leverage end-to-end encryption and decentralized architectures. These methods help ensure private and secure messaging. They prioritize user privacy by preventing unauthorized access to communication data and enabling confidential conversations without compromising user data.

Privacy-Enhancing Technologies for Smart Contracts

Because of the increased focus on personal data privacy and the increased regulations around it, several tools and technologies called Privacy-Enchancing Technologies (PET) have emerged. The emergence of specialized blockchain tools such as privacy-preserving smart contracts (PPSC) can help application developers to build use cases and applications around the concept (Qi et al., 2023).

Enigma is one such platform that focuses on improving privacy and scalability by integrating PETs into smart contracts. Oasis Labs is another platform focusing on privacy-oriented smart contracts, though not many technical details are available in the public domain. Most platforms working in this space use secure computation methods to enable computations on encrypted data, allowing for the execution of smart contracts while maintaining data privacy. Status is an end-to-end encrypted protocol that provides a private channel for discussion transactions, concealing metadata and contents of messages from intermediaries through cryptographic schemes.

PETs often have a tough challenge. On one side, they have to preserve the confidentiality of user identities and behaviors. On the other side, they have to provide personalized experiences. The surveillance of user data within a decentralized system presents a difficult task, particularly in data protection. Even anonymized profiles are not completely safe and have the risk of reidentification. Studies have shown that an average internet user has a 83 percent risk of reidentification despite his date being anonymized. Adoption promotion could get delayed if the technologies are not congruent with prevalent behaviors such as social media usage, or if they necessitate substantial modifications to interfaces and tools that users have become familiar with. Addressing such obstacles will be necessary for PETs to fulfill their promise in the next generation of the online world.

Access Management

Consent-based data sharing is enabled through tools like Ocean, allowing granular control over who can access specific personal information and revoking access whenever desired without intermediaries.

Decentralized Storage and Data Privacy

IPFS (InterPlanetary File System) and Filecoin are the best solutions for decentralized storage requirements for the Web3 era. They give priority to data privacy. These platforms use distributed storage mechanisms and encryption to ensure data is stored securely without compromising user privacy. More stronger data storage mechanisms have evolved to cater to the needs of Web 3 user needs as blockchain and other related technologies gets together (Pham et al., 2020).

INTEROPERABILITY AND WEB 3

An important goal of Web 3.0 is to improve interoperability between decentralized applications and platforms. The systems are currently mainly working independently as isolated islands. They are seen struggling to share data and functionality between different networks. Users face lock-in without options to efficiently move profiles, content, and digital assets. For Web 3.0 to realize its vision of an open network, technical standards must emerge, allowing distributed apps and services built on separate blockchains to connect and exchange information seamlessly.

Further, the systems would turn complex and have a complex mix of technologies. Developers wish to be incentivized for their additional efforts in adopting and implementing standards that ensure compatibility. Cross-compatible interoperability poses complex technical challenges but is essential for the long-term growth and usability of the decentralized web.

Cross-Chain Asset Transfers

One of the visions of Web 3.0 is that technologies collaborate to provide the next-generation experience to the users. As a part of this, it aspires that different blockchains and protocols communicate and transact with each other seamlessly, encouraging a more connected ecosystem. Platforms like Cosmos and Polkadot provide an interface between state machines to communicate with each other. Though both follow different architectures and models, both focus on allowing interoperability between blockchains. They enable cross-chain asset transfers, allowing tokens and data to move seamlessly between otherwise isolated blockchain networks. This leads to a culture of connected systems.

Decentralized Finance (DeFi) Interoperability

Projects such as Wormhole and Ren Protocol aim to facilitate interoperability within the DeFi space. They enable assets from one blockchain to be utilized on another. Users will thus be able to get access to various DeFi applications and services across multiple chains. Wormhole is an example of protocol that supports secure cross-chain transfers of tokens or data. Though not many details of Ren Protocol are available in the public domain, the protocol is perceived to have kept privacy and interoperability in the DeFi at its core.

Interoperable Identity and Authentication

One of the viewpoints of Web3 is to give individuals control over their personal data. Numerous tools like decentralized identifiers (DIDs), verifiable credentials, blockchain-based solutions, and interoperable identity systems collaborate to achieve this.

Open industry initiatives like the DID Alliance are working on standardizing interoperable decentralized identity solutions. They attempt to create standards for interoperable identity protocols which allow users to manage their identities across various platforms and services securely. Sovrin, uPort, SelfKey, Civic, and Hyperledger Indy are examples of some Web3 tools that work in this area.

Cross-Chain Communication Protocols

Technologies like Atomic Swaps and Interledger Protocol (ILP) allow cross-chain communication. Atomic Swaps enable peer-to-peer exchange of different cryptocurrencies without an intermediary. Through the use of a "virtual vault" known as a time-bound smart contract, funds can only be unlocked when both parties deposit the correct amount of assets (Chainlink, 2023). On the other hand, ILP aims to connect different ledgers and payment systems and allow for seamless exchange of value across various payment networks. Future research can advance how data is stored, processed, and exchanged.

Multi-Chain DApp Ecosystems

Ethereum-compatible chains and ecosystems focus on compatibility with Ethereum's infrastructure. Some examples of such networks are Binance Smart Chain and Polygon. Through enabling interoperability, decentralized applications (DApps) will have the ability to function across multiple blockchain networks by capitalizing on the network effects inherent to the Ethereum platform, while drawing upon alternative chains to address issues of scalability and cost. Development frameworks such as the Cosmos SDK help in development of applications with cross-chain functionality from diverse blockchains. The removes the need for end-users to maintain separate digital wallets or to develop specialized knowledge pertaining to individual networks. Interoperability promises to allow DApps to leverage established infrastructure like Ethereum for adoption and usability reasons.

Bridging Chains

Bridging chains use protocols that allow easy movement of tokens between principal blockchains and side networks. Polygon Proof-of-Stake is one such bridge chain that enables smooth transfers of cryptocurrency holdings between platforms such as Ethereum and sidechains. They improve transaction throughput and providing access to other environments. This reduces barriers for developers and users by connecting separate ecosystems, expanding the reach of decentralized applications and liquidity options for digital assets across multiple systems. Bridge chains and the secure cross-chain interoperability that it provides is essential for real-world usability of blockchain technology on a larger scale.

Decentralized Storage and Computing

Web 3.0 uses blockchain and peer-to-peer networks to offer decentralized storage solutions. With this, the way data is stored and processed drastically changes. Dependency on centralized cloud services comes down. Data security gets enhanced. There is no single controlling entity or authority. Data is not stored in a single computer or a server but is distributed across all or multiple nodes on the network. The data is encrypted with cryptographic technologies, making it very hard to access it without the availability of the right keys. However, the validity or authentication of data is easily possible because of the usage of hash functions. Some places where these concepts are used include InterPlanetary File System (IPFS), Ethereum Swarm, Filecoin, Golem Network, and DFINITY.

CONCLUSION

In conclusion, Web 3 applications demonstrate vast potential across various domains, from finance and social media to the arts. The management case studies use cases, and examples presented have shown how blockchain technologies like smart contracts, decentralized networks, and tokenized assets reinvent old industries and create new ones. While challenges around scalability, usability, and regulations remain, continued technical progress and real-world implementations will help realize the vision of a more open and transparent internet. Web 3 promises distributed systems that are decentralized, more resilient, inclusive, and empowering for all. Since the topic is still evolving, it has the potential for impactful research and development in the future.

REFERENCES

Boussada, R., Elhdhili, M. E., Hamdane, B., & Azouz Saidane, L. (2022). Privacy Preserving in the Modern Era: A Review of the State of the Art. In A. K. Tyagi (Ed.), Advances in Information Security, Privacy, and Ethics. IGI Global. doi:10.4018/978-1-6684-5250-9.ch001

Brennecke, M., Guggenberger, T., Schellinger, B., & Urbach, N. (2022). *The De-Central Bank in Decentralized Finance: A Case Study of MakerDAO. Hawaii International Conference on System Sciences.* 10.24251/HICSS.2022.737

Chainlink. (2023, November 30). *What Is an Atomic Swap?* https://chain.link/education-hub/atomic-swaps

Chen, Y., Liu, C., Wang, Y., & Wang, Y. (2021). A Self-Sovereign Decentralized Identity Platform Based on Blockchain. *2021 IEEE Symposium on Computers and Communications (ISCC)*, 1–7. 10.1109/ISCC53001.2021.9631518

Compound, D. A. O. (2023). *Compound DAO.* https://compound.finance

Cui, P., Dixon, J., Guin, U., & Dimase, D. (2019). A Blockchain-Based Framework for Supply Chain Provenance. *IEEE Access : Practical Innovations, Open Solutions*, *7*, 157113–157125. doi:10.1109/ACCESS.2019.2949951

Damodaran, A. (2023). From non fungible tokens to metaverse: Blockchain based inclusive innovation in arts. *Innovation and Development*, 1–20. doi:10.1080/2157930X.2023.2180709

Dasaklis, T. K., Voutsinas, T. G., Tsoulfas, G. T., & Casino, F. (2022). A Systematic Literature Review of Blockchain-Enabled Supply Chain Traceability Implementations. *Sustainability (Basel)*, *14*(4), 2439. doi:10.3390/su14042439

Davies, R., Randall, D., & West, R. E. (2015). Using Open Badges to Certify Practicing Evaluators. *The American Journal of Evaluation*, *36*(2), 151–163. doi:10.1177/1098214014565505

Dhillon, V., Metcalf, D., & Hooper, M. (2017). The DAO Hacked. In Blockchain Enabled Applications (pp. 67–78). Apress. doi:10.1007/978-1-4842-3081-7_6

Francisco, K., & Swanson, D. (2018). The Supply Chain Has No Clothes: Technology Adoption of Blockchain for Supply Chain Transparency. *Logistics*, *2*(1), 2. doi:10.3390/logistics2010002

Guidi, B. (2021). An Overview of Blockchain Online Social Media from the Technical Point of View. *Applied Sciences (Basel, Switzerland)*, *11*(21), 9880. doi:10.3390/app11219880

Guidi, B., & Michienzi, A. (2022). How to reward the Web: The social dApp Yup. *Online Social Networks and Media*, *31*, 100229. doi:10.1016/j.osnem.2022.100229

Harvey, C. R., Ramachandran, A., & Santoro, J. (2021). *DeFi and the future of finance.* Wiley.

Huang, J., He, D., Obaidat, M. S., Vijayakumar, P., Luo, M., & Choo, K.-K. R. (2022). The Application of the Blockchain Technology in Voting Systems: A Review. *ACM Computing Surveys*, *54*(3), 1–28. doi:10.1145/3439725

Jyothi, C., & Supriya, M. (2023). Decentralized Application (DApp) for Microfinance Using a Blockchain Network. In G. Ranganathan, R. Bestak, & X. Fernando (Eds.), *Pervasive Computing and Social Networking* (Vol. 475, pp. 95–107). Springer Nature Singapore. doi:10.1007/978-981-19-2840-6_8

Kameshwara, K. K., Sandoval-Hernandez, A., Shields, R., & Dhanda, K. R. (2020). A false promise? Decentralization in education systems across the globe. *International Journal of Educational Research*, *104*, 101669. doi:10.1016/j.ijer.2020.101669

Karanjai, R., Xu, L., Diallo, N., Chen, L., & Shi, W. (2023). DeFaaS: Decentralized Function-as-a-Service for Emerging dApps and Web3. *2023 IEEE International Conference on Blockchain and Cryptocurrency (ICBC)*, 1–3. 10.1109/ICBC56567.2023.10174945

Khaleel Ibrahim, A. (2021). Evolution of the Web: From Web 1.0 to 4.0. *Qubahan Academic Journal*, *1*(3), 20–28. doi:10.48161/qaj.v1n3a75

Khaliq, L. N., & Manda, V. K. (2023). Customer Experience in the Web 3.0 Era: The Meeting of Blockchain and the Metaverse. In M. Majeed, K. S. Ofori, G. K. Amoako, A.-R. Alolo, & G. Awini (Eds.), Advances in Marketing, Customer Relationship Management, and E-Services. IGI Global. doi:10.4018/978-1-6684-7649-9.ch015

Kirkpatrick, K. (2022). Applying the metaverse. *Communications of the ACM*, *65*(11), 16–18. doi:10.1145/3565470

Koerhuis, W., Kechadi, T., & Le-Khac, N.-A. (2020). Forensic analysis of privacy-oriented cryptocurrencies. *Forensic Science International Digital Investigation*, *33*, 200891. doi:10.1016/j.fsidi.2019.200891

Konashevych, O., & Khovayko, O. (2020). Randpay: The technology for blockchain micropayments and transactions which require recipient's consent. *Computers & Security*, *96*, 101892. doi:10.1016/j.cose.2020.101892

Kondova, G., & Barba, R. (2020). Governance of Decentralized Autonomous Organizations. *Journal of Modern Accounting and Auditing*, *15*(8). https://papers.ssrn.com/sol3/papers.cfm?abstract_id=3549469

Korpal, G., & Scott, D. (2022). *Decentralization and web3 technologies*. https://gkorpal.github.io/files/drewscott_gkorpal_web3.pdf

Kwon, S. (2023). Regulation of DeFi Lending: Agency Supervision on Decentralization. *The Columbia Science and Technology Law Review*, *24*(2), 379–413. doi:10.52214/stlr.v24i2.11629

Li, J. (2021). DeFi as an Information Aggregator. In M. Bernhard, A. Bracciali, L. Gudgeon, T. Haines, A. Klages-Mundt, S. Matsuo, D. Perez, M. Sala, & S. Werner (Eds.), *Financial Cryptography and Data Security. FC 2021 International Workshops* (Vol. 12676, pp. 171–176). Springer Berlin Heidelberg. doi:10.1007/978-3-662-63958-0_15

Lucena, P., Binotto, A. P. D., Momo, F. da S., & Kim, H. (2018). *A Case Study for Grain Quality Assurance Tracking based on a Blockchain Business Network* (arXiv:1803.07877). arXiv. http://arxiv.org/abs/1803.07877

MandaV. K.AnuradhaY. (2023). *The Aftermath of the FTX Cryptocurrency Exchange Collapse*. doi:10.5281/ZENODO.10207831

Manda, V. K., & Nihar, L. K. (2023). Lessons From the FTX Cryptocurrency Exchange Collapse. In S. Saluja, D. Kulshrestha, & S. Sharma (Eds.), Advances in Business Strategy and Competitive Advantage. IGI Global. doi:10.4018/978-1-6684-8488-3.ch002

Manoj Kumar, T., Mukunthan, K., Reena, R., & Bhuvaneswari, S. (2022). Decentralized Social Media Platform using Blockchain. *International Journal of Advanced Research in Science. Tongxin Jishu, 54–58*. Advance online publication. doi:10.48175/IJARSCT-4979

Mathilde, G. og R. R. (2022). *Impact of the decentralized economy of the WEB3 on the business strategies* [Master Thesis, Norwegian Business School]. https://biopen.bi.no/bi-xmlui/bitstream/handle/11250/3037617/Master%20Thesis%20-%20Impact%20of%20the%20decentralized%20economy%20of%20the%20WEB3%20on%20the%20business%20strategies.pdf

Momtaz, P. P. (2022). Some Very Simple Economics of Web3 and the Metaverse. *FinTech*, *1*(3), 225–234. doi:10.3390/fintech1030018

Nabben, K. (2023). Web3 as 'self-infrastructuring': The challenge is how. *Big Data & Society*, *10*(1), 205395172311590. doi:10.1177/20539517231159002

Pham, V.-D., Tran, C.-T., Nguyen, T., Nguyen, T.-T., Do, B.-L., Dao, T.-C., & Nguyen, B. M. (2020). B-Box—A Decentralized Storage System Using IPFS, Attributed-based Encryption, and Blockchain. *2020 RIVF International Conference on Computing and Communication Technologies (RIVF)*, 1–6. 10.1109/RIVF48685.2020.9140747

Phan, L., Li, S., & Mentzer, K. (2019). Blockchain Technology and the current discussion on Fraud. *Issues in Information Systems*. Advance online publication. doi:10.48009/4_iis_2019_8-20

Qi, H., Xu, M., Yu, D., & Cheng, X. (2023). SoK: Privacy-preserving smart contract. *High-Confidence Computing*, *100183*. Advance online publication. doi:10.1016/j.hcc.2023.100183

SEC. (2017). *SEC Issues Investigative Report Concluding DAO Tokens, a Digital Asset, Were Securities*. US Securities and Exchange Commission. https://cdn.lawreportgroup.com/hflr-files/2017/10/11/aca_press-release_sec-issues-investigative-report-concluding-dao-tokens.pdf

Shahbazi, Z., & Byun, Y.-C. (2021). Fake Media Detection Based on Natural Language Processing and Blockchain Approaches. *IEEE Access : Practical Innovations, Open Solutions*, *9*, 128442–128453. doi:10.1109/ACCESS.2021.3112607

Sharma, T., Kwon, Y., Pongmala, K., Wang, H., Miller, A., Song, D., & Wang, Y. (2023). *Unpacking How Decentralized Autonomous Organizations (DAOs) Work in Practice* (arXiv:2304.09822). arXiv. http://arxiv.org/abs/2304.09822

Tennakoon, D., Hua, Y., & Gramoli, V. (2023). Smart Redbelly Blockchain: Reducing Congestion for Web3. *2023 IEEE International Parallel and Distributed Processing Symposium (IPDPS)*, 940–950. 10.1109/IPDPS54959.2023.00098

Truong, N., Lee, G. M., Sun, K., Guitton, F., & Guo, Y. (2021). A blockchain-based trust system for decentralised applications: When trustless needs trust. *Future Generation Computer Systems*, *124*, 68–79. doi:10.1016/j.future.2021.05.025

Tsai, W.-T., He, J., Wang, R., & Deng, E. (2020). Decentralized Digital-Asset Exchanges: Issues and Evaluation. *2020 3rd International Conference on Smart BlockChain (SmartBlock)*, 1–6. 10.1109/SmartBlock52591.2020.00024

Tyagi, A. K. (2023). Decentralized everything: Practical use of blockchain technology in future applications. In *Distributed Computing to Blockchain* (pp. 19–38). Elsevier. doi:10.1016/B978-0-323-96146-2.00010-3

Wu, X., & Lin, Y. (2019). Blockchain recall management in pharmaceutical industry. *Procedia CIRP*, *83*, 590–595. doi:10.1016/j.procir.2019.04.094

Xiao, Y., Liu, Y., & Li, T. (2020). Edge Computing and Blockchain for Quick Fake News Detection in IoV. *Sensors (Basel)*, *20*(16), 4360. doi:10.3390/s20164360

Yousaf, I., Abrar, A., & Yarovaya, L. (2023). Decentralized and centralized exchanges: Which digital tokens pose a greater contagion risk? *Journal of International Financial Markets, Institutions and Money*, *89*, 101881. doi:10.1016/j.intfin.2023.101881

KEY TERMS AND DEFINITIONS

Cross-Chain: A term used to describe the ability of a blockchain or distributed ledger technology (DLT) to interoperate with other blockchains or DLTs, allowing for seamless communication and value transfer between different networks.

Cryptocurrencies: Digital or virtual currencies that use cryptography for security and are decentralized, meaning they are not controlled by any government or financial institution. Examples include Bitcoin, Ethereum, and Litecoin.

Decentralized Exchanges (DEXs): Platforms that enable peer-to-peer trading of cryptocurrencies in a trustless and permissionless manner, without the need for intermediaries.

Decentralized Identity: A system of managing and verifying individual identities using blockchain technology, allowing for secure and privacy-preserving identity verification and authentication.

Decentralized Storage: A network of distributed storage nodes that work together to provide a secure and decentralized storage solution, ensuring that data is not controlled by any single entity.

Knowledge Marketplace: A platform that enables the buying and selling of knowledge and expertise, using blockchain technology to facilitate transparent and trustworthy transactions.

Peer-to-Peer Lending: A decentralized lending platform that connects borrowers directly with lenders, eliminating intermediaries and allowing for more efficient and cost-effective lending.

Privacy Enhancement Technologies: Technologies that are designed to enhance the privacy and security of blockchain transactions, such as zero-knowledge proofs and homomorphic encryption.

Stablecoins: Cryptocurrencies that are pegged to the value of a fiat currency or other stable asset, in order to reduce the volatility associated with other cryptocurrencies.

Tokenization: The process of converting assets or rights into a digital token, which can be traded, stored, and managed on a blockchain. This can include everything from real estate to artwork to voting rights.

Chapter 14
Guide Material Study for the Use of Web Tools in Science Lessons:
Example of Physical and Chemical Change

Fatma Alkan
https://orcid.org/0000-0003-2784-875X
Hacettepe University, Turkey

Melih Erkan Doğan
https://orcid.org/0009-0009-8224-8678
Hacettepe University, Turkey

ABSTRACT

The use of computers in education has brought about developments in web technology, and Web 2.0 tools have begun to be used frequently in science lessons. Web 2.0 tools are a technology that allows materials to be developed without space and time limitations, and these materials can be easily shared with students. This study was prepared as a guide material on how to develop the lesson content of the eighth-grade science lesson on physical and chemical change using Web 2.0 tools. All contents about eighth grade physical and chemical change were prepared with Web 2.0 tools, and it was emphasized how to benefit from Web 2.0 tools. With Web 2.0 tools, various tools have been introduced for use in interactive presentations, animations, videos, concept maps, and measurement and evaluation. It is thought that lessons taught with Web 2.0 tools increase students' motivation, permanent learning occurs, and contribute to collaborative learning, and students will actively participate in the process.

DOI: 10.4018/979-8-3693-1532-3.ch014

INTRODUCTION

Science Teaching

Science is studies events in nature, trying to recognize and explain it. The aim of the science lesson is to cultivate environmentally sensitive individuals who explore, investigate, produce solutions to problems, make logical decisions, open to technological developments, produce new technology, use technology (MEB, 2000). Teaching science is useful in enabling people to know themselves better, as well as being able to describe the events and developments around them (Uzuner, 2018). It is possible to keep up with the current pace of scientific developments through qualified science teaching. Skilled science teaching allows the student to study knowledge in depth, relate it with old knowledge, become aware of responsibility, cooperate with those around him, and strive to overcome the difficulties that arise (Uzuner, 2018). Research and inquiry are at the core of the curriculum of the sciences (Mone, 2018). Together with the transition from traditional teaching management to constructivist approach, project-based learning environments with students at the center of science teaching and promoting cooperation were envisaged (Mone, 2018). The constructivist approach is mainly aimed at the teacher's ability to access and bridge the knowledge with previous knowledge, by preparing appropriate learning environments, so that the teacher can access the knowledge and build bridges with previous knowledge, structuring the knowledge. The science lesson focuses on 3 main skills, namely scientific process skills, life skills, engineering, and design skills (Mone, 2018). It would be appropriate to use time-appropriate, methodological techniques that are engaging, capable of addressing multiple sense organs to gain access to the achievements of the science lesson (Karahan, 2022). When the specific objectives of the science lesson are examined, they have gained basic knowledge in the fields of biology, physics, chemical engineering, are able to explore nature and produce solutions to problems encountered in nature, developed awareness of sustainable development, can solve everyday life problems, have career awareness and entrepreneurial skills, understand scientific knowledge, are curious about the surrounding events, universal ethics It can be considered to educate individuals with moral values who have adopted scientific ethical principles (Mone, 2018).

The basic principles outlined in the science curriculum, the skills desired to be acquired and the specific purposes can only be possible with appropriate educational environments. Instead of continuing to use traditional teaching methods in science teaching, taking advantage of the evolving technological possibilities can contribute more to achieving the objectives in the program. The science lesson collaborates with other disciplines and adopts an active learning approach based on research and inquiry. With the development of computer technology, it can be said that science teaching is more effective, interesting and an environment in which research and inquiry are easier with the Internet environment. Among the many concepts and knowledge that will enable students to produce solutions to problems that may be encountered during their life adventures, the lesson of science from the bar is an important lesson (Erdoğan & Yıldırım, 2023).

Technology in Science Education

Rapid developments in the field of technology have also jumped into the field of education, especially advances in computer technology have directly affected education. Progress in technology is the most important indicator of the degree of development of countries (Akbaba & Kılıç, 2022). In the field of science, it has been concluded that when computer-assisted teaching is used instead of traditional methods (Akdeniz et al., 2002). The science lesson is presented as a lesson that arouses curiosity in students, aims to explore, and aims to make students think rather than memorize. For this reason, traditional teaching methods fall short in meeting these goals. In education using computer-aided instruction, it is seen that the student can progress at his own pace, the student can work in groups, understand abstract topics better, and his experimental processes that are difficult to do can be carried out in a computer environment (Bal, 2015).

A science lesson is one that requires more practice. With the transition from traditional teaching to constructivist approach, it is expected that the topic will be better understood by learning by living by doing, designing products, and giving examples from everyday life. For this reason, it is inevitable to use Technology support in science lessons to provide environments that allow the development of high-level cognitive process skills. In education using technology-assisted teaching, the motivation of the student increases, the education is individualized, and equality of opportunity is achieved. Active participation of the student in educational and educational processes is ensured (Akbaba & Ertaş, 2022). Unlike traditional learning methods, in technology-assisted science teaching, students take responsibility, investigate why they learn, and make learning easier and lasting by making abstract topics more concrete with tools such as animation, simulation, interactive videos. Computer-generated animations help to visually memorize information, making it easier to connect with old information.

With advanced communication technologies using technology in science education, first-hand resources can be easily accessed regardless of time and place. With Web 2.0 tools, productivity can be achieved in the virtual environment, individual and group teaching environments can be created, fluid learning can take place, the subject to be learned can be made more concrete, and an engaging and motivating environment can be created (Gürlüoğlu, 2019). The use of technology with education, which began with television in the 1950s, today, together with the developments in the Internet infrastructure and speed, but also with the developments in computer technology, makes it possible to easily access information in any environment, in parallel with the developments in computer technology. With advances in web technology, people can not only consume information but also produce it (Çelik, 2021). Web 2.0 tools are among the tools used in science education. It enables people using Web 2.0 tools to be involved in content creation processes (Akbaba & Ertaş, 2022). Thanks to these tools, students have come to the position of not only reading information, but also generating and sharing it. Today, web 2.0 tools are very diverse. Web 2.0 tools, which are emerging with rapid developments in computer technologies, offer interactive learning possibilities and allow designing learning environments and content independent of time and space (Çelik, 2021). In a time when we live in the age of technology, it is inevitable that students are relevant to technology and the use of technology in the educational environment due to the intensive use of technology (Erdoğan & Yıldırım, 2023)

BACKGROUND

Computer-Assisted Instruction

Learning is a process, and the more sensory organs are addressed in this process, the more students remember the information they have learned. With the rapid development of computers, learning environments have now become more effective with computer support. Today's computers have become faster, cheaper, and easier to transport than they used to be. In addition, storage capabilities and processing speeds have also advanced (Kayacı, 2023). It is conceivable to use computers during the presentation of content in computer-aided training in general. Computer software and content can be prepared in a virtual environment so that students can interact.

With computer-aided training, motivation increases, time is saved because the tasks that teachers do in a long time are done in a short time. Collaborative learning environments can be created with computer-aided training (Bediroğlu, 2021).

Stages of Educational Situations

Gagne, one of the pioneers of the theory of information processing, treats learning as both a product and a process (Özkök 2010). According to the model of teaching situations introduced by Gagne, educational situations are evaluated in 3 stages. Introductory activities include attracting attention, informing about the goal, motivating, reminding of prerequisite information. The development activities include information transfer, effective participation, return and correction, hint, reinforcement, monitoring type evaluation. The result is summarization, re-motivation, and closure within the scope of the activities.

According to Gagne, learning depends on internal factors as well as external factors. Internal factors are counted as previously learned information, cognitive strategies, and mental abilities. Gagne's Teaching Activities Model comes to the fore in the organization of the learning environment as a model conducive to planning the teaching process in computer and internet-based programs (Özkök, 2010).

Web Tools

The World Wide Web is generally known as the web and is used in our daily lives in the same sense as the Internet. But the web and the internet are not the same thing. The web appears as a system that allows people to communicate (İbrahim, 2021). Named the world's largest information medium, the web is a virtual environment where information can be changed and published with web browsers (İbrahim, 2021) Tim Berners-Lee designed the World Wide Web to share his work with colleagues in other countries during his work at CERN (European Center for Nuclear Research). In the last 20 years, there have been significant developments in Web technologies (Candan, 2022). The web adventure that started with web 1.0 continues today with web 4.0.

Advances in Web Technology

In this section, developments in web technology are described. Web technology, which started with Web 1.0, continues today with Web 4.0.

Web 1.0

It is the first period of development of the web. Web 1.0 uses html (Hyber Text Markup Language). With Web 1.0, users can passively use the web network without interacting with each other. With Web 1.0, a user reaches the information by searching and can only read it. The user cannot communicate with another user, make changes to the data. Web 1.0 has evolved with advances in technology, web 2.0.

Web 2.0

Web 2.0 is a name given to community-based and collaborative internet tools (Efe et al., 2022). The name Web 2.0 was used for the first time in a web conference organized by O'Reilly and MediaLive International in 2004 (İncekar, 2023). Web 2.0 differs from web 1.0 in terms of the technologies used and the people who use it. Because Web 1.0 is read-only, people are identified as visitors, and web 2.0 is defined as users (Incekar, 2023). Web 2.0 creates a user-oriented and share-based environment. During this period, an intensive flow of information is provided on social networks such as wiki, Facebook, Instagram, blog, Twitter (X), youtube. Web 2.0 is an internet service that can evolve the more people it is used by, sharing data from multiple sources, constantly updated with its participation architecture (O'Reilly, 2007). With Web 2.0, users have gained a virtual environment where they can create content, modify it, share their thoughts freely (İncekar, 2023). Today, with web 2.0 technology, we are presented with Web 2.0 tools, especially in the field of education. The operations that can be done with the computer thanks to the necessary software can be done easily with simple web 2.0 tools. These tools are usually available in free versions and are notable for the fact that they can be used from anywhere there is internet with different devices (computers, tablets, phones, etc.). Web 2.0 tools can be used in science lessons to attract students' interest, embody abstract concepts, simulate, measure, and evaluate activities (Erdoğan & Yıldırım, 2023).

Web 2.0 tools, which are often used in the field of education, offer students active experiences in the learning process. The web 2.0 tools available in each lesson also support the configuration approach (Çelik, 2021). Because content produced with Web 2.0 tools is easily shared with students and teachers, web 2.0 tools make a significant contribution to education in accordance with the collaborative approach (Arslantaş et al., 2022). It also allows content preparation in collaboration with the collaborative working environment. A study with Web 2.0 tools concluded that web 2.0 tools are easy to use (Gencer et al., 2023). It should be noted that there are various difficulties in the use of Web 2.0 tools by teacher candidates (Bower, 2007).

Advantages of Web 2.0 for Teachers

- Can create a meaningful learning environment with Web 2.0 tools, feedback, and an active student experience.
- The introduction of the lesson can be used in the development outcome stages.
- It can be used effectively in measurement and evaluation processes.
- Thanks to its dynamic infrastructure, web 2.0 tools can keep content constantly up to date.
- Does not require a high level of computer hardware.
- Does not require any software, content can be generated with a web browser.

Advantages of Web 2.0 for Students

- Web 2.0 tools can support students' technological literacy,
- Students can develop a product in a virtual environment with web 2.0 tools,
- They can learn in accordance with their own learning styles.
- By following each other's work, they can give feedback to each other.
- Through feedback, they can improve their products or become aware of missing learnings.
- It contributes to collaborative learning as Web 2.0 tools enable group work.
- Provides fun learning environments,
- Can contribute to the development of cognitive skills (Efe, et al., 2022)

Limitations of Web 2.0 Tools

- To use Web 2.0 tools, teachers must be trained in the relevant tools.
- Requires Internet infrastructure.
- While free use of Web 2.0 tools is possible, many of the advanced features are available for a fee.
- Web 2.0 tools often have a foreign language interface.

Some of the Web 2.0 Tools Used in Education

Web 2.0 tools that teachers can easily use for many lessons are presented in Table 1 using the relevant literature.

Table 1. Web 2.0 tools used in education

Category	Web 2.0 Tools
Website/Blog tools	Kidblog, Weebly, Wix, Blogger
Social Media Tools	Lesson Hero, Beyazpano, Edmodo, Eba, Classkick, Moodle, X, Facebook, Google Clasroom, Educlipper
Photo and Video Editing Tools	Adobe Spark, Explain Everything, Toondoo, Movenote, Pixlr, We Video, Youtube, Adobe Comp Cc, Screencast-O-Matic, Showme
Concept Map and Diagram Tools	Miro, Buble.Us, Cacoo, Popplet, Mindmup, Drawa.İo Midomo, Gliffy, Scribblar
Infographic Tools	Piktochart, Easelly, Genial.Ly, Canva
Word Cloud and Presentation Preparation	Wordle, Wordclouds, Worldart, Worditout, Way, Prezi, Nearpod, Emaze,
Animation Preparation Tools	Voki, Powtoon, Braınpop, Toontastıc, Explanıa, Tellagamı, Wıdeo
Video Production and Dissemination Tools	Khan Academey, Ted Ed, Youtube, Pindex, Voscreen, Spral,
Measurement and Evaluation Tools	Quizbean, Quiziz, Quizlet, Synap.Ac, Opninstage, Testmoz, Kahoot, Socrative, Quiznetic, Wordwall
Collaborative Working Tools	Sutori, Padlet, Remind, Deekit, Trello, Doodle, Bascamp, Gotomeeting, Meetinword, Zoom
Flipped Classroom Tools	Edpuzzle, Tes Teach with Blendspace, Vialohues, Plickers, Lessonpaths, Vıdeonot.Es, Blobbr, Drive, Dpopbox, Pixiclip, Wixer.Me
Game and Gamification Tools	Funbrain, Pixel Press, Badgestack, Creaza, Dustbin
Augmented and Virtual Reality Tools	Aurasma, Taleblazer, Blippar, Augment, Spacecraft 3d, Quiver, Second Life, Tincercad

Source: 101 Tools web 2.0, Pegem Akademi, 2019

As can be seen from Table 1, there are a lot of web 2.0 tools, and the number of these tools is increasing. Teachers need to identify appropriate web 2.0 tools and train interest with these tools so that they can integrate web 2.0 tools with their lessons (Steel, 2021). With Web 2.0 tools that can easily adapt to the lessons, the content of a lesson can be created, and favorable learning environments can be provided to it (Çelik, 2021). For teachers to benefit from web 2.0 technologies, they first need to be familiar with web 2.0 varieties (Bower, 2016). While Web 2.0 tools are easy to use, most web 2.0 tools guide users and facilitate content creation. There are also several training videos related to web 2.0 tools.

Web 3.0 (Semantic Web)

Web 1.0 presents itself as an integrated web experience in which web 3.0 machines can make sense of data, while web 1.0 presents itself as an integrated web experience in which web 2.0 machines can make sense of data (Candan, 2022). Can interpret by understanding machines in Web 3.0 technology. Blockchain technology, metaverse applications, artificial intelligence applications, smart assistants have entered our web 3.0 technology life (Kaplan, 2020) web 2.0 tools are evolving into web 3.0 technology together. Most web 2.0 tools have started hosting AI-powered applications in beta versions.

Web 4.0

There is no more precise definition of Web 4.0. However, with the development of Web 3.0, it is predicted that it could become a Web-based operating system. Web 4.0 correlates with Industry 4.0 (Ersöz, 2020).

Problem Status

How to explain the subject of eighth grade Science physical and chemical change using Web 2.0 tools?

Purpose and Importance of Research

This study aims to explain eighth grade physical and chemical change topic using web 2.0 tools using web 2.0 tools. In a study, it was determined that science teacher candidates experience difficulties due to the fact that web 2.0 tools are mostly foreign languages and lack computer skills (Erdoğan and Yıldırım, 2023). It is important that teachers and teacher candidates have basic knowledge in technology and have digital literacy in order to capture the requirements of the digital age (Arslantas, Tabak and Tabak, 2022). Improper application of Web 2.0 tools by teachers can generate negative effects in students rather than benefit them in the learning process (Bower, 2016). Teachers often have difficulty adapting to the rapid change in the web 2.0 environment and understanding the opportunities presented by web 2.0 technologies (Bower, 2016). Therefore, in this study, it was tried to increase the awareness of web 2.0 tools with various activities that can be done with web 2.0 technologies.

They Counted

It is considered that tools such as computers, tablets, smart boards, etc. which are a prerequisite for the use of Web 2.0 tools are ready and available. It is assumed that students have the equipment and internet connection necessary to participate in activities with web 2.0 tools.

Limitations

This study was limited to the subject of eighth grade physical and chemical change. This study is limited to the web 2.0 tools used in the study.

Definitions

Web: It is an information system made up of hypertext documents that are interrelated on an Internet network. In a simpler sense, the web is a network that brings together computers around the world.

Web 2.0: Technologies and applications in which users can produce and share content and whose active participation is ensured.

Computer-aided teaching: Computer-aided teaching covers many applications that computers can be exploited with different objectives in the educational process.

Web-assisted teaching: Defined as the use of web technologies in education, it hosts various web resources such as websites, web applications, and web-based educational systems.

METHODOLOGY

In this study, the process of preparing a guide material for the preparation of these events was discussed in detail by preparing various events with web 2.0 tools for the topic of eighth grade science physical and chemical changes. Prepared for Web 2.0 tools for the acquisition listed in Table 2.

Table 2. Physical and chemical change, subjects, and achievements

Unit	Subjects	Acquisition
F.8.4. Material and Industry	F.8.4.2. Physical and chemical changes	F.8.4.2.1. Explains the differences between physical and chemical changes by observing various phenomena.

In the process of event development with Web 2.0 tools, the primary science curriculum was examined, and literature review was carried out. The eighth-grade science lesson was planned as introductory events, development events, outcome events using the physical and chemical changes subject web 2.0 tools. Regarding the prepared events, first of all the web 2.0 tool was introduced, and the preparation stages of the event and the related web 2.0 tool were described in detail. Ease of use and familiarity are paramount in the selection of Web 2.0 tools.

Event Development Process With Web 2.0 Tools

In this study, the activity developed while developing content for the subject of eighth grade science in physical change and chemical change was designed in accordance with Gagne's educational situations. There are many web 2.0 tools available for content creation, and each stage introduces a different web 2.0 tool.

Figure 1.Gagne's stages of education

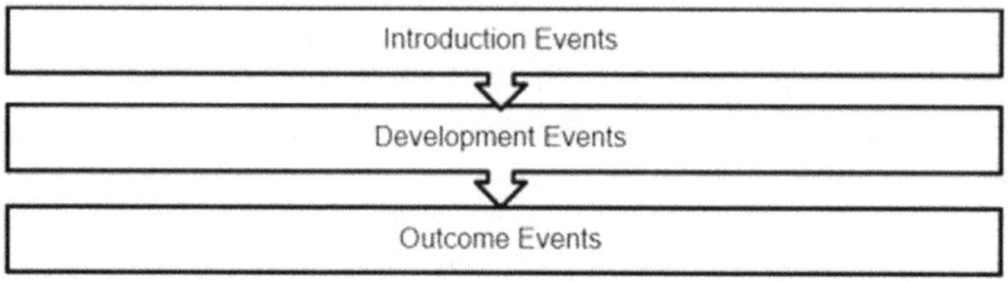

Introduction Events

According to the teaching situations model, introductory activities are activities carried out in the first phase of the lesson. These activities are presented as attracting attention, informing about the goal, motivating, and reminding of prerequisite information.

Figure 2. Introduction activities

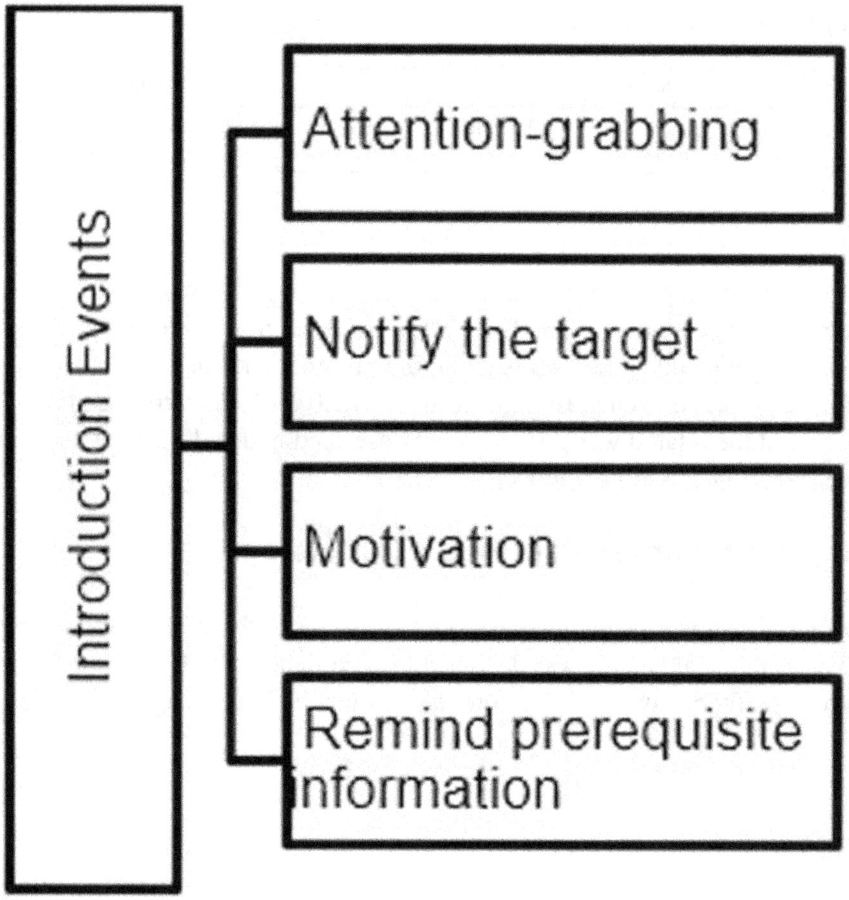

Introduction events can be prepared using Web 2.0 tools. Attraction is the interest of students by using an event, souvenir, question, cartoon, joke, joke, movie, picture, etc., when their teacher starts class. Informing the goal is telling the student what you will learn at the end of the lesson. Motivation is the student being told how to use the interests they have learned in everyday life. The prerequisite for remembering information, on the other hand, refers to information that must be known before in order to learn the current topic. In this study, Pixton and canva applications were used within the scope of introduction activities.

Pixton

Pixton is a design tool with graphic features and comics with which to prepare different lesson contents (Şahin & Erol, 2022). Pixton is available in free and paid versions, with educator and parent options. The Pixton tool includes a comic book maker, avatar creator, classrooms, staff photos, and content packs sections. It allows students to prepare comics by creating a class in the classrooms department. With Pixton, students' imagination can be developed, and their creativity supported. With Pixton you can turn a boring learning environment into a fun and interactive way of learning (Orellana & Mayorga, 2021). The cartoon was created with the Pixton app to draw attention at the beginning of the lesson on the subject of eighth grade physical and chemical change.

A remarkable scenario about physical and chemical change in grade 8 has been prepared and caricatured with the Pixton app. Caricature can be created simply by selecting the desired background, weather, characters, words, faces, objects, movements in Pixton application. Sharing, printing, voicing and some other features are offered in their paid versions. Pixton can be considered a useful tool because it allows creating cartoons or comics without requiring any software and software knowledge, without requiring high hardware features.

Figure 3. Caricature preparation with Pixton

Canva

Canva is a web 2.0 tool used to design graphics. A person with average knowledge of design can design various graphics with Canva. Canva stands out for its features such as a choice of over 100 languages, operation on all operating systems, ease of use, accessibility from anywhere (Gehred, 2020). It is enough to enter canva.com in the address bar of the browser to be able to access Canva. Canva is a web-based application with a Turkish interface. There are paid and free versions. The paid version offers more advanced options. While software knowledge and appropriate software are required to prepare engaging infographics, canva is a useful application in that it is easier to use and does not require software. The necessary corrections can be made in a simple way by selecting the appropriate one among the keywords entered in the search section and the templates. Teachers, students can create their own materials, share the materials they create, and download them with various download options.

In this study, a poster was prepared to inform the students about the goal related to the eighth grade physical and chemical change topic.

Figure 4. Preparation of poster with Canva

Development Events

Development activities include activities that will be carried out to achieve the goal. The presentation of the subject content takes place at this stage, active participation of students, hinting, reinforcement, reversal and correction are used, measuring evaluation activities are utilized to address learning deficiencies. In this study, quiziz, powtoon, wordwall, Miro, H5P and Lumi Education tools were used as part of the development activities.

Figure 5. Development activities

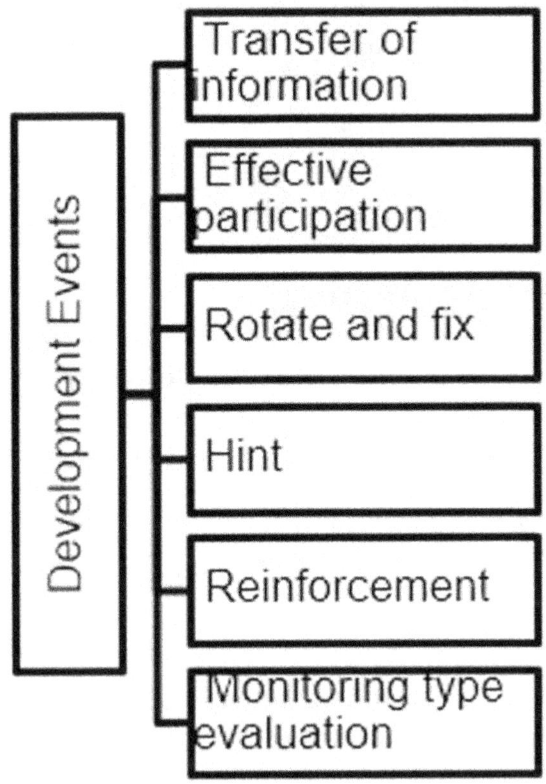

Quiziz

Quiziz is a web-based application that is used by teachers in measurement evaluation processes and to prepare impressive presentations. Quiziz can be said to be a useful and fun tool in learning processes (Değirmenci, 2021). The application, available at Quiziz.com, has a simple interface and Turkish language support. It consists of two parts as exam and lecture.

In Quiziz's quiz section, it is possible to create quizzes from scratch, text, by uploading documents and url. Some of these features are supported by artificial intelligence and are in the testing phase. Teachers can also share the tests they create with the students in a code in different formats, so that the tests can be completed by the students.

Slides can be created in the lesson section. Slide, text, media, shapes, tables are available from the menu located in the left section, images can be searched with its own image search and can be easily added to slides.

The paid version of Quiziz, which has paid and free versions, offers more advanced features. Content prepared by other teachers can be used in the Quiziz app. Quiziz is a very useful application for teachers in teaching science. (Darmawan et al., 2020).

An eighth grade presentation with the subject of physical and chemical changes with quiziz application was prepared.

Figure 6. Preparation of presentation with Quiziz

Powtoon

Powtoon is a transformative web tool for creating animated video content (Puspitarini & Akhyar, 2019). Powtoon is an application designed with the help of cartoon characters. With Powtoon, a student who does not have any knowledge of animation preparation can create an animation suitable for the lesson content. The Powtoon application can be accessed from the web address Powtoon.com. The Turkish language interface of Powtoon is not to be missed, which is easy to use. The lesson content prepared with the application of Powtoon contains cartoons and animations, which are important for the maintenance of the student's drawing (Puspitarini & Akhyar, 2019). The effect of animations is greater than that of pictures and visuals, also increases students' motivation for learning (İşbulan et al., 2019). Free and extended versions of Powtoon are available. Upgraded versions have a more phased feature. Animation, storyboard, content creation can be created. With Powtoon, lesson content can be shown to students in an interactive way, prompting students to convert their work into animations with powtoon. Students can develop their creativity while creating animations with Powtoon. Powtoon helps students create interesting learning materials. In this issue, students can be more focused (Susanti et al., 2020).

With Powtoon web 2.0 tool, you can create animated explainer, video, social media, character creator, whiteboard layout, screen slider, animated content.

Figure 7. Content preparation process with Powtoon

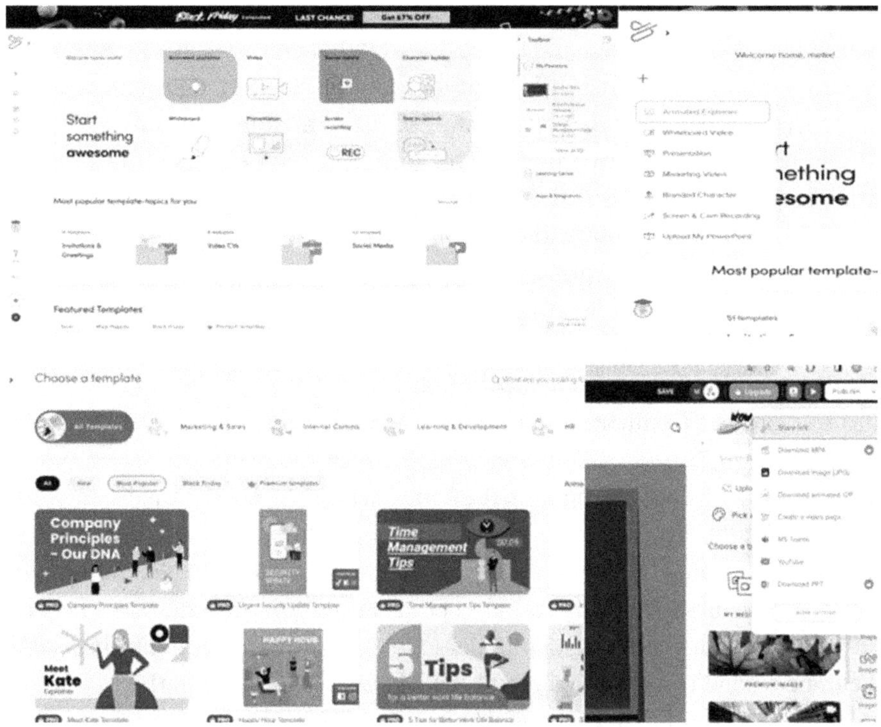

In this study, eighth grade physical and chemical changes subject content was prepared as animation using Powtoon.

Figure 8. Preparing animation with Powtoon

Wordwall

Wordwall is a game-based learning tool and a web 2.0 tool that contributes to creating student-centered educational learning environments that can be used at every stage of the course, including measurement evaluation processes (Novianti & Mufaridah, 2023). Available at Wordwall.com Interactive and printable events can be created with Wordwall. The ability to print events allows low-income students to do the activities without a device and the activities can also be played with the entire class using an interactive board, classroom computer, group or individual tablet computers (Moorhouse & Kohnke, 2022). Wordwall, which can be used from any device, has an easy-to-use interface that does not require software knowledge and has Turkish language support. Events prepared with Wordwall can be shared online and can also be used in the classroom environment with smart boards.

With Wordwall, a template is selected before preparing an event, wordwall has paid and free versions. The 19 templates of wordwall application, which has 37 ready-made templates, are printable contents. The templates available in the free version are limited. After the event is created, you can switch to a different template, so that the content remains the same, while increasing the interest of students in the course. Events prepared with Wordwall can be presented in different themes, with each theme changing graphics, sounds and appearance. Activities prepared with Wordwall can be shared with students in an interactive environment as homework. It can also be used by other teachers as a ready-made activity. Events prepared with Wordwall can be added to personal websites thanks to html code. Events prepared with Wordwall can be reached from anywhere in the My events section. In the My Results section, you can see the results of the activities shared with the students.

In this study, activities related to the 8th grade physical and chemical change were prepared.

Figure 9. Wordwall homepage screenshot

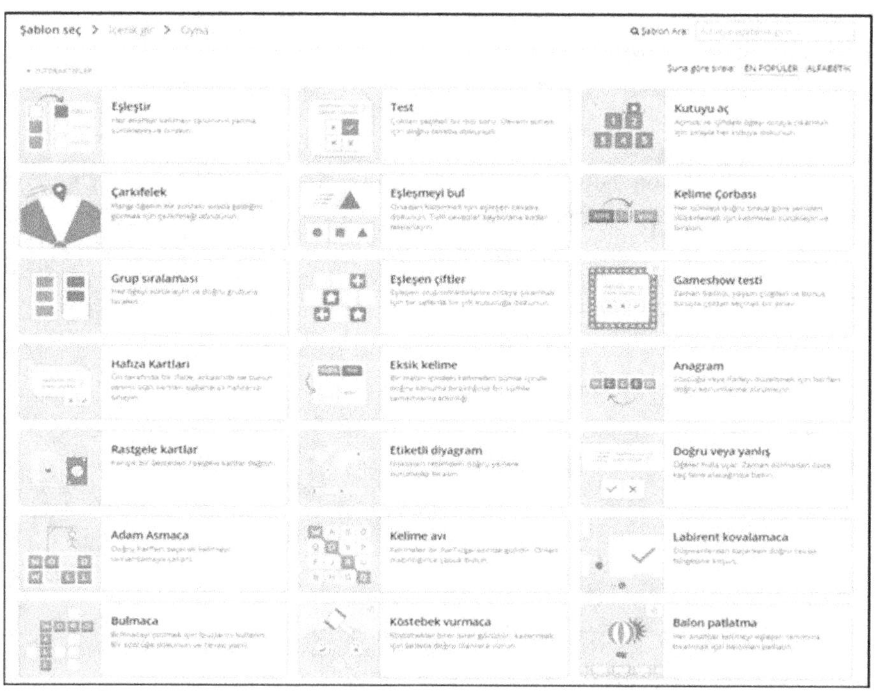

Figure 10. Wordwall content preparation templates

Wordwall event preparation process can be sorted into create event, choose template, input information about content, add images, finish and share.

Figure 11. Wordwall content preparation process

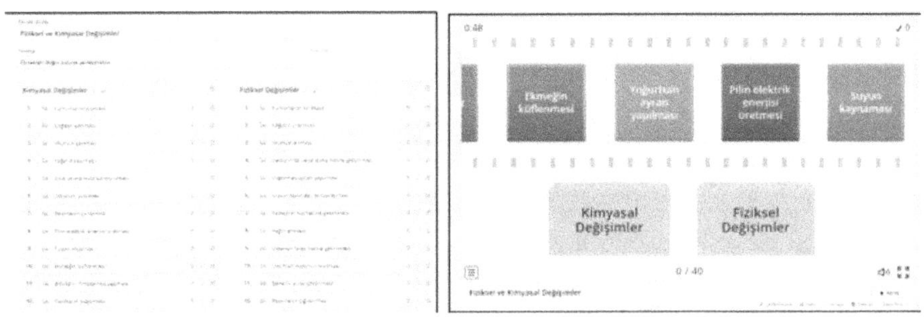

An interactive activity about physical and chemical change has been prepared. To prepare the event, after the user login is made, enter the Create event section to select the matching from the ready-made templates. Each event is written into relevant chapters to be matched with physical or chemical change. Content can be enriched using Wordwall image search or taking advantage of ready-made images. Finally, by pressing the done button, the interactive activity is completed.

Figure 12. Matching activity prepared with Wordwall

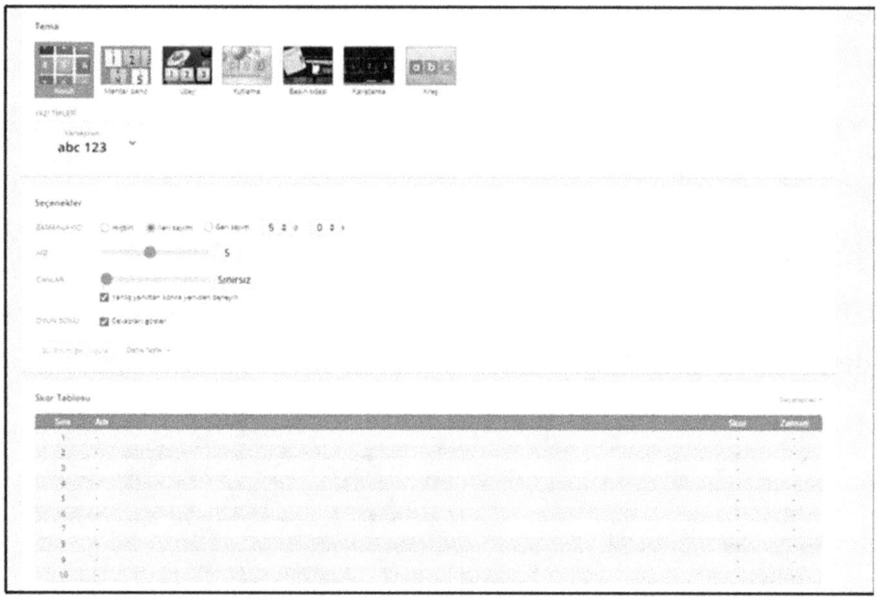

In the events we prepare with Wordwall, you can set the timer, forward count, countdown and display the answers at the end of the game, and also the score of the students can be monitored with the scoreboard.

Figure 13. The matchmaking activity settings section prepared with Wordwall

Activities prepared with Wordwall related to the subject of physical and chemical change can be used in the introductory, development and outcome activities section of the lesson. With Wordwall, events on different themes related to physical and chemical changes have been prepared.

Figure 14. Events prepared with Wordwall

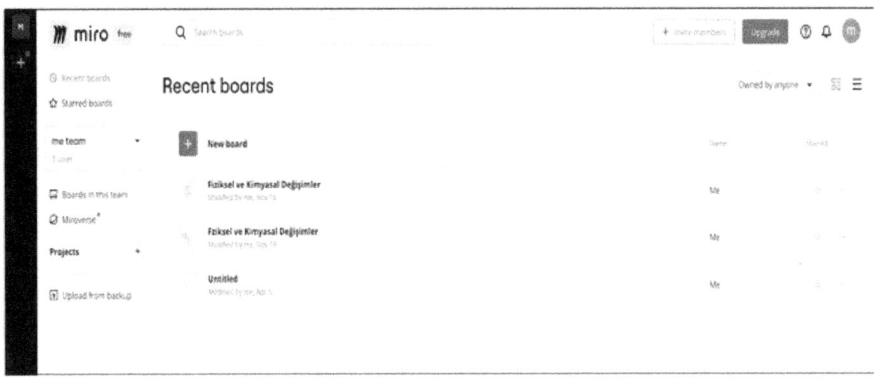

Miro

Miro is an online web 2.0 tool that can be used collaboratively for brainstorming, concept maps and workflows, accessible through web browsers, and downloaded as an application to a computer, tablet or mobile phone (Chan et al., 2023).

Concept maps are used to show the relationship of concepts related to a topic with each other. Concept maps developed by Novak in 1970 support meaningful learning (Kaptan, 1998).

Login is made at Miro.com. There are paid and free versions of Miro. The Miro app, which supports five languages, does not have Turkish language support. Miro supports teamwork, enabling collaboration over the web. It can be used for various purposes, such as brainstorming, idea development, research development. It can also be used in different fields, such as education, education, financial services, healthcare, industry.

The eighth grade concept map on the subject of physical and chemical change was prepared with the application of Miro.

Figure 15. Miro homepage view

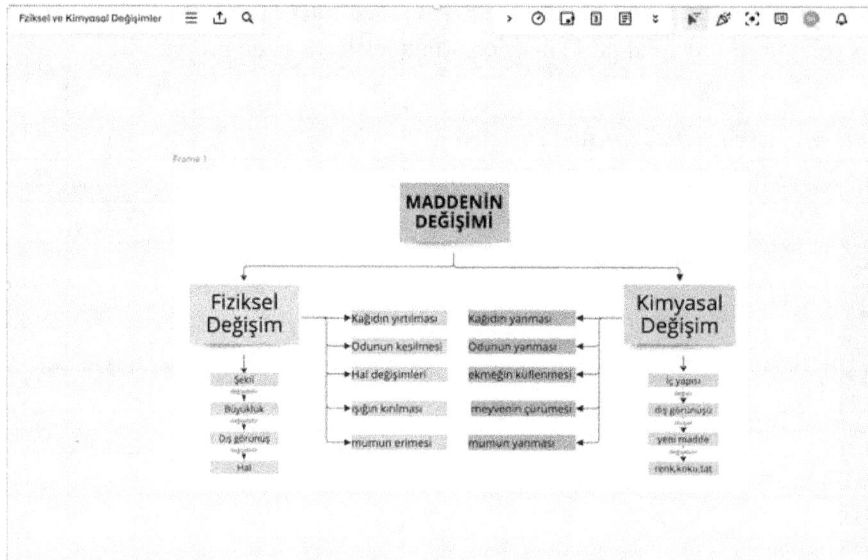

Figure 16. Concept map prepared with Miro

H5P: Lumi Education

H5P is a free script with open source code (Amali et al., 2019). H5P.com is reachable from the internet address. However, the H5P, which can be used through a scanner, can be used with the Lumi Education application. The H5P supports 4 languages, but the Turkish language option is not available, but it can be used in Turkish with the application of Lumi. H5P is a web2.0 tool that can be used to create impactful environments, engage learners, and master. With H5P you can create tutorials, quizzes, interactive videos, and content over the gibi 50. Those who do not have sufficient technical knowledge of H5P are required to prepare content for a lesson that does not have sufficient technical knowledge. Without the need for high hardware, users have access to content from anywhere. The generated content can be accessed from any location via mobile devices. The prepared contents can also be used by other people. The prepared contents can be viewed in a platform integrated form that supports H5P. The contents can be stored by obtaining results and statistical information. In the number of open source code, development by other users is obvious. H5P provides training in related content for content creation requests. The stages of preparation of content with H5P are generally given in the following figure.

Figure 17. Stages of content preparation with H5P

Activities have been prepared with H5P and Lumi Education related to the subject of eighth grade physical and chemical changes.

Figure 18. H5P.com homepage image

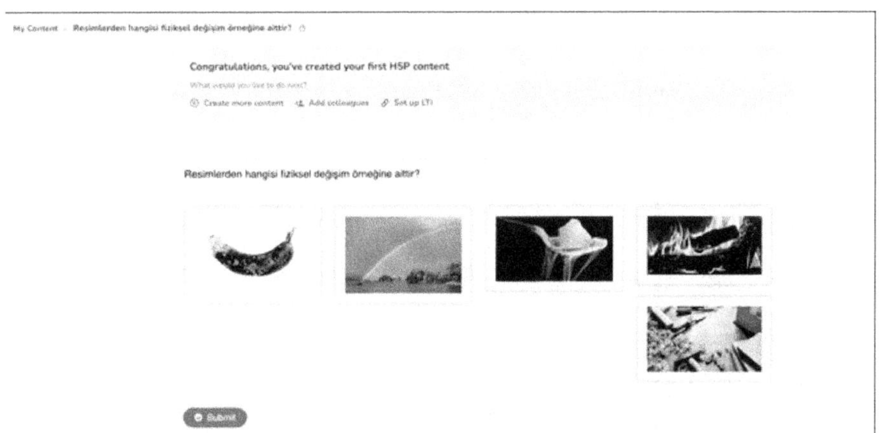

Figure 19. Let's find the physical change activity with H5P

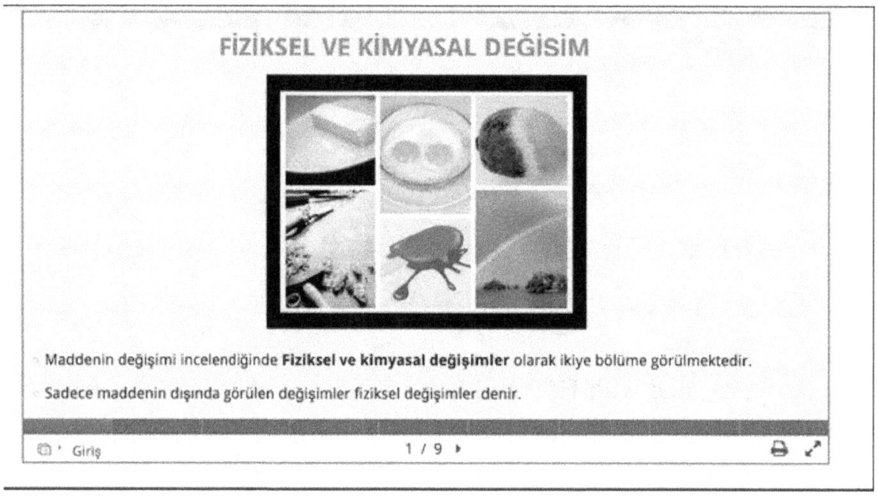

Figure 20. Physical and chemical change presentation with H5P

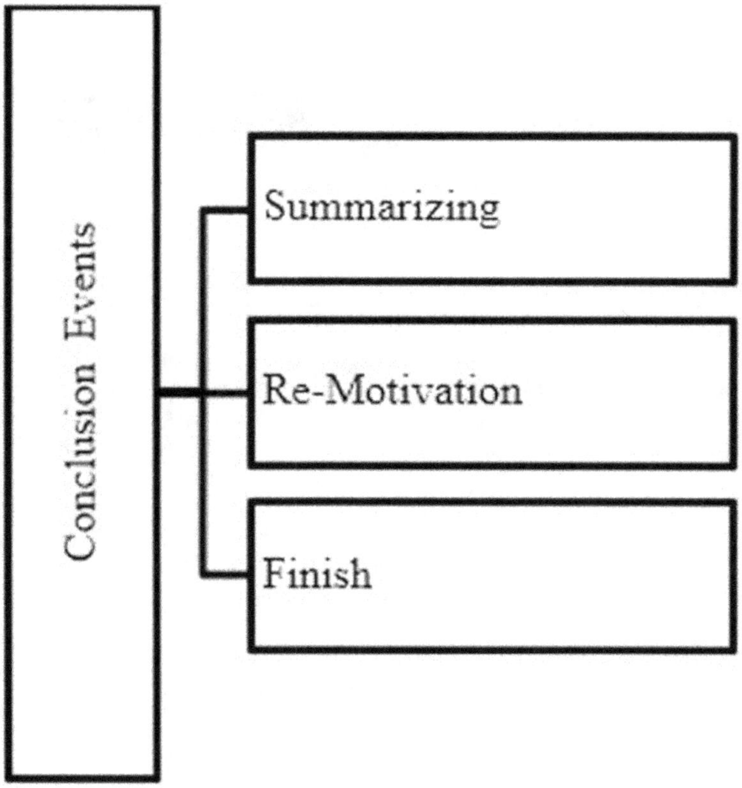

CONCLUSION EVENTS

Outcome activities are the section in which the important places of the subjects are indicated, the learning desires are continued against the learned topics, as well as the connection with the previous knowledge and the newly learned information. It consists of summarizing, re-motivating and closing sections.

Figure 21. Conclusion events

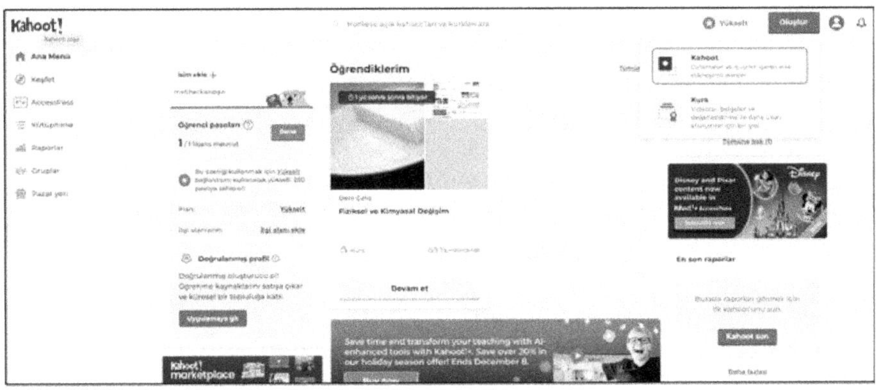

Kahoot!

Kahoot is a web 2.0 tool that offers fun teaching environments. It can be accessed at Kahoot.com. Kahoot! is available in free and paid versions, with limited content available in the free version. With Kahoot, mini-exams and questionnaires can be created, as well as course presentations. In the exam preparation section, there are options from exam creator, blank canvas and templates with artificial intelligence. In the presentation preparation section, mini exams, documents, stories, videos prepared can be brought together and a long course presentation can be arranged. With the Kahoot library menu, it is possible to access the previously prepared contents, the groups prepared from the group section, and the ready-made contents from the marketplace menu. In addition, it is possible to offer the contents prepared in the kahoot vehicle on the marketplace for a fee. Students do not need to open a user account to benefit from the contents in Kahoot, students can access the contents with the pin code given to them.

Kahoot is basically designed to present content in a way that can be of interest to students. A learning environment with fun content can increase students' motivation by providing a different learning experience to students (Yapıcı & Karakoyunlu, 2017). Students do not want to participate in activities that do not make sense to them and do not interest them (Ar, 2016). Kahoot also helps students focus on the content by bringing their content to the screen with impressive music. Increases motivation in students by giving feedback. Activities prepared with Kahoot can be assigned to students and can be implemented live at the same time. In Kahoot application, users can specify nicknames, so that a game environment is created between users, it contributes to motivation, and also contributes to learning with cooperation.

This section includes Kahoot activities prepared in relation to eighth grade physical and chemical change.

Figure 22. Kahoot homepage view

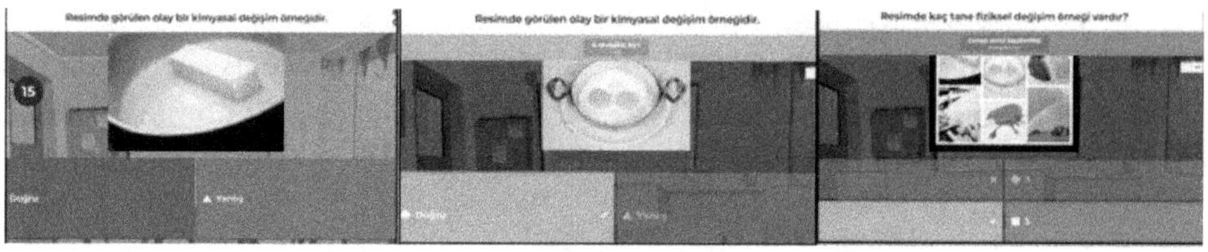

Figure 23. Correct or incorrect activity prepared with Kahoot

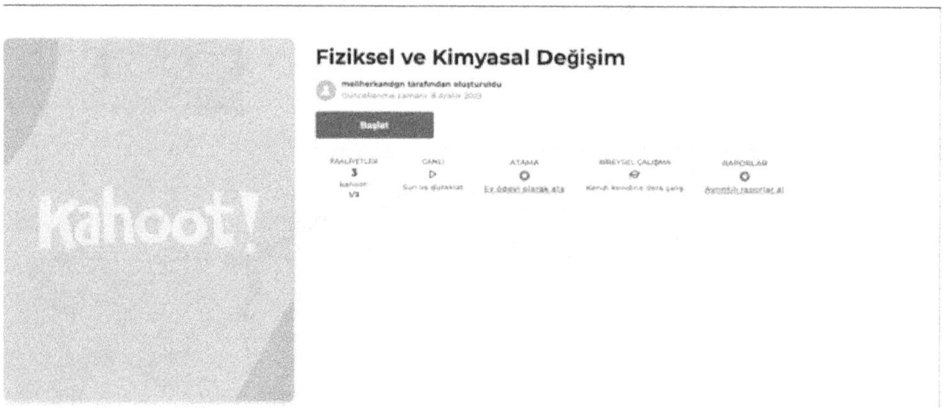

Figure 24. Event visualization prepared with Kahoot

FINDINGS AND COMMENTS

Today, the variety of Web 2.0 tools is increasing. Web 2.0 tools contribute to the permanence of learned knowledge in the realization of meaningful learning.

The most important benefit of using Web 2.0 tools in teaching activities is that it simplifies concept teaching (Erdoğan & Yıldırım, 2023). Pürbudak (2020) concluded in his study that web 2.0 tools are effective in consolidating the subjects and obtaining more permanent information. In their study, Erdoğan and Yıldırım (2023) concluded that as a result of the training given to teacher candidates on web 2.0 tools, their ability to develop interactive learning materials, their awareness of web 2.0 tools increased, their use of web 2.0 tools ensured permanence, and they realized the importance of web 2.0 tools.

Language is seen as an obstacle for preparing Web 2.0 activities. It is stated that there are few web 2.0 tools with Turkish language support. In order to overcome this situation, it was suggested that web 2.0 tools course should be given as an elective course at undergraduate level (Erdoğan & Yıldırım, 2023). The reason why teachers are reluctant to use web 2.0 tools is that they do not know web 2.0 tools sufficiently and have not received training on this subject (Alhassan, 2017). It is emphasized that the use of Web 2.0 tools in their lessons will enable teachers to allocate more time to students (Timur et al., 2020). According to the study conducted by Uçak and Saka (2022), the importance of web 2.0 tools is seen as contributing to permanent learning. In a 9th grade study on matter passage through cell membranes, it was determined that teaching using web 2.0 tools increased students' academic achievement and was an effective tool in permanent learning (Çelik, 2022). The use of web tools in science teaching ensures students' participation in the lesson and the permanence of learning (Alkan & Kurtoğlu, 2023). Web tools such as Wordwall and Scrath are useful for teachers in associating science course content with daily life (Altundağ Koçak & Koçer, 2023).

With the constructivist approach, it has replaced traditional teaching methods with a student-centered approach. Advances in internet speed, increase in computer use, widespread use of mobile computing tools have necessitated the effective use of computer-assisted teaching processes. Students are very interested in IT tools, and students who are introduced to computers at a very early age are interested in content developed with web 2.0 tools. Web 2.0 tools also include artificial intelligence-supported applications. In this way, it becomes easier to prepare content. It is a fact that Web 2.0 tools are developed by for-profit companies. A fee must be paid to use advanced features. For this reason, web 2.0 tools are designed to serve users in other areas such as advertising, marketing, as well as education-themed content. For example, it is possible to create an advertising poster with a tool that helps create infographics, such as Canva.

CONCLUSION, DISCUSSIONS, AND RECOMMENDATIONS

The topic of physical and chemical change in the 8th grade is explained with content prepared using web 2.0 tools. Web 2.0 tools are developing rapidly today and new web 2.0 tools are being released every day. Especially with the transition to distance education with the Covid-19 pandemic, interest in the use of web 2.0 tools has increased. While most Web 2.0 tools offer free basic packages, many are designed to offer more options on a paid basis. In this study, pixton, quiziz, powtoon, canva, wordwall, H5P, miro, kahoot, tools were used.

Within the scope of the research, sample materials were prepared using pixton and canva web tools for the introductory activities of the 8th grade physical and chemical change course.

The Pixton tool has been used in the preparation of conceptual cartoons. The conceptual cartoon prepared with the free features of the Pixton tool can be used in the introductory part of the course in order to draw students' attention to the topic. Conceptual cartoons increase students' attention and motivation in science teaching. Conceptual cartoons supported by Web 2.0 tools have been determined to be more effective than traditional methods (Can & Usta, 2021). It is also emphasized that comics made with Pixton web 2.0 tool have a positive effect on science course academic success according to traditional teaching (Arslan & Akçay 2022).

Within the scope of the introduction events, a poster was prepared using the canva tool. Creating a product using infographics in concept teaching is interesting for students to create a product using text and images. In this way, at the stage of teaching abstract concepts, the active participation of students can be ensured (Coruhlu et al., 2023). The Canva web 2.0 tool stands out as the most used web tool by teacher candidates (Saka & Uçak, 2022). The result that the use of the Canva tool in the learning environment improves student success reveals the importance of web tools (Maryunani, 2021).

Within the scope of development activities, events with quiziz, powtoon, wordwall, miro, h5p, Lumi Education web 2.0 tools have been prepared.

A presentation was prepared with the quiz web 2.0 tool with the subject of 8th grade physical and chemical change. With Quiziz, impressive presentations can be prepared from anywhere on the internet without requiring high hardware features with the help of web browsers. Quiziz draws attention because it is a web 2.0 tool that can be used both as a presentation and assessment and evaluation tool. Content prepared with quiz can be shared with students and feedback can be received. It can be said that the activities prepared with quiz are very useful, students can remember the information they have learned better, contribute to motivation, and attract the attention of students with features such as the result table (Agustia et al., 2021).

Within the scope of the development activities, an animation on the subject of physical and chemical change was prepared using powtoon web 2.0 tool. Animations are important in keeping students interested in the lesson. Powtoon is a web 2.0 tool that can be easily used by teachers and is based on animating individually created slides, it is interesting for students. In addition, content prepared with powtoon can be easily shared by uploading to platforms such as youtube (Indriani et al., 2023).

Within the scope of the development activities, seven game-based events were prepared within the scope of the development activities using wordwall web 2.0 tool. These events are the matching activity, crossword puzzles, drag and drop, learn with cards, anagram balloon popping, play time Links to these activities are presented in the appendix to the study. Wordwall, a web-based learning tool, contributes to students' meaningful learning by increasing motivation with entertaining content (Novianti & Mufaridah, 2023).

Within the scope of development activities, a concept map of the Miro web 2.0 tool was created to show the relationship between concepts related to the subject. The concept map can be prepared before the lesson or in collaboration with the students. The Miro tool supports collaborative learning, saves time, and allows the work done in the classroom to be displayed as a whole (Chan et al., 2023).

Within the scope of development activities, a Let's Find Physical and Chemical Change activity and an interactive presentation on the subject were prepared using H5P and Lumi Education. H5p is a web 2.0 tool that can be used for free. Since the teaching material developed with H5p contains HTML packages, there is no need for any software to use it. Contents can be accessed with a web browser. With Lumi Education, it is possible to develop content in places where there is no internet connection. In this respect, h5p differs from other web tools. Content prepared with H5p can be published on websites such as Moodle and WordPress (Avcı & Atik 2022). H5p attracts attention as a preferred web 2.0 tool due to its constant updating, simple structure, free use, no need for software knowledge and the large number of content that can be produced (Avcı & Atik, 2022).

Within the scope of the concluding activities, a summary presentation on physical and chemical change using the kahoot web 2.0 tool was prepared for summarizing the lesson, re-motivation and closure, and a true-false activity was prepared for measurement and evaluation.

It is noted that the use of kahoot practice for evaluation purposes provides motivation and increases students' academic performance. It is important to draw on the possibilities of Kahoot and similar game-themed tools to teach abstract topics (Mdlalose et al., 2021). Kahoot is effective in capturing students' attention with its rich visuals and sound effects. With gamified content, students' motivation can be increased. It is possible to use the kahoot tool at each stage of the course. Kahoot provides information to teachers by reporting the answers given by students. AI-powered content can be created. Students can access content prepared with Kahoot without having to sign up with a pin code. With Kahoot, an entire course can be created with introduction, presentation of course content and measurement evaluation activities. Kahoot can be used to guide students to activities suitable for them by measuring students' readiness at the beginning of the course (Gündeniz & Akkoyunlu, 2020). Kahoot stands out for its contribution to educational and instructional learning in the cognitive dimension, providing understanding and permanence of topics, its fun aspect in the affective dimension, its motivating nature and relevance to the lessons, and in the social dimension, by providing a competitive environment and providing an interactive learning environment (Candan, 2022).

Teacher candidates and teachers should be trained on Web 2.0 tools. It is necessary to introduce these tools to teachers with in-service trainings and to explain their ease of use. A course on web 2.0 tools can be given as an elective course in undergraduate education. Using web tools in undergraduate courses such as micro teaching increases the proficiency of teacher candidates in using web tools (Alkan & Mustafaoğlu, 2023).

It is important to provide ease of use and Turkish language support in the selection of Web 2.0 tools. In addition, what it offers in terms of free features in vehicle selection should be checked before use. For example, sharing or printing content prepared with a web 2.0 tool with students can be a paid feature. In such cases, the time and effort spent on developing content may be wasted.

With this study, it is aimed to introduce web 2.0 tools and to explain the methods of use in teaching processes. The study is thought to be a guide for teachers and teacher candidates.

In this study, the contents and links prepared with web 2.0 tools are given in Annex-1.

REFERENCES

Agustia, M., Aprilia, C., Sari, J., Hikmah, D., & Risnita, R. (2021). Using Quizizz in learning assessment with science literacy oriented in science learning. *International Journal of Engineering, Science, and Information Technology*, *1*(1), 86–90. doi:10.52088/ijesty.v1i1.213

Akbaba, K., & Ertaş-Kılıç, H. (2022). The effect of Web 2.0 applications on students' attitudes towards the use of science and technology. Erzincan University Faculty of Education Journal, 24(1), 130-139.

Akdeniz, A. R., & Yiğit, N. (2001). The effect of computer-aided materials on student achievement in science teaching: The example of frictional force. *Symposium on Science Education in Turkey at the Beginning of the New Millennium, Maltepe University, Istanbul, Proceedings Book*, 229-234.

Alhassan, R. (2017). Exploring the relationship between Web 2.0 Tools Self-Efficacy and Teachers' Use of these Tools in their teaching. *Journal of Education and Learning*, *6*(4), 217–228. doi:10.5539/jel.v6n4p217

Alkan, F., & Kurtoğlu, H. (2023). Computer-Aided Instruction in a Science Lesson Slowmation Development Study: Example of Phases of the Moon. In K. Walters (Ed.), *Dynamic Curriculum Development and Design Strategies for Effective Online Learning in Higher Education* (pp. 250–274). IGI Global. doi:10.4018/978-1-6684-8646-7.ch013

Alkan, F., & Mustafaoğlu, F. M. (2023). Using Web Tools in Lecture: Example of Micro Teaching Lesson. In R. Queirós, M. Cruz, C. Pinto, & D. Mascarenhas (Eds.), *Fostering Pedagogy through Micro and Adaptive Learning in Higher Education: Trends, Tools, and Applications* (pp. 261–286). IGI Global. doi:10.4018/978-1-6684-8656-6.ch012

Altundağ, Koçak, C., & Koçer, M. Y. (2023). Web 2.0 Tools Supported Innovative Applications in Science Education Based on the Context-Based Learning Approach. In J. Braun & G. Trajkovski (Eds.), Designing Context-Rich Learning by Extending Reality (pp. 179-204). IGI Global. doi:10.4018/978-1-6684-7644-4.ch010

Amali, L. N., Kadir, N. T., & Latief, M. (2019). Development of e-learning content with H5P and iSpring features. *Journal of Physics: Conference Series*, *1387*(1), 012019. doi:10.1088/1742-6596/1387/1/012019

Ar, N. A. (2016). *The effect of learning by gamification on academic achievement and the use of learning strategies by vocational high school students* [Unpublished Master's Thesis]. Sakarya University, Institute of Educational Sciences.

Arslan, K., & Akçay, H. (2022). The Effect of Science Teaching with Comics on Student Achievement. *Journal of Science Education Art and Technology*, *6*(1), 14–31.

Arslantas, T. K., Tabak, B. Y., & Tabak, H. (2022). Learning mediation via web 2.0 tools in the context of school health and safety. *Research in Pedagogy*, *12*(1), 127–146. doi:10.5937/IstrPed2201127K

Avcı, F., ve Atik, H. (2022). An innovative application in educational technology: The H5P project. *School Administrator*, *2*(1), 57–69.

Bediroğlu, R. (2021). *Self-competencies of science teacher candidates to develop digital teaching materials* [Master's Thesis]. Yıldız Technical University, Institute of Social Sciences, Istanbul.

Bower, M. (2016). Deriving a typology of Web 2.0 learning technologies. *British Journal of Educational Technology*, *47*(4), 763–777. doi:10.1111/bjet.12344

Can, B., & Usta, E. (2021). The effect of Web 2.0 supported conceptual cartoon on achievement and attitude. *Turkish Journal of Academic Publications*, *5*(1), 51–69.

Candan, F. (2022). *Meta-thematic analysis of the use of technology-oriented gamification practices in the learning process: kahoot*! Example [Master's Thesis]. Gaziantep University Institute of Educational Sciences.

Çoruhlu, Ş. T., Altunsoy, Y., & Sağlam, A. (2023). Infographics Influence on Students' Conceptual Developments: The Case of the Conscious Consumer. *İnönü University Faculty of Education Journal*, *24*(2), 1442-1466. doi:10.17679/inuefd.1213344

Darmawan, M. S., Daeni, F., & Listiaji, P. (2020). The use of Quizizz as an online assessment application for science learning in the pandemic era. *Unnes Science Education Journal*, *9*(3), 144–150. doi:10.15294/usej.v9i3.41541

Değirmenci, R. (2021). The use of Quizizz in language learning and teaching from the teachers' and students' perspectives: A literature review. *Language Education and Technology*, *1*(1), 1–11.

Efe, H., Gül, R., & Topsakal, Ü. U. (2022). Use of web 2.0 tools in science education: examining primary school students' perceptions on self-regulation. In *Elementary School Forum* (Vol. 9, No. 3, pp. 552-568). Indonesia University of Education.

Erdogan, A., & Yildirim, N. (2023). Evaluation of the Training to Make Preservice Science Teachers Use Web 2.0 Tools during Teaching. *Educational Policy Analysis and Strategic Research, 18*(1), 77–97. doi:10.29329/epasr.2023.525.4

Erol Şahin, A. N., & Kara Erol, H. (2022). A digital educational tool experience in history lesson: Creating digital comics via Pixton Edu. *Journal of Educational Technology & Online Learning : The Official Journal of the Online Learning Consortium, 5*(1), 223–242. doi:10.31681/jetol.983861

Ersöz, B. (2020). New generation web paradigm: Web 4.0. *Journal of Computer Science and Technologies, 1*(2), 58–65.

Gehred, A. P. (2020). Canva. *Journal of the Medical Library Association: JMLA, 108*(2), 338. doi:10.5195/jmla.2020.940

Gencer, S., Turan-Oluk, N., Kadayıfçı, H., & Yalçin Çelik, A. (2023). The Purposes and Justifications for Preferences of Web 2.0 Tools Used by Pre-Service Chemistry Teachers in Their Teaching Practices in Distance Education Environment. *Shanlax International Journal of Education, 11*(S1-Jan), 61–75. doi:10.34293/education.v11iS1-Jan.5908

Gündüz, A. Y., & Akkoyunlu, B. (2020). Gamification tool for classroom response systems: Kahoot. *Hacettepe University Journal of Education, 35*(3), 480–488. doi:10.16986/HUJE.2019052870

Gürlüoğlu, L. (2019) *Examining the effects of science teaching carried out with web 2.0 applications in accordance with the 5E model on student success, motivation, attitude, and digital literacy* [Master's Thesis]. Ankara University, Institute of Educational Sciences.

İbrahim, A. K. (2021). Evolution of the Web: From Web 1.0 to 4.0. *Qubahan Academic Journal, 1*(3), 20–28. doi:10.48161/qaj.v1n3a75

İncekar, O. (2023) *Kahoot Effect on motivation and student opinions with success in teaching English vocabulary* [Master's Thesis]. Ankara University, Institute of Educational Sciences.

İşbulan, O., Kaymak, Z., & Kıyıcı, M. (2019). *Web 2.0 with 101 Tools.* Pegem A Yayıncılık.

Kaplan, K. (2020). The impact of developing web technologies (web 1.0, web 2.0, web 3.0) on Turkey's tourism. *Safran Journal of Culture and Tourism Research, 3*(3), 276–289.

Kaptan, F. (1998). Use of concept map method in science teaching. Hacettepe University Faculty of Education Journal, 14(14)

Karahan, M. (2022) *The effect of simulation-assisted science teaching on the academic success of 6th grade students: Systems in our body unit* [Master's Thesis]. Akdeniz University Institute of Educational Sciences.

Mdlalose, N., Ramaila, S., & Ramnarain, U. (2022). Using Kahoot! as a formative assessment tool in science teacher education. *International Journal of Higher Education, 11*(2), 43–51. doi:10.5430/ijhe.v11n2p43

Mertha, i. w., & Mahfud, m. (2022). History learning based on wordwall applications to improve student learning results class x ips in ma as'adiyah ketapang. *International Journal of Educational Review, Law, and Social Sciences, 2*(5), 507–612.

Mone. (2000). Primary School Science Lesson (grades 4-8) Curriculum. *Journal of Announcements.*

Moorhouse, B. L., & Kohnke, L. (2022). Creating the conditions for vocabulary learning with wordwall. *RELC Journal.* doi:10.1177/00336882221092796

Novianti, F. A., & Mufaridah, F. (2023). Literature review: wordwall game application in English language learning to develop a disciplined character in the millennial era. In *Proceeding the Second English National Seminar Exploring Emerging Technologies in English Education* (pp. 29-34). Lppm Press Stkip Pgri Pacitan.

O'Reilly, T. (2007). What is Web 2.0 design patterns and business models for the next generation of software. *Communications & Stratégies, 65*(1), 17–37.

Ortiz Orellana, X. G., & Mena Mayorga, J. I. (2021). Pixton as a digital teaching tool to encourage the writing skill. *Ciancia Digital, 5*(3), 20–35. doi:10.33262/cienciadigital.v5i3.1621

Özkök, E. (2010*). The effect of Gagne's instructional software on the academic success and student attitudes of elementary eighth grade students in mathematics lesson on square root numbers and student attitudes* [Unpublished Master Thesis]. Gazi University Institute of Educational Sciences.

Şahin, A. N., & Kara Erol, H. (2022). A digital educational tool experience in history course: Creating digital comics via Pixton Edu. *Journal of Educational Technology & Online Learning, 5*(1), 223–242. doi:10.31681/jetol.983861

Susanti, V. D., Andari, T., & Harenza, A. (2020). Web based learning media assisted by powtoon in basic mathematics lesson. *Al-Jabar: Jurnal Pendidikan Matematika, 11*(1), 11–20. doi:10.24042/ajpm.v11i1.5308

Timur, S., Timur, B., & Arcagök, S., & Öztürk, G. (2020). Opinions of science teachers towards web 2.0 tools. *Kırşehir Faculty of Education Journal, 21*(1), 63–108.

Uzuner, Ö. (2018). *The effect of slow animation technique on secondary school students' achievements, scientific thinking skills and goal orientation in science lessons* [Master's Thesis]. Amasya University Institute of Science and Technology.

Yapıcı, İ., & Karakoyun, F. (2017). Gamification in Biology teaching: A sample of Kahoot application. *Turkish Online Journal of Qualitative Inquiry, 8*(4), 396–414. doi:10.17569/tojqi.335956

KEY TERMS AND DEFINITIONS

Computer-Aided Teaching: Computer-aided teaching covers many applications that computers can be exploited with different objectives in the educational process.

Web: It is an information system made up of hypertext documents that are interrelated on an Internet network. In a simpler sense, the web is a network that brings together computers around the world.

Web 2.0: Technologies and applications in which users can produce and share content and whose active participation is ensured.

Web-Assisted Teaching: Defined as the use of web technologies in education, it hosts various web resources such as websites, web applications, and web-based educational systems.

APPENDIX

List of contents developed with web 2.0 tools and QR code links

Content Name	Name of the web 2.0 tool	QR code link
Cartooning with Pixton	Pixton	
Preparing posters with Canva	Canva	
Preparing a presentation with Quiziz	Quiziz	
Preparing animation with Powtoon	Powtoon	
Pairing activity with Wordwall	Wordwall	
Let's find the physical changes event	Wordwall	
Drag and drop the correct answer	Wordwall	
Anagram activity	Wordwall	

Balloon popping activity	Wordwall
Playtime	Wordwall
Preparing a concept map	Miro
Preparing a presentation with H5P	H5P-Lumi Education
Let's find the physical change event with H5P	H5P-Lumi Education
Kahoot evaluation activity	Kahoot
Kahoot course activity	Kahoot

Chapter 15
Web 3 Privacy and Security

Puneett Bhatnagr
https://orcid.org/0000-0002-9281-1809
Amity University, India

ABSTRACT

In the rapidly evolving landscape of Web 3, where the very fabric of the internet undergoes profound transformation, the paramount significance of privacy and security emerges as the guiding light of this new era. This chapter encapsulates a multifaceted exploration of the importance of privacy and security in Web 3, delving into its historical context, technological foundations, challenges, and ethical considerations. From the retrospective examination of the web's evolution from Web 1 to Web 3, with its emphasis on decentralization and user-centric control, to the in-depth analysis of key technologies like blockchain, smart contracts, and privacy-enhancing tools, this chapter uncovers the critical infrastructure of a more secure and private digital world. The challenges and threats that loom in this decentralised landscape, from regulatory and legal considerations to security vulnerabilities, were elucidated, highlighting the need for transparent and ethical development practices. Real-world case studies serve as poignant illustrations of both the transformative potential and pitfalls of Web 3, providing valuable lessons for future research. In conclusion, the call for action resonates with readers, urging them to stay informed, vigilant, and engaged in the Web 3 era. Advocating for privacy, supporting ethical development, engaging in regulatory discussions, and actively educating and innovating are the pathways that contribute to safer and more private Web 3. In essence, this chapter is a holistic journey through the nuances of Web 3, underscoring its transformative potential and pivotal role of privacy and security in shaping a digital future that empowers individuals and safeguards their rights in the digital realm.

INTRODUCTION

The digital landscape has transformed through a series of evolutionary leaps, each marked by distinct shifts in technology and philosophy. The emergence of Web3 represents the latest chapter in this ever-unfolding story, which promises to revolutionise the way we interact with the digital world. In this chapter, we delve into the concept of Web3, explore the pivotal shift from Web2 to Web3, and underscore the paramount importance of privacy and security in this emerging paradigm.

DOI: 10.4018/979-8-3693-1532-3.ch015

To understand the significance of Web3, we must first establish a clear understanding of what it entails. Web3, often referred to as the “third generation of the Internet,” is a decentralised and trustless digital ecosystem. At its core, Web3 seeks to empower users with greater control over their digital life. Unlike its predecessors, Web3 is not controlled by a central authority, be it a tech giant or a government. Instead, it leverages blockchain technology to operate as a global, peer-to-peer network.

Blockchain, which is a distributed ledger technology, forms the backbone of Web3. This enables the creation of decentralized applications (DApps) and the execution of smart contracts. These digital agreements automatically enforce the terms and conditions of various transactions without the need for intermediaries, thereby fostering transparency and trust.

Web3 extends beyond blockchain, encompassing a range of emerging technologies, including decentralised identity, decentralised finance (DeFi), and nonfungible tokens (NFTs). These innovations collectively reshape how individuals interact with the Internet and transfer control from centralised corporations to users.

The Shift From Web 2 to Web 3

The transition from Web2 to Web3 represents a profound shift in both ideology and technology. Web2, the second generation of the Internet, is characterised by the dominance of a handful of powerful corporations that have become the gatekeepers of information and services. Social media platforms, search engines, and e-commerce giants have amassed enormous power, and they often wield them without sufficient consideration of users’ privacy and security.

Web3, on the other hand, seeks to dismantle this hierarchical structure. It champions decentralisation as an antidote to the centralised control exerted by Web2 entities. In Web3, individuals take the central stage as sovereign digital citizens with the ability to control their own data and online interactions. This decentralisation promises to break the silos that have characterised the Internet for years, reducing the monopolistic grip of major corporations.

Blockchain technology is a key enabler of this shift. The blockchain’s transparent and immutable ledger provides a foundation of trust that negates the need for intermediaries. This, in turn, facilitates peer-to-peer transactions and, most significantly, hands back ownership and control of data to the user.

Web3 also reimagines the way we view digital assets. NFTs, which have gained considerable attention, allow for the ownership and provenance of digital content, thereby creating new economic models for artists and content creators. DeFi platforms enable access to and management of financial services without intermediaries, making finance more inclusive and efficient. All of these innovations contribute to the dethronement of Web2 giants, redistributing power in favour of the individual.

The Importance of Privacy and Security in the New Web Paradigm

The concepts of privacy and security take new dimensions in the Web3 landscape. With great power over data, digital assets are responsible for safeguarding them. Let us examine why privacy and security have become paramount concerns in this emerging paradigm.

1. **Ownership of Personal Data**: Web3 grants individuals ownership of their data, but this also makes them responsible for their protection. Decentralisation of data storage implies that if users

lose access to their private keys, they may lose their data forever. This necessitates heightened data-protection measures and user education.

2. **Trust in Smart Contracts**: In a Web3 environment, smart contracts are at the heart of many transactions, ranging from managing finances to authenticating digital identities. Users must place trust in the code rather than in centralised intermediaries. Ensuring the security of smart contracts is a fundamental concern for preventing exploitation and vulnerabilities.
3. **Privacy in the Transparent World**: Web3's transparency poses challenges for user privacy. While transactions are recorded on a public blockchain, it is vital to implement privacy-enhancing technologies, such as zero-knowledge proofs and confidential transactions, to protect sensitive information.
4. **Regulatory Complexities**: The regulatory landscape of Web3 is still evolving. Legal frameworks vary by jurisdiction and governments are navigating how to address decentralised systems. This dynamic regulatory environment underscores the importance of understanding and complying with local laws.
5. **Protecting Digital Assets**: As importance of NFTs and digital assets increases, so does the risk of theft or loss. The security of digital wallets and asset management is paramount. Users must be educated on the best practices to protect valuable digital assets.

The move to Web3 promises increased empowerment, autonomy, and innovation. However, this is not without challenges. Privacy and security are fundamental to the success of Web3. Individuals need to be aware of the risks and be equipped with knowledge and tools to navigate this new digital frontier safely.

In conclusion, Web3 represents a fundamental transformation of the digital landscape driven by decentralisation, blockchain technology, and a renewed focus on user sovereignty. This shift from Web2 to Web3 empowers individuals but also places a substantial burden of responsibility on them. Privacy and security are no longer optional considerations but imperative pillars of this new web paradigm. As we embrace the possibilities of Web3, it is crucial to do so with a commitment to safeguard our data and digital lives.

Understanding Web 3: A Paradigm Shift in the Digital World

The evolution of the World Wide Web is characterised by continuous transformation and innovation. The transition from Web1 to Web2 marked a significant leap from static content to user-generated dynamic interaction. However, Web3 was the most recent and arguably the most profound shift in this narrative. In this study, we aim to provide a comprehensive understanding of Web3 by tracing the evolution of the Web through Web1 and Web2 and delving into the key technologies and concepts that define Web3.

Web3 is not merely a sequel to Web2, nor is it a buzzword. This represents a fundamental reimagination of the Internet, changing the way we interact with digital spaces. At its core, Web3 is a decentralised and trustless ecosystem that leverages blockchain technology and other innovative concepts to empower users with control over their digital lives. It is a movement away from centralised control and towards a peer-to-peer network.

A BRIEF HISTORY OF THE WEB (WEB 1, WEB 2, WEB 3)

Web 1: The Static Web (1990s)

Web1, also known as the "Static Web", marked the inception of the World Wide Web in the early 1990s. During this era, web pages were rudimentary and primarily composed of static text and images. Hypertext Markup Language (HTML) is the foundational technology used to create web pages, and web browsers such as Mosaic and Netscape Navigator have brought the web to the masses.

Key Characteristics of Web 1

- **Static Content**: Web1 is primarily characterised by static web pages that present information in a read-only format. Users can view content, but have limited opportunities for interaction or contribution.
- **Early Websites**: Early websites were text-heavy and lacked the multimedia elements that we see today. The graphics and animations were limited.
- **Limited Interactivity**: Interactivity was minimal, with basic hyperlinks connecting webpages. There is no concept of user-generated content or social interactions.

Web 2: The Social Web (Early 2000s)

Web2, often referred to as the "Social Web" or "Web 2.0," emerged in the early 2000s and represented a significant paradigm shift. This introduced a new era of dynamic, user-centric, and interactive web experiences. Key developments during this period included the rise of social media platforms, cloud computing, and proliferation of web applications.

Key Characteristics of Web 2

- **User-Generated Content**: Web2 brought about a fundamental shift by enabling users to create, share, and interact with content. Social media platforms, such as Facebook, blogging, and online communities, have facilitated this user-generated content.
- **Rich Multimedia**: Web2 saw the integration of rich multimedia elements, including images, videos, and interactive applications. This enriches the user experience.
- **Interactivity**: Websites have become more interactive, with features such as comments, forums, and online collaboration. Users can actively participate in discussions and engage with others.
- **Cloud Computing**: The emergence of cloud computing has allowed for the storage and accessibility of data and applications from anywhere, fostering collaboration and accessibility.
- **Web Applications**: Web2 brought the concept of web applications, with tools such as Google Docs, Gmail, and other cloud-based services that revolutionised how people work and communicate online.

Web 3: The Decentralized Web (Emerging)

Web3 is the latest generation of the Internet and is still in the process of being fully realised. This represents a paradigm shift from the centralised control of Web2 to a decentralised, trustless digital ecosystem. The core of Web3 is blockchain technology, which enables transparency, security, and user empowerment.

Key Characteristics of Web 3

- **Decentralisation**: Web3 is characterised by decentralisation, which means that there is no central authority that controls the Internet. Instead, power and decision-making are distributed among the participants in the network.
- **Blockchain Technology**: Blockchain, the foundational technology of Web3, provides a transparent and immutable ledger for recording transactions. This enabled trust in a trustless environment.
- **Smart Contracts**: Smart contracts are self-executing agreements written in codes operating on the blockchain. They automate processes and transactions without intermediaries.
- **Decentralised Applications (DApps)**: DApps run on a blockchain, offering users greater control over their data and interactions. They span various industries, including finance and gaming.
- **Cryptocurrencies**: Cryptocurrencies, such as Bitcoin and Ethereum, serve as digital assets and facilitate transactions within decentralised systems, eliminating the need for traditional financial intermediaries.
- **Decentralised Identity**: Web3 introduces the concept of decentralised identity, which allows users to control their digital identity without relying on centralised entities.

Web3 represents a fundamental reimagining of the Internet that aims to empower individuals with greater control over their digital lives, data, and assets. It seeks to address issues related to data privacy, censorship, and digital inequality, thereby promising a more transparent, secure, and user-centric online environment. While the transition to Web3 is ongoing, it holds the potential to reshape the Internet.

Key Technologies and Concepts in Web 3

Web3 is not just an abstract concept, but a collection of groundbreaking technologies and concepts that collectively redefine the Internet. The following are the core components that underpin the Web3 paradigm.

1. **Blockchain Technology**: At the core of Web3 lies a distributed ledger that records transactions across a network of computers. This technology introduces transparency and immutability, thus enabling trust in a trustless environment. Blockchains can be public (accessible to all) or private (restricted to a selected group).
2. **Decentralisation**: Decentralisation is the cornerstone principle of Web3. Unlike Web2, where a few dominant entities controlled the web, Web3 promotes a decentralized network where there is no central authority. Instead, power and decision-making are distributed among the participants in the network.
3. **Smart Contracts**: Smart contracts are self-executing agreements with the terms of the contract written directly into the code. These contracts operate on the blockchain, automating processes and

transactions without the need for intermediaries. Ethereum is one of the most prominent blockchain platforms and popularised smart contracts.

4. **Decentralised Applications (DApps)**: DApps are applications that run on a blockchain rather than on centralised servers. They leverage the transparency and security of blockchain technology, while offering users greater control over their data and interactions. DApps span a wide range of industries from finance to gaming.
5. **Cryptocurrencies**: Cryptocurrencies, such as Bitcoin and Ethereum, are a vital part of Web3. They serve as digital assets and can be used for various transactions in decentralised systems. Cryptocurrencies eliminate the need for traditional financial intermediaries.
6. **Decentralised Identity**: Web3 introduces the concept of decentralised identity, which allows users to control their digital identity without relying on centralised entities. This shift holds promise in enhancing privacy and security in the digital realm.
7. **Non-Fungible Tokens (NFTs)** are unique digital assets that represent the ownership and authenticity of digital content, such as art, music, or collectibles. NFTs have gained popularity in Web3 by offering new opportunities for creators and collectors.

Web 3's Promise and Potential

Web3 is not merely an upgrade, but a profound transformation of the digital landscape. This promises greater user autonomy, data ownership, and security. Owing to its transparent and trustless nature, Web3 has the potential to address many issues that have plagued the Internet for years, including data-privacy violations, censorship, and digital inequality.

Web3's decentralised model disrupts existing power structures and offers a path to reclaiming control over digital life. It fosters innovation and entrepreneurial opportunities, particularly in emerging areas such as decentralised finance (DeFi), blockchain gaming, and decentralised autonomous organisations (DAOs). Moreover, the transparent nature of Web3 drives accountability and trust in various industries.

In conclusion, understanding Web3 necessitates recognising it as a profound paradigm shift, not just an incremental advancement of the Web. It is a journey from static and controlled Web1 to interactive but centralised Web2, culminating in decentralised, trustless, and user-centric Web3. Key technologies and concepts, including blockchain, decentralisation, smart contracts, and cryptocurrencies, collectively redefine the digital landscape and offer unprecedented opportunities and challenges. Web3 is not just a technological progression, but a transformative shift that holds the potential to reshape the Internet and empower users in ways previously unimaginable.

Challenges to Privacy in Web 3: Safeguarding Digital Sovereignty

The advent of Web3 represents a revolutionary paradigm shift in the digital world. It aims to deliver a decentralised, user-centric Internet, empowering individuals with greater control over their data and digital interactions. However, as Web3 gains momentum, it also ushers in a new set of challenges, particularly in the realm of privacy. This study delves into the multifaceted landscape of privacy in Web3, emphasising the formidable challenges it poses, the indispensable role of encryption in preserving user confidentiality, the rise of privacy-focused cryptocurrencies and technologies, and the invaluable lessons learned from real-world case studies of privacy breaches and their far-reaching consequences.

Challenges to Privacy in Web 3

The transition to Web3 introduced a unique set of privacy challenges, setting it apart from its predecessors. The challenges are as follows:

1. **Public Blockchain Transparency**: The foundational technology of Web3, public blockchains, offers unparalleled transparency and immutability. While these attributes enhance trust, they simultaneously expose transaction data to anyone with access to blockchain. Maintaining privacy in a public ledger, where every transaction is visible, poses a formidable challenge.
2. **Decentralised identity**: Decentralised identity solutions promise greater control over personal data. However, their successful implementation must carefully balance privacy and security. Managing identity without compromising user privacy is a complex endeavour, as it requires robust protocols and user-friendly interfaces.
3. **Smart Contract Auditing**: Smart contracts central to Web3 must undergo thorough auditing for security and privacy vulnerabilities. Mishandled or flawed contracts can expose sensitive data or assets, posing a significant risk to privacy. The audit process must be meticulous to ensure that such vulnerabilities are identified and rectified.
4. **Regulatory Uncertainty**: Web3 operates in a rapidly evolving regulatory landscape. Balancing compliance with data protection regulations, such as GDPR, while maintaining the core principles of decentralisation and user control is an ongoing and intricate challenge. Navigating these complexities is vital for sustainable growth of Web3 without undue regulatory friction.

The Role of Encryption in Web 3

Encryption, often touted as the guardian of digital privacy, plays a pivotal role in mitigating privacy concerns within Web3:

- **End-to-End Encryption**: End-to-end encryption is the cornerstone of privacy in communication within Web3. It secures the transmission of data between users, ensuring that even the service provider cannot access the content of messages or shared data. Technologies such as Signal and WhatsApp implement end-to-end encryption, preserving privacy in digital conversations.
- **Privacy-Preserving Protocols**: Privacy-preserving protocols, including zero-knowledge proofs and homomorphic encryption, are indispensable to ensure that users can interact with blockchain data without exposing the specifics of their transactions. These technologies are instrumental in safeguarding transaction privacy and reducing the potential for data correlations.
- **Private Key Management**: Properly managing private keys is vital to ensuring the security and privacy of digital assets in Web3. Loss of a private key can result in permanent data or asset loss, making key management a crucial aspect of privacy protection.
- **Confidential Transactions**: Privacy-focused cryptocurrencies and technologies, such as Monero and Zcash, employ confidential transactions to shield the details of transactions, making them private by default. These technologies bolster transaction privacy and enhance user confidentiality by obscuring transaction amounts and sender and receiver information.

Privacy-Focused Cryptocurrencies and Technologies

Privacy-focused cryptocurrencies and technologies are emerging as potent tools for addressing privacy concerns in Web3.

- **Monero**: Monero is at the forefront of privacy-focused cryptocurrencies, employing ring signatures and confidential transactions to obfuscate transaction details. This innovative approach makes it nearly impossible to trace sender, receiver, or transaction amounts, thereby preserving user privacy.
- **Zcash**: Zcash utilizes zero-knowledge proofs to enable private transactions. Users can choose between transparent and shielded addresses, affording them greater control over their transaction privacy. This dual approach demonstrates the adaptability of privacy technologies within Web3.
- **Mixnets**: Mixnets, such as the Nym platform, aim to anonymises user interactions with the blockchain. By routing transactions and communications through a series of nodes, mixnets make it challenging for third parties to correlate data and activities with specific users, thereby further strengthening user privacy.
- **Decentralised VPNs**: Decentralised VPNs offer an additional layer of privacy within Web3. They allow users to route their Internet traffic through a network of peers, effectively concealing their IP addresses and enhancing their online privacy.

Case Studies on Privacy Breaches and Their Consequences

Real-world case studies serve as powerful illustrations of the importance of privacy in Web3 and the dire consequences of neglecting it.

- **De-anonymisation attacks on privacy costs**: Several instances have highlighted the risks of de-anonymisation attacks on privacy-focused cryptocurrencies. These attacks have exploited vulnerabilities to trace transactions and compromise user privacy, thereby undermining the essence of privacy coins. Case studies in this regard emphasise the need for ongoing research and vigilance to improve privacy technologies.
- **Data Leaks on Decentralized Networks**: Decentralized applications, when not designed with privacy in mind, may inadvertently expose user data. Case studies of data leaks in Web3 applications underscore the importance of robust security measures and privacy-by-design principles. They emphasised that the promise of decentralisation should not come at the expense of data privacy.
- **Regulatory actions and fines**: Organisations and projects operating in the Web3 space must navigate a complex regulatory landscape. Noncompliance with data protection laws can result in severe fines and legal consequences. Case studies of regulatory actions against Web3 entities serve as a stark reminder of the importance of understanding and adhering to legal requirements, while balancing privacy and innovation.
- **Blockchain Analysis and Deanonymization**: Blockchain analysis firms have developed increasingly sophisticated techniques to deanonymize users by tracing their transactions. The case studies of these analyses shed light on the vulnerabilities within public blockchains and underscore

the importance of privacy-enhancing technologies to counteract these challenges. The balance between transparency and privacy is an ongoing debate in the Web3 community.

Privacy is a fundamental concern in the Web3 era and is characterised by decentralised user-centric interactions and blockchain technology. Understanding multifaceted challenges, harnessing encryption, embracing privacy-focused cryptocurrencies and technologies, and learning from real-world case studies are essential for safeguarding digital sovereignty. As Web3 continues to evolve, addressing these privacy challenges will be paramount for realising the full potential of this transformative digital paradigm. Users, developers, and regulators must work collaboratively to strike a balance between innovation and privacy protection in the Web3 landscape, ensuring that the benefits of decentralised, user-centric Web3 are achieved, while respecting and preserving the privacy of individuals and organisations.

Security in Web 3: Safeguarding Decentralized Systems

Web3, the next evolutionary phase of the Internet, brings forth a revolutionary shift towards decentralisation, user empowerment, and transparency. Although this transition offers numerous benefits, it also presents a host of novel security challenges. This chapter explores the intricate landscape of security in Web3, shedding light on the diverse threats and vulnerabilities intrinsic to decentralised systems, essential security best practices for fortifying Web3 applications, pivotal role of decentralised identity and authentication, and imperative need to ensure the security of smart contracts through thorough audits and best practices.

Threats and Vulnerabilities in Decentralized Systems

The adoption of Web3, characterised by decentralisation and trustless interactions, ushers in a unique set of security challenges.

- **51% Attacks**: Public blockchains, the backbone of Web3, are susceptible to 51% attacks, where a single entity or coalition of entities gains control over the majority of the network's computational power. This can potentially enable them to rewrite the transaction history of the blockchain, thereby undermining the security and integrity of the network.
- **Front-Running**: In the context of decentralised finance (DeFi) and other applications, front running has become a concern. Front-running occurs when an attacker exploits price information to trade before legitimate users, thereby impacting the integrity of transactions.
- **Smart Contract Bugs**: Vulnerabilities in smart contracts can lead to significant financial loss. Issues such as re-entrancy attacks, integer overflow/underflow, and logic errors can result in exploits. Notable incidents such as the DAO hack serve as stark reminders of the perils associated with smart-contract vulnerabilities.
- **Phishing and Social Engineering**: Malicious actors can employ phishing and social engineering tactics to deceive users by revealing their private keys or sensitive information, compromising their digital assets and identity.
- **Decentralised Identity Challenges**: While decentralised identity holds the promise of user-controlled data, its implementation confronts challenges in areas such as identity management, user-friendliness, and protection against identity theft, thus demanding comprehensive solutions.

Security Best Practices for Web 3 Applications

To fortify the security of Web3 applications, developers and users must adhere to a set of best practices:

- **Code Auditing**: Rigorous code auditing is indispensable for identifying vulnerabilities and bugs in smart contracts and decentralised applications. Third-party audits and comprehensive testing are essential for preventing exploits and security breaches.
- **Decentralized Autonomous Organizations (DAOs) Governance**: Implementing robust governance mechanisms in DAOs can help mitigate the risk of malicious proposals and actions. Multisignature wallets, transparent decision-making processes, and dispute resolution mechanisms enhance the security of DAOs.
- **Hardware Wallets**: Users should consider using hardware wallets to safeguard their private keys and digital assets. Hardware wallets offer an additional security layer against phishing and malware attacks.
- **Multi-Signature Wallets**: Multi-signature wallets require multiple signatures or approvals to authorise transactions, thereby reducing the risk of unauthorised access to digital assets.
- **Web3 Browser Extensions**: Users should exercise caution when installing Web3 browser extensions because these extensions can access sensitive information. They should only be obtained from reputable sources and kept up-to-date.
- **Secure Development Practices**: Developers should follow secure coding practices, adhere to established security standards, and conduct thorough security reviews before deploying smart contracts or applications. Formal verification tools and static code analysis can provide additional security layers.

The Role of Decentralized Identity and Authentication

Decentralised identity and authentication systems play a pivotal role in enhancing the security within Web3.

- **Self-sovereign identity**: Decentralised identity empowers individuals with self-sovereign control over their identity information. Users can selectively disclose data without relying on centralised authorities, thereby reducing the risk of identity theft and data breach. Protocols like DID (decentralised identifiers) and Verifiable Credentials offer robust solutions in this context.
- **Decentralised Authentication**: Decentralised authentication mechanisms, such as the use of blockchain-based digital signatures and public-private key pairs, enable secure access to Web3 applications and services. Users can authenticate themselves without relying on third-party identity providers, thus reducing the risk of single points of failure.
- **Privacy-Enhancing Protocols**: Privacy-focused technologies such as zero-knowledge proofs enable authentication and identity verification without revealing unnecessary personal information. These protocols enhance user privacy while maintaining security and ensuring that sensitive user data remain confidential.
- **Immutable Identity**: Blockchain-based decentralised identity ensures the immutability of user data, reducing the risk of identity fraud and unauthorised alterations of personal information. Blockchain immutability ensures that once identity data are recorded, they remain tamper-proof.

Smart Contract Security and Audits

Smart contracts, which are the building blocks of Web3 applications, must undergo rigorous security measures.

- **Smart Contract Audits**: Third-party audits by reputable security firms are essential for identifying vulnerabilities, logic errors, and other security risks in smart contracts. Audits provide a comprehensive evaluation of the contract code, functionality, and adherence to best security practices.
- **Formal Verification**: Formal verification techniques, which involve mathematical proofs of smart contract correctness, can significantly enhance the security of smart contracts. These techniques help ensure that contracts behave precisely as intended and are resistant to vulnerabilities and exploits.
- **Bug Bounty Programs**: Developers can encourage a community to participate in bug bounty programs, rewarding individuals who discover and report vulnerabilities. These programs incentivise security researchers and white-hat hackers to identify and address potential issues, and enhance the overall security of smart contracts and applications.
- **Upgradable Contracts**: The ability to upgrade smart contracts is a double-edged sword, offering the flexibility to fix vulnerabilities but introducing centralisation risks. Developers should exercise caution when creating upgradable contracts, carefully considering the balance between security and decentralisation.
- **Immutable contracts**: Once deployed, they cannot be changed. Developers must be cautious when creating immutable contracts and should conduct thorough testing and auditing to prevent irreversible vulnerabilities. Immutable contracts provide assurance against unauthorised changes but also require enhanced vigilance during development.

Security in Web3 is a multifaceted challenge arising from the unique characteristics of decentralisation and trustlessness. To ensure the safety and integrity of Web3 applications and systems, addressing threats and vulnerabilities in decentralised environments, adhering to security best practices, embracing decentralised identity and authentication, and prioritising smart contract security are critical steps. Users, developers, and the broader Web3 community must collaborate diligently to build a secure and resilient ecosystem that leverages the advantages of decentralisation, while mitigating the security risks inherent to this transformative digital paradigm. Security in Web3 is an ongoing and evolving effort that requires continuous innovation and vigilance to provide a secure and trustworthy digital environment for all stakeholders.

Regulatory and Legal Considerations in Web3: Navigating the Evolving Landscape

Web3, a revolutionary evolution of the Internet, introduced a decentralised paradigm that grants individuals greater control over their digital interactions and assets. However, this transformation presents a complex array of regulatory and legal challenges that require careful consideration. This chapter embarks on an extensive exploration of the intricate landscape of regulatory and legal considerations in Web3, with a focus on the evolving legal framework, profound implications of data protection regulations, and the nuanced intersection between Web3 and government control.

The Web3 ecosystem operates within a dynamic and rapidly shifting legal framework as governments and regulatory bodies grapple with understanding and adapting to this transformative digital paradigm. Several pivotal factors have contributed to the evolution of the legal landscape.

- **Decentralisation vs. Centralisation**: At the heart of Web3 lies the principle of decentralisation, which challenges the traditional models of centralised authority. This shift necessitates the development of innovative legal structures capable of accommodating decentralised systems, trustless transactions, and autonomous organisations. The unique nature of Web3 demands the reimagining of traditional legal definitions and frameworks to align with decentralised principles.
- **Smart Contracts and Legal Validity**: The ascendancy of smart contracts and self-executing agreements executed on blockchains presents a profound challenge to existing legal definitions and interpretations. The legal recognition and enforceability of these contracts have been subject to continuous evolution and refinement. Legal authorities worldwide are actively working to define the boundaries of smart contract legality and are exploring frameworks that allow digital contracts to coexist within traditional legal structures.
- **Tokenomics and Digital Assets**: The proliferation of digital assets and cryptocurrencies within Web3 raises questions regarding their classification and regulation. Governments worldwide are grappling with categorising these assets as securities, commodities, or a novel asset class. The evolving landscape of digital asset regulation requires a flexible legal framework capable of adapting to the rapidly changing tokenomics and the emergence of novel financial instruments.
- **Cross-Border Nature**: Web3 operates on a global scale, transcending geographic boundaries. This cross-border nature challenges the traditional jurisdictional framework, leading to enquiries into which legal authorities have jurisdiction and how conflicts must be resolved. In the Web3 world, the concept of traditional territorial borders has become less relevant, necessitating international cooperation and the development of cross-border legal mechanisms.
- **Decentralised autonomous organisations (DAOs)**: DAOs, which are entities governed by decentralised decision-making mechanisms, introduce new challenges for legal recognition and liability. Defining legal responsibility and decision making within these entities is a complex and evolving process that necessitates careful legal consideration. Legal scholars and authorities are actively exploring mechanisms for establishing the legal status of DAOs and accountability of their stakeholders.

The Implications of Data Protection Regulations

The advent of data protection regulations, exemplified by the European Union's General Data Protection Regulation (GDPR), has exerted a significant influence on Web3 and its management of user data. Thus, numerous critical implications have emerged.

- **User Data Ownership**: Web3 seamlessly aligns with the principle that individuals are the rightful owners and controllers of their data. Data protection regulations reinforce this concept by granting users greater control over their personal information, including the right to access, modify, and delete data. The evolving legal landscape acknowledges the user-centric nature of Web3, in which individuals have sovereign control over their data.

- **Data Transparency**: The transparent nature of Web3 aligns harmoniously with the transparency and accountability principles of data-protection regulations. Users have the right to know how their data are processed, providing natural synergy with Web3's principles. Legal authorities worldwide are actively embracing the idea of data transparency, ensuring that users are well informed about data-processing practices.
- **Data Portability**: Data protection regulations often empower users with the right to port data between services. In the Web3 context, this translates to the ability of users to seamlessly transfer their data across applications and services, ensuring interoperability. This evolving legal framework acknowledges the importance of data portability and the need for interoperable data systems.
- **Consent Mechanisms**: Web3 applications must adhere to stringent consent mechanisms to process user data. The principles of explicit consent and granular control over data align precisely with the user-centric ethics of Web3. Legal authorities recognise the need for robust consent mechanisms that respect individual privacy and data autonomy.
- **Challenges in Deidentification**: Data protection regulations impose stringent requirements on the deidentification and anonymisation of data. In a Web3 environment, ensuring the complete removal of personally identifiable information is crucial for compliance with these regulations. The evolving legal landscape emphasises the importance of protecting user privacy using effective de-identification methods.

The Intersection of Web 3 and Government Control

The convergence of Web3 and government control represents a contentious and continually evolving domain that gives rise to several critical considerations.

- **Regulatory Clarity**: Achieving regulatory clarity is paramount to striking a delicate balance between innovation and security. Governments must provide clear and adaptable regulatory frameworks that promote responsible Web3 development and use while safeguarding the public interest. Legal authorities recognise the need for proactive regulation that fosters innovation while addressing potential risks and challenges.
- **Taxation**: The emergence of decentralised financial systems within Web3 challenges the traditional taxation models. Governments are actively exploring ways to tax cryptocurrency transactions, DeFi income, and other digital assets, necessitating the development of innovative tax frameworks. Taxation within the Web3 ecosystem requires legal authorities to create frameworks that can adapt to the dynamic nature of digital assets.
- **Censorship and Content Regulation**: The decentralised nature of Web3 challenges governments' conventional methods for regulating content and communication. Striking the right balance between freedom of expression and the need to prevent illegal or harmful activities is an ongoing debate. Legal authorities worldwide are actively exploring content regulation frameworks that respect freedom of speech, while addressing potential threats to public safety.
- **KYC and AML Compliance**: Governments are increasingly focusing on Know Your Customer (KYC) and Anti-Money Laundering (AML) regulations within the Web3 space. This requires decentralised platforms to implement robust measures for identity verification and transaction monitoring, ensuring compliance with regulatory requirements. The evolving legal landscape em-

phasises the need for robust KYC and AML mechanisms to prevent illicit activity within the Web3 ecosystem.

- **National Digital Currencies**: Some governments are actively exploring the development of national digital currencies, a move that significantly affects the use of decentralised cryptocurrencies within their jurisdiction. The integration of national digital currencies with Web3 introduces new regulatory challenges and opportunities. Legal authorities recognise the potential impact of national digital currencies on the Web3 ecosystem and are actively exploring the legal implications of these initiatives.

Self-regulation initiatives have emerged within the Web3 community in response to an evolving legal landscape. These initiatives aim to establish industrial standards, best practices, and codes of conduct. Self-regulation can play a pivotal role in shaping the legal framework and demonstrating an industry's commitment to responsible innovation. The evolving legal landscape acknowledges the importance of self-regulation as a means of promoting responsible behaviour within the Web3 ecosystem.

The regulatory and legal considerations in Web3 are multifaceted, intricate, and constantly evolving. As Web3 continues to mature, it will require a dynamic and adaptable legal framework that accommodates its unique characteristics such as decentralisation, smart contracts, and decentralised identity. Achieving regulatory clarity, addressing taxation, and defining the boundaries of content regulation are complex challenges that necessitate thoughtful and informed decision making.

In navigating this evolving legal landscape, self-regulation initiatives play a pivotal role in shaping industry standards and best practices. The future of Web3 relies on collaborative efforts between governments, regulatory bodies, industry stakeholders, and the broader Web3 community to foster innovation, while ensuring the responsible and secure growth of this transformative digital paradigm. Finding equilibrium between decentralisation, user empowerment, and compliance with legal and regulatory standards is a journey that will shape the digital landscape for years to come. The evolving legal landscape in Web3 reflects the dynamic nature of digital innovation, in which legal authorities and industry stakeholders must work together to strike a harmonious balance between innovation and security.

Privacy-Enhancing Technologies (PETs) in Web 3: Guarding Digital Freedom

The advent of Web3 represents a transformative shift in the digital landscape, emphasising the principles of decentralisation, trustless interactions, and user empowerment. The cornerstone of this paradigm is privacy, a fundamental right in the digital age. To safeguard this right, Privacy-Enhancing Technologies (PETs) have gained prominence, offering a diverse set of tools and techniques designed to protect and enhance user privacy in digital spaces. This chapter provides a comprehensive exploration of PETs, offering an overview of key PETs such as Zero-Knowledge Proofs, Homomorphic Encryption, and Mixnets. It delves into how these technologies can be applied within the Web3 context and provides illustrative case studies of successful PET implementation.

An Overview of Privacy-Enhancing Technologies (PETs)

Privacy-Enhancing Technologies include a wide range of tools and techniques designed to safeguard user privacy in the digital domain. Within this expansive landscape, several PETs have played a pivotal role in preserving privacy.

- **Zero-Knowledge Proofs**: Zero-Knowledge Proofs (ZKPs) are cryptographic methods that allow a prover to demonstrate knowledge of a fact without revealing the fact itself. This means that one party can verify the authenticity of certain information without being privy to sensitive data itself. A notable example of ZKPs is zk-SNARKs (Zero-Knowledge Succinct Non-Interactive Argument of Knowledge), which have been applied in blockchain systems. One remarkable illustration of ZKPs in action is Zcash, a privacy-focused cryptocurrency that employs zk-SNARKs to shield transaction details while proving the validity of these transactions.
- **Homomorphic Encryption**: Homomorphic encryption is a cryptographic technique that enables computations to be performed on encrypted data without the need for decryption. In Web3 applications, this technology serves as a protective shield for data and computation. For example, Enigma, a privacy-preserving computation platform, utilises homomorphic encryption to execute smart contracts while keeping the contract data private.
- **Mixnets**: Mixnets are systems that shuffle and re-route messages to provide anonymity to participants. These networks obfuscate the link between the sender and receiver, making it exceedingly challenging to trace the communication back to its source. Mixnets are extensively used in decentralised communication protocols, particularly in Web3 applications. A tangible example of a mixnet in action is Nym, which provides mixnet-based privacy for blockchain transactions.

How PETs Can Be Applied to Web 3

The application of Privacy-Enhancing Technologies in Web3 is both nuanced and multifaceted.

- **Decentralised Identity**: Within the Web3 context, decentralised identity solutions benefit significantly from the ZKPs. These technologies allow users to prove attributes without revealing them themselves. This enables secure and privacy-preserving identity verification in various contexts, from age verification for accessing adult content to KYC (Know Your Customer) processes in the financial sector.
- **Private Transactions**: Privacy-focused cryptocurrencies such as Monero implement ring signatures and confidential transactions, which are based on ZKPs and confidential transactions. These features obscure transaction details and enhance privacy in Web3's financial interactions.
- **Secure Data Sharing**: In the Web3 ecosystem, applications often require data sharing while preserving user privacy. ZKPs and homomorphic encryption enable secure sharing of data, such as medical records, without revealing sensitive information. For instance, MedicalChain applies a blockchain and encryption to protect patient data.
- **Privacy-Preserving Smart Contracts**: Privacy-focused blockchain networks such as Oasis Network incorporate PETs to enable privacy-preserving smart contracts. This allows for confidential computation and data sharing, while maintaining the privacy of a public ledger.
- **Decentralized Messaging**: Mixnets and other PETs are integrated into decentralized messaging platforms like Cwtch to ensure private and anonymous communication.

Case Studies of Successful PET Implementations

- **Zcash**: Zcash stands as a prominent example of a privacy-focused cryptocurrency. It leverages zk-SNARKs to enable fully shielded transactions in which the sender, recipient, and transaction amounts remain confidential. Zcash demonstrates the practical application of Zero-Knowledge Proofs in preserving financial privacy within a blockchain context.
- **Oasis Network**: Oasis Network is a blockchain platform designed for privacy and security. It incorporates secure enclaves and homomorphic encryption to enable confidential smart contracts and data-sharing. Oasis Labs demonstrated the practical application of Homomorphic Encryption and secure enclaves in Web3.
- **Nym**: Nym is a mixnet-based privacy infrastructure for Web3. It offers a decentralised and anonymous means of sending cryptocurrency transactions. Nym's implementation shows how Mixnets can be seamlessly integrated into Web3 applications to safeguard user privacy.
- **Cwtch**: Cwtch is a decentralised messaging platform that uses Mixnets to protect user privacy. By routing messages through a series of nodes, Cwtch ensures that the content and metadata of the messages remain confidential, exemplifying the importance of mixnets in decentralised communication.
- **Enigma**: Enigma is a privacy-preserving computation platform that employs a combination of secure Multi-Party Computation (SMPC) and Homomorphic Encryption. This allows users to perform computations on encrypted data while preserving data privacy, making it a prime example of PETs in action.

CONCLUSION

Privacy-Enhancing Technologies served as guardians of digital freedom in the Web3 era. Zero-Knowledge Proofs, Homomorphic Encryption, and Mixnets provide the tools and techniques necessary to secure data, transactions, and communication in a trustless and decentralised environment. These technologies empower users to control their digital identities, securely share data, execute confidential smart contracts, and communicate privately. Case studies of successful PET implementations such as Zcash, Oasis Network, Nym, Cwtch, and Enigma demonstrate the practical application of PETs in diverse Web3 contexts.

In the Web3 world, where decentralisation and user control are paramount, Privacy-Enhancing Technologies serve as safeguards for digital freedom. As Web3 applications continue to proliferate, the seamless integration of PETs is instrumental in preserving the fundamental principles of privacy and security that underpin the decentralised digital landscape. Through a harmonious blend of PETs, Web3 users can confidently embrace the digital future, knowing that their privacy and autonomy are safeguarded in the ever-evolving digital paradigm.

Web3 Projects: Navigating the Frontier of Privacy and Security

Web3, the next evolution of the Internet, promises a decentralised, user-centric digital landscape. The key to its success is protecting user privacy and security. In this section, we delve into real-world examples of Web3 projects that prioritise privacy and security, offering valuable case studies and lessons learned from successful and unsuccessful ventures.

Privacy-First Web 3 Projects

Zcash: Zcash, a privacy-focused cryptocurrency, employs advanced cryptographic techniques like Zero-Knowledge Proofs (ZKPs) to protect transaction data. Zcash's implementation of zk-SNARKs allows for fully shielded transactions, where sender, recipient, and amount remain confidential. This project highlights how privacy-enhancing technologies can be effectively integrated into a blockchain, setting a high standard for financial privacy within the Web3 ecosystem.

- **Lessons Learned**: Zcash's success underscores the importance of privacy in digital transactions. The user demand for confidentiality is a powerful driver of Web3 projects. The effective implementation of privacy-enhancing technologies is key, but regulatory compliance and user adoption remain challenges.

Oasis Network: The Oasis Network aims to provide a secure and private platform for decentralised applications. It leverages Homomorphic Encryption and secure enclaves to enable confidential smart contracts and data-sharing. The approach of Oasis Labs showcases how Encryption can be used to protect sensitive data while maintaining the advantages of a public blockchain.

- **Lessons Learned**: The Oasis Network's endeavour highlights the potential of combining security and privacy in Web3 applications. This emphasises the importance of transparent and efficient encryption methods, as well as secure enclaves, in maintaining user trust. Collaboration with other projects is crucial for promoting interoperability.

Nym: Nym, a privacy infrastructure for Web3, provides decentralised and anonymous means of sending cryptocurrency transactions. It employs mixnets to protect the user privacy. Nym's commitment to decentralisation and privacy in communication exemplifies Mixnets' power in safeguarding user anonymity.

- **Lessons Learned**: Nym's project showcases the potential of Mixnets to secure decentralised communication. This emphasises that user privacy is a fundamental concern within the Web3 space. The challenges include routing efficiency, scalability, and incentivising participation in the network.

Monero: Monero is another privacy-focused cryptocurrency that uses ring signatures and confidential transactions to obscure transaction details, including sender, recipient, and amount. This exemplifies the robust application of privately focused features in Web3.

- **Lessons Learned**: Monero's success highlights the importance of providing users with strong privacy options. It also emphasises the challenge of balancing privacy with regulatory compliance because privacy features can make some authorities uneasy.

Security-Centric Web 3 Projects

Chainlink: Chainlink focuses on decentralised oracles that facilitate data transfer between blockchain smart contracts and external sources. Its success is based on a strong emphasis on security through decentralisation. By using multiple nodes to fetch and validate data, Chainlink prevents a single point of failure.

- **Lessons Learned**: Chainlink's journey teaches us that security is paramount in Web3 projects. Decentralisation is a key strategy to prevent vulnerabilities. However, this also highlights the need for comprehensive security audits and continuous vigilance to maintain a robust system.

Avalanche: An avalanche is a platform for creating custom blockchains and decentralised applications. This emphasises the importance of network security. Avalanche uses a unique consensus algorithm that divides nodes into multiple subnets, thereby enabling more efficient parallel processing and greater security.

- **Lessons Learned**: Avalanche's innovative consensus mechanism showcases the significance of security-focused innovations in the Web3 ecosystem. While introducing new concepts can enhance security, they should undergo rigorous testing and evaluation to ensure that they function as intended.

Polkadot: Polkadot introduced a novel approach for interoperability by connecting various blockchains. It prioritises security through its relay chain and parachain structure, allowing customisable and secure connections between the blockchains.

- **Lessons Learned**: Polkadot illustrates the importance of secure interoperability solutions in the Web3 environment. However, this also highlights the complexity of implementing and maintaining such networks. Comprehensive security measures are vital, particularly when connecting multiple blockchains.

Tezos: Tezos is a blockchain platform that places strong emphasis on security and upgradability. This allows for on-chain governance, enabling the network to evolve without hard forks. Tezos demonstrated the importance of flexibility in maintaining secure and adaptable blockchains.

- **Lessons Learned**: Tezos' on-chain governance mechanism highlights the significance of adaptability in Web3 projects. Security is not just about the present; it is also about ensuring future resilience and evolution of the system.

Unsuccessful Endeavors and Their Lessons

The decentralised autonomous organization (DAO) is a promising project but suffers from a critical security breach due to vulnerabilities in its smart contract code. It was a stark reminder that even in a decentralised environment, code quality and security audits were paramount.

- **Lessons Learned**: The DAO's collapse emphasises the necessity of rigorous code audits and the importance of transparency in smart contract development. This shows that, while decentralisation offers many advantages, it does not negate the need for robust security practices.

Parity Multi-Sig Wallet: Parity, a blockchain technology company, faced multiple security breaches, resulting in the loss of significant cryptocurrency funds. These incidents highlighted the critical role of secure key management in Web3 projects.

- **Lessons Learned**: Parity's security incidents underscore the importance of rigorous security measures, including secure key storage and recovery mechanisms. Effective security education for users is crucial for preventing losses.

QuadrigaCX: QuadrigaCX is a Canadian cryptocurrency exchange that faced insolvency after the sudden death of its founder and CEO, who was the sole holder of the exchange's private keys. This incident underlines the critical importance of secure key management, transparency, and legal compliance.

- Lessons Learned: QuadrigaCX's tragic story highlights the need for transparent key management practices, including contingency planning for the unexpected. This also emphasises the significance of regulatory compliance in exchange spaces.

Real-world examples of Web3 projects that focus on privacy and security reveal essential lessons for the future. Successful projects such as Zcash, Oasis Network, Nym, Monero, Chainlink, Avalanche, Polkadot, and Tezos demonstrate the potential of privacy-enhancing technologies and security-focused innovations in the Web3 ecosystem. These case studies emphasise the significance of user demand, need for robust privacy-enhancing technologies, transparent encryption methods, secure key management, and importance of interoperability.

Even unsuccessful endeavours such as The DAO, Parity Multi-Sig Wallet, and QuadrigaCX provide valuable lessons. They highlighted the importance of rigorous code audits, secure key management, security education for users, transparency, and regulatory compliance. These case studies remind us that in a Web3 environment, while decentralisation brings significant advantages, security remains a critical concern.

In navigating the Web3 frontier, these case studies and their lessons serve as beacons, illuminating the path to a decentralised, secure, and privately focused digital future. Web3 projects must draw upon the wisdom gleaned from both successes and failures to chart a course that truly safeguards user privacy and security in an evolving digital paradigm. As the Web3 ecosystem continues to expand, commitment to privacy and security remains paramount, ensuring that the principles of a user-centric, decentralised Internet are upheld.

The Future of Web 3 Privacy and Security: Empowering Individuals in a Decentralized Era

As Web3 continues to gain momentum, it is evolving into a groundbreaking paradigm that places privacy, security, and user empowerment at its forefront. In this section, we explore the future of Web3 privacy and security, predict the evolving landscape, and discuss how Web3 has the potential to empower individuals to control their data. We also consider the ethical considerations that must guide the development of Web3 to ensure that it aligns with our values and principles.

The Future of Web 3 Privacy and Security

There are several promising developments in the future of Web3 privacy and security.

1. **Privacy-Preserving Protocols**: The adoption of privacy-preserving protocols will continue to increase. Projects are increasingly implementing Zero-Knowledge Proofs (ZKPs), Homomorphic Encryption, and Mixnets to ensure that user data remain confidential. These protocols can be extended to decentralised identity solutions, making it possible to verify user attributes without revealing the actual attributes themselves.
2. **Enhanced Smart Contract Security**: Smart contracts will undergo major overhaul in terms of security. Formal verification methods are widely employed to ensure that self-executing agreements are free from vulnerabilities. Security audits and bug bounties will become standard practices, thereby significantly reducing the risk of exploitable flaws in smart contracts.
3. **Decentralised identity revolution**: Decentralised identity systems become the norm, giving individuals complete control over their personal information. Users have the power to selectively share attributes with service providers while keeping other information private. This will not only enhance security, but also reduce reliance on centralised identity providers.
4. **Secure Data Marketplaces**: Web3 fosters the development of secure data marketplaces where individuals can choose to monetise their data while maintaining strict control over its usage. Users are able to define who has access to their data and under what circumstances.
5. **Privacy-Preserving Tokens**: Privacy-focused cryptocurrencies, such as Monero and Zcash, will continue to gain popularity. These cryptocurrencies provide the robust privacy features that are essential for transactions in a decentralised economy.
6. **Federated Learning**: In Web3, federated learning becomes a key component of privacy-conscious data analysis. This approach allows machine-learning models to be trained on decentralised data sources without the data itself, leaving the control of the user.

Predictions and Trends in Web 3

Several trends and predictions have shaped the Web3 landscape.

1. **Interoperability**: Web3 networks will increasingly strive for interoperability, enabling seamless communication between different blockchains and protocols. Cross-chain integration will become a common practice, allowing assets and data to move rapidly between different Web3 platforms.
2. **User-Centric Data Control**: The concept of "self-sovereign identity" will gain traction, allowing users to control their digital identities and personal data. This will not only empower individuals, but also disrupt the current data broker model, where centralised entities profit from the sale of personal information.
3. **Regulatory Evolution**: Governments and regulatory bodies will work to establish a framework for Web3 technologies. This complex and evolving process is driven by the need to balance inno-

vation and privacy with legal and regulatory requirements. There will be a push for more flexible regulations that can adapt to rapid changes in the Web3 space.

4. **Privacy by Default**: Web3 applications adopt privacy by default as a standard, ensuring that user data remain private unless explicitly shared. Transparency in data usage and policies will become a crucial part of these applications. Users are informed about the data they generate and how they are used, giving them greater control and insight into their digital footprint.
5. **Ethical Development**: The ethical development of Web3 will gain prominence. Developers and project leaders will be held accountable for the ethical implications of their work, including issues related to data privacy, security, and inclusivity. There is a growing emphasis on open-source development and community-driven governance in Web3 projects.

The Potential for Web 3 to Empower Individuals in Controlling Their Data

Web3 has the immense potential to empower individuals by putting them in controlling their data.

1. **Self-Sovereign Identity:** Individuals have the freedom to own, manage, and share their digital identities. This eliminates the need for centralised identity providers, thereby reducing the risk of identity theft and data breaches. Users will have portable identities that they can use across various Web3 platforms.
2. **Data monetisation:** Web3 enables users to monetise their data directly. Rather than having data brokers profit from personal information, individuals are compensated for allowing limited and consent-based access to their data. Users can set the terms and conditions for sharing their data, thereby ensuring that their privacy is respected and rewarded.
3. **Privacy-Centric Economies:** Web3 paves the way for privacy-centric economies, where individuals can participate in transactions and interactions with confidence in the security of their personal information. This can extend to financial transactions, healthcare data sharing, etc. Users will be assured that their sensitive information is protected and not exploited.
4. **User-Centric Applications:** Web3 applications are designed with the user in mind. These applications prioritise data privacy, security, and transparency, giving individuals assurance that their personal information is respected. Users have granular control over their data and can choose how, when, and with whom to share it.

Ethical Considerations in the Development of Web 3

The development of Web3 has brought forth several ethical considerations.

1. **Data Ownership:** Developers and organisations must respect the principle that individuals own their data. Data collection and use should be based on clear and informed consent, with users having the ability to revoke access or delete their data. Developers must create mechanisms that allow users to maintain control over their data even when it's used in various Web3 applications.
2. **Inclusivity:** Efforts should be made to ensure that Web3 technologies are both accessible and inclusive. Developers must consider the needs of all users, including those with disabilities, and avoid creating digital divides. Web3 projects should invest in making their platforms usable and accessible to global audiences.

3. **Transparency:** Transparency is paramount. Developers should provide clear information about how data is used and offer easy-to-understand privacy settings. This transparency builds trust and allows users to make informed decisions. Users should gain insight into how their data are used, and this information should be presented in a way that is easy to understand.
4. **Security:** Security of Web3 applications is a critical ethical concern. Developers must prioritise security, conducting regular audits and addressing vulnerabilities promptly. User data must be safeguarded against breaches and projects should invest in robust security practices to maintain user trust. Security should not be an afterthought, but an integral part of Web3 development.
5. **Compliance with Regulations:** The development of Web3 should align with existing legal and regulatory frameworks. Ethical developers should work to ensure compliance with data protection laws and financial regulations and acknowledge the importance of operating within the law. This involves working with legal experts to navigate the complex regulatory landscape and advocating the development of sensible and balanced regulations in the Web3 space.

The future of Web3 privacy and security is promising, with a clear shift towards privacy-enhancing technologies, user-centric data control, and ethical development. Web3 is poised to empower individuals to control their data and provide tools and frameworks for a more secure and private digital world. However, this journey must be guided by strong ethical principles that prioritise data ownership, inclusivity, transparency, security, and compliance with regulations.

As Web3 continues to shape our digital future, it is our collective responsibility to ensure that it evolves in a manner that respects individual rights, enhances security, and maintains the highest ethical standard. This commitment is the foundation upon which Web3 establishes itself as a transformative force for privacy, security, and user empowerment in the decentralised era. The evolution of Web3 is not just a technological shift; it is also a societal shift that holds the potential to redefine how individuals interact with the digital world. It is crucial to do so in a way that is ethical, secure, and empowering.

Recap of the Importance of Privacy and Security in Web 3

In the ever-evolving landscape of the digital realm, where the Internet has undergone several transformative phases, Web3 has emerged as a paradigm shift of paramount significance. Throughout this chapter, we traverse the historical context of the Web's evolution, dissect the core technologies underpinning Web3, examine the multifaceted challenges and vulnerabilities it faces, and explore the profound ethical considerations that must guide its development. Now, as we conclude our journey through the intricacies of Web3, let us recap the pivotal takeaways underscoring the critical importance of privacy and security in this burgeoning era.

1. **Web3 Evolution**: Web3 represents a pivotal juncture in the evolution of the Internet. It marks a notable departure from the centralised surveillance-driven approach of Web2, embracing a new paradigm that centres on individual privacy and data security. In Web3, the digital landscape becomes decentralised, user-centric, and privately focused. The importance of this transition cannot be overstated; it is a digital renaissance that empowers individuals and redefines their relationships with the online world.
2. **Privacy and Security Technologies**: Web3 hinges on a set of foundational technologies that form the bedrock of privacy and security. Blockchain, decentralisation, smart contracts, and a host of

privacy-enhancing technologies, such as Zero-Knowledge Proofs (ZKPs), Homomorphic Encryption, and Mixnets, are integral to Web3's promise to enhance data security and safeguard user privacy. These technologies act as enablers of a digital world, where data is no longer a commodity for surveillance but a sovereign asset for individuals.

3. **Challenges and Threats**: While potential of Web3 is immense, it is not without its share of challenges and vulnerabilities. Regulatory and legal considerations are significant, as the legal framework for this new digital landscape is still in its infancy. Security vulnerabilities in decentralised systems present ongoing challenges that demand innovative solutions. The need for transparent ethical development practices to ensure users' privacy and security is more significant than ever.
4. **Case Studies**: Throughout this chapter, we delve into real-world examples that serve as poignant illustrations of both the potential and pitfalls of Web3. Successful endeavours, such as Zcash, Oasis Network, Nym, Monero, Chainlink, Avalanche, Polkadot, and Tezos, underscore the transformative power of privacy and security technologies in Web3. They demonstrate that commitment to user privacy and the effective implementation of privacy-enhancing technologies can set new standards in the digital realm.
5. **Lessons Learned from Unsuccessful Endeavors**: Equally instructive are the lessons gleaned from unsuccessful projects like The DAO, Parity Multi-Sig Wallet, and QuadrigaCX. These case studies highlight the critical importance of rigorous code audits, secure key management, security education for users, and regulatory compliance. They serve as stark reminders that, even in a decentralised environment, the tenets of security must be diligently upheld.

Encouragement for Readers

As we move forward into the heart of the Web3 era, it is imperative that we remain vigilant and well informed. The digital landscape is evolving at an unprecedented pace, and with this evolution comes a dynamic interplay of threats and opportunities that significantly influence online experiences. We offer encouragement to all the readers.

1. **Stay Informed**: The Web3 landscape is continually evolving, and staying informed is your best defence. This chapter provides a snapshot of the current state; however, it is your responsibility to remain updated. Follow reputable sources, engage with online forums, attend conferences, and keep their fingers on the pulse of Web3 development.
2. **Be Vigilant**: In era where privacy and security are paramount, it is incumbent upon each of us to take personal responsibility for our digital well-being. Understand the tools and technologies at your disposal and be vigilant in your online actions. Scrutinise the permission you grant and the data you share.
3. **Ask Questions**: Do not hesitate to seek clarification and ask questions. Engage with the vibrant Web3 community to gain insights, share your knowledge, and raise your concerns. The Web3 community is a diverse and knowledgeable network, and by actively participating, one can enhance one's understanding and contribute to collective knowledge.

Call to Action

Web3's success is contingent on the collective efforts of its users, developers, advocates, and stakeholders. To ensure that the vision of a safer and more private Web3 becomes a reality, we urge you to take active steps and contribute to the ongoing transformation:

1. **Advocate for Privacy**: Be advocate for privacy-centric practices and technologies. Promote privacy-preserving protocols, secure data sharing, and user-centric control over personal information. Engage in discussions, both online and offline, to raise awareness of the importance of privacy in the digital age.
2. **Support Ethical Development**: Participate in and support Web3 projects that prioritise ethical development, transparency, and security. Contribute to open-source initiatives that uphold these values and actively collaborate with projects that embody the principles you believe.
3. **Engage in Regulatory Discussions**: Get involved in discussions about regulatory frameworks for Web3. The legal and regulatory landscapes of this transformative technology are still being defined. It participates in the creation of sensible, balanced regulations that protect user rights while fostering innovation.
4. **Educate and Raise Awareness**: Educate others about the importance of privacy and security in Web3. Raising awareness of the potential risks and benefits of this new digital era. Share your knowledge and insights to help create a more informed and cautious user base.
5. **Innovate and Create**: If you are a developer or technologist, consider how you can contribute to the development of privacy and security solutions in Web3. Create tools and applications that empower users to protect their digital identities and data. Champion causes digital privacy and security within the developer community.

In conclusion, the advent of Web3 holds the promise of a more private and secure digital future, where individual empowerment and data protection are paramount. However, to make this a reality, we must actively participate in shaping the future. Privacy and security are not just principles; they are our shields and rights in the digital world. Together, let us forge Web3 that empowers individuals, safeguards their digital lives, and preserves the cherished values of privacy and security in the digital age. This is our collective responsibility and opportunity in the Web3 era, and the journey has just just begun.

Chapter 16
Exploring Web 3 Benefits and Challenges

Munir Ahmad
https://orcid.org/0000-0003-4836-6151
Survey of Pakistan, Pakistan

Muhammad Awais Ali
Bahria University, Pakistan

Muhammad Arslan
Chenab College of Advance Studies. Faisalabad, Pakistan

ABSTRACT

This chapter delved into the multifaceted benefits and challenges characterizing the Web 3 paradigm. Web 3, operating on decentralized networks, fortifies digital ecosystems against cyber threats and unauthorized access, exemplified by the resilience of Bitcoin's decentralized blockchain. Rooted in blockchain technology, web 3 introduces transparency to transactions, fostering trust and eliminating intermediaries. User empowerment takes center stage as Web 3 enables unprecedented control over digital assets through blockchain-based smart contracts. Tokenization stimulates collaboration, fostering a more inclusive digital economy, while interoperability connects diverse blockchain networks seamlessly. The metaverse's integration into Web 3 faces challenges due to a lack of industry standards, exposing users to potential financial security risks. Scalability, regulatory uncertainty, and environmental impact present hurdles, emphasizing the need for innovative solutions.

INTRODUCTION

Web3 has originated from its ancestor, Web2. It marks a transformative paradigm shift in the expansive empire of the digital landscape. This advancement is not only a linear progression but also a dynamic and multifaceted shift in human interaction with information and technology. Web3 describes the evolution of the Internet through the submission of decentralized apps and blockchain technology. Its objective is to improve upon the centralized Web2 of today by aiming for higher levels of security, openness, and

DOI: 10.4018/979-8-3693-1532-3.ch016

transparency. Extensive research endeavours have been conducted to meticulously explore the emerging narrative of Web3. Both technologists and academics have set out to unravel the complex web of advantages and difficulties that are woven into this new digital frontier. This collective effort aims to shed light on the possible implications and advantages that may surface with the introduction of Web 3.

Ray (2023) underscored the various benefits of Web3 such as scalability, better governance, stronger security, higher transparency, interoperability, user authorization, and enticements, in addition to data protection and privacy. Along with benefits, the study also endorsed several obstacles to the prevalent use of Web3, such as regulatory compliance, environmental sustainability, and scalability. Web3 utilities such as Decentralized Autonomous Organization (DAO) can benefit researchers in implementing and testing research results, as noted by Filipcic (2022) while studying Web3 in the context of research and education. Hanswal et al. (2023) underscored that despite challenges like scalability and interoperability, Web3 envisions creating a more open, decentralized, and equitable Internet. The development of blockchain technology and DAOs in Web3 communities provides new insights for participatory grassroots co-creation (Zhang et al., 2023).

In the business context, Murray et al., (2023) endorsed that Web3 can increase peer-to-peer interactions, reduce large companies' control, and provide cost-effective access to user networks. Whereas potential challenges in building a Web3 e-commerce platform include scalability, user adoption, and interoperability (Bahadure et al., 2023). The complex and evolving tech stack of Web3 makes it hard to showcase its benefits, whereas that decentralized nature presents unique marketing challenges without a central controlling entity as noted by Chicotsky, (2023) in marketing research. Furthermore, Park et al., (2023) underpinned the technical, organizational, and regulatory interoperability for Web3 to deliver on its promises of value.

Nabben (2023) underscored that the fundamental challenge for Web3 lies in negotiating technical and governance experiments to achieve effective self-infrastructure. According to (Sable et al., 2023) Web3 can empower consumers with ownership and authority. It can offer enhanced security and transparency, prioritize user privacy, and provide users with more control over personal data; however, challenges of scalability and regulatory issues are associated with Web3. Even decentralized marketplaces can make construction data more uniform and usable to solve the challenges of data fragmentation and scattered data islands (F. Bucher & M. Hall, 2022). Decentralized science (DeSci) is an emerging topic linked to Web3 and DAOs. However, DeSci faces hurdles like scaling, participant quality balancing, system suboptimal loops, and a lack of accountability mechanisms (Ding et al., 2022).

Stablecoins contain blockchain technology and decentralized finance (DeFi). Stablecoins are essential for real-time, inexpensive, programmable payments, financial inclusion, and decentralized finance (DeFi). However, stablecoins may affect financial stability, market integrity, and consumer protection which can lead to regulatory issues (Momtaz, 2022). Using blockchain technology and smart contracts, non-fungible tokens (NFTs) are also essential components of the Web3 ecosystem because they make it possible to tokenize physical or digital assets. Some of the key qualities of NFTs that ensure unique and secure ownership of assets are scarcity, interoperability, security, traceability, and indivisibility (Guidi & Michienzi, 2023).

Another key component of Web3, the Metaverse, offers the ability to use augmented and virtual reality technology to expand the boundaries of the physical world. Trust, privacy, bias, misinformation, the application of the law, psychological aspects of addiction, and the effects on vulnerable people are some of the challenges associated with the metaverse (Dwivedi et al., 2022). Similarly, the lack of industry standards and regulatory rules are emphasized as the main threats to the Web3-empowered metaverse by Wu et al., (2023). These threats can lead to financial security challenges such as scams, code exploits, wash trading, money laundering, and illegal services. The mentioned studies show that studies have been looking at different parts of Web3 without seeing the whole picture. Many studies focus on specific aspects, like its good features or tough challenges, but end up creating separate understandings of the overall digital world of Web3.

Against this backdrop, the main purpose of this chapter is to comprehensively explore the benefits and challenges intricately woven into the fabric of Web 3. To address this objective, the chapter is structured as follows: Section 2 provides the historical background of the Web3 landscape, unraveling its roots and highlighting its diverse applications. Section 3 outlines the diverse advantages connected with Web3, whereas Section 4 critically examines the challenges integral to the adoption and implementation of Web3. Section 5 underpins the ethical, policy, financial, and technical implications. The last section synthesizes the key insights gleaned from the exploration of Web3 benefits and challenges. Additionally, it provides valuable suggestions for future research avenues, pointing toward areas that warrant further investigation.

BACKGROUND

This section explores the historical development of Web3, unveiling its origins and emphasizing its varied applications in today's digital environment.

Introduction to Web 3

Web3 is not merely an upgrade but a revolutionary departure from its predecessor, Web2, which is characterized by centralized control and data ownership by tech giants. Unlike the traditional client-server model, Web3 envisions a decentralized internet architecture, often powered by blockchain technology (Swan, 2015). Blockchain, a distributed ledger that records transactions across a network of computers, serves as the backbone of Web3, providing a secure and transparent foundation for the next generation of digital interactions. Key to the ethos of Web3 is the concept of decentralization. In Web3, power is distributed among participants rather than concentrated in the hands of a few centralized authorities (Tapscott & Tapscott, 2018). This decentralized model not only enhances security by eliminating single points of failure but also empowers users with greater control over their data, redefining the relationship between individuals and the digital platforms they engage with.

At the heart of Web3 is the vision of a trustless and transparent digital ecosystem facilitated by smart contracts (Mougayar, 2016). Smart contracts, self-executing code deployed on blockchain networks, automate and enforce contractual agreements, reducing the need for intermediaries and fostering a more efficient and secure exchange of value. Web3 also embraces the concept of tokenization, representing digital or real-world assets as tokens on the blockchain (Swan, 2015). This tokenization opens up new possibilities for decentralized finance, digital ownership, and novel models of incentivization, creating a more inclusive and democratized digital economy.

As we embark on the journey into the era of Web3, it is essential to understand the foundational principles that underpin this transformative vision. This article will delve deeper into the benefits, challenges, and emerging trends within the Web3 landscape, exploring its potential to reshape the internet and redefine our digital interactions.

Web 3 Applications

In the ever-evolving landscape of the internet, Web3 applications emerge as pioneers of a decentralized future, reshaping how we interact with digital technologies. This comprehensive text delves into the diverse realms of Web3 applications, shedding light on their multifaceted nature, revolutionary potential, and the transformative impact they can have on industries across the globe.

Non-Fungible Tokens (NFTs)

NFTs are digital assets representing objects like art, collectibles, and in-game items, traded online and encoded within smart contracts on a blockchain (Nadini et al., 2021; Pinto-Gutiérrez et al., 2022). NFTs' unique digital assets have transformed the art, gaming, and entertainment industries. Through blockchain's immutability and transparency, NFTs authenticate and prove ownership of digital content, providing creators with new avenues for monetization and audience engagement (Guidi & Michienzi, 2023). The crypto-collectible game CryptoKitties is a prime example, where players can buy, sell, and breed unique digital cats as NFTs. Each CryptoKitty is a distinct NFT, emphasizing ownership and scarcity. This game showcases the creative and entertainment potential of NFTs within the Web3 ecosystem. Figure 1 shows the example code written in Solidity for NFT.

Figure 1. Sample code for NFT

```
// SPDX-License-Identifier: MIT
pragma solidity ^0.8.0;

import "@openzeppelin/contracts/token/ERC721/ERC721.sol";
import "@openzeppelin/contracts/access/Ownable.sol";

contract MyNFT is ERC721, Ownable {

    // Counter to keep track of token IDs
    uint256 private tokenIdCounter;

    // Base URI for metadata
    string private baseTokenURI;

    constructor(string memory _name, string memory _symbol, string memory _baseTokenURI) ERC721(_name, _symbol) {
        baseTokenURI = _baseTokenURI;
    }

    // Mint a new NFT
    function mintNFT(address to) external onlyOwner {
        uint256 newTokenId = tokenIdCounter;
        _safeMint(to, newTokenId);
        tokenIdCounter++;
    }

    // Set the base URI for metadata
    function setBaseTokenURI(string memory _baseTokenURI) external onlyOwner {
        baseTokenURI = _baseTokenURI;
    }

    // Return the URI for a given token ID
    function tokenURI(uint256 tokenId) public view override returns (string memory) {
        return bytes(baseTokenURI).length > 0
            ? string(abi.encodePacked(baseTokenURI, tokenId.toString()))
            : "";
    }
}
```

Decentralized Autonomous Organizations (DAOs)

Web3 applications have given rise to the concept of Decentralized Autonomous Organizations (DAOs), which are new organization forms with management and operational rules encoded on blockchain in the form of smart contracts, autonomously operating without centralized control or third-party intervention (Wang et al., 2019). DAOs operate on a consensus mechanism, allowing members to participate in governance without the need for traditional hierarchical structures (Ding et al., 2022). This can enable a more democratic and transparent approach to organizational management. MakerDAO, a prominent DeFi DAO, uses blockchain technology to create a stablecoin pegged to the US Dollar for decentralized financial services (Ellinger et al., 2023). Similarly, the Global Research Decentralized Autonomous Organization (GR-DAO) is an anticipated global community of researchers devoted to mutually generating knowledge and sharing it with the world (L. Page & Elmessiry, 2021).

Decentralized Applications (DApps)

DApps, or decentralized applications, represent distributed and trusted applications leveraging blockchain technology. These applications are comprised of various services, including transaction scalability protocols, decentralized storage, and distributed computing solutions (Besancon et al., 2022). One notable DApp is Brave, a privacy-focused browser built on blockchain technology. Brave rewards users with

Basic Attention Tokens (BAT) for viewing ads, challenging the traditional advertising model and providing users with greater control over their online experiences. On https://ethereum.org/, plenty of DApps have been hosted, that are classified into six categories such as finance, arts & collectibles, technology, metaverse, gaming, and social. Figure 2 shows a snip of a few DApps featured on the website.

Figure 2. Sample DApps

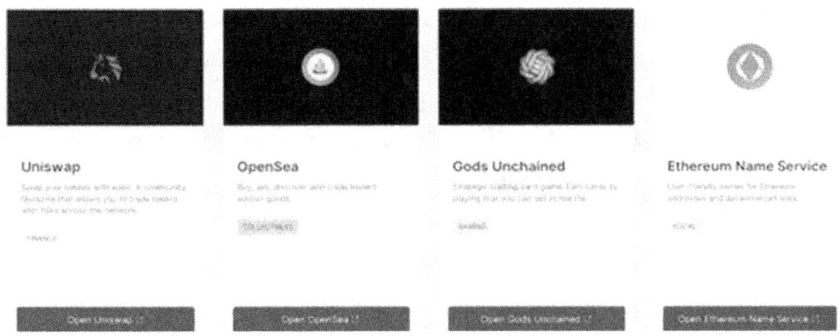

Decentralized Finance (DeFi)

Web3 applications are at the forefront of revolutionizing the financial landscape through decentralized finance, or DeFi (Salami, 2021; Zetzsche et al., 2020). DeFi platforms, built on blockchain technology, facilitate peer-to-peer financial services, including lending, borrowing, and trading, without the need for traditional intermediaries (Majumdar & Gochhait, 2022; Mougayar, 2016). Smart contracts can enable automated and transparent financial transactions, fostering a more inclusive and accessible financial ecosystem. For instance, Aave, a DeFi lending platform, allows users to lend and borrow assets directly from one another through smart contracts (Aave, 2023). This eliminates the need for a central authority and provides users with greater control over their finances. Figure 3 shows Aave Community Treasury amounting to $ 126,411,516 dated 24 December 2023 fetched from https://aave.com/. DeFi with a mushrooming ecosystem has a total value of around 150bn USD as of April 2022 (Werner et al., 2022).

Figure 3. Aave community treasury

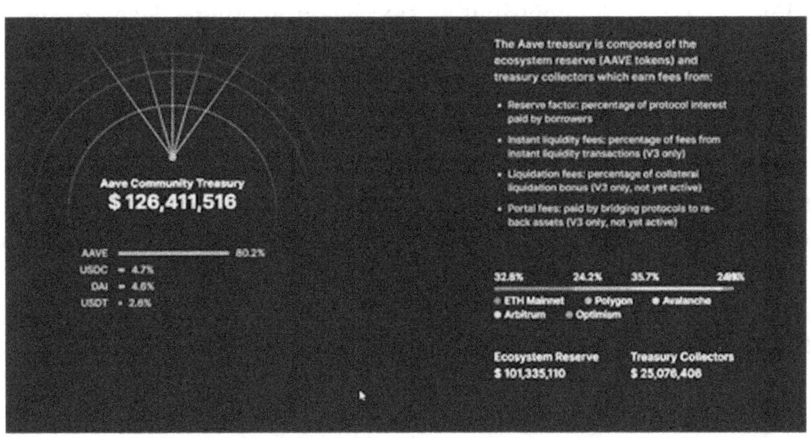

Web 3 Gaming

The gaming industry is transforming with the integration of Web3 technologies. Web3 gaming involves decentralized systems with NFTs, IPFS, and blockchains that enable new business models and support the evolvability of in-game assets (Karapapas et al., 2022). Web3 gaming entails crafting incentive structures for cryptocurrency-driven services through the application of behavioral economics. This includes the utilization of concepts like cumulative prospect theory, particularly in the context of cryptographic lottery games (Toyoda, 2023). Blockchain-based games leverage NFTs for digital asset ownership, and decentralized platforms enhance in-game economies through transparent and secure transactions (Mougayar, 2016). Games like Axie Infinity utilize NFTs to allow players to truly own and trade their in-game items, fostering a new paradigm of digital ownership within the gaming ecosystem. Similarly, the Dark Forest game emulates social systems, offering insights into the consistency of behavioral patterns both within and beyond the confines of the simulated gaming environment (Lin et al., 2022). The emergence of blockchain and Non-Fungible Tokens (NFTs) has paved the way for platforms such as Decentraland. Here, users can delve into immersive 3D virtual realms, fostering communication and interaction in novel and engaging ways (Guidi & Michienzi, 2022b).

Decentralized Social Media

Web3 applications are reshaping the landscape of social media by emphasizing user control and content ownership. Steemit, a blockchain-based social media platform, exemplifies how Web3 applications prioritize user control and content ownership. Users on Steemit are rewarded with cryptocurrency for their contributions, shifting the power dynamic away from centralized platforms (Ba et al., 2022). Minds is another example, offering a blockchain-based social network focused on privacy and user empowerment (Guidi & Michienzi, 2022a).

Decentralized Cloud Computing

Web3 introduces decentralized cloud computing platforms that leverage blockchain technology to create distributed, secure, and censorship-resistant cloud infrastructures. Filecoin, a decentralized storage network, allows users to rent out their excess storage space. This peer-to-peer approach challenges traditional cloud service providers by creating a distributed and secure cloud infrastructure. Users are incentivized with Filecoin tokens for contributing storage, promoting a decentralized and collaborative cloud ecosystem (Khalid et al., 2023).

Cross-Border Payments and Remittances

Web3 applications are disrupting the traditional financial system by providing more efficient and cost-effective cross-border payment solutions. Ripple, a Web3 application, has disrupted cross-border payments by enabling faster and more cost-effective international money transfers. Financial institutions and banks utilize Ripple's blockchain technology to facilitate real-time settlements, reducing the reliance on traditional correspondent banking networks and enhancing financial inclusivity.

FOCUS OF THE CHAPTER

This chapter examines the transformative impact of Web3 on the digital landscape, highlighting its dual nature by exploring both benefits and challenges. The multifaceted benefits of Web3, such as enhanced security through decentralization, user empowerment, and tokenization-driven collaboration, contribute to creating a more secure, transparent, and inclusive digital ecosystem. Real-life examples like Bitcoin, Ethereum-based NFTs, and Steem's incentivization model illustrate the practical successes of Web3 applications. Conversely, the chapter delves into challenges, including scalability concerns, interoperability issues, regulatory uncertainties, user experience challenges, and environmental impacts. Real-life instances, like Ethereum's scalability issues and regulatory variances in DeFi, underscore the practical hurdles that necessitate resolution for the widespread adoption of Web3. By juxtaposing these aspects, the chapter aims to provide a comprehensive understanding of the intricate dynamics influencing the decentralized Web3 paradigm's future trajectory.

BENEFITS OF WEB 3

In recent years, the emergence of Web3 has marked a transformative epoch in the digital realm, offering a decentralized and user-centric approach to online interactions. This paradigm shift brings forth a myriad of benefits, each contributing to a more secure, transparent, and inclusive digital ecosystem.

Enhanced Security

Web3 operates on decentralized networks, significantly reducing the susceptibility to cyber threats and unauthorized access. As opposed to traditional centralized models, the distributed nature of Web3 ensures that there is no single point of failure, thus enhancing the overall security of digital transactions (Murray et al., 2023). An example of this is Bitcoin, the pioneering cryptocurrency, which operates on a decentralized blockchain network, making it resistant to centralized control and security vulnerabilities.

Increased Transparency

Blockchain, a foundational technology of Web3, introduces transparency by recording transactions in an immutable ledger. This transparency builds trust among users and eliminates the need for intermediaries in various processes, fostering a more trustworthy digital environment (Hamilton, 2020; Tariq et al., 2019). For instance, in supply chain management, IBM's Food Trust leverages blockchain to enhance transparency, allowing consumers to trace the origin and journey of food products, thereby ensuring the integrity of the supply chain (IBM, 2023).

User Empowerment

Web3 enables users to have greater control over their digital assets and data (Chicotsky, 2023; Sable et al., 2023). Through the use of blockchain-based smart contracts, individuals can interact with digital platforms without relinquishing ownership of their personal information, empowering them with unprecedented control (Hamilton, 2020; Hewa et al., 2021). A notable example is Ethereum-based NFTs, where artists retain ownership and control over their digital artwork, even after it has been sold or traded.

Incentivization

Tokenization, a key feature of Web3, introduces digital assets that represent real-world value. This facilitates new economic models, incentivizing collaboration and contribution within decentralized ecosystems. Users are rewarded with tokens for their participation, creating a more inclusive and value-driven digital economy (Voshmgir, 2020). Murray et al., (2023) emphasized how these incentives can drive peer-to-peer interactions and reduce central control in business contexts. Steem, a blockchain-based social media platform, rewards content creators with its native cryptocurrency, Steem, encouraging active participation and content creation (Steem, 2023).

Interoperability

Web3 promotes interoperability by enabling different blockchain networks to communicate and share data seamlessly. This interoperability fosters a more connected digital landscape, eliminating silos and promoting collaborative innovation (Chi et al., 2023; Hanswal et al., 2023). The Interledger Protocol (ILP) is an exemplar, facilitating cross-ledger transactions and promoting interoperability between different blockchain networks (Interledger Foundation, 2023).

Privacy Preservation

Web3 incorporates decentralized identity systems that allow users to maintain control over their personal information. This shift from centralized identity management enhances privacy, reducing the risks associated with large-scale data breaches (Bahri et al., 2018; Friebe et al., 2018). Sovrin, a decentralized identity platform, empowers users to control and share their digital identity securely, minimizing the reliance on centralized entities for identity verification (Sovrin, 2023).

Scalability

While scalability undeniably poses a challenge within the realm of Web3, it simultaneously emerges as a pivotal benefit. The vision articulated by (Hanswal et al., 2023), envisioning a more open and equitable Internet, accentuates the imperative need for scalable solutions. Scalability, in this context, becomes not merely an obstacle but a requisite feature for the widespread adoption of Web3 technologies.

Improved Governance

Ray, (2023) posits a compelling perspective on the transformative potential of Web3 in governance. Through the deployment of decentralized mechanisms such as Decentralized Autonomous Organizations (DAOs), Web3 can empower individuals with ownership and authority. This empowerment, according to Ray, establishes a foundation for a more democratic and transparent decision-making process. By leveraging these decentralized structures, Web3 can contribute to reshaping governance paradigms, fostering inclusivity, and enhancing the overall integrity of decision-making within digital ecosystems.

CHALLENGES OF WEB 3

As the digital landscape transitions towards Web3, a decentralized paradigm, it is essential to acknowledge and address the challenges that accompany this transformative shift. This section explores key challenges associated with Web3.

Scalability Concerns

Web3, often built on blockchain technology, faces inherent scalability challenges. As decentralized networks grow, the scalability of blockchain systems becomes a critical bottleneck (Gupta et al., 2022; Zarrin et al., 2021). Transaction speeds and throughput may be hindered, impacting the user experience and overall efficiency of the network. An illustrative example is Ethereum, a widely used blockchain for decentralized applications. Ethereum has faced scalability issues, leading to delays and higher transaction fees during periods of high network activity, hindering user experience.

Interoperability Issues

While interoperability is a touted advantage of Web3, achieving seamless collaboration among different blockchain networks and decentralized applications (DApps) remains a challenge (Belchior et al., 2022). Incompatible protocols and standards hinder the effective exchange of data and value between diverse decentralized ecosystems. An example is the interoperability challenge between Ethereum and BNB Smart Chain (BSC). Users often face difficulties moving assets between these blockchains due to differences in their underlying architectures.

Regulatory Uncertainty

The decentralized nature of Web3 raises regulatory challenges, as existing frameworks struggle to adapt to this evolving paradigm (Lai et al., 2023; Murray et al., 2023). Ambiguities in legal frameworks and varying regulatory approaches across different jurisdictions can impede the widespread adoption of Web3 technologies. Some countries embrace DeFi, while others are still navigating regulatory frameworks, creating uncertainty for developers and users alike. Defi is also facing the challenges of market manipulation and money laundering (Chohan, 2021).

User Experience and Accessibility

For Web3 to gain mass adoption, user interfaces and experiences must be intuitive and accessible. However, the current state of decentralized applications often requires users to manage complex cryptographic keys and navigate unfamiliar interfaces, posing a barrier to entry for non-technical users (Aria et al., 2023; Wen et al., 2023). An example is the decentralized wallet MetaMask, which, while powerful, can be challenging for users unfamiliar with blockchain concepts, impacting the accessibility of associated DApps.

Environmental Impact

The energy consumption associated with certain consensus mechanisms, such as Proof-of-Work (PoW), poses environmental concerns in Web3 systems (Kshetri, 2022). As sustainability becomes a focal point globally, addressing the environmental impact of decentralized technologies is imperative. Bitcoin, as a PoW-based blockchain, has faced scrutiny due to its energy-intensive mining process. This example underscores the importance of exploring and adopting more environmentally friendly consensus mechanisms in the Web3 landscape, such as Proof-of-Stake (PoS).

Lack of Industry Standards

The integration of the metaverse into the Web3 landscape presents a noteworthy obstacle in the form of a lack of industry standards (Wu et al., 2023). This deficiency not only hampers the smooth evolution of the metaverse but also exposes users to potential financial security challenges, ranging from deceptive scams to the proliferation of illegal services. Establishing robust industry standards and regulatory guidelines is imperative to mitigate these risks and create a more secure and reliable metaverse ecosystem.

Privacy and Ethical Concerns

As an extension of Web3, the metaverse introduces a multifaceted set of challenges encompassing trust, privacy, bias, disinformation, and psychological impacts (Dwivedi et al., 2022). Effectively addressing these concerns is fundamental to cultivating a safe and inclusive digital environment within the metaverse. The intricate interplay of these factors necessitates comprehensive strategies that not only safeguard user privacy but also combat biases, misinformation, and psychological repercussions. By prioritizing privacy and ethical considerations, stakeholders can contribute to shaping a metaverse that aligns with the principles of trust, transparency, and responsible digital engagement.

IMPLICATIONS

This section outlines the ethical, policy, financial, and technical implications of the benefits and challenges of Web3.

Ethical Implications

Web3, characterized by its commitment to decentralization, transparency, and user empowerment, introduces a range of ethical considerations that redefine our digital landscape. One of the primary concerns revolves around privacy and security, with the potential for enhanced user control over data balanced against the challenges of securing decentralized networks and safeguarding sensitive information. The decentralized nature of Web3 is seen as positive for fostering inclusivity, yet ethical challenges emerge in ensuring equitable access and preventing the creation of new digital divides. Decentralized governance models aim to distribute decision-making power, but ethical challenges persist in ensuring fairness and preventing the concentration of power. Education and awareness are crucial ethical dimensions, where

Web3 has the potential to drive awareness about digital rights, but misinformation and the need for comprehensive education efforts pose challenges.

Policy Implications

The advent of Web3 carries profound policy implications, necessitating a reevaluation of regulatory frameworks to accommodate decentralized structures. Policymakers must grapple with the challenge of crafting adaptive regulations that foster innovation and protect users while addressing the decentralized nature of Web3. Striking a balance between regulatory certainty and the flexibility required for technological evolution is crucial. Collaborative efforts across jurisdictions are essential to harmonize regulatory approaches, ensuring a cohesive and globally applicable framework. This may involve the creation of international standards and agreements to navigate the cross-border nature of decentralized technologies, fostering regulatory certainty and promoting responsible development within the Web3 ecosystem.

Technical Implications

From a technical standpoint, the transition to Web3 demands innovative solutions to address scalability, interoperability, and user experience challenges. Scalability concerns call for the exploration and implementation of novel consensus mechanisms, such as sharding or layer 2 solutions, to enhance transaction speeds and throughput. Interoperability issues require the development of standardized protocols that enable seamless communication between diverse blockchain networks and DApps. Enhancing user experience and accessibility necessitates the creation of user-friendly interfaces and educational tools to demystify complex cryptographic processes. Additionally, the pursuit of environmentally sustainable consensus mechanisms, such as Proof-of-Stake, becomes a technical imperative to mitigate the environmental impact of Web3. Collaborative research initiatives and open-source development can drive the innovation needed to overcome these technical challenges and ensure the robustness of Web3 technologies.

Financial Implications

The financial landscape is intricately tied to the success of Web3, and addressing challenges in this domain requires strategic planning and investment. Venture capitalists and financial institutions must recognize the potential of decentralized technologies and actively support projects that contribute to scalability, interoperability, and user accessibility. Furthermore, the establishment of industry standards in the metaverse necessitates collaborative financial initiatives to fund research, development, and the implementation of secure and reliable metaverse ecosystems. Sustainable investment practices can incentivize the adoption of eco-friendly consensus mechanisms, aligning financial interests with environmental responsibility. As regulatory uncertainty poses a challenge, financial institutions need to adapt by developing risk management strategies that account for evolving legal frameworks, fostering stability and confidence in the Web3 financial landscape.

CONCLUSION

In conclusion, the exploration of Web3 in this chapter unveils a transformative epoch in the digital landscape, marked by a decentralized and user-centric approach that fosters a more secure, transparent, and inclusive digital ecosystem. The multifaceted benefits of Web3, including enhanced security through decentralization, user empowerment, incentivized collaboration, interoperability, and privacy preservation, showcase the paradigm's potential to reshape digital interactions. Examples, such as Bitcoin, Ethereum-based NFTs, and Steam's incentivization model, illustrate practical successes.

However, alongside these benefits, the chapter delves into critical challenges that Web3 encounters scalability concerns, interoperability issues, regulatory uncertainties, user experience challenges, and environmental impacts. Instances, such as Ethereum's scalability issues and varying regulatory approaches towards DeFi, underscore practical hurdles that necessitate resolution for the widespread adoption of Web3.

The implications of successful resolution extend beyond technology, impacting global economies, governance structures, and individual empowerment. Web3 has the potential to reshape how we trust, collaborate, and transact in the digital era, ushering in an era where users have unprecedented control over their digital interactions. As stakeholders navigate the complexities of Web3, collaboration across academia, industry, and regulatory bodies will be essential in shaping a sustainable and inclusive future for decentralized technologies.

Moving forward, addressing these challenges will be pivotal in unlocking the full potential of Web3. Future research should focus on developing scalable solutions to enhance network efficiency, refining interoperability standards, and navigating the regulatory landscape to ensure a conducive environment for innovation. Improving user interfaces and accessibility of decentralized applications can play a crucial role in driving mass adoption, necessitating user-friendly tools and educational initiatives. Moreover, exploring environmentally friendly consensus mechanisms, such as Proof-of-Stake, can mitigate the environmental impact of Web3 technologies.

REFERENCES

Aave. (2023). *Aave: Empowering Users with DeFi Aggregation and Efficient Token Swaps.* https://aavve.github.io/

Aria, R., Archer, N., Khanlari, M., & Shah, B. (2023). Influential Factors in the Design and Development of a Sustainable Web3/Metaverse and Its Applications. In Future Internet (Vol. 15, Issue 4). doi:10.3390/fi15040131

Ba, C. T., Zignani, M., & Gaito, S. (2022). The role of cryptocurrency in the dynamics of blockchain-based social networks: The case of Steemit. *PLoS ONE, 17*(6). doi:10.1371/journal.pone.0267612

Bahadure, M., Khasare, M. R., Mahure, M. S., Rathod, M. L., Junghare, M. S., & Rathi, P. N. G. (2023). Thr3ebay: E-commerce Dapp using Blockchain. *International Journal for Research in Applied Science and Engineering Technology, 11*(5), 1435–1438. Advance online publication. doi:10.22214/ijraset.2023.51813

Bahri, L., Carminati, B., & Ferrari, E. (2018). Decentralized privacy preserving services for Online Social Networks. In Online Social Networks and Media (Vol. 6). doi:10.1016/j.osnem.2018.02.001

Belchior, R., Vasconcelos, A., Guerreiro, S., & Correia, M. (2022). A Survey on Blockchain Interoperability: Past, Present, and Future Trends. In ACM Computing Surveys (Vol. 54, Issue 8). doi:10.1145/3471140

Besancon, L., Da Silva, C. F., Ghodous, P., & Gelas, J. P. (2022). A Blockchain Ontology for DApps Development. *IEEE Access : Practical Innovations, Open Solutions*, *10*, 49905–49933. Advance online publication. doi:10.1109/ACCESS.2022.3173313

Bucher, D., & Hall, D. (2022). *New Ways of Data Governance for Construction? Decentralized Data Marketplaces as Web3 Concept just around the Corner*. doi:10.7146/aul.455.c224

Chi, Y., Duan, H., Cai, W., Wang, Z. J., & Leung, V. C. M. (2023). Networking Parallel Web3 Metaverses for Interoperability. *IEEE Network.*

Chicotsky, B. (2023). Web3 and marketing: The new frontier. *Applied Marketing Analytics, 9*(2).

ChohanU. W. (2021). Decentralized Finance (DeFi): An Emergent Alternative Financial Architecture. *Econometric Modeling: International Financial Markets - Foreign Exchange EJournal*. doi:10.2139/ssrn.3791921

Ding, W., Hou, J., Li, J., Guo, C., Qin, J., Kozma, R., & Wang, F. Y. (2022). DeSci Based on Web3 and DAO: A Comprehensive Overview and Reference Model. In IEEE Transactions on Computational Social Systems (Vol. 9, Issue 5). doi:10.1109/TCSS.2022.3204745

Dwivedi, Y. K., Hughes, L., Baabdullah, A. M., Ribeiro-Navarrete, S., Giannakis, M., Al-Debei, M. M., Dennehy, D., Metri, B., Buhalis, D., Cheung, C. M. K., Conboy, K., Doyle, R., Dubey, R., Dutot, V., Felix, R., Goyal, D. P., Gustafsson, A., Hinsch, C., Jebabli, I., ... Wamba, S. F. (2022). Metaverse beyond the hype: Multidisciplinary perspectives on emerging challenges, opportunities, and agenda for research, practice and policy. *International Journal of Information Management*, *66*, 102542. Advance online publication. doi:10.1016/j.ijinfomgt.2022.102542

Ellinger, E. W., Mini, T., Gregory, R. W., & Dietz, A. (2023). Decentralized Autonomous Organization (DAO): The case of MakerDAO. *Journal of Information Technology Teaching Cases*. doi:10.1177/20438869231181151

Filipcic, S. (2022). Web3 & DAOs: an overview of the development and possibilities for the implementation in research and education. *2022 45th Jubilee International Convention on Information, Communication and Electronic Technology, MIPRO 2022 - Proceedings*. 10.23919/MIPRO55190.2022.9803324

Friebe, S., Sobik, I., & Zitterbart, M. (2018). DecentID: Decentralized and Privacy-Preserving Identity Storage System Using Smart Contracts. *Proceedings - 17th IEEE International Conference on Trust, Security and Privacy in Computing and Communications and 12th IEEE International Conference on Big Data Science and Engineering, Trustcom/BigDataSE 2018*. 10.1109/TrustCom/BigDataSE.2018.00016

Guidi, B., & Michienzi, A. (2022a). How to reward the Web: The social dApp Yup. *Online Social Networks and Media*, *31*, 100229. Advance online publication. doi:10.1016/j.osnem.2022.100229

Guidi, B., & Michienzi, A. (2022b). Social games and Blockchain: exploring the Metaverse of Decentraland. *Proceedings - 2022 IEEE 42nd International Conference on Distributed Computing Systems Workshops, ICDCSW 2022*. 10.1109/ICDCSW56584.2022.00045

Guidi, B., & Michienzi, A. (2023). From NFT 1.0 to NFT 2.0: A Review of the Evolution of Non-Fungible Tokens. In Future Internet (Vol. 15, Issue 6). doi:10.3390/fi15060189

Gupta, N. K., Jain, A., Sharma, P. C., & Vishwakarma, S. K. (2022). State of the Art and Challenges in Blockchain Applications. *Smart Innovation. Systems and Technologies*, *235*, 311–320. Advance online publication. doi:10.1007/978-981-16-2877-1_28

Hamilton, M. (2020). Blockchain distributed ledger technology: An introduction and focus on smart contracts. In Journal of Corporate Accounting and Finance (Vol. 31, Issue 2). doi:10.1002/jcaf.22421

Hanswal, G., Jain, S., & Thankachan, B. (2023). The Potential of Web3 for Shaping the Digital Landscape. *International Journal of Advanced Research in Science. Tongxin Jishu*, 27–35. Advance online publication. doi:10.48175/IJARSCT-10715

Hewa, T., Ylianttila, M., & Liyanage, M. (2021). Survey on blockchain based smart contracts: Applications, opportunities and challenges. In Journal of Network and Computer Applications (Vol. 177). doi:10.1016/j.jnca.2020.102857

IBM. (2023). *Food manufacturing on blockchain*. https://www.ibm.com/blockchain/resources/food-trust/manufacturing/

Interledger Foundation. (2023). *The modern way to make payments*. https://interledger.org/

Karapapas, C., Syros, G., Pittaras, I., & Polyzos, G. C. (2022). Decentralized NFT-based Evolvable Games. *2022 4th Conference on Blockchain Research and Applications for Innovative Networks and Services, BRAINS 2022*. 10.1109/BRAINS55737.2022.9909178

Khalid, M. I., Ehsan, I., Al-Ani, A. K., Iqbal, J., Hussain, S., Ullah, S. S., & Nayab. (2023). A Comprehensive Survey on Blockchain-Based Decentralized Storage Networks. *IEEE Access : Practical Innovations, Open Solutions*, *11*, 10995–11015. Advance online publication. doi:10.1109/ACCESS.2023.3240237

Kshetri, N. (2022). Policy, Ethical, Social, and Environmental Considerations of Web3 and the Metaverse. In IT Professional (Vol. 24, Issue 3). doi:10.1109/MITP.2022.3178509

Lai, Y., Yang, J., Liu, M., Li, Y., & Li, S. (2023). Web3: Exploring Decentralized Technologies and Applications for the Future of Empowerment and Ownership. *Blockchains*, *1*(2), 111–131. doi:10.3390/blockchains1020008

Lin, Z., Yao, N., Wu, X., & Wang, L. (2022). A Peek at Metaverse Society from Web 3.0 Games: A Preliminary Case Study of Dark Forest. *2022 IEEE 24th International Workshop on Multimedia Signal Processing, MMSP 2022*. 10.1109/MMSP55362.2022.9949551

Majumdar, S., & Gochhait, S. (2022). Risks and Solutions in Islamic Decentralised Finance. *2022 International Conference on Sustainable Islamic Business and Finance, SIBF 2022*. 10.1109/SIBF56821.2022.9939821

Momtaz, P. P. (2022). Some Very Simple Economics of Web3 and the Metaverse. SSRN *Electronic Journal*. doi:10.2139/ssrn.4085937

Mougayar, W. (2016). The Business Blockchain: Promise, Practice, and Application of the Next Internet Technology. John Wiley & Sons.

Murray, A., Kim, D., & Combs, J. (2023). The promise of a decentralized internet: What is Web3 and how can firms prepare? *Business Horizons*, *66*(2), 191–202. doi:10.1016/j.bushor.2022.06.002

Nabben, K. (2023). Web3 as 'self-infrastructuring': The challenge is how. In Big Data and Society (Vol. 10, Issue 1). doi:10.1177/20539517231159002

Nadini, M., Alessandretti, L., Di Giacinto, F., Martino, M., Aiello, L. M., & Baronchelli, A. (2021). Mapping the NFT revolution: Market trends, trade networks, and visual features. *Scientific Reports*, *11*(1), 20902. Advance online publication. doi:10.1038/s41598-021-00053-8 PMID:34686678

Page, K., & Elmessiry, A. (2021). *Global Research Decentralized Autonomous Organization (GR-DAO): A DAO of Global Researchers*. doi:10.5121/csit.2021.111708

Park, A., Wilson, M., Robson, K., Demetis, D., & Kietzmann, J. (2023). Interoperability: Our exciting and terrifying Web3 future. *Business Horizons*, *66*(4), 529–541. Advance online publication. doi:10.1016/j.bushor.2022.10.005

Pinto-Gutiérrez, C., Gaitán, S., Jaramillo, D., & Velasquez, S. (2022). The NFT Hype: What Draws Attention to Non-Fungible Tokens? *Mathematics*, *10*(3), 335. Advance online publication. doi:10.3390/math10030335

Ray, P. P. (2023). Web3: A comprehensive review on background, technologies, applications, zero-trust architectures, challenges and future directions. In Internet of Things and Cyber-Physical Systems (Vol. 3). doi:10.1016/j.iotcps.2023.05.003

Sable, N. P., Sonkamble, R., Rathod, V. U., Shirke, S., Deshmukh, J. Y., & Chavan, G. T. (2023). Web3 Chain Authentication and Authorization Security Standard (CAA). *International Journal on Recent and Innovation Trends in Computing and Communication*, *11*(5), 70–76. Advance online publication. doi:10.17762/ijritcc.v11i5.6526

Salami, I. (2021). Challenges and approaches to regulating decentralized finance. *AJIL Unbound*, *115*, 425–429. Advance online publication. doi:10.1017/aju.2021.66

Sovrin. (2023). *Sovrin*. https://sovrin.org/

Steem. (2023). *Powering Communities and Opportunities - Steem*. https://steem.com/

Swan, M. (2015). Blockchain: Blueprint for a new economy. O'Reilly Media, Inc.

Tapscott, D., & Tapscott, A. (2018). Blockchain Revolution: How the Technology Behind Bitcoin and Other Cryptocurrencies Is Changing the World. Sage Publications, Inc.

Tariq, U., Ibrahim, A., Ahmad, T., Bouteraa, Y., & Elmogy, A. (2019). Blockchain in internet-of-things: A necessity framework for security, reliability, transparency, immutability and liability. *IET Communications*, *13*(19), 3187–3192. Advance online publication. doi:10.1049/iet-com.2019.0194

Toyoda, K. (2023). Web3 meets behavioral economics: An example of profitable crypto lottery mechanism design. *2023 IEEE International Conference on Metaverse Computing, Networking and Applications (MetaCom)*, 678–679. 10.1109/MetaCom57706.2023.00122

Voshmgir, S. (2020). *Token Economy: How the Web3 reinvents the internet* (Vol. 2). Token Kitchen.

Wang, S., Ding, W., Li, J., Yuan, Y., Ouyang, L., & Wang, F. Y. (2019). Decentralized Autonomous Organizations: Concept, Model, and Applications. *IEEE Transactions on Computational Social Systems*, *6*(5), 870–878. Advance online publication. doi:10.1109/TCSS.2019.2938190

Wen, M. H., Huang, C. Y., Chen, Y. C., & Lin, I. C. (2023). Exploring Factors Influencing Community Consensus Building of Web3 Decentralized Apps. Lecture Notes in Computer Science (Including Subseries Lecture Notes in Artificial Intelligence and Lecture Notes in Bioinformatics), 14032 LNCS. doi:10.1007/978-3-031-35702-2_29

Werner, S., Perez, D., Gudgeon, L., Klages-Mundt, A., Harz, D., & Knottenbelt, W. (2022). *SoK: Decentralized Finance*. DeFi. doi:10.1145/3558535.3559780

Wu, J., Lin, K., Lin, D., Zheng, Z., Huang, H., & Zheng, Z. (2023). Financial Crimes in Web3-Empowered Metaverse: Taxonomy, Countermeasures, and Opportunities. *IEEE Open Journal of the Computer Society*, *4*, 37–49. Advance online publication. doi:10.1109/OJCS.2023.3245801

Zarrin, J., Wen Phang, H., Babu Saheer, L., & Zarrin, B. (2021). Blockchain for decentralization of internet: Prospects, trends, and challenges. *Cluster Computing*, *24*(4), 2841–2866. Advance online publication. doi:10.1007/s10586-021-03301-8 PMID:34025209

Zetzsche, D., Arner, D., & Buckley, R. P. (2020). Decentralized Finance. *Journal of Financial Regulation*. doi:10.1093/jfr/fjaa010

Zhang, M., Wang, J., & Ji, D. (2023). Between Institutioning and Commoning: Grassroots Co-creation in Web3 Communities. Lecture Notes in Computer Science (Including Subseries Lecture Notes in Artificial Intelligence and Lecture Notes in Bioinformatics), 14022 LNCS, 317–329. doi:10.1007/978-3-031-35936-1_23

KEY TERMS AND DEFINITIONS

Decentralized Applications (DApps): Are web applications that distribute key components across peer-to-peer (P2P) networks, diminishing the risk of a single point of failure and enhancing the overall user experience.

Decentralized Autonomous Organizations (DAOs): Are organizational structures enabled by smart contracts on blockchain networks, empowering decentralized decision-making and governance.

Decentralized Financial Applications (DeFi): Are a new breed of consumer-facing financial applications composed of smart contracts on permissionless blockchain technologies.

Metaverse: Is a collective virtual shared space that is created by the convergence of physical and virtual reality.

Non-Fungible Tokens (NFTs): Are unique digital assets such as music, videos, and images that represent ownership or proof of authenticity of a specific item or piece of content using blockchain technology.

Virtual Reality (VR): Allows users to experience real-life situations in a computer-simulated environment.

Chapter 17
Web3 Forward:
Trends and Predictions

Anitha Kumari
https://orcid.org/0000-0002-8343-8926
GITAM University (Deemed), Bengaluru, India

ABSTRACT

The digital landscape is poised for a transformative shift with the advent of Web3. This dynamic and ever-evolving realm provides a comprehensive overview of the chapter, offering insights into the trends shaping the internet's future. Web3 represents a paradigm shift in how society interacts with the digital world, characterized by decentralization, blockchain technology, and user empowerment. This chapter explores the emerging trends that are set to define the Web3 ecosystem in the coming years. The future of Web3 is crucial to understanding the trends and predictions that will shape our digital world. This chapter equips individuals and organizations with valuable insights to anticipate and harness the unfolding transformations in our digital future.

INTRODUCTION

The internet has undergone significant transformations since its inception, evolving from a static information repository to an interactive, dynamic space. Web3 represents the next phase in this evolution, promising a decentralized and user-centric digital landscape. As we navigate through the complexities of Web3, it becomes essential to dissect the technologies underpinning it, understand its evolving ecosystem, and anticipate the future applications that will shape our online experiences. In the early days of the internet, often referred to as Web 1.0, the digital landscape was characterized by static, read-only web pages. These pages, powered by early versions of HTML and supported by data transmission protocols like TCP/IP, SMTP, and HTTP, allowed users to perform basic functions such as transferring data between applications, sending and receiving emails, and reading hypertext online (Choudhury, 2014).

However, despite the functional aspects, Web 1.0 faced notable challenges. One major hurdle was its highly technical nature, acting as a barrier for the average user to actively contribute to online content creation. The intricacies of web development made it a domain accessible primarily to those with tech-

DOI: 10.4018/979-8-3693-1532-3.ch017

nical expertise. Another significant limitation of this era was the absence of a mechanism to monetize content. Websites struggled to find viable ways to generate revenue, impacting their overall success. The dotcom bust of the late 90s served as a harsh reality check, revealing that the value propositions of websites needed to be more clearly defined and developed (McCormick, 2021). In observation, Web 1.0 can be seen as a foundational stage that laid the groundwork for the internet's evolution. The challenges faced during this period prompted a shift towards more user-friendly interfaces, dynamic content creation, and innovative business models in subsequent phases of the internet's development. The lessons learned during these early years continue to influence and shape the digital landscape we navigate today.

In the transition from Web 1.0 to Web 2.0, HTML improvements and the introduction of XML technology were pivotal. Web 2.0 addressed the web designer bottleneck by democratizing content creation. Now, anyone could actively participate in consuming and contributing to dynamic web pages and blogs. This transformative era led to the emergence of a platform economy dominated by tech giants like Google, Amazon, Apple, Meta (Facebook), and Microsoft, alongside smaller players. These platforms operated as walled gardens, tightly regulating user data and activities within their ecosystems (Kietzmann et al., 2011). While Web 2.0 facilitated greater accessibility and user engagement, it was not without its challenges. The centralized storage of data raised concerns about cybersecurity, privacy, and transparency issues along the supply chain. Unintended consequences highlighted the need for careful consideration and regulation in the rapidly evolving landscape of the internet. Web 2.0 marked a significant leap forward, yet it also brought forth complex issues that required thoughtful solutions (Demetis, 2020; Montecchi et al., 2019).

Web 2.0 revolutionized the front end, allowing non-tech users to create online content and revealing new communication channels. In contrast, Web3, distinct from Web 2.0, focuses on a back-end revolution. It replaces centralized data storage with widely distributed data, offering a fresh approach to information organization. Coined by Ethereum's Gavin Wood, Web3 disintermediates data governance, storing data on blockchains and P2P networks. This decentralized model empowers everyone to monetize their data through tokens, representing assets or access to them, from precious materials to event tickets or incentives for eco-friendly actions (Voshmgir, 2020). Web3 not only transforms data storage but also introduces innovative ways for individuals to harness the value of their data through tokenization. Web3 is not new but a continuation of the cyberpunk and cryptopunk spirit from the 1980s and 1990s. This current revolution injects cyberspace with native economic flows, envisioning a future blockchain-based web that includes cryptocurrencies, NFTs, DAOs, and DeFi (Sheridan et al., 2022). Exploring the positive and negative aspects of Web3 technologies, as well as their organizational influences, is crucial for shaping a positive Web3 future (Part et al., 2023). This chapter equips individuals and organizations with valuable insights to anticipate and harness the unfolding transformations in our digital future.

WEB3 TECHNOLOGIES

In Web3.0, HTML remains foundational, but data connections shift from centralized databases to decentralized blockchains, offering users greater control over information and personal data usage. Web3 signifies a paradigm shift in internet functionality, emphasizing decentralization, blockchain integration, and user-centric empowerment. It serves as a compass for readers navigating the promising, complex, and ever-evolving terrain of Web3. It equips individuals and organizations with valuable insights to anticipate and harness the unfolding transformations in our digital future. Web3.0 is poised to leverage

AI to understand users' intentions, personalizing content based on user-controlled data. This automated curation is expected to enhance efficiency and reduce costs for companies (Essex et al, 2023). With blockchain as its foundation, Web3.0 will usher in new applications:

- **NFTs:** Unique cryptographic assets authenticating digital asset ownership will play a pivotal role in creating and exchanging valuable items on Web3.0.
- **DeFi:** The emerging blockchain technology of decentralized finance (DeFi) may serve as the cornerstone for Web3.0's financial services.
- **Cryptocurrency:** Blockchain-based digital currencies like Bitcoin, secured by cryptography, are envisioned as the primary currency in the Web3.0 realm.
- **dApps:** Open-source applications on decentralized blockchains, such as middleware, charitable donations, and social media platforms, will contribute to the diverse landscape of Web3.0.
- **Smart Contracts:** As the foundation for emerging blockchain applications, smart contracts, though not legally binding, will be crucial in executing responsive business logic in Web3.0.
- **Cross-Chain Bridges:** With numerous blockchains in the Web3.0 landscape, cross-chain bridges will facilitate interoperability across these networks.
- **DAOs:** Decentralized Autonomous Organizations (DAOs) may serve as organizing entities, providing the necessary structure and governance for practical decentralized Web3.0 services.

DIGITAL PARADIGM SHIFT (DPS)

The Digital Paradigm Shift (DPS) within Web3 technologies signifies a transformative change in the digital landscape. This shift is characterized by a departure from traditional models, introducing novel approaches to data management, user experiences, and the very foundations of digital interactions. In Web3, DPS encompasses the decentralization of power structures, challenging the dominance of major tech companies. It introduces new possibilities for users, allowing them to actively engage with and monetize their data in ways previously unseen. This shift also addresses issues related to inefficient data processing, aiming for more streamlined and effective digital operations.

Figure 1. Digital paradigm shift

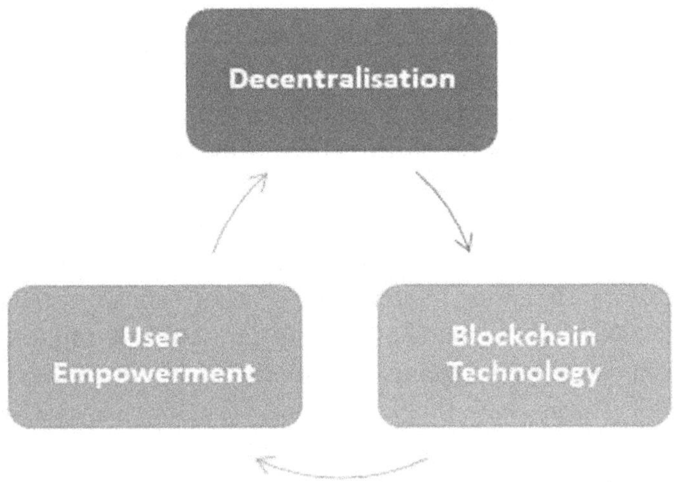

- **Decentralisation:** At the core of Web3 is the principle of decentralization, challenging the traditional models where power and control are concentrated in the hands of a few entities. Web3 envisions a distributed architecture, empowering users by eliminating single points of failure and reducing the influence of intermediaries. This shift towards decentralization promotes transparency, security, and fosters a more inclusive digital environment.

In contrast to the first two generations of the web, characterized by centralized governance and applications, Web3.0 will provide applications and services through a distributed approach, free from reliance on a central authority (Essex et al., 2023).

- **Blockchain Technology:** Blockchain serves as the backbone of Web3, providing the trust and security needed for decentralized systems. The immutability and transparency of blockchain facilitate secure transactions, smart contracts, and decentralized applications (DApps). By managing and validating data on a widely distributed peer-to-peer network, blockchain establishes a foundation for trust. The use of an ostensibly immutable ledger of transactions and activities enhances authenticity, fostering trust among participants in the blockchain ecosystem (Essex et al., 2023). As Web3 continues to evolve, the integration of blockchain technology will be pivotal in reshaping how data is managed and transactions are conducted online.
- **User Empowerment:** Web3 empowers users by granting them control over their data and digital identities. Web3 is not just a technological shift; it's a movement towards empowering users. Individuals regain control over their digital identities, data, and online experiences. The shift towards user-centric platforms ensures that the internet serves the needs of its users rather than exploiting their data. This empowerment is central to the ethos of Web3 and underlines its departure from the centralized models of Web1 and Web2.

WEB3 ECOSYSTEM

As Web3 gains momentum, its ecosystem is expanding rapidly. New platforms, protocols, and communities are emerging, each contributing to the diverse tapestry of the decentralized web. From decentralized finance (DeFi) platforms to decentralized autonomous organizations (DAOs), the Web3 ecosystem is a dynamic and interconnected web of innovation. Empowering the Web3 movement, blockchain introduces trust, transparency, and efficiency in ecosystems, connecting members, data, and machines intelligently. Its decentralized structure ensures democratic decision-making, with varying influence among Web3 participants. Decentralized Autonomous Organizations (DAOs), such as Braintrust, redefine governance by prioritizing value creators. Braintrust, functioning as a DAO, links freelance workers with major brands, enabling over 50,000 freelancers to collectively earn USD 60 million since its 2020 launch. Smart contracts streamline venture contracting, as demonstrated by Boundaryless's open-source tools inspired by Haier's model. Tokens, both fungible and non-fungible, play a crucial role in reinforcing identity and fostering community growth, as illustrated by Braintrust's innovative approach (TCS, 2023).

The rise of Web3 marks a shift towards decentralized, user-centric, and blockchain-powered interactions, revolutionizing the digital landscape. This transformative ecosystem prioritizes enhanced privacy, digital asset ownership, and seamless peer-to-peer interactions, reshaping industries and redefining our tech engagement (Kumar, 2023).

- **DeFi Maturation:** The DeFi sector in Web3 matures, democratizing access to financial instruments through lending, borrowing, and yield farming. Rising user adoption transforms traditional finance models.
- **NFT Evolution and Innovation:** NFTs undergo innovation, expanding beyond art to virtual real estate, gaming, and real-world assets. Reshaping ownership concepts, NFTs open new monetization avenues.
- **Interoperability Among Blockchains:** Interoperability becomes crucial as the Web3 ecosystem grows, facilitating seamless communication between different blockchains.
- **Enhanced Privacy with Decentralized Identity (DID):** Web3 prioritizes user privacy, with decentralized identity solutions gaining prominence, allowing individuals control over digital identities while ensuring privacy.
- **Metaverse Development and Virtual Reality (VR):** The metaverse gains momentum, driven by advancements in virtual and augmented reality. The Web3-powered metaverse transforms social interactions, work dynamics, and digital content experiences.
- **DAOs and Decentralized Governance:** DAOs become integral, enabling decentralized decision-making, resource allocation, and project management within the Web3 ecosystem.
- **Web3 Browsers and Infrastructure:** Specialized Web3 browsers and infrastructure enhance user experiences, providing seamless access to blockchain-based applications, services, and assets.
- **Sustainability and Energy Efficiency:** Addressing environmental concerns, Web3 embraces sustainability through eco-friendly consensus mechanisms like Proof-of-Stake (PoS), reducing the carbon footprint of blockchain networks.
- **Decentralized Content Platforms:** Web3 fosters decentralized content platforms, empowering creators with direct ownership and control, eliminating intermediaries.

- **Regulatory Challenges and Adaptations:** As the Web3 ecosystem expands, regulatory frameworks evolve to navigate the unique challenges and opportunities of decentralized technologies, emphasizing collaboration for a balanced approach between innovation and compliance.

THE FUTURE OF WEB3 APPLICATIONS

The applications of Web3 extend far beyond the current landscape. DApps are becoming more sophisticated, addressing issues of scalability and usability. The integration of virtual reality (VR) and augmented reality (AR) into the Web3 experience is on the horizon, offering immersive and interactive online environments. The future of Web3 applications holds promise for redefining how we collaborate, transact, and engage with digital content. Augmented Reality (AR) and Virtual Reality (VR) stand out as prominent themes in the Web3 landscape. AR enriches our physical reality by overlaying digital information, encompassing sound, video, graphics, haptics, and text. A practical example involves a real estate app leveraging AR to provide users with property details, such as square footage and property tax, by simply viewing it through a mobile phone camera. On the other hand, VR creates a fully immersive 3D virtual environment, either replicating the real world or crafting entirely fictitious digital realms.

For instance, individuals can personalize a virtual supermarket with their favourite products and navigate through its virtual aisles using a VR headset. In the context of real estate, VR facilitates a virtual tour experience, enabling potential buyers to explore a property remotely through a 3D video, offering a realistic feel of the building and its surroundings without physically visiting the location. Mixed reality seamlessly blends aspects of the actual physical environment with the immersive capabilities of VR. This integration enhances the user experience by combining the tangible elements of reality with the transformative potential of virtual environments, creating a dynamic and engaging interface (Park et al., 2023). AR, VR, and Mixed Reality represent the forefront of Web3, opening up new possibilities for immersive and interactive experiences. Whether enhancing our everyday encounters with augmented information, transporting us to virtual realms, or seamlessly blending the real and digital, these technologies are shaping the future of how we perceive and interact with our surroundings. The journey into Web3 realities has just begun, and the potential for innovation and transformative experiences is boundless.

TRENDS AND PREDICTIONS

As we embark on this journey into the future of Web3, it is crucial to understand the trends and predictions that will shape our digital world. This chapter offers readers a roadmap for navigating the evolving landscape of Web3, empowering them to anticipate, adapt to, and leverage the transformative trends on the horizon.

- **Rise of Decentralized Finance (DeFi):** DeFi platforms are at the forefront of Web3, revolutionizing traditional financial services. The coming years will witness the continued growth of DeFi, with increased adoption and innovative financial products reshaping the global financial landscape.
- **Interoperability:** Interoperability is crucial as it enables seamless connection and meaningful data exchange among systems, devices, and organizations without requiring extra user interven-

tion (Park et al., 2023). Seamless communication and interaction between different blockchain networks will be a key trend. Interoperability solutions will play a crucial role in connecting various decentralized systems, fostering a more connected and collaborative Web3 ecosystem.

- **Web3 and Artificial Intelligence (AI):** The integration of AI with Web3 technologies will lead to intelligent and adaptive decentralized systems. Smart contracts and DApps infused with AI capabilities will enhance automation, decision-making, and overall user experience.
- **Privacy-Centric Solutions:** With the growing concerns around data privacy, Web3 will see the rise of privacy-centric solutions. Zero-knowledge proofs, decentralized identity management, and privacy-focused DApps will become integral components of the Web3 landscape.
- **Blockchain's Ascendance:** Blockchain technology lies at the heart of Web3, enabling trustless transactions and decentralized applications (dApps). The chapter delves into the expanding use cases of blockchain beyond cryptocurrencies, such as supply chain management, voting systems, and decentralized finance (DeFi).
- **Decentralized Identity:** As concerns over data privacy and security mount, Web3 is driving the development of decentralized identity solutions. The abstract discusses the potential of self-sovereign identity and its implications for user control over personal data.
- **NFTs and Digital Ownership:** Non-Fungible Tokens (NFTs) have garnered widespread attention, and reshaping the concept of digital ownership, from art and collectibles to virtual real estate and in-game assets. NFT represent a pivotal development in the Web3 timeline. Commonly known as NFTs, these serve as digital certificates of ownership, leveraging blockchain technology to secure digital files and transform them into tradeable assets (Wilson et al., 2021). In stark contrast to replicable digital data, NFTs provide an innovative means to unequivocally establish ownership of distinctive digital assets.
- **Web3 in Education:** The chapter discusses the potential of Web3 to revolutionize education through decentralized learning platforms, credential verification, and tokenized incentives for lifelong learning.
- **Governance and DAOs:** Decentralized Autonomous Organizations (DAOs) are at the forefront of Web3 governance. The abstract examines their role in decision-making and community governance.
- **Web3's Impact on Industries:** Web3 is poised to disrupt various industries, including finance, healthcare, entertainment, and more. The chapter provides insights into how these sectors are evolving in response to Web3 technologies.

ETHICAL IMPLICATIONS AND SOCIETAL IMPACTS OF WEB3

The advent of Web3 brings forth not only technological innovations but also a myriad of ethical considerations and societal impacts that demand careful examination. While the transformative potential of Web3 is evident, it is imperative to navigate the ethical dimensions to ensure that the deployment of these technologies aligns with values, inclusivity, and societal well-being.

- **Decentralization and Power Dynamics:** While decentralization is a cornerstone of Web3, the redistribution of power raises ethical questions. Understanding the implications of shifting control from centralized entities to a more distributed model is crucial. Striking a balance between empowering individuals and preventing potential misuse of this newfound power is an ongoing ethical challenge (Guan et al., 2023).

- **Data Ownership and Monetization:** Web3's promise to empower users with control over their data introduces ethical questions around ownership, consent, and fair compensation. Ensuring that individuals are not exploited in the process of monetizing their data requires robust ethical frameworks and transparent practices.
- **Environmental Sustainability:** The energy consumption associated with blockchain technologies, especially in the case of Proof-of-Work consensus mechanisms, poses ethical concerns. As Web3 evolves, prioritizing sustainability through eco-friendly consensus mechanisms becomes imperative to mitigate the environmental impact of decentralized systems.
- **Privacy and Decentralized Identity:** The shift towards decentralized identity solutions and enhanced privacy in Web3 is commendable. However, the ethical challenge lies in striking the right balance between privacy and accountability. Ensuring that decentralized identity systems do not become tools for illicit activities while safeguarding individual privacy is a delicate ethical consideration.
- **Financial Inclusion and DeFi:** While decentralized finance (DeFi) has the potential to revolutionize traditional financial services, ethical considerations arise regarding accessibility and potential risks for vulnerable populations. Ensuring that DeFi platforms prioritize financial inclusion and adhere to ethical lending and borrowing practices is paramount.
- **NFTs and Digital Ownership:** The rise of Non-Fungible Tokens (NFTs) introduces ethical questions surrounding digital ownership, copyright, and cultural appropriation. Balancing the democratization of digital assets with ethical considerations of cultural sensitivity and originality becomes crucial in the NFT space.
- **Governance and Decentralized Autonomous Organizations (DAOs):** The emergence of DAOs in Web3 governance introduces ethical challenges related to decision-making, transparency, and accountability. Establishing ethical guidelines for DAOs to ensure inclusive governance and prevent the concentration of influence in the hands of a few is a vital consideration.
- **Education and Lifelong Learning:** Web3's potential to revolutionize education through decentralized learning platforms raises ethical questions related to accessibility and equity. Ensuring that the benefits of decentralized education are accessible to diverse populations and do not exacerbate existing inequalities is an ethical imperative.
- **Regulatory Frameworks:** As Web3 expands, the development of ethical regulatory frameworks becomes crucial. Striking a balance between fostering innovation and safeguarding against potential misuse or exploitation requires continuous ethical reflection and collaboration between industry stakeholders and regulators (Allen et al., 2023).
- **Inclusive Innovation:** Ethical innovation in the Web3 space requires a commitment to inclusivity. Ensuring that the benefits of Web3 technologies are accessible across diverse demographics, cultures, and socio-economic backgrounds is essential to prevent the exacerbation of existing digital divides.

As Web3 reshapes the digital landscape, stakeholders must actively engage with the ethical implications and societal impacts of these technologies. Balancing innovation with ethical considerations is not only a responsibility but a necessity to foster a digital future that prioritizes transparency, inclusivity, and societal well-being. Continuous dialogue, ethical frameworks, and collaborative efforts are essential to navigate the intricate ethical landscape of Web3.

CHALLENGES

While Web3 holds immense potential, it is not without its challenges. Scalability issues, regulatory uncertainties, and the environmental impact of certain blockchain technologies are hurdles that must be addressed. Achieving widespread adoption and overcoming the inertia of existing centralized systems present additional challenges that the Web3 community must navigate. As Web3 matures, it also faces challenges related to scalability, energy consumption, and regulatory scrutiny. Web3.0 brings with it considerable potential challenges that enterprise leaders should be aware of, including:

- **Complexity:** The adoption of decentralized networks and smart contracts introduces substantial learning curves and management challenges for IT professionals and everyday web users alike.
- **Security:** The intricate nature of foundational technologies in Web3.0 poses a real challenge to security. Incidents of hacked smart contracts and security breaches on blockchains and cryptocurrency exchanges frequently make national headlines.
- **Regulatory Concerns:** The absence of a central authority renders the regulatory and compliance frameworks, crucial for ensuring the safety of online commerce and other web activities, ineffective or non-existent.
- **Technical Requirements:** Blockchains and decentralized applications (dApps) often demand significant resources and expensive hardware upgrades. The environmental and monetary costs associated with their energy consumption further add to the challenges.
- **Technology Selection:** Companies developing Web3.0 applications may face challenges in selecting the right technologies, given the proliferation of tools for blockchain, cryptocurrency, NFTs, and smart contracts. Additionally, there is an alternative decentralized data technology called Solid, proposed by none other than Berners-Lee, the inventor of the web. He contends that blockchains are too slow, expensive, and public for storing personal information, leading him to establish a company, Inrupt, to commercialize Solid (Essex et al., 2023).

SOLUTIONS

Collaboration and innovation are key to overcoming the challenges facing Web3. Continuous research and development, community engagement, and a commitment to sustainable and scalable solutions will drive the evolution of Web3. Open dialogue with regulators and the development of frameworks that balance innovation with accountability will be crucial for the long-term success of Web3. The emergence of Web3 brings with it a mix of excitement and apprehension due to its vast possibilities and implications. These encompass a shift towards the decentralization of power currently consolidated within major tech entities. The potential for novel user experiences and the prospect for users to monetize their data add further layers to this transformative narrative. However, concerns arise in the form of issues related to inefficient data processing and the looming possibility of environmental repercussions. As we navigate this evolving landscape, it becomes imperative to balance the optimism with a thoughtful consideration of the challenges at hand.

CONCLUSION

This chapter emphasizes the transformative potential of Web3.0 in revolutionizing the internet and associated applications. Central to this new paradigm are decentralized technologies and the blockchain, protocol, concepts summarized within this study (Guan et al., 2023). The future of cryptocurrency finance demands immediate global regulations to address criminal activity. The inadequacy of the current regulatory framework for the digital realm necessitates the creation of new rules, laws, and frameworks. In this transition from the Web2.0 to the Web3.0 world, researchers play a crucial role in ensuring a smooth and effective evolution. It is imperative that regulatory efforts align with the transformative nature of these technologies to usher in a secure and prosperous digital future. Web3 is not just a technological upgrade, it is a transformative force shaping the future of the internet. The decentralized, user-centric nature of Web3 is redefining how we perceive and interact with the digital world. In this journey, understanding the emerging trends and predictions is paramount. Navigating the challenges and implementing innovative solutions will be instrumental in realizing the full potential of Web3 and building a more inclusive, transparent, and user-empowered digital future.

REFERENCES

Allen, D., Frankel, E., Lim, W., Siddarth, D., Simons, J., & Weyl, G. E. (2023). *Ethics of Decentralized Social Technologies: Lessons from Web3, the Fediverse, and Beyond.* Justice, Health & Democracy.

Chaudhry, P. (2017). The looming shadow of illicit trade on the internet. *Business Horizons*, *60*(1), 77e89.

Demetis, D. (2020). Breaking bad online: A synthesis of the darker sides of social networking sites. *European Management Journal*, *38*(1), 33e44.

Essex, D., Kerner, S. M., & Gillis, A. S. (2023). What is Web3.0 (Web3), Definition, Guide and History. *TechTarget.* https://www.techtarget.com/whatis/definition/Web-30

Guan, C., Ding, D., Guo, J., & Teng, Y. (2023). An ecosystem approach to Web3. 0: A systematic review and research agenda. *Journal of Electronic Business & Digital Economics*, *2*(1), 139–156. doi:10.1108/JEBDE-10-2022-0039

Kietzmann, J., Hermkens, K., McCarthy, I., & Silvestre, B. (2011). Social media? Get serious! Understanding the functional building blocks of social media. *Business Horizons*, *54*(3), 241-251.

Kumar, N. (2023). Web3 Ecosystem: 10 Key Trends in 2023. *Analytics Insight.* https://www.analyticsinsight.net/web3-ecosystem-10-key-trends-in-2023/

McCormick, P. (2021). The value chain of the open metaverse. *Not Boring*. Available at https://www.notboring.co/p/the-value-chain-of-the-open-metaverse

Montecchi, M., Plangger, K., & Etter, M. (2019). It's real, trust me! Establishing supply chain provenance using blockchain. *Business Horizons*, *62*(3), 283-293.

Murray, A., Kuban, S., Josefy, M., & Anderson, J. (2021). Contracting in the smart era: The implications of blockchain and decentralized autonomous organizations for contracting and corporate governance. *Academy of Management Perspectives*, *35*(4), 622-641.

Park, A., Wilson, M., Robson, K., Demetis, D., & Kietzmann, J. (2023). Interoperability: Our exciting and terrifying Web3 future. *Business Horizons*, *66*(4), 529–541. doi:10.1016/j.bushor.2022.10.005

Sheridan, D. A. H., Wear, F., Cowell, J., Wong, E., & Yazdinejad, A. (2022). *Web3 challenges and opportunities for the market.* doi: /arXiv.2209.02446. doi:10.48550

TCS. (2023). Building value by building community. *Tata Consultancy Services.* https://www.tcs.com/insights/article/organizations-expand-with-web3-ecosystems

Voshmgir, S. (2020). *Token economy: How the Web3 reinvents the internet.* Blockchain Club Berlin.

Wilson, M., Robson, K., & Pitt, L. (2022). Consumer subversion and its relationship to anti-consumption, deviant and dysfunctional behaviors, and consumer revenge. *Psychology and Marketing*, *39*(3), 598-611.

KEY TERMS AND DEFINITIONS

Blockchain Technology: Blockchain is a decentralized ledger system leveraging cryptographic principles to secure and validate transactions across a distributed network, ensuring transparency and trust.

Decentralization: Decentralization involves distributing authority and decision-making across a network, reducing reliance on central entities. In technology, it enhances security, transparency, and resilience.

Digital Paradigm Shift (DPS): The Digital Paradigm Shift denotes a transformative change in societal operations due to widespread digital technology adoption, with blockchain playing a key role in reshaping traditional systems.

Future of Web3: The Future of Web3 envisions a decentralized internet where users have greater control over data and interactions, facilitated by technologies like blockchain, smart contracts, and decentralized applications.

User Empowerment: User Empowerment in Web3 signifies users gaining control and ownership of their data and digital assets, fostering autonomy and privacy through blockchain and decentralized technologies.

Web3 Ecosystem: The Web3 Ecosystem comprises interconnected decentralized technologies, platforms, and applications, forming the infrastructure for the next generation of the internet.

Web3 Technologies: Web3 Technologies encompass decentralized solutions, including blockchain, smart contracts, and cryptographic protocols, aiming to create a more secure, private, and user-centric online experience.

Compilation of References

Aave. (2023). *Aave: Empowering Users with DeFi Aggregation and Efficient Token Swaps*. https://aavve.github.io/

Abdelmaboud, A., Ahmed, A. I. A., Abaker, M., Eisa, T. A. E., Albasheer, H., Ghorashi, S. A., & Karim, F. K. (2022). Blockchain for IoT applications: Taxonomy, platforms, recent advances, challenges and future research directions. *Electronics (Basel)*, *11*(4), 630. doi:10.3390/electronics11040630

AbendscheinR.DesaiS.AstellA. J. (2023). Towards Accessibility Guidelines for the Metaverse: A Synthesis of Recommendations for People Living With Dementia. doi:10.25972/OPUS-32019

Abou Jaoude, J., & Saade, R. G. (2019). Blockchain applications–usage in different domains. *IEEE Access : Practical Innovations, Open Solutions*, *7*, 45360–45381. doi:10.1109/ACCESS.2019.2902501

Abrol, N., Shaifali, Rattan, M., & Bhambri, P. (2005). Implementation and performance evaluation of JPEG 2000 for medical images. *International Conference on Innovative Applications of Information Technology for Developing World*.

Agarwal, A., & Alathur, S. (2023). *Metaverse revolution and the digital transformation: Intersectional analysis of Industry 5.0. Transforming Government: People*, Process and Policy. doi:10.1108/TG-03-2023-0036

Aggarwal, S., & Kumar, N. (2021). Blockchain 2.0: smart contracts. In Advances in Computers (Vol. 121, pp. 301-322). Elsevier. doi:10.1016/bs.adcom.2020.08.015

Aghaei, H., Naderibeni, N., & Karimi, A. (2021). Designing a tourism business model on block chain platform. *Tourism Management Perspectives*, *39*, 100845. doi:10.1016/j.tmp.2021.100845

Agrawal, T. K., Angelis, J., Khilji, W. A., Kalaiarasan, R., & Wiktorsson, M. (2023). Demonstration of a blockchain-based framework using smart contracts for supply chain collaboration. *International Journal of Production Research*, *61*(5), 1497–1516. doi:10.1080/00207543.2022.2039413

Agustia, M., Aprilia, C., Sari, J., Hikmah, D., & Risnita, R. (2021). Using Quizizz in learning assessment with science literacy oriented in science learning. *International Journal of Engineering, Science, and Information Technology*, *1*(1), 86–90. doi:10.52088/ijesty.v1i1.213

Ahmadi, M., Moghaddam, F. F., Jam, A. J., Gholizadeh, S., & Eslami, M. (2014). A 3-level re-encryption model to ensure data protection in cloud computing environments. *2014 IEEE Conference on Systems, Process and Control (ICSPC 2014)*.

Akbaba, K., & Ertaş-Kılıç, H. (2022). The effect of Web 2.0 applications on students' attitudes towards the use of science and technology. Erzincan University Faculty of Education Journal, 24(1), 130-139.

Akdeniz, A. R., & Yiğit, N. (2001). The effect of computer-aided materials on student achievement in science teaching: The example of frictional force. *Symposium on Science Education in Turkey at the Beginning of the New Millennium, Maltepe University, Istanbul, Proceedings Book*, 229-234.

Al Breiki, H., Al Qassem, L., Salah, K., Habib Ur Rehman, M., & Sevtinovic, D. (2019). Decentralized Access Control for IoT Data Using Blockchain and Trusted Oracles. *2019 IEEE International Conference on Industrial Internet (ICII)*, 248–257. 10.1109/ICII.2019.00051

Albizri, A., & Appelbaum, D. (2021). Trust but Verify: The Oracle Paradox of Blockchain Smart Contracts. *Journal of Information Systems*, *35*(2), 1–16. doi:10.2308/ISYS-19-024

Alcón, A. P. (2023). The acquisition (or not) of property in the metaverse: The tokenization of real estate assets. *Revista de Derecho Civil*, *10*(2), 163–185.

Aldasoro, I., Doerr, S., Gambacorta, L., Garratt, R., & Wilkens, P. K. (2023). *The tokenisation continuum*. BIS. https://www.bis.org/publ/bisbull72.htm

Aleks, G. (2023, September 13). *Compound founder Robert Leshner says 'institutions aren't coming' to DeFi*. DLNews. https://www.dlnews.com/articles/defi/robert-leshner-says-institutional-investors-arent-coming-to-defi/

Alford, H. (2021). *Crypto's networked collaboration will drive Web 3.0*. TechCrunch.

Alharby, M., Aldweesh, A., & Van Moorsel, A. (2018, November). Blockchain-based smart contracts: A systematic mapping study of academic research. In *2018 International Conference on Cloud Computing, Big Data and Blockchain (ICCBB)* (pp. 1-6). IEEE. https://doi.org/10.5121/csit.2017.71011

Alhassan, R. (2017). Exploring the relationship between Web 2.0 Tools Self-Efficacy and Teachers' Use of these Tools in their teaching. *Journal of Education and Learning*, *6*(4), 217–228. doi:10.5539/jel.v6n4p217

Ali, M. S., Vecchio, M., Pincheira, M., Dolui, K., Antonelli, F., & Rehmani, M. H. (2018). Applications of blockchains in the Internet of Things: A comprehensive survey. *IEEE Communications Surveys and Tutorials*, *21*(2), 1676–1717.

Alkan, F., & Kurtoğlu, H. (2023). Computer-Aided Instruction in a Science Lesson Slowmation Development Study: Example of Phases of the Moon. In K. Walters (Ed.), *Dynamic Curriculum Development and Design Strategies for Effective Online Learning in Higher Education* (pp. 250–274). IGI Global. doi:10.4018/978-1-6684-8646-7.ch013

Alkan, F., & Mustafaoğlu, F. M. (2023). Using Web Tools in Lecture: Example of Micro Teaching Lesson. In R. Queirós, M. Cruz, C. Pinto, & D. Mascarenhas (Eds.), *Fostering Pedagogy through Micro and Adaptive Learning in Higher Education: Trends, Tools, and Applications* (pp. 261–286). IGI Global. doi:10.4018/978-1-6684-8656-6.ch012

Alkhatib, Y. J., Forte, A., Bitelli, G., Pierdicca, R., & Malinverni, E. (2023). Bringing Back Lost Heritage into Life by 3D Reconstruction in Metaverse and Virtual Environments: The Case Study of Palmyra, Syria. In L. T. De Paolis, P. Arpaia, & M. Sacco (Eds.), *Extended Reality* (Vol. 14219, pp. 91–106). Springer Nature Switzerland. doi:10.1007/978-3-031-43404-4_7

Allen, D. W., & Potts, J. (2023). Web3 toolkits: A user innovation theory of crypto development. *Journal of Open Innovation*, *9*(2), 100050. doi:10.1016/j.joitmc.2023.100050

Allen, D., Frankel, E., Lim, W., Siddarth, D., Simons, J., & Weyl, G. E. (2023). *Ethics of Decentralized Social Technologies: Lessons from Web3, the Fediverse, and Beyond*. Justice, Health & Democracy.

Almeida, F., Santos, J. D., & Monteiro, J. A. (2013). E-Commerce business models with the context of Web 3.0 paradigm. *International Journal of Advanced Information Technology*, *3*(6), 1–12. doi:10.5121/ijait.2013.3601

Altundağ, Koçak, C., & Koçer, M. Y. (2023). Web 2.0 Tools Supported Innovative Applications in Science Education Based on the Context-Based Learning Approach. In J. Braun & G. Trajkovski (Eds.), Designing Context-Rich Learning by Extending Reality (pp. 179-204). IGI Global. doi:10.4018/978-1-6684-7644-4.ch010

Amali, L. N., Kadir, N. T., & Latief, M. (2019). Development of e-learning content with H5P and iSpring features. *Journal of Physics: Conference Series*, *1387*(1), 012019. doi:10.1088/1742-6596/1387/1/012019

Androulaki, E., Barger, A., Bortnikov, V., Cachin, C., Christidis, K., De Caro, A., Enyeart, D., Ferris, C., Laventman, G., & Manevich, Y. (2018). Hyperledger fabric: a distributed operating system for permissioned blockchains. *Proceedings of the Thirteenth EuroSys Conference.*

Androulaki, E., Barger, A., Bortnikov, V., Cachin, C., Christidis, K., De Caro, A., ... Yellick, J. (2018). Hyperledger Fabric: A Distributed Operating System for Permissioned Blockchains. In *Proceedings of the Thirteenth EuroSys Conference* (pp. 30:1-30:15). 10.1145/3190508.3190538

Ante, L., Wazinski, F.-P., & Saggu, A. (2023). Digital real estate in the metaverse: An empirical analysis of retail investor motivations. *Finance Research Letters*, *58*, 104299. doi:10.1016/j.frl.2023.104299

Antoniadis, I., Spinthiropoulos, K., & Kontsas, S. (2020). Blockchain applications in tourism and tourism marketing: A short review. Strategic Innovative Marketing and Tourism: 8th ICSIMAT. *Northern Aegean, Greece*, *2019*, 375–384.

Antonopoulos, A. M. (2014). *Mastering Bitcoin: Unlocking Digital Cryptocurrencies*. O'Reilly Media.

Ar, N. A. (2016). *The effect of learning by gamification on academic achievement and the use of learning strategies by vocational high school students* [Unpublished Master's Thesis]. Sakarya University, Institute of Educational Sciences.

Aria, R., Archer, N., Khanlari, M., & Shah, B. (2023). Influential Factors in the Design and Development of a Sustainable Web3/Metaverse and Its Applications. In Future Internet (Vol. 15, Issue 4). doi:10.3390/fi15040131

Armknecht, F., Karame, G. O., Mandal, A., Youssef, F., & Zenner, E. (2015). Ripple: Overview and outlook. *Trust and Trustworthy Computing: 8th International Conference, TRUST 2015, Heraklion, Greece, August 24-26, 2015, Proceedings, 8.*

Arroyo, A. (2023). *Beyond Realms: Navigating the Metaverse and Web3*. Academic Press.

Arslan, E., & Güzel, G. (2021). Development of crypto coins and their place in the economy. [PAP]. *PressAcademia Procedia*, *14*(1), 80–83. doi:10.17261/Pressacademia.2021.1491

Arslan, K., & Akçay, H. (2022). The Effect of Science Teaching with Comics on Student Achievement. *Journal of Science Education Art and Technology*, *6*(1), 14–31.

Arslantas, T. K., Tabak, B. Y., & Tabak, H. (2022). Learning mediation via web 2.0 tools in the context of school health and safety. *Research in Pedagogy*, *12*(1), 127–146. doi:10.5937/IstrPed2201127K

Aslam, A. M., Chaudhary, R., Bhardwaj, A., Budhiraja, I., Kumar, N., & Zeadally, S. (2023). Metaverse for 6G and Beyond: The Next Revolution and Deployment Challenges. *IEEE Internet of Things Magazine*, *6*(1), 32–39. doi:10.1109/IOTM.001.2200248

Aslan, Ö., Aktuğ, S. S., Ozkan-Okay, M., Yilmaz, A. A., & Akin, E. (2023). A comprehensive review of cyber security vulnerabilities, threats, attacks, and solutions. *Electronics (Basel)*, *12*(6), 1333.

Aspris, A., Foley, S., Svec, J., & Wang, L. (2021). Decentralized exchanges: The "wild west" of cryptocurrency trading. *International Review of Financial Analysis*, *77*, 101845. doi:10.1016/j.irfa.2021.101845

Avcı, F., ve Atik, H. (2022). An innovative application in educational technology: The H5P project. *School Administrator*, *2*(1), 57–69.

Axelsen, H., Jensen, J. R., & Ross, O. (2022). When is a DAO Decentralized? *Complex Systems Informatics and Modeling Quarterly*, *31*(31), 51–75. doi:10.7250/csimq.2022-31.04

Ba, C. T., Zignani, M., & Gaito, S. (2022). The role of cryptocurrency in the dynamics of blockchain-based social networks: The case of Steemit. *PLoS ONE, 17*(6). doi:10.1371/journal.pone.0267612

Badri, N., Nasraoui, L., & Saidane, L. A. (2022, May). Blockchain for WSN and IoT Applications. In *2022 IEEE 9th International Conference on Sciences of Electronics, Technologies of Information and Telecommunications (SETIT)* (pp. 543-548). IEEE. 10.1109/SETIT54465.2022.9875746

Baggio, R., Micera, R., & Del Chiappa, G. (2020). Smart tourism destinations: A critical reflection. *Journal of Hospitality and Tourism Technology, 11*(3), 407–423. doi:10.1108/JHTT-01-2019-0011

Bahadure, M., Khasare, M. R., Mahure, M. S., Rathod, M. L., Junghare, M. S., & Rathi, P. N. G. (2023). Thr3ebay: E-commerce Dapp using Blockchain. *International Journal for Research in Applied Science and Engineering Technology, 11*(5), 1435–1438. Advance online publication. doi:10.22214/ijraset.2023.51813

Bahri, L., Carminati, B., & Ferrari, E. (2018). Decentralized privacy preserving services for Online Social Networks. In Online Social Networks and Media (Vol. 6). doi:10.1016/j.osnem.2018.02.001

Balakrishnan, N., Aruna, S., Akshaya, D., Karthikeyan, P. C., & Dharshini, G. D. (2023, May). Smart Contracts and Blockchain based E-Voting. In *2023 7th International Conference on Intelligent Computing and Control Systems (ICICCS)* (pp. 1394-1399). IEEE. 10.1109/ICICCS56967.2023.10142675

Balcerzak, A. P., Nica, E., Rogalska, E., Poliak, M., Kliestik, T., & Sabie, O. M. (2022). Blockchain technology and smart contracts in decentralized governance systems. *Administrative Sciences, 12*(3), 96. doi:10.3390/admsci12030096

Ball, M. (2022). *Web 3.0 and the Future of Media*. The Metaverse.

Bamakan, S. M. H., Motavali, A., & Bondarti, A. B. (2020). A survey of blockchain consensus algorithms performance evaluation criteria. *Expert Systems with Applications, 154*, 113385. doi:10.1016/j.eswa.2020.113385

Bambacht, J., & Pouwelse, J. (2022). Web3: A decentralized societal infrastructure for identity, trust, money, and data. *arXiv preprint arXiv:2203.00398*. https://arxiv.org/abs/2203.00398

Band Protocol. (2023). *Band Protocol—Secure, Scalable Blockchain-Agnostic Decentralized Oracle*. https://www.bandprotocol.com/

Baninemeh, E., Farshidi, S., & Jansen, S. (2023). A decision model for decentralized autonomous organization platform selection: Three industry case studies. *Blockchain: Research and Applications, 4*(2), 100127. doi:10.1016/j.bcra.2023.100127

Bansal, P., Bhambri, P., & Gupta, O. P. (2012). *GOR Method to Predict Protein Secondary Structure using Different Input Formats*. Paper presented at the International Conference on Advanced Computing and Communication Technologies, Delhi, India.

Bartels, N., & Hahne, K. (2023). Teaching Building Information Modeling in the Metaverse—An Approach Based on Quantitative and Qualitative Evaluation of the Students Perspective. *Buildings, 13*(9), 2198. doi:10.3390/buildings13092198

Bartholic, M., Burger, E. W., Matsuo, S., & Jung, T. (2023). Reputation as Contextual Knowledge: Incentives and External Value in Truthful Blockchain Oracles. *2023 IEEE International Conference on Blockchain and Cryptocurrency (ICBC)*, 1–9. 10.1109/ICBC56567.2023.10174903

Bartholic, M., Laszka, A., Yamamoto, G., & Burger, E. W. (2022). A Taxonomy of Blockchain Oracles: The Truth Depends on the Question. *2022 IEEE International Conference on Blockchain and Cryptocurrency (ICBC)*, 1–15. 10.1109/ICBC54727.2022.9805555

Bathla, S., Jindal, C., & Bhambri, P. (2007, March). Impact of Technology On Societal Living. In *International Conference on Convergence and Competition* (p. 14). Academic Press.

Bathla, S., Jindal, C., & Bhambri, P. (2007, March). Impact of Technology On Societal Living. In *International Conference on Convergence and Competition* (pp. 14). Academic Press.

Bediroğlu, R. (2021). *Self-competencies of science teacher candidates to develop digital teaching materials* [Master's Thesis]. Yıldız Technical University, Institute of Social Sciences, Istanbul.

Behal, P. (2022). Listen-To-Earn: How Web3 Can Change the Music Industry. SSRN *Electronic Journal*. doi:10.2139/ssrn.4150998

Belchior, R., Vasconcelos, A., Guerreiro, S., & Correia, M. (2022). A Survey on Blockchain Interoperability: Past, Present, and Future Trends. In ACM Computing Surveys (Vol. 54, Issue 8). doi:10.1145/3471140

Bellavitis, C., Fisch, C., & Momtaz, P. P. (2023). The rise of decentralized autonomous organizations (DAOs): A first empirical glimpse. *Venture Capital, 25*(2), 187–203. doi:10.1080/13691066.2022.2116797

Benduch, D. (2019, September). Risks And Opportunities for Tourism Using Smart Contracts. In *26th Geographic Information Systems Conference and Exhibition "GIS ODYSSEY 2019"* (p. 12). Academic Press.

Benji, M., & Sindhu, M. (2019). A study on the Corda and Ripple blockchain platforms. Advances in Big Data and Cloud Computing: *Proceedings of ICBDCC18*.

Béres, F., Seres, I. A., Benczúr, A. A., & Quintyne-Collins, M. (2021, August). Blockchain is watching you: Profiling and deanonymizing ethereum users. In *2021 IEEE international conference on decentralized applications and infrastructures (DAPPS)* (pp. 69-78). IEEE. https://ieeexplore.ieee.org/abstract/document/9566179/

Berners-Lee, T., Hendler, J., & Lassila, O. (2001). Web3.0: A vision for personalized, decentralized web. In *Proceedings of the 12th international conference on World Wide Web* (pp. 1-4). Academic Press.

Besancon, L., Da Silva, C. F., Ghodous, P., & Gelas, J. P. (2022). A Blockchain Ontology for DApps Development. *IEEE Access : Practical Innovations, Open Solutions, 10*, 49905–49933. Advance online publication. doi:10.1109/ACCESS.2022.3173313

Bhambri, P., & Thapar, V. (2009, May). *Power Distribution Challenges in VLSI: An Introduction*. Paper presented at the International Conference on Downtrend Challenges in IT.

Bhambri, P., Hans, S., & Singh, M. (2008, November). Bioinformatics - Friendship between Bits & Genes. In *International Conference on Advanced Computing & Communication Technologies* (pp. 62-65). Academic Press.

Bhambri, P., Hans, S., & Singh, M. (2009). Inharmonic Signal Synthesis & Analysis. *Technia-International Journal of Computing Science and Communication Technologies, 1*(2), 199-201.

Bhambri, P., Sinha, V. K., & Jaiswal, M. (2019). Change in iris dimensions as a potential human consciousness level indicator. *International Journal of Innovative Technology and Exploring Engineering*, *8*(9S), 517–525. doi:10.35940/ijitee.I1082.0789S19

Bhambri, P., & Thapar, V. (2009, May). Power Distribution Challenges in VLSI: An Introduction. *International Conference on Downtrend Challenges in IT*, 63.

Bhandari, B. (2018). Supply Chain Management, Blockchains and Smart Contracts. SSRN *Electronic Journal*. doi:10.2139/ssrn.3204297

Bhutta, M. N. M., Khwaja, A. A., Nadeem, A., Ahmad, H. F., Khan, M. K., Hanif, M. A., Song, H., Alshamari, M., & Cao, Y. (2021). A survey on blockchain technology: evolution, architecture and security. *IEEE Access : Practical Innovations, Open Solutions*, *9*, 61048–61073.

Bodemer, O. (2023). *Corporate Asset Management in the Digital Age: A Blockchain Perspective.* https://doi.org/doi:110.36227/techrxiv.24220675.v1

Bodkhe, U., Bhattacharya, P., Tanwar, S., Tyagi, S., Kumar, N., & Obaidat, M. S. (2019, August). BloHosT: Blockchain enabled smart tourism and hospitality management. In *2019 international conference on computer, information and telecommunication systems* (CITS) (pp. 1-5). IEEE.

Bodkhe, U., Tanwar, S., Parekh, K., Khanpara, P., Tyagi, S., Kumar, N., & Alazab, M. (2020). Blockchain for industry 4.0: A comprehensive review. *IEEE Access : Practical Innovations, Open Solutions*, *8*, 79764–79800. doi:10.1109/ACCESS.2020.2988579

Boeing. (2023). https://www.Boeing.com/

Bojic, L. (2022). Metaverse through the prism of power and addiction: What will happen when the virtual world becomes more attractive than reality? *European Journal of Futures Research*, *10*(1), 22. doi:10.1186/s40309-022-00208-4

Bosamia, M., & Patel, D. (2018). Current trends and future implementation possibilities of the Merkel tree. *International Journal on Computer Science and Engineering*, *6*(8), 294–301.

Boussada, R., Elhdhili, M. E., Hamdane, B., & Azouz Saidane, L. (2022). Privacy Preserving in the Modern Era: A Review of the State of the Art. In A. K. Tyagi (Ed.), Advances in Information Security, Privacy, and Ethics. IGI Global. doi:10.4018/978-1-6684-5250-9.ch001

Bouzid, A., Narciso, P., & Wood, S. (2023). *NFTs for Business: A Practical Guide to Harnessing Digital Assets*. APress.

Bower, M. (2016). Deriving a typology of Web 2.0 learning technologies. *British Journal of Educational Technology*, *47*(4), 763–777. doi:10.1111/bjet.12344

Braeckman, Y. (2022, February 18). *Philanthropy DAOs—The future of giving?* Medium.Com. https://medium.com/impact-shakers/philanthropy-daos-the-future-of-giving-608cc7a829b4

Breidenbach, L., Cachin, C., Coventry, A., Ellis, S., Juels, A., Miller, A., Magauran, B., Nazarov, S., Topliceanu, A., Zhang, F., Chan, B., Koushanfar, F., Moroz, D., & Tramer, F. (2021). *Chainlink 2.0: Next Steps in the Evolution of Decentralized Oracle Networks*. https://naorib.ir/white-paper/chinlink-whitepaper.pdf

Breitner, J., & Heninger, N. (2019). Biased nonce sense: Lattice attacks against weak ECDSA signatures in cryptocurrencies. *International Conference on Financial Cryptography and Data Security*.

Brennecke, M., Guggenberger, T., Schellinger, B., & Urbach, N. (2022). *The De-Central Bank in Decentralized Finance: A Case Study of MakerDAO. Hawaii International Conference on System Sciences*. 10.24251/HICSS.2022.737

Brown, C., & Jones, D. (2018). Securing Web3 Wallets: Best Practices for Users. *Journal of Blockchain Technology*, *5*(2), 112–130.

Bucher, D., & Hall, D. (2022). *New Ways of Data Governance for Construction? Decentralized Data Marketplaces as Web3 Concept just around the Corner*. doi:10.7146/aul.455.c224

Buhalis, D., & Amaranggana, A. (2015). Smart tourism destinations enhancing tourism experience through personalisation of services. In *Information and Communication Technologies in Tourism 2015: Proceedings of the International Conference in Lugano, Switzerland, February 3-6, 2015* (pp. 377-389). Springer International Publishing. 10.1007/978-3-319-14343-9_28

Buhalis, D., Leung, D., & Lin, M. (2023). Metaverse as a disruptive technology revolutionising tourism management and marketing. *Tourism Management*, *97*, 104724. doi:10.1016/j.tourman.2023.104724

Buonincontri, P., & Micera, R. (2016). The experience co-creation in smart tourism destinations: A multiple case analysis of European destinations. *Information Technology & Tourism*, *16*(3), 285–315. doi:10.1007/s40558-016-0060-5

Buterin, V. (2013). *Ethereum whitepaper: A next-generation smart contract and decentralized application platform* [White Paper]. Ethereum.

Buterin, V. (2016). Ethereum: platform review. *Opportunities and Challenges for Private and Consortium Blockchains, 45.* https://files.gitter.im/cyberFund/cyber.fund/P8Xb/314477721-Ethereum-Platform-Review-Opportunities-and-Challenges-for-Private-and-Consortium-Blockchains-_1_.pdf

Buterin, V. (2019). *On public and private blockchains (2015).* https://blog. ethereum. org/2015/08/07/on-public-and-private-blockchains

Buterin, V. (2017). Ethereum: A Next-Generation Smart Contract and Decentralized Application Platform. *Ledger*, *1*, 63–75. doi:10.5195/ledger.2017.23

Cachin, C. (2016, July). Architecture of the hyperledger blockchain fabric. *Workshop on distributed cryptocurrencies and consensus ledgers, 310*(4), 1-4.

Caldarelli, G. (2020a). Real-world blockchain applications under the lens of the oracle problem. A systematic literature review. *2020 IEEE International Conference on Technology Management, Operations and Decisions (ICTMOD)*, 1–6. 10.1109/ICTMOD49425.2020.9380598

Caldarelli, G. (2020b). Understanding the Blockchain Oracle Problem: A Call for Action. *Information (Basel)*, *11*(11), 509. doi:10.3390/info11110509

Cambridge Dictionary. (n.d.). https://dictionary.cambridge.org/dictionary/english/driving-force

Can, B., & Usta, E. (2021). The effect of Web 2.0 supported conceptual cartoon on achievement and attitude. *Turkish Journal of Academic Publications*, *5*(1), 51–69.

Candan, F. (2022). *Meta-thematic analysis of the use of technology-oriented gamification practices in the learning process: kahoot*! Example [Master's Thesis]. Gaziantep University Institute of Educational Sciences.

Cant, B., Khadikar, A., Ruiter, A., Bronebakk, J. B., Coumaros, J., Buvat, J., & Gupta, A. (2016). *Smart Contracts in Financial Services: Getting from Hype to Reality*. Capgemini Consulting. https://www.capgemini.com/consulting-de/wp-content/uploads/sites/32/2017/08/smart_contracts_paper_long_0.p

Carapella, F., Chuan, G., Gerszten, J., Hunter, C., & Swem, N. (2023). Tokenization: Overview and Financial Stability Implications. *Finance and Economics Discussion Series, 60*, 1–29. doi:10.17016/feds.2023.060

Cassatt, A. (2023). *Web3 Marketing: A Handbook for the Next Internet Revolution*. Wiley.

Catalini, C., & Gans, J. S. (2016). *Some Simple Economics of the Blockchain*. MIT Sloan Research Paper No. 5191-16.

Chainlink. (2021, December 14). *Blockchain in Insurance*. https://blog.chain.link/blockchain-insurance

Chainlink. (2023). *Chainlink.* https://chain.link

Chainlink. (2023, November 30). *What Is an Atomic Swap?* https://chain.link/education-hub/atomic-swaps

Chainstack. (2023). https://chainstack.com/

Chalaemwongwan, N., & Kurutach, W. (2018). Notice of Violation of IEEE Publication Principles: State of the art and challenges facing consensus protocols on blockchain. *2018 International Conference on Information Networking (ICOIN).*

Chao, C.-H., Ting, I.-H., Tseng, Y.-J., Wang, B.-W., Wang, S.-H., Wang, Y.-Q., & Chen, M.-C. (2022). The Study of Decentralized Autonomous Organization (DAO) in Social Network. *The 9th Multidisciplinary International Social Networks Conference*, 59–65. 10.1145/3561278.3561293

Chaudhry, P. (2017). The looming shadow of illicit trade on the internet. *Business Horizons*, *60*(1), 77e89.

Chen, Y. (2018). Blockchain tokens and the potential democratization of entrepreneurship and innovation. *Business Horizons*, *61*(4), 567–575.

Chen, C., Zhang, K. Z. K., Chu, Z., & Lee, M. (2023). Augmented reality in the metaverse market: The role of multimodal sensory interaction. *Internet Research.* Advance online publication. doi:10.1108/INTR-08-2022-0670

Chen, H.-J. (2023). Gather in the metaverse: Learning outcomes, virtual presence, and perceptions of high- and low-achieving pre-service teachers of English as a Foreign Language. *Education and Information Technologies.* Advance online publication. doi:10.1007/s10639-023-12135-3

Chenna, S. (2023). Augmented Reality and AI: Enhancing Human-Computer Interaction in the Metaverse. SSRN *Electronic Journal.* doi:10.2139/ssrn.4324629

Chen, Y., Liu, C., Wang, Y., & Wang, Y. (2021). A Self-Sovereign Decentralized Identity Platform Based on Blockchain. *2021 IEEE Symposium on Computers and Communications (ISCC)*, 1–7. 10.1109/ISCC53001.2021.9631518

Chi, Y., Duan, H., Cai, W., Wang, Z. J., & Leung, V. C. M. (2023). Networking Parallel Web3 Metaverses for Interoperability. *IEEE Network.*

Chicotsky, B. (2023). Web3 and marketing: The new frontier. *Applied Marketing Analytics, 9*(2).

Chohan, R., & Paschen, J. (2023). NFT marketing: How marketers can use nonfungible tokens in their campaigns. *Business Horizons*, *66*(1), 43–50. doi:10.1016/j.bushor.2021.12.004

ChohanU. W. (2017). The decentralized autonomous organization and governance issues. *Available at* SSRN 3082055. doi:10.2139/ssrn.3082055

ChohanU. W. (2021). Decentralized Finance (DeFi): An Emergent Alternative Financial Architecture. *Econometric Modeling: International Financial Markets - Foreign Exchange EJournal.* doi:10.2139/ssrn.3791921

Chorey, P., & Sahu, N. (2024). Enhancing efficiency and scalability in Blockchain Consensus algorithms: The role of Checkpoint approach. *J. Integr. Sci. Technol.*, *12*(1), 1–7.

Choudhury, T., Khanna, A., Chatterjee, P., Um, J. S., & Bhattacharya, A. (Eds.). (2023). *Blockchain Applications in Healthcare: Innovations and Practices.* John Wiley & Sons. doi:10.1002/9781394229512

Christidis, K., & Devetsikiotis, M. (2016). Blockchains and Smart contracts for the Internet of Things. *IEEE Access : Practical Innovations, Open Solutions*, *4*, 2292–2303. doi:10.1109/ACCESS.2016.2566339

Cloots, A. S. (2019). Blockchain and the Law: The Rule of Code. *The Cambridge Law Journal*, *78*(1), 213–217. doi:10.1017/S0008197319000084

CoinGecko. (2023, July 17). *2023 Q1 Crypto Industry Report*. https://www.coingecko.com/research/publications/2023-q1-crypto-report

Coingecko. (2023, September 9). *Top Liquid Staking Governance Tokens Coins by Market Cap*. https://www.coingecko.com/en/categories/liquid-staking-governance-tokens

Coita, D. C., & Ban, O. (2020). Revolutionizing marketing in tourism industry through blockchain technology. In Strategic Innovative Marketing and Tourism: 8th ICSIMAT, Northern Aegean, Greece, 2019 (pp. 789-797). Springer International Publishing. doi:10.1007/978-3-030-36126-6_87

Compound, D. A. O. (2023). *Compound DAO*. https://compound.finance

Cong, L. W., Tang, K., Wang, Y., & Zhao, X. (2023). *Inclusion and democratization through web3 and defi? initial evidence from the ethereum ecosystem* (No. w30949). National Bureau of Economic Research. https://www.nber.org/papers/w30949

Çoruhlu, Ş. T., Altunsoy, Y., & Sağlam, A. (2023). Infographics Influence on Students' Conceptual Developments: The Case of the Conscious Consumer. *İnönü University Faculty of Education Journal*, *24*(2), 1442-1466. doi:10.17679/inuefd.1213344

Cosares, S., Kalish, K., Maciura, T., & Spieler, A. C. (2021). Blockchain applications in finance. In *The Emerald Handbook of Blockchain for Business* (pp. 275–291). Emerald Publishing Limited. doi:10.1108/978-1-83982-198-120211022

Croman, K., Decker, C., Eyal, I., Gencer, A. E., Juels, A., Kosba, A. E., ... Wattenhofer, R. (2016). On Scaling Decentralized Blockchains. In *International Conference on Financial Cryptography and Data Security* (pp. 106-125). Academic Press.

Cui, P., Dixon, J., Guin, U., & Dimase, D. (2019). A Blockchain-Based Framework for Supply Chain Provenance. *IEEE Access : Practical Innovations, Open Solutions*, *7*, 157113–157125. doi:10.1109/ACCESS.2019.2949951

Dai, W., & Vasileiou, I. (2020). Exploring the Security Landscape of Web3 Wallets. *International Journal of Cybersecurity*, *14*(3), 245–263.

Damodaran, A. (2023). From non fungible tokens to metaverse: Blockchain based inclusive innovation in arts. *Innovation and Development*, 1–20. doi:10.1080/2157930X.2023.2180709

DAOmatch. (2023). *Grants & Funding from DAOs*. https://daomatch.xyz/grants-investments

Darmawan, M. S., Daeni, F., & Listiaji, P. (2020). The use of Quizizz as an online assessment application for science learning in the pandemic era. *Unnes Science Education Journal*, *9*(3), 144–150. doi:10.15294/usej.v9i3.41541

Dasaklis, T. K., Voutsinas, T. G., Tsoulfas, G. T., & Casino, F. (2022). A Systematic Literature Review of Blockchain-Enabled Supply Chain Traceability Implementations. *Sustainability (Basel)*, *14*(4), 2439. doi:10.3390/su14042439

Davies, R., Randall, D., & West, R. E. (2015). Using Open Badges to Certify Practicing Evaluators. *The American Journal of Evaluation*, *36*(2), 151–163. doi:10.1177/1098214014565505

Davis, M. (2021). *10 DAOs to Follow in the Social Impact and Environmental Space*. https://www.onegreenplanet.org/human-interest/10-daos-to-follow-in-the-social-impact-space/

De Marco, E. L., Longo, A., & Zappatore, M. (2023). Game Engine Platforms Supporting Metaverse-Linking Process: A Proposed Case Study on Virtual 3D Printing. In L. T. De Paolis, P. Arpaia, & M. Sacco (Eds.), *Extended Reality* (Vol. 14218, pp. 198–209). Springer Nature Switzerland. doi:10.1007/978-3-031-43401-3_13

DeFi Llarma. (2023). *DeFi Llarma*. https://defillama.com/

Defidao, Lee, D. K. C., Guan, C., & Ding, D. (2023). *Global Web3 Eco Innovation*. Singapore University of Social Sciences.

Değirmenci, R. (2021). The use of Quizizz in language learning and teaching from the teachers' and students' perspectives: A literature review. *Language Education and Technology*, *1*(1), 1–11.

Del Vecchio, P., Mele, G., Ndou, V., & Secundo, G. (2018). Creating value from social big data: Implications for smart tourism destinations. *Information Processing & Management*, *54*(5), 847–860. doi:10.1016/j.ipm.2017.10.006

Delgado-Segura, S., Pérez-Sola, C., Navarro-Arribas, G., & Herrera-Joancomartí, J. (2018). Analysis of the Bitcoin UTXO set. International Conference on Financial Cryptography and Data Security, Di Pierro, M. (2017). What is the blockchain? *Computing in Science & Engineering*, *19*(5), 92–95.

Demetis, D. (2020). Breaking bad online: A synthesis of the darker sides of social networking sites. *European Management Journal*, *38*(1), 33e44.

Demirel, E., & Zeren, S. K. (2021). Developing smart contracts for financial payments as innovation. In Research Anthology on Blockchain Technology in Business, Healthcare, Education, and Government (pp. 1870-1889). IGI Global. doi:10.4018/978-1-7998-5351-0.ch102

Demirel, E. (2023). Application of Blockchain-Based Smart Contract in Sustainable Tourism Finance. In *Blockchain for Tourism and Hospitality Industries* (pp. 122–138). Routledge. doi:10.4324/9781003351917-9

Demirel, E., Karagöz Zeren, S., & Hakan, K. (2022). Smart contracts in tourism industry: A model with blockchain integration for post pandemic economy. *Current Issues in Tourism*, *25*(12), 1895–1909. doi:10.1080/13683500.2021.1960280

Deng, X., Zhao, Z., Beillahi, S. M., Du, H., Minwalla, C., Nelaturu, K., Veneris, A., & Long, F. (2023). A Robust Front-Running Methodology for Malicious Flash- Loan DeFi Attacks. *2023 IEEE International Conference on Decentralized Applications and Infrastructures (DAPPS)*, 38–47. 10.1109/DAPPS57946.2023.00015

Dezfouli, M. (2023). *Ultraverse City: Delve into a world where the boundaries between reality and fantasy are blurred*. Academic Press.

Dhillon, V., Metcalf, D., & Hooper, M. (2017). The DAO Hacked. In Blockchain Enabled Applications (pp. 67–78). Apress. doi:10.1007/978-1-4842-3081-7_6

Dimitri, N. (2023). Voting in DAOs. *Distributed Ledger Technologies: Research and Practice*, *3624574*(4), 1–12. Advance online publication. doi:10.1145/3624574

Ding, W., Hou, J., Li, J., Guo, C., Qin, J., Kozma, R., & Wang, F. Y. (2022). DeSci Based on Web3 and DAO: A Comprehensive Overview and Reference Model. In IEEE Transactions on Computational Social Systems (Vol. 9, Issue 5). doi:10.1109/TCSS.2022.3204745

Dinh, T. T. A., Wang, J., Chen, G., Liu, R., Ooi, B. C., & Tan, K.-L. (2017). Blockbench: A framework for analyzing private blockchains. *Proceedings of the 2017 ACM International Conference on Management of Data.*

Duffey, C. (2023). *Decoding the Metaverse: Expand Your Business Using Web3*. Kindle Edition.

Dutta, H., Nagesh, S., Talluri, J., & Bhaumik, P. (2023). A Solution to Blockchain Smart Contract Based Parametric Transport and Logistics Insurance. *IEEE Transactions on Services Computing*, *16*(5), 3155–3167. doi:10.1109/TSC.2023.3281516

Dwivedi, V., Norta, A., Wulf, A., Leiding, B., Saxena, S., & Udokwu, C. (2021). A formal specification smart-contract language for legally binding decentralized autonomous organizations. *IEEE Access : Practical Innovations, Open Solutions*, *9*, 76069–76082. doi:10.1109/ACCESS.2021.3081926

Dwivedi, V., Pattanaik, V., Deval, V., Dixit, A., Norta, A., & Draheim, D. (2021). Legally enforceable smart-contract languages: A systematic literature review. *ACM Computing Surveys*, *54*(5), 1–34. doi:10.1145/3453475

Dwivedi, Y. K., Hughes, L., Baabdullah, A. M., Ribeiro-Navarrete, S., Giannakis, M., Al-Debei, M. M., Dennehy, D., Metri, B., Buhalis, D., Cheung, C. M. K., Conboy, K., Doyle, R., Dubey, R., Dutot, V., Felix, R., Goyal, D. P., Gustafsson, A., Hinsch, C., Jebabli, I., ... Wamba, S. F. (2022). Metaverse beyond the hype: Multidisciplinary perspectives on emerging challenges, opportunities, and agenda for research, practice and policy. *International Journal of Information Management*, *66*, 102542. Advance online publication. doi:10.1016/j.ijinfomgt.2022.102542

Eberhardt, J., & Tai, S. (2017). On or off the blockchain? Insights on off-chaining computation and data. *European Conference on Service-Oriented and Cloud Computing.*

Edelman, G. (2021). *What Is Web3, Anyway?* Wired.

Efe, H., Gül, R., & Topsakal, Ü. U. (2022). Use of web 2.0 tools in science education: examining primary school students' perceptions on self-regulation. In *Elementary School Forum* (Vol. 9, No. 3, pp. 552-568). Indonesia University of Education.

El Jaouhari, A., Arif, J., Samadhiya, A., Kumar, A., & Trinkūnas, V. (2023). Are we there Or Do we have more to do? Metaverse in Facility Management and Future Prospects. *International Journal of Strategic Property Management*, *27*(3), 159–175. doi:10.3846/ijspm.2023.19516

Ellinger, E. W., Mini, T., Gregory, R. W., & Dietz, A. (2023). Decentralized Autonomous Organization (DAO): The case of MakerDAO. *Journal of Information Technology Teaching Cases*. doi:10.1177/20438869231181151

Emurgo. (2023). *Emurgo—Supporting Adoption Of Cardano And Blockchain Tech.* https://www.emurgo.io/

Erdogan, A., & Yildirim, N. (2023). Evaluation of the Training to Make Preservice Science Teachers Use Web 2.0 Tools during Teaching. *Educational Policy Analysis and Strategic Research*, *18*(1), 77–97. doi:10.29329/epasr.2023.525.4

Erol Şahin, A. N., & Kara Erol, H. (2022). A digital educational tool experience in history lesson: Creating digital comics via Pixton Edu. *Journal of Educational Technology & Online Learning : The Official Journal of the Online Learning Consortium*, *5*(1), 223–242. doi:10.31681/jetol.983861

Ersöz, B. (2020). New generation web paradigm: Web 4.0. *Journal of Computer Science and Technologies*, *1*(2), 58–65.

Essex, D., Kerner, S. M., & Gillis, A. S. (2023). What is Web3.0 (Web3), Definition, Guide and History. *TechTarget.* https://www.techtarget.com/whatis/definition/Web-30

Eternal. (2023). https://eternal.gg/

Ethereum Project. (2022). *Ethereum White Paper*. Retrieved from https://ethereum.org/whitepaper/

Etherspot. (2023). https://etherspot.io/

ETHGlobal. (2023). *Supply Chain Dapp*. https://ethglobal.com/showcase/supply-chain-dapp-crcvh

European Securities and Markets Authority. (2021). *TRV, ESMA Report on Trends, Risks and Vulnerabilities* (Vol. 1). Publications Office. https://data.europa.eu/doi/10.2856/723305

Eyal, I., & Sirer, E. G. (2014). Majority is not enough: Bitcoin mining is vulnerable. In *International conference on financial cryptography and data security* (pp. 436-454). Academic Press.

Eyal, I., & Sirer, E. G. (2014). Majority is not enough: Bitcoin mining is vulnerable. *International Conference on Financial Cryptography and Data Security.*

Fan, X., & Chai, Q. (2018). Roll-DPoS: a randomized delegated proof of stake scheme for scalable blockchain-based internet of things systems. *Proceedings of the 15th EAI International Conference on Mobile and Ubiquitous Systems: Computing, Networking and Services.*

Fantazzini, D. (2022). Crypto-coins and credit risk: Modelling and forecasting their probability of death. *Journal of Risk and Financial Management*, *15*(7), 304. doi:10.3390/jrfm15070304

FB. (2021, October 28). *Introducing Meta: A Social Technology Company*. https://about.fb.com/news/2021/10/facebook-company-is-now-meta/

Fenwick, M., & Jurcys, P. (2022). *The Contested Meaning of Web3 and Why it Matters for (IP)*. Lawyers. doi:10.2139/ssrn.4017790

Fernandez-Carames, T. M., & Fraga-Lamas, P. (2019). A review on the application of blockchain to the next generation of cybersecure industry 4.0 smart factories. *IEEE Access : Practical Innovations, Open Solutions*, *7*, 45201–45218.

Ferreira, A. (2021). Regulating smart contracts: Legal revolution or simply evolution? *Telecommunications Policy*, *45*(2), 102081. doi:10.1016/j.telpol.2020.102081

Ferro, E., Saltarella, M., Rotondi, D., Giovanelli, M., Corrias, G., Moncada, R., & Favenza, A. (2023). Digital assets rights management through smart legal contracts and smart contracts. *Blockchain: Research and Applications*, *100142*(3). Advance online publication. doi:10.1016/j.bcra.2023.100142

Filieri, R., D'Amico, E., Destefanis, A., Paolucci, E., & Raguseo, E. (2021). Artificial intelligence (AI) for tourism: An European-based study on successful AI tourism start-ups. *International Journal of Contemporary Hospitality Management*, *33*(11), 4099–4125. doi:10.1108/IJCHM-02-2021-0220

Filipcic, S. (2022). Web3 & DAOs: an overview of the development and possibilities for the implementation in research and education. *2022 45th Jubilee International Convention on Information, Communication and Electronic Technology, MIPRO 2022 - Proceedings*. 10.23919/MIPRO55190.2022.9803324

Filipova, I. A. (2023). Creating the Metaverse: Consequences for Economy, Society, and Law. *Journal of Digital Technologies and Law*, *1*(1), 7–32. doi:10.21202/jdtl.2023.1

Finney, H. (2004). *Reusable Proof of Work (RPOW)*. Retrieved from https://www.finney.org/~hal/rpow/

Fiorentino, S., & Bartolucci, S. (2021). Blockchain-based smart contracts as new governance tools for the sharing economy. *Cities (London, England)*, *117*, 103325. doi:10.1016/j.cities.2021.103325

Flaumenhaft, Y., & Ben-Assuli, O. (2018). Personal health records, global policy and regulation review. *Health Policy (Amsterdam)*, *122*(8), 815–826. doi:10.1016/j.healthpol.2018.05.002 PMID:29884294

Flynn, B., & Ferreira, E. (2021). Web 3.0: Decentralized Apps and the Future of the Web. *IEEE Software*, *38*(5), 78–85.

Foggan, L. A., & Cwiertny, C. E. (2018). *Blockchain, smart contracts and parametric insurance: Made for each other*. Academic Press.

Foundry. (2023). https://www.foundry.com/

Francisco, K., & Swanson, D. (2018). The Supply Chain Has No Clothes: Technology Adoption of Blockchain for Supply Chain Transparency. *Logistics*, *2*(1), 2. doi:10.3390/logistics2010002

Friebe, S., Sobik, I., & Zitterbart, M. (2018). DecentID: Decentralized and Privacy-Preserving Identity Storage System Using Smart Contracts. *Proceedings - 17th IEEE International Conference on Trust, Security and Privacy in Computing and Communications and 12th IEEE International Conference on Big Data Science and Engineering, Trustcom/BigDataSE 2018*. 10.1109/TrustCom/BigDataSE.2018.00016

Friesendorf, C., & Blütener, A. (2023a). Decentralized Finance: Concept and Characteristics. In Decentralized Finance (DeFi) (pp. 29–36). Springer Nature Switzerland. doi:10.1007/978-3-031-37488-3_3

Friesendorf, C., & Blütener, A. (2023b). Decentralized Finance: Empirical Analysis of Customer Willingness. In Decentralized Finance (DeFi) (pp. 75–94). Springer Nature Switzerland. doi:10.1007/978-3-031-37488-3_10

Friesendorf, C., & Blütener, A. (2023c). Decentralized Finance: Regulation. In Decentralized Finance (DeFi) (pp. 55–59). Springer Nature Switzerland. doi:10.1007/978-3-031-37488-3_7

Frtisch, R., Käser, S., & Wattenhofer, R. (2022). The Economics of Automated Market Makers. *Proceedings of the 4th ACM Conference on Advances in Financial Technologies*, 102–110. 10.1145/3558535.3559790

Gandal, N., Hamrick, J. T., Moore, T., & Vasek, M. (2021). The rise and fall of cryptocurrency coins and tokens. *Decisions in Economics and Finance, 44*(2), 981-1014. https://link.springer.com/article/10.1007/s10203-021-00329-8

Gandal, N., Hamrick, J., Moore, T., & Vasek, M. (2021). The rise and fall of cryptocurrency coins and tokens. *Decisions in Economics and Finance*, *44*(2), 981–1014. doi:10.1007/s10203-021-00329-8

Ganeshkumar, C., Sankar, J. G., & David, A. (2023). Impact of Artificial Intelligence on Agriculture Value Chain Performance: Agritech Perspective. In Blockchain, IoT, and AI Technologies for Supply Chain Management (pp. 71-98). CRC Press.

García, F. A. C. (2008). *The third generation web is coming*. https://methainternet.wordpress.com/2008/01/25/the-third-generation-web-is-coming/

Garrigos-Simon, F. J., Lapiedra-Alcamí, R., & Ribera, T. B. (2012). Social networks and Web 3.0: Their impact on the management and marketing of organizations. *Management Decision*, *50*(10), 1880–1890. doi:10.1108/00251741211279657

Garzik, J. (2014). *BIP 32: Hierarchical Deterministic Wallets*. Retrieved from https://github.com/bitcoin/bips/blob/master/bip-0032.mediawiki

Gaži, P., Kiayias, A., & Zindros, D. (2019). Proof-of-stake sidechains. *2019 IEEE Symposium on Security and Privacy (SP)*.

Gehred, A. P. (2020). Canva. *Journal of the Medical Library Association: JMLA*, *108*(2), 338. doi:10.5195/jmla.2020.940

Gencer, S., Turan-Oluk, N., Kadayıfçı, H., & Yalçin Çelik, A. (2023). The Purposes and Justifications for Preferences of Web 2.0 Tools Used by Pre-Service Chemistry Teachers in Their Teaching Practices in Distance Education Environment. *Shanlax International Journal of Education*, *11*(S1-Jan), 61–75. doi:10.34293/education.v11iS1-Jan.5908

General Electric. (2023). https://www.ge.com/

Gennaro, M. D., Italiano, L., Meroni, G., & Quattrocchi, G. (2022). DeepThought: A Reputation and Voting-Based Blockchain Oracle. In J. Troya, B. Medjahed, M. Piattini, L. Yao, P. Fernández, & A. Ruiz-Cortés (Eds.), *Service-Oriented Computing* (Vol. 13740, pp. 369–383). Springer Nature Switzerland. doi:10.1007/978-3-031-20984-0_26

George, A. S. H., George, A. S., & Hameed, A. S. (2023). *The Web3 Revolution: Navigating the Future of Decentralized Networks*. Book Rivers.

Gervais, A., Karame, G. O., Wüst, K., Glykantzis, V., Ritzdorf, H., & Capkun, S. (2016). On the Security and Performance of Proof of Work Blockchains. In *Proceedings of the 2016 ACM SIGSAC Conference on Computer and Communications Security (CCS '16)* (pp. 3-16). 10.1145/2976749.2978341

Giaccardi, E., & Zaga, C. (2021). Web 3.0 and the Future of Social Networks. *Journal of Computer-Mediated Communication*, *26*(2), 89–102.

Gilbert, S. (2022). *Crypto, web3, and the Metaverse. Bennett Institute for Public Policy*. Policy Brief. https://www.bennettinstitute.cam.ac.uk/wp-content/uploads/2022/03/Policy-brief-Crypto-web3-and-the-metaverse.pdf

Gilcrest, J., & Carvalho, A. (2018, December). Smart contracts: Legal considerations. In *2018 IEEE International Conference on Big Data (Big Data)* (pp. 3277-3281). IEEE.

Gitcoin. (2023). *Gitcoin Grants*. https://grants.gitcoin.co/

Gramlich, V., Guggenberger, T., Principato, M., Schellinger, B., & Urbach, N. (2023). A multivocal literature review of decentralized finance: Current knowledge and future research avenues. *Electronic Markets*, *33*(1), 11. doi:10.1007/s12525-023-00637-4

Grigg, I. (2018). *Web3: A Platform for Decentralized Applications*. Retrieved from https://medium.com/@i.m.grigg/web3-a-platform-for-decentralised-applications-17a46b2caf1

Grinberg, R. (2012). Bitcoin: An Innovative Alternative Digital Currency. *Hastings Science & Technology Law Journal*, *4*, 159–207.

Guan, C., Ding, D., Guo, J., & Teng, Y. (2023). An ecosystem approach to Web3. 0: A systematic review and research agenda. *Journal of Electronic Business & Digital Economics*, *2*(1), 139–156. doi:10.1108/JEBDE-10-2022-0039

Guidi, B., & Michienzi, A. (2022b). Social games and Blockchain: exploring the Metaverse of Decentraland. *Proceedings - 2022 IEEE 42nd International Conference on Distributed Computing Systems Workshops, ICDCSW 2022*. 10.1109/ICDCSW56584.2022.00045

Guidi, B. (2021). An Overview of Blockchain Online Social Media from the Technical Point of View. *Applied Sciences (Basel, Switzerland)*, *11*(21), 9880. doi:10.3390/app11219880

Guidi, B., & Michienzi, A. (2022). How to reward the Web: The social dApp Yup. *Online Social Networks and Media*, *31*, 100229. doi:10.1016/j.osnem.2022.100229

Guidi, B., & Michienzi, A. (2023). From NFT 1.0 to NFT 2.0: A Review of the Evolution of Non-Fungible Tokens. *Future Internet*, *15*(6), 189. doi:10.3390/fi15060189

Gündüz, A. Y., & Akkoyunlu, B. (2020). Gamification tool for classroom response systems: Kahoot. *Hacettepe University Journal of Education*, *35*(3), 480–488. doi:10.16986/HUJE.2019052870

Gupta, S., & Sadoghi, M. (2019). Blockchain Transaction Processing (pp. 366–376). doi:10.1007/978-3-319-77525-8_333

Gupta, N. K., Jain, A., Sharma, P. C., & Vishwakarma, S. K. (2022). State of the Art and Challenges in Blockchain Applications. *Smart Innovation. Systems and Technologies*, *235*, 311–320. Advance online publication. doi:10.1007/978-981-16-2877-1_28

Gupta, O. P., & Bhambri, P. (2012). Protein Secondary Structure Prediction. *PCTE Journal of Computer Sciences*, *6*(2), 39–44.

Gupta, S., Modgil, S., Lee, C. K., & Sivarajah, U. (2023). The future is yesterday: Use of AI-driven facial recognition to enhance value in the travel and tourism industry. *Information Systems Frontiers*, *25*(3), 1179–1195. doi:10.1007/s10796-022-10271-8

Gürlüoğlu, L. (2019) *Examining the effects of science teaching carried out with web 2.0 applications in accordance with the 5E model on student success, motivation, attitude, and digital literacy* [Master's Thesis]. Ankara University, Institute of Educational Sciences.

Hamid, R. A., Albahri, A. S., Alwan, J. K., Al-Qaysi, Z. T., Albahri, O. S., Zaidan, A. A., Alnoor, A., Alamoodi, A. H., & Zaidan, B. B. (2021). How smart is e-tourism? A systematic review of smart tourism recommendation system applying data management. *Computer Science Review*, *39*, 100337. doi:10.1016/j.cosrev.2020.100337

Hamilton, M. (2020). Blockchain distributed ledger technology: An introduction and focus on smart contracts. In Journal of Corporate Accounting and Finance (Vol. 31, Issue 2). doi:10.1002/jcaf.22421

Hanna, G. (1995). Challenges to the importance of proof. *For the Learning of Mathematics*, *15*(3), 42–49.

Hanswal, G., Jain, S., & Thankachan, B. (2023). The Potential of Web3 for Shaping the Digital Landscape. *International Journal of Advanced Research in Science. Tongxin Jishu*, 27–35. Advance online publication. doi:10.48175/IJARSCT-10715

Hardhat. (2023). https://hardhat.org/

Harvey, C. R., Ramachandran, A., & Santoro, J. (2021). *DeFi and the future of finance*. Wiley.

Hassan, A., Makhdoom, I., Iqbal, W., Ahmad, A., & Raza, A. (2023). From trust to truth: Advancements in mitigating the Blockchain Oracle problem. *Journal of Network and Computer Applications*, *217*, 103672. doi:10.1016/j.jnca.2023.103672

Hassan, S., & De Filippi, P. (2021). Decentralized Autonomous Organization. *Internet Policy Review*, *10*(2). Advance online publication. doi:10.14763/2021.2.1556

Havele, A., Polys, N., Benman, W., & Brutzman, D. (2022). The Keys to an Open, Interoperable Metaverse. *The 27th International Conference on 3D Web Technology*, 1–7. 10.1145/3564533.3564575

He, L., Kang, T., & Guo, L. (2021). Blockchain based Distributed Oracle in Time Sensitive Scenario. *2021 the 7th International Conference on Communication and Information Processing (ICCIP)*, 103–111. 10.1145/3507971.3507990

Hedayati, A., & Hosseini, H. A. (2021). A Survey on Blockchain: Challenges, Attacks, Security, and Privacy. *International Journal of Smart Electrical Engineering*, *10*(03), 141–168.

Heilman, E., Kendler, A., Zohar, A., & Goldberg, S. (2015). Eclipse Attacks on Bitcoin's Peer-to-Peer Network. In *24th USENIX Security Symposium (USENIX Security 15)* (pp. 129-144). USENIX.

Hemphill, T. A. (2023). The 'Metaverse' and the challenge of responsible standards development. *Journal of Responsible Innovation*, *10*(1), 2243121. doi:10.1080/23299460.2023.2243121

Henry, C. D., & Shannon, L. (2023). *Virtual Natives: How a New Generation is Revolutionizing the Future of Work, Play, and Culture*. Wiley.

He, S. (2023). *Spartan Price Oracle: A Schelling-point Based Decentralized Pirce Oracle* [Master of Science, San Jose State University]. doi:10.31979/etd.y8qv-myun

Hewa, T., Ylianttila, M., & Liyanage, M. (2021). Survey on blockchain based smart contracts: Applications, opportunities and challenges. *Journal of Network and Computer Applications*, *177*, 102857. doi:10.1016/j.jnca.2020.102857

Hileman, G., & Rauchs, M. (2017). *Global Blockchain Benchmarking Study: 2017*. Cambridge Centre for Alternative Finance.

Huang, D., Ma, X., & Zhang, S. (2019). Performance analysis of the raft consensus algorithm for private blockchains. *IEEE Transactions on Systems, Man, and Cybernetics. Systems*, *50*(1), 172–181. doi:10.1109/TSMC.2019.2895471

Huang, H., Wu, J., & Zheng, Z. (Eds.). (2023). *From Blockchain to Web3 & Metaverse*. Springer. doi:10.1007/978-981-99-3648-9

Huang, J., He, D., Obaidat, M. S., Vijayakumar, P., Luo, M., & Choo, K.-K. R. (2022). The Application of the Blockchain Technology in Voting Systems: A Review. *ACM Computing Surveys*, *54*(3), 1–28. doi:10.1145/3439725

Huckle, S., Bhattacharya, R., White, M., & Beloff, N. (2016). Internet of things, blockchain and shared economy applications. *Procedia Computer Science*, *98*, 461–466. doi:10.1016/j.procs.2016.09.074

Hundreds, B. (2023). *NFTs Are a Scam / NFTs Are the Future: The Early Years: 2020-2023*. MCD.

Hussain, F. (2012). E-learning 3.0=E-learning 2.0 + Web 3.0? *Proceedings of the IADIS International Conference on Cognition and Exploratory Learning in Digital Age*, 11-17.

Hyun, W. (2023). Study on standardization for Interoperable Metaverse. *2023 25th International Conference on Advanced Communication Technology (ICACT)*, 319–322. 10.23919/ICACT56868.2023.10079642

IBM. (2023). *Food manufacturing on blockchain*. https://www.ibm.com/blockchain/resources/food-trust/manufacturing/

IDC FutureScape. (2023). https://www.idc.com/events/futurescape

Idrees, S. M., Nowostawski, M., Jameel, R., & Mourya, A. K. (2021). Security aspects of blockchain technology intended for industrial applications. *Electronics (Basel)*, *10*(8), 951. doi:10.3390/electronics10080951

Immunebytes. (2023, March 20). *Explained: Blockchain Oracles & Their Use Cases*. https://www.immunebytes.com/blog/explained-blockchain-oracles-their-use-cases/

İncekar, O. (2023) *Kahoot Effect on motivation and student opinions with success in teaching English vocabulary* [Master's Thesis]. Ankara University, Institute of Educational Sciences.

Interledger Foundation. (2023). *The modern way to make payments*. https://interledger.org/

İşbulan, O., Kaymak, Z., & Kıyıcı, M. (2019). *Web 2.0 with 101 Tools*. Pegem A Yayıncılık.

Ismailisufi, A., Popović, T., Gligorić, N., Radonjic, S., & Šandi, S. (2020). A private blockchain implementation using multichain open source platform. *2020 24th International Conference on Information Technology (IT)*.

Jack, W. (2023, July 18). *Tokenization of Real Estate: The Ultimate Guide to Invest in Tokenized Real Estate*. https://faun.pub/tokenization-of-real-estate-the-ultimate-guide-to-invest-in-tokenized-real-estate-59c5c89f3658

Jafar, R. M. S., & Ahmad, W. (2023). Tourist loyalty in the metaverse: The role of immersive tourism experience and cognitive perceptions. *Tourism Review*. Advance online publication. doi:10.1108/TR-11-2022-0552

Jánszky, S. G., & Pinker, A. (2021). *Web 3.0: The Next Generation of the Internet*. The Futures Agency.

Jeganathan, G. S., David, A., & Ganesh Kumar, C. (2022). Adaptation of Blockchain Technology In HRM. *Korea Review of International Studies*, 10-22.

Jeganathan, G. S., David, A., & Ilangovan, K. (2022). Determination of Hospitality Services Quality and Customer Satisfaction–a Holserv Approach. In *AU Virtual International Conference on" Entrepreneurship & Sustainability in Digital Era" under the theme of" Challenges of Organizational & Business Management in Dynamic Digital Dimension"* (Vol. 3, No. 1, pp. 325-334). Academic Press.

Jeganathan, G. S., & Srinivasulu, Y. (2014). Growth Drivers of Tourism Industry in India. *International Journal of Business and Management*, *2*(11), 100.

Jeong, W.-J., Oh, G.-S., Oh, S.-H., & Whangbo, T.-K. (2023). Establishment of Production Standards for Web-based Metaverse Content: Focusing on Accessibility and HCI. *Journal of Web Engineering*. Advance online publication. doi:10.13052/jwe1540-9589.2181

Johnson, D., Menezes, A., & Vanstone, S. (2001). The elliptic curve digital signature algorithm (ECDSA). *International Journal of Information Security*, *1*(1), 36–63.

Jones, A. (2021). NFTs: Ownership, Distribution, and the Digital Frontier. *Journal of Digital Media & Policy*, *13*(1), 7–23.

Joo, J., Park, J., & Han, Y. (2021). Applications of blockchain and smart contract for sustainable tourism ecosystems. *Evolutionary Computing and Mobile Sustainable Networks Proceedings of ICECMSN*, *2020*, 773–780.

Juels, A., Kosba, A., & Shi, E. (2016, October). The ring of gyges: Investigating the future of criminal smart contracts. In *Proceedings of the 2016 ACM SIGSAC Conference on Computer and Communications Security* (pp. 283-295). 10.1145/2976749.2978362

Jyothi, C., & Supriya, M. (2023). Decentralized Application (DApp) for Microfinance Using a Blockchain Network. In G. Ranganathan, R. Bestak, & X. Fernando (Eds.), *Pervasive Computing and Social Networking* (Vol. 475, pp. 95–107). Springer Nature Singapore. doi:10.1007/978-981-19-2840-6_8

Kaal, W. A. (2020). Decentralized Corporate Governance via Blockchain Technology. *Annals of Corporate Governance*, *5*(2), 101–147. doi:10.1561/109.00000025

Kachniewska, M. (2021). Smart Tourism: Towards the Concept of a Data-Based Travel Experience. Handbook of Sustainable Development and Leisure Services, 289-302.

Kameshwara, K. K., Sandoval-Hernandez, A., Shields, R., & Dhanda, K. R. (2020). A false promise? Decentralization in education systems across the globe. *International Journal of Educational Research*, *104*, 101669. doi:10.1016/j.ijer.2020.101669

Kang, J., Yu, R., Huang, X., Maharjan, S., Zhang, Y., & Hossain, E. (2017). Enabling localized peer-to-peer electricity trading among plug-in hybrid electric vehicles using consortium blockchains. *IEEE Transactions on Industrial Informatics*, *13*(6), 3154–3164. doi:10.1109/TII.2017.2709784

Kaplan, A. M., & Haenlein, M. (2010). Users of the world, unite! The challenges and opportunities of Social Media. *Business Horizons*, *53*(1), 59–68. doi:10.1016/j.bushor.2009.09.003

Kaplan, K. (2020). The impact of developing web technologies (web 1.0, web 2.0, web 3.0) on Turkey's tourism. *Safran Journal of Culture and Tourism Research*, *3*(3), 276–289.

Kaptan, F. (1998). Use of concept map method in science teaching. Hacettepe University Faculty of Education Journal, 14(14)

Karagoz Zeren, S., & Demirel, E. (2020). Blockchain based smart contract applications in tourism industry. *Digital business strategies in blockchain ecosystems: Transformational design and future of global business*, 601-615.

Karahan, M. (2022) *The effect of simulation-assisted science teaching on the academic success of 6th grade students: Systems in our body unit* [Master's Thesis]. Akdeniz University Institute of Educational Sciences.

Karanjai, R., Xu, L., Diallo, N., Chen, L., & Shi, W. (2023). DeFaaS: Decentralized Function-as-a-Service for Emerging dApps and Web3. *2023 IEEE International Conference on Blockchain and Cryptocurrency (ICBC)*, 1–3. 10.1109/ICBC56567.2023.10174945

Karapapas, C., Syros, G., Pittaras, I., & Polyzos, G. C. (2022). Decentralized NFT-based Evolvable Games. *2022 4th Conference on Blockchain Research and Applications for Innovative Networks and Services, BRAINS 2022*. 10.1109/BRAINS55737.2022.9909178

Karim, R., Ishrat, M., & Rahman, M. A. (2022). Blockchain Technology and Its Untapped Potentials in the Hospitality Industry. *Journal of Technology Management and Business*, *9*(1), 1–10. doi:10.30880/jtmb.2022.09.01.001

Kastrenakes, J. (2021). *Jack Dorsey says VCs really own Web3 (and Web3 boosters are pretty mad about it)*. The Verge.

Kaur, G., Habibi Lashkari, A., Sharafaldin, I., & Habibi Lashkari, Z. (2023a). DeFi Platforms. In Understanding Cybersecurity Management in Decentralized Finance (pp. 57–70). Springer International Publishing. doi:10.1007/978-3-031-23340-1_3

Kaur, G., Habibi Lashkari, A., Sharafaldin, I., & Habibi Lashkari, Z. (2023b). The Origin of Modern Decentralized Finance. In Understanding Cybersecurity Management in Decentralized Finance (pp. 1–28). Springer International Publishing. doi:10.1007/978-3-031-23340-1_1

Kaur, J., Bhambri, P., & Goyal, F. (2012). Phylogeny: Tree of Life. *International Conference on Sports Biomechanics, Emerging Technologies and Quality Assurance in Technical Education*, 350-354.

Kausar MA, & Nasar M (2021). SQL versus NoSQL databases to assess their appropriateness for big data application. *Recent Advances in Computer Science and Communications, 14*(4), 1098–1108.

Khaleel Ibrahim, A. (2021). Evolution of the Web: From Web 1.0 to 4.0. *Qubahan Academic Journal*, *1*(3), 20–28. doi:10.48161/qaj.v1n3a75

Khalid, M. I., Ehsan, I., Al-Ani, A. K., Iqbal, J., Hussain, S., Ullah, S. S., & Nayab. (2023). A Comprehensive Survey on Blockchain-Based Decentralized Storage Networks. *IEEE Access : Practical Innovations, Open Solutions*, *11*, 10995–11015. Advance online publication. doi:10.1109/ACCESS.2023.3240237

Khaliq, L. N., & Manda, V. K. (2023). Customer Experience in the Web 3.0 Era: The Meeting of Blockchain and the Metaverse. In M. Majeed, K. S. Ofori, G. K. Amoako, A.-R. Alolo, & G. Awini (Eds.), Advances in Marketing, Customer Relationship Management, and E-Services. IGI Global. doi:10.4018/978-1-6684-7649-9.ch015

Khan, S. N., Loukil, F., Ghedira-Guegan, C., Benkhelifa, E., & Bani-Hani, A. (2021). Blockchain smart contracts: Applications, challenges, and future trends. *Peer-to-Peer Networking and Applications*, *14*(5), 2901–2925. doi:10.1007/s12083-021-01127-0

Khettry, A. R., Patil, K. R., & Basavaraju, A. C. (2021). A detailed review on blockchain and its applications. *SN Computer Science*, *2*(1), 1–9. doi:10.1007/s42979-020-00366-x PMID:34723205

Khoshafian, S. (2021). *Can the Real Web 3.0 Please Stand Up?* RTInsights.

Kiayias, A., Miller, A., & Zindros, D. (2020). Non-interactive proofs of proof-of-work. *International Conference on Financial Cryptography and Data Security.*

Kietzmann, J., Hermkens, K., McCarthy, I., & Silvestre, B. (2011). Social media? Get serious! Understanding the functional building blocks of social media. *Business Horizons*, *54*(3), 241-251.

Kim, J. (2020). Blockchain technology and its applications: Case studies. *Journal of System and Management Sciences*, *10*(1), 83–93.

Kim, H. (2023). An Analysis of Domestic and International Research Trends on Metaverse. *Journal of the Korean Society for Library and Information Science*, *57*(3), 351–379. doi:10.4275/KSLIS.2023.57.3.351

Kim, H., & Kahng, M. (2020). Web 3.0: From Web to Blockchain. *IEEE Internet Computing*, *24*(5), 10–16.

Kirkpatrick, K. (2022). Applying the metaverse. *Communications of the ACM*, *65*(11), 16–18. doi:10.1145/3565470

Koerhuis, W., Kechadi, T., & Le-Khac, N.-A. (2020). Forensic analysis of privacy-oriented cryptocurrencies. *Forensic Science International Digital Investigation*, *33*, 200891. doi:10.1016/j.fsidi.2019.200891

Konashevych, O., & Khovayko, O. (2020). Randpay: The technology for blockchain micropayments and transactions which require recipient's consent. *Computers & Security*, *96*, 101892. doi:10.1016/j.cose.2020.101892

Kondova, G., & Barba, R. (2020). Governance of Decentralized Autonomous Organizations. *Journal of Modern Accounting and Auditing*, *15*(8). https://papers.ssrn.com/sol3/papers.cfm?abstract_id=3549469

Kong, L., Chen, C., Zhao, R., Chen, Z., Wu, L., Yang, Z., Li, X., Lu, W., & Xue, F. (2022). When permissioned blockchain meets IoT oracles: An on-chain quality assurance system for off-shore modular construction manufacture. *2022 IEEE 1st Global Emerging Technology Blockchain Forum: Blockchain & Beyond (iGETblockchain)*, 1–6. 10.1109/iGETblockchain56591.2022.10087164

Kontogianni, A., & Alepis, E. (2020). Smart tourism: State of the art and literature review for the last six years. *Array (New York, N.Y.)*, *6*, 100020. doi:10.1016/j.array.2020.100020

Korpal, G., & Scott, D. (2022). *Decentralization and web3 technologies*. https://attachment.victorlampcdn.com/article/content/20220824/drewscott_gkorpal_web3.pdf

Korpal, G., & Scott, D. (2022). *Decentralization and web3 technologies*. https://gkorpal.github.io/files/drewscott_gkorpal_web3.pdf

Kosba, A., Miller, A., Shi, E., Wen, Z., & Papamanthou, C. (2016). Hawk: The blockchain model of cryptography and privacy-preserving smart contracts. *2016 IEEE Symposium on Security and Privacy (SP)*.

Kraski, J., & Shenkarow, J. (2023). *The Future of Community: How to Leverage Web3 Technologies to Grow Your Business*. Wiley.

Kreminski, M. (2019). The Future of the Web: Decentralization, Interoperability, and Intelligence. XRDS: Crossroads. *The ACM Magazine for Students*, *26*(2), 10–14.

Kshetri, N. (2022). Policy, Ethical, Social, and Environmental Considerations of Web3 and the Metaverse. In IT Professional (Vol. 24, Issue 3). doi:10.1109/MITP.2022.3178509

Kshetri, N., & Voas, J. (2018). Blockchain in developing countries. *IT Professional*, *20*(2), 11–14.

Kumar, N. (2023). Web3 Ecosystem: 10 Key Trends in 2023. *Analytics Insight*. https://www.analyticsinsight.net/web3-ecosystem-10-key-trends-in-2023/

Kumar, S., Kumar, B., Nagesh, Y., & Christian, F. (2022). Application of blockchain technology as a support tool in economic & financial development. *Manager-The British Journal of Administrative Management*.

Kumar, S., Patel, R., Iqbal, N., & Gubareva, M. (2023). Interconnectivity among cryptocurrencies, NFTs, and DeFi: Evidence from the Russia-Ukraine conflict. *The North American Journal of Economics and Finance*, *68*, 101983. doi:10.1016/j.najef.2023.101983

Kurniawan, W. (2022). *Voting Mechanism Selection for Decentralized Autonomous Organizations*. https://secureseco.org/wp-content/uploads/2022/08/Voting_Mechanism_Selection_for_Decentralized_Autonomous_Organizations-3-1.pdf

Kwon, S. (2023). Regulation of DeFi Lending: Agency Supervision on Decentralization. *The Columbia Science and Technology Law Review*, *24*(2), 379–413. doi:10.52214/stlr.v24i2.11629

Lai, Y., Yang, J., Liu, M., Li, Y., & Li, S. (2023). Web3: Exploring Decentralized Technologies and Applications for the Future of Empowerment and Ownership. *Blockchains*, *1*(2), 111–131. doi:10.3390/blockchains1020008

Laroiya, C., Saxena, D., & Komalavalli, C. (2020). Applications of blockchain technology. In *Handbook of research on blockchain technology* (pp. 213–243). Elsevier. doi:10.1016/B978-0-12-819816-2.00009-5

Lashkari, B., & Musilek, P. (2021). A comprehensive review of blockchain consensus mechanisms. *IEEE Access : Practical Innovations, Open Solutions*, *9*, 43620–43652. doi:10.1109/ACCESS.2021.3065880

Lassila, O., & Hendler, J. (2007). Embracing Web 3.0. *IEEE Internet Computing*, *11*(3), 90–93. doi:10.1109/MIC.2007.52

Lee, T. B. (2006). *Data growth and Web 3.0*. Retrieved March 10, 2018, from http://www.expertsystem.com /web-3-0/

Lee, W. (2023). *Beginning Ethereum Smart Contracts Programming: With Examples in Python, Solidity, and JavaScript*. APress.

Lekhi, P., & Kaur, G. (Eds.). (2023). *Concepts, Technologies, Challenges, and the Future of Web 3*. IGI Global. doi:10.4018/978-1-6684-9919-1

Lemieux, V. L. (2016). Trusting records: Is Blockchain technology the answer? *Records Management Journal*, *26*(2), 110–139. doi:10.1108/RMJ-12-2015-0042

Lemieux, V., Hofman, D., Batista, D., & Joo, A. (2019). *Blockchain technology & recordkeeping*. ARMA International Educational Foundation.

Levis, D., Fontana, F., & Ughetto, E. (2021). A look into the future of blockchain technology. *PLoS One*, *16*(11), e0258995. doi:10.1371/journal.pone.0258995 PMID:34788307

Lewis, G. (2023). *Web 3.0: Simple Guide*. Kindle Edition.

Li, A., Tan, S., & Jia, Y. (2019). A method for achieving provable data integrity in cloud computing. *The Journal of Supercomputing*, *75*(1), 92–108. doi:10.1007/s11227-015-1598-2

Li, C., Xu, R., & Duan, L. (2023). Liquid Democracy in DPoS Blockchains. *Proceedings of the 5th ACM International Symposium on Blockchain and Secure Critical Infrastructure*, 25–33. 10.1145/3594556.3594606

Li, J. (2021). DeFi as an Information Aggregator. In M. Bernhard, A. Bracciali, L. Gudgeon, T. Haines, A. Klages-Mundt, S. Matsuo, D. Perez, M. Sala, & S. Werner (Eds.), *Financial Cryptography and Data Security. FC 2021 International Workshops* (Vol. 12676, pp. 171–176). Springer Berlin Heidelberg. doi:10.1007/978-3-662-63958-0_15

Lim, Y. Q. (2023, June 26). *DeFi Ecosystem: Categories by Market Share*. https://www.coingecko.com/research/publications/defi-categories-market-share

Lin, Z., Yao, N., Wu, X., & Wang, L. (2022). A Peek at Metaverse Society from Web 3.0 Games: A Preliminary Case Study of Dark Forest. *2022 IEEE 24th International Workshop on Multimedia Signal Processing, MMSP 2022*. 10.1109/MMSP55362.2022.9949551

LinkedIn. (2023). *What are the benefits of decentralized gaming in Web3?* https://www.linkedin.com/advice/1/what-benefits-decentralized-gaming-web3-skills-blockchain-lqvjf

Lin, S. Y., Zhang, L., Li, J., Ji, L. L., & Sun, Y. (2022). A survey of application research based on blockchain smart contract. *Wireless Networks*, *28*(2), 635–690. doi:10.1007/s11276-021-02874-x

Lisdorf, A. (2023). *Still Searching for Satoshi: Unveiling the Blockchain Revolution*. Academic Press.

Liu, C., Zhang, X., & Medda, F. (2021). Plastic credit: A consortium blockchain-based plastic recyclability system. *Waste Management (New York, N.Y.)*, *121*, 42–51. doi:10.1016/j.wasman.2020.11.045 PMID:33348229

Liu, Z., Xiang, Y., Shi, J., Gao, P., Wang, H., Xiao, X., & Hu, Y. C. (2021). Make web3. 0 connected. *IEEE Transactions on Dependable and Secure Computing*, *19*(5), 2965–2981. doi:10.1109/TDSC.2021.3079315

Li, W., Bu, J., Li, X., Peng, H., Niu, Y., & Zhang, Y. (2022). A survey of DeFi security: Challenges and opportunities. *Journal of King Saud University. Computer and Information Sciences*, *34*(10), 10378–10404. doi:10.1016/j.jksuci.2022.10.028

Li, W., Feng, C., Zhang, L., Xu, H., Cao, B., & Imran, M. A. (2020). A scalable multi-layer PBFT consensus for blockchain. *IEEE Transactions on Parallel and Distributed Systems*, *32*(5), 1146–1160. doi:10.1109/TPDS.2020.3042392

Lo, Y. C., & Medda, F. (2022). Do DEXs work? Using Uniswap V2 to explore the effectiveness of decentralized exchanges. *Journal of Financial Market Infrastructures*. doi:10.21314/JFMI.2022.004

Logesh, R., Subramaniyaswamy, V., Vijayakumar, V., & Li, X. (2019). Efficient user profiling based intelligent travel recommender system for individual and group of users. *Mobile Networks and Applications*, *24*(3), 1018–1033. doi:10.1007/s11036-018-1059-2

Lopez, R. A. (2023). *The rise of the metaverse: A must-have guide on How virtual reality, augmented reality, and mixed reality are transforming the way we work, learn, and play in the world of artificial intelligence*. Academic Press.

Lotti, L. (2016). Contemporary art, capitalization and the blockchain: On the autonomy and automation of art's value. *Finance and Stochastics*, *2*(2), 96–110.

Lucena, P., Binotto, A. P. D., Momo, F. da S., & Kim, H. (2018). *A Case Study for Grain Quality Assurance Tracking based on a Blockchain Business Network* (arXiv:1803.07877). arXiv. http://arxiv.org/abs/1803.07877

Lumineau, F., Wang, W., & Schilke, O. (2021). Blockchain governance—A new way of organizing collaborations? *Organization Science*, *32*(2), 500–521. doi:10.1287/orsc.2020.1379

Luo, L., & Zhou, J. (2021). BlockTour: A blockchain-based smart tourism platform. *Computer Communications*, *175*, 186–192. doi:10.1016/j.comcom.2021.05.011

Luong, D. H. (2019). *The Ethereum blockchain: Use cases for social finance applications*. https://trepo.tuni.fi/bitstream/handle/123456789/27245/Luong.pdf?sequence=4

Madhani, P. M. (2022). Effective marketing strategy with blockchain implementation: Enhancing customer value propositions. *IUP Journal of Business Strategy*, *19*(1), 7–35.

Maesa, D. D. F., & Mori, P. (2020). Blockchain 3.0 applications survey. *Journal of Parallel and Distributed Computing*, *138*, 99–114. doi:10.1016/j.jpdc.2019.12.019

Magaki, I., Khazraee, M., Gutierrez, L. V., & Taylor, M. B. (2016). Asic clouds: Specializing the datacenter. *2016 ACM/IEEE 43rd Annual International Symposium on Computer Architecture (ISCA).*

Majumdar, S., & Gochhait, S. (2022). Risks and Solutions in Islamic Decentralised Finance. *2022 International Conference on Sustainable Islamic Business and Finance, SIBF 2022.* 10.1109/SIBF56821.2022.9939821

Mak, A. (2021). *What Is Web3 and Why Are All the Crypto People Suddenly Talking About It?* Slate.

Makarov, I., & Schoar, A. (2022). *Cryptocurrencies and decentralized finance (DeFi).* Academic Press.

Mammadzada, K., Iqbal, M., Milani, F., García-Bañuelos, L., & Matulevičius, R. (2020). Blockchain Oracles: A Framework for Blockchain-Based Applications. In A. Asatiani, J. M. García, N. Helander, A. Jiménez-Ramírez, A. Koschmider, J. Mendling, G. Meroni, & H. A. Reijers (Eds.), *Business Process Management: Blockchain and Robotic Process Automation Forum* (Vol. 393, pp. 19–34). Springer International Publishing. doi:10.1007/978-3-030-58779-6_2

MandaV. K.AnuradhaY. (2023). *The Aftermath of the FTX Cryptocurrency Exchange Collapse.* doi:10.5281/ZENODO.10207831

Manda, V. K., & Nihar, L. K. (2023). Lessons From the FTX Cryptocurrency Exchange Collapse. In S. Saluja, D. Kulshrestha, & S. Sharma (Eds.), Advances in Business Strategy and Competitive Advantage. IGI Global. doi:10.4018/978-1-6684-8488-3.ch002

Manoj Kumar, T., Mukunthan, K., Reena, R., & Bhuvaneswari, S. (2022). Decentralized Social Media Platform using Blockchain. *International Journal of Advanced Research in Science. Tongxin Jishu, 54–58.* Advance online publication. doi:10.48175/IJARSCT-4979

Mansfield-Devine, S. (2015). The growth and evolution of DDoS. *Network Security, 2015*(10), 13–20. doi:10.1016/S1353-4858(15)30092-1

Marco, C. (2019, May 9). Provable (formerly Oraclize) joins Poseidon Group. *Cryptonomist.* https://en.cryptonomist.ch/2019/05/09/provable-oraclize-joins-poseidon-group/

MarxF. (2022). *Banking without banks? An analysis of the opportunities and threats for commercial banks resulting from DeFi, Metaverse, and Web 3.0.* doi:10.13140/RG.2.2.36020.01923

Mashinsky, A., & Krug, J. (2020). *Web 3.0: The Age of Machine Intelligence.* Celsius Network.

Mathilde, G. og R. R. (2022). *Impact of the decentralized economy of the WEB3 on the business strategies* [Master Thesis, Norwegian Business School]. https://biopen.bi.no/bi-xmlui/bitstream/handle/11250/3037617/Master%20Thesis%20-%20Impact%20of%20the%20decentralized%20economy%20of%20the%20WEB3%20on%20the%20business%20strategies.pdf

McConaghy, T. (2016). *How blockchains could transform artificial intelligence.* Dataconomy.

McCormick, P. (2021). The value chain of the open metaverse. *Not Boring.* Available at https://www.notboring.co/p/the-value-chain-of-the-open-metaverse

McGhin, T., Eyal, I., Mirhoseini, Z. S., Zhang, J., & Juels, A. (2021). Smart contracts for fair exchange: Applications to trade finance. ACM Transactions on Economics and Computation.

McGhin, T., Choo, K. K. R., Liu, C. Z., & He, D. (2019). Blockchain in healthcare applications: Research challenges and opportunities. *Journal of Network and Computer Applications, 135*, 62–75. doi:10.1016/j.jnca.2019.02.027

Mdlalose, N., Ramaila, S., & Ramnarain, U. (2022). Using Kahoot! as a formative assessment tool in science teacher education. *International Journal of Higher Education, 11*(2), 43–51. doi:10.5430/ijhe.v11n2p43

Mehar, M. I., Shier, C. L., Giambattista, A., Gong, E., Fletcher, G., Sanayhie, R., Kim, H. M., & Laskowski, M. (2021). Understanding a Revolutionary and Flawed Grand Experiment in Blockchain: The DAO Attack. In Research Anthology on Blockchain Technology in Business, Healthcare, Education, and Government (pp. 1253–1266). IGI Global. doi:10.4018/978-1-7998-5351-0.ch069

Mehraliyev, F., Chan, I. C. C., Choi, Y., Koseoglu, M. A., & Law, R. (2020). A state-of-the-art review of smart tourism research. *Journal of Travel & Tourism Marketing*, *37*(1), 78–91. doi:10.1080/10548408.2020.1712309

Mehrpouyan, H., & Sadeghian, M. A. (2021). Web 3.0: A New Era for E-commerce. *International Journal of Business and Management*, *16*(5), 1–11.

Mertha, i. w., & Mahfud, m. (2022). History learning based on wordwall applications to improve student learning results class x ips in ma as'adiyah ketapang. *International Journal of Educational Review, Law, and Social Sciences*, *2*(5), 507–612.

Metamask. (2023). https://metamask.io/

MetaversityE. (2023), https://www.ey.com/en_eg

Meyer, E., Welpe, I. M., & Sandner, P. (2021). Decentralized Finance—A systematic literature review and research directions. SSRN *Electronic Journal*. doi:10.2139/ssrn.4016497

Milutinovic, M., He, W., Wu, H., & Kanwal, M. (2016). Proof of luck: An efficient blockchain consensus protocol. *Proceedings of the 1st Workshop on System Software for Trusted Execution.*

Mingxiao, D., Xiaofeng, M., Zhe, Z., Xiangwei, W., & Qijun, C. (2017). A review on consensus algorithm of blockchain. *2017 IEEE International Conference on Systems, Man, and Cybernetics (SMC).*

Mishra, L., & Kaushik, V. (2023). Application of blockchain in dealing with sustainability issues and challenges of financial sector. *Journal of Sustainable Finance & Investment*, *13*(3), 1318–1333.

Mitra, D. (2023). *Channel Coding Techniques for Scaling Modern Data-Driven Applications: From Blockchain Systems to Quantum Communications* [Doctor of Philosophy in Electrical and Computer Engineering, University of California]. https://escholarship.org/uc/item/0cp2c3tk

Mogaji, E., Dwivedi, Y. K., & Raman, R. (2023). Fashion marketing in the metaverse. *Journal of Global Fashion Marketing*, 1–16. doi:10.1080/20932685.2023.2249483

Mogaji, E., Wirtz, J., Belk, R. W., & Dwivedi, Y. K. (2023). Immersive time (ImT): Conceptualizing time spent in the metaverse. *International Journal of Information Management*, *72*, 102659. doi:10.1016/j.ijinfomgt.2023.102659

Momtaz, P. P. (2022). Some Very Simple Economics of Web3 and the Metaverse. SSRN *Electronic Journal*. doi:10.2139/ssrn.4085937

Momtaz, P. P. (2022). Some Very Simple Economics of Web3 and the Metaverse. *FinTech*, *1*(3), 225–234. doi:10.3390/fintech1030018

Mone. (2000). Primary School Science Lesson (grades 4-8) Curriculum. *Journal of Announcements.*

Montecchi, M., Plangger, K., & Etter, M. (2019). It's real, trust me! Establishing supply chain provenance using blockchain. *Business Horizons*, *62*(3), 283-293.

Moorhouse, B. L., & Kohnke, L. (2022). Creating the conditions for vocabulary learning with wordwall. *RELC Journal*. doi:10.1177/00336882221092796

Mougayar, W. (2016). The Business Blockchain: Promise, Practice, and Application of the Next Internet Technology. John Wiley & Sons.

Mougayar, W. (2016). *The Business Blockchain: Promise, Practice, and Application of the Next Internet Technology*. John Wiley & Sons.

Mougayar, W. (2016). *The Rise of Web 3.0: Emerging Patterns in Decentralized Computing*. Coin Desk Research.

Mourtzis, D., Angelopoulos, J., & Panopoulos, N. (2023). Metaverse and Blockchain in Education for collaborative Product-Service System (PSS) Design towards University 5.0. *Procedia CIRP*, *119*, 456–461. doi:10.1016/j.procir.2023.01.008

Muhammad Khan, F., & Ullah Khan, I. (2023). *The Game-Changing Impact of 5G and Metaverse on the Future of E-Learning*. https://www.researchgate.net/publication/368397907

Mukherjee, P., & Pradhan, C. (2021). Blockchain 1.0 to blockchain 4.0—The evolutionary transformation of blockchain technology. In *Blockchain technology: applications and challenges* (pp. 29–49). Springer International Publishing. doi:10.1007/978-3-030-69395-4_3

Muratov, F., Lebedev, A., Iushkevich, N., Nasrulin, B., & Takemiya, M. (2018). YAC: BFT consensus algorithm for blockchain. *arXiv preprint arXiv:1809.00554*.

Murray, A., Kuban, S., Josefy, M., & Anderson, J. (2021). Contracting in the smart era: The implications of blockchain and decentralized autonomous organizations for contracting and corporate governance. *Academy of Management Perspectives*, *35*(4), 622-641.

Murray, A., Kim, D., & Combs, J. (2023). The promise of a decentralized internet: What is Web3 and how can firms prepare? *Business Horizons*, *66*(2), 191–202. doi:10.1016/j.bushor.2022.06.002

Murtas, G., Pedeliento, G., & Mangiò, F. (2023). Luxury fashion brands at the gates of the Web 3.0: An analysis of early experimentations with NFTs and the metaverse. *Journal of Global Fashion Marketing*, 1–25. doi:10.1080/20932685.2023.2249476

Muzammal, M., Qu, Q., & Nasrulin, B. (2019). Renovating blockchain with distributed databases: An open source system. *Future Generation Computer Systems*, *90*, 105–117. doi:10.1016/j.future.2018.07.042

Myalo, A. S. (2019). Comparative Analysis of ICO, DAOICO, IEO and STO. Case Study. *Finance: Theory and Practice*, *23*(6), 6–25. doi:10.26794/2587-5671-2019-23-6-6-25

Nabben, K. (2023). Web3 as 'self-infrastructuring': The challenge is how. *Big Data & Society*, *10*(1), 205395172311590. doi:10.1177/20539517231159002

Nadini, M., Alessandretti, L., Di Giacinto, F., Martino, M., Aiello, L. M., & Baronchelli, A. (2021). Mapping the NFT revolution: Market trends, trade networks, and visual features. *Scientific Reports*, *11*(1), 20902. Advance online publication. doi:10.1038/s41598-021-00053-8 PMID:34686678

NadlerM.BekemeierF.SchärF. (2022). *DeFi Risk Transfer: Towards A Fully Decentralized Insurance Protocol*. doi:10.48550/ARXIV.2212.10308

Nakamoto, S. (2008). Bitcoin: A peer-to-peer electronic cash system. *Decentralized Business Review*, 21260.

Nakamoto, S. (2008). *Bitcoin: A Peer-to-Peer Electronic Cash System*. Retrieved from https://bitcoin.org/bitcoin.pdf

Nandwani, A., Gupta, M., & Thakur, N. (2019). Proof-of-Participation: Implementation of Proof-of-Stake Through Proof-of-Work. In S. Bhattacharyya, A. E. Hassanien, D. Gupta, A. Khanna, & I. Pan (Eds.), *International Conference on Innovative Computing and Communications* (*Vol. 55*, pp. 17–24). Springer Singapore. 10.1007/978-981-13-2324-9_3

Napieralska, A., & Kępczyński, P. (2023a). Smart contracts and Web 3: From Automated Transactions to DAOs. In P. Lekhi & G. Kaur (Eds.), Advances in Web Technologies and Engineering. IGI Global. doi:10.4018/978-1-6684-9919-1.ch008

Narayanan, A., Bonneau, J., Felten, E., Miller, A., & Goldfeder, S. (2016). *Bitcoin and Cryptocurrency Technologies: A Comprehensive Introduction*. Princeton University Press.

Neto, J. B. S. (n.d.). *The Next Phase of Blockchain: From Cryptocurrencies to Smart Contracts and a Decentralized Future*. Academic Press.

Nguyen, C. T. (2023). *Proof-of-Stake-based Blockchain Frameworks for Smart Data Management* [Doctor of Philosophy, University of Technology]. https://www.proquest.com/dissertations-theses/proof-stake-based-blockchain-frameworks-smart/docview/2901815472/se-2?accountid=139958

Nike. (2023). https://www.nike.com/

Ni, P., Zhu, J., & Wang, G. (2023). Activity-Oriented Production Promotion Utility Maximization in Metaverse Social Networks. *IEEE/ACM Transactions on Networking*, 1–15. doi:10.1109/TNET.2023.3309624

Niranjanamurthy, M., Nithya, B., & Jagannatha, S. (2019). Analysis of Blockchain technology: Pros, cons and SWOT. *Cluster Computing*, *22*(6), 14743–14757. doi:10.1007/s10586-018-2387-5

Njoku, J. N., Ifeanyi Nwakanma, C., & Kim, D.-S. (2022). The Role of 5G Wireless Communication System in the Metaverse. *2022 27th Asia Pacific Conference on Communications (APCC)*, 290–294. 10.1109/APCC55198.2022.9943778

Nobanee, H., & Ellili, N. O. D. (2023). Non-fungible tokens (NFTs): A bibliometric and systematic review, current streams, developments, and directions for future research. *International Review of Economics & Finance*, *84*, 460–473. doi:10.1016/j.iref.2022.11.014

Nofer, M., Gomber, P., Hinz, O., & Schiereck, D. (2017). Blockchain. *Business & Information Systems Engineering*, *59*(3), 183–187. doi:10.1007/s12599-017-0467-3

Novianti, F. A., & Mufaridah, F. (2023). Literature review: wordwall game application in English language learning to develop a disciplined character in the millennial era. In *Proceeding the Second English National Seminar Exploring Emerging Technologies in English Education* (pp. 29-34). Lppm Press Stkip Pgri Pacitan.

Noyes, C. (2016). Bitav: Fast anti-malware by distributed blockchain consensus and feedforward scanning. *arXiv preprint arXiv:1601.01405.*

O'Reilly, T. (2007). What is Web 2.0 design patterns and business models for the next generation of software. *Communications & Stratégies*, *65*(1), 17–37.

Ochoa, A. M. M., Corgo, S. R., & Cristóbal, I. D. (2023). Metaverse and mental health, what about the future? *European Psychiatry*, *66*(S1). Advance online publication. doi:10.1192/j.eurpsy.2023.1171

O'Dwyer, K. J., & Malone, D. (2014). *Bitcoin mining and its energy footprint*. Academic Press.

Oliva, G. A., Hassan, A. E., & Jiang, Z. M. (2020). An exploratory study of smart contracts in the Ethereum blockchain platform. *Empirical Software Engineering*, *25*(3), 1864–1904. doi:10.1007/s10664-019-09796-5

Omar, I. A., Jayaraman, R., Salah, K., Yaqoob, I., & Ellahham, S. (2021). Applications of blockchain technology in clinical trials: Review and open challenges. *Arabian Journal for Science and Engineering*, *46*(4), 3001–3015. doi:10.1007/s13369-020-04989-3

Ortiz Orellana, X. G., & Mena Mayorga, J. I. (2021). Pixton as a digital teaching tool to encourage the writing skill. *Ciancia Digital*, *5*(3), 20–35. doi:10.33262/cienciadigital.v5i3.1621

Ottina, M., Steffensen, P. J., & Kristensen, J. (2023). *Automated Market Makers: A Practical Guide to Decentralized Exchanges and Cryptocurrency Trading*. APress.

Ozdemir, A. I., Ar, I. M., & Erol, I. (2020). Assessment of blockchain applications in travel and tourism industry. *Quality & Quantity*, *54*(5-6), 1549–1563. doi:10.1007/s11135-019-00901-w

Özkök, E. (2010). *The effect of Gagne's instructional software on the academic success and student attitudes of elementary eighth grade students in mathematics lesson on square root numbers and student attitudes* [Unpublished Master Thesis]. Gazi University Institute of Educational Sciences.

Page, K., & Elmessiry, A. (2021). *Global Research Decentralized Autonomous Organization (GR-DAO): A DAO of Global Researchers*. doi:10.5121/csit.2021.111708

Paktiti, M., & Economides, A. A. (2023). Smart contract applications in tourism. *International Journal of Technology Management & Sustainable Development*, *22*(2), 165–184. doi:10.1386/tmsd_00074_1

Panarello, A., Tapas, N., Merlino, G., Longo, F., & Puliafito, A. (2018). Blockchain and iot integration: A systematic survey. *Sensors (Basel)*, *18*(8), 2575. doi:10.3390/s18082575 PMID:30082633

Panda, S. K., Mishra, V., Dash, S. P., & Pani, A. K. (Eds.). (2023). *Recent Advances in Blockchain Technology: Real-World Applications: 237 (Intelligent Systems Reference Library)*. Springer. doi:10.1007/978-3-031-22835-3

Panwar, G., Misra, S., & Vishwanathan, R. (2019). BlAnC: Blockchain-based Anonymous and Decentralized Credit Networks. *Proceedings of the Ninth ACM Conference on Data and Application Security and Privacy*, 339–350. 10.1145/3292006.3300034

Papadouli, V., & Papakonstantinou, V. (2023). A preliminary study on artificial intelligence oracles and smart contracts: A legal approach to the interaction of two novel technological breakthroughs. *Computer Law & Security Report*, *51*, 105869. doi:10.1016/j.clsr.2023.105869

Park, A., Wilson, M., Robson, K., Demetis, D., & Kietzmann, J. (2023). Interoperability: Our exciting and terrifying Web3 future. *Business Horizons*, *66*(4), 529–541. Advance online publication. doi:10.1016/j.bushor.2022.10.005

Parker, C., Yoo, S., Lee, Y., Fredericks, J., Dey, A., Cho, Y., & Billinghurst, M. (2023). Towards an Inclusive and Accessible Metaverse. *Extended Abstracts of the 2023 CHI Conference on Human Factors in Computing Systems*, 1–5. 10.1145/3544549.3573811

Pasdar, A., Lee, Y. C., & Dong, Z. (2023). Connect API with Blockchain: A Survey on Blockchain Oracle Implementation. *ACM Computing Surveys*, *55*(10), 1–39. doi:10.1145/3567582

Pastore, F., Mariani, L., & Fraser, G. (2013). CrowdOracles: Can the Crowd Solve the Oracle Problem? *2013 IEEE Sixth International Conference on Software Testing, Verification and Validation*, 342–351. 10.1109/ICST.2013.13

Patel, D., Johnston, A., Stokesberry, J., Damak, M., Duran, C., Raziano, A., Wilkinson, L., & O'Neill, A. (2023). *Utility at a cost: Assessing the risks of blockchain oracles*. S&P Global.

Patel, V., Khatiwala, F., Shah, K., & Choksi, Y. (2020). A review on blockchain technology: Components, issues and challenges. *ICDSMLA*, *2019*, 1257–1262. doi:10.1007/978-981-15-1420-3_137

Patiño-Martínez, M., & Paulo, J. (Eds.). (2023). Distributed Applications and Interoperable Systems. In *23rd IFIP WG 6.1 International Conference, DAIS 2023, Held as Part of the 18th International*. Springer.

Paul, G., Sarkar, P., & Mukherjee, S. (2014). Towards a more democratic mining in bitcoins. *International Conference on Information Systems Security*.

Pejic, I. (2023). *Big Tech in Finance: How To Prevail In the Age of Blockchain, Digital Currencies and Web3*. Kogan Page.

Pelfrey, K. (2023). *The Pathway to Blockchain & Web3: Next Waves for Developers in Tech*. Academic Press.

Peng, X., Zhao, Z., Wang, X., Li, H., Xu, J., & Zhang, X. (2023). A review on blockchain smart contracts in the agri-food industry: Current state, application challenges and future trends. *Computers and Electronics in Agriculture*, *208*, 107776. doi:10.1016/j.compag.2023.107776

Perez Riaza, B., & Gnabo, J.-Y. (2023). Decentralized Autonomous Organizations (DAOs): Catalysts for enhanced market efficiency. *Finance Research Letters*, *58*, 104445. doi:10.1016/j.frl.2023.104445

Petcu, A., Pahontu, B., Frunzete, M., & Stoichescu, D. A. (2023). A Secure and Decentralized Authentication Mechanism Based on Web 3.0 and Ethereum Blockchain Technology. *Applied Sciences (Basel, Switzerland)*, *13*(4), 2231. doi:10.3390/app13042231

Pham, V.-D., Tran, C.-T., Nguyen, T., Nguyen, T.-T., Do, B.-L., Dao, T.-C., & Nguyen, B. M. (2020). B-Box—A Decentralized Storage System Using IPFS, Attributed-based Encryption, and Blockchain. *2020 RIVF International Conference on Computing and Communication Technologies (RIVF)*, 1–6. 10.1109/RIVF48685.2020.9140747

Phan, L., Li, S., & Mentzer, K. (2019). Blockchain Technology and the current discussion on Fraud. *Issues in Information Systems*. Advance online publication. doi:10.48009/4_iis_2019_8-20

Pilkington, M. (2016). Blockchain Technology: Principles and Applications. *Research Handbook on Digital Transformations*, 225-253.

Pinto-Gutiérrez, C., Gaitán, S., Jaramillo, D., & Velasquez, S. (2022). The NFT Hype: What Draws Attention to Non-Fungible Tokens? *Mathematics*, *10*(3), 335. Advance online publication. doi:10.3390/math10030335

Platt, M., & McBurney, P. (2023). Sybil in the Haystack: A Comprehensive Review of Blockchain Consensus Mechanisms in Search of Strong Sybil Attack Resistance. *Algorithms*, *16*(1), 34. doi:10.3390/a16010034

pNetwork Team. (2015, November 4). Oraclize, the provably-honest oracle service, is finally here! *Medium.Com*. https://medium.com/pnetwork/oraclize-the-provably-honest-oracle-service-is-finally-here-3ac48358deb8

Poon, J., & Dryja, T. (2016). *The Bitcoin Lightning Network: Scalable Off-Chain Instant Payments*. Retrieved from https://lightning.network/lightning-network-paper.pdf

Pop, C., Pop, C., Marcel, A., Vesa, A., Petrican, T., Cioara, T., Anghel, I., & Salomie, I. (2018). Decentralizing the Stock Exchange using Blockchain An Ethereum-based implementation of the Bucharest Stock Exchange. *2018 IEEE 14th International Conference on Intelligent Computer Communication and Processing (ICCP)*, 459–466. 10.1109/ICCP.2018.8516610

Popescu, A.-D. (2020). Decentralized Finance (DeFi) – The Lego of Finance. *Social Sciences and Education Research Review*, *7*(1), 321–349.

Pranata, A. R., & Tehrani, P. M. (2022). The Legality of Smart Contracts in a Decentralized Autonomous Organization (DAO). In Regulatory Aspects of Artificial Intelligence on Blockchain (pp. 112-131). IGI Global.

PrasadRao. K. V., RadhaKrishna, P. K. S., Teja, G. M. C., & Panda, S. K. (n.d.). *Blockchain based Smart Contract deployment on Ethereum Platform using Web3. js and Solidity*. https://www.researchgate.net/profile/Mani-Gaddam/publication/356988224_Blockchain_based_Smart_Contract_deployment_on_Ethereum_Platform_using_Web3js_and_Solidity/links/61f079e0dafcdb25fd501ebb/Blockchain-based-Smart-Contract-deployment-on-Ethereum-Platform-using-Web3js-and-Solidity.pdf

Prause, G. (2019). Smart contracts for smart supply chains. *IFAC-PapersOnLine, 52*(13), 2501–2506. doi:10.1016/j.ifacol.2019.11.582

Puthal, D., & Mohanty, S. P. (2018). Proof of authentication: IoT-friendly blockchains. *IEEE Potentials, 38*(1), 26–29.

Qasem, Z., Hmoud, H. Y., Hajawi, D., & Al Zoubi, J. Z. (2022). The Effect of Technostress on Cyberbullying in Metaverse Social Platforms. In A. Elbanna, S. McLoughlin, Y. K. Dwivedi, B. Donnellan, & D. Wastell (Eds.), *Co-creating for Context in the Transfer and Diffusion of IT* (Vol. 660, pp. 291–296). Springer International Publishing. doi:10.1007/978-3-031-17968-6_22

Qian, P., Cao, R., Liu, Z., Li, W., Li, M., Zhang, L., Xu, Y., Chen, J., & He, Q. (2023). *Empirical Review of Smart Contract and DeFi Security: Vulnerability Detection and Automated Repair* (arXiv:2309.02391). arXiv. http://arxiv.org/abs/2309.02391

Qi, H., Xu, M., Yu, D., & Cheng, X. (2023). SoK: Privacy-preserving smart contract. *High-Confidence Computing, 100183.* Advance online publication. doi:10.1016/j.hcc.2023.100183

Queiroz, M. M., Telles, R., & Bonilla, S. H. (2020). Blockchain and supply chain management integration: A systematic review of the literature. *Supply Chain Management, 25*(2), 241–254. doi:10.1108/SCM-03-2018-0143

Ramzan, S., Aqdus, A., Ravi, V., Koundal, D., Amin, R., & Al Ghamdi, M. A. (2022). Healthcare applications using blockchain technology: Motivations and challenges. *IEEE Transactions on Engineering Management.*

Ranganthan, V. P., Dantu, R., Paul, A., Mears, P., & Morozov, K. (2018, October). A decentralized marketplace application on the ethereum blockchain. In *2018 IEEE 4th International Conference on Collaboration and Internet Computing (CIC)* (pp. 90-97). IEEE. https://ieeexplore.ieee.org/abstract/document/8537821/

Rashideh, W. (2020). Blockchain technology framework: Current and future perspectives for the tourism industry. *Tourism Management, 80*, 104125. doi:10.1016/j.tourman.2020.104125

Rawal, B. S., Mentges, A., & Ahmad, S. (2022). The Rise of Metaverse and Interoperability with Split-Protocol. *2022 IEEE 23rd International Conference on Information Reuse and Integration for Data Science (IRI)*, 192–199. 10.1109/IRI54793.2022.00051

Ray, P. P. (2023). Web3: A comprehensive review on background, technologies, applications, zero-trust architectures, challenges and future directions. In Internet of Things and Cyber-Physical Systems (Vol. 3). doi:10.1016/j.iotcps.2023.05.003

Reed, S. L. (2014). Bitcoin cooperative proof-of-stake. *arXiv preprint arXiv:1405.5741.*

Reyna, A., Martín, C., Chen, J., Soler, E., & Díaz, M. (2018). On blockchain and its integration with IoT. Challenges and opportunities. *Future Generation Computer Systems, 88*, 173–190. doi:10.1016/j.future.2018.05.046

Rikken, O., Janssen, M., & Kwee, Z. (2019). Governance challenges of blockchain and decentralized autonomous organizations. *Information Polity, 24*(4), 397–417. doi:10.3233/IP-190154

Ritterbusch, G. D., & Teichmann, M. R. (2023). Defining the Metaverse: A Systematic Literature Review. *IEEE Access : Practical Innovations, Open Solutions, 11*, 12368–12377. doi:10.1109/ACCESS.2023.3241809

Rumbelow, J. (2023). *Building With Ethereum: Products, Protocols, and Platforms.* APress.

Russo, D. (2023). *Pioneering Sustainable Supply Chain Solutions: Green Chain Revolution.* Academic Press.

Rutskiy, V., Muda, I., Joudar, F., Ilia, F., Lyubaya, S., Kuzmina, A., & Tsarev, R. (2023). DAO Tokens: The Role for the Web 3.0 Industry and Pricing Factors. In R. Silhavy & P. Silhavy (Eds.), *Networks and Systems in Cybernetics* (Vol. 723, pp. 595–604). Springer International Publishing. doi:10.1007/978-3-031-35317-8_54

Sable, N. P., Sonkamble, R., Rathod, V. U., Shirke, S., Deshmukh, J. Y., & Chavan, G. T. (2023). Web3 Chain Authentication and Authorization Security Standard (CAA). *International Journal on Recent and Innovation Trends in Computing and Communication, 11*(5), 70–76. Advance online publication. doi:10.17762/ijritcc.v11i5.6526

Sadawi, A. A., Hassan, M. S., & Ndiaye, M. (2022). On the Integration of Blockchain With IoT and the Role of Oracle in the Combined System: The Full Picture. *IEEE Access : Practical Innovations, Open Solutions, 10*, 92532–92558. doi:10.1109/ACCESS.2022.3199007

Saengchote, K. (2023). Decentralized lending and its users: Insights from compound. *Journal of International Financial Markets, Institutions and Money, 87*, 101807. doi:10.1016/j.intfin.2023.101807

Saengchote, K., Putniņš, T., & Samphantharak, K. (2023). Does DeFi remove the need for trust? Evidence from a natural experiment in stablecoin lending. *Journal of Behavioral and Experimental Finance, 100858*, 100858. Advance online publication. doi:10.1016/j.jbef.2023.100858

Sagirlar, G., Carminati, B., Ferrari, E., Sheehan, J. D., & Ragnoli, E. (2018). Hybrid-iot: Hybrid blockchain architecture for internet of things-pow sub-blockchains. *2018 IEEE International Conference on Internet of Things (iThings) and IEEE Green Computing and Communications (GreenCom) and IEEE Cyber, Physical and Social Computing (CPSCom) and IEEE Smart Data (SmartData).*

Salami, I. (2021). Challenges and approaches to regulating decentralized finance. *AJIL Unbound, 115*, 425–429. Advance online publication. doi:10.1017/aju.2021.66

Samara, D., Magnisalis, I., & Peristeras, V. (2020). Artificial intelligence and big data in tourism: A systematic literature review. *Journal of Hospitality and Tourism Technology, 11*(2), 343–367. doi:10.1108/JHTT-12-2018-0118

Sankar, J. G., & David, A. (2023). Measuring the Service Quality of Artificial Intelligence in the Tourism and Hospitality Industry. In Handbook of Research on Innovation, Differentiation, and New Technologies in Tourism, Hotels, and Food Service (pp. 133-155). IGI Global. doi:10.4018/978-1-6684-6985-9.ch007

Sankar, J. G., Sugundan, N., & Sivakumar, S. (2018). MOOCs: A Comparative analysis between Indian scenario and Global scenario. *International Journal of Engineering & Technology, 7*(4.39), 854-857.

Sankar, J. G., Valan, P., & Siranjeevi, M. S. (2020). Various Models to Evaluate Quality in the Service Industry. In Digital Transformation and Innovative Services for Business and Learning (pp. 181-194). IGI Global.

Sankar, J.G., & Srinivasulu, Y. (2014). Growth Drivers of Tourism Industry in India. *The International Journal of Business & Management, 2*(11).

SankarJ. G.DavidA.Ganesh KumarC. (2022). Adaptation of Blockchain Technology In HRM. *Available at* SSRN 4515408.

Sankar, J. G., & Kiruba Sagar, M, V. (2020). Examining the Risk Factor Associated with UTAUT MODEL. *Solid State Technology*, 1196–1198.

Sanz Bayón, P. (2019). Key legal issues surrounding smart contract applications. *SSRN, 9*(1), 63–91. doi:10.2139/ssrn.3525778

Sata, B., Berlanga, A., Chanel, C. P. C., & Lacan, J. (2021). Connecting AI-based Oracles to Blockchains via an Auditable Auction Protocol. *2021 3rd Conference on Blockchain Research & Applications for Innovative Networks and Services (BRAINS)*, 23–24. 10.1109/BRAINS52497.2021.9569808

Saurabh, K., Rani, N., & Upadhyay, P. (2023). Towards blockchain led decentralized autonomous organization (DAO) business model innovations. *Benchmarking, 30*(2), 475–502. doi:10.1108/BIJ-10-2021-0606

Savelyev, A. (2017). Contract law 2.0:'Smart'contracts as the beginning of the end of classic contract law. *Information & Communications Technology Law*, *26*(2), 116–134. doi:10.1080/13600834.2017.1301036

Schär, F., & Finance, D. (2021). On Blockchain- and Smart Contract-Based Financial Markets Federal Reserve Bank of St. Louis Review. *Second Quarter*, *103*(2), 153–174. doi:10.20955/r.103.153-74

SEC. (2017). *SEC Issues Investigative Report Concluding DAO Tokens, a Digital Asset, Were Securities*. US Securities and Exchange Commission. https://cdn.lawreportgroup.com/hflr-files/2017/10/11/aca_press-release_sec-issues-investigative-report-concluding-dao-tokens.pdf

Sedkaoui, S., & Chicha, N. (2021). Blockchain-based smart contract technology application in the insurance industry: The case of "Fizzy". *MJBS*, (2).

Seitova, D., & Malik, G. (2023). Unlocking the Metaverse: Revolutionizing Resource Learning for Future Students. *International Journal of Educational Technology and Artificial Intelligence*, *2*(2). https://topazart.info/e-journals/index.php/ijetai/article/view/34

Sengupta, J., Ruj, S., & Bit, S. D. (2020). A comprehensive survey on attacks, security issues and blockchain solutions for IoT and IIoT. *Journal of Network and Computer Applications*, *149*, 102481.

Shahbazi, Z., & Byun, Y.-C. (2021). Fake Media Detection Based on Natural Language Processing and Blockchain Approaches. *IEEE Access : Practical Innovations, Open Solutions*, *9*, 128442–128453. doi:10.1109/ACCESS.2021.3112607

Shahbazi, Z., & Byun, Y.-C. (2022). Blockchain-Based Event Detection and Trust Verification Using Natural Language Processing and Machine Learning. *IEEE Access : Practical Innovations, Open Solutions*, *10*, 5790–5800. doi:10.1109/ACCESS.2021.3139586

Sharma, T., Kwon, Y., Pongmala, K., Wang, H., Miller, A., Song, D., & Wang, Y. (2023). *Unpacking How Decentralized Autonomous Organizations (DAOs) Work in Practice* (arXiv:2304.09822). arXiv. http://arxiv.org/abs/2304.09822

Sharma, P. K., Moon, S. Y., & Park, J. H. (2017). Block-VN: A distributed blockchain based vehicular network architecture in smart city. *Journal of Information Processing Systems*, *13*(1), 184–195.

Sheldon, M. D. (2021). Auditing the Blockchain Oracle Problem. *Journal of Information Systems*, *35*(1), 121–133. doi:10.2308/ISYS-19-049

Shen, B., Tan, W., Guo, J., Zhao, L., & Qin, P. (2021). How to Promote User Purchase in Metaverse? A Systematic Literature Review on Consumer Behavior Research and Virtual Commerce Application Design. *Applied Sciences (Basel, Switzerland)*, *11*(23), 11087. doi:10.3390/app112311087

Shen, J., Deng, C., & Gao, X. (2016). Attraction recommendation: Towards personalized tourism via collective intelligence. *Neurocomputing*, *173*, 789–798. doi:10.1016/j.neucom.2015.08.030

Sheridan, D. A. H., Wear, F., Cowell, J., Wong, E., & Yazdinejad, A. (2022). *Web3 challenges and opportunities for the market.* doi: /arXiv.2209.02446. doi:10.48550

Sheridan, D., Harris, J., Wear, F., Cowell, J., Jr., Wong, E., & Yazdinejad, A. (2022). *Web3 Challenges and Opportunities for the Market* (arXiv:2209.02446). arXiv. http://arxiv.org/abs/2209.02446

Sheridan, D., Harris, J., Wear, F., Cowell, J., Jr., Wong, E., & Yazdinejad, A. (2022). Web3 challenges and opportunities for the market. *arXiv preprint arXiv:2209.02446*. https://arxiv.org/abs/2209.02446

Sheth, A., & Subramanian, H. (2019). Blockchain and contract theory: Modeling smart contracts using insurance markets. *Managerial Finance*, *46*(6), 803–814. doi:10.1108/MF-10-2018-0510

Shi, Y., Liang, J., Li, M., Ma, T., Ye, G., Li, J., & Zhao, Q. (2022). Threshold EdDSA Signature for Blockchain-based Decentralized Finance Applications. *25th International Symposium on Research in Attacks, Intrusions and Defenses*, 129–142. 10.1145/3545948.3545977

Shoker, A. (2021). Blockchain technology as a means of sustainable development. *One Earth*, *4*(6), 795–800. doi:10.1016/j.oneear.2021.05.014

Sillaber, C., & Waltl, B. (2017). Life cycle of smart contracts in blockchain ecosystems. *Datenschutz Datensich*, *41*(8), 497–500. doi:10.1007/s11623-017-0819-7

Singh, S., & Bharti, M. (2023). *Building and Deploying Modern Web 3.0 Blockchain Application.* http://www.ir.juit.ac.in:8080/jspui/handle/123456789/9834

Singh, M., & Kim, S. (2019). Blockchain technology for decentralized autonomous organizations. In *Advances in Computers* (Vol. 115, pp. 115–140). Elsevier. doi:10.1016/bs.adcom.2019.06.001

Singh, P., Sammanit, D., Krishnan, P., Agarwal, K. M., Shaw, R. N., & Ghosh, A. (2021). Combating challenges in the construction industry with blockchain technology. In *Innovations in Electrical and Electronic Engineering* (pp. 707–716). Springer. doi:10.1007/978-981-16-0749-3_56

Singh, S., Kakkar, P., & Bhambri, P. (2013). A Study of the Impact of Random Waypoint and Vector Mobility Models on Various Routing Protocols in MANET. *International Journal of Advances in Computing and Information Technology*, *2*(3), 41–51.

Siniarski, B., Alwis, C. D., Gür, G., & Liyanage, M. (2016). *Need of 6G for the Metaverse Realization.* Academic Press.

Smaili, N., & De Rancourt-Raymond, A. (2022). Metaverse: Welcome to the new fraud marketplace. *Journal of Financial Crime.* Advance online publication. doi:10.1108/JFC-06-2022-0124

Sober, M., Scaffino, G., Spanring, C., & Schulte, S. (2021). *A Voting-Based Blockchain Interoperability Oracle* (arXiv:2111.10091). arXiv. doi:10.1109/Blockchain53845.2021.00030

Solakis, K., Katsoni, V., Mahmoud, A. B., & Grigoriou, N. (2022). Factors affecting value co-creation through artificial intelligence in tourism: A general literature review. *Journal of Tourism Futures.*

Song, A., Seo, E., & Kim, H. (2023). Anomaly VAE-Transformer: A Deep Learning Approach for Anomaly Detection in Decentralized Finance. *IEEE Access : Practical Innovations, Open Solutions*, *11*, 98115–98131. doi:10.1109/ACCESS.2023.3313448

Sovrin. (2023). *Sovrin.* https://sovrin.org/

Spherical Insights. (2023). *Global Blockchain AI Market.* https://www.sphericalinsights.com/reports/blockchain-ai-market

Stark, J. (2017). Making Sense of Blockchain Smart Contracts, 2016. *Acesso em, 13.* https://www.coindesk.com/markets/2016/06/04/making-sense-of-blockchain-smart-contracts/

Steem. (2023). *Powering Communities and Opportunities - Steem.* https://steem.com/

StepanovaV.EriņšI. (2021). Review of Decentralized Finance Applications and Their Total Value Locked. *TEM Journal*, 327–333. https://doi.org/ doi:10.18421/TEM101-41

Suarez Barcia, L. (2023). Decentralized Finance Oracles. *Journal of New Finance*, *3*(1). Advance online publication. doi:10.46671/2521-2486.1016

Subburaj, T., Shilpa, K., Sultana, S., Suthendran, K., Karuppasamy, M., Arun Kumar, S., & Jyothi Babu, A. (2023). Discover Crypto-Jacker from Blockchain Using AFS Method. In K. A. Reddy, B. R. Devi, B. George, K. S. Raju, & M. Sellathurai (Eds.), *Proceedings of Fourth International Conference on Computer and Communication Technologies* (*Vol. 606*, pp. 145–156). Springer Nature Singapore. 10.1007/978-981-19-8563-8_15

Subramanian, H., & Liu, R. (2021). Blockchain and smart contract: A review. *Journal of Database Management*, *32*(1), vii–xxvi.

Sunyaev, A., & Sunyaev, A. (2020). Cloud computing. *Internet Computing: Principles of Distributed Systems and Emerging Internet-Based Technologies*, 195-236.

Surve, T., & Khandelwal, R. (2023). The Development of Decentralized Governance Models for Web 3 Ecosystems. In P. Lekhi & G. Kaur (Eds.), Advances in Web Technologies and Engineering. IGI Global. doi:10.4018/978-1-6684-9919-1.ch006

Susanti, V. D., Andari, T., & Harenza, A. (2020). Web based learning media assisted by powtoon in basic mathematics lesson. *Al-Jabar: Jurnal Pendidikan Matematika*, *11*(1), 11–20. doi:10.24042/ajpm.v11i1.5308

Swan, M. (2015). Blockchain: Blueprint for a new economy. O'Reilly Media, Inc.

Swan, M. (2015). *Blockchain: Blueprint for a New Economy*. O'Reilly Media.

Szabo, N. (1997). *The idea of smart contracts, in: Nick Szabo's Papers and Concise Tutorials*. https://www.fon.hum.uva.nl/rob/Courses/ InformationInSpeech/CDROM/Literature/LOTwinterschool2006/szabo.best. vwh.net/smart_contracts_2.html

Szabo, N. (1997). Formalizing and Securing Relationships on Public Networks. *First Monday*, *2*(9). Advance online publication. doi:10.5210/fm.v2i9.548

Taeihagh, A. (2017). Crowdsourcing, sharing economies and development. *Journal of Developing Societies*, *33*(2), 191–222. doi:10.1177/0169796X17710072

Taghavi, M., Bentahar, J., Otrok, H., & Bakhtiyari, K. (2023). A reinforcement learning model for the reliability of blockchain oracles. *Expert Systems with Applications*, *214*, 119160. doi:10.1016/j.eswa.2022.119160

Tan, E., Mahula, S., & Crompvoets, J. (2022). Blockchain governance in the public sector: A conceptual framework for public management. *Government Information Quarterly*, *39*(1), 101625. doi:10.1016/j.giq.2021.101625

Tapscott, D., & Tapscott, A. (2018). Blockchain Revolution: How the Technology Behind Bitcoin and Other Cryptocurrencies Is Changing the World. Sage Publications, Inc.

Tapscott, D., & Tapscott, A. (2016). *Blockchain revolution: how the technology behind Bitcoin is changing money, business, and the world*. Penguin.

Tariq, U., Ibrahim, A., Ahmad, T., Bouteraa, Y., & Elmogy, A. (2019). Blockchain in internet-of-things: A necessity framework for security, reliability, transparency, immutability and liability. *IET Communications*, *13*(19), 3187–3192. Advance online publication. doi:10.1049/iet-com.2019.0194

TCS. (2023). Building value by building community. *Tata Consultancy Services*. https://www.tcs.com/insights/article/organizations-expand-with-web3-ecosystems

Tennakoon, D., Hua, Y., & Gramoli, V. (2023). Smart Redbelly Blockchain: Reducing Congestion for Web3. *2023 IEEE International Parallel and Distributed Processing Symposium (IPDPS)*, 940–950. 10.1109/IPDPS54959.2023.00098

Tern, S. (2021). Survey of smart contract technology and application based on blockchain. *Ozean Journal of Applied Sciences*, *11*(10), 1135–1148. doi:10.4236/ojapps.2021.1110085

Thabet, N. A., & Abdelbaki, N. (2021, October). Efficient querying blockchain applications. In *2021 3rd Novel Intelligent and Leading Emerging Sciences Conference (NILES)* (pp. 365-369). IEEE. https://doi.org/10.1109/NILES53778.2021.9600533

Thees, H., Erschbamer, G., & Pechlaner, H. (2020). The application of blockchain in tourism: Use cases in the tourism value system. *European Journal of Tourism Research*, *26*, 2602–2602. doi:10.54055/ejtr.v26i.1933

TheLAO. (2023). *The LAO*. https://thelao.io/

Timur, S., Timur, B., & Arcagök, S., & Öztürk, G. (2020). Opinions of science teachers towards web 2.0 tools. *Kırşehir Faculty of Education Journal*, *21*(1), 63–108.

Tokmakov, M. A. (2019). Corporate Governance Modernization: Legal Trends and Challenges. *SHS Web of Conferences*, *71*, 04011. 10.1051/shsconf/20197104011

Tolmach, P., Li, Y., Lin, S. W., Liu, Y., & Li, Z. (2021). A survey of smart contract formal specification and verification. *ACM Computing Surveys*, *54*(7), 1–38. doi:10.1145/3464421

TolmachP.LiY.LinS.-W.LiuY. (2021). Formal Analysis of Composable DeFi Protocols (arXiv:2103.00540). doi:10.1007/978-3-662-63958-0_13

Tondon, N., & Bhambri, P. (2017). Novel Approach for Drug Discovery. *International Journal of Research in Engineering and Applied Sciences*, *7*(6), 28–46.

Toyoda, K. (2023). Web3 meets behavioral economics: An example of profitable crypto lottery mechanism design. *2023 IEEE International Conference on Metaverse Computing, Networking and Applications (MetaCom)*, 678–679. 10.1109/MetaCom57706.2023.00122

Trabucchi, D., Moretto, A., Buganza, T., & MacCormack, A. (2020). Disrupting the Disruptors or Enhancing Them? How Blockchain Reshapes Two-Sided Platforms. *Journal of Product Innovation Management*, *37*(6), 552–574. doi:10.1111/jpim.12557

Treiblmaier, H., & Petrozhitskaya, E. (2023). Is it time for marketing to reappraise B2C relationship management? The emergence of a new loyalty paradigm through blockchain technology. *Journal of Business Research*, *159*, 113725. doi:10.1016/j.jbusres.2023.113725

Truong, N., Lee, G. M., Sun, K., Guitton, F., & Guo, Y. (2021). A blockchain-based trust system for decentralised applications: When trustless needs trust. *Future Generation Computer Systems*, *124*, 68–79. doi:10.1016/j.future.2021.05.025

Tsai, W.-T., He, J., Wang, R., & Deng, E. (2020). Decentralized Digital-Asset Exchanges: Issues and Evaluation. *2020 3rd International Conference on Smart BlockChain (SmartBlock)*, 1–6. 10.1109/SmartBlock52591.2020.00024

Tsung-ChihH.HsiehN. K.ChangC. Y.ChenT. L. (2023). Research on the Application of Smart Contracts in Travel Insurance Claims. *Available at* SSRN 4480435. doi:10.2139/ssrn.4480435

Tyagi, A. K. (2023). Decentralized everything: Practical use of blockchain technology in future applications. In *Distributed Computing to Blockchain* (pp. 19–38). Elsevier. doi:10.1016/B978-0-323-96146-2.00010-3

Um, T., Kim, H., Kim, H., Lee, J., Koo, C., & Chung, N. (2022). Travel Incheon as a Metaverse: Smart Tourism Cities Development Case in Korea. In J. L. Stienmetz, B. Ferrer-Rosell, & D. Massimo (Eds.), *Information and Communication Technologies in Tourism 2022* (pp. 226–231). Springer International Publishing. doi:10.1007/978-3-030-94751-4_20

Unal, D., Hammoudeh, M., & Kiraz, M. S. (2020). Policy specification and verification for blockchain and smart contracts in 5G networks. *ICT Express*, *6*(1), 43–47. doi:10.1016/j.icte.2019.07.002

UnblockTalent. (2023). *Top 19 global ranking of consensus mechanisms*. UnblockTalent. https://www.unblocktalent.com/topics/building-blocks/consensus/consensus-ranking/

Unnikrishnan, K. N., & Victer Paul, P. (2022). A Survey on Layer 2 Solutions to Achieve Scalability in Blockchain. In R. R. Rout, S. K. Ghosh, P. K. Jana, A. K. Tripathy, J. P. Sahoo, & K.-C. Li (Eds.), *Advances in Distributed Computing and Machine Learning* (Vol. 427, pp. 205–216). Springer Nature Singapore. doi:10.1007/978-981-19-1018-0_18

Upadhyay, U., Kumar, A., Sharma, G., Gupta, B. B., Alhalabi, W. A., Arya, V., & Chui, K. T. (2023). Cyberbullying in the Metaverse: A Prescriptive Perception on Global Information Systems for User Protection. *Journal of Global Information Management*, *31*(1), 1–25. doi:10.4018/JGIM.325793

Uriarte, R. B., Tiezzi, F., & De Nicola, R. (2016). Dynamic slas for clouds. In *Service-Oriented and Cloud Computing: 5th IFIP WG 2.14 European Conference, ESOCC 2016, Vienna, Austria, September 5-7, 2016, Proceedings 5* (pp. 34-49). Springer International Publishing. 10.1007/978-3-319-44482-6_3

Urquhart, A. (2022). Under the hood of the Ethereum blockchain. *Finance Research Letters*, *47*, 102628. doi:10.1016/j.frl.2021.102628

Ushida, R., & Angel, J. (2021). Regulatory Considerations on Centralized Aspects of DeFi Managed by DAOs. In M. Bernhard, A. Bracciali, L. Gudgeon, T. Haines, A. Klages-Mundt, S. Matsuo, D. Perez, M. Sala, & S. Werner (Eds.), *Financial Cryptography and Data Security. FC 2021 International Workshops* (Vol. 12676, pp. 21–36). Springer Berlin Heidelberg. doi:10.1007/978-3-662-63958-0_2

Usmani, S. S., Sharath, M., & Mehendale, M. (2022). Future of mental health in the metaverse. *General Psychiatry*, *35*(4), e100825. doi:10.1136/gpsych-2022-100825 PMID:36189180

Uzuner, Ö. (2018). *The effect of slow animation technique on secondary school students' achievements, scientific thinking skills and goal orientation in science lessons* [Master's Thesis]. Amasya University Institute of Science and Technology.

Vacca, A., Di Sorbo, A., Visaggio, C. A., & Canfora, G. (2021). A systematic literature review of blockchain and smart contract development: Techniques, tools, and open challenges. *Journal of Systems and Software*, *174*, 110891. doi:10.1016/j.jss.2020.110891

Van Molken, R., & van Molken, R. (2018). *Blockchain across Oracle*. Packt Publishing.

Varfolomeev, A. A., Alfarhani, L. H., & Oleiwi, Z. C. (2021). Secure-reliable smart contract applications based blockchain technology in smart cities environment. *Procedia Computer Science*, *186*, 669–676. doi:10.1016/j.procs.2021.04.188

Velmurugan, T. A., & Sankar, J. G. (2017). A comparative study on motivation theory with Maslow's hierarchy theory and two factor theory in organization. *Indo-Iranian Journal of Scientific Research*, *1*(1), 204–208.

Vero, K. (2023). *From Pixels to Portals: Exploring the Future of the Metaverse through the Evolution of Videogames*. Academic Press.

Vijayalakshmi, J., & Murugan, A. (2017, February). Crypto Coins: The Future of Transactions. In *Proceedings of International Conference on Communication, Computing and Information Technology*. https://www.researchgate.net/profile/Dr-J-Vijayalakshmi/publication/333310695_Crypto_Coins_The_Future_of_Transactions/links/5e4b792ea6fdccd965aef3b9/Crypto-Coins-The-Future-of-Transactions.pdf

Viriyasitavat, W., & Hoonsopon, D. (2019). Blockchain characteristics and consensus in modern business processes. *Journal of Industrial Information Integration*, *13*, 32–39. doi:10.1016/j.jii.2018.07.004

Volk, D. (2008). Co-creative game development in a participatory Metaverse. *Proceedings of the Tenth Anniversary Conference on Participatory Design 2008*, 262–265.

Voshmgir, S. (2020). *Token Economy: How the Web3 reinvents the internet* (Vol. 2). Token Kitchen.

Voshmgir, S. (2020). *Token economy: How the Web3 reinvents the internet*. Blockchain Club Berlin.

Wang, Q., Li, R., Wang, Q., Chen, S., Ryan, M., & Hardjono, T. (2022). Exploring web3 from the view of blockchain. *arXiv preprint arXiv:2206.08821*. https://arxiv.org/abs/2206.08821

Wang, Y., Liu, H., Wang, J., & Wang, S. (2020). Efficient Data Interaction of Blockchain Smart Contract with Oracle Mechanism. *2020 IEEE 9th Joint International Information Technology and Artificial Intelligence Conference (ITAIC)*, 1000–1003. 10.1109/ITAIC49862.2020.9338784

Wang, H., Guo, C., & Cheng, S. (2019). LoC—A new financial loan management system based on smart contracts. *Future Generation Computer Systems*, *100*, 648–655. doi:10.1016/j.future.2019.05.040

Wang, H., Moon, S., & Han, N. (2020). A study on the applications of blockchain transactions and smart contracts in recordkeeping. *Journal of Korean Society of Archives and Records Management*, *20*(4), 81–105.

Wang, H., & Yang, D. (2021). Research and Development of Blockchain Recordkeeping at the National Archives of Korea. *Computers*, *10*(8), 90. doi:10.3390/computers10080090

Wang, J., Makowski, S., Cieslik, A., Lv, H., & Lv, Z. (2023). Fake News in Virtual Community, Virtual Society, and Metaverse: A Survey. *IEEE Transactions on Computational Social Systems*, 1–15. doi:10.1109/TCSS.2022.3220420

Wang, S., Ding, W., Li, J., Yuan, Y., Ouyang, L., & Wang, F.-Y. (2019). Decentralized Autonomous Organizations: Concept, Model, and Applications. *IEEE Transactions on Computational Social Systems*, *6*(5), 870–878. doi:10.1109/TCSS.2019.2938190

Wang, W., Kumar, N., Chen, J., Gong, Z., Kong, X., Wei, W., & Gao, H. (2020). Realizing the potential of the internet of things for smart tourism with 5G and AI. *IEEE Network*, *34*(6), 295–301. doi:10.1109/MNET.011.2000250

Wang, Y., Siau, K. L., & Wang, L. (2022). Metaverse and Human-Computer Interaction: A Technology Framework for 3D Virtual Worlds. In J. Y. C. Chen, G. Fragomeni, H. Degen, & S. Ntoa (Eds.), *HCI International 2022 – Late Breaking Papers: Interacting with eXtended Reality and Artificial Intelligence* (Vol. 13518, pp. 213–221). Springer Nature Switzerland. doi:10.1007/978-3-031-21707-4_16

Wei, P., Wang, D., Zhao, Y., Tyagi, S. K. S., & Kumar, N. (2020). Blockchain data-based cloud data integrity protection mechanism. *Future Generation Computer Systems*, *102*, 902–911. doi:10.1016/j.future.2019.09.028

Wen, M. H., Huang, C. Y., Chen, Y. C., & Lin, I. C. (2023). Exploring Factors Influencing Community Consensus Building of Web3 Decentralized Apps. Lecture Notes in Computer Science (Including Subseries Lecture Notes in Artificial Intelligence and Lecture Notes in Bioinformatics), 14032 LNCS. doi:10.1007/978-3-031-35702-2_29

Wenhua, Z., Qamar, F., Abdali, T.-A. N., Hassan, R., Jafri, S. T. A., & Nguyen, Q. N. (2023). Blockchain technology: Security issues, healthcare applications, challenges and future trends. *Electronics (Basel)*, *12*(3), 546. doi:10.3390/electronics12030546

Werner, S., Perez, D., Gudgeon, L., Klages-Mundt, A., Harz, D., & Knottenbelt, W. (2022). *SoK: Decentralized Finance*. DeFi. doi:10.1145/3558535.3559780

Weyl, E. G. (2017). Quadratic Vote Buying. SSRN *Electronic Journal*. doi:10.2139/ssrn.2003531

Wikipedia. (n.d.). https://en.wikipedia.org/wiki/Smart_contract

Willie, P. (2019). Can all sectors of the hospitality and tourism industry be influenced by the innovation of blockchain technology? *Worldwide Hospitality and Tourism Themes*, *11*(2), 112–120. doi:10.1108/WHATT-11-2018-0077

Wilson, M., Robson, K., & Pitt, L. (2022). Consumer subversion and its relationship to anti-consumption, deviant and dysfunctional behaviors, and consumer revenge. *Psychology and Marketing*, *39*(3), 598-611.

Wintermeyer, L. (2021, October 14). *Oracles: The invisible backbone of DeFi and applied Blockchain apps*. Forbes. Com. https://www.forbes.com/sites/lawrencewintermeyer/2021/10/14/cryptohacks-oraclesthe-invisible-backbone-of-defi-and-applied-blockchain-apps/

Wood, G. (2014). Ethereum: A Secure Decentralised Generalised Transaction Ledger. *Ethereum Project Yellow Paper*, *151*. Advance online publication. doi:10.1007/s10203-008-0041-7

Wright, C. S. (2020). Decentralized Autonomous Corporations. In X.-S. Yang, S. Sherratt, N. Dey, & A. Joshi (Eds.), *Fourth International Congress on Information and Communication Technology* (*Vol. 1027*, pp. 153–167). Springer Singapore. 10.1007/978-981-32-9343-4_14

Wu, J., Lin, K., Lin, D., Zheng, Z., Huang, H., & Zheng, Z. (2023). Financial Crimes in Web3-Empowered Metaverse: Taxonomy, Countermeasures, and Opportunities. *IEEE Open Journal of the Computer Society*, *4*, 37–49. Advance online publication. doi:10.1109/OJCS.2023.3245801

Wüst, K., & Gervais, A. (2018). Do you need a blockchain? *2018 Crypto Valley Conference on Blockchain Technology (CVCBT)*.

Wu, X., & Lin, Y. (2019). Blockchain recall management in pharmaceutical industry. *Procedia CIRP*, *83*, 590–595. doi:10.1016/j.procir.2019.04.094

Xiao, Y., Liu, Y., & Li, T. (2020). Edge Computing and Blockchain for Quick Fake News Detection in IoV. *Sensors (Basel)*, *20*(16), 4360. doi:10.3390/s20164360

Xu, L., Shah, N., Chen, L., Diallo, N., Gao, Z., Lu, Y., & Shi, W. (2017). Enabling the sharing economy: Privacy respecting contract based on public blockchain. *Proceedings of the ACM Workshop on Blockchain, Cryptocurrencies and Contracts*.

Yadav, J. K., Verma, D. C., Jangirala, S., & Srivastava, S. K. (2021). An IAD type framework for Blockchain enabled smart tourism ecosystem. *The Journal of High Technology Management Research*, *32*(1), 100404. doi:10.1016/j.hitech.2021.100404

Yang, X., & Li, W. (2020). A zero-knowledge-proof-based digital identity management scheme in blockchain. *Computers & Security*, *99*, 102050.

Yapıcı, İ., & Karakoyun, F. (2017). Gamification in Biology teaching: A sample of Kahoot application. *Turkish Online Journal of Qualitative Inquiry*, *8*(4), 396–414. doi:10.17569/tojqi.335956

Yavuz, E., Koç, A. K., Çabuk, U. C., & Dalkılıç, G. (2018, March). Towards secure e-voting using ethereum blockchain. In *2018 6th International Symposium on Digital Forensic and Security (ISDFS)* (pp. 1-7). IEEE. https://ieeexplore.ieee.org/abstract/document/8355340/

Yildiz, H. (2023). *The Web3, Metaverse and AI Handbook: How to leverage new technologies to create unique brands and drive new lanes of revenue*. Academic Press.

Yıldız, İ., & Tanyıldızı, N. İ. (2022). An Analysis of News Containing Cyberbullying in the Metaverse. In G. Sarı (Ed.), Advances in Social Networking and Online Communities. IGI Global. doi:10.4018/978-1-6684-5426-8.ch012

Yli-Huumo, J., Ko, D., Choi, S., Park, S., & Smolander, K. (2016). Where is current research on blockchain technology?—A systematic review. *PLoS One*, *11*(10), e0163477. doi:10.1371/journal.pone.0163477 PMID:27695049

Yoo, B., Kim, A., Moon, H. S., So, M.-K., Jeong, T.-D., Lee, K. E., Moon, B.-I., & Huh, J. (2024). Evaluation of Group Genetic Counseling Sessions via a Metaverse-based Application. *Annals of Laboratory Medicine*, *44*(1), 82–91. doi:10.3343/alm.2024.44.1.82 PMID:37665289

Young, S. (2018). Changing governance models by applying blockchain computing. *Catholic University Journal of Law and Technology*, *26*(2), 87–128.

Yousaf, I., Abrar, A., & Yarovaya, L. (2023). Decentralized and centralized exchanges: Which digital tokens pose a greater contagion risk? *Journal of International Financial Markets, Institutions and Money*, *89*, 101881. doi:10.1016/j.intfin.2023.101881

Zarrin, J., Wen Phang, H., Babu Saheer, L., & Zarrin, B. (2021). Blockchain for decentralization of internet: Prospects, trends, and challenges. *Cluster Computing*, *24*(4), 2841–2866. Advance online publication. doi:10.1007/s10586-021-03301-8 PMID:34025209

Zavratnik, J. (2022). *Analysis of web3 solution development principles* (Master's thesis, Universitat Politècnica de Catalunya). https://upcommons.upc.edu/handle/2117/379908

Zeren, S. K. (2023). Revolutionizing Tourism Payments: The Formation of Decentralized Tourism Financial Systems. In Blockchain for Tourism and Hospitality Industries (pp. 66-83). Routledge.

Zetzsche, D. A., Arner, D. W., & Buckley, R. P. (2020). Decentralized Finance. *Journal of Financial Regulation*, *6*(2), 172–203. doi:10.1093/jfr/fjaa010

Zhang, J., & Quoquab, F. (2023). Metaverse in the urban destinations in China: Some insights for the tourism players. *International Journal of Tourism Cities*. doi:10.1108/IJTC-04-2023-0062

Zhang, M., Wang, J., & Ji, D. (2023). Between Institutioning and Commoning: Grassroots Co-creation in Web3 Communities. Lecture Notes in Computer Science (Including Subseries Lecture Notes in Artificial Intelligence and Lecture Notes in Bioinformatics), 14022 LNCS, 317–329. doi:10.1007/978-3-031-35936-1_23

Zhang, X., Qin, R., Yuan, Y., & Wang, F.-Y. (2018). An analysis of blockchain-based bitcoin mining difficulty: Techniques and principles. *2018 Chinese Automation Congress (CAC).*

Zhang, B., Li, X., Ren, H., & Gu, J. (2020). Semantic Knowledge Sharing Mechanism Based on Blockchain. In Y. Liu, L. Wang, L. Zhao, & Z. Yu (Eds.), *Advances in Natural Computation, Fuzzy Systems and Knowledge Discovery* (Vol. 1075, pp. 115–127). Springer International Publishing. doi:10.1007/978-3-030-32591-6_13

Zheng, J., & Lee, D. K. C. (2023). Understanding the Evolution of the Internet: Web 1.0 to Web3. 0, Web3 and Web 3. *Handbook of Digital Currency: Bitcoin, Innovation, Financial Instruments, and Big Data.* https://papers.ssrn.com/sol3/papers.cfm?abstract_id=4431284

Zheng, Z., Xie, S., Dai, H., Chen, X., & Wang, H. (2017). An overview of blockchain technology: Architecture, consensus, and future trends. *2017 IEEE International Congress on Big Data (Big Data Congress).*

Zheng, Z., Xie, S., Dai, H., Chen, X., & Wang, H. (2018). An Overview of Blockchain Technology: Architecture, Consensus, and Future Trends. In *2017 IEEE International Congress on Big Data (Big Data Congress)* (pp. 557-564). Academic Press.

Zheng, Z., Xie, S., Dai, H. N., Chen, W., Chen, X., Weng, J., & Imran, M. (2020). An overview on smart contracts: Challenges, advances, and platforms. *Future Generation Computer Systems*, *105*, 475–491. doi:10.1016/j.future.2019.12.019

Zichichi, M., Ferretti, S., & Rodríguez-Doncel, V. (2022). Decentralized Personal Data Marketplaces: How Participation in a DAO Can Support the Production of Citizen-Generated Data. *Sensors (Basel), 22*(16), 6260. doi:10.3390/s22166260 PMID:36016019

Ziegler, T., Shneor, R., Wenzlaff, K., Wang, B., Kim, J., Paes, F. F. d. C., Suresh, K., Zhang, B. Z., Mammadova, L., & Adams, N. (2021). The global alternative finance market benchmarking report. *Available at SSRN 3771509.*

Zohar, A. (2015). Bitcoin: Under the hood. *Communications of the ACM, 58*(9), 104–113. doi:10.1145/2701411

Zohar, A., & Abbe, A. (2020). The Tokenization of Assets and Potential Implications for Artists. *International Journal of Blockchain and Cryptocurrency, 1*(1), 67–81.

Zou, W., Lo, D., Kochhar, P. S., Le, X. B. D., Xia, X., Feng, Y., Chen, Z., & Xu, B. (2019). Smart contract development: Challenges and opportunities. *IEEE Transactions on Software Engineering, 47*(10), 2084–2106. doi:10.1109/TSE.2019.2942301

Zwitter, A. J., Gstrein, O. J., & Yap, E. (2020). Digital identity and the blockchain: Universal identity management and the concept of the "Self-Sovereign" individual. *Frontiers in Blockchain, 3*, 26. doi:10.3389/fbloc.2020.00026

Zyskind, G., & Nathan, O. (2015). Decentralizing privacy: Using blockchain to protect personal data. *2015 IEEE Security and Privacy Workshops*,

Zyskind, G., Nathan, O., & Pentland, A. (2015). Decentralizing Privacy: Using Blockchain to Protect Personal Data. In 2015 IEEE Security and Privacy Workshops (pp. 180-184). IEEE.

About the Contributors

Dina Darwish is currently a Professor of Artificial Intelligence for Ahram Canadian University. She is also Vice Dean of Faculty of Computer Science & IT.

* * *

Adnan Ahmad holds a BS (Hons) and MS in Computer Science from GCU and LUMS, Pakistan, respectively. He also acquired PhD in Computer Science from Massey University, Auckland, New Zealand and Post-Doc from Saint Louis University, Madrid, Spain. He has around eighteen years of teaching and research experience at various educational and research institutes. More than 45 peer-reviewed articles in renowned conferences and journals are on his credit including Trustcom, Computers & Security, ACM transactions, and IEEE Communication Magazine. He is an associate editor of 3 international journals, a reviewer of various IEEE, Elsevier, IET, and springer journals, and part of TPC of several prestigious conferences. He is also an external evaluator for National Ignite R&D fund, PITB research fund, DICE-IET, and many other international funding agencies. Moreover, he has organized multiple international workshops in Belgium, Kazakhstan, Pakistan, Portugal, and Spain. He has supervised 9 PhD, 16 MS thesis students, and several startup projects. He has also co-authored two books on emerging technologies in distributed systems. He is the founding in-charge of Center of Advance Research in Distributed Systems and Security (CARDS) research group & Cybersecurity Research Group (CSRG) at COMSATS University Islamabad, Pakistan. His research interests include Cyber Security, Digital Forensics, Penetration Testing, Distributed Systems, and Internet of things (IoT). Currently, he is performing his duties as Tenured Associate Professor at COMSATS University Islamabad, Lahore Campus, Pakistan.

Munir Ahmad, Ph.D. in Computer Science, brings over 24 years of invaluable expertise in the realm of spatial data development, management, processing, visualization, and quality assurance. His unwavering commitment to open data, crowdsourced data, volunteered geographic information, and spatial data infrastructure has solidified him as a seasoned professional and a trusted trainer in cutting-edge spatial technologies. With a profound passion for research, Munir has authored more than 30 publications in his field, culminating in the award of his Ph.D. in Computer Science from Preston University Pakistan in 2022. His dedication to propelling the industry forward and sharing his extensive knowledge defines his mission. Connect with Munir to delve into the world of Spatial Data, GIS, and GeoTech.

Muhammad Ahmed is a PhD scholar at COMSATS University Islamabad (Lahore Campus) Pakistan. He is also serving as Senior Lecturer in Department of Software Engineering at Superior University

Lahore, Pakistan. He got his MS degree in Information Security at COMSATS University Islamabad, Pakistan. His main research focuses on Blockchain, Cyber Security and Privacy concerns.

Muhammad Arslan is a dedicated individual currently affiliated with the School of Computer Science at Chenab College of Advance Studies in Faisalabad.

V. R. Balasaraswathi works as an Assistant Professor in the School of Computer Science and Engineering, Vellore Institute of Technology, Chennai, India. She received her Bachelor's degree in Computer Science and Engineering from Madras University in 2002 and a Master's in Computer Science and Engineering from Anna University in 2008. Her area of interest includes Machine Learning, Data Mining, and Artificial intelligence.

Pankaj Bhambri is affiliated with the Department of Information Technology at Guru Nanak Dev Engineering College in Ludhiana. Additionally, he fulfills the role of the Convener for his Departmental Board of Studies. He possesses nearly two decades of teaching experience. His research work has been published in esteemed worldwide and national journals, as well as conference proceedings. Dr. Bhambri has garnered extensive experience in the realm of academic publishing, having served as an editor for a multitude of books in collaboration with esteemed publishing houses such as CRC Press, Elsevier, Scrivener, and Bentham Science. In addition to his editorial roles, he has demonstrated his scholarly prowess by authoring numerous books and contributing chapters to distinguished publishers within the academic community. Dr. Bhambri has been honored with several prestigious accolades, including the ISTE Best Teacher Award in 2023 and 2022, the I2OR National Award in 2020, the Green ThinkerZ Top 100 International Distinguished Educators award in 2020, the I2OR Outstanding Educator Award in 2019, the SAA Distinguished Alumni Award in 2012, the CIPS Rashtriya Rattan Award in 2008, the LCHC Best Teacher Award in 2007, and numerous other commendations from various government and non-profit organizations. He has provided guidance and oversight for numerous research projects and dissertations at the postgraduate and Ph.D. levels. He successfully organized a diverse range of educational programmes, securing financial backing from esteemed institutions such as the AICTE, the TEQIP, among others. Dr. Bhambri's areas of interest encompass machine learning, bioinformatics, wireless sensor networks, and network security.

Arokiaraj David serves as an Associate Professor of Al Tareeqah Management Studies in UAE. He has successfully cleared the UGC-National Eligibility Test for Lectureship (NET) and has been honored with the Junior and Senior Research Fellow (JRF & SRF) titles. With over a decade of teaching and research experience, his areas of expertise include Green Marketing, Consumer Behavior, Product & Brand Management, Global Marketing, Retail Management, Strategic Management, Data Analytics, Sustainable Practices, Resources Management, Product Development, Environmental Responsibility, and General Management. Dr. David has authored more than 60 research articles, including 11 published in Scopus, 08 in ABDC, and 05 in Web of Science. He has also contributed to 07 book chapters, published 04 books, registered 07 patents, and received 01 copyright and 01 consultant project. He is proficient in various research tools and techniques such as SPSS, AMOS, E-Views, STATA, and PLS-SEM and has hands-on experience in both primary and secondary data analysis. Recently, Dr. David has been recognized with the Best Research Award, Young Academician Award, and Young Scientist Award.

Jeganathan Gomathi Sankar is a highly experienced and dedicated educationist with a passion for marketing. He has over 10 years of teaching and research experience, and his work has been recognized by Scopus and ABDC journals. He is a member of the BSSS Institute of Advanced Studies, Faculty of Marketing, and his research interests include marketing technology, marketing information systems, and diffusion of technology in marketing. Dr. Sankar is a strong advocate for using technology to enhance marketing education and practice. He is also a leading expert in the field of diffusion of technology in marketing, and his research has helped to inform the development of new marketing strategies and tactics. A dedicated teacher, Dr. Sankar is committed to providing his students with the knowledge and skills they need to succeed in the ever-changing field of marketing. He is a popular lecturer and is known for his ability to make complex concepts easy to understand. In addition to his teaching and research duties, Dr. Sankar is also an active member of the marketing community. He is a regular speaker at conferences and workshops, and he has published numerous articles in leading marketing journals.

Vivek Gupta has served corporate and Government sector for about 14 years in various capacities at senior/ middle management levels, before joining IIM Lucknow in May 2001. He is with the I.T. & Systems Group at IIM Lucknow and is involved in teaching and research activities. His areas of interest in teaching and research include managing networking environment, IS/IT usage, applications, and outsourcing in organization, network security and managing various IT related information systems and data analysis.

Vedavathi Katneni is the Principal of the GITAM School of Science and a Professor at the Department of Computer Science at GITAM (Deemed to be University), Visakhapatnam. She started a humble beginning as a Computer Programmer and entered into teaching which now spans to over three decades of experience. She has numerous journal publications and has presented at seminars and conferences worldwide. She handled various research projects and is also guiding research scholars. She is an exemplary example of how the roles of academic administrative work and classroom teaching should be balanced. She has membership in various professional bodies.

Anitha Kumari works at the Department of Business Analytics & Fintech, GITAM (Deemed University), Bengaluru, Karnataka. She is currently a Doctoral Fellow at the School of Management, Hindustan Institute of Technology and Science, where she was doing her teaching and research. Her Bachelor's degree was in Computer Applications, while she obtained a Master's in Business Administration with a specialization in finance and systems. She is interested in business, management, operations, information technology, data analysis, accounts, and finance. Her current research focuses on new technologies, business analytics, blockchain, fintech, information systems, and digital banking services. She has conference presentations and published journal articles to her record. She has 6 years of teaching experience in finance and systems.

Jhansi Madavarapu is a highly experienced Principal EAI/EDI Consultant project delivery for Cloud migration, Digital transformation, and EDI/B2B legacy modernization and API integration projects with a demonstrated history of working in the information technology and services industry. For over 10+ years, Jhansi has helped complex multinational organizations across the globe to overcome their business integration challenges by designing and implementing business process solutions and integration platforms. Jhansi has helped businesses achieve their business objectives through technology-driven solution offerings that drive sustainable results. Main areas of expertise include Cloud Authentication and Authorization, Customer Identity and Access Management (CIAM), and Data Integrity and Access and have a strong understanding of Secure protocols such as OAuth2 and OpenIDConnect, and have experience in audit and other related areas.

Vijaya Kittu Manda has nearly 13+ years of experience in capital markets, financial planning, and investing. He is an Advocate, a technocrat, an academician, a book writer, and a stock market enthusiast. He has 11 University Postgraduate Degrees in various subjects. He is a Ph.D. in Management and is currently pursuing his second Ph.D. in Computer Science with a focus on Blockchain. He has written over 730 newspaper articles to various outlets. He is the Chief Editor for a Management Book Series, writers research papers and case studies, a guest faculty for for colleges and universities, resource person for academic conferences, peer reviewer for various journals, and sits in session chair to evaluate research presentations.

L. Mary Shamala is currently working as an Assistant Professor in the School of Computer Science and Engineering, Vellore Institute of Technology, Chennai, India. She received her Bachelor of Engineering Degree with distinction in Information Technology from Manonmanium Sundaranar University, Tirunelveli, India. She pursued her M.Tech and Ph.D. in Computer Science and Engineering from Pondicherry University, Puducherry, India. She has more than 12 years of teaching experience at undergraduate and postgraduate levels. Her areas of interest include Internet of Things Cryptography, Network and Information Security, Blockchain technologies, and Privacy in Online Social Networks.

Arnold Mashud Abukari holds a PhD in Computational Mathematics (Computer Science) with Expertise in Cloud Computing Security using Homomorphic Encryption Schemes. He is a Senior Lecturer in the Computer Science Department of Tamale Technical University in Ghana. His reseearch interests are Cyber Security, Cloud computing, IoT, ERP Systems, Information Systems Auditing and encryption as well as Telecommunication solutions. He has worked in various capacities in several industries including Oil and Gas, Telecommunication, Information Technology and others. He combines industry skills with academics to propose solutions and has won the hearts of many in the field of research with over 56000 reads on research gate.

Kaushikkumar Patel is a distinguished leader known for his exceptional contributions at the intersection of finance and technology. As a key figure at TransUnion, he leverages Big Data to transform decision-making processes and financial strategies, with expertise spanning Data Analytics, FinTech, and Digital Transformation. Based in the United States, Mr. Patel is renowned for his strategic insights in addressing complex challenges like data privacy and risk assessment, ensuring compliance in dynamic financial landscapes. An influential thought leader, Mr. Patel's work has been internationally recognized, earning him the prestigious ET Leadership Excellence Award for his groundbreaking achievements in Data-Driven Financial Strategies. His unique blend of technical prowess and strategic acumen establishes him as a visionary in his field, continually pushing the boundaries of what's possible in finance and technology.

Gayathri Rajakumaran is currently affiliated with Vellore Institute of Technology (VIT), Chennai as Associate Professor in the department of Computer Science and Engineering. She received her Ph.D in Vellore Institute of Technology (VIT), Chennai in 2020 under cloud security specialization. Her specialization domains include cloud security, information and cyber security, IoT and machine learning. She received her UG and PG degrees from Rajiv Gandhi College of Engineering and Technology (2009), Pondicherry Engineering College (2011) respectively. She published numerous journals in high indexed journals and holding 2 patents related to domains agriculture, IoT. She is a reviewer for Journal of Super Computing. She played the role of editor and author for publishing the books "Grid and Cloud Computing", "Cloud Computing" and "Cloud Security". She was a sponsorship chair in International Conference on Big data and Cloud Computing (ICBCC) 2018 and attracted fund from a government funding agency. She is the current Linux Club Co-coordinator in VIT Chennai.

Srikantalahari Sagi currently serves as the Principal of Avinash College of Commerce. She has an MBA, M.Com, LLB, FDA (IIM-K), PGDC (IIMN), and a PhD in Management (Finance). She is a SAP FiCo Trainer. She is a role model and leads by example. She authored several research papers published in leading journals and is a resource person at National and International Conferences and workshops on various topics - motivation to women empowerment, skill-building, and advanced finance topics.

Bikkina Srinivas is a Director at Vingas Industries Private Limited. He has over two decades of industrial experience in dealing with industrial gases. He has special interest in computer science and information technology and has several initiatives that help in the industrial gases industry. He is a Ph.D. with specialization in Operations. He is the author of several journal articles.

Hamid Turab Mirza earned his PhD in Computer Science from Zhejiang University, China in 2012 and his MSc in Information Systems with a Distinction from The University of Sheffield, UK in 2005. Overall Dr. Turab has more than 20 years of research, teaching and software development experience in corporate and academic sectors of both Pakistan and UK. Currently he is serving as a Tenured Associate Professor and is In-Charge of the Computer Science Program at the Department of Computer Science, COMSATS University Islamabad, Lahore Campus. He has continously been a recipient of Research Productivity Awards and Honorarium's for his performance in research, teaching and other departmental responsibilities. Previously he has served in the capacity of Assistant Professor at National University of Sciences and Technology (NUST) for six years. Moreover, he has five years of hand-on software development experience in large organizations including Pakistan Aeronautical Complex, Leeds Metropolitan University UK and British Telecommunication (BT) UK. Dr. Turab's research interest lies within the areas of Data Mining and Context-Aware Computing. He has established and led Knowledge Discovery & Data Mining (KDDM) Research Group at COMSATS Lahore campus since 2012 and has been actively publishing research findings at prestigious impact factor journals (DKE, KAIS, IJGIS, IJHCI) and top ranked international conferences (CIKM, WWW, AAAI) with 800 plus citations so far. His co-authored work on Spatio-temporal data mining was selected as "Best Paper" of Data & Knowledge Engineering Journal for year 2015. Up till now a total of 68 alumni of KDDM research group have successfully completed their degrees by conducting their research under supervision of Dr. Turab. Among them are 2 PhD's, 16 MS and 50 BS Final Year Project students; currently 6 PhD students are pursuing their research with him.

Adinarayana Rao U. V. is a Professor at the Department of Operations, GSB, GITAM (Deemed to be University), India. He is an award-winning teacher and has worked at Addis Ababa University before turning to be a Professor at GITAM. He has numerous publications in reputed journals, published books, resents papers at seminars and conferences, and is guiding research scholars in the areas of Business and Industrial Operations.

Anuradha Yadav is an Assistant Professor at the Department of MBA at Dayananda Sagar College of Engineering (DSCE), a premium institution at Bengaluru, India. She is an MBA, MA, PGDJM and a Ph.D. in Marketing. Her teaching and research focus is on Product and Brand Management, Strategic Management, and Marketing Management. She is a prolific author of several research papers and book chapters. She is a resource person to various research conferences.

Furkh Zeshan is a Tenured Associate Professor in the Department of Computer Science, COMSATS University Islamabad (CUI), Lahore Campus, Pakistan. He is working as an In-charge of Software Engineering Program in the Department. He received Ph.D. degree from the Department of Software Engineering, Universiti Teknologi Malaysia (UTM). He has around 13 years of teaching and research experience at various educational and research institutes along with 2.5 years of software development experience in the software industry as a software engineer. He has published more than 35 peer-reviewed articles (cumulative IF 60+ with more than 450 citations and 14 H-index) and has supervised 20+ students (Master + Ph.D.). Moreover, he has also served different public sector universities as a member of the selection and board of studies along with delivering a keynote talk on various topics at the national and international conferences. His research interests include Service-Oriented Computing, Intelligent Recommender Systems, Software Engineering, Software Project Management, Knowledge Management, and Self-Organizing Systems.

Index

D

E

O

P

R

S

T

U

V

W

Y

www.ingramcontent.com/pod-product-compliance
Lightning Source LLC
LaVergne TN
LVHW080121011026
849160LV00013B/1149

* 9 7 9 8 3 6 9 3 4 5 6 6 5 *